To my parents and to Mary Freda

Many thanks, Brendan

INJUNCTIONS

Law and Practice

UNITED KINGDOM
Sweet & Maxwell Ltd
London

AUSTRALIA
Law Book Co.
Sydney

CANADA AND USA
Carswell
Toronto

HONG KONG
Sweet & Maxwell Asia

NEW ZEALAND
Brookers
Wellington

SINGAPORE AND MALAYSIA
Sweet & Maxwell Asia
Singapore and Kuala Lumpur

INJUNCTIONS
LAW AND PRACTICE

BRENDAN KIRWAN
LL.B. (DUB), M. JURIS (OXON), LL.M. (EUI),
BARRISTER-AT-LAW

THOMSON ROUND HALL
2008

Published in 2008 by
Thomson Round Hall Ltd
43 Fitzwilliam Place
Dublin 2
Ireland

Typeset by
Carrigboy Typesetting Services

Printed by
MPG Books, Cornwall

ISBN 978–1–85800–503–4

A catalogue record for this book
is available from the British Library.

The Author and Publisher of this book accept no responsibility whatsoever
for any loss, damage or liability, direct or indirect including consequential
loss, arising from any errors contained herein. Readers are advised that
this book should not be treated as a substitute for legal consultation.

FOREWORD

The term "injunction" is familiar to both lay people and lawyers alike. Newspapers are full of court reports setting out successful and failed injunction applications. However, the complexities of the law in relation to injunctions only becomes apparent to those who, whether as practitioners or as clients, become directly involved in those types of litigation to which the injunction is relevant.

It is of course the case, as is ably demonstrated by the author's comprehensive work, that injunctions can have application to a whole range of different areas of the law. In a way, much of the textbook treatment of injunctions to date has been found in specialist text books devoted to those areas of law (such as employment or intellectual property, for example) where injunctions play an important role.

However, it is fair to say that the wide range of areas to which an injunction may be relevant and the natural evolution of the factual circumstances in which injunctions may be sought, necessarily gives rise to a significant degree of evolution in the law relating to injunctions. For that reason, it is particularly important that the author has embarked upon this most wide ranging textbook which seeks (successfully) to bring together the various strands of the law relating to injunctions.

It seems to me that the drawing together of all of the law in relation to injunctions in Ireland in one book is useful in two very different respects. Firstly, the earlier chapters of the book which deal with the general principles applicable to injunctions, draw (as some of the specialist textbooks, for obvious reasons, do not) on decisions from the myriad of areas to which the injunction jurisdiction applies. Secondly, the author sets out in the later chapters, the specific manner in which the general jurisdiction of the courts in relation to injunctions is applied to particular areas. It seems to me that a practitioner faced with a legal problem concerning an injunction will find both of these approaches useful and is likely to be most grateful to find both addressed within the covers of a single book.

While the treatment of injunctions in specific areas will be obviously useful for practitioners, there is much ground for cross-fertilisation in the broader considerations of the general principles. New views on how to approach the application of the injunction jurisdiction in a particular field may be usefully found in the established approach of the courts in other fields. In that context, it would be wrong in my opinion, to view the law relating to injunctions in each separate specialist area as being almost a stand alone topic. The general principles under which injunctions are granted or refused apply in all cases and across all areas. It is of course the case that the application of those general principles to particular areas of law is likely to be significantly influenced by the practical situations which commonly arise in the areas concerned. Employment contracts and the facts surrounding employment disputes are very different from those relating to a patent or copyright and an allegation of breach of the Intellectual Property rights concerned. It is hardly surprising, therefore, that the courts have worked out practical ways in which to implement the general principles, which may differ, depending on the area of law involved. However, the fact that the courts have worked out somewhat different ways of applying general principles in those different areas, should not cause one to lose sight of the fact that the underlying basis for the application of the injunction jurisdiction is universal and applies across all areas. The author has done a particularly valuable service by bringing together both the general and the particular in one comprehensive book.

A further commendable feature of the author's work is the fact that all due prominence has been given to recent developments in injunction law generally. As I have pointed out, it is an evolving area of law. Practitioners are at the cutting edge of that evolution and are required to advise their clients, not on the law as it might once have been, or even, in one sense, as it now is, but rather as to how it might be next week when the injunction application comes on for hearing. Identifying trends in judicial thinking is a vital part of the practitioners' art. The author has, in my view, given a very clear picture, not only of where the law stands as of today, but also the direction in which it might reasonably be expected to evolve further, in the future. This will, in my view, give practitioners very valuable food for thought. The practitioner, who only needs to know the current state of the law, will find it set out clearly; both its general principles and its specific applications. The practitioner who may be forced to consider making a case which pushes the boundaries of the law (because, on one view, the law as currently understood may not be very favourable to his case) will find valuable food for thought as to how an argument might be mounted for the relevant evolution.

As a minor contribution to this latter process, can I suggest that judicial thinking on the reasoning behind the grant or refusal of interim or interlocutory injunctions is beginning to show some signs of moving towards adopting, as an overall approach, a view which will place a high value on assessing where the greatest risk of injustice might lie. It is implicit in a hearing at which an interim or interlocutory injunction is sought, that either the grant or refusal of that injunction may amount to an injustice. The traditional balance of convenience test is predicated on the undoubted fact that the grant of an injunction after a short hearing may amount to an injustice to a defendant, just as its refusal may amount to an injustice to the plaintiff. There is, therefore, a real risk of injustice. In my view, there is much sense in an overall approach to interim or interlocutory injunctions which applies a standard of attempting to minimise that risk while acknowledging that some not insignificant risk is an inevitable consequence of the temporary and summary nature of the application.

There can be little doubt that the author's textbook will become a standard book of reference for all practitioners who may be required to consider the injunction as part of their armoury or defence. In truth, that definition encompasses any practitioner who has even a remote connection with possible litigation. It will also, I am sure, provide a most valuable reference work for judges who are often, necessarily, faced with making quick decisions, particularly at the interim or interlocutory stage and for whom ready access to a considered view of existing authority is a more than valuable asset. The gratitude of judges and practitioners alike is due to the author for this most splendid addition to the Irish legal library.

Frank Clarke
The High Court
May 2, 2008

PREFACE

"What readers ask nowadays in a book is that it should improve, instruct and elevate."

Jerome K Jerome, *Idle Thoughts of an Idle Fellow*, 1886

Jerome K Jerome felt that his book "wouldn't elevate a cow". Whether, over one hundred and twenty years on, the reader still wants to be elevated by a book, in particular by a law book, is not entirely certain. However, I hope that in using this book the reader will, in some measure, be improved and instructed in their knowledge of injunctions. It is to my mind a curious anomaly that in a system which is now well served by many excellent textbooks in so many different areas of the law, injunctions have never really had a discrete text of their own. Hilary Delany consistently produces a clear, erudite and accessible chapter on injunctions in her book, *Equity and the Law of Trusts in Ireland*, now in its fourth edition. Mr Justice Ronan Keane in his older book on *Equity and the Law of Trusts in the Republic of Ireland* also brings his considerable learning and experience to bear on injunctions. In both instances, however, injunctions are treated as a subset of equity, with the attendant unavoidable constraints on range and depth. Both texts are also primarily academic in nature, and do not as such deal with the practical and procedural aspects of applying for injunctions. Thomas B. Courtney's excellent work, *Mareva Injunctions and Related Interlocutory Orders*, strikes the perfect balance between being both scholarly and practical, but is confined to the field suggested by the title. The twenty fifth anniversary of the Supreme Court decision in the *Campus Oil* case seemed like an appropriate time to produce a book which would treat injunctions as a discrete subject, both from an academic and from a practical and procedural perspective.

The flexibility of the injunction as a remedy is a huge asset in terms of achieving a just result in any given case. It also provides a unique headache for anyone attempting to catalogue and analyse the various decisions handed down by the courts. This is particularly so given that I took the view that the book would be incomplete without considerable reference to foreign judgments, particularly from the English courts. Although latterly the courts in both Ireland and England tread very different procedural paths, they share a history in the context of the substantive development of injunctions. The considerable volume of injunction applications flowing through the English courts, particularly those relating to commercial and intellectual property matters, has led to much thought and development in those courts. It is thus somewhat inevitable that the Irish courts have had frequent regard to how the courts in England have faced up to the challenges posed by injunction applications in new and unusual situations. I have endeavoured throughout the text to identify Irish cases which either approach injunctions from first principles, or which at a minimum analyse and then accept the principles formulated in England. In that regard, Mr Justice Clarke, who has very kindly taken the time to write the foreword to this book, has performed an invaluable task since his appointment to the Bench. Building on the work of Ms Justice Laffoy and the other Chancery judges, he has, through his clear and comprehensive written judgments, made the job of analysing, dissecting and understanding the law relating to injunctions a much easier one. As a practitioner, it is a pleasure to appear before him.

I am aware that the fact that injunctions cut across all aspects of the law means that there is an element, to adapt a phrase, of being a jack of all areas of the law, yet master of none. A significant issue I faced is that an application for an injunction presupposes a good understanding of the underlying substantive law. In that regard, the practitioner in Ireland is fortunate that there are so many textbooks available dealing with different areas of the law. Where appropriate, I have attempted to reference those textbooks, as it is well beyond the scope of this book to detail the substantive law in each different area. In his preface to the leading English work, *Injunctions*, the author, David Bean Q.C., notes that he has avoided extensive discussion of substantive law, on the basis that such would make the book intolerably long and diffuse. I have tried to address that particular issue by, in Chapter Ten, identifying and detailing a number of key cases in different areas in which injunction applications were made. However, that chapter is not intended to be a law-lite version of, or substitute for, a more detailed knowledge of the law in any given area. This is far from a perfect solution, but I would ask for the reader's understanding that this was, to my mind, the best way of approaching things if I was ever to bring this work to publication. Similarly, the various pieces of legislation considered in Chapter Eleven are looked at in relatively narrow terms, namely by way of juxtaposing them to the equitable injunction. That does leave me open to the suggestion that the chapter really only rakes across significant areas of the law; again, I am aware of that, but felt that for the purposes of the exercise, it represented the most logical way of dealing with the various issues associated with forms of injunction specifically created by statute.

I am very conscious that as a more junior practitioner at the Bar writing a book, there are those who will take the view that it is somewhat presumptuous of me to be writing about the law, and particularly the practice, in an area such as injunctions. In an attempt to address this, I have canvassed a wide-ranging group of colleagues and friends for their input from an early stage, drawing on their collective experience and wisdom. To all the people who generously provided their input, insight and assistance, I am extremely grateful. Some did so unwittingly, as I lurked in the back of courtrooms watching various injunction applications being made. Some simply sparked ideas in my head as they discussed various aspects of applications they were involved in. However, there is another group which went out of its way to assist when approached with more specific requests. Not only can the genesis of this book be traced to a conversation with Declan McGrath B.L. over two years ago, Declan took the time out from his practice and authoring career to read chapters, deal with specific questions and offer ongoing support and much-needed encouragement throughout the life of the project. To him I am most grateful. I would also like to express my sincere thanks to Brian Kennedy B.L., who not only found the time in his crowded schedule to read through one of the longest chapters in the book, namely that on interlocutory applications, but also kept in touch with me on a regular basis, providing ongoing insightful observations, updates and suggestions arising out of his own experience and practice.

Other friends and colleagues to whom I am extremely grateful, who read through draft chapters and dealt with my queries with characteristic generosity of time and spirit, are George Brady S.C., John Donnelly B.L., Mairéad McKenna B.L. and Oisín Quinn B.L. Within the group of people who read through chapters is a subset who were (or were leant on to be) sufficiently enthusiastic that they got to read two chapters, or indeed the same chapter twice, but at different stages. A double dose of thanks to Kelley Smith B.L., Ray Ryan B.L., and Emily Egan B.L. for their input, suggestions and advice.

I would also like to thank those who gave their time to deal with my more general questions over the past two years. I suspect that I tested the old saw that there is no such thing as a stupid question a little too rigorously on occasion. Those who dealt with those questions, and who offered extremely useful and practical suggestions, advice and assistance are Ciaran Kelly, the former Principal Registrar of the Central Office; Susan Ryan, the County Registrar for Dublin; David Barniville S.C., Brian McGuckian B.L., Hilary Delany of Trinity College Dublin and Kieran Kelly of Fanning and Kelly Solicitors.

In terms of production, once Catherine Dolan at Thomson Roundhall had endorsed my proposal for this book, she passed me over to the capable and supportive hands of Susan Rossney, Frieda Donohue and my editor, Nicola Barrett. I am extremely grateful to them all, and indeed to all the staff at Thomson Round Hall involved in the production of this book. To a person, they were never anything less than patient, courteous and helpful. Any slippage in terms of deadlines was down to my own misplaced ambition and misguided enthusiasm.

My parents have always supported me in my various endeavours, no less so than during the two years I have been working at this book, and I am most grateful to them for their support and encouragement. More immediately, my wife Mary Freda has borne the brunt of my working somewhat unorthodox hours, scattering numerous drafts around the house and causing general disruption to family life. I would be tempted to say that, as a non-lawyer, she has benefited from learning all about injunctions by osmosis; that would be to trivialise her love and support, to which a few words in a preface do scant justice, and for which I am greatly indebted.

When writing the book, I had in mind a broad span of intended readers who might benefit from it. I would hope that it will be of benefit to both barristers and solicitors, and that students will also be able to access it in order to better appreciate the development and ongoing growth of this area of the law. It is an area which continues to grow. However, I adopt and endorse the disclaimer which appears a few pages before this in relation to reliance on the book; no book is a substitute for proper legal advice. I have endeavoured to state the law as at January 31, 2008. Any inaccuracies or errors are, of course, my own.

Brendan Kirwan
February 2008

CONTENTS

TABLE OF CASES

IRELAND

NORTHERN IRELAND

ENGLAND AND WALES

SCOTLAND

EUROPE

AUSTRALIA

CANADA

NEW ZEALAND

TABLE OF LEGISLATION

CONSTITUTIONAL PROVISIONS

IRISH STATUTES

PRE-1922 STATUTES

IRISH STATUTORY INSTRUMENTS

IRISH RULES OF COURT

IRISH BILLS

EUROPEAN UNION LEGISLATION

OTHER EUROPEAN AND INTERNATIONAL LEGISLATION

UK LEGISLATION

CHAPTER 1

DOMESTIC JURISDICTION

A. INTRODUCTION

1. Definition

1–01 A concise, comprehensive legal definition of an injunction is harder to formulate than might be expected. An injunction is, in broad terms, an order of the court by virtue of which a party is compelled to perform, or to desist from performing, a particular act. An injunction is described in the glossary to the English Civil Procedure Rules as "a court order prohibiting a person from doing something or requiring a person to do something".[1] However, such definitions admit of a wide range of court orders which would never be classed as injunctions.[2] It is in fact easier to describe an injunction than to define it.

1–02 The injunction has been described as a "formidable legal weapon".[3] It is a remedy rather than a cause of action.[4] It developed as an equitable remedy, with various principles governing whether the court should exercise its discretion to grant such a remedy.[5] The power to grant injunctions was subsequently put on a statutory footing. A growing number of injunctions are now specifically provided for or governed by statute.[6]

2. Identification of a Right/Standing

1–03 In order to seek the remedy of an injunction from a court, a right or interest—be it a legal, equitable, statutory or constitutional right—must be

---

[1] Glossary, October 1, 2007, 45th update. As noted by Gee, *Commercial Injunctions*, 5th edn (London: Sweet & Maxwell, 2004), p.5, the glossary is a "guide" to meanings and does not give an expression "... any meaning in the Rules which they do not have in law generally".

[2] The difficulties inherent in providing an exact definition are evident from the observation that an "award of damages in a personal injuries action is in the form of an order of the court requiring the defendant to pay the plaintiff money and yet no lawyer would dream of describing it as an injunction." per Keane, *Equity and the Law of Trusts in the Republic of Ireland* (London: Butterworths, 1988), p.205, echoing Meagher, Gummow & Lehane, *Equity*, 4th edn (Australia: Butterworths, 2002), p.703.

[3] *Llandudno Urban Council v Woods* [1899] 2 Ch. 705 at 710, per Cozens-Hardy J.

[4] See *Martin v Bannister* (1879) 4 Q.B.D. 491 at 492, per Brett L.J.

[5] As stated by Lindley L.J. in *Holmes v Millage* [1893] 1 Q.B. 551 at 555: "Courts of equity proceeded upon well-known principles capable of great expansion; but the principles themselves must not be lost sight of."

[6] Such as, for example, by s.160 of the Planning and Development Act 2000. See generally, Ch.11, Specific Statutory Injunctions.

established, and a breach—or imminent breach—of such right identified. As such, party must be in a position to demonstrate that s/he has the standing to seek an injunction.[7] It is normally a plaintiff who seeks an injunction, although a defendant is not precluded from seeking an injunction on foot of a counterclaim, as indeed was the position in the seminal Irish case of *Campus Oil Ltd v Minister for Industry and Energy (No. 2)*.[8]

3. Immediate, Effective Orders

1–04 A considerable volume of injunctions is sought every year.[9] One of the reasons for the usefulness of an injunction order is that it can be sought on an interim or interlocutory basis, i.e. a temporary basis, as well as on a perpetual basis. As such, it can offer a measure of immediate relief, even in a limited form, in circumstances where years can elapse before a substantive hearing is held in relation to a given matter. From a tactical perspective, an injunction secured on an interim or interlocutory basis is also useful in so far as it can bring matters to a head, and any order arising out of such an application may ultimately determine, or assist in determining, the substantive proceedings as well.

1–05 However, the courts will not make "idle and ineffectual" orders.[10] It is also important to bear in mind the dictum of Megaw L.J. in the case of *Hubbard v Vosper*[11] that "fairness, justice and common sense in relation to the whole issues of fact and law which are relevant to the particular case"[12] should form the basis for any decision.

4. Jurisdiction of the Courts

1–06 A court must have jurisdiction to grant the injunction sought. A court's jurisdiction is in general terms founded on the authority vested in the courts:

> "over persons within the limits of their jurisdiction, and amenable to process to restrain them from doing acts which work wrong and injury to others, and are therefore contrary to equity and good conscience."[13]

---

[7]   See generally, Ch.3, Standing.

[8]   [1983] 2 I.R. 88; [1984] I.L.R.M. 45.

[9]   According to the Courts Service Annual Report 2006, (available at *www.courts.ie*), in 2006, 145 interim injunction orders were made; 54 interlocutory injunction orders were made; and 53 injunction orders were sought in judicial review cases. See Ch.6 of the report, "Court Statistics", pp.106 and 107.

[10] *Attorney General v Colney Hatch Lunatic Asylum* (1868) L.R. 4 Ch. App. 146 at 154, per Lord Hatherley L.C.

[11] [1972] 2 Q.B. 84.

[12] [1972] 2 Q.B. 84 at 98.

[13] per Porter M.R. in *Lett v Lett* [1906] 1 I.R. 618 at 629, quoting from *Kerr on Injunctions*.

1–07 Proceedings in personam (directed against a specific person)[14] are only possible against persons served with a writ. Service is thus the formal basis for the jurisdiction of the Irish courts.[15] A court cannot hear a claim for an injunction which it has no jurisdiction to grant, notwithstanding that the defendant might not object to such an application.[16]

1–08 This chapter considers the jurisdiction of the Irish courts to grant injunctions, starting with a historical overview of the development of the injunction. It proceeds to look at the statutory bases for the granting of injunctions before setting out the key provisions of the Rules of Court in that regard. The aspects of the injunction which make it a distinct remedy will then be set out before the domestic jurisdiction of the Irish courts and the initiation of proceedings is detailed. Finally, this chapter will briefly consider domestic anti-suit injunctions and alternative means of stopping proceedings before the Irish courts.

1–09 The extent to which an Irish court can grant an injunction in relation to extra-jurisdictional matters, and the extent to which the jurisdiction of the Irish courts can be invoked in order to enforce an injunction obtained outside the jurisdiction, will both be considered in Ch.2, Extraterritorial Jurisdiction.

B. Development of the Injunction

1. Introduction

1–10 Originally a creature of the Courts of Chancery,[17] and evolving around the 16th century, the equitable injunction in use in the courts today is in many ways similar to that developed by the Courts of Chancery. This means that an understanding of the development of the injunction can be instructive in terms of analysing injunctions as sought and granted today.

2. Primary Statutory Basis

1–11 The primary basis for the granting of equitable injunctions in this jurisdiction is the Supreme Court of Judicature Act (Ireland) 1877. A considerable body of jurisprudence dating back to the earliest years of injunction orders is

---

[14] See Ch.4, Equitable and General Principles, para.4–07.
[15] For an overview as to jurisdiction generally, see Delany & McGrath, *Civil Procedure in the Superior Courts*, 2nd edn (Dublin: Thomson Round Hall, 2005), particularly Ch.1.
[16] See, for example, *Simpson v Crowle* [1921] 3 K.B. 243.
[17] As to which, see para.1–13.

still of relevance to injunction applications today. Explaining this relevance, Lindley L.J. stated in the case of *Holmes v Millage*[18] that:

> "Although injunctions are granted and receivers are appointed more readily than they were before the passing of the Judicature Acts, and some inconvenient rules formerly observed have been very properly relaxed, yet the principles on which the jurisdiction of the Court of Chancery rested have not been changed."[19]

3. Development of Equity

1–12 Injunctions as popularly understood are an equitable remedy. The development of injunctions has therefore to be considered having regard to the development of equity.[20] In its broad sense, equity refers to the legal principles developed by the courts in England in order to supplement the strict rules of law when the courts viewed their operation as harsh. In the narrower sense, equity refers to the branch of law over which the Courts of Chancery had jurisdiction prior to the Supreme Court of Judicature (Ireland) Act 1877, but which law was not recognised by the common law courts.

(a) The Role of the Courts of Chancery

1–13 Prior to the enactment of the Common Law Procedure Act (Ireland) 1856, there was effectively no jurisdiction in the common law courts—which were the royal courts, deriving their authority from the King—to grant injunctions. The award of damages was the remedy at the disposal of the common law courts. However, the common law was becoming increasingly rigid, with a series of fixed grounds of complaint upon which a writ could be issued. These factors led to relief being sought directly from the King. The King began to delegate petitions for such relief to the Lord Chancellor, to the point where people began to seek relief from the Lord Chancellor directly.

---

[18] [1893] 1 Q.B. 551.

[19] [1893] 1 Q.B. 551 at 557. The basic principles on which the jurisdiction of the Court of Chancery rested were considered by Lord Esher M.R. in *Manchester and Liverpool District Banking Co. v Parkinson* (1888) 22 Q.B.D. 173 at 175.

[20] For a clear and comprehensive overview of the historical development of equity, see Hanbury & Martin, *Modern Equity*, 17th edn (London: Sweet & Maxwell, 2005), Ch.1. For an overview in the specific context of Ireland, see O'Neill Kiely, *The Principles of Equity* (Dublin: Fodhla, 1936), Ch.1. See also Delany, *Equity and the Law of Trusts in Ireland*, 4th edn (Dublin: Thomson Round Hall, 2007), Ch.1; Keane, *Equity and the Law of Trusts in the Republic of Ireland* (London: Butterworths, 1988), Ch.2; and Meagher, Gummow & Lehane, *Equity*, 4th edn (Australia: Butterworths, 2002), Ch.1, especially pp.1–11.

(b) The Lord Chancellor

1–14 The Lord Chancellor had much greater freedom as to how he wished to exercise his discretion in relation to the petitions before him. With an increase in the number of claimants seeking relief from the Lord Chancellor, the Courts of Chancery—which were the Lord Chancellor's courts—developed into a distinct judicial system with their own staff and procedures. A petition or bill would be presented to the Courts of Chancery. If the courts thought that there was a case to answer, the courts would issue a writ, ordering the defendant to appear and answer the complaint.[21] Hardship or unfairness were key considerations for the Courts of Chancery in determining what orders to make on foot of the petitions presented.

1–15 Prior to the Reformation, the Chancellor was generally a church dignitary. He tended to import from the ecclesiastical courts and from canon law a number of ideas, such as "conscience", which informed his approach to, inter alia, injunctions. As stated by the Earl of Selborne, L.C. in the case of *Ewing v Orr Ewing*[22]:

> "The courts of Equity in England are, and always have been, courts of conscience, operating *in personam* and not *in rem*; and in the exercise of this personal jurisdiction they have always been accustomed to compel the performance of contracts and trusts as to subjects which were not either locally or *ratione domicilii* within their jurisdiction."

1–16 The fact that equity acts in personam is still a key feature of injunction orders.[23] Indeed, the language of injunctions still bears traces of the religious aspect of the Chancellor's jurisdiction; for example, contempt is "purged", prison terms may be deemed necessary by way of "expiation" and so on.

(c) Common and Special Injunctions

1–17 The Courts of Chancery would grant, as necessary, an injunction preventing a person from proceeding with an action before the common law courts, or from executing a judgment obtained in the common law courts. These injunctions were known as "common injunctions". A "special injunction" would be granted as necessary in aid of an equitable right, and it is this latter type of injunction which evolved into what is now recognised as an equitable injunction.

---

[21] As noted by Gee, *Commercial Injunctions*, 5th edn (London: Sweet & Maxwell, 2004), p.1, writs could be either "remedial", issued before a decree as a restraint upon a party, or "judicial", in the nature of an execution.

[22] (1883) 9 App. Cas. 34 at 40.

[23] See, for example, *Moore v Attorney General* [1930] I.R. 471 at 486, per Kennedy C.J.

1–18 The evolving power of the Courts of Chancery and the power to grant injunctions meant that they could essentially circumnavigate, or indeed override, the strictures of the common law in individual cases. Primarily through the use of the common injunction, common law actions could in effect be restrained by the Courts of Chancery.[24] In the circumstances, it was perhaps inevitable that tension between the two systems would flourish. However, it was ultimately determined that the Courts of Chancery had the jurisdiction to restrain actions at common law.[25]

(d) Exclusive, Auxiliary and Concurrent Jurisdiction

1–19 There is also a (historical) distinction between different forms of jurisdiction exercised by the courts. The first form of injunction was granted in what was termed the "exclusive jurisdiction", namely injunctions granted in aid of an equitable right. In the "auxiliary jurisdiction", the injunction protected a legal right. In the "concurrent jurisdiction", a claim could be brought in a court of equity or another court.[26] The passing of the Judicature Acts, considered below, largely consigned the distinction to being primarily of historical interest.[27] One commentator observed in 1902 that to use the terminology which defined the relationship between the old Court of Chancery and the old common law courts in the context of the modern administration of equity "is to assign too great an importance to distinctions, which, although in fact still existing in practice, are in point of principle and in theory altogether abolished."[28]

(e) Legislative Developments

1–20 Subsequent legislative intervention set out the bases on which injunctions could be granted and ultimately clarified the positions of the common law courts and Courts of Chancery relative to each other. The evolving statutory basis for the granting of injunctions will thus be considered, culminating with the passing of the Supreme Court of Judicature Act (Ireland) 1877.

---

[24] See Meagher, Gummow & Lehane, *Equity*, 4th edn (Australia: Butterworths, 2002), p.706.

[25] A determination arrived at following a dispute which arose in the *Earl of Oxford's case* (1615) 1 Ch. Rep. 1. See Smith, *The Principles of Equity*, 3rd edn (London: Stevens & Sons, 1902), p.749.

[26] A categorisation described in 1886 by *Story's Commentaries on Equity Jurisprudence*, as analysed by Gee, *Commercial Injunctions*, 5th edn (London: Sweet & Maxwell, 2004), p.1. As observed by Gee, "[Justice] Story's classification has been adopted by judges and writers but also has been vigorously criticised."

[27] See para.1–27. See *Habib Bank Ltd v Habib Bank AG Zurich* [1981] 1 W.L.R. 1265 at 1285, per Oliver L.J, who referred to such distinctions as "both archaic and arcane", and with "little significance for anyone but a legal historian." However, *cf. Cahill v Irish Motor Traders' Association* [1966] I.R. 430 at 449, in which Budd J. appeared to make a distinction between legal and equitable rights in the context of an injunction. See the criticism of the distinction in Meagher, Gummow & Lehane, *Equity*, 4th edn (Australia: Butterworths, 2002), p.111.

[28] See Smith, *The Principles of Equity*, 3rd edn (London: Stevens & Sons, 1902), p.2.

(i) Common Law Procedure Amendment Act (Ireland) 1856

1–21 The entitlement of the common law courts to grant injunctions was enshrined in statute in the form of the Common Law Procedure Amendment Act (Ireland) 1856.[29] Section 81 of the Act provided that:

> "In all Cases of Breach of Contract or other Injury, where the Party injured is entitled to maintain and has brought an Action, he may, in like Case and Manner as herein-before provided with respect to Mandamus, claim a Writ of Injunction against the Repetition or Continuance of such Breach of Contract or other Injury, or the Committal of any Breach of Contract or Injury of a like kind, arising out of the same Contract, or relating the same Property or Right; and he may also in the same Action include a Claim for Damages or other Redress."

1–22 Although the common law courts now had the power, based on statute, to grant injunctions, s.81 referred only to "breach of contract or other injury". This was a relatively narrow set of circumstances within which such power could be exercised. Furthermore, the use of the phrase "repetition or continuance" placed the emphasis on future acts and injury.[30] It has also been noted that:

> "it has been assumed in the material authorities that common law injunctions are ordinarily granted or refused according to the same discretionary considerations, such as hardship or unfairness, that move courts of equity in analogous applications."[31]

1–23 Section 83 of the 1856 Act provided the formal criterion for the exercise of power under s.81, namely "as justice may require", leaving a significant degree of discretion to the common law judges.

1–24 Procedurally, s.84 of the 1856 Act provided that a writ of injunction could be applied for at any stage after the commencement of an action, on an ex parte basis (in other words, in the absence of the other side). Section 84 reads:

> "It shall be lawful for the Plaintiff, at any Time after the Commencement of the Action, and whether before or after Judgment, to apply ex parte to the Court or a Judge for a Writ of Injunction to restrain the Defendant in such Action from the Repetition or Continuance of the wrongful Act or Breach of Contract complained of, or the Committal of any Breach of Contract or Injury

---

[29] For further detail, specifically on s.81, see Wylie, *The Judicature Acts (Ireland)* (Dublin: Sealy, Bryers and Walker, 1906), p.71. The equivalent English provision was s.79 of the Common Law Procedure Act 1854.

[30] For a consideration of this point, see *Frearson v Loe* (1879) 9 Ch D 48 at 65, per Sir George Jessel M.R.

[31] Spry, *The Principles of Equitable Remedies*, 6th edn (London: Sweet & Maxwell, 2001), p.326.

of a like kind, arising out of the same Contract, or relating to the same Property or Right; and such Writ may be granted or denied by the Court or Judge, upon such Terms as to the Duration of the Writ, keeping an Account, giving Security, or otherwise, as to such Court or Judge shall seem reasonable and just, and in case of Disobedience such Writ may be enforced by Attachment: Provided always, that any Order for a Writ of Injunction made by a Judge, or any Writ issued by virtue thereof, may be discharged or varied or set aside by the Court, on Application made thereto by any Party dissatisfied with such Order."

1–25 As can be seen, the writ[32] could be granted or denied upon such terms "as to such court or judge shall seem reasonable and just". In relation to the equivalent sections in the English legislation,[33] Jessel M.R. observed in *Quartz Hill Consolidated Gold Mining Co v Beall*[34] that, "if the Court can grant an injunction ex parte, *à fortiori* it can grant it on notice."[35]

(ii) Chancery Amendment Act 1858

1–26 Also significant was the passing of what is more commonly known as Lord Cairns' Act, namely the Chancery Amendment Act 1858. This Act provided the Courts of Chancery with the right to award damages in addition to, or substitution for, an injunction. The impact of this Act is still as important and relevant today as it was at the time, as will be seen when considering the principles upon which a perpetual injunction may be granted.[36]

(iii) Chancery (Ireland) Act 1867

1–27 Whilst the 1856 Act provided the statutory basis for the granting of an equitable injunction, the legislature also intervened and provided for injunctions specific to certain areas. For example, s.171 of the Chancery (Ireland) Act 1867 provided that anyone with an interest in government stock transferable at the Bank of Ireland could claim an injunction to restrain the Bank of Ireland from permitting the transfer of stock or payment of dividends thereof.[37] Such legislative intervention has continued and provision has been made in a number of areas for specific statutory injunctions.[38]

---

[32] Order L r.12 of the Rules of the Supreme Court (Ireland) 1905 provided that: "No writ of injunction shall be issued. An injunction shall be by a judgment or order, and any such judgment or order shall have the effect which a writ of injunction previously had."

[33] Common Law Procedure Act 1854.

[34] (1882) 20 Ch D 501.

[35] (1882) 20 Ch D 501 at 507.

[36] See Ch.5, Perpetual Injunctions.

[37] As observed Laffoy J. in *Lee v Buckle* [2004] 3 I.R. 544 at 549, s.171 was repealed by the Statute Law Revision (No. 2) Act 1893.

[38] See Ch.11, Specific Statutory Injunctions.

(iv) Supreme Court of Judicature Act (Ireland) 1877

1–28 Notwithstanding these legislative developments, two systems of law, operated by the common law courts and the Courts of Chancery, were still in operation, complete with their own courts and staff. This situation was addressed by the Supreme Court of Judicature Act (Ireland) 1877.[39] By virtue of this Act, the common law and the rules of equity were fused from an administrative point of view.[40] The existing courts which exercised common law and equitable jurisdiction were thereby replaced by a single Supreme Court of Judicature.

1–29 The Judicature Act was essentially administrative in nature. The accepted view is that the Act was not intended to effect any change in the law.[41] Nor did it in any way enlarge the jurisdiction of the courts to grant injunctions. In *North London Railway Co. v Great Northern Railway Co.*[42] Brett L.J. stated that he was inclined to hold that "if no court had the power of issuing an injunction before the Judicature Act, no part of the High Court has the power to issue an injunction now."[43] However, by virtue of s.28(11) of the 1877 Act, where there was a conflict between the rules of equity and the common law, equity was to prevail.[44]

1–30 Section 28(8) of the Supreme Court of Judicature Act (Ireland) 1877 empowered the High Court to grant interlocutory injunctions. It reads:

> "A mandamus or an injunction may be granted or a receiver appointed by an interlocutory order of the Court in all cases in which it shall appear to the Court to be just or convenient that such order should be made, and any such order may be made either unconditionally or upon such terms and conditions as the Court shall think just; and if an injunction is asked, either before, or at, or after the hearing of any cause or matter, to prevent any threatened or

---

[39] The English equivalent being the Supreme Court of Judicature Acts 1873 and 1875, repealed and replaced by the Supreme Court of Judicature (Consolidation) Act 1925, in turn replaced by the Supreme Court Act 1981.

[40] See in particular ss.27(5) and 27(7) of the 1877 Act.

[41] The extent to which there was (or, more pertinently, was not) a fusion of principles as well as procedures is discussed by Delany, *Equity and the Law of Trusts in Ireland*, 4th edn (Dublin: Thomson Round Hall, 2007), pp.7–12.

[42] (1883) 11 Q.B.D. 30.

[43] (1883) 11 Q.B.D. 30 at 36; *cf. Beddow v Beddow* (1878) 9 Ch D 89 at 93, which seems to suggest an extension of the principles upon which jurisdiction was formerly exercised, per Jessel M.R. In *Moore v Attorney General* [1927] I.R. 569 at 580, FitzGibbon J. stated in the Supreme Court that the relevant section "extends the principles upon which jurisdiction was formerly exercised by the Court of Chancery". However, this is a view "which does not seem to be consistent with the generally accepted view of the effect of the section", per Keane in *Equity and the Law of Trusts in the Republic of Ireland* (London: Butterworths, 1988), p.209.

[44] See the dictum of Jessel M.R. in *Walsh v Lonsdale* (1882) 21 Ch D 9 at 14.

apprehended waste or trespass, such injunction may be granted, if the Court shall think fit, whether the person against whom such injunction is sought is or is not in possession under any claim of title or otherwise, or (if out of possession) does or does not claim a right to do the act sought to be restrained under any colour of title, and whether the estates claimed by both or by either of the parties are legal or equitable."[45]

1–31 Two key points arise out of the wording of s.28(8): the use of the term "interlocutory order" and the criterion of "just and convenient".

Interlocutory Order
1–32 In analysing the wording of s.28(8) in the case of *McKenna v AF*,[46] Geoghegan J. dealt with the use of the phrase "interlocutory order". Observing that the section "by its terms does not use the expression 'interlocutory injunction' but rather "interlocutory order", Geoghegan J. considered what was meant by an interlocutory order. He stated that:

> "it is well known to all lawyers that 'an interlocutory order' within the meaning of the Judicature Act and of the Rules of the Superior Courts in their various forms over the years means an order which is not a final order".

1–33 Geoghegan J. then referred to the dictum of Jessel M.R. in *Re Stockton Iron Furness Company*,[47] in which the Master of the Rolls had explained that:

> "The rules appear to contemplate two classes of orders: final orders which determine the rights of the parties, and orders which do not determine the rights."[48]

1–34 As such, s.28(8) makes provision for an interlocutory order which is not a final order.

Basis for a Final Order
1–35 That leaves open the question of whether s.28(8) in fact provides the legislative basis for final injunction orders. On its face it would seem not to. However, the dictum of Cotton L.J. in the case of *North London Railway Co v*

---

[45] Wylie, *The Judicature Acts (Ireland)* (Dublin: Sealy, Bryers and Walker, 1906), p.73 refers to this section using the term "statutory injunction". In the context of the instant work, this should not be confused with the term used in Ch.11, Specific Statutory Injunctions, which deals with injunctions provided for by the legislature in very specific areas of the law. As to the specific references to "waste" and "trespass" in s.28(8), see generally Wylie at p.74. The author also deals with applications for injunctions in specific situations.

[46] [2002] 1 I.R. 242 at 245.
[47] (1879) 10 Ch D 334.
[48] (1879) 10 Ch D 334 at 349.

Great Northern Railway Co[49] makes clear that it does. In relation to the equivalent section in England,[50] he stated that:

> "If it was intended to give the enormously increased power which it is contended is given by this section, it is remarkable that it empowers it to be done by interlocutory order. It is said if it can be done by interlocutory order, of course it can be done by a final order at the hearing of the cause or judgment; no doubt that is true."[51]

1–36 On the basis of this, and the fact that the Supreme Court of Judicature Act (Ireland) 1877 is still law in this jurisdiction,[52] s.28(8) of the 1877 Act provides the legislative basis for both final and interlocutory equitable injunctions. The Common Law Procedure Amendment Act (Ireland) 1856 was not repealed and, as such, is also still relevant, although it is probably fair to say that its role is greatly diminished.[53] The Chancery Amendment Act 1858 (Lord Cairns' Act) also has a very important role to play in the context of injunction applications. As will be seen, these statutory provisions have been supplemented by rules of court.[54]

Just and Convenient
1–37 As is clear from the wording of s.28(8), an injunction is granted if the court feels that it would be "just" and "convenient", and on such terms and conditions as the court thinks just. The use of the two words was considered by Jessel M.R. in *Beddow v Beddow*.[55] The Master of the Rolls observed that:

> "in the Judicature Act you have 'just or convenient': not that that would be convenient which was unjust; but that in ascertaining what is 'just' you must have regard to what is convenient."[56]

---

[49] (1883) 11 Q.B.D. 30.

[50] Judicature Act 1873, s.25(8).

[51] (1883) 11 Q.B.D. 30 at 39.

[52] As was acknowledged by Kearns J. in the case of *O'Neill v O'Keeffe* in the context of a *Bayer* order [2002] 2 I.R. 1; [2003] 2 I.L.R.M. 40. See generally, Ch.8, Commercial Injunctions, para.8–184.

[53] See, for example, *Re Sweeney and Kennedy's Arbitration* [1950] I.R. 85, dealing with a special case stated pursuant to s.8 of the Common Law Procedure Amendment Act (Ireland) 1856 (now repealed by the Arbitration Act 1954). In the context of arbitration, see also, *Keenan v Shield Insurance Co. Ltd* [1988] I.R. 89. See also, *McConn v Laing* [1939] I.R. 403, dealing with the question of whether an action was maintainable. However, large sections of the Act were repealed by, inter alia, the Arbitration Act 1954, the Statute of Limitations Act 1957 and the Statute Law Revision Act 1983. See also the various references to the 1857 Act in the Rules of the Superior Courts 1986.

[54] See para.1–47.

[55] (1878) 9 Ch D 89.

[56] (1878) 9 Ch D 89 at 93.

1–38 The use of the words "just" and "convenient" means that, in practical terms, the courts have a considerable degree of latitude in terms of how they wish to deal with an application for an injunction. In *Bacon v Jones*,[57] Lord Cottenham L.C. made observations on the powers of the Courts of Chancery to grant an interlocutory injunction, "either during the progress of the suit, or at the hearing; and in both cases, I apprehend, great latitude and discretion are allowed to the court in dealing with an application."[58]

1–39 However, the courts must exercise their discretion according to established principles. This was made clear by Lord Blackburn in the case of *Doherty v Allman*.[59] He stated that:

> "the discretion is not one to be exercised according to the fancy of whoever is to exercise the jurisdiction of Equity, but is a discretion to be exercised according to the rules which have been established by a long series of decisions, and which are now settled to be the proper guide to Judges in courts of Equity."[60]

(f) Evolving Jurisdiction

1–40 The power of the courts to grant injunctions is extremely wide and covers a significant range of situations and circumstances. Indeed, the injunction has been described as "equity's most wide-ranging remedy since it is one which can be invoked in most areas of the law, private and public".[61] Furthermore, it is a feature of equity generally, and injunctions specifically, that they can be developed. As stated by Jessel M.R. in *Re Hallett's Estate, Knatchbull v Hallett*,[62] equity and its principles have been "altered, improved and refined from time to time".[63]

1–41 In *Mercedes Benz v Leiduck*,[64] Lord Nicholls referred to previous House of Lords decisions and stated that:

---

[57] (1839) 4 M. & C. 433.

[58] (1839) 4 M. & C. 433 at 436. Cited in *Department of Social Security v Butler* [1995] W.L.R. 1528 at 1532, per Evans L.J.

[59] (1878) 3 App. Cas. 709.

[60] (1878) 3 App. Cas. 709 at 728. See also *Harris v Beauchamp Bros* [1894] 1 Q.B. 801 and *Morgan v Hart* [1914] 2 K.B. 183.

[61] Wylie, *Irish Land Law*, 3rd edn (Dublin: Butterworths, 1997), p.153. For example, in *Aranwell Ltd v Pura Food Products Ltd* [2004] 2 I.L.R.M. 147 at 157, Herbert J. cautioned that the use of information about the plaintiff's "potential customers" furnished by way of replies of particulars without the express permission of the court "would be restrained by injunction".

[62] (1880) 13 Ch D 696.

[63] (1880) 13 Ch D 696 at 710.

[64] [1996] A.C. 284; [1995] 3 W.L.R. 718.

"These are highly persuasive voices that the jurisdiction to grant an injunction, unfettered by statute, should not be rigidly confined to exclusive categories by judicial decision."[65]

1–42 The need to avoid injustice was, according to Lord Nicholls, a key consideration in that regard. He also referred to the fact that as circumstances change, so must the situations in which the courts will exercise their discretion to grant injunctions. Such exercise:

"must be principled, but the criterion is injustice. Injustice is to be viewed and decided in the light of today's conditions and standards, not those of yester-year."[66]

1–43 It is this flexibility which has enabled the courts to develop, inter alia, forms of injunctions such as the *Mareva* injunction, the *Anton Piller* order, the "rolling" *Anton Piller* order and the *Bayer* order,[67] and which provides the basis for the development of injunctions to address developments and circumstances which are not as yet anticipated. As other areas of the law develop, related injunctions also develop, such as in the case of breach of confidence, an area which has grown exponentially in recent years.[68] As some forms of injunctions develop, others, such as the "common injunction", have to all intents and purposes fallen into abeyance. The common injunction was effectively rendered redundant by the Supreme Court of Judicature Act (Ireland) 1877, specifically s.27(5).[69]

(g) European Convention on Human Rights

1–44 Although the impact of the European Convention on Human Rights and the European Convention on Human Rights Act 2003 in the context of injunctions has, at a general level, been more muted in this jurisdiction, its influence is growing, and has the potential to grow much further, in discrete areas of the law. The impact of the Convention has been particularly pronounced in England in areas such as breach of confidence and privacy, and there is evidence to suggest that its influence is also growing in this jurisdiction,[70] subject to any relevant constitutional considerations.

---

[65] [1996] A.C. 284 at 308; [1995] 3 W.L.R. 718 at 736.
[66] [1996] A.C. 284 at 308; [1995] 3 W.L.R. 718 at 736; [1995] 3 All E.R. 929 at 946.
[67] As to which, see Ch.8, Commercial Injunctions.
[68] See Ch.10, General Application, specifically para.10–147.
[69] O'Neill Kiely, *The Principles of Equity* (Dublin: Fodhla, 1936), p.356 observes that the subsection only applies to proceedings which are actually pending in the High or Supreme Courts (citing ss.17 and 18) and notes that, in consequence, "it does not interfere with the inherent jurisdiction of the Court, acting *in personam*, to restrain by injunction proceedings in a foreign Court or in an inferior Court," referencing *Hedley v Bates* (1880) 13 Ch. Div. 498. As such, Keane, *Equity and the Law of Trusts in the Republic of Ireland* (London: Butterworths, 1988), p.207 observes that the common injunction "cannot be said to have completely disappeared".
[70] See Ch.10, General Application, para.10–166.

4. Role of English Authority

1–45 Due to the fact that injunction orders such as *Mareva* orders and *Anton Piller* orders have primarily been developed in a commercial context in the courts in England, relevant English authorities effectively carry a greater degree of persuasiveness in this jurisdiction than might be the case in other areas of the law. Quite often, the lead is provided by the courts in England, with this lead then relied on, wholly or in a modified form, in this jurisdiction. In so far as there are differences in approach between the courts in this jurisdiction and in England, the impact of the provisions of the Constitution is a significant factor. Caution must also be exercised in relation to English cases decided since 1999, certainly in so far as aspects of procedure are concerned. This is due to the passing in that year of the Civil Procedure Rules in England. These rules effected both changes to procedure and to terminology.

1–46 It is not just modern English authority which is relied upon by the courts in this jurisdiction. What is also evident is that there is considerable reliance on early authority. This is due to the development of injunctions at a time when the Irish legal system was under the aegis of that in England. There is therefore a considerable degree of commonality in approach by the Irish and English courts both pre- and post-independence.

5. Rules of Court

1–47 The Rules of both the Superior and Circuit Courts supplement and enhance the legislative foundations for the granting of injunctions. The wording of Ord.50 rr.6(1)–(3) of the Rules of the Superior Courts (RSC) is very similar in form to s.28(8) of the Supreme Court of Judicature Act (Ireland) 1877. Rules of the Superior Courts Ord.50 r.6(1) reads:

> "The Court may grant a mandamus or an injunction or appoint a receiver, by an interlocutory order in all cases in which it appears to the Court to be just or convenient so to do."[71]

1–48 Again, the applicable test is that a court believes it to be "just or convenient" to grant the injunction.[72]

---

[71] There would appear to be no direct equivalent in the Rules of the Circuit Court (RCC). However, RCC Ord.20 refers to the granting of ex parte interim injunctions, and RCC Ord.39 provides for the appointment of a receiver by way of equitable execution. RCC Ord.67 r.16 provides that where no rule is set out to govern the practice and procedure of the Circuit Court, "the practice and procedure in the High Court may be followed".

[72] See para.1–37.

1–49 Rules of the Superior Courts Ord.50 r.6(2) provides that "any such order may be made either unconditionally or upon such terms and conditions as the Court thinks just." Rules of the Superior Courts Ord.50 r.6(3) deals with threatened or apprehended waste or trespass.

1–50 Rules of the Superior Courts Ord.50 r.12 is similar to s.54 of the Common Law Procedure Amendment Act (Ireland) 1856. The rule provides that:

> "In any cause or matter in which an injunction has been or might have been claimed, the plaintiff may, before or after judgement, apply for an injunction to restrain the defendant or respondent from the repetition or continuance of the wrongful act or breach of contract complained of, or from the commission of any injury or breach of contract of a like kind relating to the same property or right, or arising out of the same contract; and the Court may grant the injunction, either upon or without terms, as may be just."

1–51 The actual procedures involved in making an application for an injunction will be considered in subsequent chapters.

C. The Injunction as a Distinct Remedy

1. Introduction

1–52 There are other remedies available which share a number of characteristics with injunctions. However, differences can be identified between injunctions and such remedies, specifically declarations, specific performance and public law remedies. These differences will now be considered.

2. Injunction or Declaration

1–53 A declaration merely states the rights and legal position of parties to an action. Section 155 of the Chancery (Ireland) Act 1867 provided that no suit in the court should be open to objection on the ground that a merely declaratory decree or order was sought, and that it was lawful for the court to make binding declarations of right without granting consequential relief. A declaration rather than an injunction may be appropriate if it was felt that an injunction order would, for example, be oppressive.[73]

1–54 That a declaration is different from an injunction is clear from the decision of Lynch J. in the case of *Stelzer v Wexford North Slob Commissioners*.[74] He made

---

[73] See, for example, *Islington Vestry v Hornsey UDC* [1900] 1 Ch. 695.
[74] [1988] I.L.R.M. 279.

a series of declarations as well as awarding damages, but felt it "inappropriate to make any order by way of mandatory or other injunctions"[75] on the facts. However, the reality is that declarations are often the first step in seeking an injunction. For example, having secured a declaration from the court in relation to ownership, the further relief of an injunction may be sought in order to secure possession; parties will often seek both reliefs, namely a declaration and an injunction, in relation to the same matter and on the same pleadings.

3. Injunction or Specific Performance

1–55 Underlying the doctrine of specific performance is the idea that:

> "a man is entitled in equity to have *in specie* the specific article for which he has contracted, and is not bound to take damages instead."[76]

1–56 In other words, specific performance is essentially an order of the court requiring performance of the terms of a contract.[77] As noted by Snell:

> "The commonest case in which the court specifically enforces a contract is where the contract is for the sale of land or for the granting of a lease."[78]

1–57 There are a number of similarities between injunctions and specific performance.[79] Both are discretionary equitable remedies, based on established principles. As with injunctions, the remedy of specific performance will not be granted if damages would provide an adequate remedy.[80] Indeed, an enforcing mandatory injunction, which requires positive action on the part of the person to whom it is directed, is often equated with a decree for specific performance.[81] However, as observed by Keane, the relevance of the distinction really arises when dealing with contracts, in particular when a court is asked to enforce a single term of a contract. In such circumstances, he notes that that court will:

---

[75] [1988] I.L.R.M. 279 at 289.
[76] per Farwell J. in *Hexter v Pearce* [1900] 1 Ch. 341 at 346, approved by O'Connor L.J. in *O'Regan v White* [1919] 2 I.R. 339 at 392.
[77] Wylie, *Irish Land Law*, 3rd edn (Dublin: Butterworths, 1997), p.160 identifies five of the main types of contracts in which specific performance will be granted: sale of land, chattels, building contracts, separation deeds and partnership agreements. However, this list is not finite.
[78] Snell, *Equity*, 31st edn (London: Thomson Sweet & Maxwell, 2005), p.352.
[79] See generally, Farrell, *Irish Law of Specific Performance* (Dublin: Butterworths, 1994), Ch.2.
[80] See *Ryan v Mutual Tontine Westminster Chambers Association* [1893] 1 Ch. 116 at 125, per Lopes L.J.
[81] In *Dowty Boulton Paul Ltd v Wolverhampton Corporation* [1971] 1 W.L.R. 204, Pennycuick V.C. considered that there was no difference between an order for specific performance and a mandatory injunction, as stated by Millett L.J. in *Co-Operative Insurance v Argyll Stores* [1998] A.C. 1; [1996] 1 Ch. 286 at 302; [1997] 2 W.L.R. 898.

> "have to consider whether the term would be capable of being specifically performed if it stood alone and whether in all the circumstances it should be enforced on its own."[82]

Furthermore, injunctions have a much wider scope than specific performance. They may also be granted in aid of or ancillary to a claim for specific performance or in tandem with a claim for specific performance, particularly at the interim or interlocutory stage.[83]

4. Injunction or Public Law Remedy

1–58 The principal remedies sought in relation to the decision of an administrative body or inferior court are certiorari, prohibition and mandamus, all generally categorised as "public law remedies". Declarations, injunctions and damages are often termed "private law remedies".[84] Prior to the introduction of the Rules of the Superior Courts in 1986, this could lead to some confusion, as the lines between the remedies and the appropriateness of seeking them were blurred. Further complicating the area was the need to specify the correct remedy required; failure to do so could lead to no remedy being granted at all, or simply a limited remedy. For example, in the case of *O'Doherty v Attorney General*,[85] Gavan Duffy J. took the view that mandamus was the appropriate remedy, but could not grant it because it had not been sought.

1–59 However, the 1986 Rules established a comprehensive procedure for judicial review,[86] providing for the grant of an injunction if the court felt it to be "just and convenient" to do so.[87] Furthermore, by virtue of RSC Ord.84 r.25(1), "any interlocutory application may be made to the Court in proceedings on an application for judicial review". In relation to the latter provision, it was accepted in *Fitzpatrick v Commissioner of An Garda Síochána*[88] that the principles applicable to the grant of an injunction on an application for judicial review are identical to those which apply in ordinary civil litigation.[89]

---

[82] See Keane, *Equity and the Law of Trusts in the Republic of Ireland* (London: Butterworths, 1988), p.232.

[83] See, for example, *Preston v Luck* (1884) 27 Ch D 497, in which an injunction was granted to preserve a patent pending the resolution of a claim for specific performance.

[84] See generally, Scannell "Procedural Exclusivity in the UK and Ireland—Can Ireland properly claim to have taken the more enlightened approach?" (2000) 8 I.S.L.R. 1.

[85] [1941] I.R. 569.

[86] See generally, Hogan and Morgan, *Administrative Law in Ireland*, 3rd edn (Dublin: Round Hall Sweet & Maxwell, 1998), Ch.13.

[87] RSC Ord.84 r.18(2). See also RSC Ord.84 r.25(1). See generally, Ch.10, General Application, specifically para.10–103.

[88] [1996] E.L.R. 244.

[89] As per the decision of the Supreme Court in *Garda Representation Association v Ireland*, unreported, Supreme Court, December 18, 1987.

1–60 However, in general terms, it appears that as:

> "the specialist public law remedies of prohibition and mandamus often fulfil
> the role which might otherwise be discharged by the injunction, applications
> for injunctions in public law are not very common".[90]

1–61 That said, there is still a use for injunctions in this area. This is
particularly so as "mandatory and prohibitory injunctions are wider in scope
than mandamus and prohibition."[91]

D. JURISDICTION OF THE DOMESTIC COURTS

1. Introduction

1–62 The Supreme,[92] High[93] and Circuit[94] Courts can all deal with applications
for relief by way of equitable injunction. Sections 7 and 8 of the Courts
(Supplemental Provisions) Act 1961 vested in the Supreme and High Courts
respectively the jurisdiction vested in their predecessor.[95] Section 22 of the 1961
Act provides for the equivalent jurisdiction of the Circuit Court. As such, the
equitable jurisdiction of the courts to grant injunctions endures, and has been
added to in certain areas of the law by statutory provisions.[96]

1–63 The Circuit and High Courts act as courts of first instance, with the
Supreme Court acting as the ultimate court of appeal. Applications for equitable
injunctions cannot be brought in the District Court, as it is not a court with
equitable jurisdiction.[97] The criteria and considerations which apply in relation
to determining whether to bring an injunction application in the Circuit or High

---

[90] Hogan and Morgan, *Administrative Law in Ireland*, 3rd edn (Dublin: Round Hall Sweet &
      Maxwell, 1998), p.701.
[91] per Collins and O'Reilly, *Civil Proceedings and the State*, 2nd edn (Dublin: Thomson Round
      Hall, 2004), p.107.
[92] See s.18 of the Courts of Justice Act 1924 which, inter alia, transferred prior jurisdiction. See
      also the Courts (Supplemental Provisions) Act 1961, s.7.
[93] See s.17 of the Courts of Justice Act 1924 which, inter alia, transferred prior jurisdiction. See
      also the Courts (Supplemental Provisions) Act 1961, s.8.
[94] See s.51 of the Courts of Justice Act 1924. See also the Courts (Supplemental Provisions) Act
      1961, s.22.
[95] With the enactment of the 1922 and 1937 Constitutions, all pre-existing law was adopted as
      part of the law of the Irish State except to the extent that it was inconsistent with the
      Constitution. See Keane, *Equity and the Law of Trusts in the Republic of Ireland* (London:
      Butterworths, 1988), p.22.
[96] See Ch.11, Specific Statutory Injunctions.
[97] Although as will be seen in Ch.11, though statutory intervention, the District Court may in
      certain circumstances make orders which, broadly speaking, are similar in form and effect to
      equitable injunctions.

Court (other than where this is prescribed by statute) include in the first instance the monetary value of the claim concerned, although as will be seen, the power of the Circuit Court to hear injunction applications is circumscribed by statute.[98] As with any litigation, the costs of bringing a case in either the Circuit or High Court will often be another relevant factor in determining where to bring an application.

2. The Superior Courts

(a) The Supreme Court

1–64 The Courts (Supplemental Provisions) Act 1961 confirms that the present Supreme Court has equitable jurisdiction, with s.7(2) of the 1961 Act stating that:

> "There shall be vested in the Supreme Court—
> (a) all jurisdiction which was, immediately before the commencement of Part I of the Act of 1924, vested in or capable of being exercised by the former Court of Appeal in Southern Ireland[99] or any judge or judges thereof and was, immediately before the operative date, vested in or capable of being exercised by the existing Supreme Court,
> (b) all jurisdiction which, by virtue of any enactment which is applied by section 48 of this Act, was, immediately before the operative date, vested in or capable of being exercised by the existing Supreme Court."[100]

1–65 The Supreme Court will deal with any injunction applications by way of appeal from a determination of the High Court. It does not consider injunctions as a court of first instance.

(b) The High Court

1–66 As has been seen,[101] jurisdiction was conferred on the High Court to grant interlocutory and perpetual injunctions by virtue of s.28(8) of the Supreme Court of Judicature Act (Ireland) 1877.

1–67 The provisions of s.28(8) are applied to the present High Court by ss.8(2) and 8(3) of the Courts (Supplemental Provisions) Act 1961. These subsections of s.8 state that:

---

[98] See para.1–74.
[99] Wylie, *The Judicature Acts (Ireland)* (Dublin: Sealy, Bryers and Walker, 1906), p.24 observes in relation to s.24 of the Judicature Act (Ireland) 1877 that: "In *Jones v Chennell*, 8 Ch D 501, it was held that under the Judicature Act every order is appealable unless we find some provision that it is not to be subject to appeal."
[100] See the general analysis of this section by Delany, *The Courts Acts 1924–1997*, 2nd edn (Dublin: Round Hall Ltd, 2000), p.226.
[101] See para.1–30.

"(2) There shall be vested in the High Court—

(a) all jurisdiction which was, immediately before the commencement of Part I of the Act of 1924 vested in or capable of being exercised by the former High Court of Justice in Southern Ireland or any division or judge thereof and was, immediately before the operative date, vested in or capable of being exercised by the existing High Court,

(b) all jurisdiction which, by virtue of any enactment which is applied by section 48 of this Act, was, immediately before the operative date, vested in or capable of being exercised by the existing High Court.

(3) The jurisdictions vested in the High Court shall include all powers, duties and authorities incident to any and every part of the jurisdictions so vested."

1–68 The present High Court thus has the power to grant equitable injunctions. However, it should be noted that applications for injunctions may not be brought before the Master of the High Court. This is because of the provisions of s.25(2) of the Courts and Courts Officers Act 1995, which provides that:

"Without prejudice to the powers of the Master of the High Court under the Jurisdiction of the Courts and the Enforcement of Judgements (European Communities) Act, 1988, the Master of the High Court shall not exercise any function, power or jurisdiction in respect of any of the following matters:

...

(c) the granting of injunctions;"

(c) Role of the High Court Commercial Division: The Commercial Court

1–69 The Commercial Court commenced operation on January 12, 2004.[102] It deals with "commercial proceedings". These are defined in RSC Ord.63A r.1, as including:

"claims in contract or tort arising out of business transactions where the value of the claim is not less than €1 million, intellectual property cases (including passing off), certain types of arbitration claims and appeals from, or judicial review applications in respect of, any statutory body where the judge in charge of the list considers that, having regard to the commercial or any other aspect of such an application, it is one appropriate for entry into the commercial list."[103]

1–70 One of the aims of the Commercial Court upon its inception was to provide an expeditious means of bringing disputes to a resolution or determination. The functioning of the court has borne witness to the achievement of

---

[102] See generally, Dowling, *The Commercial Court* (Dublin: Thomson Round Hall, 2007).
[103] For a clear, comprehensive overview of the aims and objectives of the Commercial Court, see Mr Justice Peter Kelly, "The Commercial Court" (2004) 9(1) Bar Rev. 4.

this aim. This is important from the point of view of injunctions. Prior to the operation of the Commercial Court, most interlocutory injunctions in particular would have been sought on the basis that it could take a number of years before a matter came to trial. However, for matters which can be defined as "commercial proceedings", seeking entry into the commercial list brings with it the considerable advantage that a matter can be speedily case-managed to a hearing date. This in effect diminishes the need to seek an interlocutory injunction.

1–71 A somewhat analogous situation developed in England after the introduction of the Civil Procedure Rules (CPR). This can be explained by reference to a discrete area of the law, namely passing off. As observed by one English author,[104] prior to the introduction of the CPR, most passing-off actions brought in their wake an application for an interlocutory injunction. Full trials were relatively rare. Since the introduction of the CPR "it is noticeable that the situation is almost precisely reversed. Full trials in passing-off actions are now commonplace ...". This is explained in the following terms:

> "... it is now assumed that even a substantial passing-off action can be brought to trial within a few months from issue of the claim form, rather than the two or three years which might have been typical previously ... One result of this is that a claimant seeking an interim injunction has to convince the court of two propositions which will not easily be satisfied: first, that the damage he will suffer over a period measured in weeks or months, rather than years, will truly be irreparable in the sense of *American Cyanamid*[105]; and secondly that the effort expended on both sides on the application for the interim injunction, including evidence on the balance of convenience, would not have been better spent in going to full trial on an expedited basis."[106]

1–72 Another result of the accelerated process arising out of the change of regime in England is the fact, from a defendant's point of view, that:

> "From the defendant's point of view too, the prospect of having an interim injunction or undertaking discharged in a few months' time, and of being able to recover on the cross-undertaking in damages, means that interim undertakings are likely to be offered more willingly ... and the offer of an undertaking or the grant of an interim injunction are not the near-certain conclusions of the litigation which they were previously."[107]

---

[104] Wadlow, *The Law of Passing Off* (London: Sweet and Maxwell, 2004), p.795.
[105] As to which, see Ch.6, Interlocutory Applications.
[106] Wadlow, *The Law of Passing Off* (London: Sweet and Maxwell, 2004), pp.795–796.
[107] Wadlow, *The Law of Passing Off* (London: Sweet and Maxwell, 2004), p.796. Wadlow also observes that contested injunctions are now dealt with on a much more abbreviated timescale, are consequently more "rough and ready" and, as such, pre-C.P.R. decisions awarding or refusing interim injunctions are no longer of much value, even analogically.

1–73 The commercial list is by its nature a small one relative to the significant number of non-"commercial proceedings" which come before the courts day to day. However, in appropriate circumstances, bringing a case to the Commercial Court does provide a de facto alternative to interlocutory applications. It may also influence the considerations as to whether an interlocutory injunction should be sought, by analogy with the reasons set out above. As appropriate, interim and interlocutory injunctions may be sought and granted in accordance with the usual principles,[108] even when proceedings have been entered into the commercial list.

3. The Circuit Court

1–74 Under s.33(1) of the County Officers and Courts (Ireland) Act 1877, the "Civil Bill Courts" in Ireland had the same powers as the Chancery Division of the High Court to grant injunctions.[109] However, such jurisdiction to grant an injunction only enabled County Court judges to grant an injunction as ancillary relief, as distinct from dealing with a suit in which an injunction was the primary relief.[110] Therefore, by virtue of s.51 of the Courts of Justice Act 1924 transfer provisions, the Circuit Court did not have jurisdiction to grant a primary injunction unrelated to property.[111]

1–75 The key section in terms of the jurisdiction of the Circuit Court is s.22(1)(a) of the Courts (Supplemental Provisions) Act 1961, which reads:

> "Subject to paragraphs (b)[112] and (c)[113] of this subsection, the Circuit Court shall, concurrently with the High Court, have all the jurisdiction of the High Court to hear and determine any proceedings of the kind mentioned in column (2) of the Third Schedule to this Act at any reference number."[114]

---

[108] See Ch.6, Interlocutory Applications and Ch.7, Interim Applications.

[109] See generally, Babington, *The Jurisdiction and Practice of County Courts in Ireland* (Abingdon: Professional Books, 1910; 1980 reprint), p.8.

[110] *Sligo Corporation v Gilbride* [1929] I.R. 351.

[111] per Geoghegan J. in *Rodgers v Mangan,* unreported, High Court, Geoghegan J., July 15, 1996, citing "the Babington edition of Osborne's County Court Practice and the enactments and case law therein referred to."

[112] Which provides that: "Unless the necessary parties to the proceedings in a cause sign, either before or at any time during the hearing, the form of consent prescribed by rules of court, the Circuit Court shall not, by virtue of paragraph (a) of this subsection, have jurisdiction to hear and determine any cause of the kind mentioned in column (2) of the Third Schedule to this Act at a particular reference number in the case mentioned in column (3) of the said Schedule at that reference number." Column 2 is headed "Civil proceedings in respect of which jurisdiction is conferred on the Circuit Court." Column 3 is headed "Exclusion of jurisdiction (except by consent of necessary parties) in certain cases."

[113] Which provides that: "The Circuit Court shall not, by virtue of paragraph (a) of this subsection, have jurisdiction to hear and determine any matter of the kind mentioned in column (2) of the Third Schedule to this Act at a particular reference number in the case mentioned in column (3) of the said Schedule at that reference number." Column Three deals with exclusion of jurisdiction.

[114] See the general analysis of this section by Delany, *The Courts Acts 1924–1997*, 2nd edn (Dublin: Round Hall Ltd, 2000), p.242.

1–76 The relevant part of Column (2) of the Third Schedule of the 1961 Act provides, at reference 27, for "an action (in relation to property) claiming an injunction, otherwise than as ancillary to other relief".

1–77 In other words, the jurisdiction of the Circuit Court to grant injunctive relief as a primary relief is limited to the class of cases set out in the relevant section of the Third Schedule. These cases can in essence be summarised as cases involving property, within the applicable value.[115] However, the power of the Circuit Court to grant injunctive relief where such relief is ancillary to other relief is not limited in this way. This leads to a consideration of what is meant by "property" in the context of the legislation.

(a) The Meaning of "Property"

1–78 The word "property" as used in the 1961 Act has a more expansive interpretation than might at first seem apparent. For example, as could be divined from the name, it would appear to contemplate intellectual property[116] (although the value of such cases is such that it is more likely that the monetary jurisdiction of the High Court is more appropriate in a lot of intellectual property cases). There are various cases in which it has been made clear that the right to employment falls within the word "property". As such, if the value of a contract of employment is within the jurisdiction of the Circuit Court, an injunction related to a contract of employment may be sought from that court[117] (again, however, many contracts of employment in relation to which injunctions are sought are in excess of the monetary jurisdiction of the Circuit Court and, as such, the injunction application is brought in the High Court). However, caution needs to be exercised in that regard. This is evident from the case of *Rodgers v Mangan*.[118] In that case the injunction by way of primary relief to which the plaintiff was entitled was an injunction to restrain wrongful interference with his business. Geoghegan J. felt that this was not an action in relation to property, albeit acknowledging that "one could argue that the goodwill of the business has a value and that in that sense it might be said to be an action relating to property." However, he determined that the injunction concerned the "wrongful causing of financial loss by a wrongful activity."

1–79 If the matter which it is sought to remedy by way of injunction (as a primary relief) is not one which falls within the term of the Third Schedule of

---

[115] The applicable rateable valuation of land is now the euro equivalent of IR£200.
[116] In *Phonographic Performance (Ireland) Ltd v Cody* [1994] 2 I.L.R.M. 214 at 247, Keane J. stated that: "The right of the creator of a literary, dramatic, musical or artistic work not to have his or her creation stolen or plagiarised is a right of private property within the meaning of Articles 40.3.2 and 43.1 of the Constitution, as is the similar right of a person who has employed his or her technical skills and/or capital in the sound recording of a musical work."
[117] As occurred, for example, in *Doyle v Grangeford Precast Concrete Ltd* [1998] E.L.R. 260.
[118] unreported, High Court, Geoghegan J., July 15, 1996.

the 1961 Act, then the Circuit Court does not have jurisdiction to deal with it. In such circumstances, the application will have to be brought in the High Court.

1–80 An illustration of the importance of this point is the *Rodgers* case. In that case, an injunction was sought in the High Court to prohibit the defendant from operating a bus service along a specified route. An interlocutory injunction was granted, but at the full hearing an injunction was no longer necessary and the plaintiff was awarded £3,000 (these were damages within the jurisdiction of the District Court) and the costs of the action. Geoghegan J. had to determine, following an argument from the defendant, and having regard to the damages awarded, whether the costs of the injunction application should be Circuit Court costs (and whether the costs of the plenary hearing—by which time injunctions were no longer necessary—should be District Court costs).

1–81 Geoghegan J. held, as seen above,[119] that the injunction to which the plaintiff would have been entitled was not an injunction to restrain interference with property or the enjoyment of property but with the wrongful causing of financial loss by a wrongful activity. This was not included in the category of actions referred to in the Third Schedule of the 1961 Act. Noting that the Circuit Court did not have jurisdiction to grant an injunction by way of primary relief in an action not relating to property, he held that the High Court was the lowest court having jurisdiction to grant the reliefs to which the plaintiff was entitled at the commencement of the action. That being so, Geoghegan J. held that the plaintiff was entitled to the full costs of the injunction application, taxed as High Court costs.

1–82 A not dissimilar issue arose in *Beaumont v Figgis*.[120] In that case the court was faced with the question of whether, having regard to the terms of the applicable legislation dealing with costs in the context of jurisdictional thresholds (s.12 of the Courts of Justice Act 1936), an amount of damages awarded in lieu of an injunction was the equivalent to holding that the plaintiff was entitled to an injunction. The Supreme Court held that the sum of £35 awarded as damages in lieu of an injunction was the equivalent to so holding. As such, Murnaghan J. stated that he found it "impossible to say that the amount recovered by the appellant did not exceed £300",[121] that being the statutory threshold in the context of the recovery of costs.[122]

---

119 See para.1–78.
120 [1945] I.R. 78.
121 [1945] I.R. 78 at 96.
122 Although *cf. Buckley v Healy* [1965] I.R. 618 at 635, in which despite the fact that damages of £30 were awarded, Walsh J. observed that it was "quite clear that the learned trial Judge was not saying that the plaintiff had any ground for obtaining an injunction."

4. Inherent Jurisdiction

1–83 It has been argued in the context of a *Mareva* injunction[123] that a court also possesses an inherent jurisdiction to, "make any order which it deems necessary to protect, vindicate and safeguard its authority."[124]

1–84 In his decision in *Bambrick v Cobley*[125] Clarke J. observed that the "true basis" of the jurisdiction of the court to grant a *Mareva* injunction:

> "is the exercise by the court of its inherent power to prevent parties from placing their assets beyond the likely reach of the court in the event of a successful action."[126]

1–85 This dictum certainly suggests, although perhaps not definitively, that there is some form of inherent jurisdiction in the courts in terms of their ability to grant injunctions.

1–86 Although there appears to be no definitive judicial pronouncement on this point in the wider context of equitable injunctions generally, there appears to be no objection in principle to a court exercising its inherent jurisdiction to grant an injunction if the need to do so arises. It appears to be accepted in England that this is possible. For example, in *Re C*,[127] the amputation of the plaintiff's leg against his will was prevented by means of a *quia timet* injunction, on the basis, according to Thorpe J., that the court had an inherent jurisdiction to rule by way of injunction that an individual is capable of refusing or consenting to medical treatment.

5. The District Court

1–87 The jurisdiction of both the Circuit and Superior Courts to grant injunctions derives from statute and is to be exercised in accordance with the same principles of law and equity which governed those courts' predecessors before 1924, subject to the fact that such principles must of course be consistent with the Constitution.

1–88 The District Court has no such statutory power. The District Court's jurisdiction derived primarily from s.77 of the Courts of Justice Act 1924, which gave the court:

---

123 As to which, see generally, Ch.8, Commercial Injunctions.
124 Courtney, *Mareva Injunctions* (Dublin: Butterworths, 1998), p.57.
125 [2006] I.L.R.M. 81.
126 [2006] I.L.R.M. 81 at 90.
127 [1994] 1 W.L.R. 290.

"all powers, jurisdictions, and authorities which immediately before the 6th day of December, 1922, were vested by statute or otherwise in Justices or a Justice of the Peace sitting at Petty Sessions."[128]

1–89 This did not include the power to grant an injunction, nor was such power conferred by the 1924 Act.

1–90 Section 33 of the Courts (Supplemental Provisions) Act 1961 provided that there is vested in and transferred to the District Court all jurisdiction under ss.77 and 78 of the 1924 Act. Prior to 1961, the District Court did not have the jurisdiction to grant injunctions (or indeed equitable jurisdiction) and so, by virtue of the provisions of the 1961 Act, there was no such jurisdiction to carry over.[129]

1–91 The basic rule is thus that the District Court is restricted to dealing with whatever has been expressly conferred on it by legislation.[130] Although the District Court does not have equitable jurisdiction to grant injunctions, statutory provisions exist which provide that the District Court may make certain orders in, for example, family law matters. Such orders are in many respects similar in effect to injunctions.[131]

1–92 Thus, even if the injunctive relief sought is in the nature of secondary relief, any proceedings seeking such injunctive relief must be brought in the Circuit Court given that the District Court will not be able to grant equitable injunctive relief. This is the case even if the amount claimed is below the Circuit Court's jurisdictional threshold. For example, if damages for breach of contract are sought in the District Court on the basis that the amount sought falls within the monetary jurisdiction of the District Court, and an injunction is sought as a secondary relief, the entire claim will have to be brought in the Circuit Court if the injunctive relief is to be granted.

E. Initiating Proceedings

1. The Superior Courts

1–93 There are a number of originating documents in the Superior Courts on foot of which an injunction may be sought. As will be seen,[132] however, there is

---

[128] See also s.78, which transferred "all jurisdiction which at the commencement of this Act was vested in or capable of being exercised by District Justices under the provisions of the District Justices (Temporary Provisions) Act 1923."

[129] See, for example, the decision of Geoghegan J. in *Rodgers v Mangan*, unreported, High Court, Geoghegan J., July 15, 1996, in which he made reference to the fact that the District Court has no jurisdiction to grant injunctions.

[130] Byrne & McCutcheon, *The Irish Legal System*, 4th edn (Dublin: Butterworths, 2001) p.172.

[131] See further, Ch.8, Specific Statutory Injunctions.

[132] See para.1–95.

a residual question as to whether an injunction may be claimed on foot of all originating documents.

(a) Plenary Summons

1–94 In the High Court, an injunction is usually sought by means of a plenary summons. Such a summons is used for the commencement of plenary proceedings with pleadings and a hearing on oral evidence.[133]

(b) Summary/Special Summons

1–95 A summary summons is used where proceedings can be disposed of summarily without pleadings.[134] In *Re Greendale Developments Ltd (No. 2)*,[135] Keane J. suggested that *Mareva* injunctions[136]—and indeed injunctions generally—might be appropriately sought only on foot of a plenary summons. He stated that:

> "the notice of motion … claimed … an injunction in the *Mareva* form. No issue appears to have been raised as to the court's jurisdiction to grant such an injunction, although as a general rule it is only in proceedings commenced by a plenary summons, that relief in the form of an injunction may be granted, but no argument was addressed to us on this point."[137]

1–96 This appears to have been the first time that such a concern was explicitly raised. A few years previously, a *Mareva* injunction was sought on foot of a summary summons in the case of *Deutsche Bank AG v Murtagh*.[138] The injunction was granted by Costello J., with no issue taken in relation to the fact that the action had been brought on foot of a summary summons. It is of course a very valid concern in so far as the Rules of the Superior Courts are very prescriptive about the matters which may be brought by way of summary summons (and indeed by special summons). These matters do not include injunctions.[139]

1–97 In the later case of *Criminal Assets Bureau v Hunt*,[140] decided some years after the *Greendale Developments* case, the question arose again, albeit in a different, statutory, context. The plaintiffs had brought an action by way of

---

[133] See Delany & McGrath, *Civil Procedure in the Superior Courts*, 2nd edn (Dublin: Thomson Round Hall, 2005), p.69.

[134] See Delany & McGrath, *Civil Procedure in the Superior Courts*, 2nd edn (Dublin: Thomson Round Hall, 2005), p.70.

[135] [1998] 1 I.R. 8.

[136] See Ch.11, Commercial Injunctions.

[137] [1998] 1 I.R. 8 at 32.

[138] [1995] 2 I.R. 122; [1995] 1 I.L.R.M. 381.

[139] As to what is included, see generally Delany & McGrath, *Civil Procedure in the Superior Courts*, 2nd edn (Dublin: Thomson Round Hall, 2005), Ch.2.

[140] [2003] 2 I.R. 168.

plenary summons, whereas the defendants argued that the relevant applicable legislative provision prescribed that actions should only be brought by way of summary summonses. The provision in question was s.966 of the Taxes Consolidation Act 1997 which provides, inter alia, that, "the proceedings may be commenced by summary summons ...". Keane C.J. stated that:

> "It can be inferred from the written submissions on behalf of the plaintiff in the present case that this form of proceeding was adopted by them in the present case because it wished to obtain a *Mareva* injunction freezing the assets of the first and second defendants while the extent of their liability to tax was determined and it considered it to be at least doubtful whether such relief could be obtained in proceedings commenced by way of summary summons. That is perfectly understandable, but it is for the Oireachtas, and not for the courts, to fill any lacuna that there may be in the powers of the plaintiff in this area."[141]

1–98 This dictum must of course be viewed in the specific legislative context within which it was delivered.

1–99 It is clear from this that there is still a measure of uncertainty as to whether an injunction may be sought on foot of a summary summons.[142] Courtney takes the view that a consideration of the Rules of the Superior Courts does not support Keane J.'s suggestion in *Greendale Developments* that injunctions must be sought on foot of a plenary summons.[143] A variation on this argument is that in the normal course, unless otherwise prescribed by statute, an injunction should be sought on foot of a plenary summons, with a *Mareva* injunction being a limited exception to this.

1–100 The approach by Peart J. in *Limerick County Council v Tobin*[144] evidences a very practical approach to the matter, albeit in a somewhat different context. In that case Peart J. indicated that whether the proceedings are commenced by originating notice of motion or by plenary summons, the task (in that case, in the context of determining whether to grant an injunction pursuant to s.160 of the Planning and Development Act 2000) of the court is broadly similar. Peart J. found it "reasonable" to avail oneself of the prescribed procedure under s.160 of the Planning and Development Act 2000 in the first instance. He felt that if an issue arose subsequently in relation to pleadings, oral evidence and discovery, the court could make any directions as to pleadings and

---

[141] [2003] 2 I.R. 168 at 185. The headnote to this case appears to incorrectly make reference to s.966 providing for the commencement of proceedings by plenary summons.

[142] Or, by extension, a special summons, which is used for a set of prescribed claim where pleadings are not necessary: see Delany & McGrath, *Civil Procedure in the Superior Courts*, 2nd edn (Dublin: Thomson Round Hall, 2005), p.71.

[143] *Mareva Injunctions* (Dublin: Butterworths, 1998), p.296.

[144] unreported, High Court, Peart J., August 15, 2005.

mode of trial as necessary. By extrapolation, it might be argued that if an injunction is sought on foot of a summary summons, but issue is taken with this, the court can make any directions in relation to pleadings as necessary.

1–101 However, based on the uncertainty surfaced by the dictum of Keane J. in *Greendale*, if a party has commenced proceedings by way of summary summons, not believing that an injunction was necessary, yet finds himself in a position whereby an injunction is subsequently required, the prudent course in the circumstances would seem to be to issue new plenary proceedings seeking the injunction in question. Such an approach should minimise any risk that an injunction might not be granted simply by virtue of the format of the proceedings (albeit that would be a very harsh outcome).

(c) Originating Notice of Motion

1–102 At a broader level, injunctions may also be granted on foot of an originating notice of motion. For example, an injunction may be granted on foot of an application pursuant to s.205 of the Companies Act 1963, as occurred in the case of *McGilligan v O'Grady*.[145] In the circumstances, and although obiter, it would seem that Keane J.'s dictum in *Greendale Developments* is, on its face, unduly broad. However, he did refer to his observations being a "general rule".

(d) Judicial Review

1–103 A declaration or injunction may be sought by way of an application for judicial review. This is provided for by the Rules of the Superior Courts, specifically RSC Ord.84 r.18(2). Rules of the Superior Courts Ord.84 r.25 makes provision for interlocutory applications in proceedings on an application for judicial review. In *Harding v Cork Co. Council (No. 1)*,[146] Kelly J. held that the phrase "interlocutory applications" was wide enough to contemplate interlocutory injunctions.

1–104 *Gannon v Minister for Defence*[147] concerned an application for an interlocutory injunction pending a determination in relation to various declarations and a claim for damages. The plaintiff alleged that the defendants had acted unlawfully, in breach of his statutory contract of employment, ultra vires the Defence Forces Regulations and in breach of the principles of natural and constitutional justice in relation to his purported discharge from the Defence Forces. Peart J. had to deal with the argument that the plaintiff ought to have proceeded by way of judicial review under RSC Ord.84 (with the attendant

---

[145] [1999] 1 I.R. 346 at 362; [1999] 1 I.L.R.M. 303 at 319. See in particular the dictum of Keane J. in the Supreme Court. See Ch.10, General Application, para.10–19.

[146] [2006] 1 I.R. 294; [2006] 2 I.L.R.M. 292.

[147] unreported, High Court, Peart J., August 8, 2005.

implications in terms of needing to seek leave to bring judicial review proceedings) rather than by way of plenary summons. However, Peart J. found that the plaintiff, a member of the armed forces, even though "engaged upon an occupation which has a clear public dimension, and … engaged by virtue of a contract prescribed by statute" was challenging a decision which affected only him. As such, Peart J. believed it to be "so akin to a claim for wrongful dismissal as to make no distinction". In the circumstances, he found no need to order that the proceedings be discontinued or replaced.

2. The Circuit Court

1–105 In terms of seeking an injunction in the Circuit Court, the matter must fall within the matters specified in the Third Schedule of the 1961 Act if the injunction is sought by way of primary relief, as considered above. Regard should also be had to the monetary limits of the Circuit Court.

1–106 When an injunction is sought by way of relief in a civil bill, an equity civil bill,[148] as distinct from an ordinary civil bill, should be drafted.[149] The equity civil bill must disclose such facts as may be necessary to identify the jurisdiction of the court. The question arose in *Kearns v Deery*[150] as to whether the fact that an injunction was sought on an ordinary civil bill was fatal to a claim. In that case a mandatory injunction had been sought and granted on foot of an ordinary civil bill. The applicants sought to set aside the injunction order for this reason, claiming that the "wrong" procedure had been used. However, the respondent judge ruled that he had the power to amend the civil bill to an equity civil bill and did so, thus continuing the injunction. In refusing leave to apply for judicial review, Blayney J. determined that whether the pleadings could be amended or not was a matter of discretion for the individual Circuit Court judge, and that the Circuit Court Rules suggested that an equity civil bill is a derivative of a civil bill. Notwithstanding this, the best practice is ensure that an equity civil bill is drafted when seeking injunctive relief.

F. DOMESTIC ANTI-SUIT INJUNCTIONS

1. Introduction

1–107 Anti-suit injunctions are a device by which a party can apply for an injunction in his own jurisdiction to restrain his opponent, who is bringing

---

[148] See RCC Ord.5 r.1, Commencement of Proceedings. See also RCC Ord.46.
[149] See the dictum of Geoghegan J. in *Rodgers v Mangan*, unreported, High Court, Geoghegan J., July 15, 1996.
[150] [1993] I.L.R.M. 496.

proceedings in a foreign jurisdiction, from continuing with his action.[151] Layton and Mercer identify two situations in which anti-suit injunctions are of relevance in the context of foreign proceedings. The first is to restrain a breach of an exclusive jurisdiction or arbitration agreement. The second is to restrain a defendant:

> "whose conduct in pursuing the proceedings falls within a nebulous class of wrongful conduct, variously described as 'unconscionable', 'vexatious and oppressive' or an abuse of process."[152]

1–108 Infrequently invoked in Ireland in that context, the theory underlying such an injunction is that the jurisdiction is exercised "where it is appropriate to avoid injustice".[153]

2. Domestic Anti-Suit Injunction

1–109 However, an application may also be brought to injunct proceedings in an inferior court in this jurisdiction. For example, in *Colmey v Pinewood Developments Ltd*,[154] an injunction was sought restraining the defendant from doing any act or thing in purported pursuance of any similar proceedings or any proceedings of the same nature as ejectment proceedings which had been commenced in the District Court. An injunction was granted on an ex parte basis by Morris J. in the High Court.[155]

1–110 An application may not in general terms be brought to injunct proceedings in a court of like jurisdiction. However, there are a number of alternatives to seeking an injunction where it is sought to bring a halt to court proceedings. These include a stay on proceedings; an application to prevent a winding-up petition; and an *Isaac Wunder* order. These will briefly be considered in turn.

3. Stay

1–111 An application may be sought pursuant to s.5 of the Arbitration Act 1980 in circumstances where a party to an arbitration agreement seeks to stay

---

151 See, for example, *Lett v Lett* [1906] 1 I.R. 618 at 630. See generally, Ch.2, Extraterritorial Jurisdiction.
152 Layton and Mercer, *European Civil Practice Volume 1*, 2nd edn (London: Thomson Sweet and Maxwell, 2004), p.142.
153 *Castanho v Brown & Root (UK) Ltd* [1981] A.C. 557 at 573; [1980] 3 W.L.R. 991 at 998, per Lord Scarman. See also *Hedley v Bates* (1880) 13 Ch D 498 at 504, per Jessel M.R. in the context of the equivalent provision of s.28(8) of the Supreme Court of Judicature Act (Ireland) 1877.
154 [1994] 3 I.R. 360; [1995] 1 I.L.R.M. 331.
155 On the interlocutory application, Carroll J. refused the injunction on the basis that the court could assume that the District Court judge would administer justice in accordance with the

proceedings commenced in the courts in order that a matter be remitted to arbitration.[156]

4. Restraining a Petition

1–112 The courts may also restrain a winding-up petition, "where the plaintiff company has established at least a prima facie case that its presentation would constitute an abuse of process".[157]

5. Isaac Wunder Order

1–113 An application may also be brought to restrain a plaintiff from instituting suits against particular defendants without the leave of the court. An order granted on such an application is commonly known as an *Isaac Wunder* order, after the case in which such a form of order was acknowledged, *Wunder v Hospitals Trust (1940) Ltd*.[158] The purpose of such an order is, in essence, to prevent an abuse of court processes.

1–114 The inherent jurisdiction of the courts to make such an order was explained by Keane C.J. in *Riordan v Ireland (No. 4)*[159] in the following terms:

> "It is, however, the case that there is vested in this Court, as there is in the High Court, an inherent jurisdiction to restrain the institution of proceedings by named persons in order to ensure that the process of the court is not abused by repeated attempts to reopen litigation or to pursue litigation which is plainly groundless and vexatious. The court is bound to uphold the rights of other citizens, including their right to be protected from unnecessary harassment and expense, rights which are enjoyed by the holders of public office as well as by private citizens. This court would be failing in its duty, as would the High Court, if it allowed its processes to be repeatedly invoked in order to reopen issues already determined or to pursue groundless and vexatious litigation."[160]

---

law. Carroll J. felt that the balance of convenience lay in preserving free access to the District Court.

[156] See further, Ch.10, General Application, para.10–08.

[157] per Keane J. in *Truck and Machinery Sales Ltd v Marubeni Komatzo Ltd* [1996] 1 I.R. 12 at 27. See further, Ch.10, General Application, para.10–34.

[158] unreported, Supreme Court, January 24, 1967. See also unreported, Supreme Court, February 22, 1972. For a more detailed analysis, see Delany & McGrath, *Civil Procedure in the Superior Courts*, 2nd edn (Dublin: Thomson Round Hall, 2005), p.428.

[159] [2001] 3 I.R. 365.

[160] [2001] 3 I.R. 365 at 370. Quoted by Denham J. in *Kiely v Creative Labs (Irl) Ltd*, unreported, Supreme Court, June 19, 2002. See also *London and Global Ltd (In Liquidation) v Lamb*,

1–115 However, it is important to note that such an order should only be made in very rare circumstances, "but should be made when a court comes to the conclusion that its processes are being abused".[161]

1–116 The circumstances in which an order might be justified were set out in detail in *Riordan v Ireland (No. 5)*[162] by O'Caoimh J. and, as summarised by MacMenamin J. in *McMahon v WJ Law & Co. LLP*,[163] are:

"1. The habitual or persistent institution of vexatious or frivolous proceedings against parties to earlier proceedings.

2. The earlier history of the matter, including whether proceedings have been brought without any reasonable ground, or have been brought habitually and persistently without reasonable ground.

3. The bringing up of actions to determine an issue already determined by a court of competent jurisdiction, when it is obvious that such action cannot succeed, and where such action would lead to no possible good or where no reasonable person could expect to obtain relief.

4. The initiation of an action for an improper purpose including the oppression of other parties by multifarious proceedings brought for purposes other than the assertion of legitimate rights.

5. The rolling forward of issues into a subsequent action and repeated and supplemented, often with actions brought against the lawyers who have acted for or against the litigant in earlier proceedings.

6. A failure on the part of a person instituting legal proceedings to pay the costs of successful proceedings in the context of unsuccessful appeals from judicial decisions. Prima facie a number of these factors may be present in the instant case."[164]

unreported, High Court, Peart J., November 15, 2004 and *Devrajan v KPMG*, unreported, High Court, Hanna J., January 20, 2006.

[161] per Costello J. in *O'Malley v Irish Nationwide Building Society*, unreported, High Court, Costello J., January 21, 1994.

[162] [2001] 4 I.R. 463.

[163] unreported, High Court, MacMenamin J., March 2, 2007.

[164] See also, *London and Global Ltd v Lamb*, unreported, High Court, Peart J., November 15, 2004.

CHAPTER 2

EXTRATERRITORIAL JURISDICTION

A. INTRODUCTION

2–01 Courts have traditionally been reluctant to grant injunctions which would affect defendants outside of the jurisdiction.[1] Factors such as deference to, and respect for, foreign sovereigns have tended to act as a brake on courts' willingness to make orders granting leave to effect service on such defendants.[2] The principle of international comity—practices adopted by states for reasons of courtesy—has also played an important role.[3] However, situations arise in which a defendant is not present within the jurisdiction but in which the case is so closely connected with Ireland or with Irish law that there is a justification for their being tried within this jurisdiction.[4] This chapter will consider the issues arising in the context of injunctions with an extraterritorial dimension.

2–02 Some background to the concept of extraterritorial applications will be set out, specifically the development of various Conventions and Regulations at European level. This will provide the basis for a more detailed consideration of how provisional and protective measures—a term which encompasses injunctions—are treated in European legal instruments. This will be followed by an overview of the rules relating to recognition and enforcement in so far as they relate to injunctions. The practical element of the various applications which can be made, as set out in the Rules of the Superior Courts (RSC), will then be considered. Finally, there will be an analysis of anti-suit injunctions. Under this form of injunction, a party can apply for an injunction in his own jurisdiction to restrain his opponent, who is bringing proceedings in a foreign jurisdiction, from continuing with his action.

---

[1] See O'Floinn & Gannon, *Practice and Procedure in the Superior Courts* (Dublin: Butterworths, Dublin, 1996) and its treatment of RSC Ord.11 r.1(g).

[2] Service is the basis for the jurisdiction of the Irish courts. See generally, Cassidy, "Service out of the jurisdiction-Part I" (2005) 1(3) J.C.P.P. 8a.

[3] See *Shipsey v British and South American Steam Navigation Company* [1936] I.R. 65 at 83. In *Mackender v Feldia* [1967] 2 Q.B. 590 at 599; [1967] 2 W.L.R. 119 at 124; [1966] 3 All E.R. 847 at 850 Lord Diplock stated that that the assertion of jurisdictional competence under the English RSC Ord.11 represented a conflict "with the general principles of comity between civilised nations", adopting the dictum of Scott L.J. in *George Monro Ltd v American Cyanamid & Chemical Corporation* [1944] K.B. 432 at 437; [1944] 1 All E.R. 386 at 388.

[4] See, for example, *Grehan v Medical Incorporated* [1986] I.R. 528; [1986] I.L.R.M. 627.

2–03 A word of caution should be sounded at the outset. The sources of the law in this area are many and varied, and it is an area which is not without complexity. There is a relatively small number of reported Irish decisions in which the courts address the relevant issues in any great detail. This means that a certain amount of guidance must be gleaned from the considerable body of English jurisprudence in this area.

B. BACKGROUND

1. Introduction

2–04 Before looking at the specific rules related to injunctions in the context of extraterritorial jurisdiction, it is important to understand the background context in which such measures were developed.

2. The Common Law and *Forum Non Conveniens*

2–05 For many years the predominant approach to extraterritorial jurisdiction in common law countries was to have regard to the concept of *forum non conveniens*. By virtue of this principle, a court would stay proceedings in favour of what was deemed to be a more appropriate forum.[5]

2–06 However, this did not mean that Irish courts could never deal with matters involving a defendant outside the jurisdiction. In *Grehan v Medical Incorporated*,[6] Walsh J. considered the circumstances in which jurisdiction may be assumed where the defendant is not present within the jurisdiction, but in which the case is so closely connected with Ireland or with Irish law that there is a justification for its being tried within this jurisdiction. Reviewing the circumstances in which provision is made for service out of the jurisdiction, Walsh J. explained that:

> "This form of procedure was first provided for in the Common Law Procedure Act, 1852, and the cases in which it could be exercised were specified in the rules of court. This was a modification of the common law position whereby courts exercised jurisdiction only where the defendant was served with the process within the jurisdiction or submitted to the jurisdiction. It was clear that such a rigid system would not always work justice for the plaintiff in such cases."[7]

---

5 See, for example, *Atlantic Star v Bona Spes (The Atlantic Star)* [1974] A.C. 436 at 475; [1973] 2 W.L.R. 795 at 820; *Spiliada Maritime Corporation v Cansulex Ltd* [1987] A.C. 460; [1986] 3 W.L.R. 972; [1986] 3 All E.R. 843.
6 [1986] I.R. 528; [1986] I.L.R.M. 627.
7 [1986] I.R. 528 at 531; [1986] I.L.R.M. 627 at 629.

2–07 Although this represented the approach in common law systems, a difference of approach in civil law jurisdictions led to a concomitant need to avoid clashes between various Member States of what is now the European Union.[8] This led to the promulgation of various Conventions at European level which have an important role to play in determining whether an application can be brought in relation to a defendant situated outside the jurisdiction.

3. European Conventions and Regulations

2–08 Although what is commonly known as the Brussels I Regulation—or Judgments Regulation—2000 is now a key element in any consideration of extraterritorial application, a number of Conventions were operative prior to 2000. The first of these conventions was the Brussels Convention of 1968.

(a) The Brussels Convention

2–09 The 1968 Brussels Convention on Jurisdiction and the Enforcement of Judgments in Civil and Commercial Matters[9] ("the Brussels Convention") was designed to "strengthen in the [European] Community the legal protection of persons therein established".[10] The Brussels Convention was introduced in order to determine the international jurisdiction of the courts of the various Contracting States, to facilitate recognition and to introduce an expeditious procedure for securing the enforcement of judgments, authentic instruments and court settlements.[11]

2–10 Simplified rules governing the jurisdiction of the Contracting States' courts in civil litigation are set out in Title II of the Brussels Convention. The Convention applies in civil and commercial matters,[12] whatever the nature of the court or tribunal, but does not extend to revenue, customs or administrative matters.[13] If the matter in question is not civil or commercial, the Convention

---

[8] See the Schlosser Report [1979] OJ C59, p.97, which identifies the fact that the idea that a national court has discretion in the exercise of its jurisdiction does not generally exist in civilian systems.

[9] Convention 72/454 on Jurisdiction and the Enforcement of Judgments in Civil and Commercial Matters of September 27, 1968, as amended by the Accession Conventions under the successive enlargements of the European Communities. For a consolidated text, see [1998] OJ C27, p.1. The text of the Convention is also scheduled to the Jurisdiction of Courts and Enforcement of Judgments Act 1988.

[10] As expressed in the Preamble.

[11] Useful guidance is provided by the Jenard and Schlosser Reports, both at [1979] OJ C59.

[12] Interpreted, according to the European Court of Justice in Case 133/78 *Gourdian v Nadler* [1979] E.C.R. 733, according to the general legal principles common to the law of the contracting states.

[13] Article 1. It also does not apply to (i) the status or legal capacity of natural persons, rights in property arising out of a matrimonial relationship, wills and succession; (ii) bankruptcy, proceedings relating to the winding-up of insolvent companies or other legal persons, judicial arrangements, compositions and analogous proceedings; (iii) social security; (iv) arbitration.

has no application. In *Babanaft International v Bassatne*[14] Kerr L.J. had the following to say in relation to the Brussels Convention:

> "… it contains the most extensive code evidencing international reciprocity in the recognition and enforcement of judgments and orders issued in foreign jurisdictions, and … it includes article 24 dealing with provisional and protective measures. The forerunner of the European Judgments Convention had been a network of bilateral conventions, and among the original six member states nearly all of these had included a provision corresponding to article 24 … So the judgments convention is now the widest embodiment of international consensus in this field, founded on decades of bilateral conventions."[15]

2–11 As will be seen, Art.24 of the Brussels Convention is a key provision in terms of "provisional and protective measures", a term which incorporates injunctions.[16]

2–12 It has been emphasised that in construing the Brussels Convention it is important to put aside pre-conceptions based on traditional common law rules. The Convention has been characterised as a "radical new regime governing the international legal relationships of the contracting states."[17] This is particularly evident from the fact that the concept of *forum non conveniens* is not a feature of the Brussels Convention.[18] In the case of *Owusu v Jackson*[19] it was held by the European Court of Justice (ECJ) that the doctrine of *forum non conveniens* was in fact incompatible with the Brussels Regulation.[20] The ECJ stated that:

> "article 2 of the Brussels Convention is mandatory in nature and that, according to its terms, there can be no derogation from the principle it lays down except in the cases expressly provided for by the Convention."[21]

---

[14] [1990] Ch.13; [1989] 1 All E.R. 433.

[15] [1990] Ch.13 at 29; [1989] 1 All E.R. 433 at 442.

[16] As noted by Layton & Mercer, *European Civil Practice Vol. I*, 2nd edn (London: Thomson Sweet & Maxwell, 2004), p.134, "the term 'interim relief' … is more familiar to English practitioners than the term "provisional measures" which is used in the Brussels-Lugano regime. For practical purposes the two terms are synonymous and, together with the term 'protective measures,' they are used to describe the wide range of order which courts may make in the course of proceedings …."

[17] per Steyn L.J. in *Continental Bank NA v Aeakos Compania Naviera SA* [1994] 1 W.L.R. 588 at 596, referring to the Jenard Report [1979] OJ C59, p.19.

[18] See the overview of Lord Goff in *Airbus Industrie GIE v Patel* [1999] 1 A.C. 119 at 131; [1998] 2 W.L.R. 686 at 692; [1998] 2 All E.R. 257 at 263.

[19] Case C–281/02 [2005] 2 W.L.R. 942; [2005] Q.B. 801.

[20] Cases such as *Intermetal Group Ltd v Worslade Trading Ltd* [1998] 2 I.R. 1, an urgent application determined on the basis of *forum non conveniens*, would now appear to have been superseded by the interpretation provided by the ECJ in *Owusu*.

[21] See also Case C-256/00 *Besix SA v Wasserreinigungsbau Alfred Kretzschmar GmbH & Co KG (Wabag)* [2003] 1 W.L.R. 1113 at 1130, para.24, and Case C-116/02 *Erich Gasser GmbH v MISAT Srl.* [2005] 1 Q.B. 1 at 35, para.72, and *Turner v Grovit* (Case C–159/02) [2005] 1 A.C. 101 at 113, para.24.

(b) The Lugano Convention

2–13 The Lugano Convention on Jurisdiction and the Enforcement of Judgments in Civil and Commercial Matters[22] ("the Lugano Convention") was adopted to supplement the Brussels Convention, and was made between the states of the European Union and the members of the European Free Trade Association (EFTA).

2–14 In *Babanaft* Kerr L.J. also referred to what would become the Lugano Convention, noting that:

> "It will probably result in the adoption of article 24 throughout virtually the whole of western Europe, and with it the decisions of the European Court concerning it."[23]

(c) Protocol on Interpretation

2–15 A 1971 Protocol on the interpretation of the Convention by the European Court of Justice was also drawn up and entered into force in 1975. By virtue of this protocol, the ECJ has the power to interpret the Brussels Convention and to give rulings thereon.[24] However, it has no such power in relation to the Lugano Convention, although Protocol 2 does provide for the exchange of information on interpretation.

(d) Brussels I Regulation

2–16 Council Regulation 44/2001 of December 22, 2000[25] on Jurisdiction and the Recognition and Enforcement of Judgments in Civil and Commercial Matters, (otherwise known as the Brussels I Regulation, or the Judgments Regulation) largely supersedes the Brussels and Lugano Conventions, except in relation to proceedings instituted prior to March 1, 2002. However, Ch.VII of the Regulation contains saving provisions for the continued operation of the Brussels and Lugano Conventions (to the extent that they are not superseded),[26] other conventions[27] and other Community instruments.[28]

---

[22] Convention 88/592, The Lugano Convention on Jurisdiction and the Enforcement of Judgments in Civil and Commercial Matters of September 16, 1988.

[23] [1990] Ch.13 at 30; [1989] 2 W.L.R. 232 at 244; [1989] 1 All E.R. 433 at 442.

[24] Useful guidance is provided by the Jenard-Moller Report on the Convention, Protocols and Declarations: [1990] OJ C189.

[25] [2001] OJ L12/1, developed on the basis that the Council of the European Union took the view that it had the power to legislate directly in the field of civil jurisdiction and judgments under Art.65 of the Treaty establishing the European Community (Art.73m of the Treaty of Rome). Although the Regulation is directly effective, the Oireachtas nonetheless passed S.I. No. 52 of 2002, the European Communities (Civil and Commercial Judgments) Regulations 2002, to give the Regulation full effect in this jurisdiction.

[26] Article 68.

[27] Article 71.

[28] Article 67.

2–17 Much of the case law on the interpretation of the Brussels and Lugano Conventions is still valid in terms of analysing the later Brussels Regulation. Indeed, the provision applicable to provisional and protective measures, including injunctions,[29] contained in the Brussels Regulation is to all intents and purposes identical to those contained in the Brussels and Lugano Conventions. Before looking at this provision in more detail,[30] some key elements of the Brussels Regulation, as well as the applicability of the various Conventions and Regulations, should be set out.

(i) Article 1

2–18 Although applicable to civil and commercial matters, Art.1 of the Regulation specifically excludes "revenue, customs or administrative matters" from its scope.[31]

2–19 The Regulation aims to promote legal certainty,[32] with jurisdiction again allocated on the basis of a set of well-defined rules. In that regard, Arts 2 and 3 of the Regulation are the significant Articles.

(ii) Article 2

2–20 The guiding principle of jurisdiction, as set out in Art.2 of the Brussels I Regulation, is that persons domiciled in a Member State are, regardless of their nationality, to be sued in the courts of that Member State. As to what is meant by domicile, it is made clear at Art.11 of the European Communities (Civil and Commercial Judgments) Regulations 2002, which sets out the domestic effect of the Brussels I Regulation, that domicile is determined by whether an individual is ordinarily resident in another Member State. In *Deutsche Bank AG v Murtagh*[33] (albeit in the context of the Brussels Convention), Costello J. held that:

> "the traditional common law principles relating to the concept of domicile are not to be applied; instead the court will consider whether the defendant is 'ordinarily resident' in the State."[34]

(iii) Article 3

2–21 Article 3 clarifies the scope of the general rule laid down in Art.2. It provides that a defendant domiciled in a Member State may be sued in the

---

[29] See in particular Art.31.
[30] See para.2–27.
[31] As with the Brussels and Lugano Conventions.
[32] Jenard Report [1979] OJ C59/1, p.15.
[33] [1995] 2 I.R. 122; [1995] 1 I.L.R.M. 381.
[34] [1995] 2 I.R. 122 at 128; [1995] 1 I.L.R.M. 381 at 385.

courts of another Member State "only by virtue of the rules set out in Sections 2 to 7 of this Chapter". Sections 2 to 7 cover, in short:

> section 2: special jurisdiction. This covers contract, maintenance, tort, damages arising from criminal proceedings, branch operations, trust and salvage (Art.5)[35];
> section 3: insurance (Arts 8–14);
> section 4: consumer contracts (Arts 15–17);
> section 5: individual contracts of employment (Arts 18–21);
> section 6: exclusive jurisdiction (Art.22);
> section 7: prorogation of jurisdiction (Arts 23–24).

(e) Brussels II Regulation

2–22 Council Regulation 2201/2003[36] Concerning Jurisdiction and the Recognition and Enforcement of Judgments in Matrimonial Matters and Matters of Parental Responsibility is more commonly known as the Brussels II Regulation. It governs the specific area of rights in property arising out of a matrimonial relationship, as well as the enforcement of matrimonial judgments. As this is a relatively discrete and specialised area of the law, the focus in this chapter will be on the Brussels and Lugano Conventions as well as the Brussels I Regulation.

(f) Applicable Laws

2–23 The regulation of jurisdiction and the enforcement of judgments is governed at present as follows:

*   The Brussels I Regulation applies between the Member States of the EU. The relevant Member States of the EU are Austria, Belgium, Cyprus, Czech Republic, Denmark,[37] Estonia, Finland, France, Germany, Greece, Ireland, Italy, Latvia, Lithuania, Luxembourg, Malta, the Netherlands, Poland, Portugal, Slovakia, Slovenia, Spain, Sweden and the UK.
*   The Brussels Convention applies between the Member States of the EU and Denmark.[38]

---

[35] These rules of special jurisdiction amount to a derogation from the general rule of jurisdiction based on domicile. The ECJ has held on a number of occasions that they should be interpreted restrictively. See, for example, *Kalfelis v Bankhaus Schroeder* [1988] E.C.R. 5565; *Freistaat Bayern v Blijdensten* [2004] All E.R. (EC) 591; *Kronhofer v Maier* [2004] All E.R. (EC) 939. See also, *Burke v UVEX* [2005] 4 I.R. 452.

[36] OJ L338, as amended by Council Regulation 2116/2004/EC of December 2, 2004, OJ L367.

[37] See Rules of the Superior Courts (Jurisdiction, Recognition, Enforcement and Service of Proceedings) 2007 (S.I. No. 407 of 2007), which extends the application of Regulation 44/2001 to Denmark, "to the extent permitted".

[38] Although see Rules of the Superior Courts (Jurisdiction, Recognition, Enforcement and Service of Proceedings) 2007 (S.I. No. 407 of 2007), which extends the application of Regulation 44/2001 to Denmark, "to the extent permitted".

- The Lugano Convention applies between the Member States of the EU (including Denmark) and the EFTA States (Switzerland, Norway and Iceland but not Liechtenstein).
- Domestic rules apply in relation to other countries not covered by the foregoing categories.

(g) Domestic Implementation

(i) Jurisdiction of Courts and Enforcement of Judgments Act 1998

2–24 The Brussels and Lugano Conventions are in force in this jurisdiction by virtue of the implementation of the Jurisdiction of Courts and Enforcement of Judgments (European Communities) Act 1998. By virtue of s.5 of the Act, "judicial notice" is to be taken of the Conventions. The 1998 Act makes provision in relation to the reciprocal recognition and enforcement of judgments in civil and commercial matters as between Ireland and certain Member States of the European Communities.[39] It is primarily a consolidating measure which repeals and re-enacts the Jurisdiction of Courts and Enforcement of Judgments (European Communities) Act 1988[40] and the Jurisdiction of Courts and Enforcement of Judgments Act 1993.[41] It also amends certain sections of the Maintenance Act 1994, which had been absorbed into the consolidated text.[42]

(ii) European Communities (Civil and Commercial Judgments) Regulations 2002

2–25 In relation to the Brussels I Regulation, it is the provisions of the European Communities (Civil and Commercial Judgments) Regulations 2002 ("the 2002 Regulations") which apply.

4. Procedural Aspects

2–26 Rules of the Superior Courts Ords 11–11E, considered below,[43] deals with the procedural aspects of applying for injunctions.

---

[39] The Act has two main objectives: to enable Ireland to ratify the Accession Convention of Austria, Finland and Sweden to the 1968 Convention and to consolidate the provisions of the Jurisdiction of Courts and Enforcement of Judgments Acts 1988 and 1993, as well as providing the opportunity to make minor procedural adjustments: per the Minister of State at the Department of Justice, Equality and Law Reform, Seanad Éireann, Vol.154, April 2, 1998.

[40] Which brought into law the Brussels Convention and two subsequent accession conventions.

[41] Which gave force of law to the Accession Convention of Spain and Portugal to the 1968 Convention.

[42] The Act also enabled the State to ratify the 1996 Accession Convention dealing with the accession of the three new Member States to the Judgments Convention. Whilst in the 1998 Act the procedural provisions of the 1988 Act, as amended by the 1994 Act, are largely re-enacted, applications for the recognition and enforcement of authentic instruments and courts settlements falling within Title IV of the Brussels and Lugano Conventions which previously had to be made to the High Court can now be made to the Master of the High Court.

[43] See para.2–62.

C. Provisional and Protective Measures

1. Introduction

2–27 This section will look firstly at the concept of provision and protective measures in European legal instruments, before turning to consider the domestic equivalents.

2. Provisional and Protective Measures in European Legal Instruments[44]

2–28 In relation to interim and interlocutory injunctions, the key provisions in the two Conventions, Art.24 of the Brussels Convention and Art.24 of the Lugano Convention, are identical to each other. The courts, including the European Court of Justice, have handed down a number of decisions in relation to Art.24 which provide useful guidance in relation to these articles which deal with "provisional and protective measures". For the purposes of this analysis, the jurisprudence which has evolved in relation to Art.24 is to all intents and purposes equally applicable to Art.31, the former being almost identical in its terms to the latter.

(a) Article 24/Article 31

2–29 Article 24 of both the Brussels and Lugano Conventions, entitled "Provisional, including protective, measures", states:

> "Application may be made to the courts of a Contracting State for such provisional, including protective, measures as may be available under the law of that State, even if, under this Convention, the courts of another Contracting State have jurisdiction as to the substance of the matter."

2–30 Article 31 of the Brussels I Regulation is almost identical, save that it refers to "this Regulation" rather than "this Convention".

2–31 In short, Art.24 of the Conventions (Art.31 of the Brussels I Regulation) provides that provisional, including protective, measures may be sought from the courts of any Contracting State as may be available under the law of that state, even if the courts of another contracting state have jurisdiction over the substance of the matter. However, Art.24 (Art.31 of Brussels I) does not create

---

[44] It is not the place of this work to provide a full review of the European Conventions and Regulations and their scope and application, rather to consider them in the context of injunctions only. For a much broader treatment of the Conventions and Regulations, see in particular Briggs & Rees, *Civil Jurisdiction and Judgments*, 4th edn (London: LLP, 2005). See also Layton & Mercer, *European Civil Practice Vol. I*, 2nd edn (London: Thomson Sweet & Maxwell, 2004).

any new type of relief itself, nor does it confer any new power to grant interim or interlocutory relief.

(b) Meaning of Provisional or Protective Measures

2–32 The meaning of the term "provisional, including protective measures" was considered by the European Court of Justice in the case of *Reichert v Dresdner Bank AG (No. 2)*.[45] The ECJ stated that it must be understood as referring to:

> "measures which, in matters within the scope of the Convention, are intended to preserve a factual or legal situation so as to safeguard rights the recognition of which is sought elsewhere from the court having jurisdiction as to the substance of the matter."[46]

2–33 This dictum clearly contemplates interim relief. As such, injunctions in interim and interlocutory form, being available under the law of the State, are such that they come within the terms of Art.24 (Art.31 of Brussels I).[47] As explained by Dicey and Morris[48]:

> "It is clear that applications for provisional measures, such as preservation of property or interim injunctions, are within the scope of the Judgments Regulation and the Conventions."

2–34 In practice, this means that a measure such as a *Mareva* injunction[49] may be granted by an Irish court even though the Irish courts do not possess jurisdiction over the substantive proceedings between the parties concerned, and vice versa in relation to another Contracting State. However, it is not necessary for the court hearing an application for provisional or protective measures to have recourse to Art.24 where it already has jurisdiction as to the substance of a case in accordance with Arts 2 and 5–18 of the Convention (and by extension of Brussels I).[50]

---

[45] Case C–261/90 [1992] E.C.R. I–2149.

[46] Case C–261/90 [1992] E.C.R. I–2149, para.34.

[47] See generally, Kennett, *The Enforcement of Judgments in Europe* (Oxford: OUP, 2000), p.129. It seems that on the basis of the decision in Case 99/96 *Mietz v Intership Yachting Sneek BV* [1999] E.C.R. I-2277 that a *Mareva* injunction would have been dealt with under Art.24 (Art.31 of the Brussels I Regulation). See also *Babanaft International Co SA v Bassatne* [1990] Ch.13; [1989] 2 W.L.R. 232; [1989] 1 All E.R. 433.

[48] Dicey, Morris & Collins, *The Conflict of Laws*, 14th edn (London: Sweet & Maxwell, 2006), p.321.

[49] As to which, see Ch.8, Commercial Injunctions.

[50] Case C–99/96 *Mietz v Intership Yachting Sneek BV* [1999] E.C.R. I–2277 para.40; Case C–391/95 *Van Uden v Deco-Line* [1998] E.C.R. I–7091, para.19.

(c) Real Connecting Link

2–35 It was made clear in the case of *Van Uden Maritime BV v Firma Deco-Line*[51] that the granting of provisional or protective measures on the basis of the Conventions is conditional on the existence of a real connecting link[52] between the subject-matter of the measures sought and the territorial jurisdiction of the Contracting State of the court before which those measures are sought.[53] *De Cavel v De Cavel (No. 1)*[54] is authority for the proposition that Art.24 (Art.31 of Brussels I) cannot be relied on to bring within the scope of the Convention provisional or protective measures relating to matters which are excluded from it. The ECJ also declared in *De Cavel* that as provisional or protective measures may serve to safeguard a variety of rights, their inclusion is determined, not by their own nature, but by the nature of the rights which they serve to protect. This is to ensure that the provisional or protective measures must relate to a substantive action within the scope of the Convention.

2–36 In *Mietz v Intership Yachting Sneek BV*[55] the ECJ considered the extent to which a court must enquire whether a decision is one that attracts Art.24 (Art.31 of Brussels I). The ECJ held that a national court called upon to recognise and enforce a provisional measure should undertake a preliminary assessment of the measure prior to ruling on the criteria for recognition and enforcement; it is important to note that the court is evaluating the nature of the order made rather than the jurisdiction of the court which made it.[56]

3. Provisional and Protective Measures in Domestic Legislation

2–37 By virtue of s.13(1) of the Jurisdiction of Courts and Enforcement of Judgments Act 1998 (Art.10(1) of the European Communities (Civil and Commercial Judgments) Regulations 2002) the High Court is empowered to grant any provisional, including protective, measures which are normally

---

[51] C–391/95 [1998] E.C.R. I–7091, para.40.

[52] Briggs & Rees pose the question as to what is meant by "a "real connecting link" when the remedy being applied for is a freezing injunction" (i.e. a *Mareva* injunction): Briggs & Rees, *Civil Jurisdiction and Judgments*, 4th edn (London: LLP, 2005), p.468.

[53] A less stringent regime appeared to be espoused in the earlier case of Case 125/79 *Denilauler v SNC Couchet Freres* [1980] E.C.R. 1553, which simply referred at para.15 to "particular care" and "detailed knowledge" on the part of the court. In so far as that was the case, it now appears to be superseded by *Van Uden*.

[54] Case 143/78 [1979] E.C.R. 1055, para.9.

[55] C–99/96 [1999] E.C.R. I–2277.

[56] Article 39 of the Convention (Art.47 of Brussels I) provides that: "During the time specified for an appeal pursuant to Article 36 and until any such appeal has been determined, no measures of enforcement may be taken other than protective measures taken against the property of the party against whom enforcement is sought. The decision authorizing enforcement shall carry with it the power to proceed to any such protective measures."

available to it even if the substantive matter of the case falls to be heard by the courts of another state which is a contracting party to the 1968 Brussels Convention. In practical terms, the measure most likely to be applied for would be an injunction to restrain a defendant transferring assets out of the jurisdiction in order to prevent a judgment, in other words a *Mareva* injunction. However, as can be seen from the case of *Oblique Financial Services Ltd v The Promise Production Co Ltd*,[57] considered below,[58] the section is broad enough that it is not confined to such applications and any provisional measure appears to be contemplated by it.

2–38 Section 13(1) of the 1998 Act (Art.10(1) of the 2002 Regulations) provides that on application pursuant to Art.24 of the Brussels Convention (Art.31 of Brussels I), the High Court may grant any provisional, including protective, measures of any kind that the court has power to grant in proceedings that, apart from the Act, are within its jurisdiction, if two conditions are satisfied, namely that:

    (a)   proceedings have been or are to be commenced in a Contracting State other than the State; and

    (b)   the subject-matter of the proceedings is within the scope of the 1968 Convention as determined by Art.1 (whether or not that Convention has effect in relation to the proceedings).

2–39 It is provided at s.13(3) of the 1998 Act (Art.10(3) of the 2002 Regulations) that, subject to Art.39 of the Brussels Convention (Art.47(3) of Brussels I), an application to the Master of the High Court for an enforcement order in respect of a judgment may include an application for any protective measures the High Court has power to grant in proceedings that, apart from the 1998 Act, are within its jurisdiction.

2–40 Section 13(4) of the 1998 Act (Art.10(4) of the 2002 Regulations) provides that where an enforcement order is made, the Master of the High Court shall grant any protective measures referred to in subs. (3) that are sought in the application for the enforcement order. This is mandatory and the Master has no discretion in that regard.[59] This is a crucial difference to an application for protective measures where an application is pending or about to be instituted in another Contracting State, in which case the High Court can exercise its discretion in arriving at any decision.

---

[57]   [1994] 1 I.L.R.M. 74.
[58]   See para.2–42.
[59]   per Carroll J. in *Elwyn (Cottons) v Pearle Designs* [1989] I.R. 9; [1989] I.L.R.M. 162.

(a) Applicable Test: Section 13(1)/Article 10(1)

2–41 The normal guidelines and principles applied in the granting of interim and interlocutory injunctions, namely the *Campus Oil* guidelines, will inform whether or not the injunction should be granted.[60] In practice, however, this type of application will frequently concern *Mareva* injunctions, and the test peculiar to these injunctions applies.[61] These *Campus Oil* guidelines are, in brief:

- The party seeking the injunction must show that there is a fair/bona fide/serious question to be tried. If he can:
- The court must consider two aspects of the adequacy of damages:
  (i) First, it must consider whether, if it does not grant an injunction at the interlocutory stage, a plaintiff who succeeds at the trial of the substantive action will be adequately compensated by an award of damages for any loss suffered between the hearing of the interlocutory injunction and the trial of the action. If the plaintiff would be adequately compensated, the interlocutory injunction should be refused. This is subject to the proviso that the defendant would be in a position to pay such damages.
  (ii) Secondly, the court must consider whether, if it does grant an injunction at the interlocutory stage, a plaintiff's undertaking as to damages will adequately compensate the defendant, should the latter be successful at the trial of the action, in respect of any loss suffered by him due to the injunction being in force pending the trial. If the defendant would be compensated, the injunction may be granted. This is also subject to the proviso that the plaintiff would be in a position to pay such damages.
- If damages will not fully compensate either party, then the court may consider the balance of convenience. The matters relevant to determining where the balance of convenience lies will vary from case to case.
- If all other matters are equally balanced, the court should attempt to preserve the status quo.[62]

(b) Application of Provisions in Practice

2–42 The case of *Oblique Financial Services Ltd v The Promise Production Co Ltd*[63] provides a good example of the operation of s.13(1) of the 1998 Act (Art.10(1) of the 2002 Regulations) in practice. In that case an application for an interlocutory injunction was made by the plaintiff pursuant to s.11 of the Jurisdiction of Courts and Enforcement of Judgments (European Communities)

---

[60] See generally, Ch.6, Interlocutory Applications.
[61] See generally, Ch.8, Commercial Injunctions, particularly para.8–31.
[62] Based on the dicta of McCracken J. in *B & S Ltd v Irish Auto Trader Ltd* [1995] 2 I.R. 142 at 145; [1995] 2 I.L.R.M. 152 at 156 and Quirke J. in *Clane Hospital Ltd v Voluntary Health Insurance Board*, unreported, High Court, Quirke J., May 22, 1998.
[63] [1994] 1 I.L.R.M. 74.

Act 1988 (replaced by s.13 of the 1998 Act). The injunction sought was to prevent the publication by *The Phoenix* magazine (an Irish publication) of information as to the identity of a finance investor. An interim injunction had been granted to the plaintiff in the proceedings, which it indicated that it intended to issue in the High Court of Justice of England and Wales, as against all the defendants. It was accepted by counsel on both sides that the substantive proceedings were being instituted in an English court, and would fall to be decided by that court in accordance with English law. However, it was also accepted that the s.11 (now s.13) application fell to be determined by the court in Ireland, in accordance with the principles of Irish law applicable to the granting or withholding of an interlocutory injunction. In the circumstances, Keane J. felt that there would be serious and irreparable damage if the photos concerned were published, and felt that he should issue the injunction sought without having to proceed to a consideration of where the balance of convenience in relation to other aspects of the case might lie. However, he also felt that such balance lay in favour of granting the interlocutory injunction sought.

(c) Exercise of the Court's Discretion

2–43 By virtue of s.13(2) of the 1998 Act (Art.10(2) of the 2002 Regulations) the High Court may refuse to grant the measures under s.13(1) (Art.10(1)):

> "if, in its opinion, the fact that, apart from this section, that Court does not have jurisdiction in relation to the subject matter of the proceedings makes it inexpedient for it to grant those measures."

2–44 The English courts had to consider the equivalent English legislative provision[64] in the case of *Crédit Suisse Fides Trust v Cuoghi*.[65] Although the case involved a consideration of Art.24 of the Lugano Convention, it is equally applicable to the identically worded Art.24 of the Brussels Convention (and Art.31 of Brussels I). Asked to grant an order for the disclosure of extra-territorial assets held by the English resident defendant, which order the Swiss court concerned could not grant against an English-resident defendant, Bingham L.J. provided some useful guidelines as to the extraterritorial exercise of the Art.24 (Art.31 of Brussels I) jurisdiction. Having cautioned that the relief should not be "granted routinely or without very careful consideration", he continued:

> "It would be unwise to attempt to list all the considerations which might be held to make the grant of relief under s.25 inexpedient or expedient, whether on a municipal or a worldwide basis. But it would obviously weigh heavily,

---

[64] Civil Jurisdiction and Judgments Act 1982, s.25.
[65] [1998] Q.B. 818; [1998] 1 W.L.R. 871; [1997] 3 All E.R. 724.

probably conclusively, against the grant of interim relief if such grant would obstruct or hamper the management of the case by the court seised of the substantive proceedings (the primary court), or give rise to a risk of conflicting, inconsistent or overlapping orders in other courts. It may weigh against the grant of relief by this court that the primary court could have granted such relief and has not done so, particularly if the primary court has been asked to grant such relief and declined. On the other hand, it may be thought to weigh in favour of granting such relief that a defendant is present in this country and so liable to effective enforcement of an order made *in personam*, always provided that by granting such relief this court does not tread on the toes of the primary court or any other court involved in the case. On any application under s.25 this court must recognise that its role is subordinate to and must be supportive of that of the primary court."[66]

2–45 The *Crédit Suisse* case rejected the earlier view expressed by the courts that extraterritorial relief should be granted pursuant to Art.24 (Art.31 of Brussels I) only in exceptional circumstances, and instead focuses on the concept of "inexpediency", derived from s.25(2) of the English Civil Jurisdiction and Judgments Act.

2–46 In the case of *Refco v Eastern Trading*,[67] Morritt L.J. distilled the elements of the *Crédit Suisse* decision into two steps:

"it was implicit in all the judgments that the approach of the court in this country to an application for interim relief under s.25 is to consider first if the facts would warrant the relief sought if the substantive proceedings were brought in England. If the answer to that question is in the affirmative then the second question arises, whether, in the terms of s.25(2), the fact that the court has no jurisdiction apart from the section makes it inexpedient to grant the interim relief sought."[68]

2–47 The equivalent provision in Ireland is s.13(2) of the 1998 Act (Art.10(2) of the Regulations) and so Bingham L.J.'s guidelines set out above should be of some assistance to the courts in this jurisdiction.

4. Provisional and Protective Measures Other than Under the Conventions/ Regulation

2–48 The courts may of course make orders which have an effect beyond the countries bound by the Brussels and Lugano Conventions and the Brussels I Regulation. For example, the courts may make a worldwide *Mareva* order.[69]

---

[66] [1998] Q.B. 818 at 831; [1998] 1 W.L.R. 871 at 882; [1997] 3 All E.R. 724 at 734.
[67] [1999] 1 Lloyd's Rep. 159.
[68] [1999] 1 Lloyd's Rep 159 at 170–171.
[69] See generally, Ch.8, Commercial Injunctions.

However, the courts approach such applications cautiously; as summarised by Tuckey L.J. in *Bank of China v NMB LLC*[70]:

"(i) The limit of the court's territorial jurisdiction and the principle of comity require that the effectiveness of *Mareva* injunctions operating upon third parties holding assets abroad should normally derive only from their recognition and enforcement by the local courts;

(ii) Third parties amenable to the English jurisdiction should be given all reasonable protection."[71]

2–49 The decision of the English Court of Appeal in *Dadourian Group International Inc. v Simms*[72] has provided guidance as to how a court should exercise its discretion when considering whether to permit a party to enforce a worldwide *Mareva* injunction. Arden L.J. set out eight guidelines in relation to the enforcement of a *Mareva* injunction abroad. The decision is considered in greater detail in Ch.8, which deals with commercial injunctions, including *Mareva* injunctions.[73]

5. Procedural Aspects

2–50 Rules of the Superior Courts Ord.42A, considered below,[74] deals with the procedural aspects of applying for provisional and protective measures.

D. RECOGNITION AND ENFORCEMENT

1. Introduction

2–51 Provision is also made in the Brussels and Lugano Conventions and the Brussels I Regulation for the recognition and enforcement of judgments.[75] There is an important distinction between recognition and enforcement; a judgment must be recognised before it is enforced.

2–52 The first consideration is what constitutes a "judgment", and in that regard the Brussels and Lugano Conventions are much more expansive than the common law.[76] The common law is concerned with liquidated sums. As

---

[70] [2002] 1 W.L.R. 844; [2002] 1 All E.R. 717.
[71] [2002] 1 W.L.R. 844 at 851; [2002] 1 All E.R. 717 at 723.
[72] [2006] 1 W.L.R. 2499.
[73] See para.8–108.
[74] See para.2–113.
[75] See generally, Briggs & Rees, *Civil Jurisdiction and Judgments*, 4th edn (London: LLP, 2005), Ch.7.
[76] Dicey, Morris & Collins, *The Conflict of Laws*, 14th edn (London: Sweet & Maxwell, 2006),

observed by Dicey & Morris,[77] "[t]he historical explanation of this limitation is that the form of action appropriate for a foreign judgment was originally debt." That being so, the recognition and enforcement of injunction orders is not contemplated by the common law.[78]

2. Judgments Defined

2–53 Article 25 of the Brussels and Lugano Conventions (Art.32 of Brussels I) provides that a judgment means "any judgment given by a court or tribunal of a Contracting State, whatever the judgment may be called, including a decree, order, decision or writ of execution, as well as the determination of costs or expenses by an officer of the court."

2–54 Briggs and Rees provide a clear summary of what is contemplated by the word "judgments" as used in the Conventions and Regulation[79]:

"This term has a wide, but not unlimited, meaning: it applies to many, but not all, judicial orders … It includes many interlocutory orders, and injunctions and decrees of specific performance."

2–55 It is also important to note that an ex parte order is not a "judgment" for the purposes of the Conventions and Regulation.[80]

3. Recognition and Enforcement under European Conventions and Regulations

(a) Recognition

2–56 By virtue of Art.26 of the Brussels and Lugano Conventions (Art.33 of Brussels I), judgments given in Member States "shall be recognised" without any special procedure being required. Articles 27–30 of the Brussels and Lugano Conventions (Arts 34–37 of Brussels I) set out a number of qualifications to this. First, a judgment might not be recognised if:

---

p.651 refers to the fact that one of the most notable features of enforcement under the Judgements Regulation and in which respect it and the Conventions differ from the regime established by the common law is "that enforcement under the Judgments Regulation or Conventions is not limited to money judgments …".

[77] Dicey, Morris & Collins, *The Conflict of Laws*, 14th edn (London: Sweet & Maxwell, 2006), p.574.

[78] This is reflected in the fact that the usual procedure for enforcement is to issue a summary summons seeking an Irish judgment in terms of the foreign judgment: see generally Newman, "Enforcement of Foreign Judgments in Non-Convention Cases" (2000) 5(7) Bar Rev. 354. See also *McDonnell v McDonnell* [1921] 2 I.R. 148.

[79] Briggs & Rees, *Civil Jurisdiction and Judgments*, 4th edn (London: LLP, 2005), p.492.

[80] See Case 125/79 *Denilauler v SNC Couchet Freres* [1980] E.C.R. 1553, in which an order of attachment obtained in France on an ex parte basis could not be enforced in Germany.

- it is contrary to public policy; given in default of appearance; irreconcilable with a judgment given in a dispute between the same parties in the State in which recognition is sought; a preliminary question as to capacity has been decided or if the judgment is irreconcilable with an earlier judgment given in a Non-Contracting State involving the same cause of action and between the same parties (Art.27 of the Brussels and Lugano Conventions (Art.34 of Brussels I));
- it conflicts with the provisions of ss.3, 4 or 5 of Title II of the Brussels and Lugano Conventions, ss.3, 4 or 6 of Ch.II of Brussels I (insurance, consumer contracts and exclusive jurisdiction respectively) or in a case provided for in Art.59 (Brussels and Lugano)/Art.72 (Brussels I) (assumption of obligations towards a third State not to recognise judgments given in other Contracting States against defendants domiciled or habitually resident in the third state, for the reasons specified) (Art.35 of the Brussels and Lugano Conventions (Art.35 of Brussels I)).

2–57 Under Art.29 of the Brussels and Lugano Conventions (Art.36 of Brussels I), a foreign judgment may not be reviewed as to its substance. Under Art.30 of the Brussels and Lugano Conventions (Art.37 of Brussels I), the court in the recognising state may stay the proceedings if an ordinary appeal against the judgment has been lodged

(b) Enforcement

2–58 Article 31 of the Brussels and Lugano Conventions (Art.38 of Brussels I) provides that:

> "A judgment given in a Contracting State and enforceable in that State shall be enforced in another Contracting State when, on the application of any interested party, it has been declared enforceable there."

2–59 Article 34 of the Brussels and Lugano Conventions (Art.40 of Brussels I) provides that, "the procedure for making the application shall be governed by the law of the State in which enforcement is sought."

4. Recognition and Enforcement under Domestic Legislation

2–60 Section 7(1)(a) of the 1998 Act (Art.4(1) of the 2002 Regulations) states that an application under the Conventions for the recognition or enforcement in the state of a judgment shall be made to the Master of the High Court. Section 7(1)(b) of the 1998 Act (Art.4(2) of the 2002 Regulations) provides that the application shall be determined in accordance with the Conventions.

2–61 Rules of the Superior Courts Ord.42A, considered below,[81] deals with the procedural aspects of enforcement.

E. Rules of the Superior Courts Orders 11–11E

1. Introduction

2–62 In seeking an injunction order in this jurisdiction against a defendant who is not present within the jurisdiction, it is necessary in the first instance to have identified Ireland as a proper forum, based on the facts of the case and having regard to the provisions of the relevant Conventions and Regulations, as considered above.[82] Once this is established, it is then necessary to have regard to the relevant procedures relating to service as set out in the Rules of the Superior Courts.

2–63 There are three different aspects to this depending on which legal instrument applies:

 (i) RSC Ord.11 sets out the applicable rules and procedures if there is a justification for the issue being tried in Ireland, but the matter is one to which the various European legal instruments outlined above do not apply.
 (ii) If the defendant is domiciled in a country other than Ireland to which the Brussels Regulation applies, RSC Ord.11A sets out the applicable rules and procedures.
 (iii) If the defendant is domiciled in a country other than Ireland to which the Brussels Regulation does not apply, but to which the Brussels and Lugano Conventions apply, RSC Ord.11B sets out the applicable rules and procedures.

2–64 If the matter concerns matrimonial matters and matters of parental responsibility, then reference should be made to RSC Ord.11C for the applicable rules and procedures. Rules of the Superior Courts Ord.11D and 11E deal with the service of documents within another country.

2–65 The relevant Rules under each of these Orders relating to service of an originating document will be considered in turn.

2. Rules of the Superior Courts Order 11[83]

2–66 In order to grant an injunction, a court had to be satisfied that it had jurisdiction over the person against whom the injunction was

---

[81] See para.2–113.
[82] See para.2–04.
[83] See also Rules of the Circuit Court (RCC) Ord.13.

sought.[84] Proceedings in personam are brought by serving a party with an originating summons or motion.[85] Service of process is, in simple terms, the basis of the court's jurisdiction in Ireland. In the normal course, such service will take place within the State. However, leave to serve proceedings out of the jurisdiction may be granted under RSC Ord.11. As a fundamental preliminary point, there must be a sound basis for the contention that a party to be served out of the jurisdiction is a proper party. There must also be a reality in law and in fact to the case being made against such a party.[86] The inclusion of a party within the jurisdiction must not simply be a device to contrive a situation whereby a foreign defendant is brought before an Irish court.

2–67 Once it has been established that the party concerned is a proper one, RSC Ord.11 r.1[87] provides that service out of the jurisdiction of an originating summons or notice of an originating summons may be allowed in a number of defined circumstances. To be covered by RSC Ord.11, a cause of action must come within the terms of RSC Ord.11 r.1, which sets out a series of causes of action to which the rule applies, and must not be covered by the Conventions and Regulations outlined above. The importance of ensuring that a cause of action comes within the terms of RSC Ord.11 r.1 is evident from the case of *Adams v DPP*,[88] in which a submission was made on behalf of the applicant that "notwithstanding the absence of judicial review from the purview of Order 11 the Court can still order the service of proceedings out of the jurisdiction" under an alleged inherent jurisdiction. However, Kelly J. in the High Court held that this was "clearly in conflict with decisions of the Supreme Court."[89]

(a) Application to Injunctions

2–68 Rules of the Superior Courts Ord.11 r.1(g) provides that service out of the jurisdiction may be allowed by the court whenever:

> "Any injunction is sought as to anything to be done within the jurisdiction, or any nuisance within the jurisdiction is sought to be prevented or removed whether damages are or are not sought in respect thereof."[90]

---

[84] See, for example *Lett v Lett* [1906] 1 I.R. 618 at 629, per Porter M.R.

[85] See Ch.4, Equitable and General Principles, para.4–07 in relation to the difference between proceedings in personam and in rem.

[86] See the comments of Fennelly J. in *Analog Devices BV v Zurich Insurance Co* [2002] 1 I.R. 272 at 286; [2002] 2 I.L.R.M. 366 at 379 and of Barrington J. in *Short v Ireland* [1996] 2 I.R. 188 at 216. See also the comments of Lindley L.J. in *Massey v Heynes* (1888) 21 Q.B.D. 330 at 338, and of Dillon L.J. in *Multinational Gas and Petrochemical Co v Multinational Gas and Petrochemical Services Ltd* [1983] Ch. 258 at 286. [1983] 3 W.L.R. 492 at 517.

[87] As amended by S.I. No. 14 of 1989; by S.I. No. 243 of 1995 and by S.I. No. 506 of 2005.

[88] unreported, High Court, Kelly J., April 12, 2000.

[89] Citing the cases of *Brennan v Lockyer* [1932] I.R. 100 and *Fusco v O'Dea* [1994] 2 I.R. 93.

[90] The rule in so far as it relates to injunctions is identical to RSC Ord.11 r.1 of the Rules of the Supreme Court (Ireland) 1905 and the Rules of the Superior Courts 1962. The equivalent provision in the Circuit Court Rules is Ord.13 r.1(h).

2–69 In general terms, the injunction must be an injunction properly and necessarily sought in the originating summons as a primary, rather than an ancillary, relief.[91]

2–70 Consideration of the provisions of RSC Ord.11 must be undertaken in each individual case. Whether a court grants leave to effect service out of the jurisdiction is a matter of discretion, as is clear from the provisions of RSC Ord.11 r.5. That rule states, inter alia, that:

> "no leave shall be granted unless it shall be made sufficiently to appear to the Court that the case is a proper one for service out of the jurisdiction under this Order."[92]

(b) Operation of the Rule in Practice

2–71 In *Joynt v M'Crum*[93] the plaintiff sought an injunction against the vendor of bicycles within the jurisdiction and also the manufacturer of those bicycles in England, alleging that they infringed his patent. He also claimed damages. It was held that service out of the jurisdiction was properly allowed as the claim for an injunction could not be regarded as merely ancillary to that for damages.[94]

2–72 The need for the injunctive relief sought to be substantive and not merely ancillary is also evident from the decision of Costello J. in *Taher Meats (Ireland) Ltd v State Company for Foodstuff Trading*.[95] In that case the plaintiff sought to restrain the second named defendant by injunction from demanding payment from a bank on foot of a counter-indemnity within the jurisdiction. The plaintiff argued that as this was a substantive claim against the second defendant and not merely ancillary to other relief, it fell within the terms of RSC Ord.11 r.1(g), giving the Irish courts jurisdiction. Costello J. held that the injunctive relief claimed against the second defendant was not merely ancillary to a substantive claim. He further held that the injunction sought against the second defendant related to "something to be done within the jurisdiction" within the meaning of

---

[91]	Although the necessity for the injunction being the primary relief had been determinative of a number of cases (see, for example, *Caudron v Air Zaire* [1985] I.R. 716; [1986] I.L.R.M. 10) the passing of s.13 of the Jurisdiction of Courts and Enforcement of Judgments Act 1998 has changed the position to a degree; see para.2–78.

[92]	See the dictum of Fennelly J. in *Analog Devices BV v Zurich Insurance Co* [2002] 1 I.R. 272 at 287; [2002] 2 I.L.R.M. 366 at 380 that: "An order granting leave to effect service out of the jurisdiction is a matter of discretion. The court should grant leave only after careful consideration, not only of the existence of grounds upon which the court is empowered to grant leave, but of the appropriateness of the courts of this jurisdiction to try the case."

[93]	[1899] 1 I.R. 217.

[94]	See also, *Dunlop Rubber Co v Dunlop* [1921] 1 A.C. 367; *Rosler v Hilbery* [1925] 1 Ch. 250.

[95]	[1991] 1 I.R. 443.

the rule. As such, he refused to discharge the order granting leave to the plaintiff to serve notice of proceedings on both defendants out of the jurisdiction.

2–73 A more celebrated case in which RSC Ord.11 fell to be considered is that of *Caudron v Air Zaire*,[96] in which ex-employees of the national airline of Zaire brought an action arising from their periods of employment with Air Zaire. All the ex-employees had an exclusive jurisdiction clause in their contracts of employment providing that litigation of all disputes could only take place in Zaire.

2–74 The plaintiffs first pursued proceedings against the defendant airline in Belgium, but then learned that a plane belonging to Air Zaire was grounded at Dublin airport following repairs. The plaintiffs believed that if they could successfully pursue their litigation against the defendants in Ireland, then, with the assistance of a *Mareva* injunction,[97] they might realise any unsatisfied judgments in their favour against the grounded airplane. Key to this was demonstrating that the Irish courts had jurisdiction to deal with the matter. The defendant had no place of business in Ireland and was unlikely to submit to the jurisdiction of the Irish court by accepting service. The exclusive jurisdiction clauses in the ex-employees' contracts also militated against bringing proceedings in Ireland. In a draft plenary summons, the plaintiffs thus applied for a *Mareva* injunction and based the application on RSC Ord.11 r.1(g).

2–75 Costello J. acceded to the ex parte application, and granted the plaintiffs liberty to issue and serve a plenary summons, as well as granting an interim injunction. The defendants then sought to have Costello J.'s order set aside.

2–76 That application was dealt with in the High Court by Barr J., who accepted that a *Mareva* injunction was in the nature of ancillary relief. However, having reviewed both RSC Ord.11 and s.28(8) of the Judicature (Ireland) Act 1877,[98] he did not accept that this precluded it from being a valid jurisdictional basis within RSC Ord.11, and the defendant's appeal was refused.

2–77 However, on appeal to the Supreme Court by the defendants, it was held that to come within RSC Ord.11 r.1(g) the injunction sought in the action had to be part of the substantive relief to which the plaintiffs' cause of action entitled them. It had to be properly and necessarily sought in the indorsement of claim contained in the originating summons. Finlay C.J. held that the phrase "any injunction is sought" as used in RSC Ord.11 r.1(g) must be viewed in the light of the provisions of RSC Ord.11 r.1, which provides for service out of the

---

[96] [1985] I.R. 716; [1986] I.L.R.M. 10.
[97] See Ch.8, Commercial Injunctions.
[98] Section 28(8) gives the court power to grant injunctions "in all cases in which it shall appear to the court to be just or convenient". See generally, Ch.1, Domestic Jurisdiction, para.1–30.

jurisdiction of an originating summons or a notice of an originating summons. As such, the Chief Justice felt the injunction sought must thus be an injunction necessarily and properly sought in the originating summons. It could not be an injunction which is properly sought, not as part of the indorsement of claim on the summons, but rather by means of a motion ex parte or on notice. In other words, in order to attract the provisions of the rule, the injunctive relief sought must be the primary relief sought, as distinct from ancillary relief. The *Mareva* injunction sought was in the nature of ancillary relief.

2–78 However, s.13 of the Jurisdiction of Courts and Enforcement of Judgments Act 1998 effectively modified the position as determined in *Caudron*. That section, which deals with "provisional, including protective, measures", provides for the granting of such measures, including injunctions, pursuant to the Brussels Convention, even where the plaintiff has no independent cause of action within the jurisdiction.[99]

(c) Application of RSC Order 11 to Statutory Injunctions

2–79 It is clear that the word "injunction" as used in RSC Ord.11 r.1(g) is not confined to those orders which would be granted by the courts of equity directing a person to do or to refrain from doing an act. As determined by Finnegan J. in *McKenna v EH*,[100] the word "injunction" also encompasses statutory injunctions, whatever may be the statute in which they have their origin.

2–80 Furthermore, in *McKenna v BM*[101] Finnegan P. observed in relation to "extraterritorial legislation" that "extra territorial legislation simply means legislation which attaches significance for Courts within the jurisdiction to facts and events occurring outside the jurisdiction." In finding that such legislation did not per se offend against the comity of courts, the President observed that extraterritorial legislation did not imply that "one State can pass laws for another State or that several systems of law will be in operation regulating a particular sphere within any given State."

(d) Application to Companies with Assets Within the State

2–81 The fact that a company has assets within the State (without being domiciled in the State) may make it amenable to the jurisdiction of the State.

---

[99]   See Delany & McGrath, *Civil Procedure in the Superior Courts*, 2nd edn (Dublin: Thomson Round Hall, 2005), p.802.
[100] [2002] 1 I.R. 72; [2002] 2 I.L.R.M. 117. Reference was also made to the fact that it is the function of procedural law to give effect to the intent of the Oireachtas, and that the courts must construe the Rules widely. See also, *McKenna v RM* [2003] 3 I.R. 1 in relation to s.3 of the Proceeds of Crime Act 1996.
[101] unreported, High Court, Finnegan P., November 3, 2006.

This is clear from the case of *Kutchera v Buckingham*,[102] in which the plaintiff was a non-Irish citizen, the defendant a Canadian company. In a contract for a loan agreement between the two, it was expressly provided that the proper law of the contract should be that of Ireland, and that the parties, in the event of any dispute, would irrevocably submit to the jurisdiction of the Irish courts exclusively. The plaintiff was primarily seeking declarations and injunctive relief in the nature of a *quia timet* injunction. The plaintiff issued a plenary summons and served notice of it upon the defendant pursuant to RSC Ord.11 r.1. In the High Court, the defendant obtained an order pursuant to RSC Ord.12 r.26, setting aside the service of the summons on the ground that Irish law was unconnected with the realities of the contract.

2–82 In allowing the plaintiff's appeal, Henchy J. in the Supreme Court observed that where the defendant is a limited company, it is nonetheless amenable to the court's jurisdiction if it is registered in this State, even if it only has assets within the State. This is because the court could give effect to its orders by, for example, processes such as the sequestration of the company's assets. Similarly, in *Hospital for Sick Children (Board of Governors) v Walt Disney Productions Inc.*,[103] the fact that the defendants in question were incorporated in California was held not to be a good ground for refusing to grant an injunction. Lord Denning M.R. took the view that an injunction against a company could be enforced by sequestration of its assets within the jurisdiction, and thus could be granted.

(e) Applying for Service Out Under RSC Order 11 Rule 1

2–83 Where RSC Ord.11 applies, the leave of the High Court must be sought before documents can be served out of the jurisdiction. An application for service under RSC Ord.11 r.1 is made ex parte before the issue of the summons.[104] It is grounded on an affidavit sworn by the plaintiff in the action. The affidavit should be entitled as between the parties to the intended proceeding and headed: "In the Matter of the Courts of Justice Acts, 1924 to 1961, and the Courts (Supplemental Provisions) Acts, 1961 to 1981". The parties should be referred to as "intended", viz. the "intended plaintiff" and "intended defendant".

2–84 Although RSC Ord.11 r.6 stipulates that an application for leave to serve a summons or notice of a summons must be made before the issue of the summons, in practice a summons may be issued before the application for leave to serve out is brought. That this is permissible is clear from the decision of *Traynor v Fagan*.[105] In that case Barrington J. held that, having regard to RSC

---

[102]   [1988] I.L.R.M. 501.
[103]   [1968] Ch. 52; [1967] 2 W.L.R. 1250; [1967] 1 All E.R. 1005.
[104]   per RSC Ord.11 r.6.
[105]   [1985] I.R. 586.

Ord.11 r.6, the Central Office should not refuse to issue proceedings in circumstances where a proposed defendant was outside the jurisdiction unless a court order had already been obtained. However, the better practice is to exhibit a draft copy of a summons in the affidavit grounding the application under RSC Ord.11.

2–85 The provisions of RSC Ord.11 r.5 set out comprehensively what should be contained in the grounding affidavit. It should be in the following form:

- It must set out the nature of the cause of action.
- It must state which provisions of RSC Ord.11 r.1(a)–(q) apply; as has been considered, in the context of an application for an injunction, RSC Ord.11, r.1(g) is the appropriate provision.
- The plenary summons or notice thereof must be exhibited, and reference made to it to show precisely what orders are being sought.
- It must state the belief that the intended plaintiff has a "good cause of action",[106] although the plaintiff will also have to show that he has a "good arguable case".[107]
- It must state the place or country where the intended defendant is or is likely to be found.[108]
- It must state whether the intended defendant is an Irish citizen or not.[109]
- It must state the particulars necessary to enable the court to exercise its discretion.[110]
- It must specify why Ireland is a convenient forum, and in that regard the words of RSC Ord.11 r.2 refer to the court having regard "to the comparative cost and convenience of proceedings in Ireland, or in the place of the defendant's residence".[111]
- It must contain a prayer for relief.

(i) Applicable Provision of Rule

2–86 In *Brennan* v *Lockyer*[112] Kennedy C.J. pointed out that it is necessary when seeking an order for service out of the jurisdiction for the applicant to show that he can bring himself within one or other of the enumerated cases set out in the relevant rule. This point was effectively repeated by the Chief Justice in *Shipsey v British and South American Steam Navigation Company*,[113] in which he stated that:

---

[106] per RSC Ord.11 r.5.
[107] See para.2–88.
[108] per RSC Ord.11 r.5.
[109] per RSC Ord.11 r.5. If this is not known, the court will generally assume that the intended defendant is not an Irish citizen.
[110] per RSC Ord.11 r.5.
[111] per RSC Ord.11 r.2.
[112] [1932] I.R. 100 at 107.
[113] [1936] I.R. 65.

"in a matter of the international comity of Courts, the High Court, when making an order giving leave for service out of the jurisdiction, should specifically mention in the order the particular class of action within which the Court decides the intended action to fall ...".[114]

(ii) Remedying Breaches in Procedure

2–87 This dictum was approved by O'Hanlon J. in the High Court in the case of *Short v Ireland*.[115] However, it is clear from that case that the courts do have a measure of discretion when there are such procedural defects. In *Short*, O'Hanlon J. decided to overlook for the most part the breaches in procedural requirements.

(iii) Good Arguable Case

2–88 It must be established that there is a "good arguable case".[116] It was argued in *Analog Devices BV v Zurich Insurance Co*[117] that the appropriate test in such circumstances was the need to show a "fair arguable case", with any disputes to be resolved at the trial of the action. However, Fennelly J. rejected this argument, referring to the fact that such a test needed to be applied "with special circumspection in a case where the issue in contention is whether the court can take upon itself jurisdiction over a foreign person or corporation."[118] He acknowledged that similarly worded tests were used in determining whether or not to grant interlocutory injunctions, but observed that in such cases "the position of the opposing party is not irrevocably affected."[119] That being so, Fennelly J. held in relation to the plaintiff in *Analog Devices* that:

> "It is not sufficient that he assert that he has a cause of action. The court judges the strength of the cause of action on a test of a 'good arguable case'."[120]

(iv) A Proper Case for Service Out

2–89 The court must also be satisfied that Ireland is the convenient forum and it must sufficiently appear to the court that "the case is a proper one for service

---

[114] [1936] I.R. 65 at 83. In *Johnson v Taylor Brothers* [1920] A.C. 144 at 153 which dealt with the English equivalent of RSC Ord.11, Viscount Haldane stated that the case before the court must come within the spirit and the letter of the rule.

[115] [1996] 2 I.R. 188 at 198–199.

[116] See the dictum of Fennelly J., delivering the judgment of the Supreme Court, in the case of *Analog Devices BV v Zurich Insurance Co* [2002] 1 I.R. 272 at 281; [2002] 2 I.L.R.M. 366 at 375. Fennelly J. made reference to the confusion the English courts experienced in considering this matter, citing the decision in *Vitkovice Horni A Hutni Hezirstvo v Korner* [1951] A.C. 869, as reviewed by Lord Goff in *Seaconsar Far East Ltd v Bank Markazi Jomhouri Islami Iran* [1994] 1 A.C. 438.

[117] [2002] 1 I.R. 272; [2002] 2 I.L.R.M. 366.

[118] [2002] 1 I.R. 272 at 281; [2002] 2 I.L.R.M. 366 at 375.

[119] [2002] 1 I.R. 272 at 281; [2002] 2 I.L.R.M. 366 at 375.

[120] [2002] 1 I.R. 272 at 281; [2002] 2 I.L.R.M. 366 at 375.

out of the jurisdiction under [the] order".[121] The court will have regard to the amount or value of the claim or property affected and to the comparative cost and convenience of proceedings in Ireland, or in the place of the defendant's residence.[122] The courts have previously held that any doubts are to be resolved in favour of the absent defendant.[123]

(v) Disclosure of All Material Facts

2–90 As with any application made ex parte, all material facts must be disclosed to the court.[124] An application under RSC Ord.11 will be examined with "care and circumspection" due to the principle of international comity of the courts.[125]

(vi) Time for an Appearance

2–91 In accordance with the provisions of RSC Ord.11 r.7, the order of the court should specify a time within which an appearance must be entered in response to the summons. Once the order is made, and where the defendant is not, or is not known or believed to be, a citizen of Ireland, notice of the summons, not the summons itself, should be served upon the party concerned. Again, this practice has its origins in the notion of exercising judicial deference towards foreign sovereigns,[126] and is provided for in RSC Ord.11 r.8. A defendant may enter a conditional appearance purely for the purposes of contesting the jurisdiction of the Irish courts to deal with the matter.[127]

3. Rules of the Superior Courts Order 11A[128]

2–92 Proceedings under the Brussels I Regulation are dealt with in RSC Ord.11A.[129] Order 11A provides that its application is confined to proceedings

---

[121] Ord.11 r.5.
[122] per RSC Ord.11, r.5, described by Fennelly J. in *Analog Devices BV v Zurich Insurance Co* [2002] 1 I.R. 272 at 287; [2002] 2 I.L.R.M. 366 at 380 as a "fundamental principle". In an English context, it was held that the plaintiff must satisfy the court that it is in the *forum conveniens*, defined by Lord Goff in *Spiliada Maritime Corporation v Cansulex Ltd* [1987] 1 A.C. 460 at 480; [1986] 3 W.L.R. 972 at 990; [1986] 3 All E.R. 843 at 858 as "the forum in which the case can be suitably tried for the interests of all the parties and for the ends of justice." See also *Amin Rasheed Corp. v Kuwait Insurance* [1984] A.C. 50 at 72, per Lord Wilberforce.
[123] *Freeman v Opdeheyde* (1945) Ir. Jur. Rep. 22.
[124] See generally, Ch.7, Interim Applications, para.7–64.
[125] per Fennelly J. in *Analog Devices BV v Zurich Insurance Co* [2002] 1 I.R. 272 at 281; [2002] 2 I.L.R.M. 366 at 375.
[126] See para.2–01.
[127] Although not stated in the rules, the courts have accepted that a party can make a conditional appearance: *Fox v Taher*, unreported, High Court, Costello P., January 24, 1996 and *Minister for Agriculture v Alte Leipziger Versicherung AG* [2000] 4 I.R. 32; [2001] 1 I.L.R.M. 519.
[128] See RCC Ord.14.
[129] As inserted by Rules of the Superior Courts (Jurisdiction, Recognition, Enforcement and

which are governed by the Brussels Regulation and, "so far as practicable and applicable, to any order, motion or notice in any such proceedings". As already considered, the guiding principle of jurisdiction is that persons domiciled in a Member State are, regardless of their nationality, to be sued in the courts of that Member State.[130]

(a) Service Out Under RSC Order 11A

2–93 Order 11A entitles a plaintiff to serve a summons, order or notice or motion out of the jurisdiction, without having to seek the leave of the court to do so, when:

> "(1) the claim made by the summons or other originating document is one which, by virtue of Regulation No. 44/2001, the Court has power to hear and determine, and
>
> (2) no proceedings between the parties concerning the same cause of action are pending between the parties in another Member State of the European Union (other than Denmark)."[131]

2–94 The summons must contain two statements to this effect if it is being served out of the jurisdiction under Ord.11A.[132]

2–95 In accordance with the provisions of RSC Ord.11A r.3, where an originating summons or notice of an originating summons is to be served out of the jurisdiction under r.2, the time to be inserted in the summons within which the defendant served therewith shall an enter an appearance is:

(i) five weeks after the service of the summons or notice of summons exclusive of the day of service where an originating summons or notice of an originating summons is to be served in the European territory of another Member State of the European Union (other than Denmark); or

(ii) six weeks after the service of the summons or notice of summons exclusive of the day of service where an originating summons or notice of an originating summons is to be served under r.2 in any non-European territory of a Member State of the European Union (other than Denmark).

2–96 In a situation where two or more defendants are parties to proceedings to which RSC Ord.11A applies, but not every co-defendant is domiciled in the EU

Service of Proceedings) 2005 (S.I. No. 506 of 2005). See also, Ord.5 r.14 as substituted by those rules.

[130] per Art.2 of the Regulation. For a consideration of Art.2, see the decision of the ECJ in Case C–281/02 *Owusu v Jackson*, which emphasises the mandatory nature of Art.2.

[131] RSC Ord.11A r.2. See, however, Rules of the Superior Courts (Jurisdiction, Recognition, Enforcement and Service of Proceedings) 2007 (S.I. No. 407 of 2007), which extends the application of Regulation 44/2001 to Denmark, "to the extent permitted".

[132] RSC Ord.4 r.1A.

or in a Convention Contracting State, then the provisions of RSC Ord.11, as set out above, apply to such defendants domiciled outside the EU or a Convention Contracting State.[133]

2–97 As under RSC Ord.11, where the defendant is not, or is not known or believed to be, a citizen of Ireland, it is the notice of the summons, not the summons itself, which should be served upon the party concerned; again, the idea of the exercise of judicial deference towards foreign sovereigns is the basis for this provision, which is set out at RSC Ord.11A r.6.

4. Rules of the Superior Courts Order 11B[134]

2–98 Order 11B of the Rules of the Superior Courts governs service under the Brussels and Lugano Conventions.

(a) Service Out Under RSC Order 11B

2–99 Order 11B provides that the originating summons or notice of the originating summons may be served out of the jurisdiction, without the leave of the court if, but only if[135]:

> "(1) the claim made by the summons is one which by virtue of either the 1968 Convention and Part II of the 1998 Act (and the First Schedule thereof) or the Lugano Convention and Part III of the 1998 Act and the Seventh Schedule thereof) the Court has power to hear and determine, and
> (2) no proceedings between the parties concerning the same cause of action are pending between the parties in another Contracting State of the 1968 Convention or another Contracting State of the Lugano Convention (as the case may be)."[136]

2–100 The summons must contain two statements to this effect if it is being served out of the jurisdiction under Ord.11B.[137]

2–101 In accordance with the provisions of RSC Ord.11B r.3, where an originating summons or notice of an originating summons is to be served out of the jurisdiction under r.2, the time to be inserted in the summons within which the defendant served therewith shall an enter an appearance is:

---

[133] RSC Ord.11A r.4.
[134] See RCC Ord.14.
[135] Notice is required if the defendant is not, or is not known or believed to be, a citizen of Ireland: RSC Ord.11B r.6.
[136] RSC Ord.11B r.2.

(i) five weeks after the service of the summons or notice of summons exclusive of the day of service where an originating summons or notice of an originating summons is to be served in the European territory of another Contracting State of the 1968 Convention or of another Contracting State of the Lugano Convention; or

(ii) six weeks after the service of the summons or notice of summons exclusive of the day of service where an originating summons or other originating document or notice of an originating summons or document is to be served under r.2 in any non-European territory of any Contracting State of the 1968 Convention or of any Contracting State of the Lugano Convention.

2–102 In a situation where two or more defendants are parties to proceedings to which RSC Ord.11B applies, but not every co-defendant is domiciled in the EU or in a Convention Contracting State, then the provisions of RSC Ord.11, as set out above, apply to such defendants domiciled outside the EU or a Convention Contracting State.[138]

2–103 As under RSC Ord.11, where the defendant is not, or is not known or believed to be, a citizen of Ireland, it is the notice of the summons, not the summons itself, which should be served upon the party concerned; again, the idea is that the exercise of judicial deference towards foreign sovereigns is the basis for this provision, which is set out at RSC Ord.11B, r.6.

5. Rules of the Superior Courts Order 11C[139]

2–104 Rules of the Superior Courts Ord.11C deals with proceedings under the Brussels II Regulation, namely matrimonial and parental responsibility proceedings.[140]

(a) Service Out Under RSC Order 11C

2–105 Order 11C provides that the originating summons or notice of the originating summons may be served out of the jurisdiction, without the leave of the court if, but only if[141]:

"(a) the claim made by the summons is one which, by virtue of Regulation No. 2201/2003, the Court has power to hear and determine; and

---

[137] RSC Ord.4 r.1A.
[138] RSC Ord.11B r.4.
[139] See RCC Ord.14A.
[140] Although maintenance is covered by the Brussels I Regulation.
[141] Notice is required if the defendant is not, or is not known or believed to be, a citizen of Ireland: RSC Ord.11B r.6.

(b) no proceedings

(i) relating to divorce, legal separation or marriage annulment between the same parties or, as the case may be,

(ii) relating to parental responsibility relating to the same child and involving the same cause of action

are pending in another Member State of the European Union (other than Denmark)."[142]

2–106 The summons must contain two statements to this effect if it is being served out of the jurisdiction under Ord.11C.[143]

2–107 In accordance with the provisions of RSC Ord.11C r.3, where an originating summons or notice of an originating summons is to be served out of the jurisdiction under r.2, the time to be inserted in the summons within which the defendant served therewith shall enter an appearance is:

(i) five weeks after the service of the summons or notice of summons exclusive of the day of service where an originating summons or notice of an originating summons is to be served in the European territory of another Member State of the European Union (other than Denmark); or

(ii) six weeks after the service of the summons or notice of summons exclusive of the day of service where an originating summons or notice of summons is to be served under r.2 in any non-European territory of any Member State of the European Union (other than Denmark).

2–108 In a situation where two or more defendants are parties to proceedings to which RSC Ord.11C applies, but not every co-defendant is domiciled in the EU, then the rules as to jurisdiction in Regulation 2201/2003 apply.[144]

2–109 As under RSC Ord.11, where the defendant is not, or is not known or believed to be, a citizen of Ireland, it is the notice of the summons, not the summons itself, which should be served upon the party concerned; again, the idea of the exercise of judicial deference towards foreign sovereigns is the basis for this provision, which is set out at RSC Ord.11C r.5.

6. Rules of the Superior Courts Orders 11D and E[145]

2–110 Rules of the Superior Courts Ord.11D provides for service of documents, judicial or extrajudicial, in countries within the EU (other than Denmark).[146]

---

[142] RSC Ord.11C r.2.
[143] RSC Ord.4 r.1A.
[144] RSC Ord.11C r.4.
[145] See RCC Ord.14B. See generally, Delany & McGrath, *Civil Procedure in the Superior Courts*, 2nd edn (Dublin: Thomson Round Hall, 2005), pp.101–105.
[146] See Rules of the Superior Courts (Jurisdiction, Recognition, Enforcement and Service of

2–111 Rules of the Superior Courts Ord.11E provides for service of documents, judicial or extrajudicial, in Hague Convention[147] countries.[148]

7. Rules of the Superior Courts Orders 121, 121A and B

2–112 Rules of the Superior Courts Ord.121 provides for the service of non-originating documents. Such documents do not require personal service. Rules of the Superior Courts Ord.121A deals with the service of foreign process and RSC Ord.121B regulates the service of foreign proceedings within the jurisdiction pursuant to the Hague Convention.

F. RULES OF THE SUPERIOR COURTS ORDER 42A

1. Introduction

2–113 There are two aspects to RSC Ord.42A: it makes provision for applications for provisional and protective measures and also makes provision for the enforcement in this jurisdiction of judgments obtained abroad. Each of these will be considered in turn.

2. Provisional and Protective Measures

2–114 Order 42A of the Rules of the Superior Courts sets out the relevant procedures for provisional, including protective measures brought pursuant to Art.31 or s.13 of the 1998 Act. By virtue of RSC Ord.42A r.1, an application for provisional, including protective, measures under Art.31 of the Brussels I Regulation or s.13 of the 1998 Act shall be made ex parte to the High Court.

Proceedings) 2007 (S.I. No. 407 of 2007), which extends the application of Regulation 1348/2000 to Denmark, "to the extent permitted".

[147] The stated aims of the Hague Service Convention are to create appropriate means to ensure that judicial and extrajudicial documents to be served abroad shall be brought to the notice of the addressee in sufficient time, and to improve the organization of mutual judicial assistance for that purpose by simplifying and expediting the procedure.

[148] There are 56 Contracting States to the Convention, including Ireland. They are: Albania, Antigua and Barbuda, Argentina, Bahamas, Barbados, Belarus, Belgium, Botswana, Bulgaria, Canada, China, Croatia, Cyprus, Czech Republic, Denmark, Egypt, Estonia, Finland, France, Germany, Greece, Hungary, India, Ireland, Israel, Italy, Korea, Kuwait, Latvia, Lithuania, Luxembourg, Malawi, Mexico, Monaco, Netherlands, Norway, Pakistan, Poland, Portugal, Romania, Russian Federation, Saint Vincent and the Grenadines, San Marino, Seychelles, Slovakia, Slovenia, Spain, Sri Lanka, Sweden, Switzerland, Turkey, Ukraine, United Kingdom (Great Britain and Northern Ireland), USA and Venezuela.

2–115 Rules of the Superior Courts Ord.42A r.2 provides that the affidavit required to ground the application should set out the necessary information in relation to the application, but must also:

> "(a) state the nature of the proceedings or intended proceedings and exhibit a certified true copy of the document or documents used or proposed to be used to institute the proceedings;
> (b) specify the Member State of the European Union or, in the case of applications under the Lugano Convention, the Contracting State in which the proceedings have been commenced or are to be commenced;
> (c) state the particular provisions of Regulation No. 44/2001 or of Regulation No. 2201/2003 or the 1968 Convention or the Lugano Convention by which the court of the Member State of the European Union or, in the case of an application under the Lugano Convention, of the Contracting State has assumed jurisdiction or, in the case of intended proceedings, would be entitled to assume jurisdiction."

2–116 If an order is granted pursuant to RSC Ord.42A, any such order shall be made "upon such terms as to costs or otherwise or subject to such undertaking, if any, as the Court may think just."[149]

2–117 Rules of the Superior Courts Ord.42A r.3 provides that every application for an interlocutory order pursuant to Art.31 of the Brussels I Regulation or Art.20 of the Brussels II Regulation or s.13 of the 1998 Act shall be brought by notice of motion.

3. Enforcement of Judgments

2–118 Rules of the Superior Courts Ord.42A also makes provision for applications for the enforcement of judgments pursuant to Ch.III of the Brussels I Regulation, Ch.III of the Brussels II Regulation or s.7 of the 1998 Act.

2–119 Rules of the Superior Courts Ord.42A r.4 provides that an application for enforcement shall be made ex parte to the Master. RSC Ord.42A rr.5 and 6 sets out the requirements in terms of an affidavit grounding an application for enforcement and the specific exhibits thereto which are required. RSC Ord.42A r.5 also sets out that any protective measures sought must be specified. The affidavit must also state, per RSC Ord.42A r.6:

> (1) whether the said judgment provides for the payment of a sum or sums of money;

---

[149] RSC Ord.42A r.3.

(2) whether interest is recoverable on the judgment or part thereof in accordance with the law of the state in which the judgment was given, and if such be the case, the rate of interest, the date from which the interest is recoverable, and the date on which interest ceases to accrue;

(3) an address within the State for service of proceedings on the party making the application and, to the best of the deponent's knowledge and belief, the name and usual or last known address or place of business of the person against whom judgment was given;

(4) the grounds on which the right to enforce the judgment is vested in the party making the application;

(5) as the case may require, that at the date of the application the judgment has not been satisfied, or the judgment has not been fully satisfied, and the part or amount in respect of which it remains unsatisfied.

2–120 Notice of the order granting leave to enforce a judgment is served together with the order on the person against whom the order was made by delivering it to him or her personally or in such other manner as the Master may direct.[150] An appeal to the High Court is available within one month of service.[151]

G. Anti-Suit Injunctions

1. Introduction

2–121 Anti-suit injunctions are a device by which a party can apply for an injunction in his own jurisdiction to restrain an opponent bringing proceedings in a foreign jurisdiction from continuing with his action.

2–122 A distinction can be drawn between the application of the doctrine of *forum non conveniens* and the granting of anti-suit injunctions. The former doctrine can be classified as a defensive mechanism, under which a court employs self-restraint and refuses to hear a case because it is of the opinion that there is a manifestly more convenient forum that may hear the case without engendering an injustice. An anti-suit injunction, on the other hand, is more aggressive in so far as a court seeks, on application, to restrain another court from hearing the case. This is on the basis that it is so inconvenient for the matter to be determined elsewhere. From a tactical and strategic point of view, both have the same ultimate effect, in that they can enable a party to keep litigation away from a forum that is deemed, for whatever reason, to be undesirable or unfavourable to a party's interests.

---

[150] RSC Ord.42A r.9. The contents of the notice are set out at RSC Ord.42A r.10.
[151] RSC Ord.42A r.11.

2–123 Although anti-suit injunctions have been held to be incompatible with the Brussels I Regulation,[152] they may still be applied for in relation to non-Brussels I countries. The theory underpinning these injunctions is that such jurisdiction is exercised "where it is appropriate to avoid injustice".[153] It is important to note that an anti-suit injunction does not issue against a foreign court, but is addressed to a litigant in the foreign proceedings; as with most injunctions, it acts in personam.

2. Acts In Personam

2–124 The in personam nature of the injunction was emphasised in *Lett v Lett*.[154] In that case an injunction was granted to restrain a suit in an Argentinean court where the plaintiff in that suit had covenanted not to proceed with the suit. The plaintiff was within the jurisdiction of the Irish court. At first instance, Porter M.R. quoted from *Kerr on Injunctions*:

> "In the exercise of this jurisdiction the Court does not proceed upon any claim or right to interfere with or control the course of proceedings in the tribunals of a foreign country, or to prevent them from adjudicating on the rights of the parties when drawn in controversy and duty presented for their determination. The jurisdiction is founded on the clear authority vested in Courts of Equity over persons within the limits of their jurisdiction, and amenable to process to restrain them from doing acts which work wrong and injury to others, and are therefore contrary to equity and good conscience. As the order of the Court in such cases is pointed solely at the individual, and does not extend to the tribunal where the suit or proceeding is pending, it is wholly immaterial that the party to whom it is addressed is prosecuting his action in the Courts of a foreign Country."[155]

2–125 There is a dearth of case law in this jurisdiction on anti-suit injunctions. As such, it is necessary to have regard to the development of law abroad, in particular in England, to understand the scope and range of such anti-suit injunctions.

3. Historical Development

2–126 The English courts have long exercised a jurisdiction to restrain a party from instituting or prosecuting proceedings in a foreign court.[156] However, such

---

[152] See C–159/02 *Turner v Grovit Case* [2004] E.C.R. I–3565, also reported at [2005] 1 A.C. 101, and discussed at para.2–130.
[153] *Castanho v Brown & Root* (UK) Ltd [1981] A.C. 557 at 573; [1981] 1 All E.R. 143 at 149.
[154] [1906] 1 I.R. 618.
[155] [1906] 1 I.R. 618 at 629.
[156] See generally, Dicey, Morris & Collins, *The Conflict of Laws*, 14th edn (London: Sweet & Maxwell, 2006), Ch.12.

an injunction will only be issued restraining a party who is amenable to the jurisdiction of the court, and against whom an injunction will be an effective remedy.[157] The history of such injunctions was considered by Lord Goff in *Societé Nationale Industrielle Aerospatiale v Lee Kui Jak.*[158] He stated that the jurisdiction is to be exercised when the "ends of justice" require it.[159]

2–127 It is a prerequisite to the exercise of the power to issue an anti-suit injunction that the court being requested to do so is a natural forum for the dispute.[160]

2–128 As was made clear in the 1834 case of *Portarlington v Soulby,*[161] the jurisdiction was stated to be grounded "not upon any pretension to the exercise of judicial ... rights abroad", but upon the fact that the party to whom the order is directed is subject to the in personam jurisdiction of the English court.[162] As will be seen, however, this approach must now be viewed in the light of the decision of the European Court of Justice (ECJ) in *Turner v Grovit.*[163]

4. Modern Developments

2–129 The courts had recognised in the case of *British Airways Board v Laker Airways Ltd*[164] that although an anti-suit injunction was viewed as only operating in personam against the party to the foreign litigation, the remedy was an indirect interference with the process of the foreign court and the jurisdiction to grant such injunctions had to be exercised with caution.[165]

---

[157] *Re North Carolina Estate Co Ltd* (1889) 5 T.L.R. 328, per Chitty J.
[158] [1987] A.C. 871; [1987] 3 W.L.R. 59; [1987] 3 All E.R. 510.
[159] Citing *Bushby v Munday* (1821) 5 Madd. 297 at 307, per Sir John Leach V.C.; *Carron Iron Co v Maclaren* (1855) 5 H.L. Cas 416 at 453, per Lord St Leonards, a principle reasserted by Lord Scarman in *Castanho v Brown & Root (UK) Ltd* [1981] A.C. 557; [1981] 1 All E.R. 143 and by Lord Diplock in *British Airways Board v Laker Airways Ltd* [1985] A.C. 58; [1984] 3 W.L.R. 413; [1984] 3 All E.R. 39.
[160] *Société Nationale Industrielle Aerospatiale v Lee Kui Jak* [1987] A.C. 871 at 896; [1987] 3 W.L.R. 59; [1987] 3 All E.R. 510 at 521; *Société Commerciale de Réassurance v Eras International Ltd (No. 2)* [1995] 2 All E.R. 278 at 309; *Amchem Products Inc. v British Columbia (Workers' Compensation Board)* [1993] 1 S.C.R. 897 at 931; *CSR Ltd v Cigna Insurance Australia Ltd* (1997) 189 C.L.R. 345 at 397.
[161] (1834) 3 My & K 104 at 108, per Lord Brougham L.C.
[162] See *Bushby v Munday* (1821) 5 Madd. 297 at 307.
[163] Case C–159/02 [2004] E.C.R. I–3565, also reported at [2005] 1 A.C. 101. The House of Lords decision is reported at [2002] 1 W.L.R. 107.
[164] [1985] A.C. 58; [1984] 3 W.L.R. 413; [1984] 3 All E.R. 39.
[165] [1985] A.C. 58 at 95; [1984] 3 W.L.R. 413 at 435; [1984] 3 All E.R. 39 at 57, per Lord Scarman. See also the comments of Scrutton L.J. in *Cohen v Rothfield* [1919] 1 K.B. 410 at 413; Lord Scarman in *Castanho v Brown & Root (UK) Ltd* [1981] A.C. 557 at 573; [1981] 1 All E.R. 143 at 149 and Lord Brandon in *South Carolina Insurance Co v Assurantie Maatschappij "De Zeven Provincien" NV* [1987] A.C. 24 at 40; [1983] 3 W.L.R. 398 at 408;

(a) Incompatibility with the Conventions/Brussels I Regulation

2–130 The cautionary note sounded in the *Laker Airways* case foreshadowed the decision of the ECJ in the case of *Turner v Grovit*.[166] In the latter case, anti-suit injunctions were held to be incompatible with the Brussels Convention (the case was determined in the context of the Brussels Convention, but its principles are equally applicable to the Brussels I Regulation). In coming to this conclusion, the ECJ emphasised the principle of mutual trust, one of the pillars of the Convention. It found that anti-suit injunctions were "wholly and invariably inconsistent with the relationship of mutual trust and confidence to and by which the Member States have bound themselves."[167] Lord Hobhouse, speaking for the House of Lords, had stated that when an English court makes a restraining order, it is making an order which is addressed only to a party which is before it, and that the order is not directed against the foreign court.[168] He held that the order bound a party in personam. However, the ECJ was quite explicit in rejecting this contention, and held that:

> "A prohibition imposed by a court, backed by a penalty, restraining a party from commencing or continuing proceedings before a foreign court undermines the latter court's jurisdiction to determine the dispute. Any injunction prohibiting a claimant from bringing such an action must be seen as constituting interference with the jurisdiction of the foreign court which, as such, is incompatible with the system of the Convention."[169]

2–131 The ECJ also dismissed the argument that the grant of injunctions may contribute to attainment of the objective of the Convention, namely to minimise the risk of conflicting decisions and to avoid a multiplicity of proceedings. The court held that recourse to such measures would render ineffective the specific mechanisms provided for by the Convention for cases of *lis alibi pendens* and of related actions.

2–132 The ECJ felt that allowing anti-suit injunctions would potentially give rise to situations involving conflicts for which the Convention contains no rules. It also felt that it could not exclude the possibility that even if an injunction had been issued in one Contracting State, a decision might nevertheless be given by

---

[1986] 3 All E.R. 487 at 496; *cf. Continental Bank NA v Aeakos Compania Naviera SA* [1994] 1 W.L.R. 599, in which the Court of Appeal granted an injunction restraining a group of borrowers and guarantors from bringing legal proceedings against a bank in Greece by virtue of an exclusive jurisdiction clause.

[166] Case C–159/02 [2004] E.C.R. I-3565, also reported at [2005] 1 A.C. 101. The House of Lords decision is reported at [2002] 1 W.L.R. 107.

[167] [2004] E.C.R. I-3565.

[168] Citing *Société Nationale Industrielle Aerospatiale v Lee Kui Jak* [1987] A.C. 871; [1987] 3 W.L.R.; [1987] 3 All E.R. 510.

[169] [2004] E.C.R. I-3565, para.27.

a court of another Contracting State. Similarly, it held that the possibility could not be excluded that the courts of two Contracting States that allowed such measures might issue contradictory injunctions.

2–133 The position now, based on the *Turner v Grovit* decision, would seem to be that by virtue of the Convention/Brussels I Regulation, a national court cannot grant an injunction whereby it prohibits a party to proceedings pending before it from commencing or continuing legal proceedings before a court of another Contracting State. This is the position even where that party is acting in bad faith with a view to frustrating the existing proceedings.[170]

(b) Arbitration Agreements

2–134 That there is still some lingering uncertainty as to the status of anti-suit injunctions is evident from the case of *West Tankers Inc. v RAS Riunione Adriatica di Sicurta SpA*.[171] In that case, the House of Lords requested the ECJ to consider whether:

> "it is consistent with E.C. Regulation 44/2001 for a court of a Member State to make an order to restrain a person from commencing or continuing proceedings in another Member State on the ground that such proceedings are in breach of an arbitration agreement."

2–135 The House of Lords took the view that arbitration fell outside the scope of the Brussels I Regulation and, as such, any restrictions on anti-suit injunctions should not apply.[172]

2–136 At least one author had previously suggested, based on the case of *Aggeliki Charis Compania Maritima SA v Pagnan SpA (The Angelic Grace)*,[173] that:

> "The English court can grant an anti-suit injunction in relation to proceedings on the merits of a court of another Member State for the purpose of enforcing an English arbitration clause ... ."[174]

2–137 This was on the basis that the arbitration clause was outside the scope of the Regulation.

---

[170] See generally, Flannery, "The End of Anti-Suit Injunctions?" (2004) 154 N.L.J. 798.

[171] [2007] 1 All E.R. 794.

[172] See Qureshi, "Growing Up Fast" (2007) 157 N.L.J. 586 and Qureshi, "The Rise of Anti-Suit Injunctions" (2006) 156 N.L.J. 976.

[173] [1995] 1 Lloyd's Rep. 87.

[174] Gee, *Commercial Injunctions*, 5th edn (London: Thomson Sweet & Maxwell, 2004), p.406.

2–138 Having regard to the subsequent *Turner* decision, however, the ECJ appeared concerned that allowing anti-suit injunctions would potentially give rise to situations involving conflicts for which the Conventions/Regulation contain no rules, and it will be interesting to see which course the ECJ prefers in *West Tankers*.

5. Anti-suit injunctions in a non-Convention/Brussels I Regulation country

2–139 In so far as anti-suit injunctions which may be sought in relation to a non-Convention/Brussels I country are concerned, two categories have been defined in which anti-suit injunctions can be granted:

    (i) Where an estate is being administered in one country, or a petition in bankruptcy has been presented in a country, or winding-up proceedings have been commenced in a country, and an injunction is granted to restrain a person from seeking, by foreign proceedings, to obtain the sole benefit of certain foreign assets.

    (ii) Where the plaintiff has commenced proceedings against the defendant in respect of the same subject-matter in two different jurisdictions, and the defendant has asked one court to compel the plaintiff to elect in which country he shall alone proceed.[175]

2–140 However, it is evident from the decision in *Société Nationale Industrielle Aerospatiale v Lee Kui Jak*[176] in England that the fact that the courts there take the view that a foreign forum is a *forum non conveniens* is not a sufficient basis upon which to grant an anti-suit injunction. Restraint must be exercised due to the principles of comity and an unwillingness to interfere with a foreign jurisdiction.[177]

(a) Criteria

2–141 It is not possible to set out a definitive list of criteria as to when anti-suit injunctions will be granted, for "the width and flexibility of equity are not to be undermined by categorisation".[178] In so far as it might be possible to set out a list of categories, it appears in relation to final anti-suit injunctions that these may be granted in general terms if:

---

[175] See *McHenry v Lewis* (1882) 22 Ch D 397 and *Peruvian Guano Co v Bockwoldt* (1883) 23 Ch D 225 at 230.

[176] [1987] A.C. 871; [1987] 3 W.L.R. 59; [1987] 3 All E.R. 510.

[177] Principles which also inform the approach of the courts in this jurisdiction: see, for example, *Shipsey v British and South American Steam Navigation Company* [1936] I.R. 65.

[178] *British Airways Board v Laker Airways Ltd* [1985] A.C. 58 at 81; [1984] 3 W.L.R. 413 at 422; [1984] 3 All E.R. 39 at 46.

- the applicant has a legal right not to be sued in foreign country under contract, viz. he can point to a contract which is valid and binding and which is broken by the bringing of foreign proceedings[179];
- the applicant has an equitable right not to be sued in a foreign country[180];
- the proceedings will interfere with "the due process of the court"[181];
- the foreign action is frivolous and vexatious.[182]

2–142 It was also held in *Donohoe v Armco*[183] that the remedy, to be granted, must be an "effective" one.

(b) Single/Alternative Fora

2–143 A distinction can also be made between situations involving an alternative forum and those involving a single forum. An alternative forum case involves a choice between Ireland and a foreign forum. This was considered in an English context in *Airbus Industrie GIE v Patel*,[184] wherein it was held that:

> "an anti-suit injunction will normally only be applied for in an English court where England is the natural forum for the resolution of the dispute; and, if so, there will be no infringement of comity."[185]

2–144 A single forum anti-suit injunction arises when the cause of action relied on in the foreign court cannot be advanced in Ireland and there is no cause of action available in Ireland. In *British Airways Board v Laker Airways Ltd*[186] it was held that an injunction might be granted to restrain proceedings in a foreign court even if the plaintiff had no remedy in England, but only if the bringing of proceedings in a foreign court were in the circumstances, and in the words of Lord Scarman, "so unconscionable" that it could be regarded as an "infringement of equitable right".[187]

---

[179]   *British Airways Board v Laker Airways Ltd* [1985] A.C. 58; [1984] 3 W.L.R. 413; [1984] 3 All E.R. 39; *Donohoe v Armco Inc.* [2001] 1 Lloyds Rep. 425.

[180]   *British Airways Board v Laker Airways Ltd* [1985] A.C. 58; [1984] 3 W.L.R. 413; [1984] 3 All E.R. 39.

[181]   *South Carolina Insurance Co v Assurantie Maatschappij "De Zeven Provincien" NV* [1987] A.C. 24 at 41 [1983] 3 W.L.R. 398 at 409; [1986] 3 All E.R. 487 at 497.

[182]   *Société Nationale Industrielle Aerospatiale v Lee Kui Jak* [1987] A.C. 871; [1987] 3 W.L.R. 59; [1987] 3 All E.R. 510.

[183]   [2002] 1 Lloyds Rep 526.

[184]   [1999] 1 A.C. 119; [1998] 2 W.L.R. 686; [1998] 2 All E.R. 257.

[185]   [1999] 1 A.C. 119 at 138; [1998] 2 W.L.R. 686 at 695; [1998] 2 All E.R. 257 at 265.

[186]   [1985] A.C. 58; [1984] 3 W.L.R. 413; [1984] 3 All E.R. 39.

[187]   [1985] A.C. 58 at 95; [1984] 3 W.L.R. 413 at 435; [1984] 3 All E.R. 39 at 57. As distinct from the general test of "frivolous and vexatious" as considered in *Société Nationale Industrielle Aerospatiale v Lee Kui Jak* [1987] A.C. 871; [1987] 3 W.L.R. 59; [1987] 3.

CHAPTER 3

STANDING

A. INTRODUCTION

3–01 A key consideration in applying for an injunction is to ensure that the party seeking the injunction has the locus standi, or standing, to bring such an application. In other words, they should have sufficient interest in the matter in order to bring it before the courts. As is clear from the judgment of Walsh J. in *State (Lynch) v Cooney*,[1] the courts will consider the circumstances of individual cases, and in each case "the question of sufficient interest is a mixed question of fact and law which must be decided upon legal principles."[2]

3–02 This chapter will consider standing in the context of an application for an injunction. First, the general principles related to standing will be reviewed. This will be followed by an overview of the position of a party applying for an injunction, with an emphasis on the rights which they may invoke. The particular role and standing of the Attorney General will be looked at separately. Finally, the position of the party against whom an injunction may be sought will be considered.

B. GENERAL PRINCIPLES

1. Introduction

3–03 The seminal decision of *Cahill v Sutton*,[3] which involved a challenge to the constitutionality of provisions of the Statute of Limitations 1957, crystallised the attitude of the courts to, in Henchy J.'s lively phrase, "the crank, the obstructionist, the meddlesome, the perverse, the officious man of straw and many others."[4] In setting out parameters designed to avoid the courts becoming "… the happy hunting ground of the busybody and the crank",[5] the court was affirming a long-standing practice in relation to locus standi. The key principles set out in *Cahill* continue to inform the approach of the courts towards locus

---

[1] [1982] I.R. 337.
[2] [1982] I.R. 337 at 368.
[3] [1980] I.R. 269. For a general consideration of standing pre-*Cahill*, see *East Donegal Co-operative v Attorney General* [1970] I.R. 317.
[4] [1980] I.R. 269 at 284.
[5] [1980] I.R. 269 at 277, per O'Higgins C.J.

standi. Although determined in the context of a putative constitutional challenge, the principles are also recognised as having a wider application.[6]

2. Concrete Personal Circumstances

3–04 In *Cahill*, having acknowledged that in theory an argument could be made for allowing any citizen to bring proceedings to have a particular statutory provision declared unconstitutional, Henchy J. then observed that:

> "To allow one litigant to present and argue what is essentially another person's case would not be conducive to the administration of justice as a general rule. Without concrete personal circumstances pointing to a wrong suffered or threatened, the case tends to lack the force and urgency of reality. There is also the risk that the person whose case is being put forward unsuccessfully by another may be left with the grievance that his claim was wrongly or inadequately presented."[7]

3–05 The need to identify "concrete personal circumstances pointing to a wrong suffered or threatened" is thus a key consideration when dealing with the issue of standing. However, Henchy J. also recognised that such a rule of practice could be, "subject to expansion, exception or qualification when the justice of the case so requires".[8]

3. Expansion of the Rule of Practice

3–06 This acceptance that there could be expansion was borne out in *Crotty v An Taoiseach*.[9] In that case, the plaintiff sought an injunction to prevent the Government from ratifying the Single European Act. Barrington J. found that while the case involved the constitutionality of a political measure, it was also an issue dealing with the powers of government and with constitutional rights. He felt that there were matters of law in which a responsible citizen could take a legitimate interest. Barrington J. thus held that the plaintiff had raised a fair question of law to be tried on the issues for which there were weighty and countervailing considerations justifying a departure from the received rule of practice regarding locus standi. Barrington J. also acknowledged that the plaintiff had standing to the extent that he claimed that the Constitution itself

---

[6] See Hogan and Morgan, *Administrative Law in Ireland*, 3rd edn (Dublin: Thomson Round Hall, 1998), p.744.
[7] [1980] I.R. 269 at 283.
[8] [1980] I.R. 269 at 285.
[9] [1987] I.R. 713.

was being amended in the absence of the consultation by referendum with the electorate specifically provided for by the Constitution.[10]

3–07 However, it is important to bear in mind that even if locus standi has been established, an injunction is a discretionary remedy. That being the case, there is no guarantee that an injunction will be granted simply on the basis of standing, without more.

C. The Applicant

3–08 The standing of the plaintiff or applicant will be considered first by looking in general terms at the right or interest to be established. It will be followed by a consideration of the different types of right or interest which may be established. A consideration of the position of representative bodies will then follow.

1. Establishing a Right or Interest

3–09 In order to establish their standing, a party seeking an injunction must in general terms be able to identify at a minimum an interest in the protection of a right, which right has been infringed[11] (or where such infringement is threatened, apprehended or imminent).[12] It is not necessary for that party to identify an explicit statutory right which they seek to invoke in order to apply for an injunction; such a right can be a common law, equitable or constitutional right. There must, in other words, be some cause of action.[13]

3–10 However, it is important to note that a right to interim or interlocutory relief is not in itself a cause of action.[14] As expressed by Lord Nicholls in the case of *Mercedes Benz AG v Leiduck*,[15] this is because:

---

[10] As summarised by Budd J. in *Riordan v An Tánaiste* [1995] 3 I.R. 62 at 71. The Supreme Court subsequently held that the plaintiff did have locus standi.

[11] *Directors of Imperial Gas Light and Coke Co v Broadbent* (1859) 7 H.L. Cas. 600.

[12] See Ch.5, Perpetual Injunctions, particularly para.5–16, dealing with *quia timet* injunctions.

[13] Care should be taken when using the phrase "cause of action" for, as cautioned by Lord Nicholls in *Mercedes Benz AG v Leiduck* [1996] A.C. 284 at 310; [1995] 3 W.L.R. 718 at 738; [1995] 3 All E.R. 929 at 948: "A cause of action is no more than a lawyer's label for a type of facts which will attract a remedy from the court. If the court will give a remedy, *ex hypothesi* there is a cause of action."

[14] per Lord Diplock in *Siskina (Owners of Cargo Lately Laden on Board) v Distos Compania Naviera SA* [1979] A.C. 210; [1977] 3 W.L.R. 818; [1977] 3 All E.R. 803.

[15] [1996] A.C. 284; [1995] 3 W.L.R. 718; [1995] 3 All E.R. 929.

"ordinarily proceedings bring a substantive dispute before the court. Attention is therefore focused on the cause of action involved in the substantive dispute the court is being asked to resolve. The claim to interim protective relief is ancillary to the underlying cause of action, and in that respect it has no independent existence of its own."[16]

2. Rights Which May be Invoked

(a) General Rights

3–11 The need to point to an interest in a right, which right has been or is about to be infringed, is a matter which falls to be dealt with on a case-by-case basis. The case frequently used to illustrate the need for identification of a right or interest is that of *Day v Brownrigg*.[17] In that case, the plaintiff lived in a house that had been called "Ashford Lodge" for 60 years. The defendant acquired a neighbouring house called "Ashford Villa". The defendant started to call his house "Ashford Lodge" and the plaintiff sought an injunction to prevent him from doing so. The Court of Appeal took the view that there was no violation of a legal or equitable right. On that basis, no injunction was granted. Thesiger J. cautioned that, "the judgment appealed from is founded upon a misconception of the legal maxim that where there is a wrong there is a remedy".[18]

3–12 Similarly, in *Street v Union Bank of Spain*,[19] the court refused an injunction to restrain the use of an address. Pearson J. referred to the decision in *Day v Brownrigg* and the fact that he would be "going beyond the jurisdiction of the Court" if he was to grant an injunction where there was "no attempt to interfere with trade; no legal injury done; but where there simply was a matter of inconvenience."[20]

3–13 More recently in this jurisdiction, in *Belmont Securities Ltd v Crean*[21] O'Hanlon J. declined to grant an injunction against the continued breach of a restrictive covenant by a shop in a small shopping complex. This was because the vendor of the shop had not retained any interest which had been jeopardised or damaged by the breach. In the later case of *Kennedy v Mahon*,[22] which also dealt with covenants (or more accurately, the lack thereof), Peart J. observed that:

---

[16] [1996] A.C. 284 at 311; [1995] 3 W.L.R. 718 at 738; [1995] 3 All E.R. 929 at 948. See *Caudron v Air Zaire* [1985] I.R. 716; [1986] I.L.R.M. 10 and the consideration of a *Mareva* injunction being an ancillary order; see generally, Ch.8, Commercial Injunctions.

[17] (1878) 10 Ch D 294.

[18] (1878) 10 Ch D 294 at 305.

[19] (1885) 30 Ch D 156.

[20] (1885) 30 Ch D 156 at 159. See also *Corelli v Wall* (1906) 22 T.L.R. 532 and *Sports and General Press Agency Ltd v "Our Dogs" Publishing Co Ltd* [1917] 2 K.B. 125, in which the plaintiff was unable to establish a legal right to the sole press photographic rights at a dog show.

[21] unreported, High Court, O'Hanlon J., June 17, 1988.

[22] unreported, High Court, Peart J., August 20, 2004.

"It is difficult … to identify precisely what form of injunction the Court could grant, since at this stage there is nothing about to be done by the defendants which can be restrained."

3–14 More specific considerations apply in relation to constitutional rights and statutory rights.

(b) Constitutional Rights

3–15 Locus standi/standing in the context of the invocation of constitutional rights has already been referred to above in the context of the litigation brought by Raymond Crotty to prevent the ratification of the Single European Act.[23] As has been seen,[24] *Cahill v Sutton*[25] also involved a putative constitutional challenge.

3–16 As to what test should be applied in relation to standing in such circumstances, in *SPUC v Coogan (No. 1)*[26] Finlay C.J. affirmed his view in the earlier decision of *AG (SPUC) v Open Door Counselling Ltd*[27] that the relevant test for locus standi in relation to constitutional rights was one of "*bona fide* concern and interest, interest being used in the sense of proximity or an objective interest".[28] To establish whether such an interest exists, regard must be had to the nature of the constitutional right which is sought to be protected.

3–17 It is also clear from various decisions, such as *Education Company of Ireland Company Ltd v Fitzpatrick (No. 2)*,[29] that constitutional rights may be asserted by a private individual against other private individuals.[30]

(c) Statutory Provisions

3–18 A party considering applying for an injunction should establish whether an injunction should be sought on the basis of a specific statutory provision, or procedures outlined therein. For example, s.160 of the Planning and Development Act 2000 does not contain a specific standing requirement, and

---

[23] See para.3–06.
[24] See para.3–03.
[25] [1980] I.R. 269.
[26] [1989] I.R. 734; [1990] I.L.R.M. 70.
[27] [1988] I.R. 593.
[28] [1989] I.R. 734 at 742. See also, the cases of *Crotty v An Taoiseach* [1987] I.R. 713; *McGimpsey v Ireland* [1990] 1 I.R. 110; [1990] I.L.R.M. 441 and *Riordan v An Tánaiste* [1996] 2 I.L.R.M. 107.
[29] [1961] I.R. 345 at 368, per Budd J.
[30] See also, inter alia, *Murtagh Properties Ltd v Cleary* [1972] I.R. 330; *Murphy v Stewart* [1973] I.R. 97; *Meskell v CIE* [1973] I.R. 121 and *Glover v BLN Ltd* [1973] I.R. 388.

any member of the public, regardless of whether that person has any interest in the land in question or suffered damage as a result of the particular develop-ment, can bring an application under the section.[31]

3–19 The applicant party must also ensure that that there is no statutory provision preventing such an application or dictating the procedural aspects of an application.[32] For example, in *Dunnes Stores Ltd v Mandate*[33] the plaintiff was granted an injunction on an interim basis. However, Murphy J. refused the plaintiff's application for an interlocutory injunction. This refusal was confirmed on appeal by the Supreme Court, on the basis that it was in reality an application for a final injunction under the European Communities (Misleading Advertising) Regulations 1988, and the wrong procedure, viz. seeking an interlocutory injunction, had consequently been adopted.

(i) Specific Statutory Provision: Applicable Test

3–20 The test for determining whether a party can apply for an injunction based on a specific statutory provision was considered by Ungoed-Thomas J. in the case of *Duchess of Argyll v Duke of Argyll*.[34] He made reference to, inter alia, the dictum of Atkin L.J. in *Phillips v Britannia Hygienic Laundry Co. Ltd.*[35] In that case, Atkin L.J. had stated that:

> "the question is whether these regulations, viewed in the circumstances in which they were made and to which they relate, were intended to impose a duty which is a public duty only or whether they were intended, in addition to the public duty, to impose a duty enforceable by an individual aggrieved."[36]

3–21 Ungoed-Thomas J. felt, on a review of the authorities, that the relevant question was whether a piece of legislation, on its true construction and in light of the surrounding circumstances, "was intended only for the protection of the

---

[31] See further, Ch.11, Specific Statutory Injunctions, para.11–12. This is not unique. In the English case of *SIB v Pantell S.A.* [1989] 3 W.L.R. 698; [1990] Ch. 426, in Browne-Wilkinson V.C. held in relation to s.6 of the Financial Services Act 1986 that although the plaintiff, the Securities Investment Board, had no private cause of action entitling it to *Mareva* relief against the defendant, it had a statutory right of action for the benefit of investors conferred on it by s.6.

[32] See *Tomlinson v Criminal Injuries Compensation Tribunal*, unreported, Supreme Court, January 19, 2005, in which Denham J. stated that: "While a court would lean towards requiring that the remedies available under the scheme be exhausted, the ultimate decision depends on the circumstances of the case."

[33] [1996] 1 I.L.R.M. 384.

[34] [1967] Ch. 302; [1965] 2 W.L.R. 790; [1965] 1 All E.R. 611.

[35] [1923] 2 K.B. 832.

[36] [1923] 2 K.B. 832 at 842.

public at large or also for the benefit of a class of persons." He felt that if it was also for the benefit of a class, "then any member of that class is entitled to bring not criminal proceedings for the public offence but civil proceedings in respect of injury to himself."[37]

3–22 In *McKenna v EH*,[38] Finnegan J. approved the decision in *Argyll* and adopted the test set out by Ungoed-Thomas J. Finnegan J. summarised this test as being whether the statute manifests "an intention to confer a civil right on the plaintiff: if so the possibility of an injunction arises."[39]

(ii) Enforcing Statutory Provisions Against Private Individuals

3–23 The question of a private individual enforcing statutory provisions against another individual was considered in the case of *Irish Permanent Building Society v Registrar of Building Societies*.[40] Barrington J. held that the plaintiff building society had locus standi to seek declarations to the effect that another building society did not have the status of a building society within the meaning of the Building Societies Act 1976. He also felt that the plaintiff could seek an injunction restraining Irish Life from carrying on the business of a building society within the State. Barrington J., considering the factual circumstances before him, held that:

> "… it would be wrong to treat the plaintiffs as if they were mere members of the public. They come before the court as persons with a real grievance arising out of an alleged breach of the law and with a substantial interest in the outcome of the proceedings."[41]

3–24 The question of one private individual enforcing statutory provisions and duties against another was dealt with comprehensively in *Parsons v Kavanagh*.[42] In that case, the plaintiff operated a passenger bus service pursuant to a licence under the Road Transport Acts 1932 and 1933. He sought to injunct the unlicensed defendant who was operating a similar service on the same route. The defendant argued that the plaintiff was not entitled to take proceedings to enforce the Road Transport Acts. It fell to O'Hanlon J. to consider the general principles derived from English authorities on the question of whether, and under what conditions, a duty imposed by statute may be enforced at the suit of a private individual. As identified by O'Hanlon J., these bear setting out in full:

---

[37] [1967] Ch. 302 at 341; [1965] 2 W.L.R. 790 at 817; [1965] 1 All E.R. 611 at 632.
[38] [2002] 1 I.R. 72; [2002] 2 I.L.R.M. 117.
[39] [2002] 1 I.R. 72 at 81; [2002] 2 I.L.R.M. 117 at 125. Also citing *King v Goussetis* [1986] 5 N.S.W.L.R. 89.
[40] [1981] I.L.R.M. 242.
[41] [1981] I.L.R.M. 242 at 252.
[42] [1990] I.L.R.M. 560.

"1. Whether or not an individual can bring a common law action in respect of a breach of a duty imposed by statute depends upon whether the intention of the statute considered as a whole and in the circumstances in which it was made and to which it relates was to impose a duty which is a public duty only, or to impose in addition a duty enforceable by an aggrieved individual. No universal rule can be formulated which will answer the question whether in any given case an individual can sue. (*Philips v Britannia Hygienic Laundry Co Ltd*, (1923) 2 KB 832 /841; Halsbury, Laws of England, 4 edn, Vol 4 paras. 941, 961).

2. The only rule which in all circumstances is valid is that the answer must depend on a consideration of the whole Act and the circumstances, including the existing law, in which it was enacted. In answering the question it is relevant to consider whether the statute was intended to protect a limited class of persons or the public as a whole; whether the damage suffered by the person seeking to sue was of the kind which the statute was intended to prevent; whether a special statutory remedy by way of penalty or otherwise is prescribed for breach of the statute; the nature of the obligation imposed, and the general purview and intendment of the statute. If a statute on its true construction is intended to protect a particular class it is some indication that members of that class are intended to have a right of action, as for example, in the case of statutes for the protection of factory workers. (*Cutler v Wandsworth Stadium Ltd*, (1949) AC 398.

3. Where a statutory remedy by way of criminal proceedings is provided for the breach of a statutory duty there is a strong implication that no civil action for breach of that duty lies. The imposition by a statute of a penalty for breach of a statutory duty is generally a ground for holding that no common law action for damages lies for breach of that duty. (Lord Tenterden CJ in *Doe v Bridges*, 1 B & Ad. 847, 859). It may be relevant to consider whether the penalty imposed by the statute is an adequate deterrent against breach of statutory duty. (*Groves v Lord Wimborne*, (1898) 2 QB 402)."[43]

3–25 These factors are relatively self-explanatory. O'Hanlon J. then proceeded to consider the constitutional aspect of the claim. He also considered the wider principles referred to in the decision of Costello J. in *AG v Paperlink*.[44] In that case, Costello J. had cited an extract from the English case of *AG v Chaudhury*,[45] which stated that:

---

43 [1990] I.L.R.M. 560 at 566.
44 [1984] I.L.R.M. 373.
45 [1971] 1 W.L.R. 1614.

"Whenever Parliament has enacted a law and given a particular remedy for the breach of it, such remedy being in an inferior court, nevertheless the High Court always has a reserve power to enforce the law so enacted by way of an injunction or other suitable remedy."[46]

3–26 O'Hanlon J. found that:

"the constitutional right to earn one's livelihood by any lawful means carries with it the entitlement to be protected against any unlawful activity on the part of another person or persons which materially impairs or infringes that right."[47]

3–27 The Supreme Court decision of *Lovett v Gogan*[48] involved a case which was factually similar to that in *Parsons*, the defendants again carrying on a road passenger service. In *Lovett*, Finlay C.J. found the decision of O'Hanlon J. in the *Parsons* case to be correct in law on the findings of fact made by him in that case.[49] The Chief Justice held in the case before him that the plaintiff was entitled to an injunction if he could establish that this was the only way of protecting himself from the threatened invasion of his constitutional rights. He found that, on the evidence, the only remedy that could protect the plaintiff was that of injunction; the penalty for a continuing offence by a person operating a passenger road service without a licence was limited to five pounds.[50]

3–28 In *O'Connor v Williams*,[51] Barron J. summarised the principles to be derived from *Lovett v Gogan* and *Parsons v Kavanagh* as follows:

"(1) There is no general right entitling any person to injunct the commission of a criminal offence. Such persons must come within the category of persons for whose protection the statute was passed.

(2) When the right to earn one's living by lawful means is being infringed such right may be enforced by action.

(3) The plaintiff must show damage. This may be shown by interference, actual or threatened.

(4) To obtain an injunction to restrain the interference, the plaintiff must establish that it is the only way by which he can be protected from the invasion of his constitutional rights."[52]

---

46   [1971] 1 W.L.R. 1614 at 1624, as cited in *Paperlink* at [1984] I.L.R.M. 373 at 391.
47   [1990] I.L.R.M. 560 at 566.
48   [1995] 3 I.R. 132; [1995] 1 I.L.R.M. 12
49   [1995] 3 I.R. 132 at 142; [1995] 1 I.L.R.M. 12 at 19.
50   See also, *Pierce t/a Swords Memorials v Dublin Cemeteries Committee*, unreported, High Court, Laffoy J., May 11, 2006 and her cautionary reference to English cases such as *Attorney General v Metropolitan Electric Supply Company* [1905] 1 Ch. 24.
51   [2001] 1 I.R. 248.
52   [2001] 1 I.R. 248 at 252.

(iii) Criminal Proceedings

3–29 The third principle identified by O'Hanlon J. in *Parsons* involves the provision of "a statutory remedy by way of criminal proceedings". O'Hanlon J. suggested that there was a "strong implication" that no civil action would lie for the breach of such a duty. The equivalent point was considered in England in the case of *Gouriet v Union of Post Office Workers*.[53] In that case, the House of Lords held that a private citizen cannot seek an injunction to prevent the commission of a criminal offence, unless he can point to an actionable tort giving rise to damage.

3–30 In *O'Connor v Williams*,[54] Barron J. distinguished *Lovett* and *Parsons* on the basis that implementation of the criminal law was more appropriate than injunctive relief on the facts before the court in *O'Connor*. He observed that the *Lovett* and *Parsons* cases concerned "a direct interference with the rights of the plaintiff by the defendant and by no-one else".[55] However, the defendants in *O'Connor* were "only one of several firms operating a hackney service". It was in those circumstances that Barron J. felt that the implementation of the criminal law was more appropriate "provided that it can furnish adequate protection for the plaintiffs".[56]

(iv) Validity of a Statute

3–31 It was held in *Pesca Valentia Ltd v Minister for Fisheries*[57] that in an appropriate case a party may invoke the jurisdiction of the courts to restrain the operation of a statutory provision pending a challenge to its validity. However, a cautionary note was sounded by Murphy J. in *Grange Development Ltd v Dublin Co. Council (No. 4)*.[58] He agreed with the *Pesca Valentia* approach, but made reference to:

> "the enormous onus which lies on anybody who seeks to establish that an Act of the Oireachtas is invalid having regard to the provisions of the Constitution."[59]

3. Representative Body

3–32 Some care must be taken when dealing with the locus standi of a representative body. This is clear from the decision of the Supreme Court in the

---

[53] [1978] A.C. 435; [1977] 3 W.L.R. 300; [1977] 3 All E.R. 70.
[54] [2001] 1 I.R. 248.
[55] [2001] 1 I.R. 248 at 253.
[56] [2001] 1 I.R. 248 at 253.
[57] [1985] I.R. 193; [1986] I.L.R.M. 68.
[58] [1989] I.R. 377.
[59] [1989] I.R. 377 at 383.

case of *Construction Industry Federation v Dublin City Council.*[60] Although this
was a case which did not primarily concern an injunction application (although
an injunction was sought by way of alternative relief), it is an important decision
in the context of standing generally.

3–33 Section 48 of the Planning and Development Act 2000 provides that a
planning authority can draw up a development contribution scheme and require
contributions from all applicants for planning permission. In *Construction
Industry Federation*, the applicant federation brought proceedings relating to a
specific decision of the respondent to make a development contribution scheme
pursuant to s.48. However, McCracken J. held that the court was effectively
being asked to deal with a hypothetical situation. He felt that the challenge
could have been brought by any of the members of the applicant who were
affected, in circumstances where the contribution scheme related to the
particular situation of that member. This was something which the applicant
body could not do. Nor had it shown any damage to itself.

3–34 McCracken J. contrasted previous cases in which parties with no personal
or direct interest had been granted locus standi with the facts before it. There
had been no evidence before the court that, in the absence of the purported
challenge by the plaintiff, there would have been no other challenger. Whilst
acknowledging that there was no hint of vexatiousness or irresponsibility on the
part of the plaintiff representative body, McCracken J. could not see any
"justifiable basis upon which it can be said that the Appellant has any interest
other than that of its individual members."[61] In the circumstances, the appeal
was dismissed for want of locus standi on the part of the plaintiff.

D. THE ATTORNEY GENERAL

1. Introduction

3–35 Hogan and Morgan observe that it is a

> "cardinal legal principle that, in general, an injunction may be sought by or
> on behalf of the Attorney General to enforce a statutory obligation, even
> without explicit authorisation."[62]

The Attorney General may sue in his own name as necessary.[63]

---

[60]   [2005] 2 I.R. 496.

[61]   [2005] 2 I.R. 496 at 527. However, McCracken J. did acknowledge (at 526) that "there are
       circumstances in which it may be permissible and even desirable that a representative body
       such as the applicant may be entitled to bring judicial review proceedings", citing *R. v
       Inspectorate of Pollution, Ex p. Greenpeace Ltd* [1994] 1 W.L.R. 570.

[62]   Hogan & Morgan, *Administrative Law in Ireland*, 3rd edn (Dublin: Thomson Round Hall,
       1998), p.317.

[63]   He is independent of the Government in this regard: See *Attorney General v X* [1992] 1 I.R. 1

3–36 The ability of the Attorney General to seek the protection of public rights post-independence was recognised in *Moore v Attorney General*,[64] in which Kennedy C.J. stated that:

"the law and practice as to relations of the Attorney General and his relator … is clearly settled and is not in question here. They are, of course, illustrations of the application to the bringing of actions and other proceedings of the principle which I am stating—that the Attorney General is the only legal representative of the public in the courts, and is exclusively entitled to assert or defend public interests."[65]

2. Application for Interlocutory Injunctions

3–37 It was reaffirmed in *Attorney General v Lee*[66] that the courts will enable the Attorney General to perform his role as guardian of the rights of the public by the granting of injunctions, including interlocutory injunctions, or other appropriate relief where the remedies available for ensuring that the law is observed are plainly inadequate.[67]

3–38 In *Lee* the defendant was summonsed to testify at an inquest and refused to appear. Section 38(2) of the Coroner's Act 1962 provides that where a coroner believes that a witness is in contempt, he may certify the matter for the High Court. The High Court must then embark on an inquiry and punish any witness found guilty of such contempt. There was some concern, however, that the provisions of s.38(2) could be vulnerable to constitutional challenge, and that it would be futile to invoke same to enforce compliance with the witness summons. The coroner was of the view that the defendant was a necessary witness for an inquest. In the circumstances, the Attorney General issued proceedings and applied to the High Court for an interlocutory injunction to compel the defendant to comply with the summons and the relevant provisions of the 1962 Act. The Attorney General relied upon what was claimed to be the general jurisdiction of the High Court to enforce the law by way of an injunction or other suitable remedy on his application as the guardian of the public interest "where it was just and convenient so to do".[68]

---

at 9, per Costello J. See also the discussion in relation to the Attorney General in *Attorney General v Paperlink* [1984] I.L.R.M. 373 at 389, per Costello J.

[64] [1930] I.R. 471.

[65] [1930] I.R. 471 at 497.

[66] [2000] 4 I.R. 298.

[67] Albeit that it was found in *Lee* that it had not been demonstrated that the case was an exceptional one which required the courts to exercise their residual jurisdiction in order to secure compliance with the law.

[68] See [2000] 4 I.R. 298 at 303, per Keane C.J.

3–39 The application for the interlocutory injunction was granted by Kelly J. in the High Court. On appeal to the Supreme Court, Keane C.J. held that there was "no doubt"[69] that the jurisdiction to grant an injunction in such circumstances existed. The Chief Justice stated that:

"It has for long been recognised that, in addition to the specific role assigned to him by the Constitution as legal advisor to the Government, the Attorney General is also the guardian of the rights of the public and the courts will enable him to perform that role by the granting of injunctions or other appropriate relief where the other remedies available for ensuring that the law is observed are plainly inadequate."[70]

3–40 A subsidiary question is whether any parties other than the Attorney General may bring proceedings to enforce a public right. It was held by the Supreme Court in *Incorporated Law Society of Ireland v Carroll*[71] that the only person who could bring civil proceedings to enforce a public right was the Attorney General. However, this has been described as a "discordant note",[72] which "goes against the trend of cases such as *Coogan*" [*SPUC v Coogan*].[73] It is difficult to reconcile the decision in *Carroll* with the cases identified above in which parties other than the Attorney General have brought such proceedings. Neither the cases of *Irish Permanent* and *Parsons* nor the Supreme Court decision in *Lovett* were referred to in *Carroll*. As summarised by Hogan and Morgan[74]:

"the obverse of the widening of standing rules in the context of high constitutional matters ... is the termination of the Attorney's traditional monopoly to enforce public rights."[75]

3–41 However, it has also been noted that *Carroll* dealt with a different point from that canvassed in *Parsons* and *Lovett*.[76] *Parsons* and *Lovett* concerned the question of a private individual securing injunctive relief in relation to criminal

---

[69] [2000] 4 I.R. 298 at 303.

[70] [2000] 4 I.R. 298 at 303, referring to *Moore v Attorney General (No. 2)* [1930] I.R. 471 and *Attorney General v Paperlink* [1984] I.L.R.M. 373.

[71] [1995] 3 I.R. 145.

[72] Hogan & Morgan, *Administrative Law in Ireland*, 3rd edn (Dublin: Thomson Round Hall, 1998), p.762.

[73] [1989] I.R. 734.

[74] Hogan & Morgan, *Administrative Law in Ireland,* 3rd edn (Dublin: Thomson Round Hall, 1998), p.759.

[75] In *Dunne v Dun Laoghaire-Rathdown County Council* [2003] 1 I.R. 567 at 574, Hardiman J. referred to the "learned discussion on the rights of an individual to maintain an action for breach of a public right in Hogan and Morgan, Administrative law in Ireland (3rd ed.) at pp. 758 to 764, where the evolving state of the law on this matter is traced."

[76] See Collins and O'Reilly, *Civil Proceedings and the State*, 2nd edn (Dublin: Thomson Round Hall, 2004), p.275.

matters. *Carroll*, however, concerned the question of relator/public interest questions.[77] That being so, there is still a residual question as to which approach should prevail. Perhaps there is no definitive answer to this, for as sensibly observed by O'Hanlon J. in *Parsons v Kavanagh*[78]: "No universal rule can be formulated which will answer the question whether in any given case an individual can sue."[79]

3. Relator Actions[80]

3–42 In circumstances where the public interest and rights are affected, a claimant can apply to the Attorney General to join in the proceedings for the purposes of enforcing those interests and rights. If agreement is obtained in that regard (such agreement is referred to as the "fiat" of the Attorney General), the action is brought by the Attorney General "at the relation of" the claimant. The action is thus known as a relator action. Where the Attorney General agrees to join in the proceedings, he alone is the plaintiff, with the relator's solicitors having carriage of the case. As summarised in the words of Holmes L.J. in *Attorney General (Humphries) v Governors of Erasmus Smith Schools*[81]:

> "It has been settled beyond the possibility of question that the Attorney General alone is plaintiff. It is true that he generally permits the relator to select solicitors to conduct the case; but such person is not the solicitor of the relator, but of the Attorney General, who remains *dominus litis* throughout the proceedings."[82]

3–43 However, the fiat of the Attorney General does not issue automatically. In *Dunne v Rattigan*[83] the plaintiffs sought, and were refused, the fiat of the Attorney General. Judge Sheridan observed that it was quite clear that the Attorney General had an unfettered discretion either to grant or refuse the fiat, and that such discretion was incapable of being reviewed by the courts.[84]

---

[77] See para.3–42.

[78] [1990] I.L.R.M. 560.

[79] [1990] I.L.R.M. 560 at 566.

[80] See generally Delany & McGrath, *Civil Procedure in the Superior Courts,* 2nd edn (Dublin: Thomson Round Hall, 2005), p.199. See also Collins and O'Reilly, *Civil Proceedings and the State,* 2nd edn (Dublin: Thomson Round Hall, 2004), p.611, together with associated precedents.

[81] [1910] 1 I.R. 325. See also the case of *Attorney General (FX Martin) v Dublin Corporation* [1983] I.L.R.M. 254 in the context of whether an undertaking as to damages had been given by the Attorney General in a relator action, see generally, Ch.6, Interlocutory Applications, para.6–98.

[82] [1910] 1 I.R. 325 at 331. As cited by O'Higgins C.J. in *Attorney General (FX Martin) v Dublin Corporation* [1983] I.L.R.M. 254.

[83] [1981] I.L.R.M. 365.

[84] Citing *Attorney General v Westminster County Council* [1924] 2 Ch. 416 and *London County Council v Attorney General* [1902] A.C. 168.

However, he also acknowledged that whilst normally the fiat of the Attorney General should be asked for before an action is brought, there is also authority for the proposition that the Attorney General can be joined in proceedings by amendment after the commencement of the proceedings.

E. The Respondent

1. Introduction

3–44 In the normal course, the respondent to an application for an injunction is the party identified who is alleged to have infringed, or who is about to infringe, the right which the applicant seeks to protect. In general terms,[85] this means that the respondent will be the defendant to the action, not only at the substantive hearing, but also at the interim and interlocutory stage as appropriate.[86] Of course, a defendant may seek an injunction against a plaintiff, but to do so they will have to first deliver a counterclaim, or alternatively bring fresh proceedings.[87] For ease, this section will primarily refer to the defendant.

2. Agents

3–45 An injunction can be granted against a wrongdoer even if he is only acting as an agent. Most injunction orders are in fact framed so that they enjoin "the defendant, his servants or agents". This does of course raise the question in individual cases as to whether a party is acting as agent or in his personal capacity, which will have to be determined on the facts.[88] The relevance of this is the extent to which a party is bound by an injunction order, with the associated question of who may be found to have breached such order.[89]

---

[85] This qualification arises out of the fact that there may well be no proceedings in being in a case where, for example, it is sought to injunct a winding-up petition, or where a *Mareva* injunction is sought.

[86] It is clear from *Performing Rights Society Ltd v London Theatre of Varieties Ltd* [1924] A.C. 1 at 15, per Viscount Cave L.C., that where the grant of a perpetual injunction will prejudice rights of property, the legal owner, as well as the equitable owner, should in general be a defendant. See also *Belmont Securities Ltd v Crean*, unreported, High Court, O'Hanlon J., June 17, 1988.

[87] For example, in the case of *Campus Oil v Ltd v Minister for Industry and Energy (No. 2)* [1983] I.R. 88; [1984] I.L.R.M. 45, considered in detail in Ch.6, Interlocutory Applications, it was in fact the defendant who sought an injunction on foot of a counterclaim.

[88] For an example of a case in which this was discussed in some detail on the facts, see *Saorstat and Continental Steamship Co v De Las Morenas* [1945] 1 I.R. 291.

[89] See Ch.12, Breach of an Injunction Order, para.12–43.

3. Unknown Party

3–46 On occasion it may not in fact be possible to identify the defendant with specificity. This is particularly relevant in the context of interim injunctions, where such an injunction is generally sought at very short notice. This is something of a developing area of the law in England, with the courts there having considered the point in some detail.

3–47 There are two strands to the development of this area of the law in England. The first concerns representative defendants, the second defendants who cannot be identified at all. The position in Ireland will be considered once the development of the law in England has been looked at.

(a) Representative Defendants

3–48 The case of *Heathrow Airport Ltd v Garman*[90] demonstrates how the position of representative defendants has been addressed in England. The case arose out of the Camp for Climate Action 2007 in London in the summer of 2007. It was believed that an unholy alliance of anarchists and "eco-warriors" was planning to cause massive disruption at Heathrow Airport. The problem faced by Heathrow Airport Ltd, the company responsible for the airport, was that, "an unincorporated association is not a legal person and therefore cannot sue or be sued".[91] Heathrow Airport Ltd could not identify the leaders and members of the various groups planning to cause the disruption. In the circumstances, it identified four unincorporated associations, represented by four individuals, whom it believed were coordinators for, and whose interests were identified with, those groups. An ex parte injunction was obtained against the four named individuals "as representatives of the members of" the four unincorporated associations.

3–49 The order ultimately made by the court defined the protestors as the named individuals and:

> "all persons who are, and/or are acting as, officers, activists and/or supporters of, and/or acting in the name of, the unincorporated association known as Plane Stupid; and all persons acting in concert with any of the above persons with the purpose of disrupting the operation of Heathrow Airport."

3–50 The plaintiff was thus successful in securing an order to bind a class of people who might conduct unlawful and/or tortious activities.

---

[90] [2007] All E.R. (D) 28. See also *EMI Records Ltd v Kudhail* [1985] F.S.R. 36.
[91] See *Chitty on Contracts Vol. I General Principles*, 29th edn (London: Thomson Sweet & Maxwell, 2004), p.653.

3–51 This case needs to be treated with a measure of caution, however, in so far as under Rule 19.6 of the Civil Procedure Rules (CPR) in England, actions against unincorporated associations may be conducted through representative proceedings. There would appear to be no equivalent rule in this jurisdiction.

(b) No Defendants Identified

3–52 The modern English approach to dealing with a defendant who cannot be identified is graphically illustrated by the case of *Bloomsbury Publishing Group Ltd v News Group Newspapers Ltd*.[92] Although the reliance in England on the CPR makes a consideration of this case somewhat theoretical in terms of its application in this jurisdiction, it is not without relevance in so far as it considers the position which obtained in England prior to the introduction of the CPR. That position is broadly analogous to that pertaining in this jurisdiction.

3–53 In the *Bloomsbury* case, an urgent application was made in relation to the alleged copyright infringement of a book in the "Harry Potter" series. In circumstances where it appeared that the theft had occurred of a number of copies of the book, which copies were then offered for sale to various national newspapers, an application was made to obtain an injunction. The injunction was granted against unidentified parties, namely, "the person or persons who have offered the publishers of 'The Sun', the 'Daily Mail', and the 'Daily Mirror' newspapers a copy of the book Harry Potter and the Order of the Phoenix by J K Rowling". (Such an order is often referred to as a "John Doe" order).[93]

3–54 The claimant applied to have the injunction continued. When the matter came before Sir Andrew Morritt V.C., the court also had to deal with the question of whether it could make such an order against an unidentified party. The Vice Chancellor ultimately held that in the circumstances it could (at this stage, there had been a number of arrests and charges in relation to the theft of the various copies of the book). In coming to this conclusion, the Vice Chancellor considered two previous cases in which injunction orders had been sought against unknown persons.

3–55 The first was a Court of Appeal decision in *Friern Barnet UDC v Adams*.[94] In that case the plaintiff had issued a writ against "the owners of"

---

[92] [2003] 1 W.L.R. 1633; [2003] 3 All E.R. 736. See also *South Cambridgeshire District Council v Persons Unknown, Times Law Reports*, November 11, 2004, the latter also referring to *Hampshire Waste Services Ltd v Persons Intending to Trespass and/or Trespassing upon Incinerator Sites* (2003) E.W.H.C. 1738 (Ch.).

[93] per Eady J. in *X & Y v The Person or Persons Who Have Offered and/or Provided to the Publishers of the Mail on Sunday, Mirror and Sun Newspapers Information About the Status of the Claimants' Marriage* [2006] E.W.H.C. 2783.

[94] [1927] 2 Ch. 25.

certain land clearly identified by name. Given, inter alia, the prescriptive Rules of the Supreme Court then in force, the Court of Appeal held that the writ failed on the basis that the relevant rules required names and addresses to be specified, and also because the description used was too vague.

3–56 In *Re Wykeham Terrace*,[95] an order for possession was sought by the owner of a property against squatters whose names the owner did not know. The order sought was refused as, first, the unnamed squatters had not had the opportunity to be represented before the court and, secondly, such an order as sought would only bind parties to the proceedings, the squatters not being such parties.

3–57 Those cases would have suggested that the order sought in *Bloomsbury Publishing* could not be continued or, indeed, should not have been made in the first place. However, the Vice Chancellor had regard to the fact that the Civil Procedure Rules had introduced a different regime. He had particular regard to CPR Rule 1.1(1), which provides that the court should deal with cases justly. He also referred to CPR Rule 3.1, which allows the court to take any other step or make any other order for the purpose of managing the case and furthering the overriding objective, as set out in CPR Rule 1.1(1), of enabling the court to deal with cases justly. Noting that the CPR simply contained a direction that a defendant "should" be named, the cases of *Friern Barnet* and *Re Wykeham Terrace* were both distinguished on the basis that they were decided under the old Rules rather than the CPR. In making the order sought, the Vice Chancellor laid emphasis on the fact that he could "see no injustice to anyone if I make an order in the form sought, but considerable potential for injustice to the claimants if I do not."[96]

3–58 As will be seen in the context of *Anton Piller* orders,[97] there is also an evolving jurisdiction in some other common law countries to grant "rolling" *Anton Piller* orders ("Metallica" orders) against unnamed defendants, primarily street and other transient vendors, "where neither the identity nor the address of the persons against whom they will be executed are known."[98]

(c) Injunctions Contra Mundum ("Mary Bell" Orders)

3–59 An injunction *contra mundum*, sometimes referred to as an injunction *in rem*,[99] but more popularly known as a "Mary Bell order",[100] binds not just those

---

[95] [1971] 1 Ch. 204.
[96] [2003] 1 W.L.R. 1633 at 1641; [2003] 3 All E.R. 736 at 744.
[97] See Ch.8, Commercial Injunctions, para.8–129.
[98] per Reed J. in *Fila Canada Inc. v Doe* [1996] 3 F.C. 493.
[99] See *Re S (A Child)* [2001] 1 W.L.R. 211.
[100] Called after the case of *X (A Woman formerly known as Mary Bell) v O'Brien* [2003] 2 F.C.R. 686 and used to protect a ward of court. Also deployed in the case of the child killers of Jamie Bolger: *Venables v News Group Newspapers*; *Thompson v News Group Newspapers* [2001] 1

involved in the proceedings but anyone within the jurisdiction of the court.[101]
These actions revolve in essence around the publication of details relating to a
child's identity. They operate as a blanket ban in relation to such publication.
Such a blanket ban will, of its very nature, be granted in very limited
circumstances only. The English case of *Re G*[102] provides an example of the
wording of such an order, which in that case took the following form:

> "An injunction is hereby granted restraining until further order any person
> from taking or permitting any step likely to expose the three children of the
> family to any form of publicity arising from the current proceedings:
> including in particular the taking of or publishing photographs of the children
> whether in the company of their parents or not."[103]

3–60 Such an injunction is, by its very nature, treated as an injunction granted
ex parte, even if media organisations are represented in court when it is
granted.[104] It was held in the case of *Attorney General v Greater Manchester
Newspapers Ltd*[105] that before any party could be held to be in breach of such
an order, it had to be proved, to the criminal standard, that such party had notice
of the injunction, that the information published was "likely to lead to the
identification" of the past, present or future whereabouts of the injunction
claimants; and that the information was not already in the public domain.[106]
Again, however, it is unlikely that under the existing rules of court in this
jurisdiction that the courts here would be prepared to countenance such an
order. For the same reasons that a *Bloomsbury Publishing*-style order is unlikely
in this jurisdiction, an injunction *contra mundum* is also unlikely.

(d) Position in Ireland

3–61 As has been seen,[107] in this jurisdiction proceedings in personam are only
possible against persons served with a writ.[108] Service is thus the formal basis

Fam. 430. In relation to the latter case, see Morton, "The End of the Matter?" (2001) 151
N.L.J. 5.

[101] per Thorpe L.J. in *Re G* [1999] 1 F.L.R. 409 at 411. See also *Harris v Harris* [2001] 2 F.L.R. 895.
[102] [1999] 1 F.L.R. 409.
[103] [1999] 1 F.L.R. 409 at 410. However, Thorpe L.J. suggested that consideration should be given
       to establishing a procedure to allow those bound by a *contra mundum* order to make sub-
       missions as to where the boundary should be drawn between welfare and freedom of speech.
[104] per Munby J. in *Kelly v BBC* [2001] 1 F.L.R. 197 at 238; [2001] 2 W.L.R. 253 at 287; [2001]
       1 All E.R. 323 at 358.
[105] *Times Law Reports*, December 7, 2001.
[106] In relation to breaches generally, see Ch.12, Breach of an Injunction Order.
[107] See Ch.1, Domestic Jurisdiction, para.1–07.
[108] It should be noted that cases such as *Targe Towing Ltd and Scheldt Towage Co NV v
       The owners and all persons claiming an interest in the Vessel 'Von Rocks'* [1998] 3 I.R. 41;
       [1998] 1 I.L.R.M. 481 are admiralty actions which involve matters in rem, rather than in
       personam (see generally, Ch.4, Equitable and General Principles, para.4–07). Naming a

for the jurisdiction of the Irish courts.[109] Under the existing Irish Rules of the Superior Courts (RSC), it would appear that in principle the courts will approach the question of unknown respondents using the same principles as considered in the cases of *Friern Barnet* and *Re Wykeham Terrace*.[110]

3–62 In the case of *Moore v Attorney General*[111] Kennedy C.J., in considering the position of representative litigants,[112] observed that:

> "… an injunction can only be granted against the persons actually parties to the action. If it be necessary to obtain relief by way of injunction against a person 'represented' in, but not otherwise a party to the suit, a separate action must, in my opinion, be brought against him upon facts showing that he should be restrained by injunction."[113]

3–63 The importance of identifying parties by name in the context of injunction orders is evident by analogy with cases involving identification of parties generally. In *Roe v Blood Transfusion Service Board*,[114] Laffoy J. refused the plaintiff, Brigid McCole, leave to use a "false" name for the purposes of her action. In *Re Ansbacher (Cayman) Ltd,*[115] two un-named persons brought an

---

defendant in this jurisdiction in such a fashion is not sufficient in order to acquire in personam jurisdiction. Delany & Carolan query in their forthcoming work, *The Right to Privacy* (Dublin: Thomson Round Hall, Forthcoming 2008), at Ch.7 whether the position might be different if an injunction were sought on an ex parte basis which would not require service on a particular defendant. In the specific context of privacy, they also suggest that "The real test will come if a case similar to *X & Y [X & Y v The Person or Persons Who Have Offered and/or Provided to the Publishers of the Mail on Sunday, Mirror and Sun Newspapers Information About the Status of the Claimants' Marriage* [2006] E.W.H.C. 2783] comes before the courts in this jurisdiction where it may well be argued that in order to defend and vindicate the plaintiff's constitutional right to privacy, rather than the interest of a commercial nature at stake in *Bloomsbury,* it may be necessary to allow injunctive relief to be granted against unidentified media defendants."

[109] For a comprehensive overview as to jurisdiction generally, see Delany & McGrath, *Civil Procedure in the Superior Courts*, 2nd edn (Dublin: Thomson Round Hall, 2005), particularly Ch.1.

[110] See RSC Ord.9. r.1 and RCC Ord.11 r.6, which provide that service of any summons must be effected by personal service where reasonably practical, unless otherwise specified by the Rules.

[111] [1930] I.R. 471.

[112] As Kennedy C.J. explained: "Since the Judicature Act, 1877, the position is that some of a number of persons claiming a general right may represent all such persons for the purpose of deciding the question of the existence of the general right, if the Court is satisfied that they have been selected so as to, and do, fairly and honestly litigate the matter; and, there being no fraud or collusion in the conduct of the proceedings, the decision will bind everyone interested in the existence of the right who cannot make out a special case for exempting himself from the decision." [1930] I.R. 471 at 489.

[113] [1930] I.R. 471 at 489.

[114] [1996] 3 I.R. 67; [1996] 1 I.L.R.M. 555. See also *Re R Ltd* [1989] I.R. 126, which involved a consideration of the provisions of s.205(7) of the Companies Act 1963.

[115] [2002] 2 I.R. 517.

application in the name of their solicitors seeking to prevent disclosure of their names in a report into the affairs of the company, Ansbacher (Cayman) Ltd. McCracken J. rejected the application, stating that:

> "it seems to me that to extend the right to privacy or the right to a good name to anonymity in a court case could not possibly be said to be a practicable way for the State to defend and vindicate these rights in the light of Article 34.1."[116]

3–64 Within that general context, and based on the Rules of the Superior Courts, it would seem unlikely that the courts will embrace the *Heathrow Airport/Bloomsbury Publishing* approach in general terms.[117]

(e) Statutory Provision

3–65 Provision can be made in statute for orders against unknown respondents. For example, s.160(4)(a) of the Planning and Development Act 2000 states that, "[r]ules of court may provide for an order under this section to be made against a person whose identity is unknown." This provision has been developed by both the Rules of the Superior Courts and the Rules of the Circuit Court.[118]

3–66 If anything, that such specific statutory procedures are provided for can be interpreted as an acknowledgement that there is no general provision under the Rules of Court in relation to bringing an application for an injunction against an unknown party.

(i) Rules of the Superior Courts

3–67 Rules of the Superior Courts Ord.103 r.8(1) sets out the following:

> "Notwithstanding anything previously contained in this Order, in any case in which the identity of the person or persons alleged to be carrying on an

---

[116] [2002] 2 I.R. 517 at 529. There is a report in the Irish Times of February 11, 2008 of the case of *Doe v The Revenue Commissioners*, unreported, High Court, Clarke J., January 18, 2008. In that case, Clarke J. gave a preliminary ruling to the effect that an unidentified man and woman were not entitled to bring a High Court case aimed at stopping their names being published in a list of tax defaulters on an anonymous basis. As reported, Clarke J. summarised the relevant jurisprudence as follows: "the obligation that justice, save in special and limited circumstances, be administered in public includes an obligation that all parts of the court process, including the identities of the parties, must be made public; apart from express statutory provision, the only circumstances where publication could be restrained were where this would prejudice the right to a fair trial; the constitutional right to a good name or to privacy was not a sufficient countervailing factor to the constitutional imperative that justice be administered in public."

[117] However, a party not named in proceedings may nonetheless be found to be in breach of an injunction order: see Ch.12, Breach of an Injunction Order, para.12–74.

[118] See RSC Ord.103 r.8 and RCC Ord.56 r.3(3)(b).

unauthorised development is unknown to the applicant, the Court may, if satisfied that the applicant has made sufficient and reasonable enquiries in all the circumstances and that the order (whether interim, interlocutory or otherwise) is otherwise justified, make the order sought and shall give such directions in accordance with this rule as to service of the order and notification of the making of the order as appears reasonable and practicable in the circumstances."

3–68 Such order and notification thereof are, pursuant to RSC Ord.103 r.8(2), to be affixed to the site on which the unauthorised development is taking place.

(ii) Rules of the Circuit Court

3–69 Order 56 r.3(b) of the Rules of the Circuit Court provides that:

"An Order under Section 160 of the Act against a person whose identity is unknown to the plaintiff, shall be referred to as 'an Order under sub-rule (3)(b)', and the person against whom it is granted or sought shall be referred to as 'the defendant'."

3–70 Order 56 r.3(b) of the Rules of the Circuit Court deals with the description of such a person whose identity is unknown in the following terms:

"A plaintiff in an application for an Order under sub-rule (3)(b) shall describe the defendant by reference to:
  (i) a photograph, or
  (ii) any other means whereby the respondent can be identified with sufficient particularity to enable service to be effected; and the form of the notice of motion shall be modified accordingly."

3–71 Order 56 r.3(d) of the Rules of the Circuit Court is also instructive in that it sets out various elements which must be contained in an affidavit grounding an application in relation to a person unknown. The rule provides as follows:

"A plaintiff in an application for an Order under sub-rule (3)(b) shall, in addition to the requirements of sub-rules (4) and (7), include in the affidavit grounding the application, or shall file a separate affidavit containing, the following averments:
  (i) verifying that he was unable to ascertain, within the time reasonably available to him, the defendant's identity;
  (ii) setting out the action taken to ascertain the defendant's identity, and
  (iii) verifying the means by which the defendant has been described in the originating application and that the description is the best that the plaintiff is able to provide."

4. The State and Its Institutions

3–72 The position of the State and its institutions has fallen for consideration in various cases in the context of whether an injunction can be granted against such bodies. These will be considered in turn.

(a) Ireland as Defendant

3–73 In *Pesca Valentia Ltd v Minister for Fisheries*,[119] the Supreme Court rejected the contention that the courts should never grant an interlocutory injunction which in effect prohibited—even for a temporary period—the exercise of a statutory power contained in a post-Constitution statute. In doing so, Finlay C.J held that whereas Ireland might be an appropriate defendant in the substantive action, "it does not appear to be appropriate that any injunction should ever be given against Ireland".[120] This has been described as a "discordant note".[121] Hogan and Morgan query why Ireland should enjoy immunity in relation to a remedy such as an injunction if it can be liable for damages, especially "given that it now seems that mandamus (a very similar form of remedy to an injunction) will lie against Ireland".[122] This is circumnavigated by seeking an injunction against the relevant Minister (or indeed the DPP, Government or other agent of the State).

(b) The Government as Defendant

3–74 Whilst an injunction may in the normal course be sought against the Government, this statement must be qualified. In *Boland v An Taoiseach*,[123] an injunction was sought to restrain the Government from implementing the "Sunningdale Agreement". Fitzgerald C.J. pointed out that the court had no power, either express or implied, to supervise or interfere with the exercise by the Government of its executive functions, unless the circumstances are such as to amount to a clear disregard by the Government of the powers and duties conferred upon it by the Constitution.[124] In short, an injunction may be sought against the Government other than when it is carrying out its executive function.

3–75 Considering the *Boland* decision, it was held in *State (Christopher Sheehan) v Government of Ireland*[125] that if a statute imposes a duty on the

---

[119] [1985] I.R. 193; [1986] I.L.R.M. 68.
[120] [1985] I.R. 193 at 202; [1986] I.L.R.M. 68 at 73.
[121] See Hogan and Whyte, *J.M. Kelly: The Irish Constitution*, 4th edn (Dublin: Butterworths, 2003), p.2138.
[122] Hogan and Morgan, *Administrative Law in Ireland*, 3rd edn (Dublin: Thomson Round Hall, 1998), p.929.
[123] [1974] I.R. 338.
[124] [1974] I.R. 338 at 361.
[125] [1988] 1 I.R. 550; [1988] I.L.R.M. 437.

Government, the latter cannot claim immunity from the court's jurisdiction on the ground that in performing the duty it is carrying out an "executive function".[126]

(c) The Director of Public Prosecutions as Defendant

3–76 It is clear from the decision of the Supreme Court in *State (McCormack) v Curran*[127] that the actions of the DPP can be restrained by injunction as appropriate. As stated by Walsh J.:

> "the actions of the D.P.P. are not outside the scope of review by the courts. If he oversteps or attempts to overstep his function he can, if necessary, be restrained by injunction ...."[128]

3–77 However, it would appear that in relation to *quia timet* injunctions, when such injunctions are sought against the DPP, a higher standard obtains than would otherwise be the case. In *Szabo v Esat Digifone Ltd*,[129] the applicable test for a *quia timet* injunction was held to be the need to demonstrate a "proven substantial risk of danger". However, in his earlier decision in *Clune v DPP*[130] Gannon J. first observed that a *quia timet* injunction, to succeed "must be founded upon a genuinely apprehended threat of irreparable harm". Although the test in *Szabo* (in so far as there is any material difference between it and that suggested by Gannon J.) is now accepted to be the correct position, Gannon J. in essence added an extra element to the test for a *quia timet* injunction involving the DPP. He stated that:

> "The Director of Public Prosecutions is invested by the Legislature with the power and authority to perform some of the constitutional functions of the Attorney General. This Court must presume that the Director of Public Prosecutions will conform with the principles of justice (as would the Attorney General) in the exercise of his functions. It would require very strong and convincing evidence to displace that presumption."[131]

---

[126] [1988] 1 I.R. 550 at 555; [1988] I.L.R.M. 437 at 440, per Costello J. It should be noted that in the case of *Dudley v An Taoiseach* [1994] 2 I.L.R.M. 321, which concerned an application for leave to issue judicial review proceedings in circumstances where a by-election had not been called 14 months after a Dáil deputy had resigned his seat, Geoghegan J. refused leave as against the Dáil and the Taoiseach; in relation to the former, he found that he could not order the Dáil to vote a certain way. As for the latter, he found that the Taoiseach was not under a personal responsibility in relation to any of the matters complained of. However, the case would appear to relate to its own specific facts.

[127] [1987] I.L.R.M. 225. See also *H v DPP* [1994] 2 I.L.R.M. 285.

[128] [1987] I.L.R.M. 225 at 238.

[129] [1998] 2 I.L.R.M. 102.

[130] [1981] I.L.R.M. 17. See Ch.5, Perpetual Injunctions, para.5–16.

[131] [1981] I.L.R.M. 17 at 20.

3–78 Whilst *Szabo* did not deal with the position of the DPP, there is nothing in that case to suggest that the dictum of Gannon J. should be displaced.

(d) Foreign States as Defendant

3–79 The courts have always been very slow to allow a foreign sovereign or state to be sued in a domestic court. Spry observes that:

> "it is of no concern of the courts of equity whether a foreign sovereign acts unconscionably or not in any particular circumstances, since he is regarded for these purposes as unaccountable." [132]

3–80 The basis for such an approach in law is identified by Binchy,[133] who states that:

> "The immunity of sovereign states and their rulers from the jurisdiction of the courts of other states has long been recognised as a principle of international law and must now be accepted as part of our municipal law by reason of Article 29, section 3 of our Constitution, which provides that Ireland accepts the generally recognised principles of international law as its rule of conduct in its relations with other states."[134]

3–81 This is the case whether a plea is made against them directly or indirectly through an agent.[135] As explained by James L.J. in *Twycross v Dreyfus*,[136] it would be a "monstrous usurpation of jurisdiction" to attempt to sue a foreign government indirectly by naming local agents as defendants.[137]

3–82 In *Canada v Employment Appeals Tribunal*[138] it was held that the doctrine of sovereign immunity formed part of our law, although not in an absolute fashion. As summarised by Kelly J. in the later case of *Adams v DPP*,[139] the Supreme Court in *Canada v EAT* held that:

---

[132] Spry, *The Principles of Equitable Remedies*, 6th edn (London: Sweet and Maxwell, 2001), p.361.
[133] Binchy, *Irish Conflicts of Law* (Dublin: Butterworths, 1988), p.173.
[134] Citing *Saorstat and Continental Steamship Co v De Las Morenas* [1945] 1 I.R. 291 at 298 per O'Byrne J.
[135] See generally the case of *Saorstat and Continental Steamship Co v De Las Morenas* [1945] 1 I.R. 291.
[136] (1877) 5 Ch D 605.
[137] (1877) 5 Ch D 605 at 618.
[138] [1992] 2 I.R. 484.
[139] unreported, High Court, Kelly J., April 12, 2000.

"if the activity called in question before a court in this State truly touched the actual business or policy of the foreign government which was sought to be impleaded then immunity should be accorded to such activity."[140]

(e) Interlocutory Considerations

3–83 That an injunction is sought against a public body does not affect the relevant applicable tests at the interlocutory stage. This is clear from the decision in *Garrahy v Bord na gCon*,[141] in which O'Higgins J. rejected the argument that a different threshold for the obtaining of interlocutory relief in relation to public bodies prevailed rather than that set out in *American Cyanamid v Ethicon*.[142] In doing so, O'Higgins J. did not accept the contention that the English case of *Smith v Inner London Education Authority*[143] established a different threshold, citing the dictum of Browne L.J. in which he stated that he could not agree that in relation to the point that, "the nature of the defendant makes any difference".[144]

[140] per O'Flaherty J. in *Canada v EAT* [1992] 2 I.R. 484 at 500.
[141] [2003] 14 E.L.R. 274. See also *Crotty v An Taoiseach* [1987] I.R. 713 at 725. See Ch.6, Interlocutory Applications, para.6–173.
[142] [1975] A.C. 396; [1975] 2 W.L.R. 316; [1975] 1 All E.R. 504. See further, Ch.6, Interlocutory Applications.
[143] [1978] 1 All E.R. 411.
[144] [1978] 1 All E.R. 411 at 419.

CHAPTER 4

EQUITABLE AND GENERAL PRINCIPLES

A. INTRODUCTION

4–01 An injunction is an equitable remedy. As such, in considering whether to grant an injunction a court will have regard to equitable considerations. There are a number of general principles to which a court will also have regard in determining whether or not to grant an injunction. Although a plaintiff may establish standing in terms of seeking an injunction for the breach of an identifiable right, his conduct or other factors may ultimately disentitle him to an injunction in circumstances where he would otherwise have been granted one.[1] A knowledge of the key equitable and general principles is thus crucial in the context of seeking an injunction. However, it is important to bear in mind the cautionary words of Lord Blackburn in *Doherty v Allman*,[2] that the discretion to award an injunction is "not one to be exercised according to the fancy of whoever is to exercise the jurisdiction of Equity."[3]

4–02 The equitable and general principles to which a party must have regard will be considered in turn in this chapter. They are grouped together here for ease of reference, but it should be remembered that these principles apply regardless of the type of injunction being applied for, or the stage at which such an application is made, viz. at an interim or interlocutory stage, or at the trial of the action.

B. EQUITABLE PRINCIPLES

1. The Maxims of Equity

4–03 Fourteen fundamental equitable maxims can be identified.[4] These have been described as "trends or principles which can be discerned in many of the

---

[1] per Costello J. in *Patterson v Murphy* [1978] I.L.R.M. 85 at 99.

[2] (1878) 3 App. Cas. 709.

[3] (1878) 3 App. Cas. 709 at 728.

[4] McGhee (ed.), *Snell's Equity*, 31st edn (London: Thomson Sweet & Maxwell, 2005), p.93 lists the following 12: equity will not suffer a wrong to be without a remedy; equity follows the law; where there is equal equity, the law shall prevail; where the equities are equal, the first in time shall prevail; he who seeks equity must do equity; he who comes into equity must come with clean hands; delay defeats equities; equality is equity; equity looks to the intent rather than to the form; equity looks on that as done which ought to be done; equity imputes an intention to

detailed rules which equity has established."[5] However, caution must be exercised in having regard to these maxims, for they are just that, maxims, as distinct from hard and fast law. As has been commented:

> "All too often they appear to be little more than pithy sayings, half-truths which are just as likely to mislead and trap the unwary as they are to inform."[6]

4–04 In *Bridge v Campbell Discount Co. Ltd*,[7] Lord Radcliffe stated that equity lawyers:

> "were both surprised and discomfited by the plenitude of jurisdiction and the imprecision of rules that are attributed to 'equity' by their more enthusiastic colleagues."[8]

2. Maxims Relevant to Injunctions

4–05 With Lord Radcliffe's cautionary words in mind, five of those equitable maxims tend to play a more prominent role in the granting or otherwise of injunctions, namely:

(a) Equity acts in personam.
(b) He who seeks equity must do equity.
(c) He who comes to equity must come with clean hands.
(d) Delay defeats equity.[9]
(e) Equity, like nature, does nothing in vain.

4–06 Each of these will be considered in turn. However, in highlighting these maxims it is not intended to diminish the role which the other maxims may have to play in an appropriate case.

(a) Equity Acts In Personam

4–07 An order of the court may be made in personam or in rem. In simple terms, the former is directed against a specific person[10]; the latter applies to a specific thing or property.

---

fulfil an obligation; and equity acts in personam. Wylie, *Irish Land Law*, 3rd edn (Dublin: Butterworths, 1997), p.100 adds a further two, namely that equitable remedies are discretionary and equity, like nature, does nothing in vain.

[5] McGhee (ed.), *Snell's Equity*, 31st edn (London: Thomson Sweet & Maxwell, 2005), p.93.

[6] Wylie, *Irish Land Law*, 3rd edn (Dublin: Butterworths, 1997), p.109.

[7] [1962] A.C. 600; [1962] 2 W.L.R. 439.

[8] [1962] A.C. 600 at 626; [1962] 2 W.L.R. 439 at 455.

[9] Delay in an equitable context is more generally known as laches. Acquiescence, a related concept, will also be considered. See para.4–23.

[10] See, for example, *Lett v Lett* [1906] 1 I.R. 618.

4–08 Explaining the nature of an in personam action in *Re Flightlease (Ireland) Ltd*,[11] Clarke J. adopted a passage from the 1927 edition of Dicey's *Conflicts of Laws* which stated that:

> "An action *in personam* may be defined positively … as an action against a person with a view to enforce the doing by him of some particular thing e.g. the payment of damages for a breach of contract or for a tort; under this head comes (*inter alia*) every common-law action, whether on contract or tort, also every equitable proceeding, the objective of which is to compel the doing or not doing of a particular thing, as e.g. the specific performance of a contract
>
> …
>
> It may be well, though hardly necessary, to add that an action *in personam* does not include any proceedings which are not in strictness an 'action' at all, such as a proceeding for divorce, judicial separation, restitution of conjugal rights, or for a declaration of nullity of marriage or of legitimacy, or a proceeding in bankruptcy … ."[12]

4–09 Clarke J. held that this passage represented the law in this jurisdiction.

4–10 As is clear from decisions such as that of the Supreme Court in *Moore v Attorney General*,[13] the general principle underpinning the granting of injunctions is that an injunction is granted in personam; it will not be granted against any person not a party to the action.[14] This relates to the idea that equity concerns itself with the conscience of the parties appearing before the court.[15]

4–11 Although this basic principle still pertains in this jurisdiction, there has been a shift in recent years in England in so far as injunctions have been granted against representative and unidentified parties[16] However, such a move is based on the Civil Procedure Rules in operation in that jurisdiction. It would appear that the Rules of the Superior Courts in this jurisdiction do not specifically contemplate such an order.[17] There has also been use made in England of injunctions *contra mundum*, which bind not just those involved in the

---

[11] unreported, High Court, Clarke J., June 15, 2006.

[12] The up to date reference is Dicey, Morris & Collins, *The Conflict of Laws*, 14th edn (London: Sweet & Maxwell, London, 2006), pp.574–638.

[13] [1930] I.R. 471.

[14] See generally, *Penn v Lord Baltimore* (1750) 1 Ves. Sen. 444; *Hope v Carnegie* (1868) L.R. 7 Eq. 254 and *Ewing v Orr Ewing* (1883) 9 App. Cas. 34.

[15] See *Australian Consolidated Press Ltd v Morgan* (1965) 112 C.L.R. 483 at 498, in which it was stated that "historically the purpose of the processes of the Court of Chancery was to rectify and reform the conscience of the wrongdoer".

[16] See *Bloomsbury Publishing Group Ltd v News Group Newspapers Ltd* [2003] 1 W.L.R. 1633; [2003] 3 All E.R. 726. See in that regard, Ch.3, Standing, para.3–52; *cf. Friern Barnet UDC v Adams* [1927] 2 Ch. 25 and *Re Wykeham Terrace* [1971] 1 Ch. 204.

[17] See Ch.3, Standing, para.3–61.

proceedings but anyone within the jurisdiction of the court.[18] However, the guiding principle with regard to injunction applications in both England and in this jurisdiction is that equity acts *in personam*.

(b) He Who Seeks Equity Must do Equity

4–12 The rationale underlying this principle is self-explanatory: it is necessary for a party to act in a proper manner—or to undertake to so act—if he wishes to invoke equity in order to pursue his own claim. In such circumstances, the party's future conduct is the key consideration. The principle was considered in the case of *Chappell v Times Newspapers*,[19] in which a dispute had arisen in the printing industry between employers and unions. The plaintiff union members sought an injunction to restrain their employers from terminating their contracts of employment following industrial action in which they had not been involved. However, in seeking the injunction, the plaintiffs refused to give the undertakings sought by the employers not to engage in disruptive activities. The Court of Appeal refused the interim injunction sought on the basis that:

> "in a contract where each has to do his part concurrently with the other, then if one party seeks relief, he must be ready and willing to do his part in it."[20]

(c) He Who Comes to Equity Must Come With Clean Hands

4–13 For ease of reference, this maxim is best considered from the perspective of the plaintiff and the defendant separately.

(i) The Plaintiff

4–14 When a party seeks the equitable relief of an injunction, the maxim that, "he who comes to equity must come with clean hands" is applicable.[21] This maxim is essentially a variation on the previous one (he who seeks equity must do equity), in that the principle underlying it is the same. In this instance, however, it is a party's past conduct which is of relevance; the difference is essentially temporal. However, there must be a connection between such past conduct and the matter which is in dispute; a party will not be punished for his general behaviour.[22] This was succinctly put by Scrutton L.J. in *Moody v Cox*,[23] in which he stated that:

---

[18] Such injunctions are used in relation, for example, to the publication of details relating to a child's identity. See Ch.3, Standing, para.3–59.

[19] [1975] 1 W.L.R. 482; [1975] 2 All E.R. 233.

[20] [1975] 1 W.L.R. 482 at 502; [1975] 2 All E.R. 233 at 240, per Lord Denning M.R.

[21] See, for example, the dictum of Keane J. in *National Irish Bank Ltd v RTE* [1998] 2 I.R. 465 at 481; [1998] 2 I.L.R.M. 196 at 207.

[22] See *Dering v Earl of Winchelsea* (1787) 1 Cox 318.

[23] [1917] 2 Ch. 71.

"Equity will not apply the principle about clean hands unless the depravity, the dirt in question on the hand, has an immediate and necessary relation to the equity sued for."[24]

4–15 It is at the discretion of the court whether or not to refuse an injunction on the basis of the "clean hands" principle.[25] However, in the case of *Curust Financial Services Ltd v Loewe-Lack-Werk,*[26] Finlay C.J., in accepting that the court had a discretion to refuse an injunction on the basis that a party might come to court otherwise than "with clean hands", observed that, "this phrase must of necessity involve an element of turpitude and cannot necessarily be equated with a mere breach of contract."[27]

4–16 Although Finlay C.J. referred to "an element of turpitude", it would appear that the courts will exercise their discretion to refuse an injunction on a wider basis than "an element of turpitude". For example, in *Shell UK Ltd v Lostock Garage Ltd,*[28] Lord Denning M.R. made reference to conduct being "unfair and unreasonable".[29] This would seem to imply a somewhat lesser standard than "an element of turpitude", given the connotations of an element of baseness inherent in the latter. At the other extreme is the dictum of Megaw L.J. in *Hubbard v Vosper,*[30] in which he referred to a party attempting to safeguard his rights by "deplorable means".[31]

Reasons for Refusal of Relief
4–17 Relief may be refused under the rubric of "clean hands" for a variety of reasons. Deception has formed the basis for the refusal of injunctive relief,[32] as has deceit.[33] The non-disclosure of convictions for fraud in the context of an

---

24 [1917] 2 Ch. 71 at 87. See, for example, *Duchess of Argyll v Duke of Argyll* [1967] Ch. 302; [1965] 2 W.L.R. 790; [1965] 1 All E.R. 611, in which it was held that the conduct of the plaintiff which led to her divorce did not deprive her of an entitlement to an injunction to restrain a breach of confidence by her husband.

25 See generally, *Overton v Banister* (1844) 3 Hare 503; *Gascoigne v Gascoigne* [1918] 1 K.B. 223; *Smelter Corporation of Ireland Ltd v O'Driscoll* [1977] I.R. 305; *Parkes v Parkes* [1980] I.L.R.M. 137.

26 [1994] 1 I.R. 450; [1993] I.L.R.M. 723.

27 [1994] 1 I.R. 450 at 467; [1993] I.L.R.M. 723 at 731.

28 [1976] 1 W.L.R. 1187 at 1199.

29 However, in *Corporation of Bradford v Pickles* [1895] A.C. 587, it was held that if a defendant is performing a lawful act, his motives and objects in doing so are irrelevant.

30 [1972] 2 Q.B. 84; [1972] 2 W.L.R. 389; [1972] 1 All E.R. 1023.

31 [1972] 2 Q.B. 84 at 101; [1972] 2 W.L.R. 389 at 400; [1972] 1 All E.R. 1023 at 1033. Other examples include *Litvinoff v Kent* (1918) 34 T.L.R. 298, in which a breach of covenant was committed.

32 *Leather Cloth Co Ltd v American Leather Cloth Co Ltd* (1863) 4 D. J. & S 137.

33 *McElroy v Flynn* [1991] I.L.R.M. 294 at 300, albeit that Blayney J. did not express a formal opinion as the matter had not been argued, but stated that if "the defendants had sought to invoke equitable principles, apart from undue influence, this aspect of the facts would have been highly relevant".

election to the board of a company led to the refusal of relief in *O'Doherty v West Limerick Resources Ltd.*[34] Lynch J. refused an injunction against the defendant Minister in *Ardent Fisheries Ltd v Minister for Tourism, Fisheries and Forestry*,[35] as the plaintiff had dishonoured assurances given to the defendant in relation to operating a boat out of Irish ports and landing fish in those ports. Lynch J. noted that although the plaintiff may have had an arguable case on the legal enforceability of the applicable licensing conditions relating to crew members on board its boats, its lack of bona fides disentitled it to relief. It had not come to court with clean hands. Therefore, regardless of the merits of a case, a breach of the relevant applicable equitable principles can lead to an injunction being refused.

4–18 In essence, the court must view any behaviour in the context of the overall application, including the stage at which the application is made, and exercise its discretion on the basis of a consideration of the facts as presented to it. For example, in *Meridian Communications Ltd v Eircell Ltd*,[36] Lavan J. rejected the plaintiff's application for an interlocutory injunction on the basis that the plaintiff did not come to court with clean hands. However, in the Supreme Court McGuinness J. took the view that neither party had been free of fault and, as such, held that "this Court would not refuse the relief sought on the grounds which were relied on by the learned High Court judge."

(ii) The Defendant

4–19 As is implicit from McGuinness J.'s dictum, the behaviour of the defendant is also relevant in considering "clean hands". For example, in *Eircell Ltd v Bernstoff*,[37] Barr J., granting the injunction sought, made reference to the "reprehensible" conduct of the defendant, which he contrasted with the "fair and reasonable" behaviour of the plaintiff.[38] However, in *News Datacom Ltd v Lyons*,[39] Flood J. held that the fact that the conduct of the defendant might be questionable as a matter of ethics or morality was not in itself a reason to grant injunctive relief to the plaintiff without more.

---

[34] unreported, Supreme Court, May 14, 1999.
[35] [1988] I.L.R.M. 528.
[36] unreported, Supreme Court, May 10, 2001.
[37] unreported, High Court, Barr J., February 18, 2000.
[38] Barr J. granted the interlocutory injunction sought in light of this and the fact that damages would not constitute an adequate remedy. See also, *Howard v Commissioners of Public Works in Ireland*, unreported, High Court, O'Hanlon J., December 3, 1992, in which O'Hanlon J. referred both to the delay of the applicants in seeking injunctive relief but also to the fact that the respondents had behaved in an "irreproachable manner".
[39] [1994] 1 I.L.R.M. 450.

(iii) Maxim Extends to Hearing of an Action

4–20 The importance of coming to court with clean hands encompasses all stages at which an injunction application can be made. Although subsequently successfully appealed,[40] in the first High Court hearing of *Fanning v UCC*,[41] Lavan J. refused the relief sought on the basis that he found the plaintiff's evidence to be totally lacking in candour and clarity, and held that the plaintiff had not come to equity with clean hands. In the circumstances Lavan J. found that the plaintiff had disentitled himself to the equitable reliefs sought.[42]

(d) Delay Defeats Equity

4–21 Section 11 of the Statute of Limitations, which deals with "[l]imitation of actions of contract and tort and certain other actions", does not apply to equitable remedies except to the extent that it can be applied by analogy. Specifically, s.11(9) reads:

" (a) This section shall not apply to any claim for specific performance of a contract or for an injunction or for other equitable relief.
 (b) Paragraph (a) of this subsection shall not be construed as preventing a Court from applying by analogy any provision of this section in like manner as the corresponding enactment repealed by this Act has heretofore been applied."

4–22 However, a form of temporal limitation has been developed in equity which can be used in defence to an action seeking an equitable remedy, such as an application for an injunction. This form of limitation is termed "laches". It arises when an infringement of a person's rights takes place, but there is a period of unreasonable inaction before that party seeks a remedy for such infringement. In simple terms, the putative plaintiff effectively behaves in such a manner as to suggest that he does not intend relying on any right he may otherwise have.

4–23 Related to this is the concept of acquiescence, which can often overlap with laches, but which is nonetheless distinct. Acquiescence concerns a situation where a party does not take any action whilst the act subsequently complained of is taking place. By virtue of s.5 of the Statute of Limitations 1957 as amended, it is provided that: "Nothing in this Act shall affect any equitable jurisdiction to refuse relief on the ground of acquiescence or otherwise."

---

[40] On the basis that there was no evidence to support the assertion that the plaintiff had not come to court with clean hands.

[41] unreported, High Court, Lavan J., July 25, 2002.

[42] In *Armstrong v Sheppard & Short Ltd* [1959] 3 W.L.R. 84; [1959] 2 Q.B. 384; [1959] 2 All E.R. 651, a party attempted to mislead the court with untruthful evidence.

4–24 Each of these will now be considered in greater detail, starting with an overview of the doctrine of laches.

(i) Laches

4–25 A detailed explanation as to the meaning of laches was set out in *Lindsay Petroleum Co. v Hurd*[43] by Lord Selborne L.C.:

> "Now the doctrine of laches in courts of equity is not an arbitrary or a technical doctrine. Where it would be practically unjust to give a remedy, either because the party has, by his conduct, done that which might fairly be regarded as equivalent to a waiver of it, or where by his conduct and neglect he has, though perhaps not waiving that remedy, yet put the other party in a situation in which it would not be reasonable to place him if the remedy were afterwards to be asserted, in either of these cases lapse of time and delay are most material."[44]

4–26 More briefly, in *Sherwell v Combined Incandescent Mantles Syndicate Ltd*, it was stated that an application for an interlocutory injunction "should be made with promptness".[45]

Modern Approach

4–27 In *Frawley v Neill*,[46] Aldous L.J. held that the "modern approach" to the equitable doctrine of laches was establish whether it would in all the circumstances be unconscionable for a party to be permitted to assert his beneficial right.[47] He did not accept the approach of an inquiry as to whether the circumstances of a case could be fitted within the confines of a preconceived formula derived from earlier cases. This is a sensible approach for, as will be seen,[48] there may well be a good reason for any delay.

Establishing Laches

4–28 For a defendant to successfully establish laches, he must show two elements: first, that the plaintiff in question delayed unreasonably; and secondly,

---

[43] (1874) LR 5 P.C. 221.

[44] (1874) LR 5 P.C. 221 at 239, as cited with approval by Lord Blackburn in *Erlanger v New Sombrero Phosphate Co* (1878) 3 App. Cas. 1218 at 1279. Spry cautions that in a number of older cases from around this time, the word "laches" was used in the sense of merely unreasonable delay. As such, care should be exercised when referring to cases of this vintage, decided at a time when "the doctrine of laches had not been fully developed": Spry, *The Principles of Equitable Remedies*, 6th edn (London: Sweet and Maxwell, 2001), p.415.

[45] [1907] W.N. 110.

[46] *Times Law Reports*, April 5, 1999.

[47] It has been observed, however, that there is no consistent definition of laches. See Majumdar, "The Burden of History" (2007) 157 N.L.J. 1136.

[48] See para.4–33.

that such delay means that it would be unjust to grant an injunction to the plaintiff. Delay in itself is not sufficient. Keane J. made this clear in *JH v WJH*.[49] He held that substantial delays must be considered in the context of a plea of laches, but that there would also have to be "circumstances which would render it inequitable to enforce the claim after such a lapse of time". In other words, the mere passage of time, without more, will not bar claims for equitable relief.[50] This ties in with the dictum of Aldous L.J. in *Frawley*, in that it involves the court undertaking an inquiry into all the circumstances of a case. Indeed, as observed by O'Higgins J. in *Garrahy v Bord na gCon*,[51] there may be room for a difference of perception in relation to delay within an individual case.[52]

Time From Which Delay Runs

4–29 The time from which the delay is judged to have run is the point at which the plaintiff became aware of the facts giving rise to the relief sought.[53] Being put on suspicion of such facts has been treated as sufficient for the purposes of raising the defence of laches.[54] It has also been held that, "when the facts are known from which a right arises, the right is presumed to be known."[55]

4–30 An example of the role delay plays in practice is evident from the decision of O'Hanlon J. in *Lennon v Ganly*.[56] The plaintiff sought to prevent a rugby tour to South Africa shortly before the touring party was scheduled to travel, but some time after the tour had been announced. In refusing the injunction sought, O'Hanlon J. stated that:

> "I accept the argument ... that the court should be slow to intervene when the plaintiff has delayed until the eleventh hour before bringing his proceedings and applying for interlocutory relief ... By reason of the delay which has occurred in bringing on the application, there is no possibility of having the issues between the parties finally determined before the tour is due to commence, and the granting of interlocutory relief at this stage would give the plaintiff all he seeks by way of relief in the main proceedings ... For this reason also I would feel that the present application should not succeed, as no

---

[49] unreported, High Court, Keane J., December 20, 1979.
[50] See Brady and Kerr, *The Limitation of Actions*, 2nd edn (Law Society of Ireland, 1994), p.167.
[51] [2002] 3 I.R. 566.
[52] [2002] 3 I.R. 566 at 581.
[53] See the general discussion in *Lindsay Petroleum v Hurd* (1874) L.R. 5 P.C. 221 at 241. See also, for an example in practice, *Birmingham v Birr UDC* [1998] 2 I.L.R.M. 136, in which Morris P. had to consider the earliest date upon which the applicants could reasonably be expected to realise that a proposal to construct the halting site was becoming a reality, and the effect of s.27 of the Local Government (Planning and Development) Act 1976 in relation to an anticipated breach of the planning code.
[54] *Marquis of Clanricarde v Henning* (1861) 30 Beav. 175; 54 E.R. 855.
[55] *Stafford v Stafford* (1857) 1 De G. & J. 193 at 202; 44 E.R. 697.
[56] [1981] I.L.R.M. 84.

reason has been put forward to explain the delay which occurred before the action was brought."[57]

4–31 In *Riordan v Minister for the Environment*,[58] Finnegan P. refused the plaintiff's application for an injunction requiring the defendant to insert the plaintiff's name on the ballot paper for the European Parliament Elections. Finnegan P. pointed out that the dates for the elections were announced in December 2003 but the plaintiff did not institute proceedings until March 2004, and that this delay militated against granting the reliefs sought.

4–32 In *An Post v Irish Permanent Plc*,[59] Kinlen J., granting an interlocutory injunction, noted that a plaintiff who seeks an interlocutory injunction must move without undue delay. However, he also stated that the fact that the trial of the action was listed to take place within a relatively short time after the application for an interlocutory injunction was not a relevant consideration in determining whether the interlocutory injunction should be granted.

A Reason for the Delay

4–33 An explanation for the delay which a court would find acceptable may defeat a plea of laches.[60] For example, efforts to determine planning issues prior to bringing proceedings was of relevance in the case of *Lord Mayor of Dublin v Garland*.[61] Finlay P., dealing with an application under s.27 of the Local Government (Planning and Development) Act 1976,[62] stated that there was no conceivable question of laches or delay on the part of the applicants. The President found that the delays were:

> "no more than a reasonable approach to permitting the respondents, as a matter of concession, to exercise their rights for the determination of all legal questions concerned with the change of user, and to obtain properly arrived at decisions with regard to the planning status and user of these premises."[63]

4–34 In *Newport Association Football Club Ltd v Football Association of Wales*,[64] there had been a delay of two years before an interlocutory injunction

---

[57] [1981] I.L.R.M. 84 at 86. For a similar consideration in England, see *Bates v Lord Hailsham of St. Marylebone* [1972] 1 WLR 1373; [1972] 3 All E.R. 1019
[58] unreported, High Court, Finnegan P., May 26, 2004.
[59] [1995] 1 I.L.R.M. 336.
[60] See *Attorney General v Colney Hatch Lunatic Asylum* (1868) 4 Ch. App. 146 and *Woodhouse v Newry Navigation Co* [1898] 1 I.R. 161.
[61] [1982] I.L.R.M. 104. See also *Leigh v National Union of Railwaymen* [1970] Ch. 326; [1970] 2 W.L.R. 60; [1969] 3 All E.R. 1249, in which Goff J. refused to withhold the relief sought on the grounds of delay due to the "peculiar circumstances of the case".
[62] Now s.160 of the Planning and Development Act 2000.
[63] [1982] I.L.R.M. 104 at 107.
[64] [1995] 2 All E.R. 87.

was applied for. However, Jacob J. found the case to be wholly exceptional. He adverted to the fact that the plaintiffs, during the two years in question, had been actively seeking a solution to the problem. It had sought a reversal of the decision by the defendant association to refuse permission to the plaintiff club to play its home matches in Wales. In other words, that a party may seek to resolve a matter other than by the legal route may be looked on favourably by the court when faced with an argument that the plaintiff has delayed in bringing his case to court. A party may also be required to explore statutory resolution mechanisms before an action can be brought to court.

4–35 In O'*Kane v Campbell*,[65] Lynch J. rejected the argument that there was undue delay on the part of the plaintiff. The plaintiff had been trying to gather signatures of supporters in the neighbourhood in relation to night trading from the defendant's premises. Lynch J. observed that:

> "There are many cases such as this where a lot of neighbours will express support for the action but are then unwilling to risk the actual litigation and delays arise in trying to persuade them to support an action."[66]

4–36 He also took the view that the defendant must have been aware of the plaintiff's efforts in that regard.[67]

Extent of the Delay

4–37 The extent to which a party delays may of course provide the court with a truer view of how urgent a matter really is. For example, if the matter in relation to which an interlocutory injunction is being sought has been known about for some time, and no action has been taken in that regard, this will weigh heavily against the granting of such an injunction; questions are obviously raised about the real need for an injunction pending the substantive hearing of the matter in question. Another consideration is that the defendant may have altered his position to his detriment while there was a delay.

4–38 The extent to which delay can be established may also be referenced to the act complained of. For example, if an article is published in a Sunday newspaper, and an interlocutory injunction is sought to prevent any further publication of similar material,[68] but such application is only made the

---

[65]   [1985] I.R. 115.

[66]   [1985] I.R. 115 at 118.

[67]   See *Bula Ltd v Tara Ltd*, unreported, High Court, Murphy J., February 27, 1987, in which Murphy J., granting the relief sought, noted that although there had been a delay by the plaintiffs in instituting proceedings, the citizen must be free to institute proceedings and to invoke the procedures of the courts to present his case properly. See also *Lindsay Petroleum Co v Hurd* (1874) L.R. 5 P.C. 221.

[68]   See generally, Ch.10, General Application, particularly section L. Publication, para.10–146.

following Friday, it might be arguable that in the context of those circumstances there has been delay.

Stage of the Application

4–39 It has in fact been suggested that a "lesser" degree of laches (or acquiescence) suffices to refuse an injunction at the interlocutory stage relative to the substantive hearing; in other words, any delay may have been relatively brief. This is on the basis that the refusal of an injunction at the interlocutory stage due to laches is merely a "temporary rebuff" whereas refusal at the substantive hearing "amounts to a decision that a right which has once existed is absolutely and forever lost".[69]

4–40 This appears to have been the view taken by the court in *Cahill v Irish Motor Traders Association*.[70] Budd J. held that there was no undue delay in commencing the proceedings. He did not believe that there was anything in the nature of excessive delay in bringing the proceedings to trial, "viewing the matter in the light of the time that is usually taken to bring an action of this nature to trial."[71] In relation to applications for perpetual injunctions, he stated that it was:

> "well established that in order to deprive a person of a right to such an injunction, to which he would otherwise be entitled, there must be such delay and acquiescence as, in the view of the Court, would make it in the nature of a fraud for a plaintiff afterwards to insist upon his legal right."[72]

4–41 However, Budd J. did caution that different considerations may apply to an application for an interlocutory injunction.

4–42 The importance of moving quickly in relation to interlocutory applications and the rationale for so doing is perhaps best summarised by Keane J. in *Nolan Transport (Oaklands) Limited v Halligan*[73]:

> "In all cases of this nature, where interlocutory relief is sought, the courts expect the parties to move with reasonable expedition where they are seeking interlocutory relief, because it is of the essence of such relief that if it turns out that it has been wrongly granted, one party has suffered an injustice. It is, therefore, a remedy that should not be lightly invoked; and if invoked, it should be invoked rapidly, and where a party simply awaits events as they

---

[69] per Turner L.J. in *Johnson v Wyatt* (1863) D.G.J. & S. 18. See also *Richards v Revitt* (1877) 7 Ch D 224 at 226.
[70] [1966] I.R. 430.
[71] [1966] I.R. 430 at 449.
[72] [1966] I.R. 430 at 449.
[73] unreported, High Court, Keane J., March 22, 1994.

unfold, they cannot expect to find the Court amenable to the granting of this relief, as it would where a party moves expeditiously to protect his rights."[74]

4–43 There would also appear to be a distinction between delay at the interim stage and delay at the interlocutory stage. In *Criminal Assets Bureau v PS,*[75] the notice party, the wife of the defendant in the proceedings, applied to have an interim *Mareva* injunction obtained four-and-a-half years previously discharged. The application was brought on the grounds that the hearing of the interlocutory application had been adjourned from time to time and ultimately until the trial of the action. Finnegan J. refused to accede to the application, however, taking the view that the issues arising could only be resolved at the hearing of the action. However, Finnegan J. stressed that an interim injunction obtained by a plaintiff on an ex parte basis was more susceptible to being discharged for delay than an interlocutory injunction.

Legal or Equitable Rights

4–44 It has been argued that laches is not a ground for withholding a perpetual injunction when a legal—as distinct from an equitable—right has been breached.[76] Such a distinction was made between legal and equitable rights by Budd J. in *Cahill v Irish Motor Traders' Association.*[77] In that case Budd J. held that, unless a claim is barred by the Statute of Limitations, delay by itself will not disentitle a plaintiff to an injunction to protect a legal right.[78] However, in the English case of *Habib Bank Ltd v Habib Bank AG Zurich*[79] it was held that there was no distinction between a legal and an equitable right when laches was being pleaded. Such a distinction was viewed as "archaic and arcane", with "little significance for anyone but a legal historian".[80] Oliver L.J. summarised the position, saying that he believed that the law:

> "as it has developed over the past 20 years has now evolved a far broader approach to the problem than that suggested ... and one which is in no way dependent upon the historical accident of whether any particular right was first recognised by the common law or was invented by the Court of Chancery."[81]

---

[74] Cited with approval by Smyth J. in *Futac Services Ltd v Dublin City Council*, unreported, High Court, Smyth J., June 24, 2003. In *Futac*, delay was one of the reasons cited for not granting the injunction sought.

[75] unreported, High Court, Finnegan J., April 12, 2002.

[76] Keane, *Equity and the Law of Trusts in the Republic of Ireland* (London: Butterworths, 1988), p.36; this point was referred to by O'Sullivan J. in *McDonagh v Denton*, unreported, High Court, O'Sullivan J., April 15, 2005.

[77] [1966] I.R. 430.

[78] [1966] I.R. 430 at 449.

[79] [1981] 1 W.L.R. 1265; [1981] 2 All E.R. 650.

[80] [1981] 1 W.L.R. 1265 at 1285; [1981] 2 All E.R. 650 at 666, per Oliver L.J.

[81] [1981] 1 W.L.R. 1265 at 1285; [1981] 2 All E.R. 650 at 666, citing *Inwards v Baker* [1965] 2 Q.B. 29 and *Crabb v Arun District Council* [1976] Ch. 179.

4–45 This approach is preferable to the technical distinction which Budd J. in *Cahill* seems to have been suggesting subsisted.

Delay Generally
4–46 Even if delay is not central to the refusal of an application, the courts tend to take a dim view of delay in general terms. In *Nolan Transport (Oaklands) Ltd v Halligan*[82] O'Flaherty J. made reference to "tedious litigation" which "dragged itself out for 28 days in the High Court" and an application for an interlocutory injunction "brought with no excessive haste".

(ii) Acquiescence

4–47 Acquiescence was explained by Lord Wensleydale in *Archbold v Scully*[83]:

> "if a party, who could object, lies by and knowingly permits another to incur an expense in doing an act under the belief that it would not be objected to, and so a kind of permission may be said to be given to another to alter his condition, he may be said to acquiesce."[84]

4–48 Aldous L.J. put the matter even more succinctly in *Jones v Stones*,[85] when he stated that: "At the heart of estoppel or acquiescence lies an encouragement or allowance of a party to believe something to his detriment."[86] In short, if the plaintiff has acquiesced in the wrong complained of, this may be a ground for refusing injunctive relief.[87]

4–49 As has been seen in relation to laches, there are two elements to acquiescence: the plaintiff must be shown to have delayed unreasonably, but it must also be demonstrated that such delay means that it would be unjust to grant an injunction to the plaintiff. As with laches, so with acquiescence: there must be a standing-by on the part of the plaintiff while the acts of which he complains take place and, as a result, it would be unjust to grant the relief sought.[88]

---

[82] [1999] 1 I.R. 128 at 134.
[83] (1861) 9 H.L.C. 360.
[84] (1861) 9 H.L.C. 360 at 383. A similar definition was provided by Thesiger L.J. in *De Busche v Alt* (1878) 8 Ch D 286 at 314.
[85] [1999] 1 W.L.R. 1739.
[86] [1999] 1 W.L.R. 1739 at 1745.
[87] *Birmingham Canal Co v Lloyd* (1812) 18 Ves. 515.
[88] See generally, Spry, *The Principles of Equitable Remedies*, 6th edn (London: Sweet and Maxwell, 2001), pp.440 et seq.

Knowledge of the Act

4–50 As is clear from *Re Pauling's Settlement Trusts*,[89] the plaintiff must know that the act is actually being done. For example, in *Sayers v Collyer*[90] the plaintiff sought an injunction to restrain the use of a house as a beer shop with an off-licence, even though he had been aware of the breach for a number of years, and indeed had purchased beer there himself. Baggallay L.J., refusing the injunction sought, stated that he could "hardly imagine a stronger case of acquiescence than this". A plaintiff must also be aware that the act concerned affects his rights.[91] However, a misleading assurance might be sufficient to meet a charge of acquiescence.[92]

A Reason for the Acquiescence

4–51 As with delay, a party may be able to point to a good reason for the acquiescence in question. For example, the plaintiff may also attempt in the first instance to remedy the matter himself with the defendant.[93] That being so, it would appear sensible to approach acquiescence on the same basis as laches, in terms of considering all the circumstances of the case and whether it would be "unconscionable" [94] to allow a party who had acquiesced to assert a given right.

A Remedy in Damages Despite Acquiescence

4–52 Although acquiescence may lead to the refusal of injunctive relief, this does not in itself prevent the court ordering a remedy in damages, as occurred in *Shaw v Applegate*.[95] In that case, three years after the defendant had started to install amusement machines, the plaintiff sought an injunction to restrain a breach of covenant as to user. The Court of Appeal concluded that it had to have regard to the goodwill built up by the defendant over three years as well as the expenditure that had been incurred by him. On that basis, the court confined the plaintiff's remedy to one in damages for breach of covenant.[96]

---

[89] [1964] Ch. 303.
[90] (1884) 28 Ch D 103 at 107.
[91] *Armstrong v Sheppard & Short Ltd* [1959] 2 Q.B. 384; [1959] 2 All E.R. 651.
[92] See, for example, *Isenberg v East India House Estate Co Ltd* (1863) 3 D.G.J. & Sm. 263.
[93] See for example, *Gordon v Cheltenham and Great Western Union Rly Co* (1842) 5 Beav. 229 at 238, per Lord Langdale M.R. Halsbury sets out a number of examples of situations in which a good reason has been provided for acquiescence: *Halsbury's Laws of England* Vol.24 (reissue), para.860.
[94] per Aldous L.J., in the context of laches, in *Frawley v Neill*, *Times Law Reports*, April 5, 1999.
[95] [1977] 1 W.L.R. 970; [1978] 1 All E.R. 123. Considered in *Advanced Totes Ltd v Bord Na gCon (No. 2)* [2006] 3 I.R. 101.
[96] In *Gafford v Graham*, *Times Law Reports*, May 1, 1998, all reliefs, including damages, were refused on the basis that the plaintiff had known of his rights and had made no attempt to complain about their infringement during a three-year period. But *cf. Mortimer v Bailey* [2004] E.W.C.A. Civ 104.

(e) Equity, Like Nature, Does Nothing in Vain

(i) Futility

4–53 An injunction will not be granted if its effect would be futile.[97] As Lord Hatherley L.C. stated in *Attorney General v Colney Hatch Lunatic Asylum*,[98] the courts will "take care not to pronounce an idle and ineffectual order".[99] The Lord Chancellor offered by way of example the case of cutting down timber. As he pointed out, it would be:

> "idle when the trees have been cut down to make an order not to allow the trees to remain prostrate, and all that can be done in such a case is to leave the parties to their remedy for damages."[100]

(ii) Compliance

4–54 Closely related to this, an injunction order will not be granted if a defendant cannot comply with it. As stated by Kekewich J. in *Evans v Manchester, Sheffield and Lincolnshire Railway Co.*[101]:

> "I think it would be wrong to enjoin a company or an individual from permitting that to be done which is really beyond his control ... in the sense that he cannot by any precaution or any works with reasonable certainty comply with the order that is sought."[102]

4–55 However, that an injunction may be difficult to comply with is not in itself reason for refusing to grant such an injunction.[103]

(iii) Enforcement

4–56 In *Pride of Derby v British Celanese Ltd*,[104] Sir Raymond Evershed M.R. stated that:

---

[97] For a number of old English cases in support of this proposition, see generally, *Halsbury's Laws of England Vol. 24, Injunctions*, particularly para.829.

[98] (1868) L.R. 4 Ch. App. 146.

[99] (1868) L.R. 4 Ch. App. 146 at 154.

[100] (1868) L.R. 4 Ch. App. 146 at 154.

[101] (1887) 36 Ch D 626 at 639.

[102] This also relates directly to the issue of contempt of court, in relation to which see Ch.12, Breach of an Injunction Order. See also the dictum of Brewster L.C. in *Sheppard v Murphy* [1868] I.R. 2 Eq. 544 that "a Court of Equity cannot compel him to do that which is impossible", as referred to by Lavan J. in *Meath Co Council v Irish Shell Ltd*, unreported, High Court, Lavan J., June 12, 2006. See also *Neville & Sons Ltd v Guardian Builders Ltd* [1990] I.L.R.M. 601 at 616, in which Murphy J. stated: "If a contract is discharged by impossibility then clearly no court could compel its performance."

[103] It is not open to a party to plead that he "did his best", notwithstanding that the order was not complied with: see *Howitt Transport v Transport and General Workers Union* [1973] I.C.R. 1 at 10.

[104] [1953] Ch. 149; [1953] 2 W.L.R. 58; [1953] 1 All E.R. 179.

"Equally, of course, the Court will not impose on a local authority, or on anyone else, an obligation to do something which is impossible, or which cannot be enforced, or which is unlawful."[105]

4–57 The case of *Lennon v Ganly*[106] provides an example of a court's refusal to make an order on the basis that it could not enforce it. In that case an order was sought restraining the defendants and other members of the Irish Rugby Football Union from engaging in certain courses of conduct while abroad in South Africa. However, in refusing the order sought, O'Hanlon J. observed that if such an order were made the court would have no machinery to enforce its own order while the parties affected by it were outside the jurisdiction of the Irish courts.

4–58 In *O'Dea v O'Briain*,[107] the plaintiff nun, a teacher, claimed a mandatory injunction preventing a transfer to another school from proceeding pending full consultation with her on the issue of her transfer. Asked to make such a mandatory order, Murphy J. explained his reluctance in making the order sought on the basis that he had:

"no means of knowing or guaranteeing that that situation would come about because there is no order which I could make which would prevent the appropriate bodies taking action open to them. There is no basis on which I could direct an inquiry to be held as to the plaintiff's competence, nor could this Court conduct an inquiry as to her capacity to carry out her job. To do so, it seems to me, would be intruding on the rights of others with no prospect of achieving the purpose which the plaintiff seeks. It seems to me that I cannot guarantee the remedy on which the plaintiff's heart is set."[108]

4–59 As will be seen in the context of employment injunctions, the question of enforcement and supervision is a very live one in that area of the law,[109] as indeed it is in the area of contract. In *Noel Ó Murchú trading as Talknology v Eircell Ltd*,[110] Geoghegan J. noted that courts are:

---

[105] [1953] Ch. 149 at 181; [1953] 2 W.L.R. 58 at 82; [1953] 1 All E.R. 179 at 197. Referred to by O'Hanlon J. in *Lennon v Ganly* [1981] I.L.R.M. 84 at 86.
[106] [1981] I.L.R.M. 84.
[107] [1992] I.L.R.M. 364.
[108] [1992] I.L.R.M. 364 at 371. In *Derby & Co Ltd v Weldon (Nos 3 and 4)* [1990] 1 Ch. 65; [1989] 2 W.L.R. 412; [1989] 1 All E.R. 1002, an argument was made that, on the authorities, the maxim referred not to enforceability but to the making of orders with which it was impossible to comply, but this was not specifically addressed by Lord Donaldson M.R. See also *Attorney General v Guardian Newspapers Ltd* [1987] 1 W.L.R. 1248 at 1270; [1987] 3 All E.R. 316 at 332, per Browne-Wilkinson V.C.
[109] See Ch.9, Employment.
[110] unreported, Supreme Court, February 21, 2001.

"very slow to grant injunctions in either service contracts or trading contracts because it is very difficult to assess, at any given time thereafter, as to whether such injunctions are being obeyed or not."

4–60 Geoghegan J. also observed that it is also "usually impracticable and undesirable" to compel parties to trade with each other in circumstances where, for whatever reason, they do not wish to do so.

(iv) Supervision

4–61 Related to enforcement is the idea of supervision. The courts are very slow to grant injunctions which require ongoing supervision. Previously, the impossibility of the courts supervising the doing of work was used as a reason for refusing to grant relief.[111] However, in *Shiloh Spinners v Harding*,[112] Lord Wilberforce moved the courts away from this absolutist position, stating that:

"Where it is necessary, and, in my opinion, right, to move away from some 19th century authorities, is to reject as a reason against granting relief, the impossibility for the courts to supervise the doing of work."[113]

4–62 The Irish courts would appear to be stricter in their approach, although matters will of course have to be dealt with on a case-by-case basis. In *Lennon v Ganly*,[114] having dealt with the impossibility of enforcement, O'Hanlon J. held that it would be contrary to legal principle for the court to make an order where it had no means of supervising the enforcement of the order, and where it could have to call in aid the executive arm of the State to secure obedience to its decree.

4–63 It is evident from the foregoing that it is of cardinal importance that equitable principles inform any decision taken in relation to whether to seek an injunction, for an otherwise strong application for an injunction can still be defeated by invoking the relevant equitable principles. Once the relevant equitable principles have been addressed, the courts may still have regard to a range of general principles which will now be considered.

---

[111] See, for example, *Blackett v Bates* (1865) L.R. 1 Ch. 117 and *Powell Duffryn Steam Coal Co v Taff Vale Railway Co* (1874) L.R. 9 Ch. 331.

[112] [1973] 1 A.C. 691.

[113] [1973] 1 A.C. 691 at 724. See also, *CH Giles & Co Ltd v Morris* [1972] 1 W.L.R. 307 and *Jeune v Queens Cross Properties Ltd* [1974] Ch. 97.

[114] [1981] I.L.R.M. 84.

C. GENERAL PRINCIPLES

1. Introduction

4–64 There are a number of general principles to which the court will have regard in determining whether or not to award an injunction. One of the key considerations when determining whether or not to grant a perpetual injunction is whether damages, rather than an injunction, would provide an adequate remedy. This consideration has given rise to considerable judicial scrutiny, it will be considered separately in the chapter dealing with Perpetual Injunctions.[115]

2. Key Principles and Factors

4–65 The following, whilst not by any manner a finite list, sets out some of the other key general principles and factors to which the courts have had regard, each of which will be considered in turn:

(a) remedies available;
(b) the effect of granting an injunction on third parties;
(c) the relevance of third parties' positions on the granting of an injunction order;
(d) damage, hardship and oppression;
(e) collateral benefit;
(f) the separation of powers;
(g) the bona fides of an applicant;
(h) illegality;
(i) frivolous and vexatious applications; and
(j) status of an undertaking.

4–66 These principles will clearly inform the party applying for an injunction in terms of the factors which they will have to consider before bringing such an application, but they also provide the basis for any defences which a respondent may wish to put forward to the court.

(a) Remedies Available

4–67 There is old authority for the proposition that if a plaintiff has a remedy within his or her own power, the court will not grant the injunction sought.[116] However, as has been seen in the context of equitable principles,[117] a court may accept the argument that parties had been attempting to resolve their differences

---

[115] See Ch.5, Perpetual Injunctions.
[116] Dealt with in passing in *Elliman, Sons & Co v Carrington & Son* [1901] 2 Ch. 275 at 279.
[117] See para.4–33.

initially without having recourse to the legal system, but still be prepared to grant an injunction.

(i) More Appropriate Remedies

4–68 The granting or refusal of an injunction order is ultimately at the discretion of the court, which may take the view that it is not appropriate to grant an injunction order in the circumstances.

4–69 The courts will often attempt to ascertain whether there is any other remedy which would be more appropriate than an injunction. The reality is that the availability of such other remedy is relatively rare. However, in *Mitchell v Henry*,[118] an injunction was not granted at the interlocutory stage, but the defendant undertook to keep an account.[119] Similarly, the court in *Islington Vestry v Hornsey UDC*[120] took the view that, having regard to the conduct of the plaintiffs and to the difficulty in which an injunction would place the defendants by compelling them to close their sewers, the court ought only to make a declaration that the defendants were not entitled to send sewage from their district into the plaintiffs' sewer without the consent of the plaintiffs.

(ii) Specific Statutory Remedies

4–70 Account may also be taken of any statutory remedies which may be available to a party.[121] There are some instances where specific statutory provisions must be invoked in order to protect a right, and in certain circumstances the locus standi of parties entitled to bring such actions are also prescribed. In such circumstances, the putative plaintiff should proceed as prescribed by the relevant statute.[122]

(iii) Judicial Review Applications

4–71 More generally, and albeit more peculiar to judicial review applications, the courts have consistently held that they should be very slow to intervene by way of judicial review except to correct a final decision of a respondent body.[123]

---

[118]   (1880) 15 Ch D 181.

[119]   See also *Baily v Taylor* (1829) 1 Russ & M. 73.

[120]   [1900] 1 Ch. 695.

[121]   For example, the Domestic Violence Act 1996 regulates spousal violence and misconduct and essentially provides for a self-contained code which does not necessitate the seeking of an injunction order on an equitable basis.

[122]   For example, under the Industrial Relations Act 1990. See Ch.11, Specific Statutory Injunctions.

[123]   See, for example, *Buckley v Kirby* [2000] 3 I.R. 431 and *Garvan v Criminal Injuries Compensation Tribunal*, unreported, Supreme Court, July 20, 1993. In *Tomlinson v Criminal Injuries Compensation Tribunal*, unreported, Supreme Court, January 19, 2005, Denham J.

(b) The Effect of Granting an Injunction on Third Parties

4–72 Although previously the courts were slow to take into account the effect of granting an injunction on third parties, there has been an increasing tendency in recent years to have regard to such effect.

4–73 In *Bellew v Irish Cement Ltd*,[124] the Supreme Court rejected the argument that a court should take into account the effect of an injunction on third parties, in that case the public convenience.[125] Maguire C.J. took the view that the court:

> "was not entitled to take the public convenience into consideration when dealing with the rights of private parties. This matter is a dispute between private parties, and I think that the Court should be concerned, only, to see that the rights of the parties are safeguarded."[126]

4–74 However, a move towards considering the effect of an injunction on other parties was hinted at in the case of *McGrath v Munster and Leinster Bank Ltd*.[127] That case involved an alleged interference with the access of light into the plaintiff solicitor's office due to the construction of a building next door by the defendants. In the course of his judgment, Dixon J. referred to the fact that:

> "The necessity or desirability of having adequate lighting from the point of view of clients must be given some weight in considering whether the beneficial user of the office with natural light has been impaired."[128]

4–75 The question of the rights of third parties was more explicitly considered in *Wall v Feely*.[129] In that case, Costello J. ordered an injunction in favour of five families of Travellers, restraining a purported eviction by the old Dublin County Council from a public roadway. In finding that there would be very great hardship caused to the families if evicted, Costello J. felt he was also entitled to have regard to the public inconvenience to the defendants as a local authority (although it appears that this factor did not ultimately (of itself) determine the matter).

---

stated that: "While a court would lean towards requiring that the remedies available under the scheme be exhausted, the ultimate decision depends on the circumstances of the case."

[124] [1948] I.R. 61.

[125] In *Hartlepool Gas & Water Co v West Hartlepool Harbour & Rly Co* (1965) 12 L.T. it had been stated (at 368) that an injunction should not be granted where it would have the effect of "very materially injuring the rights of third parties".

[126] [1948] I.R. 61 at 64. Black J., dissenting, stated that whilst he accepted that the public convenience cannot justify the refusal of a remedy for nuisance, he felt that it was a different matter to say that it could or ought not to be a factor in dealing with a nuisance.

[127] [1959] I.R. 313.

[128] [1959] I.R. 313 at 327.

[129] unreported, High Court, Costello J., October 26, 1983.

4–76 Further evidence of a move towards taking into account the effect on third parties is evident in *Howard v Commissioners for Public Works*,[130] in which O'Hanlon J. considered a number of factors which tend to show that he had the wider public interest in mind. In *Dun Laoghaire Rathdown Co. Council v Shackleton*,[131] O'Sullivan J. indicated that he had been influenced by public interest considerations in granting interlocutory relief preventing an arbitrator from dealing with a compensation claim.[132]

4–77 A number of cases brought pursuant to s.160 of the Planning and Development Act 2000 have explicitly taken into account third party interests.[133] This is not entirely surprising given that, as explained by Barrington J. in *Avenue Properties Ltd v Farrell Homes Ltd*,[134] the intention of that section was that the Planning Acts "should be policed not only by the Planning Authority but also by individual citizens".[135] By virtue of the provision, citizens are acting as the "watchdog of the public".[136]

4–78 The courts in England have been somewhat divided as to the relationship between granting injunctions and their effect on third parties. In *Miller v Jackson*,[137] the Court of Appeal awarded damages in lieu of an injunction to a party who complained about cricket balls being hit from an adjoining cricket field into his property. Lord Denning M.R. took the view that the public interest in cricket outweighed the private discomfort of the plaintiff. In so far as the public interest was concerned, Cumming-Bruce L.J. quoted from *Spry on Equitable Remedies*[138]:

> "Where the plaintiff has *prima facie* a right to specific relief the Court of Equity will if occasion should arise weigh the disadvantage or hardship which he will suffer if relief were refused against any hardship or disadvantage which should be caused to third persons or to the public generally if relief were granted."[139]

---

[130] unreported, High Court, O'Hanlon J., December 3, 1992.

[131] unreported, High Court, O'Sullivan J., January 23, 2002.

[132] See also, *Clifford v Drug Treatment Centre Board*, unreported, High Court, McCracken J., November 7, 1997. However, *cf.* An *Post v Irish Permanent Plc* [1995] 1 I.R. 140, in which Kinlen J. considered *Bellew v Cement Ltd* [1948] I.R. 61, *Gibbings v Hungerford* [1904] 1 I.R. 211 and *Wall v Feeley*, unreported, High Court, Costello J., October 26, 1983. However, Kinlen J. would not express any any opinion as to whether public policy should be considered.

[133] See Ch.11, Specific Statutory Injunctions, para.11–37.

[134] [1982] I.L.R.M. 21.

[135] [1982] I.L.R.M. 21 at 26.

[136] per Barrington J. in *Stafford v Roadstone Ltd* [1980] I.L.R.M. 1 at 19.

[137] [1977] Q.B. 966; [1977] 3 W.L.R. 20; [1977] 3 All E.R. 338.

[138] [1977] Q.B. 966 at 988; [1977] 3 W.L.R. 20 at 36; [1977] 3 All E.R. 338 at 350.

[139] This extract is from the 1971 Edition, p.365. See Spry, *The Principles of Equitable Remedies*, 6th edn (London: Sweet and Maxwell, 2001), pp.201–203.

4–79 However, in *Kennaway v Thompson*[140] the Court of Appeal rejected this view and granted an injunction restraining power-boat racing on a lake other than at reasonable hours. Lawton L.J. cited the words of Lindley L.J. in *Shelfer v City of London Electric Co.*[141]:

"Neither has the circumstance that the wrongdoer is in some sense a public benefactor (e.g. a gas or water company or a sewer authority) ever been considered a sufficient reason for refusing to protect by injunction an individual whose rights are being persistently infringed."[142]

4–80 On balance, it seems that its effect on the public interest is something which should be considered in the context of granting an injunction, in so far as the principles on which injunctions are granted are not prescriptive and the courts are entitled to, and do, look at a wide range of factors in considering whether or not to grant an injunction. There would appear to be no substantive policy reason against taking the public interest into account.

4–81 Whilst a number of these factors relate to the immediate dispute between the parties concerned, there are more general factors which go beyond this. For example, public interest considerations such as freedom of expression and the right to communicate to the public are factors which may be taken into account as appropriate, as is clear from the case of *Attorney General for England and Wales v Brandon Book Publishers Ltd.*[143]

(c) The Relevance of Third Parties to the Granting of an Injunction Order

4–82 Whilst the foregoing principle deals with the effect on third parties of granting an injunction, a related matter is the extent to which the actions of third parties can be taken into account when considering an application for an injunction.

4–83 In *Phonographic Performance (Ireland) Ltd v Chariot Inns*,[144] Keane J. in the High Court had regard to the potential actions of independent third parties if he did not grant an injunction. In that case the plaintiffs sought to restrain the

---

[140] [1980] 3 W.L.R. 361; [1981] Q.B. 88; [1980] 3 All E.R. 329.
[141] [1895] 1 Ch. 287; [1891–1894] All E.R. Rep. 838.
[142] [1895] 1 Ch. 287 at 315; [1891–1894] All E.R. Rep. 838 at 844 (cited in *Kennaway v Thompson* at [1980] 3 W.L.R. 361 at 365; [1981] Q.B. 88 at 92; [1980] 3 All E.R. 329 at 332). Somewhat curiously, the decision in *Miller* ran counter to that in *Shelfer*, even though the latter was binding on the former.
[143] [1986] I.R. 597; [1987] I.L.R.M. 135. See, in relation to this case generally, Ch.10, General Application, para.10–155.
[144] unreported, High Court, Keane J., October 7, 1992.

defendants from "causing to be heard in public any of the sound recordings set out in the schedules to the plenary summons". In considering the balance of convenience, Keane J. stated that:

> "refusing the present application will probably mean that large unquantified sums will have to be recovered by them from a number of discotheque operators, since I have to assume that those other operators will be properly advised that they should adopt the same course as the present defendants."

4–84 As such, the position of third parties who were not parties to the action was explicitly taken into account by Keane J.

4–85 However, the better approach would appear to be that expressed in *Wicklow Co. Council v Fenton*,[145] in which O'Sullivan J. held that where the primary relief sought against the respondents was an injunction, the liability of the respondents in this regard could not be transferred to or diluted by reference to the third parties; there appears to be no compelling reason why a defendant should be held accountable for the actions of such third parties over whom he has no control (as distinct from servants or agents).

4–86 One exception to this appears to have been accepted, certainly implicitly, in the context of an injunction to restrain a petition to wind up a company.[146] In *Truck and Machinery Sales Ltd v Marubeni Komatsu Ltd*,[147] Keane J. had to consider the applicable test in determining whether or not to grant the injunction sought to restrain the petition in question. Holding that the normal principles did not apply in such circumstances, Keane J. made reference to the distinction between the restraint of an alleged violation of a plaintiff's right—the usual circumstances in which an injunction is sought—and the situation before him, in which a creditor's right to bring a petition was threatened by injunction. In other words, it was a third party's right which would be affected by any injunction order granted.

(d) Damage, Hardship and Oppression

4–87 It is clear from the decision of Costello J. in *Wall v Feely*,[148] considered above, that the hardship which the granting of an injunction may cause is also a factor which the courts may take into account as appropriate.[149] In *Wall*, this potential hardship played a key role in Costello J.'s consideration of the balance of convenience.

---

[145] [2002] 2 I.L.R.M. 469.
[146] See Ch.10, General Application, para.10–34.
[147] [1996] 1 I.R. 12.
[148] unreported, High Court, Costello J., October 26, 1983.
[149] See *Islington Vestry v Hornsey UDC* [1900] 1 Ch. 695.

4–88 Considering potential hardship is consistent with the much earlier English decision in *Sharp v Harrison*,[150] in which it was held that if the granting of a mandatory injunction inflicts damage on a defendant, with such damage out of all proportion to the relief which the plaintiff may claim, such an injunction will be refused. Similarly, in *Patterson v Murphy*,[151] Costello J. had regard to the fact that "relief by way of an injunction could be termed oppressive".

(e) Collateral Benefit

4–89 It was made clear by Quirke J. in *Sean Quinn Group Ltd v An Bord Pleanála*[152] that the fact that the legitimate use by a litigant of a lawful remedy such as an injunction would or might result in a collateral benefit to the applicant did not of itself affect the right of the applicant to seek such a remedy in the courts, and that the applicant could be granted such relief as was appropriate notwithstanding the accrual of such collateral benefit. Quirke J. also observed that "[t]his applies even to cases where the principle motivation for the application is a collateral benefit for the applicant."

(f) The Separation of Powers

4–90 In *Garrahy v Bord na gCon*,[153] an argument was made that the plaintiff would not be entitled to a permanent injunction as the defendant was a statutory body and its statutory obligations would make it impermissible for the court to interfere with the defendant. O'Higgins J. noted that a similar point had been made in *Howard v University College Cork*,[154] and he adopted the dictum of O'Donovan J. in the latter case:

> "While, as I have indicated, I do not think it possible that at the trial of the action the plaintiff could be awarded the permanent injunction and the declaration to which I have referred, I have little doubt but that the trial judge would accede to an application to amend the statement of claim by qualifying the claim for the permanent injunction by the addition of the words 'except in accordance with law' and by qualifying the declaration sought by the addition of the words 'unless and until lawfully terminated'."

4–91 O'Higgins thus held that the question of the separation of powers was one more properly for the trial. As such, the separation of powers may have a role to play in the granting or otherwise of an injunction, but does not of itself prevent orders for injunctions being made in accordance with the law.

---

[150] [1922] 1 Ch. 502.
[151] [1978] I.L.R.M. 85 at 99. Citing *Shelfer v City of London Electric Co* [1895] 1 Ch. 287; [1891–1894] All E.R. Rep. 838.
[152] unreported, High Court, Quirke J., October 4, 2000.
[153] [2002] 3 I.R. 566.
[154] [2001] E.L.R. 8.

(g) The Bona Fides of the Parties

4–92 Although often raised at the interlocutory stage,[155] the bona fides of a party seeking an injunction is also a relevant consideration at the hearing of an application for a perpetual injunction, as indeed the bona fides of a defendant may be.[156] For example, in *Daniel v Ferguson*,[157] Lindley L.J. disapproved of the fact that:

> "the Defendant, upon receiving notice that an injunction is going to be applied for, sets a gang of men to work and runs up his wall to a height of thirty-nine feet before he receives notice that an injunction has been granted."[158]

4–93 In the circumstances, Lindley L.J. made an order that the building in question "be pulled down at once, without regard to what the result of the trial may be."[159]

(h) Illegality

4–94 It is self-evident that a court will not grant an injunction if its effect would be to compel a party to perform an illegal act. The dictum of Sir Raymond Evershed M.R. in *Pride of Derby v British Celanese Ltd*,[160] has already been referred to above in the context of the equitable maxim that "equity, like nature, does nothing in vain". In that case, the Master of the Rolls stated that the court would not impose on anyone "an obligation to do something which is impossible, or which cannot be enforced, or which is unlawful".[161]

(i) Frivolous and Vexatious Applications

4–95 Where a capricious or trivial application is brought before the court, an injunction will generally not be granted. For example, an application to stop a clergyman preaching on the seashore was refused in *Llandudno Urban Council v Woods*[162] on the basis that an injunction was "a formidable legal weapon which ought to be reserved for less trivial occasions".[163]

---

[155] See, for example, *Garrahy v Bord na gCon* [2003] 14 E.L.R. 274.
[156] See also *Von Joel v Hornsey* [1895] 2 Ch. 774.
[157] [1891] 2 Ch. 27.
[158] [1891] 2 Ch. 27 at 29.
[159] [1891] 2 Ch. 27 at 30.
[160] [1953] Ch. 149; [1953] 2 W.L.R. 58; [1953] 1 All E.R. 179.
[161] [1953] Ch. 149 at 181; [1953] 2 W.L.R. 58 at 82; [1953] 1 All E.R. 179 at 197. Referred to by O'Hanlon J. in *Lennon v Ganly* [1981] I.L.R.M. 84 at 86.
[162] [1899] 2 Ch. 705. See also *Behrens v Richards* [1905] 2 Ch. 614 at 619, in which Buckley L. considered one aspect of the claim to be a "matter for the application of reason, common sense and ordinary forbearance, not for an injunction."
[163] [1899] 2 Ch. 705 at 710, per Cozens-Hardy J.

4–96 As with substantive proceedings, an argument can be put forward when appropriate that applications for interim and interlocutory relief are vexatious and oppressive having regard to the pertinent facts.[164] In *Twomey v Mallow Town Council*,[165] Smyth J. granted an application to strike out proceedings in which an injunction was sought restraining the second defendant from proceeding with the development of a property in accordance with planning permission obtained from the first defendant. Smyth J. found that the proceedings were frivolous, vexatious and an abuse of the process of the court.

(j) Status of an Undertaking

4–97 An undertaking given to the court in lieu of an injunction order being made will have the same status as an injunction order.[166] In *Biba Ltd v Stratford Investments Ltd*,[167] Brightman J. stated that he thought that it would be a pity to give "a lesser quality to an undertaking than to an injunction".[168]

---

164 An argument made in *Sweeney v National University of Ireland Cork t/a Cork University Press* [2001] 1 I.L.R.M. 310.
165 unreported, High Court, Smyth J., July 16, 2003.
166 *Neath Canal Co v Ynisarwed Resolven Colliery Co* (1875) 10 Ch. App. 450.
167 [1973] 1 Ch. 281; [1972] 3 W.L.R. 902; [1972] 3 All E.R. 1041.
168 [1973] 1 Ch. 281 at 287; [1972] 3 W.L.R. 902 at 907; [1972] 3 All E.R. 1041 at 1045. See also *Hussain v Hussain* [1986] 2 W.L.R. 801; [1986] 1 All E.R. 961; [1986] Fam. 134 and *Witham v Holloway* (1995) 183 C.L.R. 525. In *D v A & Co* (1900) 1 Ch. 484 it was held that undertakings given in an action are enforced by committal, not by attachment. See further, Ch.12, Breach of an Injunction.

CHAPTER 5

PERPETUAL INJUNCTIONS

A. INTRODUCTION

5–01 A perpetual injunction is a discretionary remedy which may be granted at the final determination of a case as distinct from at the interim or interlocutory stages. It is so called because of this, not because it operates in perpetuity.[1] A perpetual injunction may sometimes be referred to as a final injunction or a permanent[2] injunction. If granted, a perpetual injunction will protect a legal, equitable, constitutional or statutory right. It must be shown that a party has an interest in such a right,[3] that the right has been infringed, or there is a risk that it will be infringed and that such infringement is continuing or likely to continue.[4] A perpetual injunction provides a remedy which ensures that it is not necessary to bring a series of injunction applications every time a perceived infringement is viewed as having taken place.[5]

5–02 This chapter will look at the general principles and procedures concerning perpetual injunctions.[6] It will consider in the first instance the extent to which there is a difference between a prohibitory and a mandatory perpetual injunction, if any. It will then look at *quia timet* injunctions. The role of damages and how an assessment of the adequacy of damages informs whether or not to grant a perpetual injunction will then be considered. Next, the steps which need to be taken in applying for a perpetual injunction will be reviewed, and the terms of the relevant order will also be considered. Finally, inquiries as to damages, which may be ordered after a successful interlocutory application but where ultimately the application for a perpetual injunction does not succeed, will be discussed.

5–03 In determining whether or not to grant a perpetual injunction, it is important to note that the equitable and general principles considered in Ch.4

---

[1] See *Moore v Ullcoats Mining Co Ltd* [1908] 1 Ch. 575 at 585, in which Warrington J. referred to the fact that the plaintiffs might have asked for and obtained a perpetual injunction "that is to say, an injunction to continue so long as the lease continued in the same terms".

[2] For an example of the use of the term, see *O'Duffy v The Law Society of Ireland*, unreported, High Court, O'Neill J., March 4, 2005. Given the nature of a perpetual injunction, the use of the word "permanent" has the potential to be somewhat misleading.

[3] See generally, Ch.3, Standing.

[4] This can include circumstances where a right has already been infringed and there is a real risk of future infringement; see para.5–16.

[5] See *Pride of Derby v British Celanese Ltd* [1953] Ch. 149 at 181; [1953] 2 W.L.R. 58 at 82; [1953] 1 All E.R. 179 at 197.

may also have a role to play, and in circumstances where an injunction might otherwise have been granted it may be refused in light of such principles.

B. PROHIBITORY AND MANDATORY PERPETUAL INJUNCTIONS

1. Introduction

5–04 A perpetual injunction can be prohibitory or mandatory. It can also be in the nature of a *quia timet* injunction, sought to restrain a threatened injury. In contrast to the position at the interlocutory stage,[7] there would appear to be no difference in general terms between the applicable principles relating to prohibitory and mandatory injunctions at the substantive hearing.[8] This is notwithstanding the fact that the history of mandatory perpetual injunctions has been described as "a curious one".[9]

2. Prohibitory Injunction

5–05 A prohibitory injunction requires a party to refrain from performing or continuing to perform certain acts.[10] To obtain a prohibitory injunction it must be shown that there is something to be injuncted on an ongoing basis; a court will intervene and grant an injunction as appropriate on the basis that an injury is continuous in order to prevent the necessity of bringing a series of actions in relation to the wrong alleged.[11] As was observed in *Ronson Products Ltd v Ronson Furniture Ltd*[12] in the context of proceedings for contempt of court, the distinction in law between an order to do an act and an order prohibiting an act is not merely historical or technical, but rather depends upon practical considerations. As pointed out by Stamp J., if a man is ordered to do an act "so that his failure to do it may lead him to prison", justice requires that he should know precisely what he has to do and by what time he has to do it.[13]

---

[6] The granting of injunctions in different areas of the law is considered in Ch.10, General Application.

[7] See Ch.6, Interlocutory Applications.

[8] See the dictum of Warrington J. in *Davies v Gas Light & Coke Co* [1909] 1 Ch. 248 at 259, citing *Holland v Dickson* 37 (1888) Ch D 669 and *Mutter v Eastern and Midlands Railway Co* (1888) 38 Ch D 92.

[9] (1875) L.R. 20 Eq. 500 at 504, per Jessel M.R.

[10] These injunctions are sometimes referred to as "negative" or "restrictive" injunctions.

[11] *Attorney General v Birmingham Borough Council* (1858) 4 K. & J. 528 at 540, per Page Wood V.C.

[12] [1966] Ch. 603; [1966] 2 W.L.R. 1157.

[13] [1966] Ch. 603 at 614; [1966] 2 W.L.R. 1157 at 1164.

3. Mandatory Injunction

5–06 Whereas in broad terms a prohibitory injunction requires a party to refrain from performing or continuing to perform certain acts, it is clearly of little use if an act has already been done. The second substantive type of injunction is a mandatory injunction. This is an order requiring a party to do something, more often than not to undo the consequences of a wrongful act. As such a mandatory injunction can impose a considerable burden upon a party. It can also potentially involve the ongoing supervision of the courts.[14] In *Redland Bricks v Morris*,[15] Lord Upjohn suggested that the granting of a mandatory injunction can never be made "as of course". He was quite clear in stating that it is a jurisdiction "to be exercised sparingly and with caution but in the proper case unhesitatingly."[16]

5–07 Until the late-19th century, all injunctions were made in prohibitory form, as there was considerable doubt as to whether the courts had jurisdiction to grant mandatory injunctions.[17] In *Smith v Smith*,[18] Jessel M.R. referred to the fact that "[a]t one time it was supposed that the Court would not issue mandatory injunctions at all."[19] However, it is now accepted that mandatory injunctions may be granted by the courts, and these are in the normal course made in a positive form.[20]

5–08 The nature of a mandatory injunction is such that it is important to be able to specify with particularity what action is required. In *Bula Ltd v Tara Mines Ltd (No. 2)*,[21] Murphy J. made reference to the decision of Maugham L.J. in *Fishenden v Higgs and Hill Ltd*,[22] in particular the observation that:

> "I think a mandatory injunction, except in very exceptional circumstances, ought to be granted in such terms that the person against whom it is granted ought to know exactly what he has to do."[23]

---

[14] Which in fact may lead to the court refusing to grant a mandatory injunction: see, for example, *O'Dea v O'Briain* [1992] I.L.R.M. 364. See generally, Ch.4, Equitable and General Principles, para.4–61.

[15] [1970] A.C. 652; [1969] 2 W.L.R. 1437; [1969] 2 All E.R. 576.

[16] [1970] A.C. 652 at 665; [1969] 2 W.L.R. 1437at 1444. Although referred to in the context of an application for a *quia timet* injunction, the statement does appear to have a much more general application.

[17] *Lane v Newdigate* (1804) 10 Ves. 192, referred to in *Jackson v Normanby Brick Co* [1899] 1 Ch. 438 at 439. As noted in the latter case, for at least 95 years the courts had been exercising their jurisdiction in "a roundabout mode".

[18] (1875) L.R. 20 Eq. 500.

[19] (1875) L.R. 20 Eq. 500 at 504.

[20] *Jackson v Normanby Brick Co* [1899] 1 Ch. 438.

[21] [1987] I.R. 95; [1988] I.L.R.M. 157.

[22] (1935) 153 L.T. 128 at 142.

[23] [1987] I.R. 95 at 104; [1988] I.L.R.M. 157 at 164.

(a) Restorative and Enforcing Mandatory Injunctions

5–09 Delany identifies a distinction between the types of mandatory injunction which can be granted, namely restorative or enforcing mandatory injunctions.[24] In practice these terms are not frequently used, although there is a substantive difference between them.

(i) Restorative Mandatory Injunction

5–10 A restorative mandatory injunction, which is the more common type, requires a party to put right the consequences of his action. An example of this is the removal of a structure which has been wrongfully erected.

(ii) Enforcing Mandatory Injunction

5–11 An enforcing mandatory injunction requires positive action on the part of the person to whom it is directed, which may be on an ongoing basis. However, Keane notes that the distinction is really only of importance in one context; he compares an enforcing mandatory injunction with a decree for specific performance, subject to one difference, namely that in considering a situation where a court is asked to enforce a single term of a contract, the court will:

> "have to consider whether the term would be capable of being specifically performed if it stood alone and whether in all the circumstances it should be enforced on its own."[25]

(b) No Distinction as to Applicable Principles

5–12 Lord Upjohn stated in *Redland Bricks Ltd v Morris*[26] that a mandatory injunction can only be granted where the plaintiff shows a "very strong probability" upon the facts that grave damage will occur to him in the future. However, this statement has been criticised on the basis that it represents too stringent a test.[27] In *Smith v Smith*,[28] Jessel M.R. stated that he would have no more hesitation in granting a mandatory injunction in a proper case than he would a prohibitory injunction. The position is well summarised by Spry, who states that:

---

[24] Delany, *Equity and the Law of Trusts in Ireland*, 4th edn (Dublin: Thomson Round Hall, 2007), p.544.

[25] Keane, *Equity and the Law of Trusts in the Republic of Ireland* (London: Butterworths, 1988), p.232.

[26] [1970] A.C. 652 at 665; [1969] 2 W.L.R. 1437 at 1444; [1969] 2 All E.R. 576 at 579.

[27] Delany, *Equity and the Law of Trusts in Ireland*, 4th edn (Dublin: Thomson Round Hall, 2007), p.545, citing Spry, *The Principles of Equitable Remedies*, 6th edn (London: Sweet and Maxwell, 2001), p.547.

[28] *Smith v Smith* (1875) L.R. 20 Eq. 500 at 504.

"whenever an injury to the plaintiff is shown, being an injury that might, before it took place, have been enjoined by a prohibitory injunction if the court thought fit, a mandatory injunction may be granted unless consequent prejudice to the defendant is so disproportionate that the course is unjust in all the circumstances."[29]

5–13 In short, at the hearing of the action—different considerations arise at the interim and interlocutory stages—there would appear to be no reason in principle why the two should not be treated the same. Any perceived harshness which might be caused by the granting of a mandatory injunction will be factored into its considerations by a court for, as has been see in Ch.4, Equitable and General Principles, hardship and oppression are factors which a court will consider in arriving at any conclusion.[30]

4. Relationship to Interim and Interlocutory Applications

5–14 Regardless of whether the perpetual injunction sought is mandatory or prohibitory, it is important to note that a failure to secure an interim or interlocutory injunction does not preclude an applicant from seeking a perpetual injunction.[31] In *O'Brien v AON Insurance*,[32] Clarke J. refused to make an interlocutory order restraining a disciplinary process. However, he acknowledged that if it was ultimately found that a hearing was not conducted in accordance with fair procedures, then he believed that the plaintiff would have his remedy at that later stage.

5–15 It was emphasised by Hardiman J. in *Dunne v Lucas*[33] that, in dealing with an interlocutory motion, the court is not finally deciding any factual or legal aspect of the controversy. An application for a perpetual injunction at a substantive hearing is a full hearing with full evidence and debate of legal points as necessary. This is in contrast to an interim or interlocutory hearing which, in the normal course, will be dealt with on affidavit evidence only. That said, a failure to secure an interim or, more particularly, an interlocutory injunction, may in practical terms determine a matter.[34]

---

[29] Spry, *The Principles of Equitable Remedies*, 6th edn (London: Sweet and Maxwell, 2001), p.547.
[30] See para.4–87.
[31] *Drew v Harman* (1818) 5 Price 319 at 322.
[32] unreported, High Court, Clarke J., January 14, 2004.
[33] unreported, Supreme Court, February 24, 2003.
[34] See the dictum of Lord Denning M.R. in *Fellowes & Son v Fisher* [1976] Q.B. 122 at 129; [1975] 3 W.L.R. 184 at 189; [1975] 2 All E.R. 829 at 833, in which he stated that: "Nearly always, however, these cases do not go to trial. The parties accept the prima facie view of the court or settle the case. At any rate, in 99 cases out of 100, it goes no further." See also *Premier Dairies v Doyle* [1996] 1 I.R. 37 at 54; [1996] 1 I.L.R.M. 363 at 369, per O'Flaherty J.

C. *QUIA TIMET* INJUNCTIONS

1. Introduction

5–16 The *quia timet* injunction was described in *Frearson v Loe*[35] as being the most valuable jurisidiction of the old Court of Chancery, with no subject:

> "more frequently the cause of bills for injunction than the class of cases which were brought to restrain threatened injury as distinguished from injury which was already accomplished."

5–17 Over 100 years on, however, it was described less enthusiastically as a "somewhat arcane branch of the law".[36]

5–18 A *quia timet*[37] injunction is an injunction which will prohibit a projected actionable wrongful act where such an act is threatened, apprehended or imminent. It can also be sought to prevent the repetition of wrongful acts.[38] As explained by Lord Upjohn in *Redland Bricks Ltd v Morris*[39]:

> "*quia timet* actions are broadly applicable to two types of cases: first, where the defendant has as yet done no hurt to the plaintiff but is threatening and intending (so the plaintiff alleges) to do works which will render irreparable harm to him or his property if carried to completion. Your Lordships are not concerned with that and those cases are normally, though not exclusively, concerned with negative injunctions. Secondly, the type of case where the plaintiff has been fully recompensed both at law and in equity for the damage he has suffered but where he alleges that the earlier actions of the defendant may lead to future causes of action."[40]

5–19 However, it is important to remember that a key principle of *quia timet* injunctions is that "no one can obtain a quia timet order by merely saying *timeo*", or "I fear",[41] and that the courts will have regard to various principles before determining whether or not to grant such an injunction.

---

[35] (1879) 9 Ch D 48 at 65, per Sir George Jessel M.R.

[36] per Keane J. in *National Irish Bank Ltd v RTÉ* [1998] 2 I.R. 465 at 486; [1998] 2 I.L.R.M. 196 at 211.

[37] Which broadly translates from the Latin as "because he fears".

[38] See *Frearson v Loe* (1878) 9 Ch D 48 at 65, per Jessel M.R. See also *Litchfield-Speer v Queen Anne's Gate Syndicate (No. 2) Ltd* [1919] 1 Ch. 407 at 412, per Lawrence J., explaining the approach of the courts to an application for a *quia timet* injunction in the context of a nuisance.

[39] [1970] A.C. 652; [1969] 2 W.L.R. 1437; [1969] 2 All E.R. 576.

[40] [1969] 2 W.L.R. 1437 at 1443; [1970] A.C. 652 at 665; [1969] 2 All E.R. 576 at 579.

[41] per Lord Dunedin in *Attorney General for Dominion of Canada v Ritchie Contracting and Supply Co Ltd* [1919] A.C. 999 at 1005.

2. Applicable Principles/A Proven Substantial Risk of Danger

5–20 It has been held that there is no difference in general terms between the legal principles to be applied to an application for a substantive *quia timet* injunction (and indeed an application on an interlocutory basis)[42] and any other kind of injunction.[43] The prevailing test in this jurisdiction for determining the onus of proof involved in the granting of a *quia timet* injunction is that enunciated by Geoghegan J. in *Szabo v Esat Digifone Ltd.*[44] It is necessary to show that there is a "proven substantial risk of danger".

5–21 The plaintiff schoolchildren in Szabo sought a number of perpetual injunctions (as well as interlocutory injunctions of a similar nature) to stop the intended development and operation of a mobile phone base station in the grounds of the garda station next to their school in County Sligo. The plaintiffs claimed that the operation of such a base station and mast would be dangerous to their health. In considering the application for the interlocutory injunctions, Geoghegan J. dealt first with the applicable test for *quia timet* injunctions. He referred to *Attorney General v Manchester Corporation*[45] and the test employed in that case, namely that the plaintiff must show "a strong case of probability that the apprehended mischief" will in fact arise.[46] However, he took the view that such a test went "too far".[47]

5–22 In fact, a dilution of this test was evident a long time before *Szabo*, and in *Independent Newspapers v Irish Press*,[48] Meredith J. had shifted the test of a "strong probability" of injury to a "reasonable probability". In *Whelan v Madigan*,[49] Kenny J. referred to "probability" without any qualification. However, it is unclear whether he intended to vary the test in any way by using such a formula.

5–23 In *Szabo* Geoghegan J. stated that for a *quia timet* injunction to be granted there would have to be "a proven substantial risk of danger". He cited in support of this the case of *Attorney General (Boswell) v Rathmines and Pembroke Joint Hospital Board.*[50] That case concerned the proposed establishment of a smallpox hospital at Clonskeagh in Dublin. At the trial of the action, Chatterton V.C. set out the relevant test, in the specific context of a permanent or perpetual,

---

[42] See *Szabo v Esat Digifone Ltd* [1998] 2 I.L.R.M. 102 at 111, per Geoghegan J.
[43] *Martin v Price* [1894] 1 Ch. 276 at 285, per Lindley L.J.
[44] [1998] 2 I.L.R.M. 102.
[45] [1893] 2 Ch. 87.
[46] The test also used in the Circuit Court in *Radford v Wexford Corporation* (1955) 89 I.L.T.R. 184.
[47] [1998] 2 I.L.R.M. 102 at 110.
[48] [1932] I.R. 615.
[49] [1978] I.L.R.M. 136.
[50] [1904] 1 I.R. 161.

rather than an interlocutory, injunction, as being the necessity to show that the complainants:

"entertain a reasonable, well-grounded apprehension that the work which the defendants are carrying out would, if allowed to proceed, result in substantial damage to the complainants".[51]

5–24 However, on appeal Fitzgibbon L.J. stated that:

"To sustain the injunction, the law requires proof by the plaintiff of a well-grounded apprehension of injury–a strong probability, almost amounting to a moral certainty."[52]

5–25 Geoghegan J. was quite clear in electing for a test based on a "proven substantial risk of danger". This appears to be closer to the test set out by Chatterton V.C. rather than that employed by Fitzgibbon L.J. in the successful appeal. The latter test refers, inter alia, to a "strong probability" of danger; Geoghegan J. had already indicated he believed that this went too far. In cases such as *Minister for Arts, Heritage, the Gaeltacht and the Islands v Kennedy*,[53] the courts have approved the *Szabo* test of a "proven substantial risk of danger",[54] and that remains the test in this jurisdiction.

3. Approach in England

5–26 The courts in England take a somewhat different approach. In *Hooper v Rogers*,[55] Russell L.J. suggested that the degree of probability is not absolute and that, "what is to be aimed at is justice between the parties having regard to all the relevant circumstances".[56] This may represent a slightly better, albeit less certain, approach. Spry[57] suggests that the relevant applicable criterion to which the court should have regard is not fixed or invariable, but depends on the circumstances of the case. This is because the court must weigh the degree of probability that a material injury will occur with its gravity and likely consequences, as well as any other matters that will affect the balance of hardship or justice between parties.

---

[51] [1904] I.R. 161 at 166.
[52] [1904] 1 I.R. 161, as referred to in *Attorney General v Nottingham Corporation* [1904] 1 Ch. 673 at 677. See also the Circuit Court decision of *Radford v Wexford Corporation* (1955) 89 I.L.T.R. 184.
[53] [2002] 2 I.L.R.M. 94.
[54] The case was cited by, inter alia, Kelly J. in *Ryanair Ltd v Aer Rianta cpt,* ex tempore, High Court, Kelly J., January 25, 2001.
[55] [1975] Ch. 43.
[56] [1975] Ch. 43 at 50.
[57] Spry, *The Principles of Equitable Remedies*, 6th edn (London: Sweet & Maxwell, 2001), p.380.

5–27 That an apparently more flexible standard is applied by the courts in England is evident from *British Telecommunications Plc v One in a Million*.[58] In his decision, Jonathan Sumption Q.C. held that a final *quia timet* injunction did not require proof that damage would certainly occur; it was sufficient that what was going on was calculated to infringe the plaintiff's rights in future. However, it is also important to bear in mind the much earlier decision of *Graigola Merthyr Co Ltd v Swansea Corporation*,[59] in which Lord Buckmaster observed that a "mere vague apprehension" was not sufficient to support an action for a *quia timet* injunction, and that there had to be an "immediate threat" to do something.[60]

5–28 However, in this jurisdiction it appears to be settled that the onus of satisfying the court that there is a "proven substantial risk of danger" is the applicable test in terms of a perpetual *quia timet* injunction.[61]

D. ADEQUACY OF DAMAGES

1. Introduction

5–29 It was stated in *Isenberg v East India House Estate Co Ltd*,[62] that mandatory injunctions should be "confined to cases where the injury done to the plaintiff cannot be estimated and sufficiently compensated by a pecuniary sum."[63] However, this statement can be extrapolated to injunctions generally. A key consideration for a court in determining whether to grant a perpetual injunction is the question of the adequacy of damages rather than granting an injunction. As stated by Lindley L.J. in *London and Blackwell Railway Co v Cross*[64]:

> "The very first principle of injunction law is that *prima facie* you do not obtain injunctions to restrain actionable wrongs, for which damages are the proper remedy."[65]

---

58 [1998] F.S.R. 265 at 271. See the report of the (dismissed) appeal [1999] 1 W.L.R. 903 at 909; [1998] 4 All E.R. 476 at 482, per Aldous L.J.
59 [1929] A.C. 344 at 353.
60 Citing *Lord Cowley v Byas* (1877) 5 Ch D 944 at 950.
61 See also the consideration of *Szabo* in the context of interlocutory applications in Ch.6, Interlocutory Applications, para.6–199.
62 (1863) 3 De G.J. & S. 263.
63 (1863) 3 De G.J. & S. 263 at 271, per Lord Westbury L.C.
64 (1886) 31 Ch D 354 at 369.
65 Referred to in *Downey v Minister for Education* [2001] 2 I.R. 727 at 732. However, in the latter case, Smyth J. made reference to the defendant's submissions relating to a passage from *Bean on Injunctions* which states that: "It is comparatively unusual for the defendant to be able to say that damages are the only available remedy in the case and that the court does not even have a discretion to grant an injunction." The passage is from the 8th edn of the book. The up to date reference is Bean, *Injunctions*, 9th edn (London: Thomson Sweet & Maxwell, 2007), p.20.

The starting point for any consideration of the jurisdiction to award damages in lieu of, or in addition to, an injunction, dates back to the Chancery Amendment Act 1858, more popularly referred to as Lord Cairns' Act.[66]

2. Chancery Amendment Act 1858 (Lord Cairns' Act)

5–30 By virtue of s.2 of the Chancery Amendment Act 1858, a court could, on an application for an injunction, award and assess damages in addition to, or in lieu of, an injunction.[67] Section 2 provides that:

> "In all cases in which the Court of Chancery has jurisdiction to entertain an application for an injunction against a breach of any covenant, contract, or agreement, or against the commission or continuance of any wrongful act … it shall be lawful for the same Court, if it shall think fit, to award damages to the party injured, either in addition to or in substitution for such injunction."[68]

5–31 Lord Cairns' Act was designed to avoid the Court of Chancery having to send a party to the common law courts for the purposes of assessing damages.[69] It also enabled the courts to award damages in relation to the repetition of a wrong, or indeed future wrongs, the latter of which were not actionable at common law.[70]

5–32 As explained by Kenny J. in *Cullen v Cullen*,[71] citing Lindley L.J. in *Shelfer v City of London Electric Lighting Co.*,[72] Lord Cairns' Act was, in simple terms, passed in order to enable the Court of Chancery to administer justice between litigants more effectually than it could before the Act. However, it is important to remember that the Act does not simply make provision for one party to essentially "buy off" another, as explained by Lindley L.J. in *Shelfer*. He stated that:

---

[66] The test for the adequacy of damages under Lord Cairns' Act is only undertaken at the point where a perpetual injunction is being sought. Different considerations inform the issue of damages at the interlocutory (and interim) stage; such damages as sought at those two stages are intended to compensate a party for any loss which might be suffered in between the granting of an injunction at the interim/interlocutory stage and the final determination of the action.

[67] See, for example, *Tulk v Moxhay* (1848) 2 Ph. 774 and *Wrotham Parks Ltd v Parkside Homes Ltd* [1974] 1 W.L.R. 798; [1974] 2 All E.R. 321.

[68] See also s.28 of the Supreme Court of Judicature Act (Ireland) 1877 as referred to by Kenny J. in *Cullen v Cullen* [1962] I.R. 268.

[69] See *Jaggard v Sawyer* [1995] 1 W.L.R. 269 at 284; [1995] 2 All E.R. 189 at 204, per Millett L.J., citing Turner L.J. in *Ferguson v Wilson* (1866) L.R. 2 Ch. App. 77 at 88.

[70] *Leeds Industrial Co-Operative Society Ltd v Slack* [1924] A.C. 851 at 859, per Viscount Finlay.

[71] [1962] I.R. 268 at 287.

[72] [1895] 1 Ch. 287 at 316.

"The jurisdiction to give damages instead of an injunction is in words given in all cases ... But in exercising the jurisdiction thus given attention ought to be paid to well settled principles; and ever since Lord Cairns' Act was passed the Court of Chancery has repudiated the notion that the Legislature intended to turn that Court into a tribunal for legalising wrongful acts; or in other words, the Court has always protested against the notion that it ought to allow a wrong to continue simply because the wrongdoer is able and willing to pay for the injury he may inflict."[73]

5–33 In *Cullen v Cullen*,[74] Kenny J. set out some useful examples of when damages might be awarded instead of an injunction. Such examples included:

"trivial and occasional nuisances: cases in which a plaintiff has shown that he only wants money; vexatious and oppressive cases; and cases where the plaintiff has so conducted himself as to render it unjust to give him more than pecuniary relief."[75]

5–34 As is clear from cases such as *Evans Marshall & Co Ltd v Bertola SA*,[76] the courts have taken a fairly broad approach in this regard and will consider whether it is just in all the circumstances that a party should be confined to a remedy in damages.

(a) Application to Quia Timet Injunctions

5–35 In *Shelfer* it had been suggested that:

"the use of the word 'damages' has led to a doubt whether the Act applies to cases where no injury at all has yet been inflicted, but where injury is threatened only."[77]

5–36 This doubt does not appear to have been borne out: in *Hooper v Rogers*,[78] the plaintiff brought a successful action in the county court, inter alia, for damages in lieu of an injunction ordering the defendant to restore a slope which was supporting a farmhouse. The defendant appealed, contending that the judge had no jurisdiction to grant a mandatory *quia timet* injunction. The appeal was dismissed, with the Court of Appeal holding that justice should be done between

---

73 [1895] 1 Ch. 287 at 315.
74 [1962] I.R. 268 at 287.
75 [1962] I.R. 268 at 287. See also para.5–38.
76 [1973] 1 W.L.R. 349 at 379, per Sachs LJ.
77 [1895] 1 Ch. 287 at 315.
78 [1975] Ch. 43; [1974] 3 W.L.R. 329; [1974] 3 All E.R. 417.

the parties having regard to all the relevant circumstances. It found that on the circumstances of the case before it, it was open to the judge to hold that he could have made the mandatory order and to grant damages in lieu. Russell L.J. stated that:

> "The award of damages could only be supported as equitable damages under the Chancery Amendment Act 1858 (Lord Cairns's Act) in lieu of such an injunction. The injunction, mandatory in character, would be *quia timet*, as preventing an apprehended legal wrong ..."[79]

5–37 The courts in this jurisdiction appear to have accepted that damages can be awarded in such circumstances, and in *Rabbette v Mayo Co Council*[80] both a *quia timet* injunction and damages were awarded to the plaintiff, albeit without any detailed analysis of the applicability or otherwise of Lord Cairns' Act.

3. Circumstances in Which Damages Might be Awarded

5–38 There are a number of factors which the courts generally take into account in determining whether to award damages instead of a perpetual injunction.

(a) The Shelfer Principles

5–39 The circumstances in which damages might be given in substitution for an injunction were considered in *Shelfer v City of London Electric Lighting Co.*[81] AL Smith L.J. stated that it was a "good working rule" that:

> "(1) If the injury to the plaintiff's legal rights is small,
>   (2) And is one which is capable of being estimated in money,
>   (3) And is one which can be adequately compensated by a small money payment,
>   (4) And the case is one in which it would be oppressive to the defendant to grant an injunction:–
> then damages in substitution for an injunction may be given."[82]

---

[79] [1975] Ch. 43 at 47; [1974] 3 W.L.R. 329 at 331; [1974] 3 All E.R. 417 at 419. In *Oakacre Ltd v Claire Cleaners (Holdings) Ltd* [1982] Ch. 197 at 203; [1981] 3 W.L.R. 761 at 765; [1981] 3 All E.R. 667 at 670, no cause of action had accrued for damages for breach of contract before the relevant writ was issued. Judge Mervyn Davies Q.C. found that he could "deal with the whole case as it now stands between the parties."

[80] [1984] I.L.R.M. 156.

[81] [1895] 1 Ch. 287.

[82] [1895] 1 Ch. 287 at 322. See also the summary of the general principles made in *Coll v Home and Colonial Stores Ltd* [1904] A.C 179 at 193, as adopted by Dixon J. in *McGrath v Munster and Leinster Bank Ltd* [1959] I.R. 313 at 328.

5–40 As is clear from the terms of s.2 of Lord Cairns' Act, damages may also be awarded in addition to, or in substitution for, the granting of an injunction.[83]

(b) Acceptance of Shelfer in Ireland

5–41 The *Shelfer* principles were adopted and adapted in this jurisdiction in *Patterson v Murphy*.[84] Costello J. first identified the circumstances in which there is a right to an injunction. He agreed with the submission of the defendants that even if an infringement of the plaintiffs' rights has been established, the court has a discretion to award damages in *lieu* of an injunction. Costello J. also observed that there were "well established principles on which the court exercises this discretion", and summarised them as follows:

> "1. When an infringement of the plaintiffs' right and a threatened further infringement to a material extent has been established the plaintiff is *prima facie* entitled to an injunction. There may be circumstances however, depriving the plaintiff of this *prima facie* right but generally speaking the plaintiff will only be deprived of an injunction in very exceptional circumstances.
> 2. If the injury to the plaintiff's rights is small, and is one capable of being estimated in money, and is one which can be adequately compensated by a small money payment, and the case is one in which it would be oppressive to the defendant to grant an injunction, then these are the circumstances in which damages in lieu of an injunction may be granted.
> 3. The conduct of the plaintiff may be such as to disentitle him to an injunction. The conduct of the defendant may be such as to disentitle him from seeking the substitution of damages for an injunction.
> 4. The mere fact that a wrong-doer is able and willing to pay for the injury he has inflicted is not a ground for substituting damages."[85]

5–42 Applying those principles, Costello J. found that there were before him no circumstances which could deprive the plaintiffs of the relief to which they were prima facie entitled. He found that the infringement of their rights was a most serious one; the injury suffered was considerable and damages would not adequately compensate them.

---

[83] See, inter alia, the dictum of Lord Chelmsford L.C. in *Betts v Neilson* (1868) 3 Ch. App. 429 at 440. See also, *Leeds Industrial Co-Operative Society Ltd v Slack* [1924] A.C. 851.

[84] [1978] I.L.R.M. 85.

[85] [1978] I.L.R.M. 85 at 99; *cf.* the earlier case of *Halpin v Tara Mines Ltd* [1976–1977] I.L.R.M. 28, in which Gannon J. had awarded damages in circumstances where the defendants, who were engaged in mining activities had, since the matter had first come before the court, improved their working standards to a degree which made it unnecessary to continue the interim injunction previously granted. In *Patterson*, Costello J. pointed out that *Halpin* did not involve the substitution of damages for an injunction.

(c) Other Factors

5–43 In *Shelfer*, AL Smith L.J. stressed the fact that a defendant's conduct may disentitle him "from asking that damages may be assessed in substitution for an injunction". He offered the example of a defendant "hurrying up his buildings so as if possible to avoid an injunction".[86] Also emphasised was the fact that it was impossible to lay down rules as to what constituted a "small injury", what type of injury could be estimated in money, what adequate compensation would be, or what would be oppressive to the defendant. He stated that each case must be left to the "good sense" of the court determining it.[87]

5–44 The "good sense" of the court was evident in *Falcon Travel Ltd v Owners Abroad Group Plc*,[88] a passing-off action. The English defendant company had been in business since the early 1980s as a major tour operator, selling its product wholesale to travel agents such as the Irish plaintiff company, a retail travel agent. In 1988, the defendant company launched a brochure directed to the Irish market. It also opened an office in Ireland, where it intended to trade under the name "Falcon". Although clearly aware of the existence of the plaintiff, it did not anticipate any confusion between the two businesses operating under the "Falcon" name because of the differences between them. There was no question of fraud or deceit, nor did the defendant intend or expect to expropriate the reputation of the plaintiff or any part of its business. The plaintiff did not lose any customers to the defendant and, if anything, in fact benefited. Murphy J. found that there was passing off, and that the plaintiff company's goodwill had been appropriated by the defendant and had become submerged in that of the defendant. However, Murphy J. also found that in the circumstances of the case, where the defendant company had acted innocently, albeit wrongfully, and the fact that the grant of an immediate injunction to restrain the defendant from using the word "Falcon" in connection with its business in Ireland would cause it enormous expense and lead to potentially significant confusion among the public, it would be appropriate to grant damages in lieu of an injunction. The sum in question was held by Murphy J. to be:

> "a rough estimate of the general loss suffered and to be suffered by the plaintiff as a result of the defendant's wrongdoing. Primarily it should enable the plaintiff to mount an advertising or public relations campaign which would explain to the public and to persons in the travel agency business the very real difference between the two parties to these proceedings."[89]

---

[86] [1895] 1 Ch. 287 at 323.
[87] [1895] 1 Ch. 287 at 323.
[88] [1991] 1 I.R. 175.
[89] [1991] 1 I.R. 175 at 183.

(d) No Entitlement to Buy Way Out of Wrongdoing

5–45 Another key point about the award of damages is that a party is not entitled to buy his way out of his wrongdoing. In *Leeds Industrial Co-operative Society v Slack*,[90] Lord Sumner doubted:

> "whether it is complete justice to allow the big man, with his big building and his enhanced rateable value and his improvement of the neighbourhood, to have his way, and to solace the little man for his darkened and stuffy little house by giving him a cheque that he does not ask for."[91]

5–46 Similarly as has been seen, in *Shelfer*, Lindley L.J. stated that, Lord Cairns' Act was not designed to allow a wrongdoer buy off an injured party.[92]

5–47 However, in *Ormerod v Todmorden Mill Co.*,[93] it was held that where a plaintiff has shown by previous conduct that the injury suffered is one which in some way may be compensated by money, the court may decline to grant an injunction.[94]

(e) Wide Discretion

5–48 There is still a discretion residing with the court as to whether to grant an injunction even if the factors in *Shelfer* are met. This is clear from *Jaggard v Sawyer*.[95] In that case, Millett L.J. observed that whilst AL Smith L.J.'s check-list has stood the test of time:

> "it needs to be remembered that it is only a working rule and does not purport to be an exhaustive statement of the circumstances in which damages will be awarded instead of an injunction."[96]

5–49 An example of the wide discretion which resides in the court is evident in the case of *Regan v Paul Properties DPF No.1 Ltd.*[97] In the Court of Appeal, Mummery L.J. brought his analysis beyond the confines of *Shelfer* and undertook a review of a number of cases. Having done so, he concluded that:

---

[90] [1924] A.C. 851.
[91] [1924] A.C. 851 at 872.
[92] [1895] 1 Ch. 287 at 315.
[93] (1883) 11 Q.B.D. 155 at 162.
[94] Acquiescence by the plaintiffs was also a factor in that case.
[95] [1995] 1 W.L.R. 269; [1995] 2 All E.R. 189.
[96] [1995] 1 W.L.R. 269 at 287; [1995] 2 All E.R. 189 at 208.
[97] [2007] Ch. 135; [2006] 3 W.L.R. 1131; [2007] 4 All E.R. 48.

"the reported cases are merely illustrations of the circumstances in which particular judges have exercised their discretion. In particular all the circumstances of the case have to be considered."[98]

4. Measure of Damages

5–50 The appropriate amount of damages to award in lieu of an injunction depends on the circumstances of each individual case. In *Leeds Industrial Co-operative Society*,[99] Lord Sumner said that:

"… no money awarded in substitution can be justly awarded, unless it is at any rate designed to be a preferable equivalent for an injunction and therefore an adequate substitute for it …"[100]

5–51 The extent to which damages under Lord Cairns' Act and common law damages should be measured in the same way has caused some difficulties for the courts in England, although the Irish courts do not appear to have addressed this point with the same level of scrutiny.[101] In *Wrotham Park Estate Co v Parkshide Homes Ltd*,[102] Brightman J. identified that the plaintiff had suffered no loss. That being so, he suggested a "just substitute" for the injunction sought, rather than the nominal damages which would have flowed from the fact that there had been no loss. Similarly, in *Bracewell v Appleby*,[103] the damages awarded in lieu of an injunction to restrain trespass to land were held to be a proper and fair price for the acquisition of the right of way which the defendant had purported to extend.

5–52 The House of Lords took a somewhat different and somewhat harsh view in its decision in *Johnson v Agnew*.[104] The Lords held, albeit in the context of specific performance, that there was no difference between the measure of damages awarded under Lord Cairns' Act and those awarded at common law. However, in the later case of *Jaggard v Sawyer*,[105] Millett L.J. held that in his view Lord Wilberforce's statement in *Johnson*:

---

[98]   [2007] Ch. 135 at 146; [2006] 3 W.L.R. 1131 at 1142; [2007] 4 All E.R. 48 at 58.
[99]   [1924] A.C. 851.
[100] [1924] A.C. 851 at 870. See also *Fritz v Hobson* (1880) 14 Ch D 542 at 556, per Fry L.J.
[101] As such, this is an area which is comprehensively and clearly dealt with in Hanbury & Martin, *Modern Equity*, 17th edn (London: Sweet & Maxwell, 2005), p.813. See also Halpern, "Damages in Lieu of an Injunction: How Much?" [2001] Conv. 453.
[102] [1974] 1 W.L.R. 798; [1974] 2 All E.R. 321; *cf. Surrey County Council v Bredero Homes Ltd* [1993] 1 W.L.R. 1361; [1993] 3 All E.R. 705.
[103] [1975] Ch. 408; [1975] 2 W.L.R. 282; [1975] 1 All E.R. 993.
[104] [1980] A.C. 367.
[105] [1995] 1 W.L.R. 269; [1995] 2 All E.R. 189.

"that the measure of damages is the same whether damages are recoverable at common law or under the Act must be taken to be limited to the case whether they are recoverable in respect of the same cause of action."

5–53 He did not believe that such a statement could:

"sensibly have any application where the claim at common law is in respect of a past trespass or breach of covenant and that under the Act it is in respect of future trespasses or continuing breaches of covenant."[106]

5–54 The earlier approach in *Wrotham Park* was supported by the House of Lords in *Attorney General v Blake*,[107] albeit that Lord Cairns' Act was not applicable in that case. Lord Nicholls neatly summarised the position as being that *Wrotham Park* showed that:

"in contract as well as tort damages are not always narrowly confined to recoupment of financial loss. In a suitable case damages for breach of contract may be measured by the benefit gained by the wrongdoer from the breach. The defendant must make a reasonable payment in respect of the benefit he has gained."[108]

5–55 Although this is not a point without some complexity, this approach appears to be a lot fairer than the approach taken in Johnson. An example of the approach in practice is provided by the case of *Experience Hendrix LLC v PPX Enterprises Inc.*[109] In the Court of Appeal, Mance L.J. held that the granting of an injunction to the beneficiary of a restrictive covenant, after the defendant had gained some benefit by an infringement, did not in principle preclude the court from ordering payment of a reasonable sum in damages in compensation for that infringement. This was so even though the beneficiary could show no financial loss. The current position post-*Hendrix* has been summarised in the following way:

"So in claims for damages arising out of straightforward commercial contracts, a claim for damages will succeed based on a 'reasonable payment for use' basis, even where the claimant cannot establish any loss on conventional compensatory principles."[110]

---

[106] [1995] 1 W.L.R. 269 at 291; [1995] 2 All E.R. 189 at 211.
[107] [2001] 1 A.C. 268; [2000] 3 W.L.R. 625; [2000] 4 All E.R. 385.
[108] [2001] 1 A.C. 268 at 283; [2000] 3 W.L.R. 625at 637; [2000] 4 All E.R. 385 at 396.
[109] *Times Law Reports*, April 19, 2003, distinguishing on its facts the case of *Attorney General v Blake* [2001] 1 A.C. 268, in which it had been held that damages for breach of contract could be assessed by reference to the benefits gained by the wrongdoer rather than the loss suffered by the innocent party.
[110] See Sandy, "Spies, Rock Stars and Restitutionary Damages" (2003) 153 N.L.J. 723.

5–56 In *Lunn Poly Ltd v Liverpool & Lancashire Properties Ltd*,[111] the Court of Appeal held that there was no absolute rule that damages could not be assessed on the basis of events which arose after the breach occurred.

E. APPLYING FOR A PERPETUAL INJUNCTION

1. Introduction

5–57 An application for a perpetual injunction will often, though not always, have been preceded by an application for either an interim or interlocutory order. However, it is not a precondition of seeking a perpetual injunction to have sought an injunction on an interim or interlocutory basis; the latter applications are only necessary in situations of urgency, or in general terms to maintain the status quo pending the full hearing.

2. Pleadings

(a) Indorsement on a Plenary Summons

5–58 The originating documents upon which an injunction application can be based have already been looked at in Ch.1, Domestic Jurisdiction.[112] Where an action is being brought by way of plenary summons, an injunction should be specifically sought as a relief in an indorsement of claim if it is sought on a perpetual basis. It is not necessary, or indeed appropriate, where an injunction is sought on an interim or interlocutory basis, ancillary to substantive relief, that the interim or interlocutory injunction should be claimed in the indorsement of claim. Interim and interlocutory reliefs will be claimed as such in the relevant notice of motion. This is clear from the decision of Finlay C.J. in the case of *Caudron v Air Zaire*.[113]

5–59 In *Caudron*, the Chief Justice looked at the Rules of the Superior Courts (RSC). In particular, he set out the terms of RSC Ord.4 r.2, which deals with the indorsement of claim on a plenary summons. He then stated that there are "many forms of relief which may be sought and obtained from the court between the issue and service of the originating summons and the final determination of the claim indorsed on it", including interlocutory injunction orders. Dealing with such relief Finlay C.J. held that such interlocutory relief:

---

111 *Times Law Reports*, April 18, 2006.
112 See para.1–93.
113 [1985] I.R. 716; [1986] I.L.R.M. 10.

"Should be obtained either on an interim basis *ex parte* or on an interlocutory basis by notice of motion served after the issue of the originating summons or in the matter of an intended action. They are not, however, the relief being sought in the action and are not, in my view on the true interpretation of the Rules, matters which should be claimed by way of indorsement on the summons itself."[114]

(b) Injunction Grounded in Statute

5–60 In so far as an injunction is specifically grounded in statute, Finnegan J. was satisfied in *McKenna v EH*[115] that it would be appropriate to claim the statutory interim or interlocutory injunction in the indorsement of claim, by reference to the statutory origin of the jurisdiction to grant the same. To do otherwise would be, in the view of Finnegan J., to fail to give effect to the clear intention of the Oireachtas. However, it should be noted that this was said in the context of interim and interlocutory injunctions under the Proceeds of Crime Act 1996 which, in the view of Finnegan J., "differ in substance from interim and interlocutory relief as normally understood, albeit that they are not the ultimate substantive relief sought in the action."[116] Nonetheless, if statute provides for a specific injunction, it would seem sensible to reference the particular statutory provision concerned in the initiating document.

(c) Relationship to Interim and Interlocutory Applications

5–61 There is a related question as to whether an injunction must be specifically sought in the substantive proceedings before an interim or interlocutory application can be made for an injunction. The answer in brief is that it need not necessarily be so sought. This is clear from cases such as *McGilligan v O'Grady*,[117] albeit that such cases tend to be confined to relatively discrete areas, such as in applications for *Mareva* injunctions.[118] For example, *McGilligan* concerned an application to restrain a company from removing a director pending the hearing of a petition under s.205 of the Companies Act 1963. In the words of Keane C.J.:

"I am bound to say, with all respect, that I do not understand why it should be thought that, because the relief sought in the interlocutory proceedings is not the same as the relief which will ultimately be sought in the s.205 proceedings, an interlocutory injunction should not be granted on that ground alone. If it is desirable, in accordance with the principles laid down in the

---

[114] [1985] I.R. 716 at 721; [1986] I.L.R.M. 10 at 21. As quoted by Finnegan J. in *McKenna v EH* [2002] 1 I.R. 72 at 78; [2002] 2 I.L.R.M. 117 at 122.
[115] [2002] 1 I.R. 72.
[116] [2002] 1 I.R. 72 at 78.
[117] [1999] 1 I.R. 346; [1999] 1 I.L.R.M. 303.
[118] See further, Ch.8, Commercial Injunctions.

American Cynamid Company and *Campus Oil* cases, to preserve the plaintiff's rights pending the hearing of the s.205 proceedings and the balance of convenience does not point to a different conclusion, I see no reason why interlocutory relief should not be granted."

5–62 As has been seen, an injunction may also be sought on foot of an originating motion where appropriate.[119]

3. State of the Law

5–63 In *Application des Gaz SA v Falks Veritas Ltd*,[120] it was held that the courts must make a decision whether to grant or refuse an injunction based on the state of the law at the date when the matter is to be resolved, as distinct from the date of the issue of the writ. It was also held in *Attorney General v Birmingham, Tame, and Rea District Drainage Board*[121] that under the (then) applicable rules of court in England, the courts have power to take evidence of matters which have occurred after the date of the decision from which an appeal is brought.[122] In that case, a perpetual injunction had been granted at the hearing, but was discharged on appeal as the facts had changed in the interim and there was no longer any breach of the relevant applicable legislation.

4. Hearing of the Application

(a) Oral Evidence

5–64 In contrast to interim and interlocutory applications, a court will generally hear oral evidence as necessary in relation to an application for a perpetual injunction, and all legal points will be fully debated. However, in certain circumstances the parties will agree that the hearing of the interlocutory application will be the trial of the action.[123]

(b) Hearing in Public

5–65 The extent to which an application for an injunction should be held in public or otherwise has been an issue which the courts have had to address on various occasions. Article 34.1 of the Constitution provides that:

---

[119] See Ch.1, Domestic Jurisdiction, para.1–102.
[120] [1974] Ch. 381 at 399; [1974] 3 W.L.R. 235 at 247; [1974] 3 All E.R. 51 at 61, per Stamp L.J., referring to the speech of Lord Wright in *New Brunswick Railway Co v British and French Trust Corporation Ltd* [1939] A.C. 1 at 33.
[121] [1912] A.C. 788.
[122] Such a power is provided in this jurisdiction by RSC Ord.58 r.8, dealing with appeals to the Supreme Court. See also RSC Ord.61 r.8, dealing with appeals to the High Court.
[123] See generally, Ch.6, Interlocutory Applications.

"Justice shall be administered in courts established by law by judges appointed in the manner provided by the Constitution, and, save in such special and limited cases as may be prescribed by law, shall be administered in public."[124]

5–66 In terms of statutory exceptions, the provisions of s.45(1)(a) of the Courts (Supplemental Provisions) Act 1961 allow a matter to be dealt with otherwise than in public in certain circumstances. Section 45(1)(a) identifies four areas in which there may be a restriction on reporting and public attendance, namely urgent applications for habeas corpus, bail, prohibition or injunctions.[125]

5–67 In *Z v DPP*[126] Hamilton P., dealing with an application to have a matter dealt with *in camera*, held that the:

"applications of 'an urgent nature' for relief by way of habeas corpus, bail, prohibition or injunction, to which s.45(1) of the Courts (Supplemental Provisions) Act 1961 relates, are those which are because of their nature so urgent that they must be made to a judge in his home or some place to which the public do not directly have access and not to applications which are made in court."

5–68 As such, it is difficult to conceive of an application for a perpetual injunction of such urgency that it should be held otherwise than in public.

5. Wording of the Order

5–69 An injunction is generally only granted in personam and will not in principle be granted against any person not a party to the action.[127] In granting an injunction, a court will state "with the greatest precision the form which the order is to assume".[128] The importance of this is of course that a party against whom an injunction order is made is entitled to know as a matter of fact what it is he is meant to do in order to comply with the order of the court[129]; non-compliance could lead to an application to have him found to be in

---

[124] For a review of the terms of the Article, see the dictum of Walsh J. in *Re R Ltd* [1989] I.R. 126; [1989] I.L.R.M. 757. See also *Irish Times v Ireland* [1997] 2 I.L.R.M. 54.

[125] The term "urgent applications" applies to all four types set out, viz. habeas corpus, bail, prohibition and injunctions.

[126] [1994] 2 I.L.R.M. 481 at 488.

[127] Although in England injunctions may be made "*contra mundum*", in relation to which see Ch.3, Standing.

[128] *Ellerman Lines Ltd v Read* [1928] 2 K.B. 144 at 158, per Atkin L.J.

[129] See the dictum of Lord Upjohn in *Redland Bricks Ltd v Morris* [1970] A.C. 652 at 666; [1969] 2 W.L.R. 1437 at 1445; [1969] 2 All E.R. 576 at 580.

contempt.[130] As stated by Joyce J. in *Attorney General v Staffordshire County Council*[131]:

> "It is the necessary requisite of every injunction and every mandatory order that it should be certain and definite in its terms, and it must or ought to be quite clear what the person against whom the injunction or order is made is required to do or refrain from doing."[132]

5–70 An order will also generally state a time within which an act must be performed if it is mandatory in nature.

5–71 The words of Lord Bingham in *South Bucks District Council v Porter*[133] are also of relevance in that he stated that, when granting an injunction order:

> "the court does not contemplate that it will be disobeyed ... Apprehension that a party may disobey an order should not deter the court from making an order otherwise appropriate: there is not one law for the law-abiding and another for the lawless and truculent."[134]

5–72 How the injunction order is framed is of course a matter which depends on the facts of each individual case and the essence of the order sought. However, in a matter of some complexity such as, for example, the use of certain information, it may be more convenient, depending on the injunction sought, to attach a schedule to a summons and to specify the terms of the injunction order in such a way that it restrains a party from using any information falling within the categories described in such a schedule. This was done in the case of *National Irish Bank v RTE*.[135]

5–73 If there is any doubt or difficulty in terms of understanding the order and its terms, the parties should have sought "liberty to apply" so that they may come back to court to clarify the extent or application of the order.[136]

---

[130] The necessary precision of an order was considered by Romilly M.R. in *Crump v Lambert* (1867) L.R. 3 Eq. 409 at 414 and referred to in *Halpin v Tara Mines Ltd* [1976–1977] I.L.R.M. 28. In relation to being in contempt, see Ch.12, Breach of an Injunction Order.
[131] [1905] 1 Ch. 336.
[132] [1905] 1 Ch. 336, 342.
[133] [2003] 2 A.C. 558; [2003] 2 W.L.R. 1547; [2003] 3 All E.R. 1.
[134] [2003] 2 A.C. 558 at 580; [2003] 2 W.L.R. 1547 at 1564; [2003] 3 All E.R. 1 at 19.
[135] [1998] 2 I.R. 465; [1998] 2 I.L.R.M. 196.
[136] See *Donegal County Council v Ballantine*, unreported, High Court, McCracken J., March 20, 1998. See further, Ch.6, Interlocutory Applications.

(a) Penal Indorsements

5–74 It may be necessary to indorse the order in question. As was made clear in *The Century Insurance Co Ltd v Larkin*,[137] it is crucial to ensure that such an indorsement appears on the face of an order where it is required. In relation to mandatory orders, RSC Ord.41 r.8 provides that:

> "Every judgement or order made in any cause or matter requiring any person to do an act thereby ordered, shall state the time, or the time after service of the judgement or order, within which the act is to be done; and upon the copy of the judgement or order which shall be served upon the person required to obey the same, other than an order directing a mortgagor to deliver possession to a mortgagee, or an order under section 62 subsection (7) of the Registration of Title Act, 1964, there shall be endorsed a memorandum in the words or to the effect following, viz.:—
>
> > 'If you the within named A.B. neglect to obey this judgement or order by the time therein limited, you will be liable to process of execution including imprisonment for the purpose of compelling you to obey the same judgement or order.'"[138]

5–75 There appears to be no rule preventing the indorsement of the order by the solicitor having carriage of the proceedings concerned, in the prescribed form. Furthermore, although the requirement for an indorsement applies to mandatory orders, it is not uncommon, arising out of an abundance of caution, for such indorsement to appear on prohibitory injunction orders as well.

6. Damages

5–76 A court will usually determine all matters at the hearing of the substantive application. However, it is not unknown for the claim for an injunction to be dealt with at that hearing, but issues such as damages to be dealt with at a later date. For example, in *Rabbette v Mayo Co Council*,[139] D'Arcy J. made an order perpetually restraining the defendant from carrying out blasting operations in the vicinity of the plaintiff's property in such a way as to be a nuisance or to cause damage to the plaintiff's premises. By consent the court reserved the question of damages, and the issue of damages was brought forward for determination five years after the claim for primary relief by way of injunction was heard and determined, albeit that that was an unusually long period of time.

---

[137] [1910] 1 I.R. 91 at 94.
[138] Ord.37 r.2 of the Circuit Court Rules provides that prior to the serving of a notice for attachment, "a copy of the Court Order in respect of which obedience is sought, shall be personally served upon the party against whom the Order was made with a penal endorsement thereon." See generally, Ch.12, Breach of an Injunction Order.
[139] [1984] I.L.R.M. 156.

7. Stay and Suspension

5–77 In an appropriate case, a court may grant an injunction but suspend its operation.[140] Alternatively, the court may delay imposing the injunction until the party against whom the injunction has been granted has been given an opportunity to remedy matters. For example, in *Corporation of Dublin v Garland*,[141] an injunction was granted against the respondents using certain premises as offices. However, a 12-month stay was put on the order, so that the respondents could obtain alternative accommodation for their office purposes.

8. Qualified Injunction

5–78 A further option which found favour in the English High Court in *Sun Microsystems Inc. v Amtec Computer Corp. Ltd*[142] is a "qualified injunction". In *Sun Microsystems*, the plaintiff brought an action in relation to the parallel importing of computer servers in the European Union. Warren J. accepted that it was necessary to balance Sun's right to an injunction to prevent further infringements against Amtec's need to carry on its legitimate business. He therefore granted an injunction, but qualified it by providing that Amtec could deal with Sun products if it informed Sun of the serial numbers of the goods, and Sun had not objected to their sale within 10 days. Such an order is again testament to the flexibility of the injunction as a remedy, and represents a sound, practical approach by the courts.

9. Dissolution of the Injunction

5–79 Once granted, an injunction remains in force until such time as it is discharged, even if it ought not to have been made.[143] It may subsequently be dissolved by a court if appropriate.[144] In general terms, dissolution will frequently be sought by agreement between the parties based, for example, on a change of material circumstances. An application for such a dissolution may also be made by a third party affected by the injunction order,[145] or by a court of its own motion.[146] An order may also be varied as necessary, although this will usually happen in the context of interim or interlocutory orders.

---

140 See, for example, *Attorney General v Colney Hatch Lunatic Asylum* (1868) 4 Ch. App. 146.
141 [1982] I.L.R.M. 104.
142 [2006] E.W.H.C. 62.
143 *Isaacs v Robertson* [1985] A.C. 97; [1984] 3 W.L.R. 705; [1984] 3 All E.R. 140.
144 *Commonwealth Scientific and Industrial Research Organisation v Perry* (1988) 92 F.L.R. 182.
145 *Cretanor Maritime Co Ltd v Irish Marine Management Ltd* [1978] 1 W.L.R. 966; [1978] 3 All E.R. 164.
146 *RB Harbottle (Mercantile) Ltd v National Westminster Bank Ltd* [1978] Q.B. 146.

10. Appeal

5–80 An appeal may be brought from the Circuit Court to the High Court in relation to the granting or refusal of an injunction. An appeal may similarly be brought from the High Court to the Supreme Court

(a) Circuit to High Court

5–81 Appeals are based on Pt IV of the Courts of Justice Act 1936. Rules of the Superior Courts Ord.61 (and not the Rules of the Circuit Court) deals with the practical aspect of appeals from the Circuit to the High Court. An appeal is brought by way of notice of appeal, which must be served on the relevant parties[147] and lodged[148] within 10 days from the pronouncement of the order appealed against. Pursuant to RSC Ord.61 r.6, an appeal does not operate as a stay of execution in relation to the decision appealed from, unless ordered otherwise by the Circuit Court judge or the High Court judge in Dublin.

(b) High to Supreme Court

5–82 An appeal from the High to the Supreme Court must be brought by way of notice of appeal as provided for in RSC Ord.58. It is a 10-day notice and must be served within 21 days from the passing and perfecting of the order appealed against.[149] Pursuant to RSC Ord.58 r.4, the notice of appeal "shall in every case state the grounds of appeal and the relief sought." An appeal shall not operate as a stay of execution in relation to the decision appealed from, unless ordered otherwise by court.[150]

F. INQUIRY AS TO DAMAGES

1. Introduction

5–83 When applying for an injunction on an interim or interlocutory basis, the party seeking the injunction must also be in a position to provide an undertaking as to damages.[151] The undertaking as to damages allows a party to be compensated in circumstances where it is found at the substantive hearing of a

---

[147] RSC Ord.61 r.2.
[148] RSC Ord.61 r.3.
[149] RSC Ord.58 r.3. It is possible for the Supreme Court to abridge the relevant time limits by virtue of RSC Ord.58 r.3(3).
[150] RSC Ord.58 r.18. See generally, Delany & McGrath, *Civil Procedure in the Superior Courts*, 2nd edn (Dublin: Thomson Round Hall, 2005), Ch.20.
[151] The requirement for such an undertaking originally only applied to interim injunctions, but has now been extended to all injunction applications. See Ch.6, Interlocutory Applications and Ch.7, Interim Applications and the relevant sections on undertakings as to damages in each Chapter.

matter that the interlocutory injunction was "wrongfully" asked for. In *Graham v Campbell*,[152] James L.J., having observed that effect ought to be given to an undertaking as to damages, stated that:

> "If any damage has been occasioned by an interlocutory injunction, which, on the hearing, is found to have been wrongly asked for, justice requires that such damage should fall on the voluntary litigant who fails, not on the litigant who has been without just cause made so."[153]

5–84 In other words, if a party gives an undertaking as to damages when securing an injunction on an interim/interlocutory basis (generally referred to in England as a cross undertaking as to/in damages), but fails to secure an injunction at the substantive hearing, they are liable to pay damages to the opposing party (generally the defendant) as compensation for any loss suffered by virtue of the injunction having been secured at the interim/interlocutory stage.

5–85 There is only one detailed Irish authority on the point, *Estuary Logistics & Distribution Co Ltd v Lowenergy Solutions Ltd*,[154] but the enforcement of an undertaking as to damages has been considered in some detail in the courts in England.

2. Enforcement of the Undertaking

5–86 In *Ushers Brewery v PS King & Co (Finance) Ltd*,[155] two situations were identified in which it was held that an undertaking as to damages might be enforceable:

- where the plaintiff fails on the merits at trial[156];
- where it was established before the trial of substantive action that an injunction should never have been granted.

5–87 It should also be noted that an inquiry as to damages cannot be avoided by virtue of a plaintiff discontinuing his or her action subsequent to the undertaking having been given.[157]

---

[152] (1878) 7 Ch D 490.
[153] (1878) 7 Ch D 490 at 494.
[154] unreported, High Court, Clarke J., December 6, 2007.
[155] [1972] Ch. 148; [1971] 2 W.L.R. 1141; [1971] 2 All E.R. 468.
[156] Plowman J. citing *Newby v Harrison* (1861) 3 De G. F. & J. 287 and *Griffith v Blake* (1884) 27 Ch D 474.
[157] *Newcomen v Coulson* (1878) 7 Ch D 764.

3. Discretionary Inquiry

5–88 In *Graham v Campbell*,[158] James L.J. indicated that, unless special circumstances prevailed, effect ought to be given to the undertaking as to damages. However, the more modern view, certainly in England, is that the ordering of an inquiry into damages is discretionary.

5–89 In *F Hoffmann-La Roche & Co AG v Secretary of State for Trade and Industry*,[159] Lord Diplock observed that the court retains a discretion not to enforce the undertaking if it considers that the conduct of the defendant in relation to the obtaining or continuing of the injunction or the enforcement of the undertaking makes it inequitable to do so.

5–90 The discretionary element of enforcement was also referred to in *Financiera Avenida v Shiblaq*,[160] in which Lloyd L.J. said that the first question arising whenever there is an application by a defendant to enforce a cross-undertaking in damages is whether the undertaking ought to be enforced at all. That depended on the circumstances in which the injunction was obtained, the success or otherwise of the plaintiff at the trial, the subsequent conduct of the defendant and all the other circumstances of the case. It is thus clear that simply because an action fails at the substantive hearing, this does not inexorably lead to an undertaking as to damages being enforced.[161]

4. Options Available

5–91 The options available to a court in the context of an inquiry as to damages were dealt with in considerable detail by Neill L.J. in the English case of *Cheltenham & Gloucester Building Society v Ricketts*.[162] These are set out in full below, as this "exhaustive" review was found to be "particularly persuasive" by Clarke J. in *Estuary Logistics & Distribution Co Ltd v Lowenergy Solutions Ltd*.[163] The extract from Neill L.J. also contains six general observations as to an undertaking as to damages which also bear setting out,[164] before dealing with the enforcement of an undertaking at points (7) and (8). The principles as set out by Neill L.J. are:

---

[158] (1878) 7 Ch D 490.
[159] [1975] A.C. 295 at 361; [1974] 3 W.L.R. 104 at 127; [1974] 2 All E.R. 1128 at 1150.
[160] *Times Law Reports*, January 14, 1991.
[161] Although for a more stringent approach, see *Universal Thermosensors Ltd v Hibben* [1992] 1 W.L.R. 840; [1992] 3 All E.R. 257.
[162] [1993] 1 W.L.R. 1545; [1993] 4 All E.R. 276.
[163] unreported, High Court, Clarke J., December 6, 2007.
[164] See also, Ch.6, Interlocutory Applications, para.6–76.

"(1) Save in special cases an undertaking as to damages is the price which the person asking for an interlocutory injunction has to pay for its grant. The court cannot compel an applicant to give an undertaking but it can refuse to grant an injunction unless he does.

(2) The undertaking, though described as an undertaking as to damages, does not found any cause of action. It does, however, enable the party enjoined to apply to the court for compensation if it is subsequently established that the interlocutory injunction should not have been granted.

(3) The undertaking is not given to the enjoined but to the court.

(4) In a case where it is determined that the injunction should not have been granted the undertaking is likely to be enforced, though the court retains a discretion not to do so.

(5) The time at which the court should determine whether or not the interlocutory injunction should have been granted will vary from case to case. It is important to underline the fact that the question whether the undertaking should be enforced is a separate question from the question whether the injunction should be discharged or continued.

(6) In many cases injunctions will remain in being until the trial and in such cases the propriety of its original grant and the question of the enforcement of the undertaking will not be considered before the conclusion of the trial. Even then, as Lloyd L.J. pointed out in *Financiera Avenida v. Shiblaq*, The Times, 14 January 1991; Court of Appeal (Civil Division) Transcript No. 973 of 1990 the court may occasionally wish to postpone the question of enforcement to a later date.

(7) Where an interlocutory injunction is discharged before the trial the court at the time of discharge is faced with a number of possibilities.

(a) The court can determine forthwith that the undertaking as to damages should be enforced and can proceed at once to make an assessment of the damages. It seems probable that it will only be in rare cases that the court can take this course because the relevant evidence of damages is unlikely to be available.[165] It is to be noted, however, that in *Columbia Pictures Inc. v. Robinson* [1987] Ch. 38, Scott J. was able, following the trial of an action, to make an immediate assessment of damages arising from the wrongful grant of an *Anton Piller* order. He pointed out that the evidence at the trial could not be relied on to justify ex post facto the making of an *ex parte* order if, at the time the order was made, it ought not to have been made: see p.85H.

---

[165] Peter Gibson J. noted that "save in the most straightforward of cases where all the relevant facts are known the court is unlikely to exercise its discretion in this way." [1993] 1 W.L.R. 1545 at 1557; [1993] 4 All E.R. 276 at 287. This did in fact present itself as an option in *Estuary Logistics & Distribution Co Ltd v Lowenergy Solutions Ltd*, unreported, High Court, Clarke J., December 6, 2007, although ultimately Clarke J. felt that, for factual reasons set out in his judgment, "a decision as to whether to enforce the undertaking as to damages concerned should be reserved to the trial judge who will ... be in a much better position to take into account all appropriate factors."

(b) The court may determine that the undertaking should be enforced but then direct an inquiry as to damages in which issues of causation and quantum will have to be considered. It is likely that the order will include directions as to pleadings and discovery in the inquiry. In the light of the decision of the Court of Appeal in *Norwest Holst Civil Engineering Ltd v. Polysius Ltd*, The Times, 23 July 1987; Court of Appeal (Civil Division) Transcript No. 644 of 1987 the court should not order an inquiry as to damages and at the same time leave open for the tribunal at the inquiry to determine whether or not the undertaking should be enforced.[166] A decision that the undertaking should be enforced is a precondition for the making of an order of an inquiry as to damages.

(c) The court can adjourn the application for the enforcement of the undertaking to the trial or further order.

(d) The court can determine forthwith that the undertaking is not to be enforced.

(8) It seems that damages are awarded on a similar basis to that on which damages are awarded for breach of contract. This matter has not been fully explored in the English cases though it is to be noted that in *Air Express Ltd v. Ansett Transport Industries (Operations) Pty. Ltd* (1979) 146 C.L.R. 249, 267 Aickin J. in the High Court of Australia expressed the view that it would be seldom that it would be just and equitable that the unsuccessful plaintiff 'should bear the burden of damages which were not foreseeable from circumstances known to him at the time.' This passage suggests that the court in exercising its equitable jurisdiction would adopt similar principles to those relevant in a claim for breach of contract."[167]

5–92 Clarke J. held in *Estuary Logistics*[168] that the passage "represents the law in this jurisdiction as well".

5–93 The judgment of Peter Gibson J. in *Cheltenham & Gloucester* also bears examination; one point which Peter Gibson J. made is that the court can also refuse an application to enforce an undertaking as to damages. However, this will only be done in very straightforward cases, Peter Gibson J. giving by way of example, a case "when it is clear that the respondent has suffered no loss by reason of the order".[169]

---

[166] *cf.* the decision in *Zygal Dynamics Plc v McNulty*, unreported, Court of Appeal (Civil Division), June 20, 1989, Transcript No. 571 of 1989. In *Cheltenham & Gloucester Building Society v Ricketts* [1993] 1 W.L.R. 1545 at 1557; [1993] 4 All E.R. 276 at 287, Peter Gibson J. appears to suggest that he preferred the approach in *Norwest Holst* to that in *Zygal Dynamics*.
[167] [1993] 1 W.L.R. 1545 at 1551; [1993] 4 All E.R. 276 at 281.
[168] unreported, High Court, Clarke J., December 6, 2007.
[169] [1993] 1 W.L.R. 1545 at 1557; [1993] 4 All E.R. 276 at 287.

5. Principles of Contract Law Apply

5–94 The final point made by Neill L.J. bears highlighting; in determining whether the defendant has suffered any damage by reason of the granting of the injunction, it was held by Lloyd L.J. in *Financiera Avenida* that ordinary principles of the law of contract apply both as to causation and as to quantum.[170]

6. No Retrospective Application

5–95 It was held by the Court of Appeal in *SmithKline Beecham Plc v Apotex Europe Ltd*,[171] that undertakings in damages given to the court by the parties on the grant of an interim injunction provided no basis for a third party, who subsequently applied to be joined as a defendant but was not a defendant when the injunction was granted, to have a claim in restitution in respect of benefits which had accrued to the claimant. In other words, an undertaking as to damages cannot be applied retrospectively.

7. Form of the Inquiry

5–96 No rules are prescribed for the form of the inquiry as to damages; it appears that it is a matter in relation to which directions as to the appropriate pleadings may be given by the court. The stage at which the inquiry takes place and the judge dealing with the matter can be relevant factors; if the first of the four options identified in *Cheltenham & Gloucester* is adopted, viz. an immediate inquiry, it would not be necessary to generate any further pleadings in relation to the inquiry.

(a) Points of Claim

5–97 An immediate inquiry apart, the most appropriate format for such pleadings is, in practical terms, generally by way of points of claim, answered by points of defence.[172] The points of claim are structured in the same way as a statement of claim, with the relevant loss and damages calculated and set out. As with points of claim and points of defence generally, this approach would appear to admit of the usual sequence of steps subsequent to the delivery of points of claim and defence, namely the raising of particulars, the seeking of discovery and so on.[173]

---

[170]   Although the difficulties involved in certain inquiries are clear from *Universal City Studios Incorporated v Mulligan (No. 3)* [1999] 3 I.R. 407, specifically in that case in the context of an infringement of copyright.

[171]   [2007] Ch. 71; [2006] 3 W.L.R. 1146.

[172]   See Bullen & Leek & Jacobs, *Precedents of Pleadings*, 15th edn, Vol.2, p.771, para.42 K–6.

[173]   See generally Delany & McGrath, *Civil Procedure in the Superior Courts*, 2nd edn (Dublin: Thomson Round Hall, 2005).

(b) Notice of Motion

5–98 If an application for an inquiry as to damages is being brought before the trial of the action, however, it may be more appropriate to seek such inquiry by way of a notice of motion.[174]

(c) Motion for Directions

5–99 If there is any doubt as to how to proceed, a party may bring a motion for directions before a court, in which the main relief sought is directions from the court as to how to proceed with the application. The affidavit grounding the application will generally set out the background to the proceedings, detail the circumstances in which it is said that a need for an inquiry as to damages has arisen and set out any further information to which the court may have regard in coming to a determination as to how best to proceed.

---

[174] As happened, for example, in the case of *Estuary Logistics & Distribution Co Ltd v Lowenergy Solutions Ltd*, unreported, High Court, Clarke J., December 6, 2007.

CHAPTER 6

INTERLOCUTORY APPLICATIONS

A. INTRODUCTION

6–01 An injunction may be granted on an interlocutory basis, when proceedings are in being and before an action comes to trial.[1] As stated by Lord Diplock in *American Cyanamid v Ethicon Ltd*[2]: "The grant of an interlocutory injunction is a remedy that is both temporary and discretionary."[3] As is evident from this dictum, an interlocutory injunction is not in itself a final determination by a court of the issues in dispute. It is in general terms sought on notice to the other party, with the broad objective of maintaining the status quo between parties to an action until that final determination.[4] The interlocutory stage is not intended to provide a forum in which any disputed questions of fact or difficult issues of law are determined, for the courts have acknowledged the difficulty of trying to resolve conflicts purely on the basis of affidavit evidence at an interlocutory stage.[5] That said, the courts have recognised that in many instances disputes are resolved once the matter has been dealt with at the interlocutory stage.[6]

6–02 An interlocutory injunction can be distinguished from an interim injunction. The latter, considered in Ch.7, is normally sought in urgent situations and on an ex parte basis; the practical considerations peculiar to interim ex parte

---

[1] Under the Civil Procedure Rules (CPR) introduced in England and Wales in 1998, reference is made at CPR r.25.1(1)(a) to the power of the court to grant an "interim" injunction, which covers both interim injunctions as understood in this jurisdiction, but also interlocutory injunctions. See generally, Gee, *Commercial Injunctions*, 5th edn (London: Sweet & Maxwell, 2004), p.34.

[2] [1975] A.C. 396; [1975] 2 W.L.R. 316; [1975] 1 All E.R. 504.

[3] [1975] A.C. 396 at 405; [1975] 2 W.L.R. 316 at 320; [1975] 1 All E.R. 504 at 508.

[4] *Plimpton v Spiller* (1876) 4 Ch D 286 at 289, per James L.J.

[5] per Lord Diplock in *American Cyanamid Co v Ethicon Ltd* [1975] A.C. 396 at 407; [1975] 2 W.L.R. 316 at 323; [1975] 1 All E.R. 504 at 510. See also the dictum of Laffoy J. in *Claystone Ltd v Larking*, unreported, High Court, Laffoy J., March 14, 2007.

[6] See *Fellowes & Son v Fisher* [1976] Q.B. 122 at 129; [1975] 3 W.L.R. 184 at 189; [1975] 2 All E.R. 829 at 833, per Lord Denning M.R. On occasion, the parties may agree that the interlocutory hearing should in fact be the trial of the substantive action. Anecdotally, this in fact happens relatively infrequently. For examples of when it does, see *Macklin v Greacen* [1983] I.R. 61 [1982] I.L.R.M. 182 and *Essfood Eksportlagtiernes Sallgsforening v Crown Shipping (Ireland) Ltd* [1991] I.L.R.M. 97.

applications means that interim injunctions merit separate consideration. However, the actual legal principles upon which both interim and interlocutory injunctions are granted are, broadly speaking, similar. That said, it is not a precondition of seeking a perpetual injunction at the full hearing of an action that an application be brought for an interlocutory injunction. Nor, indeed, is it a precondition of seeking an interlocutory injunction that an interim injunction should first be sought.

6–03 This chapter will consider applications for injunctions on an interlocutory basis, looking first at the general principles applicable to such applications. It will then consider in detail applications for different types of injunctions— prohibitory, mandatory and *quia timet*—and the question of whether there is any material difference between the principles applied to the hearing of such applications. Finally, the practicalities involved in applying for an injunction on an interlocutory basis and the hearing of that application will be set out. The considerations applicable to specific areas of the law and how the courts approach applications in such individual areas are considered in Ch.10, General Application.

B. General Principles

1. Introduction

6–04 When an injunction is sought on an interlocutory basis, the question of the adequacy of damages as a remedy[7] is, in practical terms, a hugely significant consideration in determining how a court will proceed. However, in terms of the overall approach which informs the granting of interlocutory injunctions, the maintenance of the status quo between parties to an action until the final determination by a court of the issues in dispute is also a key factor[8] (though arguably more so in theory than in practice).[9] In *Campus Oil Ltd v Minister for Industry and Energy (No. 2)*,[10] O'Higgins C.J. stated that interlocutory relief is given:

> "because a period must necessarily elapse before the action can come for trial and for the purpose of keeping matters in *statu quo* until the hearing."[11]

---

[7] See para.6–56.

[8] *Jones v Pacaya Rubber and Produce Co Ltd* [1911] 1 K.B. 455 at 457.

[9] The maintenance of the *status quo* is "by no means an immutable principle", per MacMenamin J. in *Whelan Frozen Foods Ltd v Dunnes Stores*, unreported, High Court, MacMenamin J., February 17, 2006.

[10] [1983] I.R. 88; [1984] I.L.R.M. 45.

[11] [1983] I.R. 88 at 105; [1984] I.L.R.M. 45 at 60.

6–05 In other words, the party granted an injunction on an interlocutory basis is not prejudiced by reason of the delay which will necessarily occur between the issuing of proceedings and the final determination of the matter in question. This is well summarised by Zuckerman[12]:

> "The optimal balance which interlocutory remedies aim at is the bare minimum of pre-judgment interference consistent with the protection of rights. This delicate balance has to be struck in circumstances of uncertainty, because prior to judgment it cannot be legally known who is in the right. Interlocutory remedies, therefore, employ some basic fact-finding and law determining measures to minimise the risk of error. Inevitably, these measures are no more than rudimentary mechanisms dictated by the necessity of making a rough assessment of the facts and issues in dispute in order to find a timely solution, however fallible, to an inescapable and pressing problem."[13]

6–06 Although this analysis has a wide scope in so far as it concerns interlocutory remedies generally, the basic principles are equally applicable to the specific case of injunctions sought on an interlocutory basis. Before considering this and other principles to which the courts will have regard, the legislative and procedural bases for the granting of injunctions on an interlocutory basis will be reviewed. The practical consideration that proceedings must be in being before an interlocutory injunction will be granted will then be considered. First, however, it is important to consider the link between interlocutory injunctions and subtantive proceedings.

2. The Need for Substantive Proceedings

6–07 An interlocutory injunction cannot exist in isolation from substantive proceedings. The very first matter which a plaintiff bringing an application for an injunction will have to show is that they have a substantive legal, equitable, statutory or constitutional right, enforceable against a defendant.

6–08 The need to be able to identify a substantive right was explained in *Siskina (Owners of Cargo Lately Laden on Board) v Distos Compania Naviera SA*,[14] in the context of a *Mareva* injunction.[15] Lord Diplock, referring, inter alia, to the fact that an interlocutory injunction is granted to preserve the status quo pending the ascertainment by the courts of the rights of the parties, stated that:

> "A right to obtain an interlocutory injunction is not a cause of action. It cannot

---

[12] Zuckerman, "Interlocutory Remedies in Quest of Procedural Fairness" (1993) 56 M.L.R. 325.
[13] Zuckerman, "Interlocutory Remedies in Quest of Procedural Fairness" (1993) 56 M.L.R. 325 at 326.
[14] [1979] A.C. 210; [1977] 3 W.L.R. 818; [1977] 3 All E.R. 803.
[15] As to which, see Ch.8, Commercial Injunctions.

stand on is own. It is dependant on there being a pre-existing cause of action against the defendant arising out of an invasion, actual or threatened, by him of a legal or equitable right of the plaintiff for the enforcement of which the defendant is amenable to the jurisdiction of the court. The right to obtain an interlocutory injunction is merely ancillary and incidental to the pre-existing cause of action."[16]

6–09 In *Channel Tunnel Group Ltd v Balfour Beatty Construction Ltd*,[17] Lord Mustill pithily summarised the doctrine expounded in *The Siskina*, stating that:

"the right to an interlocutory injunction cannot exist in isolation, but is always incidental to and dependant on the enforcement of a substantive right."[18]

6–10 The distinction between substantive and ancillary relief has been considered in a number of cases in this jurisdiction. One of the better known ones is *Caudron v Air Zaire*.[19] Considered in Ch.2, Extraterritorial Jurisdiction, that case concerned the question of whether a *Mareva* injunction was in the nature of primary or ancillary relief.[20] The relevance of this was that the answer would determine whether proceedings could be served out of the jurisdiction.

3. Not a Determination of the Substantive Proceedings

6–11 A determination at the interlocutory stage is not a final determination of the matter in issue.[21] In *Dunne v Dun Laoghaire Rathdown Co Council*,[22] Hardiman J. emphasised that in dealing with the interlocutory motion before it, the court was not finally deciding any factual or legal aspect of the controversy.[23] The reason for this, as observed by Hardiman J., is that on a full hearing evidence may be different and more ample, with the law debated at greater length. However, Hardiman J. also acknowledged that the courts must be alive to the risk that they may determine a matter by inaction.[24] It is important to note,

---

[16] [1979] A.C. 210 at 256; [1977] 3 W.L.R. 818 at 825; [1977] 3 All E.R. 803 at 824.
[17] [1993] A.C. 334; [1993] 2 W.L.R. 262; [1993] 1 All E.R. 664.
[18] [1993] A.C. 334 at 362; [1993] 2 W.L.R. 262 at 285; [1993] 1 All E.R. 664 at 686.
[19] [1985] I.R. 716; [1986] I.L.R.M. 10.
[20] See also, *Taher Meats (Ireland) Ltd v State Company for Foodstuff Trading* [1991] 1 I.R. 443.
[21] Save where the parties agree that the interlocutory application should be treated as the trial of the action.
[22] [2003] 1 I.R. 567.
[23] [2003] 1 I.R. 567 at 581. See also the dictum of Lord Diplock in *American Cyanamid Co v Ethicon Ltd* [1975] AC 396 at 407; [1975] 2 W.L.R. 316 at 323; [1975] 1 All E.R. 504 at 510, adopted by McCarthy J. in Irish *Shell Ltd v Elm Motors Ltd* [1984] I.R. 200 at 224 and followed in, inter alia, *Ferris v Ward* [1998] 2 I.R. 194.
[24] See also the judgment of Barrington J. in *Flogas Ltd v Ergas Ltd* [1985] I.L.R.M. 221 which reviews the earlier judgment of Hamilton J. in *Reno Engrais et Produits Chimiques SA v Irish Agricultural Wholesale Society Ltd*, unreported, High Court, Hamilton J., September 8, 1976.

however, that doubt as to whether a perpetual injunction will be granted at the trial of the action does not as such preclude the granting of an interlocutory injunction.[25]

6–12 The view that an interlocutory application is not a final determination was also dealt with by Clarke J. in *Yap v Children's University Hospital Temple Street Ltd.*[26] Clarke J. noted that interlocutory applications are tried on affidavit, and the court is being asked to make an interim or interlocutory order pending a full trial. He felt that:

> "it is only in cases where either the Plaintiff has made out no case, or indeed on some occasions where the Defendant has made out no defence, that the Court is entitled to make assumptions about how the ultimate proceedings will be resolved."[27]

6–13 The courts have, however, also recognised that in many instances disputes are resolved once the matter has been dealt with at the interlocutory stage. As stated by Lord Denning M.R. in *Fellowes & Son v Fisher*[28]:

> "Nearly always, however, these cases do not go to trial. The parties accept the *prima facie* view of the court or settle the case. At any rate, in 99 cases out of 100, it goes no further."[29]

4. Legislative Basis

6–14 The legislative basis underpinning the granting of interlocutory injunctions on an equitable basis is the Supreme Court of Judicature Act (Ireland) 1877.[30] That Act confers jurisdiction on the High Court to grant injunctions in all cases where it appears just and convenient to do so, and on such terms as the court sees fit. At s.28(8) of the 1877 Act, it is provided that:

> "A mandamus or an injunction may be granted or a receiver appointed by an interlocutory order of the court in all cases in which it shall appear to the court

---

[25] See *Becker v Board of Management of St. Dominic's Secondary School*, unreported, High Court, Clarke J., April 13, 2006, in which Clarke J. stated that while it did not necessarily follow that an interlocutory injunction could not be granted where a substantive injunction could not be granted in respect of the same matter at trial, the court would have regard to the nature of the relief that might ultimately be obtained.

[26] [2006] 4 I.R. 298.

[27] [2006] 4 I.R. 298 at 300. See also the dictum of Denham J. in *ESB v Harrington*, unreported, Supreme Court, May 9, 2002.

[28] [1976] Q.B. 122; [1975] 3 W.L.R. 184; [1975] 2 All E.R. 829.

[29] [1976] Q.B. 122 at 129; [1975] 3 W.L.R. 184 at 189; [1975] 2 All E.R. 829 at 833. See also *Premier Dairies v Doyle* [1996] 1 I.R. 37 at 54; [1996] 1 I.L.R.M. 363 at 369, per O'Flaherty J.

[30] See Ch.1, Domestic Jurisdiction.

to be just or convenient that such order shall be made, and any such order may be made either unconditionally or upon such terms and conditions as the court shall think just; and if an injunction is asked, either before, or at, or after the hearing of any cause or matter, to prevent any threatened or apprehended waste or trespass, such injunction may be granted if the court shall think fit, whether the person against whom such injunction is sought is or is not in possession under any claim of title or otherwise, or (if out of possession) does or does not claim a right to do the act sought to be restrained under any colour of title, and whether the estates claimed by both or by either of the parties are legal or equitable."

6–15 As can be seen, an injunction is granted if the court feels that it would be "just" and "convenient", and on such terms and conditions as the court thinks just.[31]

5. Procedural Basis

6–16 Order 50 r.6 of the Rules of the Superior Courts (RSC) also makes provision for interlocutory injunctions. Rule of the Superior Courts Ord.50 r.6(1) states that:

"The Court may grant a mandamus or an injunction or appoint a receiver, by an interlocutory order in all cases in which it appears to the Court to be just or convenient to do so."[32]

6–17 Order 50 r.6(2) provides that "any such order may be made either unconditionally or upon such terms and conditions as the Court thinks just".

C. Prohibitory Interlocutory Injunctions

1. Introduction

6–18 A prohibitory injunction requires, in general terms, a party to refrain from performing or continuing to perform specified acts.[33]

---

[31] See Ch.1, Domestic Jurisdiction, para.1–37.
[32] There would appear to be no direct equivalent in the Rules of the Circuit Court. However, RCC Ord.20 refers to the granting of ex parte interim injunctions, and RCC Ord.39 provides for the appointment of a receiver by way of equitable execution. RCC Ord.67 r.16 provides that where no rule is set out to govern the practice and procedure of the Circuit Court, the rules of the High Court may be followed.
[33] See Ch.5, Perpetual Injunctions, para.5–05.

6–19 Prior to the seminal English case of *American Cyanamid Co v Ethicon Ltd*,[34] the key principles to which the courts had regard in determining whether to grant an interlocutory injunction, were similar in both England and Ireland. In short, the plaintiff had first to establish a strong prima facie case for the existence of the right on which he sued, after which the court would have regard to the question of balance of convenience. The governing principle was the preservation of the status quo.[35]

6–20 These principles were revisited and recast in *American Cyanamid Co v Ethicon Ltd*.[36] The *American Cyanamid* principles have also been fully endorsed in Ireland, starting with the leading case of *Campus Oil Ltd v Minister for Industry and Energy (No. 2)*.[37] The *Campus Oil* decision has been affirmed in numerous subsequent decisions, and in *Martin v Bord Pleanála*[38] O'Sullivan J. stated:

> "I do not understand our law to acknowledge principles other than those enshrined in *Campus Oil v Minister for Industry (No. 2)* for dealing with an application for an interlocutory injunction."[39]

6–21 As will be seen, however,[40] *Campus Oil* concerned a mandatory, rather than prohibitory, interlocutory injunction application. Notwithstanding this, the test set out in that case has been used many times in the context of applications for prohibitory interlocutory injunctions.

---

[34] [1975] A.C. 396; [1975] 2 W.L.R. 316; [1975] 1 All E.R. 504. For a relatively contemporaneous review of the decision, see Gore, "Interlocutory Injunctions—A Final Judgment" (1975) 38 M.L.R. 672.

[35] See, for example, *Harman Pictures NV v Osborne* [1967] 1 W.L.R. 723 at 738, per Goff J. The equivalent position in Ireland was summarised during the course of submissions, as reported in the case of *Moore v Attorney General* [1927] I.R. 569 at 570.

[36] [1975] A.C. 396; [1975] 2 W.L.R. 316; [1975] 1 All E.R. 504. And embraced after a period during which Lord Denning M.R. stated in *Fellowes & Son v Fisher*[1976] Q.B. 122 at 129; [1975] 3 W.L.R. 184 at 189; [1975] 2 All E.R. 829 at 834 that: "The *American Cyanamid* case … has perplexed the profession. It has been criticised in the legal journals. So much that counsel have appealed to us for guidance." The speech by Lord Diplock in *American Cyanamid* was described by Kelly J. in the case of *Foley v Sunday Newspapers Ltd* [2005] 1 I.R. 88 at 98 as being "considered by some commentators to have clarified and by others to have revolutionised the approach of the courts to interlocutory injunctions."

[37] [1983] I.R. 88; [1984] I.L.R.M. 45.

[38] [2002] 2 I.R. 655.

[39] [2002] 2 I.R. 655 at 663. Although curiously, in the 1998 Supreme Court decision in *Ferris v Ward* [1998] 2 I.R. 194, Blayney J. referred to both *American Cyanamid* and *Irish Shell Ltd v Elm Motors Ltd* [1984] I.R. 200; [1984] I.L.R.M. 595 in considering an appeal from an interlocutory injunction, but made no reference to *Campus Oil*.

[40] See para.6–39.

2. *Campus Oil* Guidelines

6–22 The *Campus Oil* guidelines can be summarised as follows:
- The party seeking the injunction must show that there is a fair/bona fide/serious question to be tried. If he can:
- The court must consider two aspects of the adequacy of damages:

  (i) First, it must consider whether, if it does not grant an injunction at the interlocutory stage, a plaintiff who succeeds at the trial of the substantive action will be adequately compensated by an award of damages for any loss suffered between the hearing of the interlocutory injunction and the trial of the action. If the plaintiff would be adequately compensated, the interlocutory injunction should be refused. This is subject to the proviso that the defendant would be in a position to pay such damages.

  (ii) Secondly, the court must consider whether, if it does grant an injunction at the interlocutory stage, a plaintiff's undertaking as to damages will adequately compensate the defendant, should the latter be successful at the trial of the action, in respect of any loss suffered by him due to the injunction being in force pending the trial. If the defendant would be compensated, the injunction may be granted. This is also subject to the proviso that the plaintiff would be in a position to pay such damages.

- If damages would not fully compensate either party, then the court may consider the balance of convenience. The matters relevant to determining where the balance of convenience lies will vary from case to case.
- If all other matters are equally balanced, the court should attempt to preserve the status quo.[41]

6–23 In *American Cyanamid*, it was suggested that where the arguments are finely balanced, the court may consider the relative strength of each party's case as revealed by the affidavit evidence adduced at the interlocutory stage where the strength of one party's case is disproportionate to that of the other. As will be seen,[42] this aspect of the *Cyanamid* decision does not appear to have found favour in this jurisdiction. These guidelines will be considered in greater detail after a review of the other factors to which the courts may have regard.

---

[41] Based on the dicta of McCracken J. in *B & S Ltd v Irish Auto Trader Ltd* [1995] 2 I.R. 142 at 145; [1995] 2 I.L.R.M. 152 at 156 (approved by Laffoy J. in *Symonds Cider v Showerings (Ireland) Ltd* [1997] 1 I.L.R.M. 481) and Quirke J. in *Clane Hospital Ltd v Voluntary Health Insurance Board*, unreported, High Court, Quirke J., May 22, 1998. However, in the latter case, when dealing with a bona fide question to be tried, Quirke J. referred to "whether or not the applicant has raised a fair, substantial *bona fide* question for determination." As noted by Delany, *Equity and the Law of Trusts in Ireland* 4th edn (Dublin: Thomson Round Hall, 2007), p.517, fn.137, "it is unlikely that he [Quirke J] was 4th edn trying to make the test harder to satisfy by inserting the word 'substantial'".

[42] See para.6–146.

(a) Other Factors

6–24 It was made clear in *American Cyanamid* that there may be "other special factors to be taken into consideration in the particular circumstances of individual cases".[43] In *Clane Hospital Ltd v Voluntary Health Insurance Board*,[44] Quirke J. also took the view that the court should consider any special factors which might influence the exercise of discretion and the grounds of the relief sought.[45] He referred to such factors as usually being technical in nature, but did not specify with any particularity what was meant by this.[46] As such, it is not clear whether this contemplates laches, clean hands and so on, or whether technical matters—in the truer sense of the phrase—can be considered by the court, such as, for example, the considerations relevant to an alleged breach of a patent. The latter is more likely, although the courts have a very wide discretion in any event.

6–25 There was a "special factor" in *American Cyanamid* itself, namely the risk of the commercial impracticability of seeking a permanent injunction at trial due to the damaging effect on goodwill in the market for surgical products. The commercial reality facing courts, particularly in passing-off cases, is often a relevant factor.[47]

6–26 It is obviously not possible to set out a definitive list of such factors. These will have to be identified by judges based on the facts before them. What is a little unclear is whether such special factors should displace the *American Cyanamid/Campus Oil* principles entirely. It has been argued that such factors "clearly refer to the balance of convenience", not to situations where the *American Cyanamid/Campus Oil* test can be ignored.[48] This point was also made by Stamp L.J. in *Hubbard v Pitt*.[49] However, the approach of the courts in this regard is varied. For example, in *Vogel v Cheeverstown House Ltd*,[50] Shanley J. held that the ordinary principles for interlocutory injunctions did not apply in "exceptional cases"[51] such as the one before him, which concerned a complaint of sexual abuse against the plaintiff by the resident of a centre for

---

[43] per Lord Diplock [1975] AC 396 at 409; [1975] 2 W.L.R. 316 at 324; [1975] 1 All E.R. 504 at 511.

[44] unreported, High Court, Quirke J., May 22, 1998.

[45] In fact, in *Fellowes & Son v Fisher* [1976] Q.B. 122; [1975] 3 W.L.R. 184; [1975] 2 All E.R. 829 Lord Denning M.R. appeared to try to circumnavigate the *American Cyanamid* principles by identifying special factors.

[46] Special factors were also referred to by Lord Diplock in *American Cyanamid*, but again, no explanation was given as to what was contemplated by the phrase in general terms.

[47] See, for example, the decision of Finlay Geoghegan J. in *Contech v Walsh*, ex tempore, High Court, Finlay Geoghegan J., February 17, 2006.

[48] See Gore, "Interlocutory Injunctions—A Final Judgment" (1975) 38 M.L.R. 672 at 676.

[49] [1976] Q.B. 142 at 188; [1975] 3 W.L.R. 201 at 212; [1975] 3 All E.R. 1.

[50] [1998] 2 I.R. 496.

[51] [1998] 2 I.R. 496 at 501.

persons with mental handicaps. In *Szabo v Esat Digifone Ltd*,[52] Geoghegan J. felt that there would be "something most distasteful about balancing the convenience of the first named defendant in being able to carry on its business against alleged dangers to the life and health of the plaintiff children"[53] and thus considered the matter primarily other than on the basis of the *American Cyanamid/Campus Oil* guidelines (although did indicate he would have reached the same conclusion even if he had had regard to those guidelines).[54]

(b) Equitable and General Principles

6–27 It is also important to remember that equitable and general considerations inform all applications for injunctions, including at the interlocutory stage. Where an application otherwise satisfies the *Campus Oil* principles, it may still be refused on the basis of, for example, laches, lack of clean hands or the other factors considered in greater detail in Ch.4, Equitable and General Principles.

(c) Constitutional Aspect

6–28 There is one proviso to the guidelines as set out in *American Cyanamid*. This was identified in *Oblique Financial Services Ltd v The Promise Production Co Ltd*.[55] In his decision, Keane J. accepted that there was no significant difference between the principles applied to the granting of interlocutory injunctions in this jurisdiction and in England, but pointed out that courts in this jurisdiction:

> "cannot by its order, in an application of this nature, abridge the constitutional rights, the rights enjoyed under the Irish Constitution, by any of the parties to the action."[56]

(d) Guidelines

6–29 The *American Cyanamid/Campus Oil* guidelines set out above will be considered in turn in the next section. At the outset it is important to emphasise that they are guidelines rather than binding rules.[57] That said, the guidelines tend

---

52 [1998] 2 I.L.R.M. 102. See also, Ch.5, Perpetual Injunctions, para.5–20.
53 [1998] 2 I.L.R.M. 102 at 105.
54 See also the case of *BUPA Ireland Ltd v Health Insurance Authority,* ex tempore, High Court, Finlay Geoghegan J., December 29, 2005.
55 [1994] 1 I.L.R.M. 74.
56 [1994] 1 I.L.R.M. 74 at 76.
57 As pointed out by Gee, *Commercial Injunctions*, 5th edn (London: Sweet & Maxwell, 2004), p.45: "The *American Cyanamid* case is an important statement of the principles to be applied in deciding applications for interim injunctions. But it has to be seen in the context of the facts of the case before the House of Lords. The claim was to enforce a proprietary right to a monopoly ... Notoriously damages are not an adequate remedy for the patentee because they

to be applied more frequently and more methodically by the courts than might be suggested by the fact that they are only guidelines. It should be remembered, however, that ultimately, the granting or otherwise of an interlocutory injunction is at the discretion of the court. As was stated by Kerr L.J. in the case of *Cambridge Nutrition Ltd v BBC*[58]:

> "The *American Cyanamid* case is no more than a set of useful guidelines which apply in many cases. It must never be used as a rule of thumb, let alone as a straightjacket."[59]

6–30 May L.J. similarly cautioned in *Cayne v Global Natural Resources Plc*[60] that "the words in a judgment ought not, however eminent the judge, to be construed as if they were an Act of Parliament", and that a court:

> "must be very careful to apply the relevant passages from Lord Diplock's familiar speech in the *Cyanamid* case not as rules but only as guidelines."[61]

6–31 Based on decided case law, it would be fair to say that whilst the *American Cyanamid/Campus Oil* guidelines are not in any way used as a straightjacket, they are nonetheless used as a rule of thumb.

D. THE *CAMPUS OIL* GUIDELINES

6–32 For ease of reference, it is proposed to consider the guidelines or principles applicable to equitable injunctions, as set out in *Campus Oil*, in the following order:

1. bona fide/fair/serious question to be tried;
2. the adequacy of damages;
3. balance of convenience;
4. status quo;
5. the question of the strength of the case.

1. Bona Fide/Fair/Serious Question to be Tried

6–33 The need to show a bona fide/fair/serious question to be tried—what might be termed the "threshold" criterion—was the significant change adopted

---

would be difficult to assess and because the monopoly can generate a goodwill which persists for some considerable time after the expiry of the patent."
[58] [1990] 3 All E.R. 523.
[59] [1990] 3 All E.R. 523 at 534.
[60] [1984] 1 All E.R. 225.
[61] [1984] 1 All E.R. 225 at 237.

by the courts in the *American Cyanamid* decision in 1975.[62] Prior to the decision in *American Cyanamid*, as adopted in this jurisdiction in 1983 in the *Campus Oil* decision, uncertainty existed in relation to the issue of what standard applied in relation to the plaintiff's chances of success at the trial of the action.

(a) Former test in England

6–34 Prior to the *American Cyanamid* decision, the courts in England had demonstrated a degree of inconsistency in their approaches to dealing with the test of a prima facie case. In *Donmar Productions Ltd v Bart*,[63] Ungoed-Thomas J. referred to the applicant establishing "A probability or a strong prima facie case that he is entitled to the right of whose violation he complains". Yet, in *Harman Pictures N.V. v Osborne*,[64] Goff J. held that once such a right had been established, an applicant would then have to show "that he has a case reasonably capable of succeeding".

6–35 However, as observed by Lord Diplock in *American Cyanamid*:

> "The suggested distinction between what the plaintiff must establish as respects his right and what he must show as respects its violation did not long survive."[65]

(b) Former test in Ireland

6–36 It has been noted that prior to the *Campus Oil* decision in this jurisdiction,[66] the precise requirement for the strength of the plaintiff's case was not clear.[67] The courts oscillated being diverse formulae such as "a probability"

---

62 Different criteria may apply when specific injunctions are provided for in legislation, as to which see Ch.11, Specific Statutory Injunctions.
63 [1967] 1 W.L.R. 740 at 742.
64 [1967] 1 W.L.R. 723 at 738. It has been observed by Gore, "Interlocutory Injunctions – A Final Judgment" (1975) 58 M.L.R. 672 at 674 that this appears to have in fact been a "false distinction" originating in Halsbury's *Laws of England*, notwithstanding that in *JT Stratford & Son Ltd v Lindley* [1965] A.C. 269 at 338; [1964] 3 All E.R. 102 at 116, Lord Upjohn appeared to hold that there had to be a prima facie case shown in relation to both right and breach.
65 [1975] A.C. 396 at 407; [1975] 2 W.L.R. 316 at 322; [1975] 1 All E.R. 504 at 509, citing *Hubbard v Vosper* [1972] 2 Q.B. 84.
66 See Kerr and Whyte, *Irish Trade Union Law* (Oxford: Professional Books Ltd, 1985), pp.319–329. Although written in the specific context of Trade Union Law, Ch.11, The Labour Injunction, is of interest in that it provides a relatively contemporaneous account of the lead up to the decision in *Campus Oil* and its aftermath.
67 The courts in also appeared to distinguish between cases which set out a "multi-requisite test" and those which used a "multi-factor test," the former dealing with the threshold test and the question of the balance of convenience sequentially, the latter effectively conflating the two. See *E.I. Co. Ltd v Kennedy* [1968] I.R. 69 (H.C.) (S.C.) and *Brennan v Glennon*, November 26, 1975 (S.C.) as analysed by Kerr and Whyte, *Irish Trade Union Law* (Oxford: Professional Books Ltd, 1985), at 321.

of success, "a *prima facie*" case and "a strong *prima facie*" case. Such diverse formulae could even be found within the same judgments.[68] For example, in the Supreme Court decision of *The Educational Company of Ireland Ltd v Fitzpatrick*,[69] Lavery J. had referred to passages from *Kerr on Injunctions*[70] which referred to the need to raise a "fair question", but also to show a "fair *prima facie* case". That passage also referred, in relation to the person against whom the injunction was sought, to a "probability ... in favour of his case ultimately failing in the final issue of the suit". Attempting to reconcile these apparently contradictory position in *Campus Oil Ltd v Minister for Industry and Energy (No. 2)*,[71] O'Higgins C.J. felt that the reference to "probability" in the passage from Kerr cited by Lavery J. was, "in its context", "of doubtful significance", and held that the reference to "fair question" was the "proper test."[72]

(c) Change of Test

6–37 In *American Cyanamid Co v Ethicon Ltd*,[73] Lord Diplock dealt conclusively with the issue. In admitting that the use of the different formulae led to confusion, he recast the threshold test. Lord Diplock did so in the following terms: "The court no doubt must be satisfied that the claim is not frivolous or vexatious; in other words, that there is a serious question to be tried."[74] The idea of a "serious question to be tried" is now the accepted test in England.

6–38 Although it has been suggested that the approach in *American Cyanamid* "had a mixed reception in this jurisdiction,"[75] it was ultimately approved of and adopted by both the High and Supreme Court, albeit in slightly different terms, in *Campus Oil Ltd v Minister for Industry and Energy (No. 2)*.[76]

(d) The Campus Oil Decision

6–39 The *Campus Oil* decision is widely and routinely cited as the basis for setting out the guidelines applicable to the granting of interlocutory applications in this jurisdiction. As such, it bears a degree of scrutiny. The case arose out of

[68] McMahon & Binchy, *The Irish Law of Torts*, 3rd edn (Dublin: Butterworths, 2000), p.1192.
[69] [1961] I.R. 323. A cautionary note is provided by the comments of McCarthy J. in reviewing the decision in Irish *Shell Ltd v Elm Motors Ltd* [1984] I.L.R.M. 595, in which he suggests that the headnote in the *Educational Company* case is incorrect in certain respects.
[70] 6th edn (London: Sweet and Maxwell, 1927).
[71] [1983] I.R. 88; [1984] I.L.R.M. 45. This application was by the defendants; the first reported *Campus Oil* decision concerned an application for an injunction by the plaintiffs.
[72] [1983] I.R. 88 at 106; [1984] I.L.R.M. 45 at 60.
[73] [1975] A.C. 396; [1975] 2 W.L.R. 316; [1975] 1 All E.R. 504.
[74] [1975] A.C. 396 at 407; [1975] 2 W.L.R. 316 at 323; [1975] 1 All E.R. 504 at 510.
[75] Kerr and Whyte, *Irish Trade Union Law* (Oxford: Professional Books Ltd, 1985), p.322.
[76] [1983] I.R. 88; [1984] I.L.R.M. 45. This application was by the defendants; the first reported *Campus Oil* decision concerned an application for an injunction by the plaintiffs.

the fact that the plaintiff companies, which were independent Irish-owned and controlled oil producers, were obliged by regulation to purchase a percentage of their supplies from the Whitegate refinery, owned by the State. This was known as the "mandatory regime", and operated notwithstanding the fact that oil could be purchased more cheaply elsewhere. The plaintiff companies brought a challenge to the regulation, claiming that it was contrary to the Treaty of Rome. In that regard, two questions were referred by Murphy J. to the European Court of Justice.[77]

6–40 In the meantime, the plaintiff companies ceased to comply with the regulation. Arising out of that, the defendant amended its defence by adding a counterclaim. It then applied to the High Court for interlocutory injunctions against the five plaintiffs who were refusing to comply with the mandatory regime.

6–41 In the High Court, Keane J. rejected the submission which had been made by the defendants that the guidelines propounded in *American Cyanamid* were in some way inconsistent with the criteria set out in *Educational Company of Ireland*. He observed that the test of a "fair question" to be tried, as referred to by Lavery J., was effectively the same as that adopted by Lord Diplock.[78] The Supreme Court also took this view, with O'Higgins C.J. summarising the position as follows:

> "In my view, the test to be applied is whether a fair *bona fide* question has been raised by the person seeking relief. If such a question has been raised it is not for the Court on an interlocutory application to determine that question; that remains to be decided at the trial. Once a fair question has been raised, in the manner which I have indicated, then the court should consider the other matters appropriate to the exercise of its discretion as to whether to grant interlocutory relief."[79]

6–42 O'Higgins C.J. felt that the proper test was the one laid down by Lavery J. in *Educational Company of Ireland*, to the effect that "the plaintiffs have to establish that there is a fair question raised to be decided at the trial".

---

[77] The Supreme Court declined to entertain an appeal from the determination of Murphy J. to refer the questions to the ECJ: this aspect of the case is reported at [1983] I.R. 82.

[78] This is of course correct, but ignores the section of the passage which refers to a "fair *prima facie* case". However, in the Supreme Court, Griffin J. also referred to the fact that "any such differences are more apparent than real": [1983] I.R. 88 at 111; [1984] I.L.R.M. 45 at 65.

[79] [1983] I.R. 88 at 107; [1984] I.L.R.M. 45 at 61. The "other matters" had been referred to earlier and included having regard to the "inconvenience, loss and damage might be caused to the other party" and asking "whether he who seeks relief has shown that the balance of convenience is in his favour".

6–43 What is interesting about the *Campus Oil* decision is that it was on its own terms a rather rare case in the context of the injunction application for two main reasons: first, the injunction was sought by the defendants on foot of a counterclaim, rather than by the plaintiffs.[80] Secondly, it involved an application for a mandatory injunction at the interlocutory stage, forcing the plaintiffs to comply with a ministerial order. Indeed, the plaintiffs argued that, in so far as the relief which was granted was mandatory in nature, it should not have been given by way of interlocutory relief. However, O'Higgins C.J., dealing with this point, simply stated that, "there are exceptions and, in my view, this case is one of them".[81]

6–44 Notwithstanding this convergence of factors which were of themselves relatively unusual in the context of interlocutory applications, the Supreme Court felt that the case was an appropriate one in which to adopt the *American Cyanamid* guidelines.[82] This was done almost in passing, with O'Higgins C.J. noting "the views expressed by Lord Diplock" and stating that he agreed entirely with what Lord Diplock had said.[83]

6–45 The views of Lord Diplock were accepted even though they were set out in the context of a prohibitory interlocutory injunction and the Supreme Court was dealing with an application for a mandatory interlocutory injunction. It should be noted that the *American Cyanamid* case was in itself unusual. The injunction sought in that case was a *quia timet* injunction, sought in relation to allegations of a breach of patent. This is itself arguably a type of case in which damages may not be an adequate remedy.

6–46 *American Cyanamid* and *Campus Oil* were by no means the most obvious cases from which principles of general applicability might be derived, in that they both consisted of rather atypical factual matrices. However, the principles set out in the former and adopted in the latter have been consistently applied in this jurisdiction to prohibitory interlocutory injunctions.

(i) Fair, Bona Fide Question

6–47 As enunciated by O'Higgins C.J., it is now the accepted position in this jurisdiction that the threshold test in Ireland is whether a fair, bona fide question has been raised. As to what that actually means, Butler J. suggested in *Moloney v Bolger*[84] that a "serious", "fair" and "bona fide" issue existed, "in

---

[80]   Although the plaintiffs had themselves earlier sought, and been refused, an injunction: reported as *Campus Oil Ltd v Minister for Industry and Energy* [1983] I.L.R.M. 258.
[81]   [1983] I.R. 88 at 107; [1984] I.L.R.M. 45 at 61.
[82]   [1983] I.R. 88 at 107; [1984] I.L.R.M. 45 at 61, per O'Higgins C.J.
[83]   [1983] I.R. 88 at 107; [1984] I.L.R.M. 45 at 61.
[84]   unreported, High Court, Butler J., September 6, 2000.

contradistinction" to one which was "frivolous or vexatious". This reference to a contradistinction to a "frivolous or vexatious" issue was an adoption of Lord Diplock's remarks in *American Cyanamid*.[85]

6–48 Ultimately, the actual words used are of less importance than the key idea that the test has been moved away from considering whether there is a prima facie case. That a case may be at best a very fragile one should not preclude a finding that there is a bona fide/fair question raised.[86]

(ii) Fair Question or Serious Question

6–49 As to whether there is any significant difference between the words "serious"—the word used by Lord Diplock in *American Cyanamid*—and "fair", as more commonly used in this jurisdiction, it would seem that there is not. Macken J. addressed the point in the case of *Lonergan v Salter-Townshend*.[87] Noting that the use of the term "fair question to be tried" had become more frequently used, Macken J. held that the use of such a description:

> "avoids the difficulties which arise with the use of the word 'serious', which tended to give the impression that the plaintiff had to establish that he had a case which was very strong."[88]

(iii) Lower Threshold

6–50 The *Campus Oil* test is clearly an easier one to satisfy than that of a strong prima facie case. However, although in cases such as *Pasture Properties v Evans*[89] Laffoy J. made reference to "the very low threshold to be surmounted on this type of application", it should not be assumed that a lower threshold will automatically lead to most cases satisfying the need to show a bona fide/serious question to be tried.

6–51 In *Cavankee Fishing Co Ltd v Minister for Communications, Marine and Natural Resources*,[90] Kelly J. stated that the defendants had made strong arguments to the effect that the plaintiffs did not have any serious issue for trial, and that if this was correct, there was no question of an injunction being granted

---

85 See also, *Dimbleby & Sons Ltd v National Union of Journalists* [1984] 1 W.L.R. 427 at 430; [1984] 1 All E.R. 751 at 754 per Lord Diplock.
86 *Hennessy v St Gerard's School Trust* [2004] 15 E.L.R. 230, per Smyth J.
87 [2000] E.L.R. 15.
88 [2000] E.L.R. 15 at 25. In *Nova Media Services Ltd v Minister for Posts and Telegraphs* [1984] I.L.R.M. 161 at 167, Murphy J. held that it was sufficient to say that "a stateable case has been made out"; but, there would appear to be no suggestion that this was an attempt to vary the test.
89 ex tempore, High Court, Laffoy J., February 5, 1999.
90 unreported, High Court, Kelly J., March 4, 2004.

by the court. However, in that case Kelly J. chose not to express views on that point and was prepared to assume that there was a serious question to be tried.[91]

6–52 However, various decisions such as *O'Brien v AON Insurance Managers (Dublin) Ltd*,[92] *Collen Construction Ltd v BATU*[93] and *Finlay v Laois Co Council*[94] provide examples of cases in which the courts have not been satisfied that there was a fair case to be tried. Of course, each case will ultimately turn on its own facts and, as such, it is impossible to prescribe what will represent a fair, bona fide issue to be tried.

(iv) Relationship to Substantive Proceedings

6–53 Although an application for an injunction on an interlocutory basis is not meant to be a determination of the substantive proceedings, a finding that there is no fair, bona fide case has the potential to significantly undermine any substantive proceedings. If a court holds that there is no fair, bona fide case to be tried, this would certainly suggest that the plaintiff may struggle in his claim for a perpetual injunction at the trial of the action. However, such a finding is not necessarily fatal to the substantive case. For example, in *O'Brien*,[95] Clarke J., in refusing to make an order restraining a disciplinary process, acknowledged that if it was ultimately found that a hearing was not conducted in accordance with fair procedures, the plaintiff would have his remedy at that stage. Similarly, in *Collen Construction*, which involved industrial action and the use of grievance and disputes procedures, Clarke J. accepted that the plaintiff had established a fair issue to be tried as to the unlawfulness of much of the activities directed against it. However, he did not accept that there was a fair issue to be tried as against the first named defendant. That said, he acknowledged that at the trial of the action the plaintiff might be in a position "to put before the court further evidence which would satisfy a court, by inference if necessary" that the first named defendant was involved and that a claim could be maintained against it.

6–54 In theory, if a court finds that a bona fide/fair case has not been made out, that should be the end of the matter so far as the interlocutory application is concerned. However, it is not uncommon for judges to proceed to consider the other aspects of the *Campus Oil* test regardless.[96] This safeguards against a

---

[91] It may have been of some relevance that this was one of the early cases which fell for determination by the then newly established Commercial Court, which began operating on January 12, 2004, less than two months previously.
[92] unreported, High Court, Clarke J., January 14, 2004.
[93] unreported, High Court, Clarke J., May 15, 2006.
[94] unreported, High Court, Peart J., December 20, 2002.
[95] unreported, High Court, Clarke J., January 14, 2004.
[96] See, for example, *Howberry Lane Ltd v Telecom Éireann* [1999] 2 I.L.R.M. 232.

subsequent holding that the judge may have come to the wrong conclusion as to whether there was a fair, bona fide issue to be tried.

6–55 Once a fair, bona fide case has been established, the court will then address, per the *Campus Oil* guidelines, the issue of the adequacy of damages.

2. The Adequacy of Damages

6–56 The extent to which damages would compensate the parties to an action for any losses suffered in between dealing with a matter at the interlocutory stage and the trial of the action, is addressed in the second part of the A*merican Cyanamid/Campus Oil* guidelines. There are two elements which a court must consider:

(a) whether a plaintiff who succeeds at the trial of the substantive action will be adequately compensated by an award of damages for any loss suffered between the hearing of the interlocutory injunction and the trial of the action if an injunction is not granted at the interlocutory stage[97];
(b) whether the plaintiff's undertaking as to damages will adequately compensate the defendant, should he be successful at the trial, in respect of any loss suffered by him due to the injunction being in force pending the trial.

6–57 In practical terms, the consideration of the adequacy of damages is generally the single most important factor in the analysis of whether or not to grant an interlocutory injunction.

(a) Adequate Compensation for the Plaintiff[98]

6–58 Each case will have to be looked at on its own facts in the context of the adequacy of damages from the plaintiff's perspective.[99] For example, in *Mantruck Services v Ballinlough Electrical Refrigeration Co Ltd*,[100] the

---

97 In *Re Ural Hudson Ltd*, ex tempore, High Court, Finlay Geoghegan J., January 9, 2005, Finlay Geoghegan J. held that even if a serious question is to be tried, the petitioner, following the principles as determined in *Campus Oil* "must establish, in order to obtain an interlocutory injunction, that it would suffer irreparable loss and damage unless the order which it seeks is granted pending the determination of the proceedings".

98 See generally, Keay "Whither American Cyanamid? Interim Injunctions in the 21st Century" (2004) 23 C.J.Q. 132 and Elliott, "Cyanamid Revisited", *Building*, March 12, 2004 at 51, considering the case of *Bath and North East Somerset District Council v Mowlem Plc* [2004] All E.R. (D) 337.

99 Which can of course lead to seemingly contradictory results: contrast *Miller v Jackson* [1977] Q.B. 966; [1977] 3 W.L.R. 20; [1977] 3 All E.R. 338 with *Kennaway v Thompson* [1981] Q.B. 88; [1980] 3 W.L.R. 361; [1980] 3 All E.R. 329.

100 [1992] 1 I.R. 351.

Supreme Court contrasted the position of a well-established company with that of a growing business. McCarthy J. observed that if the injunction in question was to be continued, the defendant, a growing business, would suffer damage which "would be very difficult to assess in money terms".[101]

6–59 In *Ó'Murchú t/a Talknology v Eircell Ltd*,[102] the Supreme Court held that even if the plaintiff appellant went out of business, his losses could be assessed in money terms and, as such, damages would be an adequate remedy.[103]

6–60 In circumstances where a court is satisfied that the plaintiff could be adequately compensated by an award of damages which the defendant is in a position to meet, it will invariably exercise its discretion to refuse the injunctive relief sought.[104]

(i) Probable Future Loss

6–61 Finlay C.J. held in *Curust Financial Services Ltd v Loewe-Lack-Werk*[105] that what is considered is not just the loss which could be established up to the date when damages would be assessed but also to probable future loss. The same point was also made by Clarke J. in the case of *Sheridan v Louis Fitzgerald Group Ltd*.[106]

(ii) Standard of Proof for Adequacy of Damages

6–62 In *Curust Financial Services Ltd v Loewe-Lack-Werk*,[107] Finlay C.J. touched upon the standard of proof which must be satisfied on the question of adequacy of damages. The Chief Justice referred to reaching a conclusion:

> "on the affidavit evidence as to whether it has, as a matter of probability, been established at this stage for the purposes of the interlocutory injunction that damages would not be an adequate remedy by reason of the real risk of the financial collapse of the Curust companies."[108]

---

[101] [1992] 1 I.R. 351 at 359, per McCarthy J. Although see para.6–67 in relation to whether difficulty, as opposed to impossibility, in the assessment of damages is sufficient to demonstrate that damages would not be an adequate remedy.

[102] unreported, Supreme Court, February 21, 2001.

[103] *cf.* the decision of Carroll J. in *A & N Pharmacy Ltd v United Drug Wholesale Ltd* [1996] 2 I.L.R.M. 42.

[104] However, the court can and does in appropriate cases require a defendant to make payments to the plaintiff pending the substantive hearing of a case, particularly in the context of contracts of employment. See generally, Ch.9, Employment.

[105] [1994] 1 I.R. 450 at 468.

[106] unreported, High Court, Clarke J., April 4, 2006.

[107] [1994] 1 I.R. 450.

[108] [1994] 1 I.R. 450 at 471.

Based on this decision, the onus is thus on the plaintiff to establish, as a matter of probability, that damages would not be an adequate remedy.[109]

6–63 In *Garrahy v Bord na gCon*,[110] O'Higgins J. in the High Court held that in order for the plaintiff to succeed in obtaining interlocutory relief:

> "the court must be satisfied, not that damages are not an adequate remedy, but that there is a doubt as to whether damages would be an adequate remedy."[111]

6–64 In so far as this is at odds with the dictum of Finlay C.J. in *Curust*, the decision of the Supreme Court in *Curust* is to be preferred.

(iii) Ability to Quantify Damages

6–65 The fact that damages can be quantified will generally lead to an application for an interlocutory injunction being refused. In *Ryanair Ltd v Aer Rianta cpt*,[112] Kelly J. took the view that the fact that damages had been quantified in an affidavit put before the court was fatal to the claim being made for such an interlocutory injunction.

6–66 However, the fact that an amount claimed is easily quantifiable does not inexorably lead to the conclusion that damages are an appropriate or adequate remedy. This is particularly so in employment cases. For example, in *Boyle v An Post*,[113] it was held in the context of a claim for unpaid wages and salaries that such wages and salaries were easy to ascertain, but their non-payment could cause serious inconvenience and prejudice.[114]

(iv) Difficulty in Quantification of Damages

6–67 The fact that damages would be difficult, as distinct from impossible, to assess is not an appropriate ground for a claim that damages would be an inadequate remedy. In *Curust Financial Services Ltd v Loewe-Lack-Werk*,[115] a submission was made on behalf of the plaintiff that although the loss likely to

---

[109] Referred to in *Smithkline Beecham Plc v Genthon BV*, unreported, High Court, Kelly J., February 28, 2003 and *Whelan Frozen Foods Ltd v Dunnes Stores,* unreported, High Court, MacMenamin J., February 17, 2006.

[110] [2002] 3 I.R. 566.

[111] [2002] 3 I.R. 566 at 572, referring to *Ferris v Ward* [1998] 2 I.R. 194 at 202, per Blayney J., the latter approving the observations of Lord Diplock in *American Cyanamid*.

[112] ex tempore, High Court, Kelly J., January 25, 2001.

[113] [1992] 2 I.R. 437 at 442.

[114] Although employment cases are in a sense particular in so far as they involve parties who may be left without a salary pending the trail of the action. See, for example, *Harte v Kelly* [1997] E.L.R. 125.

[115] [1994] 1 I.R. 450. See generally, the analysis of this case by Delany, (1993) 15 D.U.L.J. 228.

be sustained by it in the event of an injunction not being granted was simply commercial loss arising from a diminution in trade, damages were not an adequate remedy because of the difficulty in quantifying those damages. Rejecting that argument, Finlay C.J. stated that:

> "The loss to be incurred by Curust if it succeeds in the action and no interlocutory injunction is granted to them, is clearly and exclusively a commercial loss, in what had been, apparently, a stable and well-established market. In those circumstances, *prima facie*, it is a loss which should be capable of being assessed in damages both under the heading of loss actually suffered up to the date when such damages would fall to be assessed and also under the heading of probable future loss. Difficulty, as distinct from complete impossibility, in the assessment of such damages should not, in my view, be a ground for characterising the awarding of damages as an inadequate remedy."[116]

6–68 The Chief Justice's dictum in *Curust* has been adopted in a number of cases, including in *Cavankee Fishing Company Limited v Minister for Communication, Marine and Natural Resources*.[117] Dealing with the assessment of damages, Kelly J. said in *Cavankee Fishing* that he was bearing in mind what was said by Finlay C.J. in *Curust*, namely that:

> "difficulty, as distinct from complete impossibility, in the assessment of damages should not be a ground for characterising the awarding of damages as an inadequate remedy."[118]

6–69 Speaking for the Supreme Court in *Ó'Murchú t/a Talknology v Eircell Ltd*,[119] Geoghegan J. stated in the context of the injunction sought in relation to a breach of an agency or distribution agreement that although, "the task of assessing damages will be difficult, this does not mean that it cannot be done". In that case, the court was prepared to accept that damages could be assessed even though it had been argued that the plaintiff appellant could in fact go out of business. Geoghegan J. went so far as to say, inter alia, that "even if he does go out of business, as a result of losing the agency, his losses can be assessed in money terms".

---

[116] [1994] 1 I.R. 450 at 468, disagreeing with the determination of Barron J. in the High Court that "damages which are not readily susceptible to accurate measurements are not usually an appropriate remedy". See also, *Mantruck Services v Ballinlough Electrical Refrigeration Co Ltd* [1992] 1 I.R. 351.

[117] unreported, High Court, Kelly J., March 4, 2004.

[118] In *Oblique Financial Services Ltd v the Promise Production Co Ltd* [1994] 1 I.L.R.M. 74, it was held that although the damages in that case were necessarily hard to quantify, this was insufficient to prevent the imposition of an interlocutory injunction, since the balance of convenience clearly lay with the plaintiff.

[119] unreported, Supreme Court, February 21, 2001. See also, *BUPA Ireland Ltd v Health Insurance Authority,* unreported, High Court, Finlay Geoghegan J., December 29, 2005.

(v) Impossibility in Assessment of Damages

6–70 Impossibility in the assessment of damages can be the basis for a claim that damages would be an inadequate remedy. In *Mitchelstown Co-Op Ltd v Société des Produits Nestlé SA*,[120] the loss which the plaintiff might sustain was not quantifiable in monetary terms. In the circumstances, an interlocutory injunction was granted. Similarly, in *Sweeney v National University of Ireland Cork t/a Cork University Press*,[121] it was held by Smyth J. in granting the injunction sought that the alleged loss of the plaintiff was not quantifiable or capable of being compensated by an award of damages.

6–71 However, it can often prove difficult to satisfy a court that damages would not provide adequate compensation for the party seeking the injunction. For example, in dealing with an argument that a person could not be adequately compensated for damage to reputation, Kelly J. pointed out in *Fitzpatrick v Commissioner of An Garda Síochána*[122] that damage to reputation was regularly compensated by means of an award of damages.

(vi) Ability to Pay

6–72 Another factor which must be borne in mind when considering the role of damages in this context is the ability of a party to actually pay such damages. In *Westman Holdings Ltd v McCormack*,[123] Finlay C.J. observed that the question of the plaintiff being adequately compensated in damages in fact potentially raised two separate issues in every case. The first was whether damages would be an adequate remedy. The second was whether "there is a defendant liable to pay such damages who is able to do so, and thus the appropriate compensation could actually be realised".[124]

6–73 In *Westman Holdings*, Finlay C.J. found that damages would be an adequate remedy. However, he was also satisfied that a combination of an inability to pay on the part of some of the individual defendants and a potential immunity from liability to pay damages for the trade union made it:

> "extremely improbable that the plaintiff would, if refused an injunction, be able to obtain adequate compensation in the event of their establishing that the picket was unlawful."[125]

---

[120] unreported, Supreme Court, October 26, 1988.
[121] [2001] 1 I.L.R.M. 310.
[122] [1996] E.L.R. 244, citing the decision of Costello J. in *Kearney v Minister for Justice* [1986] I.R. 116 and Hamilton P. in *Kennedy v Ireland* [1987] I.R. 587. See also, *Foley v Aer Lingus Group* [2001] E.L.R. 193.
[123] [1992] 1 I.R. 151.
[124] [1992] 1 I.R. 151 at 158.
[125] [1992] 1 I.R. 151 at 158. See also, *DJS Meats Ltd v Minister for Agriculture and Food*,

6–74 As to how an inability to pay might be addressed, one solution was accepted in the case of *B & S Ltd v Irish Auto Trader Ltd.*[126] In that case the defendant company offered to have its parent company joined as a co-defendant, thus ensuring that the plaintiff would be able to recover damages should they be awarded by the court. That being so, McCracken J. found that "the question of the ability of either party to pay does not seem to me to enter into the issue."[127]

(b) Adequate Compensation for the Defendant

6–75 The second element in relation to damages which a court must consider is whether an interlocutory injunction should be granted if the plaintiff's undertaking as to damages would adequately compensate the defendant, should the latter be successful at the trial, in respect of any loss suffered by him due to the injunction being in force pending the trial.

(i) Undertaking as to Damages[128]

6–76 An undertaking as to damages, "invented" by Knight-Bruce L.J. in the 1800s,[129] provides that should the plaintiff's substantive claim not succeed, he can be asked to compensate the successful defendant for any damage suffered by reason of the interlocutory injunction having been secured. This may ultimately necessitate an inquiry as to damages as appropriate at the conclusion of the substantive hearing.[130]

6–77 The requirement for such an undertaking originally only applied to ex parte injunctions.[131] However, it was extended to interlocutory injunction applications "by degrees", the rationale being that due to the shortness of time:

> "it was often difficult for the defendant to get up his case properly, and as the evidence was taken by affidavit, and generally without cross-examination, it was impossible to be certain on which side the truth lay."[132]

---

unreported, High Court, Lynch J., February 17, 1993. But *cf. Moore v Attorney General* [1927] I.R. 569 in which it was argued that damages could not be recovered from the defendants owing to their poverty and that "irreparable damage" was thus being suffered. However, Kennedy C.J. took the view that the real question was whether the acts alleged were likely to cause permanent injury to the fishery in question.

126   [1995] 2 I.R. 142; [1995] 2 I.L.R.M. 152.
127   [1995] 2 I.R. 142 at 146; [1995] 2 I.L.R.M. 152 at 156.
128   Generally referred to in English cases and texts as a "cross undertaking in/as to damages".
129   See the speech of Lord Diplock in *F Hoffmann-La Roche & Co AG v Secretary of State for Trade and Industry* [1975] A.C. 295 at 360; [1974] 3 W.L.R. 104 at 126; [1974] 2 All E.R. 1128 at 1149.
130   See generally, Ch.5, Perpetual Injunctions, particularly para.5–83.
131   See *Smith v Day* (1882) 21 Ch D 421 at 423, per Jessel M.R.
132   per Jessel M.R. in *Smith v Day* (1882) 21 Ch D 421 at 423. See generally the overview of the development of the requirement by Lord Diplock in *F Hoffmann-La Roche & Co AG v*

6–78 Lord Diplock explained in *American Cyanamid* that the undertaking as to damages:

> "aided the court in doing that which was its great object, *viz.* abstaining from expressing any opinion upon the merits of the case until the hearing."[133]

6–79 The position was concisely put by Laffoy J. in the case of *Pasture Properties Ltd v Evans*,[134] in which she stated that:

> "The Plaintiff cannot get an injunction unless it can give an under-taking as to damages. If an injunction is wrongly granted at this stage and it so transpires at the hearing of the action, the Plaintiff must undertake to adequately indemnify the Defendant against any loss incurred by the Defendant by reason of the injunction being wrongly granted."

6–80 Peter Gibson L.J. made similar observations in *Cheltenham and Gloucester Building Society v Ricketts*.[135] He referred to the:

> "obvious risk of unfairness to a respondent against whom an interlocutory injunction is ordered at a time when the issues have not been fully determined and when usually all the facts have not been ascertained."[136]

(ii) Ability to Pay

6–81 A court must be satisfied as to the plaintiff's ability to pay on foot of the undertaking as to damages given. Plaintiffs are on occasion required to show that they have the financial means to honour the undertaking. In *Martin v Bord Pleanála*,[137] O'Sullivan J. held that whilst the applicant had given an undertaking as to damages, there was insufficient detail in it which would enable the court to assess it as a realistic undertaking when balanced against the prospective losses of the notice party if the stay were granted. O'Sullivan J. further took the view that the applicant's undertaking was little more than a pro forma compliance with the usual requirement of the court on such an application.

Secretary of State for Trade and Industry [1975] A.C. 295 at 360; [1974] 3 W.L.R. 104 at 126; [1974] 2 All E.R. 1128 at 1149.

[133] [1975] A.C. 396 at 407; [1975] 2 W.L.R. 316 at 323; [1975] 1 All E.R. 504 at 510, citing *Wakefield v Duke of Buccleuch* (1865) 12 L.T. 628.

[134] ex tempore, High Court, Laffoy J., February 5, 1999.

[135] [1993] 1 W.L.R. 1545; [1993] 4 All E.R. 276.

[136] [1993] 1 W.L.R. 1545 at 1554; [1993] 4 All E.R. 276 at 284. See also the decision of Neill L.J., particularly at [1993] 1 W.L.R. 1545 at 1551; [1993] 4 All E.R. 276 at 281, in which, prior to setting out the options available in relation to the enforcement of an undertaking as to damages, Neill L.J. sets out the basic principle arising in relation to an undertaking as to damages. See also, Ch.5, Perpetual Injunctions, para.5–91. See also, *Graham v Campbell* (1878) 7 Ch D 490 and *Griffith v Blake* (1884) 27 Ch D 474 at 477 and the judgment of Finlay C.J. in *Westman Holdings Limited v McCormack* [1992] 1 I.R. 151.

[137] unreported, High Court, O'Sullivan J., July 24, 2002.

6–82 In *Riordan v Minister for the Environment*,[138] Finnegan P. observed that an undertaking as to damages in that case would be worthless as the plaintiff admitted that he had not the means to satisfy such an undertaking if called upon to do so. Although the President found this fact "not determinative of the application", it was a factor which he said he had to take into account.

6–83 However, it was held in England in the case of *Allen v Jambo Holdings Ltd* that a court may still grant an injunction even when there are doubts about the plaintiff's ability to satisfy an undertaking.[139]

Impecunious Plaintiff
6–84 One issue which has been raised is whether it would be just to impose an undertaking as to damages on an impecunious plaintiff who is the clear victim of a wrong. Leaving aside the question of the court effectively pre-judging a matter at the interlocutory stage in order to consider an undertaking as to damages,[140] it has been suggested that it would seem to be "grossly unjust" if a court was to decline an undertaking on the basis of a lack of resources.[141] One way of addressing this would be to allow a third party to provide the undertaking.

Third Parties Providing the Undertaking
6–85 In certain situations a court may allow a third party to provide the undertaking. In *Moloney v Laurib Investments Ltd*,[142] the plaintiff had been left paralysed from the waist down at the age of 15. Acknowledging the injustice which would arise in not granting a *Mareva* injunction simply because the plaintiff's undertaking would be, as he described it, "worthless", Lynch J. also considered whether, if the plaintiff's parents were to join in giving the undertaking, this would be sufficient. He held on the facts that it would not, due to the potential considerable losses which would be suffered by the defendant company if they successfully defended the action after the grant of an inter-locutory injunction. However, there appears to be an acceptance by Lynch J. that a third party may, depending on the facts of a case, provide the undertaking required.[143]

---

[138]   unreported, High Court, Finnegan P., May 26, 2004.
[139]   [1980] 1 W.L.R. 1252; [1980] 2 All E.R. 502.
[140]   This is related, it is submitted, to the question of whether a court may consider the strength of the parties' respective cases at the interlocutory stage, in relation to which, see para.6–145.
[141]   Byrne & Binchy, *Annual Review of Irish Law 1993* (Dublin: Round Hall Sweet & Maxwell, 1996), p.285.
[142]   unreported, High Court, Lynch J., July 20, 1993.
[143]   See also para 6–74, above. See, however, the case of *Attorney General (FX Martin) v Dublin Corporation* [1983] I.L.R.M. 254, a relator action. It was erroneously recorded in the court order that the undertaking had been given by the Attorney General, despite counsel for Fr Martin informing the court that the Attorney General's fiat did not extend to or include such an undertaking. The court ultimately found that the Attorney General should not be liable on foot of the undertaking, nor did the court accept that he had impliedly accepted a joint and several liability to pay damages.

(iii) Dispute as to Ability to Pay

6–86 However, some caution must be exercised. If a respondent wishes to dispute the adequacy of the undertaking as to damages, he should be in a position to offer specific evidence of the loss which would be suffered if the injunction was to be granted. In *Dunne v Dun Laoghaire Rathdown County Council*,[144] Hardiman J. in the Supreme Court was quite critical of the respondent's approach of attacking the plaintiff's undertaking as to damages by mentioning huge sums of money without relating them either to the specific relief sought or to the specific liability for which the plaintiffs, by virtue of their undertaking, might become responsible.[145]

(iv) Continuing Obligation

6–87 In the English case of *Staines v Walsh*,[146] it was held, albeit in the specific context of a *Mareva* injunction, that it was inherent in the injunction order that for so long as such an order was in place, there was a continuing obligation on a claimant not only to be willing to honour his cross-undertaking in damages, but to disclose to the defendant any material change for the worse in his financial position.

(v) Fortified Undertaking

6–88 A court may require a fortified undertaking as to damages. This essentially provides a back-up to ensure payment in the event of the substantive injunction application being unsuccessful. Whether a fortified undertaking will be sought and granted is a matter which will arise on the specific facts of a case. Such an undertaking is very unusual, however, as was made clear by Herbert J. in *O'Connell v EPA*.[147] Referring to the constitutional right of access to the courts, Herbert J. noted that:

> "the occasions on which a court might properly require what is described as a fortified undertaking to pay damages must be very few."[148]

6–89 Kelly J. agreed with this approach in *Harding v Cork County Council*.[149] He added that if such a fortified undertaking as to damages is to be required then a proper evidential basis has to be set for it.

---

[144] [2003] 1 I.R. 567.
[145] [2003] 1 I.R. 567 at 579.
[146] *Times Law Reports*, August 1, 2003.
[147] [2001] 4 I.R. 494.
[148] [2001] 4 I.R. 494 at 509.
[149] unreported, High Court, Kelly J., February 28, 2006.

6–90 By way of guidance as to the circumstances in which a fortified undertaking might be required, the matter was considered in some detail in *Broadnet v ODTR*,[150] albeit in the context of an application for judicial review. Notwithstanding the nature of the application, Laffoy J. was referred to *Bean on Injunctions*,[151] the relevant passage being set out by her:

> "But where there are doubts about the plaintiff's resources, the court has discretion to require either security or the payment of money into court to '*fortify*' the undertaking, or (as an alternative) an undertaking from a more financially secure person or body. This might apply if the plaintiff is legally aided; or a minor or patient … ; or resident outside the jurisdiction (*Harman Pictures N.V. v Osborne* [1967] 1 W.L.R. 723);[152] or an unquoted company. In cases where the plaintiff is a subsidiary of a large company and apparently lacking funds it is common for the parent company to be invited to guarantee the undertaking in damages in writing."[153]

6–91 Having considered the passage, Laffoy J. found that, "it is undoubtedly the case that an undertaking from Broadnet would be worthless unless secured",[154] and sought a guarantee from Broadnet's backers in relation to the undertaking required in that case. Based on this it would seem that the principles set out in the passage referred to by Laffoy J. are accepted in this jurisdiction, and that a fortified undertaking can be sought, albeit only, in the words of Herbert J. in *O'Connell*, in "very few" circumstances.

(vi) Discretion to Dispense with the Undertaking

6–92 There may be individual circumstances in which the undertaking may also be dispensed with. For example, Lardner J. held in *Boyle v An Post*[155] that the right of the plaintiffs to recover payment of their wages and salaries was not in issue and, as such, he did not propose any undertaking as to damages. In *Keenan Brothers Ltd v CIE*,[156] Budd J. held that an undertaking may not be

---

[150] [2000] 3 I.R. 281; [2000] 2 I.L.R.M. 241.

[151] The passage is from the 7th edn of the book, p.29. The up to date reference is Bean, *Injunctions,* 9th edn (London: Thomson Sweet & Maxwell, 2007), p.32.

[152] However, requiring a fortified undertaking where a plaintiff is resident outside the jurisdiction is unlikely to survive a challenge based on European law and discrimination; see, for example, the decision of the European Court of Justice in *Boussac Saint-Freres SA v Gerstenmeier* (Case 22/80) [1980] E.C.R. 3427 at 3436 which considered Art.7 (now Art.6) dealing with non-discrimination on the basis of nationality, the court holding that the article "forbids not only overt discrimination by reason of nationality but also covert forms of discrimination which, by the application of other criteria of differentiation, lead in fact to the same result". In the 9th edition of Bean, *Injunctions,* the reference to being resident outside the jurisdiction has been excised.

[153] [2000] 3 I.R. 281 at 304; [2000] 2 I.L.R.M. 241 at 264.

[154] [2000] 3 I.R. 281 at 304; [2000] 2 I.L.R.M. 241 at 262.

[155] [1992] 2 I.R. 437 at 448.

[156] (1963) 97 I.L.T.R. 54 at 60.

required if there is evidence of clear fraud. However, he also emphasised that an undertaking as to damages is a sine qua non when an application is being made for a mandatory injunction.

6–93 It is only in exceptional cases, however, that the requirement for an undertaking as to damages should be dispensed with, particularly given the rationale for the undertaking.[157]

(vii) Requirement to Apply for an Injunction to Benefit from an Undertaking

6–94 One question which has been considered but not definitively resolved in this jurisdiction is whether a court has the ability to require a plaintiff to apply for an interlocutory injunction in order to ensure that, pending the trial, the defendants are not exposed to loss which is not compensatable, which loss flows from a claim by the plaintiffs which might be unjustified. The rationale for requiring the plaintiff to make such an application is that a defendant would thereby have the protection of an undertaking as to damages.[158]

6–95 In *Blue Town Investments v Higgs & Hill Plc*,[159] Browne-Wilkinson V.C., in order to ensure that pending the trial the defendant was not exposed to loss which was not compensatable, decided to strike out the plaintiff's claim unless it was prepared to apply for an interim injunction accompanied by an undertaking as to damages. However, in *Oxy-Electric Ltd v Zainuddin,*[160] Hoffman J. held that, since the court had no jurisdiction to strike out an action except in accordance with established principles under the Rules of the Supreme Court or the inherent jurisdiction of the court, it had no jurisdiction to impose conditions on the right to prosecute a claim.

6–96 The latter approach in *Oxy-Electric* appears—rightly, it is submitted—to have found favour in this jurisdiction. Laffoy J. considered the matter in *Broadnet v ODTR*.[161] She took the view, having regard to the decision of Hoffman J., that:

> "whether the right of a plaintiff in an ordinary plenary action, who has not sought an interlocutory injunction, to maintain a claim for a perpetual

---

[157] Although an undertaking was not given in the case of *Fitzpatrick v Commissioner of An Garda Síochána* [1996] E.L.R. 244, that it was a point which Kelly J. felt merited highlighting suggests, it is submitted, that this was very much the exception rather than the rule.

[158] See, for example, the decision of Templeman J. in *Clearbrook Property Holdings Ltd v Verrier* [1974] 1 W.L.R. 243; considered by Laffoy J. in *Broadnet v ODTR* [2000] 2 I.L.R.M. 241. See also the decision of the Court of Appeal in *Tiverton Estates Ltd v Wearwell Ltd* [1975] 1 Ch. 146.

[159] [1990] 1 W.L.R. 696; [1990] 2 All E.R. 897.

[160] [1991] 1 W.L.R. 115; [1990] 2 All E.R. 902.

[161] [2000] 3 I.R. 281; [2000] 2 I.L.R.M. 241.

injunction may be made conditional on him seeking an interlocutory injunction and giving an undertaking as to damages, must be doubtful."[162]

6–97 Laffoy J. also viewed it as questionable whether in ordinary private civil litigation in this jurisdiction, the courts have any power to inhibit or render conditional the prosecution of a claim unless it is frivolous or vexatious or clearly cannot succeed. This is a view entirely in keeping with the courts' general reluctance to strike out claims on this basis.[163]

(viii) The Attorney General

6–98 The question of whether the Attorney General must give an undertaking as to damages has caused some difficulties for the courts. The view in England, as expressed in *F Hoffman La Roche & Co AG v Secretary of State for Trade and Industry*,[164] is that the court should enquire as to whether the Attorney General should given an undertaking. In other words, there is a discretion residing with the court as to whether to require such an undertaking or not. Lord Morris referred to the earlier case of *Attorney General v Albany Hotel Co.*[165] He noted that the general practice had been not to require an undertaking as to damages from the Crown, observing that:

> "That was probably for the reason that the Crown was not liable in damages in the ordinary way and that relief against the Crown could only be obtained by a petition of right."[166]

6–99 However, Lord Reid also acknowledged that even at the time of the *Albany Hotel* case, the Crown "was not placed in an isolated position of privilege".[167] He also suggested that there seemed to be no reason for any differentiation between the Crown and "an ordinary plaintiff litigant" in more modern times.

6–100 Recognising the special role of the Crown, and the fact that a statute may provide that compliance with its provisions shall be enforceable by civil proceedings by the Crown for an injunction, Lord Diplock stated that:

---

[162]   [2000] 3 I.R. 281 at 298; [2000] 2 I.L.R.M. 241 at 256.
[163]   See Delany & McGrath, *Civil Procedure in the Superior Courts*, 2nd edn (Dublin: Thomson Round Hall, 2005), Ch.14. For a comprehensive review of the jurisdiction to strike out, in the context of specific performance proceedings which involved a related injunction, see *Claystone Ltd v Larking Ltd*, unreported, High Court, Laffoy J., March 14, 2007.
[164]   [1975] A.C. 295; [1973] 3 W.L.R. 805; [1974] 2 All E.R. 1128 See also *Kirklees Metropolitan Borough Council v Wickes Building Supplies Ltd* [1993] A.C. 227; [1992] 3 W.L.R. 170.
[165]   (1896) 2 Ch. 696.
[166]   [1975] A.C. 295 at 351; [1974] 3 W.L.R. 104 at 118; [1974] 2 All E.R. 1128 at 1142. The Crown's immunity was removed by the Crown Proceedings Act 1947, s.21.
[167]   [1975] A.C. 295 at 351; [1974] 3 W.L.R. 104 at 118; [1974] 2 All E.R. 1128 at 1142.

"I agree, therefore, with all your Lordships that the practice of exacting an undertaking in damages from the Crown as a condition of the grant of an interlocutory injunction in this type of law enforcement action ought not to be applied as a matter of course, as it should in actions between subject and subject, in relator actions, and in actions by the Crown to enforce or to protect its proprietary or contractual rights. On the contrary, the propriety of requiring such an undertaking from the Crown should be considered in the light of the particular circumstances of the case."[168]

6–101 In short, the view promoted by the House of Lords is that the circumstances of the case determine whether the Attorney General must furnish an undertaking. Where the action is for the purposes of "law enforcement", an undertaking may, depending on the circumstances, be required. However, where the action concerns, for example, the assertion of a contractual or proprietary right, the usual undertaking as to damages should be given.

6–102 The point was canvassed in this jurisdiction in the case of *Competition Authority v Avonmore Waterford Plc*.[169] However, in that case O'Sullivan J. felt that he did not need to make a determination as to whether an undertaking as to damages was something which could be required from the Competition Authority as a matter of course in an application where it was "sought by a State Authority implementing statutory policy set out in the Competition Act."

6–103 The matter was returned to in the case of *Minister for Justice v Devine*.[170] Both parties in that case are recorded in the judgment of O'Sullivan J. as having accepted the following passage from *Bean on Injunctions* to represent the common law position in this country:

"The court has a discretion to grant an interim injunction[171] without requiring an undertaking in damages. There are a number of types of case in which an undertaking is generally dispensed with. They include:

'(a) Matrimonial and domestic proceedings ...
(b) Where the Crown applies for an injunction to enforce what is *prima facie* the law of the land (*Hoffman LaRoche and Co. A.G. v Secretary of State for Trade and Industry* [1975] A.C. 295[172]; *Director General of Fair Trading v Toby Ward Limited* [1989] 1 W.L.R. 517) or to uphold

---

168 [1975] A.C. 295 at 364; [1974] 3 W.L.R. 104 at 130.
169 unreported, High Court, O'Sullivan J., November 17, 1998.
170 unreported, High Court, O'Sullivan J., June 27, 2006.
171 The word "interim" in England covers both interim and interlocutory injunctions as understood in this jurisdiction. As noted by Gee, *Commercial Injunctions*, 5th edn (London: Thomson Sweet & Maxwell, 2004), p.34, the expression "interim injunctions" as used in CPR r.25.1(1)(a) "covers all injunctions which are not granted as final relief".
172 As to which, see para.6–98.

the proper administration of justice (*Attorney General v Newsgroup Newspapers Limited* [1987] Q.B. 1): if the Crown is seeking to enforce its proprietary rights this rule does not apply …[173]

(c) Where a local authority or other public authority seeks to enforce what is *prima facie* the law of the land (*Kirklees Metropolitan Borough Council v. Wickes Building Supplies Limited* [1993] A.C. 227);

(d) Where the financial services authority seeks an injunction …'"[174]

6–104 A word of caution must be sounded in relation to this extract in so far as O'Sullivan J. accepted it in *Devine* "for the purpose of this application" only.

(ix) Company Liquidators

6–105 Although an undertaking is, in the normal course, unlimited, one possible exception to this concerns company liquidators. Snell[175] suggests that liquidators, who are performing a statutory duty, and have no personal interest in the matter, may not be required to give an unlimited undertaking, but only one commensurate with the size of the company assets, citing *Rochdale Borough Council v Anders*.[176] Such an approach appears in principle to strike a very fair balance between the need for an undertaking and the circumstances in which a company in liquidation finds itself, coupled with the liquidator's obligations.

6–106 In the case of *Re DPR Futures Ltd*,[177] Millet J. observed that the value of undertakings previously given by a company was limited in reality to the value of the company's assets. Where the company's assets were insufficient to support the undertaking, the court would require the undertaking to be fortified by a bond or payment into court. However, the undertaking:

> "would still in practice be limited in amount; that is to say, to the amount of the company's assets together with the amount of the bond or payment into court. The court would not require the creditors, still less the liquidator, to provide an unlimited guarantee that the defendant would suffer no loss from the granting of the injunction."[178]

---

[173] As pointed out by O'Sullivan J.: "The distinction between a State application which seeks to enforce the law of the land or to uphold the proper administration of justice on the one hand and on the other to enforce its own proprietary rights is readily intelligible and explains the distinction in practice at common law."

[174] The passage is from the 8th edn of the book, p.26. The up-to-date reference is: Bean, *Injunctions*, 9th edn (London: Thomson Sweet & Maxwell, 2007), p.35.

[175] Snell, *Equity*, 31st edn (London: Thomson Sweet & Maxwell, 2005), p.414.

[176] [1988] 3 All E.R. 490.

[177] [1989] 1 W.L.R. 778.

[178] [1989] 1 W.L.R. 778 at 786.

6–107 Millet J. refused to criticise a liquidator for refusing to risk his personal assets by giving an unlimited undertaking.

6–108 However, in this jurisdiction, in the case of *O'Mahony v Horgan*,[179] which concerned an application for a *Mareva* injunction, Murphy J. in the High Court had capped a liquidator's undertaking as to damages. O'Flaherty J. in the Supreme Court suggested that he did not think it right in principle that such a limit should be placed on an undertaking. Hamilton C.J. reserved the matter for future consideration. However, he also indicated that he was inclined to agree with O'Flaherty J.'s view in that regard. It is arguable that it is unfair to a liquidator to leave him potentially exposed in relation to damages arising on any undertaking given, although there is a related concern that it would be unfair on any party who succeeded on an inquiry as to damages that, in practical terms, their recovery could be capped.

(c) General Considerations

(i) Limits to the Application of the Damages Principle

6–109 A consideration of the adequacy of damages is of little assistance where the substantive relief sought does not include damages, certainly in so far as the adequacy of damages in terms of compensating the plaintiff or party seeking the injunction is concerned.

6–110 An example of a situation in which a plaintiff will not be seeking damages by way of substantive relief is an application under s.160 of the Planning and Development Act 2000, whereby no provision is made under that Act for the recovery of damages.

6–111 In *Dunne v Dun Laoghaire Rathdown Co Council*,[180] the plaintiffs applied for an interlocutory injunction to prevent the defendant from removing, as part of a road building scheme, parts of a monument on lands which the defendant owned. In considering the *Campus Oil* guidelines, Hardiman J. observed:

> "As to adequacy of damages, I cannot see how, in a case where no damages are claimed and where the right asserted is a public right, it can be said that damages would be an adequate remedy to the plaintiffs."[181]

---

[179] [1995] 2 I.R. 411.
[180] [2003] 1 I.R. 567.
[181] [2003] 1 I.R. 567 at 580.

6–112 In the case of *Limerick County Council v Tobin*,[182] Peart J. stated in relation to the questions of irreparable harm and the adequacy of damages that "it is not something which arises for consideration in an application of this kind, where the applicant is acting in the public interest rather than in order to protect some private commercial or other interest"[183] (although it should be noted that Peart J. did indicate that damages would be an adequate remedy for the respondent).[184]

6–113 A similar observation was made by Costello J. in the case of *Dublin District Milk Board v Golden Vale Co-Operative Creameries Ltd.*[185] The case involved a challenge to a statute, namely the Milk (Regulation of Supply and Price) Act 1936. Costello J. stated that:

> "If the statute is valid it is obvious that damages would not be the appropriate remedy because only an injunction would enable the Plaintiffs to carry out their statutory function and maintain the statutory regime."

(ii) Damages and Rights Normally Protected by Injunction

6–114 Although a consideration of damages is generally crucial to an application for an interlocutory injunction, there are some rights which are normally protected by injunction, although at least one more recent case indicates that this is not absolute, and that the emphasis is on "normally".

6–115 The types of rights which the court will normally protect by injunction include negative covenants, trespass and passing off.[186] In *Dublin Port and Docks Board v Britannia Dredging Company Limited*,[187] the Supreme Court accepted that where it is established that a party has agreed to a negative covenant, a court, at least at the trial of an action, will prima facie enforce that covenant even though it may be possible to measure the loss that would be attributable to its non-performance in monetary terms. In *Pasture Properties v Evans*,[188] Laffoy J. stated that "it is axiomatic in trespass cases that damages are not an adequate remedy." A similar approach would appear evident in relation to passing-off cases, as exemplified by the decision of Costello J. in *Mitchelstown Co-Operative Agricultural Society Limited v Golden Vale Food*

---

[182] unreported, High Court, Peart J., August 15, 2005.
[183] See Lewis, *Judicial Remedies in Public Law*, 3rd edn (London: Sweet & Maxwell, 2004), p.245 where it is stated that: "The balance of convenience in public law cases must take account of the wider public interest and cannot be measured simply in terms of the financial consequences to the parties."
[184] See further, Ch.11, Specific Statutory Injunctions, para.11–54.
[185] unreported, High Court, Costello J., April 3, 1987.
[186] These are considered in more detail in Ch.10, General Application.
[187] [1968] I.R. 136, following *Doherty v Allman* (1878) 3 App. Cas. 709.
[188] ex tempore, High Court, Laffoy J., February 5, 1999.

Products Ltd,[189] although in a later passing-off case, *Contech v Walsh*,[190] Finlay Geoghegan J. took the view that the court should look at the facts of each case. More recently, Clarke J. cautioned in *Jacob Fruitfield Food Group Ltd v United Biscuits (UK) Ltd*[191] that the earlier decisions, such as *Mitchelstown Co-Op*, did not establish a rule of law to the effect that:

> "a plaintiff will suffer uncompensatable damages if an injunction is refused even though the plaintiff has established a fair case to be tried and that the balance of convenience will, therefore, almost always require that an interlocutory injunction be granted in those circumstances."[192]

6–116 In his decision in *Metro International SA v Independent News & Media Plc*,[193] Clarke J. accepted that a court's primary consideration in assessing the adequacy or otherwise of damages at the interlocutory stage is the loss that might be sustained in the period between the refusal of an interlocutory injunction (or indeed its grant and the reliance by a defendant upon the undertaking as to damages given to secure it) and the trial. However, he stated that:

> "I am nonetheless of the view that in assessing the adequacy or otherwise of such damages as a remedy the court can and should have regard to the question of whether the right sought to be enforced or protected by interlocutory injunction is one which is of a type which the court will normally protect by injunction even though it might, in one sense, be possible to value the extinguishment or diminution of that right in monetary terms."[194]

6–117 This is a concise and commendable summary of the approach to take in relation to a consideration of the adequacy of damages where a right is normally protected by injunction.

(d) Distinction Between Adequacy of Damages and the Balance of Convenience

6–118 The question of the distinction—such as there is—between the adequacy of damages and the balance of convenience has never been entirely resolved by the courts. Some decisions have proceeded on the basis that the question of the adequacy of damages must be considered before looking at the balance of convenience. Others proceed on the basis that the adequacy of damages is an element of the balance of convenience. A more recent decision has viewed the

---

[189]   unreported, High Court, Costello J., December 12, 1985. See also, *DSG Retail Ltd v PC World Ltd*, unreported, High Court, Laffoy J., January 13, 1998.

[190]   unreported, High Court, Finlay Geoghegan J., February 17, 2006.

[191]   unreported, High Court, Clarke J., October 12, 2007.

[192]   See Ch.10, General Application, para.10–143.

[193]   [2006] 1 I.L.R.M. 414.

[194]   [2006] 1 I.L.R.M. 414 at 424. See also *Irish Shell Limited v JH McLoughlin (Balbriggan) Ltd*, unreported, High Court, Clarke J., August 4, 2005.

distinction, if any, as a question of semantics rather than substance. These three viewpoints will be considered in turn.

(i) Adequacy of Damages Then Balance of Convenience

6–119 In *American Cyanamid v Ethicon*,[195] having addressed the question of whether damages, rather than an interlocutory injunction, would be an adequate remedy, Lord Diplock then stated that:

> "It is where there is doubt as to the adequacy of the respective remedies in damages available to either party, or to both, that the question of balance of convenience arises."[196]

6–120 It would seem from this that the adequacy of damages should be considered in the first instance, separately from the question of the balance of convenience. A court would then proceed to consider the balance of convenience as appropriate once it has dealt with the question of the adequacy of damages. This would appear to be confirmed by the dictum of May L.J. in *Cayne v Global Natural Resources*,[197] in which, having cited the relevant section of Lord Diplock's speech in *American Cyanamid*, he stated that:

> "It is only thereafter, if damages after a trial are thought to be inadequate, that one is then enjoined to look at what is described as the 'balance of convenience' ..."[198]

6–121 A number of decisions confirm that the balance of convenience is only to be considered once the issue of damages has been dealt with. For example, in the Supreme Court decision in *Ferris v Ward*,[199] Blayney J. stated that it was only where there was doubt as to the adequacy of the respective remedies in damages available to either party or to both that the question of the balance of convenience arose. Similarly, O'Higgins J. in the High Court was quite explicit in *Garrahy v Bord na gCon*[200] in holding that it has to be established prior to any discussion on the balance of convenience whether damages are an adequate remedy or not.[201]

---

[195] [1975] A.C. 396; [1975] 2 W.L.R. 316; [1975] 1 All E.R. 504.
[196] [1975] A.C. 396 at 408; [1975] 2 W.L.R. 316 at 323; [1975] 1 All E.R. 504 at 511.
[197] [1984] 1 All E.R. 225.
[198] [1984] 1 All E.R. 225 at 237.
[199] [1998] 2 I.R. 194 at 202.
[200] [2002] 3 I.R. 566 at 572. See also, *Templeville Developments Ltd v Leopardstown Club Ltd*, unreported, High Court, O'Sullivan J., December 10, 2003.
[201] Referring to *Ferris v Ward*.

(ii) Adequacy of Damages as an Element of Balance of Convenience

6–122 In his judgment in *B & S Ltd v Irish Auto Trader Ltd*,[202] McCracken J. in the High Court suggested that the adequacy of damages was an element of the balance of convenience. Referring to Lord Diplock's dictum in *American Cyanamid*, McCracken J. stated that:

> "While Lord Diplock only used the phrase 'balance of convenience' when considering the position if damages were not an adequate remedy for either party, I would be more inclined to the view that the entire test rests on a balance of convenience, but that the adequacy of damages is a very important element, and may frequently be the decisive element, in considering where the balance of convenience lies."[203]

6–123 This approach has also been adopted in a number of cases, such as *Curust Financial Services Ltd v Loewe-Lack-Werk*.[204] In that case, O'Flaherty J. in the Supreme Court stated that the question of the balance of convenience "involves as a first inquiry whether damages would be an adequate remedy …"[205] In *Symonds Cider v Showerings (Ireland) Ltd*,[206] Laffoy J. also held, based on a consideration of *Auto Trader*, that the adequacy of damages was a "very important element" of the balance of convenience.[207]

6–124 The blurring of the lines between a consideration of damages and the question of the balance of convenience has particular traction in the context of employment injunctions.[208] For example, in *Murphy v ACC Bank,*[209] O'Sullivan J. referred to considering "the question of damages in the overall context of the balance of convenience". Referring to the decision of Laffoy J. in *Harte v Kelly*,[210] O'Sullivan J. made reference to the fact that the plaintiff was from a small close-knit community, that his only source of income was his salary from the defendant and that he had ongoing financial obligations to the members of his family. In the view of O'Sullivan J., the disruption caused by refusing an injunction would be disproportionate in the circumstances of this case.

---

[202] [1995] 2 I.R. 142; [1995] 2 I.L.R.M. 152.
[203] [1995] 2 I.R. 142 at 146; [1995] 2 I.L.R.M. 152 at 156.
[204] [1994] 1 I.R. 450.
[205] [1994] 1 I.R. 450 at 472.
[206] [1997] 1 I.L.R.M. 481.
[207] [1997] 1 I.L.R.M. 481 at 494. See also, *Miss World Ltd v Miss Ireland Beauty Pageant Ltd* [2004] 2 I.R. 394 at 404, in which Laffoy J. stated that she agreed with the dictum of McCracken J. in *Auto Trader*.
[208] As to which, see Ch.9, Employment.
[209] unreported, High Court, O'Sullivan J., February 4, 2002.
[210] [1997] E.L.R. 125. Referred to by MacMenamin J. in *Whelan Frozen Foods Ltd v Dunnes Stores*, unreported, High Court, MacMenamin J., February 17, 2006.

(iii) Semantics or Substance

6–125 An alternative view was taken by Murphy J. in *Paramount Pictures Corporation v Cablelink Ltd.*[211] He suggested that it might be a mistake to view as separate or watertight compartments the questions of balance of convenience and adequacy of damages as a remedy since one would necessarily impinge on the other. A not dissimilar view to that of Murphy J. was adopted in the case of *Metro International SA v Independent News & Media Plc.*[212] Clarke J. suggested that it was a question of "semantics" rather than "substance" whether the question of adequacy of damages and the weighing-up of balance of convenience are viewed as two separate tests, or as one in which the former is a significant part of the latter.[213] This approach in *Metro* is both pragmatic and sensible.

6–126 In any event, it is also arguable that even if damages are viewed as part of the balance of convenience, a consideration of damages should be the "first inquiry"[214] or a "very important element"[215] in such a consideration. In theory a finding that damages are adequate would relieve the need for the court to make any further determination in relation to the balance of convenience.

3. Balance of Convenience

6–127 It is for the party seeking the injunction to show that the balance of convenience is in his favour.[216] Whereas previously this was a consideration which applied to the granting of a perpetual injunction,[217] it now refers to the interlocutory (or interim) stages of an application.[218]

(a) What is the Balance of Convenience?

6–128 As to what is to be understood by the term "balance of convenience", Lord Diplock explained in *American Cyanamid* in the context of the court affording protection by means of an injunction that:

---

[211] [1991] 1 I.R. 521 at 528.

[212] [2006] 1 I.L.R.M. 414.

[213] [2006] 1 I.L.R.M. 414 at 423.

[214] per O'Flaherty J. in *Curust Financial Services Ltd v Loewe-Lack-Werk* [1994] 1 I.R. 450 at 472.

[215] per Laffoy J. in *Symonds Cider v Showerings (Ireland) Ltd* [1997] 1 I.L.R.M. 481.

[216] per O'Higgins C.J. in *Campus Oil* [1983] I.R. 88 at 106; [1984] I.L.R.M. 45 at 60. See also, the dictum of Finlay C.J. in *Mitchelstown Co-Operative Society Ltd v Société des Produits Nestlé SA* [1989] I.L.R.M. 582 at 587.

[217] See, for example, *Jenkins v Jackson* (1888) 40 Ch D 71 at 77.

[218] See, for example, *Texaxo Ltd v Mulberry Filling Station Ltd* [1972] 1 W.L.R. 814 at 830 for a consideration of this point.

"the plaintiff's need for [such] protection must be weighed against the corresponding need of the defendant to be protected against injury resulting from his having been prevented from exercising his own legal rights, for which he could not be adequately compensated under the plaintiff's undertaking in damages if the uncertainty was resolved in the defendant's favour at the trial. The court must weigh one need against the other and determine where the 'balance of convenience' lies."[219]

6–129 In *Cayne v Global Natural Resources*,[220] May L.J. referred to the term "balance of convenience" as being a "useful shorthand", and suggested that the balance which the court looks to make is more fundamental than mere convenience. May L.J. preferred the description "the balance of the risk of doing an injustice" by granting the injunction.[221] However, this was in the context of a situation where the granting or refusal of the injunction would effectively dispose of the entire action. Sir John Donaldson M.R. went further in *Francome v Mirror Group Newspapers Ltd*[222] in describing the term "balance of convenience" as "… an unfortunate expression. Our business is justice, not convenience".[223] Lord Diplock took a similar approach in the case of *NWL Ltd v Woods,*[224] in which the trial of the action was also unlikely on the facts. He observed that, "… the judge is engaged in weighing the respective risks that injustice may result from his deciding one way rather than the other at a stage when the evidence is incomplete."[225]

6–130 Regardless of whether the use of the phrase "risk of injustice" is employed or not, the understanding of the term "balance of convenience" is clearly sufficiently broad that the court may consider a wide variety of factors in determining where that balance actually lies.[226]

(b) Balance of Convenience: Factors to Consider

6–131 In *American Cyanamid*, Lord Diplock stated that it would be unwise:

---

[219] [1975] A.C. 396 at 406; [1975] 2 W.L.R. 316 at 321; [1975] 1 All E.R. 504 at 509. Approved of by McWilliam J. in *Lift Manufacturers Ltd v Irish Life Assurance Co Ltd* [1979] I.L.R.M. 277 at 280.

[220] [1984] 1 All E.R. 225 at 237. See also, *Harkins v Shannon Foynes Port Company* [2001] E.L.R. 75.

[221] Referred to with approval by O'Higgins J. in *Garrahy v Bord na gCon* [2003] 14 E.L.R. 274.

[222] [1984] 1 W.L.R. 893; [1984] 2 All E.R. 408.

[223] [1984] 1 W.L.R. 893 at 898; [1984] 2 All E.R. 408 at 413.

[224] [1979] 1 W.L.R. 1294; [1979] 3 All E.R. 614.

[225] [1979] 1 W.L.R. 1294 at 1306; [1979] 3 All E.R. 614 at 625. For a wider analysis of this case, see Clarke & Bowers "American Cyanamid—N.W.L. Ltd A Change of Heart?" (1980) 96 L.Q.R. 189.

[226] See, for example, *B & S Ltd v Irish Auto Trader Ltd* [1995] 2 I.L.R.M. 152, in particular at 157.

"to attempt even to list all the various matters which may need to be taken into consideration in deciding where the balance lies, let alone to suggest the relative weight to be attached to them. These will vary from case to case."[227]

6–132 However, McMahon & Binchy[228] refer to a number of considerations which may be of relevance in considering the balance of convenience, such as the risk of personal injury[229]; the question of public convenience[230]; and whether irreparable damage would result.[231] Two other factors to which the courts have had regard are the question of whether an injustice may be done, and also whether a statutory function is being exercised.

(i) Doing an Injustice

6–133 "The risk of doing an injustice" was a consideration in the decision in *Cayne*. The idea of justice being key was also reinforced by Laffoy J. in her decision in *Harte v Kelly*,[232] in which she felt that it would be unjust to leave a person who alleges that his dismissal has been wrongful without his salary pending the trial of the action and merely with his prospect of an award of damages at the trial of the action.

(ii) Exercise of a Statutory Function

6–134 The question of whether a statutory function is being exercised is also of relevance. In the case of *Martin v Bord Pleanála*,[233] O'Sullivan J. referred to the inconvenience which can arise on an interlocutory application, by delay of or interference with procedure by a statutory authority.[234] He also made reference to the respect which the court should afford the existing legislative regime of the State.[235] Similarly, in *Dublin District Milk Board v Golden Vale Co-Operative Creameries Ltd*,[236] Costello J. granted an interlocutory injunction against the defendant on the basis that only an injunction would enable the plaintiff to carry out its statutory function. In coming to his determination, Costello J. had regard to the public interest in considering the balance of convenience, as the plaintiff was carrying out a statutory function in the public interest.[237]

---

227 [1975] 1 A.C. 396 at 408; 1975] 2 W.L.R. 316 at 323; [1975] 1 All E.R. 504 at 511.
228 McMahon & Binchy, *The Irish Law of Torts*, 3rd edn (Dublin: Butterworths, 2000), p.1198.
229 Citing *McDonald v Feely*, unreported, Supreme Court, July 23, 1980.
230 See generally, Ch.4, Equitable and General Principles, specifically para.4–72 and the consideration of whether the public convenience is a factor which may legitimately be considered.
231 See *Moore v Attorney General* [1927] I.R. 569.
232 [1997] E.L.R. 125.
233 unreported, High Court, O'Sullivan J., July 24, 2002.
234 Citing *R v Association of Futures Brokers and Dealers Ltd* [1991] 3 Admin. L.R. 254.
235 See also, *Pesca Valentia Ltd v Minister for Fisheries* [1986] I.L.R.M. 68; [1985] I.R. 193.
236 unreported, High Court, Costello J., April 3, 1987.
237 As to the role the public interest or other third party considerations may have in the context of

4. The Status Quo

6–135 As observed by McCracken J. in *B & S Ltd v Irish Auto Trader Ltd*[238]:

> "It is normally a counsel of prudence, although not a fixed rule, that if all other matters are equally balanced, the court should preserve the *status quo*."[239]

6–136 This view echoed that expressed by O'Higgins C.J. in the *Campus Oil* case in which he had stated that "interlocutory relief is intended to keep matters in *status quo* until the trial and to do no more."[240]

6–137 Although criticised for its "ambiguity and the limited practical significance that was given to it",[241] the idea of the preservation of the status quo has nonetheless been an important consideration in determining whether or not to grant an injunction on an interlocutory basis. The court is not trying to anticipate the determination of a right but merely to determine whether an order should be granted in essence preserving a position until such time as the court can determine the rights concerned.[242] In the words of Fennelly J. in *McKenna v AF*,[243] the purpose of an interlocutory injunction is to "maintain a just equilibrium between the parties until their respective rights can be substantively determined."

6–138 Careful consideration needs to be given to the effect that the granting of an injunction on an interlocutory basis would have in terms of its impact on the status quo. For example, in *Bula Ltd v Tara Mines (No. 2)*,[244] Murphy J. took the view that the proposed injunction sought would not maintain the status quo, but would "decide, at least on some temporary or conditional basis, the legal framework within which those actions are to be taken". He felt that it would be "wrong for the Court to adopt that course at interlocutory stage".[245]

---

injunction applications, see generally, Ch.4, Equitable and General Principles, particularly para.4–72.

[238] [1995] 2 I.R. 142; [1995] 2 I.L.R.M. 152.

[239] [1995] 2 I.R. 142 at 145; [1995] 2 I.L.R.M. 152 at 156. Albeit that in that case, McCracken J. found that it was an "unusual case" where the balance of convenience lay in favour of refusing an interlocutory injunction, notwithstanding the fact that this involved altering the status quo. As to the general rule being to strive to maintain the status quo, see also, *Private Research v Brosnan* [1996] 1 I.L.R.M. 27 and *McAuley v Keating*, unreported, High Court, Kelly J., April 24, 1997.

[240] [1983] I.R. 88 at 106; [1984] I.L.R.M. 45 at 60. See also the dictum of Finlay C.J. in *SPUC v Grogan* [1989] I.R. 753 at 762.

[241] Zuckerman, "Interlocutory Remedies in Quest of Procedural Fairness" (1993) 56 M.L.R. 325 at 327.

[242] See the reference in *Bula Ltd v Tara Mines (No. 2)* [1987] I.R. 95 to a passage from *Kerr on Injunctions*.

[243] [2002] 2 I.L.R.M. 303 at 314.

[244] [1987] I.R. 95.

[245] [1987] I.R. 95 at 105. Cited with approval in *Hennessy v St Gerard's School Trust* [2004] 15 E.L.R. 230.

6–139 However, it is obviously not sufficient to simply ignore the matter and presume that this will in some way maintain the status quo. The need to reach a decision on an interlocutory application for an injunction was referred to by Finlay C.J. in the *SPUC* case, observing that deferring or postponing reaching such a decision:

> "for a period which certainly equals and probably exceeds the time necessary to bring the action to hearing is, in my view, to decline or refuse to make an interlocutory injunction."[246]

(a) Altering the Status Quo

6–140 It is still open to a court to grant an interlocutory injunction even though it will have the effect of altering the status quo. Indeed, the reality is that an injunction order such as an *Anton Piller* order[247] will affect the status quo. The position was summarised succinctly by McCracken J. in the case of *Private Research Ltd v Brosnan*.[248] He stated that whilst a court should "strive to maintain the *status quo*, this is only one element in considering the balance of convenience and there is no absolute rule that the *status quo* must be maintained."[249]

6–141 A similar view to that expressed in *Private Research* was also taken in *Dublin City Council v McGrath*.[250] Carroll J., whilst acknowledging that the court will generally preserve the status quo, also stated that the court should not be constrained ab initio from considering whether an injunction should be granted.

6–142 As is clear as well from the foregoing extract from *Private Research*, it appears that the courts take the view that the status quo should be considered as an element of the balance of convenience. This view is confirmed by MacMenamin J. in *Whelan Frozen Foods Ltd v Dunnes Stores*,[251] although McCracken J.'s dictum in the *Auto Trader* case would suggest that a consideration of the status quo only comes into play when "all other matters are equally balanced". It seems that not a lot turns on such a distinction in reality.

(b) Point of Determination of the Status Quo

6–143 The general view is that the status quo is, in the normal course, that which prevailed during the period immediately proceeding the issuing of the

---

[246] [1989] I.R. 753 at 762.
[246] As to which, see Ch.8, Commercial Injunctions, para.8–129.
[248] [1995] 1 I.R. 534; [1996] 1 I.L.R.M. 27.
[249] [1995] 1 I.R. 534 at 539; [1996] 1 I.L.R.M. 27 at 32.
[250] unreported, High Court, Carroll J., March 12, 2004.
[251] unreported, High Court, MacMenamin J., February 17, 2006.

writ claiming the permanent injunction. In *Contech v Walsh*,[252] Finlay Geoghegan J. suggested in the context of an action for passing off that "where a plaintiff moves speedily after learning of the commencement of selling of a product on a market, it appears to me that the *status quo* which the court must primarily have regard to is the position which prevailed before the commencement of the alleged wrongful acts, or the acts alleged to constitute the passing-off."

6–144 However, it has been accepted that if there is a lengthy delay in seeking an interlocutory injunction, it may be the status quo at the time immediately preceding the motion seeking the interlocutory injunction application which is of relevance.[253] This would appear to make sense having regard to Finlay Geoghegan J.'s reference to moving "speedily".

5. The Question of the Strength of the Case

6–145 In *American Cyanamid*,[254] Lord Diplock suggested that if the various arguments were finely balanced, the court could, based on the affidavit evidence adduced, consider the relative strength of each party's case. Despite this, some writers have suggested that, after the *American Cyanamid* decision, once there was a view that the plaintiff had shown that there was a serious question to be tried, "any further reference to the relative strength of the parties' cases was prohibited."[255]

(a) Not a Consideration in Ireland

6–146 This view is in fact the one which effectively still prevails in this jurisdiction. In the case of *Westman Holdings Ltd v McCormack*,[256] Finlay C.J. stated that once a conclusion had been reached that the party seeking an interlocutory injunction had raised a fair question to be tried:

> "the Court should not express any view on the strength of the contending submissions leading to the raising of such a fair and *bona fide* question."[257]

6–147 In his subsequent High Court decision in *B & S Ltd v Irish Auto Trader Ltd*,[258] McCracken J. took the view that the strength of a case may be a factor if

---

[252] ex tempore, High Court, Finlay Geoghegan J., February 17, 2006. See also *Bayzana Ltd v Galligan* [1987] I.R. 238 in which McCarthy J., dissenting, held that the status quo in the context of the picketing of a factory premises was that pertaining when the plaintiff became involved in the matter upon becoming aware of the dispute and the picket.

[253] *Garden Cottage Foods Ltd v Milk Marketing Board* [1984] A.C. 130 at 140; [1983] 2 All E.R. 770 at 775.

[254] [1975] A.C. 396; [1975] 2 W.L.R. 316; [1975] 1 All E.R. 504.

[255] Bean, *Injunctions*, 9th edn (London: Thomson Sweet & Maxwell, 2007), p.38.

[256] [1992] 1 I.R. 151.

[257] [1992] 1 I.R. 151 at 157.

[258] [1995] 2 I.R. 142; [1995] 2 I.L.R.M. 152.

all the other factors do not lead to a conclusive determination. However this view, expressed in the High Court, was obiter. When the issue was subsequently canvassed in the case of *Symonds Cider & English Wine Company Ltd v Showerings (Ireland) Ltd*[259] in the context of a passing-off action,[260] Laffoy J. explicitly stated, on the basis of the Supreme Court decision in *Westman Holdings*, that it would be inappropriate for the court to express any view on the strengths of the parties' respective cases.[261]

(b) May be Considered in England

6–148 The position in Ireland can be contrasted with the evolving position in England. In *Series 5 Software v Clarke*,[262] Laddie J. took the view that it had not been intended in *American Cyanamid* to exclude consideration of the strength of the case in applications for interlocutory relief.[263] Laddie J.'s view was that it was intended that the court should "not attempt to resolve difficult issue of fact or law" on an interlocutory application. He acknowledged that it was clearly important that the interlocutory hearing does not itself become a form of mini-trial. However, he was of the view that the court should not ignore the fact that one party's case is much stronger than the other party's. He also justified his approach in referring to the strength of the case on the basis that there was great merit in expressing a non-binding view.

6–149 Bean suggests that, certainly in England, such an approach "represents what many judges had been doing already".[264] The justification for this is perhaps best encapsulated in the statement that "A court which does not enquire into the prospect of winning on the merits would be as likely to come to the assistance of a party with no rightful claim as to assist a rightful party."[265]

---

[249]   [1997] 1 I.L.R.M. 481.

[260]   Counsel for the defendant had argued that the court could consider the strength of the case on the basis that the determination of the court at the interlocutory stage generally determined the outcome of the case overall.

[261]   *cf.* the decision of *European Paint Importers Ltd v O'Callaghan*, unreported, High Court, Peart J., August 10, 2005 in which Peart J. expressed a view as to the interpretation of a clause at the centre of a dispute between the parties "in a general way and because the parties have encouraged me to make a finding in this regard, since the Court at this stage of the case is in every bit as good a position to determine the meaning of the clause, as it would be at any more substantial hearing of the case". This would appear to be a relatively unusual dictum and is perhaps better considered as being confined to the facts of the case before the court.

[262]   [1996] 1 All E.R. 853 at 865.

[263]   A view reaffirmed by the same judge in *Cmi-Centres for Medical Innovation GmbH v Phytopharm Plc* [1999] F.S.R. 235 at 243. See also *Wyeth Holdings Corpn v Alpharma Ltd* [2003] All E.R. (D) 266, in which Laddie J. stated that he would not retract any of what he said in *Series 5 Software*.

[264]   Bean, *Injunctions*, 9th edn (London: Thomson Sweet & Maxwell, 2007), p.39.

[265]   Zuckerman, "Interlocutory Remedies in Quest of Procedural Fairness" (1993) 56 M.L.R. 325 at 328. A similar view is expressed in Bean, *Injunctions*, 9th edn (London: Thomson Sweet &

6–150 Although the *Series 5 Software* decision has stood the test of time in England, it is clear from the Supreme Court decision in *Westman Holdings*, as reviewed in *Symonds Cider*, that the *Series 5 Software* decision goes well beyond what the Irish courts are prepared to countenance. Whether there is any merit in considering the strength of a case is perhaps best considered by focusing on the point at which the strength of a case should be a relevant factor.

(i) Point of Consideration

6–151 In the case of *Ryanair v Aer Rianta cpt*,[266] counsel for the applicant had contended that the applicant's case was so strong that the court ought not to apply the "well-established" principles. Instead, it was argued that the court should "proceed to grant an injunction pending trial based on the strength of his case alone and without regard to either adequacy of damages as a remedy or balance of convenience." Kelly J. unequivocally rejected this contention in the strongest terms. He stated that:

> "such an approach is unprecedented. No case was cited in support of it. It is an invitation which is extended in the teeth of authoritative statements from the highest courts both in this jurisdiction and in England."

6–152 Such an approach would indeed have been "unprecedented". The dictum of Lord Diplock in *American Cyanamid* referred specifically to addressing the strength of the case when all the other arguments and tests had been dealt with. This implies that the "strength" test is in no way intended to displace the *American Cyanamid/Campus Oil* test. It only comes into play once the bona fide threshold has been crossed, and the issues of the adequacy of damages, the balance of convenience and the status quo have been dealt with.

6–153 In *Series 5 Software*, Laddie J. approached the matter by first considering the other factors set out in *American Cyanamid*. In so far as he was suggesting that strength might be an issue which could be addressed once all the other tests had been considered, there is some merit in this if everything else is evenly balanced (though the volume of cases in which this is the position is, one would imagine, relatively small). There is also a degree of merit in the suggestion that, by dealing with the strength of the case, a judge may in fact assist the parties concerned. As explained by Laddie J.:

Maxwell, 2007), p.28, in which the author observes that a refusal to consider the relative strengths of the parties' cases once it was established that there was a serious question to be tried "placed a weapon for injustice in the hands of the claimants with weak but arguable cases".

[266] ex tempore, High Court, Kelly J., January 25, 2001.

"In fact, as any lawyer who has experience of interlocutory proceedings will know, it is frequently the case that it is easy to determine who is most likely to win the trial on the basis of the affidavit evidence and any exhibited contemporaneous documents. If it is apparent from that material that one party's case is much stronger than the other's then that is a matter the court should not ignore. To suggest otherwise would be to exclude from consideration an important factor and such exclusion would fly in the face of the flexibility advocated earlier in *American Cyanamid* ."[267]

6–154 The flexibility of the *American Cyanamid* principles in that regard was also referred to by Walker L.J. in the Court of Appeal in the case of *Guardian Media Groups Plc v Associated Newspapers Ltd.*[268] He felt that such flexibility did not "prevent the court from giving proper weight to any clear view which the court can form at the time of the application for interim relief ... as to the likely outcome at trial." However, he also stated that he did not need to consider whether "the court's entitlement to give effect to its provisional view of the merits goes quite so far as Laddie J. sought in *Series 5 Software v Clarke.*" In brief, there is probably some merit to considering the strength of a case, but only if appropriate, once all the other *Campus Oil* factors have been considered and to some useful end, e.g. assisting the parties in analysing the merits of their respective cases and determining whether to pursue them to conclusion.

6. Prohibitory Interlocutory Injunctions: A Summary

6–155 In summary, there are a number of key points in relation to prohibitory interlocutory injunctions:

- The granting of a prohibitory interlocutory injunction is a discretionary relief, and the granting of such relief will depend on the facts of the case before the court.
- It is not a determination of the action between the parties, and a court should not attempt to resolve questions of fact or law.
- It is a flexible relief, but one which is guided by the guidelines set out in *Campus Oil.*
- The party seeking the relief will have to demonstrate that they have a fair/bona fide/serious question to be tried, as distinct from a prima facie case.
- The court will consider the adequacy of damages in relation to both parties. This, in practical terms, is the issue on which the courts focus most often.
- The courts will also consider the balance of convenience. Whether the former is distinct from, or a subset of, the latter, is a matter of semantics.

---

[267] [1996] 1 All E.R. 853 at 865.
[268] *All England Official Transcripts*, January 20, 2000.

- A court will in general terms endeavour to maintain the status quo between the parties.[269]

7. Departure from General Guidelines

6–156 The guidelines in *American Cyanamid/Campus Oil*, "have a wide but not a universal application."[270] It has been observed that the *American Cyanamid* guidelines specifically must be viewed in the context in which they were set out,[271] namely a claim to enforce a proprietary right to a monopoly, the plaintiff owning a patent for surgical sutures.

6–157 Many of the circumstances in which the *American Cyanamid/Campus Oil* guidelines are not followed are very specific areas of the law. These will be dealt with in Ch.10, General Application. They include applications to restrain a company winding up[272]; references to the European Court of Justice where a challenge is made to the validity of a Community measure[273]; and the linked situations of where defamation is pleaded[274] and prior restraint of publication.[275] In the context of applications for *Mareva* injunctions, elements of the guidelines are displaced.[276] Injunctions which are provided for in statute,[277] such as under the Industrial Relations Act 1990 which regulates, inter alia, trade disputes, may also attract specific considerations.

6–158 Distilled from case law,[278] there are certain broader circumstances in which the courts will often depart from the general principles, which is entirely consistent with the idea that the *American Cyanamid/Campus Oil* guidelines are just that, not rigid rules. These circumstances are not "special factors" as such, as considered above, but essentially bring the case beyond the need to consider the *American Cyanamid/Campus Oil* guidelines.

(a) The Interlocutory Application is the Hearing of the Substantive Matter

6–159 The parties to an action may agree that the interlocutory application should be treated as the substantive hearing. This is relatively self-explanatory:

---

[269] See also the summary by Laddie J. in *Series 5 Software v Clarke* [1996] 1 All E.R. 853 at 865.
[270] per Kelly J. in *Reynolds v Malocco* [1999] 2 I.R. 203 at 209.
[271] Gee, *Commercial Injunctions*, 5th edn (London: Thomson Sweet & Maxwell, 2004), p.45.
[272] See Ch.10, General Application, para.10–34.
[273] See Ch.10, General Application, para.10–97.
[274] See *Reynolds v Malocco* [1999] 2 I.R. 203. See Ch.10, General Application, para.10–164.
[275] Known as the rule in *Bonnard v Perryman* [1891] 2 Ch. 269, approved and followed in this jurisdiction in the case of *Sinclair v Gogarty* [1937] I.R. 377. See *Foley v Sunday Newspapers Ltd* [2005] 1 I.R. 88. See Ch.10, General Application, para.10–164.
[276] See Ch.8, Commercial Injunctions, para.8–31.
[277] See Ch.11, Specific Statutory Injunctions, para.11–56.
[278] See the synopsis of these circumstances in Delany, *Equity and the Law of Trusts in Ireland*, 4th edn, (Dublin: Thomson Round Hall, 2007), pp.518–543.

if the hearing of the substantive matter is conflated with the interlocutory action, this renders otiose the need to consider the various elements of the *American Cyanamid/Campus Oil* tests. For example, in *AG v X*,[279] Costello J. suggested to counsel that consideration be given to treating the motion as the trial of the action, with leave to call oral evidence, with counsel agreeing to this course.

6–160 However, there is old authority for the proposition that where a motion for an injunction is treated as the hearing of the action and where there is no statement of claim drafted, the plaintiff cannot seek relief on any ground not specifically claimed in the writ.[280]

(b) Prima Facie Entitlement/No Arguable Defence

6–161 In *Boyle v An Post*,[281] Lardner J. referred to the fact that in *Campus Oil* O'Higgins C.J. had said that:

> "It frequently happens that neither the applicant's right nor the fact of its violation is disputed by the person whose acts are sought to be restrained. In such a case an injunction may be given almost as of course."[282]

However, as Lardner J. pointed out, he believed that the Chief Justice "was referring to mandatory orders which had been sought."

6–162 Notwithstanding this, the courts may on occasion be prepared to grant an interlocutory injunction where there is a prima facie entitlement to such a remedy, essentially on the basis that there is no arguable defence. There are a number of qualifications to this statement. The dictum of Kelly J. in *Ryanair v Aer Rianta cpt*,[283] as set out above, must be borne in mind. This category needs to be approached on the basis that it applies to specific legal rights rather than as a general proposition.

6–163 By way of example as to when it might be appropriate to grant a prohibitory interlocutory injunction without reference to the *American Cyanamid/Campus Oil* tests, where a plaintiff clearly has good title and the defendant's trespass is indisputable, an interlocutory injunction will be granted as a matter of course. This is clear from the decision in *Patel v WH Smith (Eziot) Ltd*,[284] an English case, the *ratio* of which has been accepted in Ireland. In that case, Balcombe L.J. stated that:

---

[279] [1992] I.L.R.M. 401.
[280] *Serff v Acton Local Board* (1886) 21 Ch D 679.
[281] [1992] 2 I.R. 437.
[282] [1992] 2 I.R. 437 at 771.
[283] ex tempore, High Court, Kelly J., January 25, 2001.
[284] [1987] 1 W.L.R. 853; [1987] 2 All E.R. 569.

"It seems to me that, first, *prima facie* a landowner whose title is not in issue is entitled to an injunction to restrain trespass on his land whether or not the trespass harms him."[285]

6–164 However, Balcombe L.J. acknowledged that a defendant:

"may put in evidence to seek to establish that he has a right to do what would otherwise be a trespass. Then the court must consider the principle set out in American *Cyanamid Co v Ethicon Ltd* in relation to the grant or refusal of an interlocutory injunction."[286]

6–165 In this jurisdiction, the principle stated in the *Patel* case was repeated in virtually identical terms by Keane J. in *Keating & Co Ltd v Jervis Shopping Centre Ltd*.[287] He held that:

"It is clear that a landowner, whose title is not in issue, is *prima facie* entitled to an injunction to restrain a trespass and that this is also the case where the claim is for an interlocutory injunction only."[288]

6–166 It is important that the court is clear as to the title being asserted, however. In *Dublin Corporation v Burke*,[289] Geoghegan J. observed that he was:

"extremely doubtful that there would even be a *prima facie* case for an injunction where a defendant with some back-up evidence (if ultimately accepted) is alleging an actual tenancy in the premises and the plaintiff is for all practical purposes merely sceptical of the truth of the allegation."[290]

6–167 If there is any doubt as to whether there is an arguable defence, the usual American *Cyanamid/Campus Oil* guidelines as considered above should be applied.

(c) Where the Trial of the Substantive Action is Unlikely

6–168 In the case of *NWL Ltd v Woods*,[291] having considered the role of the balance of convenience in the *American Cyanamid* guidelines, Lord Diplock

---

[285] [1987] 1 W.L.R. 853 at 858; [1987] 2 All E.R. 569 at 573. See also *Hampstead & Suburban Properties Ltd v Diomedus* [1969] 1 Ch. 248; [1968] 3 W.L.R. 990; [1968] 3 All E.R. 545, in which a defendant was in clear breach of a binding covenant. This should be distinguished from cases where liability is arguable: *Texaxo Ltd v Mulberry Filling Station Ltd* [1972] 1 W.L.R. 814.

[286] [1987] 1 W.L.R. 853 at 859; [1987] 2 All E.R. 569 at 574.

[287] [1997] 1 I.R. 512.

[288] [1997] 1 I.R. 512 at 518. See also in relation to the construction of a contract, *Fellowes & Son v Fisher* [1976] Q.B. 122; [1975] 3 W.L.R. 184 and *Associated British Ports v Transport and General Workers' Union* [1989] 1 W.L.R. 939 at 979.

[289] unreported, Supreme Court, October 9, 2001.

[290] Cited by Carroll J. in *Dublin City Council v McGrath*, unreported, High Court, Carroll J., March 12, 2004.

[291] [1979] 1 W.L.R. 1294; [1979] 3 All E.R. 614.

then contrasted this position to that of what he termed "exceptional" cases. These were cases in which the granting or refusal of an injunction at the interlocutory stage would dispose of the action in favour of whichever party was successful in the application, because there would be nothing left on which it was in the unsuccessful party's interest to proceed to trial. He stated:

> "Where ... the grant or refusal of the interlocutory injunction will have the practical effect of putting an end to the action because the harm that will have been caused to the losing party by its grant or refusal is complete and of a kind for which money cannot constitute any worthwhile recompense, the degree of likelihood that the plaintiff would have succeeded in establishing his right to an injunction if the action had gone to trial, is a factor to be brought into the balance by the judge in weighing the risks that injustice may result from his deciding the application one way rather than the other."[292]

6–169 The Court of Appeal in England has approved and followed the approach of Lord Diplock in a number of cases.[293] There is some uncertainty as to the actual effect of such an approach, however. What is not entirely clear is whether a consideration of the trial of the substantive action being unlikely is to be considered as part of the balance of convenience or whether this essentially overrides the *American Cyanamid* test, or parts thereof, specifically the consideration of whether there is a bona fide/fair/serious question to be tried. Lord Diplock's dictum set out above refers to a factor "to be brought into the balance". However, in *Cambridge Nutrition Ltd v British Broadcasting Corporation*,[294] Kerr L.J. did not apply the *American Cyanamid* principles as the matter before him was one in which the determination of the crucial issue as between the parties would essentially depend on whether interlocutory relief was granted or refused.[295]

6–170 It is unclear whether the Irish courts would be prepared to adopt such an approach. As has been seen, in *Westman Holdings Ltd v McCormack*,[296] Finlay C.J. held that once the party seeking an injunction had demonstrated that there was a fair question to be tried, the court should not express any view on the strength of the competing submissions.[297] To find that the trial of the substantive action would be unlikely would be to, in effect, express a view.

---

292 [1979] 1 W.L.R. 1294 at 1307; [1979] 3 All E.R. 614 at 625. This is a particular concern in passing off cases: see Drysdale and Silverleaf *Passing Off—Law and Practice*, 2nd edn (London: Butterworths Tolley, 1995), p.142.

293 See, for example, *Cayne v Global Natural Resources Plc* [1984] 1 All E.R. 225.

294 [1990] 3 All E.R. 523.

295 See also *Douglas v Hello! Ltd* [2001] Q.B. 967 at 1007; [2001] 2 W.L.R. 992; [2001] 2 All E.R. 289, per Keene L.J. See also *Lansing Linde Ltd v Kerr* [1991] 1 W.L.R. 251 and *Credit Suisse Asset Management Ltd v Armstrong* [1996] I.C.R. 882.

296 [1992] 1 I.R. 151.

297 [1992] 1 I.R. 151 at 157.

6–171 However, in the case of *Benckiser GmbH v Fibrisol Services Ltd*,[298] the lack of a serious conflict between the parties on affidavit evidence and the strength of the plaintiff's case were considered by Costello J. in the High Court in refusing to grant an injunction. In doing so, he effectively determined the matter. This is an approach favoured by Byrne and Binchy, who note that such an approach is "… realistic and practical. If the issue is a purely legal one, nothing will be gained by deferring such consideration of the legal issue until a full hearing."[299] However, as cautioned by Delany, "there are inherent dangers in applying such an approach too freely."[300] She raises the legitimate concern that "allowing a judge to rule on the merits of a case on the basis of inadequate evidence should be avoided at all costs" and suggests that it is better to maintain the status quo rather than prejudging the issues unless it is "abundantly clear" that otherwise no trial of the action will take place.

(d) Statutory Requirements

6–172 There may be a statutory provision which requires the displacement, at least in part, of the *American Cyanamid/Campus Oil* guidelines. The extent to which different statutes prescribe the proofs required in order to obtain an injunction is considered further in Ch.11, Specific Statutory Injunctions.

8. The Position of Public Bodies

6–173 That fact that a public body is applying for an injunction does not constitute a reason for applying a different threshold in terms of applying for an interlocutory injunction. In *Garrahy v Bord na gCon*,[301] O'Higgins J. rejected the contention that the earlier English decision of *Smith v Inner London Education Authority*[302] established a different threshold for the obtaining of interlocutory relief in relation to public bodies than the test set out in *American Cyanamid*. However, O'Higgins J. did acknowledge that the status of the body as a public body may be of relevance in considering the balance of convenience, citing the dictum of Browne L.J. in *Smith* to that effect.[303]

---

[298] unreported, High Court, Costello J., May 13, 1988.
[299] Byrne & Binchy, *Annual Review of Irish Law* (Dublin: Thomson Round Hall, 1988), p.200. See also *Governors of Barrington's Hospital v Minister for Health* [1989] I.L.R.M. 77; [1988] I.R. 56 in which Costello J. refused to grant an interlocutory injunction to the plaintiffs, finding that there was no dispute as to the facts and thus determining the legal issue.
[300] per Delany (1993) 15 D.U.L.J. 228 at 241 in the course of her analysis of *Curust Financial Services Ltd v Loewe-Lack-Werk* [1994] 1 I.R. 450.
[301] [2002] 3 I.R. 566. See also the decision of O'Sullivan J. in *Competition Authority v Avonmore Waterford Group Plc*, unreported, High Court, O'Sullivan J., November 17, 1998.
[302] [1978] 1 All E.R. 411.
[303] [2002] 3 I.R. 566 at 579.

6–174 O'Higgins J. also referred to the fact that even if a higher standard was required it was by no means certain that this would apply to all the functions ancillary to that public body's main function. However, he did refer to the fact that the courts should be slower to grant an injunction to restrain a public body in the performance of its public functions.[304]

6–175 A related point fell to be considered by O'Donovan J. in *Howard v University College Cork*.[305] It was argued in that case that the plaintiff would not be entitled to a permanent injunction as the defendant was a statutory body with statutory obligations, making it impermissible for the court to interfere with it. However, O'Donovan J., whilst acknowledging that he did not think it possible that at the trial of the action the plaintiff could be awarded the permanent injunction (and the declaration sought), had little doubt but that the trial judge would accede to an application to amend the statement of claim by qualifying the claim for the permanent injunction by the addition of the words "except in accordance with law".[306]

6–176 It is clear, however, that there is still some scope for argument in relation to public bodies, in so far as O'Higgins J. in *Garrahy* made reference to the fact that he was not going to apply a higher standard to public bodies "without fuller argument".[307] However, there is no immediately compelling general policy argument why a public body should be subject to a higher standard in that regard, particularly if the fact of being a public body can be considered as an element of the balance of convenience.

E. MANDATORY INTERLOCUTORY INJUNCTIONS

1. Introduction

6–177 A mandatory interlocutory injunction requires a party to do something or to undo the consequences of an allegedly wrongful act. The former is known as an enforcing mandatory injunction, the latter as a restorative mandatory injunction.[308] It is rare, though not impossible, to secure a mandatory injunction at the interlocutory stage. Such injunctions, by their nature, tend to affect the status quo to a much greater degree. They are also difficult to formulate precisely and, in many cases, to supervise.[309] That said, there is no reason in principle why an interlocutory mandatory injunction cannot be granted by a

---

[304] [2002] 3 I.R. 566 at 572.
[305] [2001] E.L.R. 8.
[306] See also, Ch.4, Equitable and General Principles, para.4–90.
[307] [2002] 3 I.R. 566 at 579.
[308] See Ch.5, Perpetual Injunctions, para.5–09.
[309] See Ch.4, Equitable and General Principles, para.4–61.

court, notwithstanding very early authority which suggests that it was in fact contrary to equitable principles to grant a mandatory injunction at the interlocutory stage.[310] The *Campus Oil* case was, in fact, an example of a mandatory injunction being granted on an interlocutory basis.

2. A Mandatory or Prohibitory Order

6–178 The dividing line between mandatory and prohibitory interlocutory injunctions is not always entirely clear. For example, in the case of *Garrahy v Bord na gCon*,[311] O'Higgins J. referred to the fact that the injunctions sought were not mandatory, as has been claimed, but were in fact prohibitory. This in turn affected the relevant considerations in terms of whether or not an injunction should be granted.

6–179 To the extent that a party may perceive that it is in some way "easier" to secure a prohibitory rather than mandatory injunction on an interlocutory basis, they should not attempt to seek what amounts to a mandatory injunction by careful phrasing in relation to the prohibitory injunction sought. This could be done, for example, by seeking a putative prohibitory injunction forbidding a party from not performing an act.[312]

6–180 That there is some analysis required of the form of injunction sought before determining how to approach the application is evident from the decision of Geoghegan J. in the Supreme Court in *Ó'Murchú t/a Talknology v Eircell Ltd*.[313] In that case Geoghegan J. applied the *Campus Oil* guidelines, but on the basis that, "although the injunctions sought in this case may arguably be classified as 'mandatory' they are not of that type." Conversely, in the case of *Glenkerrin Homes v Dun Laoghaire Rathdown County Council*,[314] Clarke J. had to deal with an order sought in negative terms, but which was, in his view, a "mandatory order involving a double negative." More recently, in the case of *Bergin v Galway Clinic Doughiska Ltd*,[315] Clarke J. held that an employment injunction is to all intents and purposes mandatory even though it may be expressed in a negative form.[316]

---

[310] See, for example, *Ryder v Bentham* (1750) 1 Ves. Sen. 543.
[311] [2002] 3 I.R. 566.
[312] *Jackson v Normanby* [1899] 1 Ch. 438.
[313] unreported, Supreme Court, February 21, 2001.
[314] unreported, High Court, Clarke J., December 6, 2006.
[315] unreported, High Court, Clarke J., November 2, 2007.
[316] See Ch.9, Employment, para.9–61.

3. An Exceptional Order

6–181 It is generally accepted that it is considerably harder to secure a mandatory injunction at the interlocutory stage than it is a prohibitive one. Megarry J. observed in *Shepherd Homes Ltd v Sandham*[317] that the courts are far more reluctant to grant a mandatory injunction on an interlocutory basis. He explained that:

> "In a normal case the court must, *inter alia*, feel a high degree of assurance that at the trial it will appear that the injunction was rightly granted; and this is a higher standard than is required for a prohibitory injunction."[318]

6–182 A similar view prevails in Ireland. O'Higgins C.J. made it clear in *Campus Oil* that mandatory relief does not usually issue prior to the trial of the action, but that there are exceptions to this.[319] Consistent with this, in *O'Dea v O'Briain*,[320] Murphy J. stated that: "To make a mandatory order at an interlocutory stage is possible but it is rare."[321] In *Riordan v Minister for the Environment (No.6)*,[322] Murphy J. stated that "the granting of a mandatory injunction on an interlocutory application is exceptional though not unknown."[323] In *Boyle v An Post*,[324] although Lardner J. granted a mandatory injunction on an interlocutory basis, he stated that it was "an exceptional case where one can say with assurance that at the hearing of the substantive action the plaintiffs are bound to succeed."[325]

6–183 The reason for the reticence of the courts to grant mandatory injunctions at the interlocutory stage is clear: it is much harder to undo the consequences of a mandatory order than a prohibitory order if at the trial of the action the courts find in favour of the party against whom the mandatory order was granted. An example of the "classic form of mandatory injunction which a court will rarely grant" is that provided by Geoghegan J. in *Ó'Murchú trading as Talknology v Eircell Ltd.*[326] Geoghegan J. observed that:

---

317 [1971] Ch. 340; [1970] 3 W.L.R. 348; [1970] 3 All E.R. 402.
318 [1971] Ch. 340 at 351; [1970] 3 W.L.R. 348 at 359; [1970] 3 All E.R. 402 at 412.
319 [1983] I.R. 88 at 107. As indeed was the case in *Campus Oil* itself. The courts' reluctance to grant mandatory injunctions at the interlocutory stage is long established: see for example, *Blakemore v The Glamorganshire Canal Navigation* (1832) 1 Myl. & K. 154.
320 [1992] I.L.R.M. 364.
321 [1992] I.L.R.M. 364 at 371. See also the comments of Kelly J. in *Judge v Diageo Ireland Ltd*, unreported, High Court, Kelly J., December 21, 2004 (in the context of an employment dispute) that a mandatory interlocutory injunction is "an exceptional form of relief". See also *Irish Oil and Cake Mills Ltd v Donnelly*, unreported, High Court, Costello J., March 27, 1983.
322 [2002] 4 I.R. 404.
323 [2002] 4 I.R. 404 at 407.
324 [1992] 2 I.R. 437.
325 [1992] 2 I.R. 437 at 442.
326 unreported, Supreme Court, February 21, 2001.

"Undoubtedly, if a plaintiff is looking for a mandatory injunction requiring a wall to be knocked down he may in fact be attempting to obtain at an interlocutory stage what effectively is his final relief. Once the wall is gone it may not be practicable to rebuild it."[327]

6–184 Similarly, in *O'Donoghue v Clare County Council*,[328] Keane C.J. refused the mandatory interlocutory relief sought as it "would be wholly inappropriate on an application for an interlocutory injunction such as this. It would effectively resolve the case in favour of the plaintiffs."

6–185 An example of the type of case in which a court feels itself able to grant a mandatory injunction at the interlocutory stage is that of *Capemel Ltd v Lister (No. 2)*.[329] In that case a mandatory injunction was granted compelling the defendant to pay money to the plaintiff company. The court was faced with the competing likelihoods that the plaintiff company would go into liquidation if not paid and that the defendant would not be able to retrieve the money if it succeeded on a related appeal. However, Costello J. referred to the situation as being "very unusual"[330] and further stated that in the normal course such an order would not be made.[331]

4. The Applicability of the *American Cyanamid/Campus Oil* Guidelines

(a) England: An Unusually Sharp and Clear Case

6–186 In the case of *Shepherd Homes Ltd v Sandham*,[332] Megarry J. held that a court would be more reluctant at the interlocutory stage to grant a mandatory rather than a prohibitory injunction and that the case has to be "unusually sharp and clear" before a mandatory injunction will be granted.[333] However, Megarry J. also referred to the fact that the "subject is not one in which it is possible to draw firm lines or impose any rigid classification".

6–187 The dictum of Megarry J. was approved in the case of *Locabail International Finance Ltd v Agroexport* by Mustill L.J. He observed that although the judgment of Megarry J. predated the decision in *American*

---

[327] Although in that case Geoghegan J. found that: "Although the injunctions sought in this case may arguably be classified as "mandatory" they are not of that type. They are directed simply towards retaining the *status quo* pending the outcome of the action, which is the normal purpose of a prohibitive injunction."

[328] unreported, Supreme Court, November 6, 2003.

[329] [1989] I.R. 323.

[330] [1989] I.R. 323 at 324.

[331] [1989] I.R. 323 at 326.

[332] [1971] Ch. 340; [1970] 3 W.L.R. 348; [1970] 3 All E.R. 402. See also, *De Falco v Crawley Borough Council* [1980] Q.B. 460 at 481; [1980] 2 W.L.R. 664 at 676, per Bridge L.J.

[333] [1971] Ch. 340 at 349; [1970] 3 W.L.R. 348 at 359; [1970] 3 All E.R. 402 at 412. See also, *Bula Ltd v Tara Ltd* [1988] I.L.R.M. 149.

Cyanamid, "the statement of principle by Megarry J. in relation to the very special case of the mandatory injunction is not affected by what the House of Lords said in the *Cyanamid* case."[334] In so holding, Mustill L.J. also set out the test to be applied in relation to mandatory injunctions, citing a passage from *Halsbury's Laws of England*[335]:

> "A mandatory injunction can be granted on an interlocutory application as well as at the hearing, but, in the absence of special circumstances, it will not be granted on motion. If, however, the case is clear and one which the court thinks ought to be decided at once … a mandatory injunction will be granted on an interlocutory application."[336]

6–188 The current position in England is well set out in the English Court of Appeal decision in *Zockoll Group Ltd v Mercury Communications*[337]:

> "… the overriding consideration is which course is likely to involve the least risk of injustice if it turns out to be 'wrong' in the sense described by Hoffmann J. in [*Films Rover International and others v Cannon Film Cells Ltd* [1986] 3 All E.R. 772].
>
> Secondly, in considering whether to grant a mandatory injunction, the court must keep in mind that an order which requires a party to take some positive step at an interlocutory stage, may well carry a greater risk of injustice if it turns out to have been wrongly made than an order which merely prohibits action, thereby preserving the status quo.
>
> Thirdly, it is legitimate, where a mandatory injunction is sought, to consider whether the court does feel a high degree of assurance that the plaintiff will be able to establish his right at a trial. That is because the greater the degree of assurance the plaintiff will ultimately establish his right, the less will be the risk of injustice if the injunction is granted.
>
> But, finally, even where the court is unable to feel any high degree of assurance that the plaintiff will establish his right, there may still be circumstances in which it is appropriate to grant a mandatory injunction at an interlocutory stage. Those circumstances will exist where the risk of injustice if this injunction is refused sufficiently outweigh the risk of injustice if it is granted."[338]

---

334 [1986] 1 W.L.R. 657 at 664.
335 [1984] 1 I.R. 200 at 217; [1984] I.L.R.M. 595 at 600; Halsbury, 3rd edn, Vol.21, p.369.
336 Also referred to by Lardner J. in *Boyle v An Post* [1992] 2 I.R. 437.
337 [1998] F.S.R. 354 (which in turn accepted the approach put forward by Chadwick J. in *Nottingham Building Society v Eurodyamics Systems* [1993] F.S.R. 468 at 474).
338 Adopted in, inter alia, *Getmapping Plc v Ordnance Survey* [2003] I.C.R. 1 at 9.

(b) Ireland

6–189 In theory, the position in Ireland should be straightforward. The guidelines set out in *Campus Oil* were set out in the context of an application for a mandatory interlocutory injunction. That being so, it would seem that the courts need go no further than the *Campus Oil* test. However, there are mixed dicta from the courts in this jurisdiction in relation to what test to employ.

(i) The *Campus Oil* Guidelines

6–190 The *American Cyanamid*/*Campus Oil* guidelines have been applied in a number of cases involving applications for mandatory interlocutory injunctions. For example, in the case of *A&N Pharmacy Ltd v United Drug Wholesale Ltd*,[339] Carroll J. approached the application for a mandatory injunction at the interlocutory stage on the basis of the *American Cyanamid*/*Campus Oil* guidelines, considering whether there was a serious issue to be tried, the adequacy of damages and the balance of convenience.[340] Peart J. also adopted the same approach in the case of *Sheehy v Ryan*,[341] although he did refer to the fact that a court is in general "reluctant, save in truly exceptional circumstances, to grant mandatory interlocutory relief".[342]

6–191 In *Cronin v Minister for Education*,[343] Laffoy J. was quite explicit in rejecting the submission by counsel for the first defendant that, "as the Plaintiff is seeking mandatory relief at an interlocutory stage, the criterion which the Court should apply is whether the Plaintiff is likely to succeed at the trial." She stated that she did not consider that that was

> "the appropriate criterion to apply at this interlocutory stage. It involves making a judgement at this juncture as to the strength of the respective cases of the Plaintiff and the First Defendant, which the court is not entitled to do, as was made clear by the Supreme Court in *Westman Holdings v McCormack* …"[344]

Laffoy J. proceeded to consider the criteria in *Campus Oil* and to apply them to the case before her.

6–192 However, there are other cases to the effect that a "strong, clear case"— as distinct from a fair, bona fide question to be tried—must be shown in order to secure a mandatory interlocutory injunction.

---

[339] [1996] 2 I.L.R.M. 46.

[340] See also, *Premier International Trading House Ltd v Seamar Ltd*, unreported, High Court, Budd J., May 8, 1997.

[341] unreported, High Court, Peart J., August 29, 2002.

[342] In that regard, reference was made to the decision of Costello P. in *Fennelly v Assicurazioni Generali*, unreported, High Court, Costello P., March 12, 1985; *cf. Hennessy v St Gerard's School Trust* [2004] 15 E.L.R. 230.

[343] [2004] 3 I.R. 205.

[344] [2004] 3 I.R. 205 at 213.

(ii) A Strong, Clear Case

6–193 In *Irish Shell Ltd v Elm Motors*,[345] Costello J. confirmed that a court has jurisdiction to grant a mandatory injunction on an interlocutory application. He quoted from the same passage in *Halsbury's Laws of England* that Mustill L.J. had quoted from in *Locabail*, set out above.[346] Costello J. reiterated that the principles on which the court exercises this jurisdiction are different to those applicable in relation to prohibitory injunctions on an interlocutory application.

6–194 In the case of *Boyhan v Tribunal of Inquiry into the Beef Industry*,[347] Denham J. in the High Court, in describing a mandatory injunction as a "powerful instrument", also held that:

> "in seeking this exceptional form of relief, a mandatory injunction, it is up to the plaintiffs to establish a strong and clear case—so that the court can feel a degree of assurance that at a trial of the action a similar injunction would be granted."[348]

6–195 The *Boyhan* approach was echoed by the Supreme Court in the case of *Maha Lingam v Health Service Executive*.[349] In that case, Fennelly J. held that:

> "the implication of an application of the present sort is that in substance what the plaintiff/appellant is seeking is a mandatory interlocutory injunction and it is well established that the ordinary test of a fair case to be tried is not sufficient to meet the first leg of the test for the grant of an interlocutory injunction where the injunction sought is in effect mandatory. In such a case it is necessary for the applicant to show at least that he has a strong case that he is likely to succeed at the hearing of the action. So it is not sufficient for him to simply show a *prima facie* case, and in particular the courts have been slow to grant interlocutory injunctions to enforce contracts of employment."[350]

6–196 Both *Boyhan* and *Maha Lingam* are clear in suggesting that in order to succeed in an application for a mandatory injunction at the interlocutory stage, the party seeking the injunction must show a strong, clear case. This clearly displaces the bona fide/fair/serious question to be tried test in *Campus Oil*.

6–197 The consequences of granting such a mandatory interlocutory injunction means that the *Maha Lingam* approach, as used by the courts in England, is on balance a preferable one. However, even if the full *American Cyanamid/ Campus Oil* guidelines are applied, a consideration of the balance of convenience will lead by default to a greater degree of scrutiny of the effect of granting a mandatory interlocutory injunction.

---

[345] [1984] 1 I.R. 200; [1984] I.L.R.M. 595.
[346] See para.6–187.
[347] [1993] 1 I.R. 210; [1992] I.L.R.M. 545.
[348] [1993] 1 I.R. 210 at 223; [1992] I.L.R.M. 545 at 556.
[349] [2006] 17 E.L.R. 137.
[350] [2006] 17 E.L.R. 137 at 140.

5. Summary

6–198 In summary, it is generally the case that a mandatory injunction is harder to obtain at the interlocutory stage than a prohibitory injunction. As to the test to be applied in considering whether to grant a mandatory injunction, there are mixed dicta from the courts in this jurisdiction, and it is far from certain whether the full *Campus Oil* guidelines apply, or whether a party must show a strong, clear case. In that regard, the judgment of Hoffman J. in *Films Rover International Ltd v Cannon Film Sales Ltd*[351] is apposite, in so far as he took the view that the fundamental principle on interlocutory applications for both prohibitory and mandatory injunctions is that the court should take whatever course would carry the lower risk of injustice if it turns out to have been the "wrong" decision.[352] From a practical perspective, regardless of which test the courts apply, the fact that a mandatory injunction is being sought will inevitably be a factor in the balance of convenience.[353] However, it is arguable that a point is now being arrived at where a comprehensive restatement or fresh formulation of the *Campus Oil* principles by the courts would be of considerable benefit and guidance.

F. *QUIA TIMET* INTERLOCUTORY INJUNCTIONS

1. Applicable Test

6–199 The case of *Szabo v Esat Digifone Ltd*,[354] has already been considered in the context of the relevant test for granting a perpetual *quia timet* injunction.[355] The background facts were, in brief, that the plaintiff schoolchildren sought a

---

[351] [1987] 1 W.L.R. 670; [1986]3 All E.R. 772.

[352] [1987] 1 W.L.R. 670 at 680; [1986] 3 All E.R. 772 at 781.

[353] In *Thomas Crosbie Holdings v Webprint Concepts Ltd*, unreported, High Court, Hedigan J., January 9, 2008, Hedigan J. endorsed the summary of the approach of the courts in this regard by Delany, *Equity and the Law of Trusts in Ireland*, 3rd edn (Dublin: Thomson Round Hall, 2003), p.497 (the passage is at p.548 of the 4th edn, 2007): "On balance it would appear that in recent decisions the Courts have tended to favour the application of the traditional *Campus Oil* principles even in the context of mandatory relief and there has been some support for the proposition laid down by Murphy J in *Bula Limited v Tara Mines Limited (No. 2)*, [1987] I.R. 95, that the granting or withholding of a mandatory interlocutory injunction should not be dependent on the strength of the Applicant's case (see *De Burca v. Wicklow County Council*, High Court [2000] No. 42 Judicial Review, Ó Caoimh J., May 24, 2000). However, it is also fair to say that it is unlikely that the balance of convenience will lie in favour of granting mandatory relief save in fairly exceptional cases and to this extent it is still accurate to assert that the Courts are more reluctant to grant an interlocutory injunction where it is of a mandatory nature."

[354] [1998] 2 I.L.R.M. 102. See also, *Garrahy v Bord na gCon* [2002] 3 I.R. 566 at 580 and *Futac Services Ltd v Dublin City Council*, unreported, High Court, Smyth J., June 24, 2003, both of which approved the dicta of Geoghegan J. in *Szabo*.

[355] See Ch.5, Perpetual Injunctions, para.5–16.

number of perpetual injunctions (as well as interlocutory injunctions of a similar nature) to stop the intended development and operations of a mobile phone base station in the grounds of a garda station next to their school. The plaintiffs claimed that the operation of such a base station and mast would be dangerous to their health.

6–200 Having dealt first with the test for a perpetual *quia timet* injunction, Geoghegan J. then turned his attention to the correct principles to be applied in relation to applications for interlocutory *quia timet* injunctions. Geoghegan J. adopted and accepted the principles set out in *Spry on Equitable Remedies*.[356] It was made clear in that work that there is no difference in the legal principles to be applied to interlocutory *quia timet* injunctions and any other kind of interlocutory injunction. Geoghegan J. summarised the position in Spry by stating that:

> "The author makes clear that there is no difference in the legal principles to be applied to a *quia timet* injunction as to any other injunction and that *ipso facto* there is no difference between the principles to be applied to an interlocutory *quia timet* injunction than to the granting of any other kind of interlocutory injunction."[357]

6–201 That said, in *Szabo,* Geoghegan J. specifically doubted the appropriateness of the *American Cyanamid/Campus Oil* guidelines, given that he found it somewhat distasteful to engage in a balancing exercise between carrying on business and health. Geoghegan J. preferred to approach the case other than by the application of what he referred to as "standard guidelines". However, he did undertake a parallel exercise to confirm he would have reached the same conclusion had he applied the guidelines.[358] Having regard to the requirement of a probability that the apprehended danger would ensue before a *quia timet* injunction would be granted on a permanent basis, Geoghegan J. was "very doubtful" that there was a serious issue to be tried. He felt that even if there was, the balance of convenience required that the court should refuse any temporary injunction pending the hearing of the case.

6–202 The effective non-application of the *American Cyanamid/Campus Oil* guidelines in *Szabo* is perhaps understandable on the facts, given that Geoghegan J. found it distasteful to weigh peoples' health in the balance.

---

[356] *Spry on Equitable Remedies*, 4th edn, p.459. See now Spry, *The Principles of Equitable Remedies*, 6th edn (London: Sweet and Maxwell, 2001), pp.468–470.

[357] [1998] 2 I.L.R.M. 102 at 111.

[358] See also the decision of Clarke J. in *Collen Construction Ltd v BATU*, unreported, High Court, Clarke J., May 16, 2006, in which on the facts Clarke J. rejected the test of a "fair issue to be tried" in the circumstances before him, which concerned industrial agitation which had subsequently abated.

However, at a more general level, it is worth noting that the *American Cyanamid* case itself involved an application for a *quia timet* injunction, to restrain the threatened infringement of the plaintiff's patent, and that it was within that context that the various guidelines and principles were set out.

G. Applying for an Interlocutory Injunction

1. Introduction

6–203 It is crucial to remember that an interlocutory injunction is generally sought due to some measure of urgency which demands that a court needs to intervene prior to the substantive hearing of an action.[359] As has been seen in cases such as *Lennon v Ganley*,[360] delay in applying for such an injunction may be fatal to such an application. Delay was also critical in the case of *Futac Services Ltd v Dublin City Council*[361] in which Smyth J. held that the plaintiff had "in effect, awaited events as they unfolded and did not move with reasonable expedition".

6–204 That being so, an application for an injunction on an interlocutory basis needs to be made promptly once an identified wrong has been committed or is apprehended.[362] If there is no such urgency evident, this will mitigate against the court acceding to such an application. It is also important to remember that simply because an application for an interlocutory injunction is rejected, this does not automatically lead to the substantive action failing. As has been seen, however,[363] the reality is that the determination of the interlocutory application in many cases brings a degree of finality to the matter, particularly when an interlocutory injunction is in fact granted.

6–205 A number of considerations should be borne in mind before seeking an injunction on an interlocutory basis; although an application for an interlocutory injunction may get the parties to court quickly, it is more the exception than the norm for such applications to be concluded in a limited period of time. On the first return date, an adjournment will generally be sought in order to file any

---

[359] Depending on the value of the claim concerned and the degree of urgency, an alternative and/or additional aspect to seeking an interlocutory injunction is to seek to have a matter entered into the Commercial Court which operates a case management procedure such that matters generally come on for full determination much more quickly than would otherwise be the case. See Ch.1, Domestic Jurisdiction, para.1–69. See generally Dowling, *The Commercial Court* (Dublin: Thomson Round Hall, 2007).

[360] [1981] I.L.R.M. 84. See Ch.4, Equitable and General Principles.

[361] unreported, High Court, Smyth J., June 24, 2003.

[362] See *Nolan Transport (Oaklands Ltd) v Halligan*, unreported, High Court, Keane J., March 22, 1994.

[363] See para.6–13.

replying affidavits as necessary. However, it is often possible to secure a quid pro quo for agreement to such an adjournment, namely extracting an under- taking that the wrong complained of will not be continued or repeated pending the hearing of the interlocutory application. As such, there is considerable tactical merit in bringing an application for an interlocutory injunction.

6–206 In addition, an application for an interlocutory injunction can crystallise matters in the respective parties' minds; in the best case scenario, the initiation of interlocutory proceedings may even lead to a resolution of the substantive proceedings themselves. Even the threat of bringing an application for an injunction on an interlocutory basis may lead to a resolution of the dispute at hand, or at a minimum some form of satisfactory compromise.

2. Documentation

(a) Originating Document

6–207 Prior to an application for an interlocutory injunction being brought, proceedings must be in being. In the normal course, a plenary summons or originating motion will be drafted so that it seeks the relevant injunctions, damages, further or other orders which to the court shall seem fit, and costs, with a motion for an interlocutory injunction being issued immediately afterwards. In the Circuit Court, it is necessary to proceed by way of an equity civil bill, injunctive relief being equitable in nature.[364]

6–208 As a claim for interlocutory relief in the High Court is brought by way of notice of motion and grounding affidavit, it is not necessary to claim interlocutory (and interim) relief in the statement of claim or civil bill, but simply the substantive relief.[365]

(b) Notice of Motion

6–209 An application for an interlocutory injunction is brought by way of notice of motion, grounded on an affidavit. Order 52 r.1 of the Rules of the Superior Courts (RSC) provides that:

> "All interlocutory applications to Court and all applications authorised by these Rules to be made to the Court shall be made by motion, save as otherwise provided by these Rules."[366]

[364] See RCC Ord.5 r.1, Commencement of Proceedings. See also RCC Ord.46.
[365] See the dictum of Finlay C.J. in *Caudron v Air Zaire* [1985] I.R. 716 at 721; [1986] I.L.R.M. 10 at 21.
[366] If a defendant does not attend court having been properly served with a notice of motion, the court can proceed and, as necessary, make an order on the basis of there being an affidavit of service in court: *Davidson v Leslie* (1845) 9 Beav. 104.

6–210 Rules of the Superior Courts Ord.52 r.6 sets out the usual periods of notice, and provides that unless special leave is given by the Court to the contrary, there must be:

> "two clear days between the service of the notice of motion and the day named in the notice for hearing the motion; provided that, where the notice of motion requires to be served personally out of Court, it shall be served not less than four clear days before the hearing of the application."[367]

(i) Short Service

6–211 In some urgent circumstances, it may be necessary to seek short service, namely an abridgement of the two-/four-day requirement. This will generally be sought before an appearance is entered. By virtue of RSC Ord.52 r.10, a notice of motion can be served upon a defendant who has been served with an originating summons, but who "has not appeared within the time limited for that purpose". Short service is provided for by RSC Ord.52 r.11, which states that:

> "The plaintiff may, by leave of the Court to be obtained *ex parte*, serve any notice of motion upon any defendant along with the originating summons, or at any time after service of the originating summons and before the time limited for the appearance of such defendant."

6–212 An application for short service will generally be brought under two provisions: RSC Ord.52 r.6, as set out above, but also under RSC Ord.122 r.7,[368] which provides that:

> "The Court shall have power to enlarge or abridge the time appointed by these Rules, or fixed by any order enlarging time, for doing any act or taking any proceeding, upon such terms (if any) as the Court may direct, and any such enlargement may be ordered although the application for the same is not made until after the expiration of the time appointed or allowed."

6–213 An application for short service is made to a judge designated as a Chancery judge (as set out in the legal diary for any given day during term). There is no formal rule which prescribes what documents must be brought to court when seeking short service. The normal practice is to bring to court:

- a draft notice of motion for interlocutory relief; this is usually entitled "Notice of Motion for the Sitting of the Court", with spaces left for the

---

[367] By virtue of RSC Ord.122 r.2, Saturday, Sunday, Christmas Day and Good Friday are excluded in calculating "clear days".

[368] See RCC Ord.67 r.6.

insertion of the relevant return dates by the court registrar if short service is granted by the court;

- a copy of the affidavit grounding the application for interlocutory relief.

6–214 It is not necessary to prepare a separate ex parte notice and grounding affidavit in relation to the short service itself.

6–215 In general, it is sufficient to explain to the judge hearing the application for short service the nature of the urgency such that short service is required. It may be appropriate as necessary to point to the relevant paragraphs of the affidavit grounding the application for interlocutory relief which demonstrate such urgency. However, this happens relatively infrequently in practice.

(c) Grounding Affidavit

6–216 The application for interlocutory relief must be grounded on an affidavit, sworn by a person with the appropriate means of knowledge. This will generally be the party seeking the injunction, or a director of a plaintiff company. In extremis, and if that person is not available, in theory a party's solicitors can swear such an affidavit. A concern in that regard is that if a solicitor swears the grounding affidavit, this brings with it the risk that the solicitor might be cross-examined by the defendant/respondent in relation to matters which might otherwise be privileged.

(i) Hearsay

6–217 Although affidavits should not normally contain hearsay,[369] RSC Ord.40 r.4 provides that on interlocutory motions, statements as to a witness's belief, with the grounds thereof, may be admitted. As pointed out by Geoghegan J. in *McKenna v AF*[370]:

> "hearsay evidence can only be admitted in an interlocutory application within the traditional meaning of that expression and the name of the informant must be given."

6–218 However, as observed by Clarke J. in *Collen Construction Ltd v BATU*,[371] whilst it was permissible to include hearsay evidence in affidavits sworn for interlocutory applications, no reliance should ordinarily be placed on hearsay attributed to unnamed persons, as such evidence "could not … be regarded as meaningful evidence in any proper sense of the term."

---

[369]   See RSC Ord.40 r.4.
[370]   [2002] 1 I.R. 242; [2002] 2 I.L.R.M. 303.
[371]   unreported, High Court, Clarke J., May 15, 2006.

(ii) Content

6–219 The affidavit must set out the facts giving rise to the action as well as the facts giving rise to the motion for injunctive relief in as comprehensive a manner as possible. It should also exhibit any correspondence in relation to the matter which forms the basis of the application for the injunction, including any replies received. It is important to state in the affidavit that the matter complained of will continue or will not occur as appropriate if an injunction is not granted.

6–220 When drafting an affidavit, it is important to bear in mind the relevant applicable principles, particularly those set out in *Campus Oil*. In that regard a common, effective, way of address these principles in the body of the affidavit is to deal with each under separate sub-headings. Evidence will have to be provided to show that there is a "fair/serious/bona fide question" to be tried. As has been seen, there is a lack of consistency in the courts concerning the applicability or otherwise of the *Campus Oil* guidelines in the context of mandatory injunctions and, as such, the better course is to set out the basis of a "strong and clear case", as referred to by Fennelly J. in *Maha Lingam v Health Service Executive*.[372]

6–221 The moving party should also outline why they believe that damages would not be an adequate remedy for them in the event that they were not to be awarded the interlocutory injunction. Clearly, if they are in a position to show that the defendant would not be able to meet an award of damages, this should be averred to, together with any substantiating information in that regard.[373]

6–222 Even if the evidence in relation to the adequacy of damages is strong, it is clearly prudent to proceed to the issue of the balance of convenience.

(iii) Duty Not to Mislead the Court

6–223 Whereas at the interim stage, there is an obligation to make full and frank disclosure on an ex parte application,[374] at the inter partes interlocutory stage, there is a duty on the applicant not to knowingly mislead the court.[375]

(d) Resisting an Application for an Interlocutory Injunction

6–224 Once an application for an injunction on an interlocutory basis has been served, the responding party (generally the defendant) will usually seek time on

---

[372] [2006] 17 E.L.R. 137 at 140.
[373] See *Westman Holdings Ltd v McCormack* [1992] 1 I.R. 151 at 158.
[374] See Ch.7, Interim Applications, para.7–66.
[375] See Gee, *Commercial Injunctions*, 5th edn (London: Thomson Sweet & Maxwell, 2004), p.247.

the return date of the motion to file a replying affidavit in which they will
outline their position and address the matters raised in the affidavit grounding
the motion. A court will usually allow time to do so on foot of an undertaking
that a given action will not take place in the intervening period, or that certain
actions will be undertaken. Without such an undertaking, the defendant could
clearly use the time available in such an intervening period to do something to
affect the status quo.

6–225 The defendant will usually proceed by dealing with the individual issues
raised, but would similarly be advised to deal with all the *Campus Oil* principles
even if these have not been, or have not fully been, addressed in the grounding
affidavit. In that regard, the question of the adequacy of damages will often
form a central plank of the respondent's affidavit.

H. The Hearing of the Application and Related Matters

6–226 It has been stressed that, "interlocutory proceedings are there to hold the
ring pending the final determination of the case."[376] This was elaborated upon
by Sir John Donaldson M.R. in the Court of Appeal in *Attorney General v
Newspaper Publishing Plc.*[377] The Master of the Rolls stated that in the waiting
period before the final resolution of the dispute, the court:

> "must give each side the benefit of any doubts, it must assume that either
> party may win and it must seek to preserve the rights of both parties. In other
> words, it must undertake a damage limitation exercise for the benefit of
> whomsoever it may ultimately concern."[378]

6–227 However, it is also generally accepted that the determination of
interlocutory proceedings can often decide the fate of the main action.[379]

1. Judge Hearing the Application

6–228 In *O'Callaghan v Disciplinary Tribunal*,[380] McCracken J. pointed out that
there is no rule in the High Court that a judge who grants an interim injunction may
not hear the later interlocutory injunction application. As explained by Geoghegan
J. on appeal to the Supreme Court, the rationale for this is that the:

---

[376] per O'Flaherty J. in *Premier Dairies v Doyle* [1996] 1 I.R. 37 at 54; [1996] 1 I.L.R.M. 363
at 369.
[377] [1988] Ch. 333; [1987] 3 All E.R. 276
[378] [1988] Ch. 333 at 358.
[379] per O'Flaherty J. in *Premier Dairies v Doyle* [1996] 1 I.R. 37 at 54; [1996] 1 I.L.R.M. 363
at 369.
[380] [2002] 1 I.L.R.M. 89.

"nature of the decision to be made the second time round is quite different from the nature of the decision made on the first occasion."[381]

2. Hearing *In Camera*

6–229 In certain circumstances, an application for an injunction can be made *in camera*. Section 45(1) of the Courts (Supplemental Provisions) Act 1961 identifies four areas in which there may be a restriction on reporting and public attendance, namely urgent applications for habeas corpus, bail, prohibition or injunctions; matrimonial causes or matters; lunacy and minor matters; and proceedings involving the disclosure of a secret manufacturing process. However, the matter is ultimately at the discretion of the court. It is rare that an application for an interlocutory injunction will be made *in camera*; the provisions of the 1961 Act are more applicable where injunctions are sought on an interim basis.[382] This is evident from the decision of Hamilton P. in *Z v DPP*.[383] The President, dealing with an application to have a matter dealt with *in camera*, held that the:

> "applications of 'an urgent nature' for relief by way of habeas corpus, bail, prohibition or injunction, to which s 45(1) of the Courts (Supplemental Provisions) Act 1961 relates, are those which are because of their nature so urgent that they must be made to a judge in his home or some place to which the public do not directly have access and not to applications which are made in court."[384]

3. Referral to the European Court of Justice

6–230 The extent to which a referral to the European Court of Justice (ECJ) has the effect of postponing the granting of an injunction was considered in the case of *SPUC v Grogan*.[385] In that case Carroll J., having heard submissions on the application for an injunction, decided to refer certain questions to the ECJ for a preliminary ruling. However, she made no express order refusing or adjourning the application for an interlocutory injunction. She stated that she needed an opinion from the ECJ in order to reach a decision as to whether an injunction should be granted. The appeal to the Supreme Court was allowed on the basis that where in proceedings for an interlocutory injunction a court decided to make a reference to the ECJ, this did not automatically have the effect of

---

[381] [2002] 1 I.L.R.M. 89 at 94.
[382] See Ch.7, Interim Applications.
[383] [1994] 2 I.L.R.M. 481.
[384] [1994] 2 I.L.R.M. 481 at 488.
[385] [1990] I.L.R.M. 350.

postponing a decision on the application for an interlocutory injunction. Finlay C.J. specifically stated that it was clear, based on the *Campus Oil* guidelines, that it was open to Carroll J. to grant an interlocutory injunction at the same time as she decided to refer questions of law for the determination of the ECJ. This is also consistent with the statement by Hardiman J. in *Dunne v Dun Laoghaire Rathdown Co Council*[386] that a court must be alive to the fact that a court may determine a matter by inaction.

6–231 The Chief Justice further held in the *SPUC* case that in considering an appeal on the issue of whether an interlocutory injunction should be granted or not, the making of the reference to the European Court remained unaltered, the only matter for review being the question of the granting of an interlocutory injunction.

4. Form of the Injunction Order

6–232 An injunction generally takes effect upon its pronouncement.[387] Judges will often discuss the appropriate form of an injunction with counsel once they have determined that an injunction should be granted. However, in drafting both the motion seeking interlocutory relief (and indeed the originating writ), parties should be alive to the need for a judge to make an enforceable order, which covers all matters as appropriate. The order should thus be clear in its terms.[388] The importance of this is evident from the observations of Lord Nicholls in *Attorney General v Punch Ltd*,[389] in which he said that:

> "Here arises the practical difficulty of devising a suitable form of words. An interlocutory injunction, like any other injunction, must be expressed in terms which are clear and certain. The injunction must define precisely what acts are prohibited. The court must ensure that the language of its order makes plain what is permitted and what is prohibited. This is a well established, soundly based principle. A person should not be put at risk of being in contempt of court by any ambiguous prohibition, or a prohibition the scope of which is obviously open to dispute."[390]

6–233 In the normal course the order is addressed to a party to the proceedings, generally the defendant. However, there is nothing to prevent an injunction being sought and granted against a plaintiff on a counterclaim, as indeed was the basis for the injunction sought in *Campus Oil*.

---

[386] [2003] 1 I.R. 567 at 581.
[387] *Z Ltd v A-Z* [1982] Q.B. 558; [1982] 2 W.L.R. 288; [1982] 1 All E.R. 556.
[388] See *Iberian Trust Ltd v Founders' Trust and Investments Company Ltd* [1932] 2 K.B. 87. See also *Redland Bricks Ltd v Morris* [1970] A.C. 652; [1969] 2 W.L.R. 1437; [1969] 2 All E.R. 576 and *Hackett v Baiss* (1875) L.R. 20 Eq. 494 at 499.
[389] [2003] 1 A.C. 1046; [2003] 2 W.L.R. 49; [2003] 1 All E.R. 289.
[390] [2003] 1 A.C. 1046 at 1055. [2003] 2 W.L.R. 49 at 57; [2003] 1 All E.R. 289 at 297.

6–234 The usual formula of wording of the injunction order used encompasses a phrase enjoining "the defendant, his servants or agents". In certain circumstances, and for the sake of clarity, this phrase may also include a variant on the wording "any person acting in concert with the Defendant, and any person having notice of the making of the order". This is often used in cases involving the media, in order to ensure that those who have such notice do not attempt to evade the sanction of the courts in cases where they are alleged to have breached an injunction order.

6–235 The injunction order will usually be expressed in such terms that it continues until the trial of the action or until further order made by the court.[391] As has been seen, a court will not make an interlocutory order where it has no means of supervising and enforcing of the order.[392]

6–236 Once the injunction has been granted, it remains in force until such time as it is discharged, even if it ought not to have been made.[393]

(a) Liberty to Apply

6–237 An injunction order will usually provide that the parties have liberty to apply. The purpose and meaning of this phrase was considered in *Donegal County Council v Ballantine*.[394] In that case, McCracken J. set out the principles stated in *Halsbury's Laws of England*[395] as to the meaning of "liberty to apply" before stating that:

> "Probably the most frequent use of the phrase 'liberty to apply' is in the case where either declarations are made or injunctions are granted. In such circumstances it is always possible that events may occur which would raise the question of whether there has or has not been a breach of the Order, or whether some event does or does not come within the declaration granted. Liberty to apply allows the parties to come back into Court and clarify the extent or application of the Order."

6–238 McCracken J. also made the important observation in relation to injunctions that:

> "if there is a breach of that injunction, the proper procedure is not to reapply to the Court for a further injunction, but to bring proceedings for contempt or attachment".

---

[391] See *Hadkinson v Hadkinson* [1952] P. 285 at 288, per Romer L.J.
[392] See Ch.4, Equitable and General Principles, para.4–56.
[393] *Isaacs v Robertson* [1985] A.C. 97; [1984] 3 W.L.R. 705; [1984] 3 All E.R. 140.
[394] unreported, High Court, McCracken J., March 20, 1998.
[395] *Halsbury's Laws of England*, 4th edn, Vol. 26, para.554.

5. Renewal of an Application

6–239 An application for an interlocutory injunction may be renewed depending on whether there is a change to the factual scenario. In *Paramount Pictures Corp. v Cablelink Ltd*,[396] the plaintiffs were refused an interlocutory injunction based on a claim that the defendant breached the copyright in films by transmitting them on a cable TV system without paying the plaintiffs the appropriate royalties. The plaintiffs subsequently renewed their application for an interlocutory injunction on the basis that the defendant was now planning to transmit material through a multi-point microwave distribution system (MMDS) in addition to the cable system.

6–240 In declining to alter the previous order made, Murphy J. proceeded on the basis that the question as to whether the proposed use of the MMDS system raised new issues in the renewed application should be judged against the background of the general principles applicable in interlocutory applications.

6. Undertakings

6–241 There are, broadly speaking, three categories of undertakings which may or should be given to the court, each of which will be considered in turn. The first is the undertaking as to damages given by the plaintiff. The second is an undertaking given in lieu of an order being made by the court. The third category is a broad catchall category, by virtue of which an undertaking may be required based on the facts before the court.

(a) Undertaking as to Damages

6–242 As has been seen,[397] a party seeking and granted an injunction must generally give an undertaking as to damages. A body corporate can also give an undertaking as to damages.[398] In the normal course, it is sufficient for counsel to inform that court that the plaintiff is prepared to give "the usual (or ordinary) undertaking as to damages".

6–243 It was argued in *Harding v Cork County Council*[399] that the undertaking as to damages had to be given in the applicant's affidavit. Kelly J. rejected this argument, stating that "That is not the normal practice in this court." He found that the fact that the undertaking had been given by counsel, given "in the proper way" in open court was not such that it rendered the undertaking "either

---

[396] unreported, High Court, Murphy J., March 8, 1990.
[397] See para.6–76.
[398] *East Molesey Local Board v Lambeth Waterworks Co* [1892] 3 Ch. 289 at 300, per Kekewich J.
[399] unreported, High Court, Kelly J., February 28, 2006.

useless or worthless". Notwithstanding this, it is invariably the practice to see a paragraph in the affidavit grounding an interlocutory application stating that the plaintiff has been advised as to the meaning of the phrase "undertaking as to damages" and stating that the plaintiff is prepared to give "an undertaking as to damages" or "the usual undertaking as to damages".

6–244 The usual undertaking in full is:

> "to abide by any order which this court may make as to damages in case this court shall be of the opinion that the respondent shall have suffered any by reason of this order which the applicant ought to pay."[400]

6–245 A court cannot compel an undertaking as to damages to be given. However, if no undertaking is given, the court can refuse to grant an inter-locutory injunction, even if it would otherwise have done so.[401] Where an undertaking is not expressly given, it cannot be implied.[402] Furthermore, a court will not put a limit on the amount of damages which may be required to be paid due to the "far-reaching implications" of such a limit being imposed.[403]

6–246 As has been seen,[404] a court must also be satisfied that the plaintiff would be able to honour such an undertaking.

(i) Inquiry as to Damages

6–247 If the undertaking must subsequently be honoured, the court will assess the appropriate damages at an inquiry as to damages, which is considered in greater detail in Ch.5, Perpetual Injunctions.[405]

(b) Undertaking in Lieu of an Injunction

6–248 It is often the case that rather than granting an injunction, the court will accept an undertaking from a defendant not to perform (or indeed to perform) certain acts. This has the same binding effect as an injunction.[406] The breach of such an undertaking can similarly lead to proceedings for contempt for breach

---

[400] per Peter Gibson L.J. in *Cheltenham and Gloucester Building Society v Ricketts* [1993] 1 W.L.R. 1545 at 1554; [1993] 4 All E.R. 276 at 285.
[401] *Tucker v New Brunswick Trading Co of London* (1890) 44 Ch D 249 at 252, per Cotton L.J. See also *F Hoffmann-La Roche & Co AG v Secretary of State for Trade and Industry* [1975] A.C. 295 at 361; [1974] 3 W.L.R. 104 at 126; [1974] 2 All E.R. 1128 at 1149, per Lord Diplock.
[402] *Howard v Press Printers* (1904) 74 L.J. Ch. 100
[403] per O'Flaherty J. in *O'Mahony v Horgan* [1995] 2 I.R. 411 at 422. Although see para.6–105.
[404] See para.6–81.
[405] See para.5–83.
[406] *Neath Canal Co v Ynisarwed Resolven Colliery Co* (1875) 10 Ch. App. 450.

of the undertaking.[407] As stated by Brightman J. in *Biba Ltd v Stratford Investments Ltd*[408]:

> "I think it would be a pity to disturb that practice by giving a lesser quality to an undertaking than to an injunction."[409]

(c) Other Undertakings

6–249 Based on the wording of RSC Ord.50 r.6(2), the court "may be made either unconditionally or upon such terms and conditions as the Court thinks just". In other words, the court may require any undertaking which it sees fit, and may also grant relief on other terms and conditions. For example, in *Crotty v An Taoiseach*[410] an injunction was granted by Barrington J. to the plaintiff on the basis of an undertaking as to damages but also on the basis of an undertaking that the hearing of the matter would be expedited.

6–250 The discretion afforded the courts by RSC Ord.50 r.6(2) is evident in the decision of Peart J. in the case of *Study Group International Ltd v Millar*.[411] The plaintiff in that case sought an injunction to restrain the defendant from attending a workshop in Moscow. Peart J. allowed the defendant to attend the workshop, but only on the strict basis that he did so as he had set out in his affidavit, namely keeping complete records of any business he transacted while there. Peart J. also required the defendant to keep a complete record of all persons with whom, in a business context, he came into contact with, as well as a complete record of all conversations and meetings he had with relevant parties. Upon his return to Ireland, Peart J. required the defendant to report to the court, on affidavit, in relation to all those matters, and to serve a copy of such affidavit on the plaintiffs' solicitors, not later than ten days following his return to Ireland.[412]

7. Stay on the Injunction Order

6–251 Where appropriate, a court may make an injunction order but put a stay on such an order so that a particular activity may be undertaken.

---

[407] See Ch.12, Breach of an Injunction Order, para.12–45. See, for example, *Chanelle Veterinary Ltd v Pfizer (Ireland) Ltd* [1998] 1 I.L.R.M. 161.

[408] [1973] 1 Ch. 281; [1972] 3 W.L.R. 902; [1972] 3 All E.R. 1041.

[409] [1973] 1 Ch. 281 at 287; [1972] 3 W.L.R. 902 at 907; [1972] 3 All E.R. 1041 at 1045. See generally, Ch.12, Breach of an Injunction Order.

[410] [1987] I.L.R.M. 400.

[411] unreported, High Court, Peart J., March 28, 2002.

[412] See also, *Paramount Pictures Corp. v Cablelink Ltd*, unreported, High Court, Murphy J., March 8, 1990, in which in which the court required the defendant to lodge a certain percentage of its income from the cable system in a bank account to meet any claim which the plaintiffs might establish.

8. Costs of the Application

6–252 The costs of an application for an interlocutory injunction are generally reserved for the trial judge to determine at the conclusion of the substantive hearing, although there is a discretion to depart from this practice which is exercised by the courts.

(a) Reserving Costs

6–253 The rationale for reserving the costs of an interlocutory application was explained by Keane J. in *Dubcap Ltd v Microchip Ltd*[413]:

> "It is right to say, of course, that while there is no rule of court or even of practice to that effect, the normal procedure on the hearing of an interlocutory application is to reserve the costs to the trial judge. The reason for that is obvious: there may and very frequently will be matters which can only be resolved by the court of trial on oral evidence at a plenary hearing of the action and indeed matters may come to light by way of discovery or by way of new evidence not available to the parties at the time of the hearing of an interlocutory application which may bring about a result which seemed unlikely or improbable at the time of the hearing of the interlocutory application, so for that reason it is quite normal on the hearing of the interlocutory applications to reserve the costs."

6–254 In describing this procedure as "sensible and appropriate" in *Ryanair v Aer Rianta cpt*,[414] Keane C.J. stated that this was so because:

> "at the interlocutory injunction stage the trial judge manifestly cannot and should not arrive at any concluded determination of the issues and consequently he is not in a position to say with any degree of justice to either party who should bear the costs."

(b) Discretion to Depart from Rule

6–255 However, the rule is not absolute. It was made clear in *Ryanair Ltd v Aer Rianta cpt*[415] that a discretion existed to depart from the rule. In that case, Kelly J. in the High Court had refused the claim for an interlocutory injunction and awarded the costs of the application against the applicant airline. The issue of costs was appealed. Keane C.J. emphasised that the Supreme Court had jurisdiction to interfere with the trial judge's discretion in the issue of costs, but that this jurisdiction would be used sparingly. He concluded that no case had

---

[413] unreported, Supreme Court, December 9, 1997.
[414] *Ryanair v Aer Rianta cpt,* ex tempore, Supreme Court, October 26, 2001.
[415] *Ryanair v Aer Rianta cpt,* ex tempore, Supreme Court, October 26, 2001.

been made out for interfering with the exercise of the High Court judge's discretion. Attention should be paid, however, to the fact that, as explained by Keane C.J., Kelly J.:

> "gave his order for costs because he considered that this was an application without any foundation in law and that accordingly it was an appropriate case in which to depart from the usual practice."

6–256 The fact that the application was deemed premature and unnecessary also appears to have weighed in favour of granting costs.

6–257 The wide discretion which the courts have in relation to costs was also emphasised by Barrington J. in *Lancefort Co Ltd v Treasury Holdings Ltd*.[416] He held that the High Court was perfectly entitled to award costs against the applicant despite also finding that it had acted bona fide in bringing an application for an injunction.

6–258 Costs were also awarded after the interlocutory hearing in the case of *Davis v Walshe*.[417] In that case, the plaintiff, appealing the fact that an order for costs had been made at the interlocutory stage in favour of the defendant, argued that they should have been reserved. McGuinness J. again acknowledged the basic rule that costs are usually reserved to the substantive trial. However, she stated that in her view the interlocutory application concerned a discrete issue which would have no further relevance to trial of action and, as such, she concluded that it was correct to award costs in the High Court at the interlocutory stage.[418]

(c) The Commercial Court

6–259 By virtue of RSC Ord.63A r.30, when a matter is before the Commercial Court:

> "Upon the determination of any interlocutory application by a Judge, the Judge shall make an award of costs save where it is not possible justly to adjudicate upon liability for costs on the basis of the interlocutory application."

6–260 As such, the costs of applications for interlocutory injunctions brought before the Commercial Court may be awarded once that application has been determined, and not when the matter comes on for substantive trial.

---

[416] unreported, Supreme Court, July 17, 1998.
[417] [2003] 2 I.R. 152.
[418] [2003] 2 I.R. 152 at 154. See also, *Veolia Water UK Plc v Fingal Co. Council*, unreported, High Court, Clarke J., June 22, 2006.

(d) Substantive Hearing

6–261 At the substantive hearing, if costs have been reserved, they are generally awarded to the successful party. However, an interesting argument in relation to the awarding of reserved costs was put forward in the case of *Murnaghan v Markland Holdings Ltd.*[419] In that case Laffoy J. had found, inter alia, that the plaintiff could have tried to, but did not, resolve the problems which he encountered without resorting to the remedy of an interim injunction. In the circumstances, it was submitted on behalf of the first named defendant that the plaintiff should not be allowed the reserved costs of, inter alia, the applications for interim and interlocutory injunctions. In support of this, it was pointed out that the plaintiff had not written a preliminary letter threatening injunctive proceedings before making the application. Laffoy J. agreed with the submission, taking the view:

> "Having regard to the efforts made by the architect for the first defendant to make contact to address the problem before the interim injunction was sought, I consider that the plaintiff should not be awarded the reserved costs of the application for the interim injunction."[420]

6–262 However, Laffoy J. did award the costs reserved at the interlocutory injunction stage to the plaintiff on the basis that the construction works complained of which formed the kernel of the case had caused damage to property and "the plaintiff was entitled to pursue the remedy he sought on notice to the defendants".

6–263 There is also an argument in theory, which does not appear to have been considered by the courts in any written judgment in this jurisdiction, that if a plaintiff succeeds in securing an interlocutory injunction, and ultimately wins his case, he should not be entitled to the reserved costs of the interlocutory injunction if it is found at the substantive hearing that damages, rather than an injunction, are in fact an adequate remedy. This is based solely on first principles; if damages are an adequate remedy at the substantive hearing, then the party who has secured the injunction would essentially have obtained such an injunction "for free" if awarded the reserved costs of the interlocutory application. Whether this means that the party against whom the injunction is granted should be awarded the costs is a distinct question; if an award of damages is made against him at the substantive hearing, it would seem wrong in principle that he should benefit from an award of costs in relation to an interlocutory application. As such, the better approach would be to make no order as to the costs of the interlocutory application in such circumstances.

---

[419] [2005] 2 I.L.R.M. 161.
[420] [2005] 2 I.L.R.M. 161 at 167.

9. Appeal

(a) Role of the Appellate Court

6–264 An appeal lies from the granting or refusal of an injunction. However, an injunction will generally only be overturned or set aside on appeal in exceptional circumstances, such as where it is based on an incorrect fact or law. It is not sufficient that the judge hearing the appeal might have come to a different conclusion.

6–265 The reason why the Supreme Court is generally slow to interfere with the discretion of a trial judge in determining whether or not to grant an injunction is encapsulated in the dictum of Murphy J. in the case of *Riordan v Minister for the Environment (No. 6)*.[421] He stated that:

> "subject to the recognition of the propositions established in *Campus Oil Ltd v Minister for Industry and Energy (No. 2)* [1983] I.R. 88, the application of the general equitable principles confers upon the trial judge a wide discretion as to whether he or she will grant injunctive relief and that is a discretion with which this Court will not lightly interfere."[422]

6–266 In the *American Cyanamid* decision itself, Lord Diplock made reference to the fact that Graham J., who had originally granted the interlocutory injunction sought before being successfully appealed to the Court of Appeal, had "unrivalled experience of pharmaceutical patents" and that an appellate court, lacking such experience, "should be hesitant to overrule his exercise of his discretion, unless they are satisfied that he has gone wrong in law".[423]

6–267 The role of the Supreme Court in hearing an appeal in relation to interlocutory applications was summarised by O'Flaherty J. in the case of *Premier Dairies Ltd v Doyle*,[424] in which he stated that the duty of the court was to:

> "adjudicate in as concise a manner as possible on what is laid before us so that the main action can progress free of whatever impediment required an appellate decision in the first place. The pith and substance of the action remains to be put before the judge of trial and we should resist any temptation to give even tentative conclusions on the matters in contention in the main litigation."[425]

---

[421]   [2002] 4 I.R. 404.
[422]   [2002] 4 I.R. 404 at 407.
[423]   [1975] A.C. 396 at 489; [1975] 2 W.L.R. 316 at 324; [1975] 1 All E.R. 504 at 511. The House of Lords reversed the decision of the Court of Appeal and granted the injunction sought. See also *Hadmore Productions Ltd v Hamilton* [1983] 1 A.C. 191 at 220.
[424]   [1996] 1 I.R. 37; [1996] 1 I.L.R.M. 363.
[425]   [1996] 1 I.R. 37 at 52; [1996] 1 I.L.R.M. 363 at 368.

(b) Procedure

(i) Circuit to High Court

6–268 As has been seen in the context of perpetual injunctions,[426] appeals are based on Pt IV of the Courts of Justice Act 1936. Rules of the Superior Courts Ord.61 (and *not* the Rules of the Circuit Court) deals with the practical aspect of appeals from the Circuit to the High Court. An appeal is brought by way of notice of appeal, which must be served on the relevant parties[427] and lodged[428] within 10 days from the pronouncement of the order appealed against. Pursuant to RSC Ord.61 r.6, an appeal does not operate as a stay of execution in relation to the decision appealed from, unless ordered otherwise by the Circuit judge or the High Court judge in Dublin.

(ii) High to Supreme Court

6–269 An appeal from the High to the Supreme Court must be brought by way of notice of appeal as provided for by RSC Ord.58. It is a ten day notice and must be served within 21 days from the passing and perfecting of the order appealed against.[429] Pursuant to RSC Ord.58 r.4, the notice of appeal "shall in every case state the grounds of appeal and the relief sought". An appeal shall not operate as a stay of execution in relation to the decision appealed from, unless ordered otherwise by court.[430]

(c) Injunctions in Relation to an Appeal

6–270 An appeal shall not operate as a stay of execution in relation to the decision appealed from, unless ordered otherwise by court.[431] This is set out at RSC Ord.58 r.18, which provides that:

> "An appeal to the Supreme Court shall not operate as a stay of execution or of proceedings under the decision appealed from, except so far as the High Court or the Supreme Court may order; and no intermediate act or proceeding shall be thereby invalidated, except so far as the High Court or the Supreme Court may direct."[432]

---

[426] See Ch.5, Perpetual Injunctions, para.5–80.

[427] RSC Ord.61 r.2.

[428] RSC Ord.61 r.3.

[429] RSC Ord.58 r.3. It is possible for the Supreme Court to abridge the relevant time limits by virtue of RSC Ord.58 r.3(3).

[430] RSC Ord.58 r.18. See generally, Delany & McGrath, *Civil Procedure in the Superior Courts*, 2nd edn (Dublin: Thomson Round Hall, 2005), Ch.20.

[431] RSC Ord.58 r.3; RSC Ord.61 (and not the Rules of the Circuit Court) deals with the practical aspect of appeals from the Circuit to the High Court. See generally, Delany & McGrath, *Civil Procedure in the Superior Courts*, 2nd edn (Dublin: Thomson Round Hall, 2005), Ch.20.

[432] See RSC Ord.61 r.9 in relation to appeals from the Circuit to the High Court.

(i) Jurisdiction of the Supreme Court

6–271 The Supreme Court has an inherent power to grant an interlocutory injunction pending the hearing of an appeal to it where it is necessary to protect the rights of the parties.[433] For example, such an injunction may be appropriate in order to preserve property the subject matter of proceedings. This includes an injunction pending the appeal in circumstances where the claim for an interlocutory injunction has been dismissed. In the English case of *Erinford Properties Ltd v Cheshire Co Council*,[434] Megarry J. held that the relevant applicable test in that regard was:

> "whether the judgment that has been given is one upon which the successful party ought to be free to act despite the pendency of an appeal."[435]

6–272 He also cautioned that there would be many cases in which:

> "it would be wrong to grant an injunction pending appeal, as where any appeal would be frivolous, or to grant the injunction would inflict greater hardship than it would avoid, and so on."

6–273 However, the guiding principle recognised by Megarry J. was that set out in *Wilson v Church (No. 2)*,[436] namely:

> "when a party is appealing, exercising his undoubted right of appeal, this court ought to see that the appeal, if successful, is not nugatory".[437]

6–274 Although the court has the power to grant such an injunction, it was emphasised by McCracken J. in *Cosma v Minister for Justice, Equality and Law Reform*[438] that "such order must be made sparingly and only in circumstances where it will not conflict with the undisputed rights of any of the parties."

(ii) Jurisdiction of the High Court

6–275 The jurisdiction of the Supreme Court to grant an injunction pending an appeal to it was reaffirmed by Clarke J. in the case of *Harding v Cork County*

---

[433] per McCracken J. in *Cosma v Minister for Justice, Equality and Law Reform*, unreported, Supreme Court, July 10, 2006.

[434] [1974] Ch. 261; [1974] 2 W.L.R. 749; [1974] 2 All E.R. 448. The application was brought by way of an "opposed *ex parte* motion". See *Pickwick International Inc. (GB) Ltd v Multiple Sound Distributors Ltd (Practice Note)* [1972] 1 W.L.R. 1213 at 1214.

[435] [1974] Ch. 261 at 267; [1974] 2 W.L.R. 749 at 755; [1974] 2 All E.R. 448 at 454.

[436] 12 Ch D 454. See also, *Orion Property Trust Ltd v Du Cane Court Ltd* [1962] 1 W.L.R. 1085; [1962] 3 All E.R. 466.

[437] 12 Ch D 454 at 458. See also, *Orion Property Trust Ltd v Du Cane Court Ltd* [1962] 1 W.L.R. 1085; [1962] 3 All E.R. 466.

[438] unreported, Supreme Court, July 10, 2006.

Council.[439] However, Clarke J. held that the High Court also had the jurisdiction to grant an injunction pending an appeal. It had been argued that the High Court had no jurisdiction to grant an injunction in such circumstances, its jurisdiction being spent once it had delivered judgment. Clarke J. rejected this argument, and adopted a passage from *Gee on Commercial Injunctions*[440] in which it is stated that:

> "If an applicant wishes to appeal against a decision declining to grant or continue an injunction, he may apply for an injunction pending appeal.
>
> The High Court may refuse to grant an injunction at an *inter partes* application made either before the trial or at the end of the trial, but still grant an injunction pending an appeal. Ordinarily an application for relief pending appeal must be made in the first instance to the judge who refused the relief, although another judge of the court of first instance does have jurisdiction to deal with the application. Even if the court of first instance is not minded to grant the injunction pending an appeal, the court will normally maintain the *status quo* pending the hearing of an application to the single judge or the Court of Appeal (as the case may be).
>
> The Court of Appeal's jurisdiction to grant an injunction pending appeal is an original jurisdiction which is concurrent to that of the High Court."[441]

6–276 Clarke J. felt that although these views were set out in the context of commercial injunctions, there was no reason why they shouldn't apply to other types of injunctions. Nor did he feel that there should be any distinction between such jurisdiction as exercised in England and that in Ireland. As such, he held that "both this court and the Supreme Court have a jurisdiction to put in place any appropriate form of injunctive relief pending appeal."

6–277 The courts will seek to prevent irrevocable or serious damage arising in the period between the dismissal of a plaintiff's claim in the High Court and an application to the Supreme Court. As observed by Clarke J., having regard to the decision in *Erinford Properties Ltd v Cheshire County Council*[442]:

> "the general principle applied by the court is to seek to preserve the *status quo* so that the appeal, if successful, is not rendered nugatory."

6–278 However, one cautionary note was sounded by Clarke J. He warned that simply because a party has the benefit of interlocutory relief pending a

---

[439] unreported, High Court, Clarke J., January 31, 2007.

[440] Gee, *Commercial Injunctions*, 5th edn (London: Thomson Sweet & Maxwell, 2004), p.729.

[441] The author citing *Ketchum International Plc v Group Publications Holdings* (1997) 1 L.R. 4; *Erinford Properties v Cheshire County Council* (1974) Ch. 261; *Williams v Minister for Environment and Heritage* (2003) 199 A.L.R. 352 and *Ryan Property Trust Limited v Du Cane Court Limited* [1962] 1 W.L.R. 1085.

[442] [1974] Ch. 261.

determination in the High Court, it did not necessarily follow that such relief would automatically be available pending the subsequent appeal. As Clarke J. observed, circumstances may change, and "some of the issues which might have originally been before the court may have disappeared as a result of the trial and the judgment of the court arising from it."

10. Variation and Discharge

6–279 As considered above,[443] most injunction orders will contain the phrase "liberty to apply". Between the granting of an interlocutory injunction and the hearing of the substantive action, circumstances may arise which lead to the view that the injunction needs to be either varied or discharged.

6–280 If a variation is sought, the usual procedure would be to deal with the matter by applying to the judge who granted the injunction in the first instance, or in the High Court to the judge in charge of the Chancery list. The form which the application will take depends on the position as between the parties. If the parties cannot agree as to how and in what terms the injunction should be varied, the usual procedure would be for one party to apply to the judge in question for liberty to issue a motion in which variation would be sought. If there is urgency to the matter, short service may also be required.[444]

6–281 If the parties are agreed to the form of the variation, they have the option of setting out in draft form the varied order, then applying to the relevant judge to vary the order in those terms. No formal motion is usually required in this regard, though if there are any contentious matters, the better way to proceed is by notice of motion.

6–282 A motion seeking to vary the injunction should set out in clear terms exactly what the nature of the variation is. The grounding affidavit should set out the background to why the variation is being sought.

6–283 An interlocutory injunction may be discharged at any time before judgment in the action where the interests of justice so demand, and on whatever terms the court deems appropriate. It is usual that if an injunction is discharged, this is done on the basis that an undertaking in relation to specified behaviour or actions is given.[445] An application for such a discharge may in

---

[443] See para.6–237.

[444] As to which, see above, para.6–211.

[445] See, for example, *Radio Limerick One Ltd v IRTC* [1997] 2 I.L.R.M. 1, in which the Supreme Court observed that the interlocutory injunction granted in the High Court restraining the IRTC pending the hearing of the proceedings from terminating the licence and contract of the plaintiffs had been discharged by Smyth J., the latter having noted an undertaking by the

certain circumstances also be made by a third party affected by the injunction order.[446]

11. Breach of an Interlocutory Injunction

6–284 As stated by Kindersley V.C. in the case of *Harding v Tingey*[447]:

> "it is of the greatest importance that either an order for an injunction or an interim order should be implicitly observed, and every diligence exercised to observe it."[448]

6–285 There are a variety of remedies available to a party when an injunction has been breached, and these are considered in detail in Ch.12, Breach of an Injunction Order.

12. Delivery of Pleadings

6–286 In the High Court, where a plaintiff issues a motion seeking an interlocutory injunction, he is generally not required to deliver a statement of claim in advance of the determination of that application (although a statement of claim may well have been delivered already). However, if an application for an interlocutory injunction is successful, it is important that the successful applicant should issue and serve any pleadings which may be outstanding. This is clear from the decision of Denham J. in *Irish Family Planning Association v Youth Defence*,[449] in which she stated that where a plaintiff has obtained an interlocutory injunction on foot of a plenary summons (but without a statement of claim having been served), she found it wholly inappropriate that having achieved the benefit of the equitable jurisdiction of the court the plaintiff should be dilatory in serving the statement of claim. In so holding, Denham J. agreed with the approach of Lawton L.J. in the case of *Hytrac Conveyors v Conveyors International*,[450] in which he had observed that:

> "In this case, as a result of the attempt to get an interlocutory injunction before the delivery of the statement of claim, weeks passed and by the middle

---

commission to permit the applicant to continue to operate under the terms of the contract pending the next appointment by the commission of a local sound broadcasting operator for the Limerick area.

[446] *Cretanor Maritime Co Ltd v Irish Marine Management Ltd* [1978] 1 W.L.R. 966; [1978] 3 All E.R. 614; in that case, the party seeking the discharge was a debenture holder and was the equitable assignee under Irish law of a fund deposited in England.

[447] (1864) L.R. 1 Eq. 42.

[448] (1864) L.R. 1 Eq. 42 at 48.

[449] [2004] 1 I.R. 374; [2004] 2 I.L.R.M. 19.

[450] [1983] 1 W.L.R. 44; [1982] 3 All E.R. 415.

of July still no statement of claim had been delivered. This was particularly unfortunate from the point of view of the fourth, fifth, sixth and seventh, defendants, who said that they were on the fringes of the case and did not know what allegations were being made against them at all."[451]

6–287 Having set out the relevant section of Lawton L.J.'s decision, Denham J., whilst acknowledging that the *Hytrac* case related to *Anton Piller* orders, held that its principles applied equally to "situations where an injunction has been granted". She emphasised that "those who make charges must state at an early stage what they are and on what facts they are based." Denham J. also referred to the fact that as a general principle "the rules of court should not be utilised, or facilitated by court orders, to ambush parties." She also held that extensive delay should not be condoned and cautioned that the court should not facilitate the service of defective documents.[452]

6–288 The need to prosecute proceedings promptly was also emphasised by Finnegan P. in *Criminal Assets Bureau v PS*,[453] both in relation to the interlocutory injunction and substantive hearing of the action. In that case, the trial of the action and the motion for interlocutory relief, having been listed for hearing, were adjourned on application by the plaintiff. The notice party pointed out that no motion for an interlocutory *Mareva* injunction had been moved by the plaintiff in the four and a half years since the interim order had been granted. It was also pointed out that when the date fixed for the hearing of the motion for interlocutory relief was reached, the plaintiff had applied to have it adjourned to an unascertained date in the distant future, namely the trial of the action.

6–289 There is no defined timescale within which the proceedings should be prosecuted. However, in the *PS* case, Finnegan P. referred to the fact that there had not been culpable delay on the part of the plaintiff and that the notice party had not shown that by reason of lapse of time that the justice of the case required that the interim order be discharged. Culpability in terms of delay and the general "justice of the case" are thus two factors which will be of relevance. Presumably the extent to which a party may or may not be prejudiced by virtue of the delay is also a significant factor.

---

[451] [1983] 1 W.L.R. 44 at 47; [1982] 3 All E.R. 415 at 417. See also *Newsgroup Newspapers Ltd v Mirror Group Newspapers (1986) Ltd* [1991] F.S.R. 487, which emphasises that a plaintiff may not sit upon an interlocutory injunction and effectively treat it as a de facto perpetual injunction if the other side does not formally complain.

[452] See also, *Dun Laoghaire Rathdown County Council v Shackleton*, unreported, Supreme Court, June 17, 2002.

[453] unreported, High Court, Finnegan P., April 12, 2002.

13. Early Trial

6–290 The court may also make an order for an early trial in circumstances where it takes the view that the matter is one which can be conveniently dealt with in this manner. This is provided for by RSC Ord.50 r.2, which states that:

> "Whenever an application shall be made before trial for an injunction or other order, and on the opening of such application, or at any time during the hearing thereof, it shall appear to the Court that the matter in controversy in the cause or matter is one which can be most conveniently dealt with by an early trial, without first going into the whole merits on affidavit or other evidence for the purposes of the application, the Court may make an order for such trial accordingly, and in the meantime make such order as the justice of the case may require".

CHAPTER 7

INTERIM APPLICATIONS

A. INTRODUCTION

7–01 An interim injunction is sought in circumstances where there is an element of urgency. It is in broad terms designed to maintain the status quo, and will normally last for a very short period, generally until the next motion day.[1] It is normally applied for in the absence of the party against whom it is sought—on an ex parte basis—usually because that party is unobtainable.[2]

7–02 It has been stated that, "any order made ex parte must be regarded as an order of a provisional nature only."[3] It is important to note that the mere fact that interim relief has been granted against a party to litigation should not be allowed to tilt the balance of that litigation in any way against that party.[4] Nor is the bringing of an application for an injunction on an interim basis a necessary precursor per se to bringing an application for either interlocutory or perpetual relief.

7–03 This chapter will consider the circumstances in which an injunction is sought on an interim basis and the procedure for applying for such an injunction. That the application for an interim injunction is usually made in the absence of the party against whom it is sought has led to the development of a number of guidelines and criteria which are designed to ensure that the court has, to the best of the moving party's ability, sufficient information on which to base its decision whether or not to grant an interim injunction.

7–04 The steps to be taken once an injunction has been secured on an interim basis will then be considered. At the outset, however, it should be noted that in terms of the applicable principles to which the courts have regard when

---

[1] See, inter alia, the dictum of Keane C.J. in *Keating v Crowley* [2002] 2 I.R. 744 at 758; [2003] 1 I.L.R.M. 88 at 102. However, the statement must be qualified somewhat in so far as, for example, the granting of an *Anton Piller* order (see Ch.8, Commercial Injunctions, para.8–129), although leading to the preservation of evidence, will in effect change the status quo.

[2] Although the terms "interim" and "ex parte" are sometimes used interchangeably, they are in fact discrete; not all interim applications are made ex parte, nor do they have to be.

[3] per Hardiman J. in *Adam v Minister for Justice* [2001] 3 I.R. 53 at 77; [2001] 2 I.L.R.M. 452 at 473, albeit that this was in the context of judicial review proceedings.

[4] per Hardiman J. in *Goold v Collins* [2005] 1 I.L.R.M. 1 at 12.

determining whether or not to grant an injunction on an interim basis, there is a significant degree of commonality with applications for injunctions on an interlocutory basis. As such, reference should also be made to Ch.6, Interlocutory Applications.

B. GENERAL PRINCIPLES

1. Introduction

7–05 The nature of the application for an interim injunction, given its urgency, is such that there are very few reported cases which consider such applications in a comprehensive manner. In many cases, the relevant principles relating to the granting of an interim injunction are only later discussed in written decisions concerning the hearing of the interlocutory application or the substantive proceedings. A note of caution must thus be sounded at the outset, as the lack of written decisions can lead to difficulties in fully capturing the approach of the courts to injunctions granted on an interim basis.[5]

2. The Need for Substantive Proceedings

7–06 A party seeking the injunction will have to establish their standing to bring such an application.[6] An interim injunction cannot exist in isolation from substantive proceedings.[7] This is considered in greater detail in Ch.6, Interlocutory Applications. As explained by Lord Mustill in *Channel Tunnel Group Ltd v Balfour Beatty Construction Ltd*[8] in the context of an interlocutory injunction, a right to an injunction "cannot exist in isolation, but is always incidental to and dependant on the enforcement of a substantive right."[9]

---

[5] Caution should also be exercised when considering cases decided in English courts since the introduction and under the Civil Procedure Rules (CPR) in 1999, under which both interim and interlocutory injunction applications are now referred to as applications for interim injunctions. It has also been observed by Wadlow, *The Law of Passing Off* (London: Sweet and Maxwell, 2004), p.796 that the abbreviated timescale now operating in England since the introduction of the CPR means that there is a much more "rough and ready" approach to interim applications. As such, Wadlow cautions that pre-CPR decision on awarding or refusing interim injunctions are no longer of much value, even analogically.

[6] As to which, see Ch.3, Standing.

[7] Although in appropriate circumstances an order may be granted before substantive proceedings have been formally instituted: see *Fourie v Le Roux* [2007] 1 W.L.R. 320; [2007] 1 All E.R. 1087. See generally, Ch.8, Commercial Injunctions, para.8–36.

[8] [1993] A.C. 334; [1993] 2 W.L.R. 262; [1993] 1 All E.R. 664.

[9] [1993] A.C. 334 at 362; [1993] 2 W.L.R. 262 at 285; [1993] 1 All E.R. 664 at 686.

3. Not a Determination of the Substantive Proceedings

7–07 In *Dunne v Dun Laoghaire Rathdown Co Council*,[10] Hardiman J. emphasised that in dealing with an interlocutory motion the court is not finally deciding any factual or legal aspect of the controversy.[11] Similar principles apply by extrapolation in relation to an application for an interim injunction.[12]

4. Departure from the Principle of *Audi Alteram Partem*

7–08 The principle of *audi alteram partem* refers to the fact that the other side to an action should be heard. The power of the court to exercise ex parte jurisdiction is a departure from the *audi alteram partem* principle. As stated in the case of *Thomas A Edison Ltd v Bullock*[13] by Isaacs J.:

> "There is a primary precept governing the administration of justice, that no man is to be condemned unheard; and, therefore, as a general rule, no order should be made to the prejudice of a party unless he has the opportunity of being heard in defence."[14]

7–09 Clarke J. made a similar observation in *JRM Sports Ltd v Football Association of Ireland*.[15] He stated that:

> "Allowing people to go into Court and get an order without the other side being told in advance is a departure from the normal rule that both sides are entitled to be heard."

7–10 However, the exercise of ex parte jurisdiction has been held to be justified where there is an immediate risk of significant harm.[16] In the English case of *Ansah v Ansah*,[17] the applicable principle was clearly summarised by Ormrod L.J., who stated that:

---

[10] [2003] 1 I.R. 567.
[11] [2003] 1 I.R. 567 at 581. See also the dictum of Lord Diplock in *American Cyanamid Co v Ethicon Ltd* [1975] A.C. 396 at 407; [1975] 2 W.L.R. 316 at 323; [1975] 1 All E.R. 504 at 510, adopted by McCarthy J. in Irish *Shell Ltd v Elm Motors Ltd* [1984] I.R. 200 at 224 and followed in, inter alia, *Ferris v Ward* [1998] 2 I.R. 194.
[12] Reference should be made to Ch.6, Interlocutory Applications, for a fuller consideration of this point.
[13] (1912) 15 C.L.R. 679.
[14] (1912) 15 C.L.R. 679 at 681, as cited by Slade L.J. in *Bank Mellat v Nikpour* [1985] F.S.R. 87 at 92, and by Whitford J. in *Jeffrey Rogers Knitwear Productions Ltd v Vinola (Knitwear) Manufacturing Co* [1985] F.S.R. 184 at 187.
[15] unreported, High Court, Clarke J., January 31, 2007.
[16] As stated in the context of an action involving domestic violence by Kelly J. in *Keating v Crowley*, unreported, High Court, Kelly J., June 2, 2000, although the decision was successfully appealed to the Supreme Court.
[17] [1977] Fam. 138.

"Orders made *ex parte* are anomalies in our system of justice which generally demands service or notice of the proposed proceedings on the opposite party: see *Craig v Kanssen* [1943] K.B. 256, 262. None the less, the power of the court to intervene immediately and without notice in proper cases is essential to the administration of justice. But this power must be used with great caution and only in circumstances in which it is really necessary to act immediately."[18]

5. Legislative Basis for the Application

7–11 As has been seen,[19] s.82 of the Common Law Procedure Act (Ireland) 1856 provided that a writ of injunction could be applied for on an ex parte basis. A plaintiff might, at any time after the commencement of proceedings:

"apply *ex parte* to the court or a judge for a writ of injunction to restrain the defendant in such action from the repetition or continuance of the wrongful act or breach of contract complained of, or the committal of any breach of contract or injury of a like kind, arising out of the same contract, or related to the same property or right."

7–12 As with interlocutory applications, the legal basis underpinning the granting of injunctions on an equitable basis is s.28(8) of the Supreme Court of Judicature (Ireland) Act 1877.[20] That section provides that:

"A mandamus or an injunction may be granted or a receiver appointed by an interlocutory order of the Court in all cases in which it shall appear to the Court to be just or convenient that such order should be made, and any such order may be made either unconditionally or upon such terms and conditions as the Court shall think just; and if an injunction is asked, either before, or at, or after the hearing of any cause or matter, to prevent any threatened or apprehended waste or trespass, such injunction may be granted, if the Court shall think fit, whether the person against whom such injunction is sought is or is not in possession under any claim of title or otherwise, or (if out of possession) does or does not claim a right to do the act sought to be restrained under any colour of title, and whether the estates claimed by both or by either of the parties are legal or equitable."

7–13 Although there is no reference to interim orders contained in the section, there appears to be nothing to suggest that interim orders are not contemplated by s.28(8). Furthermore, ex parte applications are provided for procedurally in the Rules of the Superior Courts.[21]

---

[18] [1977] Fam. 138 at 142. See also *Re First Express Ltd, Times Law Reports*, October 10, 1991, per Hoffman J.
[19] See Ch.1, Domestic Jurisdiction.
[20] Often referred to in shorthand as the Judicature (Ireland) Act.
[21] And the Rules of the Circuit Court: see para.7–15.

6. Procedural Basis for the Application

7–14 It has been a long-standing principle that an order will not be made ex parte other than in cases of urgency.[22] As such, it is important for a party seeking an interim order to consider whether the matter is so urgent that an application must be made ex parte. Consideration should also be given to whether an interim, rather than an interlocutory, injunction is required in the first instance,[23] or whether short service of a notice of motion for an interlocutory injunction might be more appropriate.

7–15 Ex parte applications are provided for by Ord.52 r.3 of the Rules of the Superior Courts (RSC), which states:

> "In any case the Court, if satisfied the delay caused by proceedings by motion on notice under this Order would or might entail irreparable or serious mischief, may make any order *ex parte* upon such terms as to the costs or otherwise and subject to such undertaking, if any, as the Court may think just; and any part affected by such order may move to set it aside."[24]

7–16 In relation to injunctions, RSC Ord.50 r.6(1) provides that:

> "The Court may grant a mandamus or an injunction or appoint a receiver, by an interlocutory order in all cases in which it appears to the Court to be just or convenient so to do."[25]

7–17 That this contemplates interim orders as well appears clear from RSC Ord.50 r.7, which provides that an application under, inter alia, RSC Ord.50 r.6 "may be made either *ex parte* or on notice".

7. Short Service

7–18 An alternative to an interim application is to seek short service of a motion for an interlocutory application.[26] An application for short service

---

[22] See further Wylie, *The Judicature Acts (Ireland)* (Dublin: Sealy, Bryers and Walker, 1906), p.692.

[23] It was reported in the Irish Times of June 14, 1990 that Costello J. warned that an ex parte interim injunction will be considered "in exceptional circumstances only" and that applications for interim injunctions were now sought virtually automatically 'and in my experience about 90 per cent of them, wrongly". As cited by Courtney, *Mareva Injunctions* (Dublin: Butterworths, 1998), p.290, fn.19.

[24] See RCC Ord.20 r.2.

[25] There would appear to be no direct equivalent in the Rules of the Circuit Court. However, RCC Ord. 20 refers to the granting of ex parte interim injunctions, and RCC Ord.39 provides for the appointment of a receiver by way of equitable execution. Pursuant to RCC Ord.67 r.16, where no rule is set out to govern the practice and procedure of the Circuit Court, the rules of the High Court may be followed.

[26] See, inter alia, the dictum of Keane C.J. in *Keating v Crowley* [2002] 2 I.R. 744 at 759; [2003] 1 I.L.R.M. 88 at 102. See Ch.6, Interlocutory Applications, para.6–211.

benefits the moving party from the perspective of time. It also allows the other side to appear before the court on the return date to set out their position on affidavit as necessary and to give as necessary any undertakings which may be required.

7–19 It is the requirement to comply with the principle of *audi alteram partem* and the ability of the court to hear the "other side of the story" which is a key consideration in terms of providing for short service. It is also open to a judge who hears an application for an interim injunction, and who is not minded to grant the interim injunction on an ex parte basis, to direct that short service be granted so that the matter can be dealt with on an interlocutory basis.

7–20 There is no prescribed time for the period which must elapse between short service being granted and the matter being back before the court on notice. Anecdotally, there have been occasions when the court has heard an application for short service at 11am and returned the motion on notice for 12.30pm. Such an approach is more likely if the other party already has solicitors on record and the need for an interim injunction arises during the course of litigation which is already in train. However, such an accelerated timeframe is comparatively rare.

(a) Benefit to Moving Party

7–21 Short service is a potent tactical move in the context of attempting to secure an injunction, in that serving notice of the motion will put the other side on notice that the application is being brought. The other side is then at risk that if it continues the act complained of whilst on such notice, this will weigh against it at any subsequent hearing before the court. As has been seen in the context of equitable and general principles in Ch.4, the bona fides of a defendant may be a relevant consideration. In *Daniel v Ferguson*,[27] Lindley L.J. made reference to the fact that upon receiving notice that an injunction was going to be applied for, the defendant set:

> "a gang of men to work and runs up his wall to a height of thirty-nine feet before he receives notice that an injunction has been granted."

7– 22 In those circumstances, Lindley L.J. held that:

> "It is right that buildings thus run up should be pulled down at once, without regard to what the result of the trial may be."[28]

---

[27]   [1891] 2 Ch. 27. See also, *Von Joel v Hornsey* [1895] 2 Ch. 774.
[28]   [1891] 2 Ch. 27 at 30.

(b) Benefit to Respondent

7–23 Short service can, of course, also benefit a defendant/respondent. If an injunction application is made ex parte, that defendant/respondent's side of the case will be filtered through the prism of the plaintiff/applicant's presentation. However, if a motion is returnable on foot of an order for short service, the defendant will be able to appear in court to put their side of the case.

7–24 The procedural basis for brining an application for short service will be considered below.[29]

8. Ambush Injunctions

7–25 The courts will also be alert for any opportunistic attempts to seek an injunction, often referred to as "ambush" injunctions.[30] As stated by Denham J. in *Irish Family Planning Association v Youth Defence*[31]:

> "As a general principle the Rules of the Superior Courts 1986 should not be utilised, or facilitated by court orders, to ambush parties."[32]

7–26 This is a difficult exercise for the courts, in that a party may be able to point to a genuine right which needs to be protected. In the absence of the other party, however, a court will have to determine whether the grievance the plaintiff has is in fact more opportunistic than genuine. An example of such considerations is provided by the case of *Kinane v Turf Club*.[33] In that case the plaintiff, a jockey, had been banned from riding for two days. He applied for, and obtained, an interim injunction against the decision of the Appeal Committee of the Turf Club. This injunction enabled him to ride in (and win) a prestigious race, subsequent to which he served his ban.

C. Prohibitory and Mandatory Interim Injunctions

1. Introduction

7–27 In theory both prohibitory and mandatory injunctions may be granted at the interim stage. However, it is generally accepted that it is rare to obtain a

---

[29] See para.7–92.
[30] See Byrne and Binchy, *Annual Review of Irish Law 2001* (Dublin: Round Hall, 2002), p.45. See generally, Anderson "Sports and the Courts—Time for a Sports Disputes Tribunal of Ireland?" (2005) 23 I.L.T. 149.
[31] [2004] 1 I.R. 374.
[32] [2004] 1 I.R. 374 at 383.
[33] unreported, High Court, McCracken J., July 27, 2001.

mandatory injunction at the interim stage on foot of an ex parte application,[34] as the courts are reluctant to make an order compelling an action which may be difficult to undo on the basis of hearing one party to an action only. A mandatory injunction was refused at an ex parte hearing in the case of *Felton v Callis*.[35] Megarry J. stated that to grant such an injunction would be a "vigorous new jurisidiction ...". However, this would seem to be overstating the position, for it would not appear correct to say that it is never possible to secure a mandatory injunction at an ex parte hearing. A better, more modern statement of the law is that set out by Keane C. J. in the case of *Keating v Crowley*.[36] The Chief Justice stated in relation to "interim or interlocutory injunctions typically granted in civil proceedings" that:

> "While they may on occasions be mandatory in nature, that is unquestionably the exception rather than the rule. It is even rarer for mandatory injunctions to be granted on an interim basis on the *ex parte* application of the plaintiff."[37]

7–28 That mandatory injunctions may be granted on an interim basis is clear from decisions such as *Daniel v Ferguson*[38] in which, as seen above,[39] Stirling J. ordered a wall to be pulled down in circumstances where the defendant, having received notice of an application for an injunction, built the wall before receiving notice that an ex parte interim injunction had been granted.[40] The appeal was refused.

7–29 As with applications for interlocutory injunctions, the courts consider a number of factors and principles when determining whether or not to grant an interim injunction. As with interlocutory injunctions, it is not just the principles specifically applicable to interim injunctions which are relevant; the court may also have regard to wider equitable and general principles, considered in Ch.4, in coming to its determination.

2. Applicable Tests

(a) Prohibitory Injunctions

7–30 The test which should be applied by the courts in determining whether or not to grant a prohibitory injunction at the interim stage is that applied at the

---

[34] See the dictum of Keane C.J. in *Keating v Crowley* [2002] 2 I.R. 744 at 758; [2003] 1 I.L.R.M. 88 at 102.

[35] [1969] 1 Q.B. 200 at 219; [1968] 3 W.L.R. 951 at 968; [1968] 3 All E.R. 673 at 684.

[36] [2002] 2 I.R. 744.

[37] [2002] 2 I.R. 744 at 758.

[38] [1891] 2 Ch. 27.

[39] See para.7–21.

[40] Spry, *The Principles of Equitable Remedies*, 6th edn (London: Sweet and Maxwell, 2001), p.559 suggests that an injunction in such circumstances might be appropriate where a structure

interlocutory stage, namely the guidelines set out in England in the case of *American Cyanamid v Ethicon Ltd*,[41] as endorsed in this jurisdiction in *Campus Oil Ltd v Minister for Industry and Energy (No.2)*.[42] Although the lack of written judgments concerning ex parte injunction applications means that this is not analysed in any great detail in reported case law concerning interim injunctions, there is no reason why a different standard should be applied at the interim stage than is applied at the interlocutory stage.

7–31 That an application is brought on an ex parte basis, implying some form of urgency, does not mean that it should be subject to any diminished scrutiny. In terms of the preparation of the affidavit, the party moving the application would therefore be well advised to ensure that the relevant principles/guidelines as set out in the *Campus Oil* principles are considered and dealt with in the affidavit as necessary.

7–32 As has been seen in the context of interlocutory injunctions,[43] the relevant applicable principles derived from *American Cyanamid/Campus Oil* in relation to a prohibitory injunction are as follows:

- The party seeking the injunction must show that there is a fair/bona fide/serious question to be tried.
- The court must consider two aspects of the adequacy of damages:
    (i) First, it must consider whether, if it does not grant an injunction at the interlocutory stage, a plaintiff who succeeds at the trial of the substantive action will be adequately compensated by an award of damages for any loss suffered between the hearing of the interlocutory injunction and the trial of the action. If the plaintiff would be adequately compensated, the interlocutory injunction should be refused. This is subject to the proviso that the defendant would be in a position to pay such damages.
    (ii) Secondly, the court must consider whether, if it does grant an injunction at the interlocutory stage, a plaintiff's undertaking as to damages will adequately compensate the defendant, should the latter be successful at the trial of the action, in respect of any loss suffered by him due to the injunction being in force pending the trial. If the defendant would be compensated, the injunction may be granted. This is also subject to the proviso that the plaintiff would be in a position to pay such damages.
- If damages would not fully compensate either party, then the court may consider the balance of convenience. The matters relevant to determining where the balance of convenience lies will vary from case to case.

---

on a piece of land is causing immediate and extremely serious interference with the conduct of a business or else personal inconvenience of an extremely serious nature.

[41]   [1975] A.C. 396; [1975] 2 W.L.R. 316; [1975] 1 All E.R. 504.
[42]   [1983] I.R. 88; [1984] I.L.R.M. 45.
[43]   See Ch.6, Interlocutory Applications, para.6–22.

- If all other matters are equally balanced, the court should attempt to preserve the status quo.[44]

(b) Mandatory Injunctions

7–33 As has been seen in the context of interlocutory applications,[45] there is a divergence between judgments in this jurisdiction in relation to the principles applicable to mandatory injunctions. Some judges have taken the view that the *Campus Oil* guidelines should be adhered to in their entirety,[46] whereas others have suggested that, in the first instance, the party seeking the injunction must be able to demonstrate a strong, clear case.[47] This is notwithstanding the fact that the *Campus Oil* guidelines were set out in the context of an application for a mandatory interlocutory injunction. In circumstances where an injunction is being applied for on an interim ex parte basis, it would seem that the better approach would be the more rigorous one. Given the courts' reluctance to grant mandatory interim injunctions, a prudent applicant for an injunction would be well advised to approach the matter on the basis that they should be able to identify a strong, clear case. Even if the *Campus Oil* "fair case" guideline is applied, however, the nature of an interim injunction, particularly when applied for on an ex parte basis, means that a judge will be very aware of the effect of any order in the context of a consideration of the balance of convenience. As such, there will effectively be a heightened requirement by default before a mandatory injunction is granted at the interim stage.

D. Applying for an Ex Parte Interim Injunction

1. Exchange of Correspondence

7–34 When an application is being made for an interim injunction, given the urgency of the situation it is quite often not possible to notify the other party to

---

[44] Based on the dicta of McCracken J. in *B & S Ltd v Irish Auto Trader Ltd* [1995] 2 I.R. 142 at 145; [1995] 2 I.L.R.M. 152 at 156 (approved by Laffoy J. in *Symonds Cider v Showerings (Ireland) Ltd* [1997] 1 I.L.R.M. 481) and Quirke J. in *Clane Hospital Ltd v Voluntary Health Insurance Board*, unreported, High Court, Quirke J., May 22, 1998. However, in the latter case, when dealing with a bona fide question to be tried, Quirke J. referred to "whether or not the applicant has raised a fair, substantial *bona fide* question for determination." As noted by Delany, *Equity and the Law of Trusts in Ireland* (Dublin: Thomson Round Hall, 2007), p.517, fn.137, "it is unlikely that he [Quirke J.] was trying to make the test harder to satisfy by inserting the word 'substantial'".

[45] See Ch.6, Interlocutory Applications, para.6–190.

[46] See, for example, *A & N Pharmacy Ltd v United Drug Wholesale Ltd* [1996] 2 I.L.R.M. 46 and *Cronin v Minister for Education* [2004] 3 I.R. 205 at 213, per Laffoy J.

[47] See, for example, *Boyhan v Tribunal of Inquiry into the Beef Industry* [1993] 1 I.R. 210 at 223; [1992] I.L.R.M. 545 at 556, per Denham J. and *Maha Lingam v Health Service Executive* [2006] 17 E.L.R. 137 at 140, per Fennelly J.

the action in advance of such an application. A solicitor will frequently have previously written to a party against whom an interim injunction application is subsequently brought, putting them on notice that if a stated act takes place or continues, an application for an injunction will be made "without further notice".[48]

7–35 Given the requirement of full and frank disclosure by any party seeking an interim injunction on an ex parte basis,[49] any correspondence relating to a matter must be disclosed by the moving party. From a respondent's perspective, it is therefore crucial when threatened with an injunction to reply to any such correspondence with a letter setting out clearly and rationally why, in essence, there is no basis for such an order. If, as it should be,[50] such a letter is exhibited to the affidavit grounding the application for interim relief, a judge can take a view as to its merits and either refuse the injunction at the interim stage, or alternatively grant short service so that the motion is returnable on notice. Either option is clearly to the benefit of the respondent.

2. Application

7–36 Although there is a 1999 Practice Direction entitled "Urgent *Ex Parte* Applications for Interim Relief—Practice Direction",[51] this has been complemented, and indeed overtaken to a degree, by day-to-day practice. The terms of the Practice Direction are as follows[52]:

> "Urgent *ex-parte* applications for injunctions or other interim relief in chancery, family law, judicial review matters and under the Companies Acts should be made during term to the Judge assigned for the time being to hear such matters as indicated in the Legal Diary. During Vacation such application should be made to the Duty Judge.
>
> Where it is intended to make an *ex-parte* application other than a formal application in a matter which has not been listed in the Legal Diary or mentioned in Court prior to the making of the application, the following practice should be adopted:
>
> (i) The advice of the Chief Registrar may be obtained to ascertain the appropriate Judge to whom the application should be made and the application should be made to that Judge.

---

[48] See the case of *Graham v Campbell* (1878) 7 Ch D 490 (see para.7–97) in which the question of the relevant procedure once an appearance has been entered is considered.

[49] As to which see para.7–66.

[50] Given the requirement for full and frank disclosure: see para.7–66.

[51] February 16, 1999, by Morris P.

[52] As reproduced at Appendix 5.3 of Collins and O'Reilly, *Civil Proceedings and the State*, 2nd edn (Dublin: Thomson Round Hall, 2004), p.468; the 1999 Practice Direction does not appear to be otherwise readily accessible.

(ii) It should be indicated to the Judge at the sitting of the Court or if that is not possible as soon thereafter as is possible, that it is intended to make this application so as to ascertain the time at which the Court will entertain the application.

(iii) The papers relevant to the application should be handed into Court when the matter is mentioned to the Court or at the first possible opportunity thereafter.

At times when no Court is sitting, Counsel should telephone the appropriate Judge to make arrangements for the time and place for the hearing, and to ascertain the name of the Registrar to be contacted by the Solicitor for the Moving Party."

7–37 The Practice Direction applies to ex parte applications generally. As will be seen, the point set out at (i) is in practice too broad in relation to applications for injunctions. However, the points set out at (ii) and (iii) are still very valid in terms of applying for an interim injunction on an ex parte basis.

7–38 In practical terms, there are at present different systems in operation in the High Court when applying for an interim injunction, depending on whether the matter arises during the legal term and, if so, whether the courts are sitting.[53]

(a) The High Court

(i) During the Legal Term, Courts are Sitting

7–39 An application for an interim injunction should be sought in the first instance from a Chancery judge. Specifically, the best practice is to approach the judge who is in charge of the Chancery list for that day (and who will be named as such in the legal diary for the day). If there is any doubt as to this, the provisions of the 1999 Practice Direction are of relevance in terms of obtaining the advice of the chief registrar.

7–40 As per the terms of the Practice Direction, a judge should ideally be approached at the initial sitting of the court. Ideally, the registrar of the court will have been informed of the application in advance and will have been handed the relevant papers, so that these can be handed in to the judge, who can then adjudicate as to how s/he wishes to proceed.

7–41 If that judge is not available to deal with the matter, s/he will frequently be able to indicate which judge might be in a position to do so. If this is not the

---

[53] See generally, the letter from Chief Registrar and Director, Supreme and High Court Operations printed in (2006) 100(7) L.S. Gazette 45 (Aug/Sept 2006), albeit written in reply to the Criminal Law Committee.

case, then any judge assigned to deal with Chancery matters (again, as set out in the legal diary) should be approached. If no Chancery judges are available, then any High Court judge can be approached with a view to dealing with the matter.

(ii) During the Legal Term, Out of Hours

7–42 If an urgent interim application has to be made during the legal term, but out of hours when the courts are not sitting (including at weekends), then counsel acting for the party seeking the injunction should contact the Four Courts. The duty registrar, who will have in their possession an officially supplied mobile, will be contacted and will then call back the relevant representative.

7–43 Duty judges are nominated by the President of the High Court and that judge, upon being contacted by the duty registrar, will then deal with the matter.

(iii) During Vacation

7–44 When an urgent injunction is sought outside of the legal terms, during vacation, there is a duty registrar on call. The Four Courts should be contacted in the first instance,[54] with contact details being passed on to the designated duty registrar, who will then contact the representatives for the party seeking the injunction.

(b) The Circuit Court

7–45 Order 20 r.2 of the Rules of the Circuit Court provides that:

> "Applications in connection with any of the matters hereinafter mentioned may be made to the Judge by any party, without notice to any other party, on lodging with the County Registrar a copy of the Civil Bill, an *ex parte* docket in accordance with Form 27 of the Schedule of Forms annexed hereto and filing an affidavit in support of the application."[55]

7–46 Included in the "matters hereinafter mentioned" is "(i) an *ad interim* injunction".

(c) Granting an Injunction over the Telephone

7–47 It has been recognised in England that, in exceptional cases, injunctive relief may be sought over the telephone.[56] However, Nourse J cautioned in the

---

54 Not the duty registrar directly at the officially supplied mobile number. See www.courts.ie for contact details.
55 The practice in the Circuit Court is not as structured as in the High Court, and different practices may obtain on different circuits. If there is difficulty identifying a judge able to deal with the matter, contact should be made in the first instance with the relevant Circuit Court office.
56 For example, in *Allen v Jambo Holdings Ltd* [1980] 1 W.L.R. 1252; [1980] 2 All E.R. 502, the

case of *PS Refson & Co Ltd v Saggers*[57] that in cases where relief is being sought on the telephone:

> "the material part or parts of the draft indorsement should normally be read to the judge. Only in cases of exceptional urgency should the court be asked to act without sight or hearing of the material part or parts of a draft endorsement."[58]

7–48 Such a practice in extremis has never been disavowed in Ireland,[59] although the cautionary words of Nourse J. would appear to be equally applicable in this jurisdiction. However, it will be necessary to have a registrar involved in the telephone call in order to record any order made.

(d) Documentation Required

7–49 Regardless of whether the application for an interim injunction is moved on an ex parte basis or otherwise, the following documents should in the normal course be brought to court when the application is being made:

- an originating summons/other originating document;
- ex parte motion / notice of motion, as appropriate;
- grounding affidavit.

(i) Originating Summons/Document

7–50 An action will be grounded on an originating summons or other originating document, such as a motion or petition.[60] The substantive proceedings should not be drafted so as to specifically claim relief on an interim or interlocutory basis; these are more properly claimed in the documentation grounding the interim or interlocutory application.[61]

7–51 Some situations may be of such urgency that an originating document may not be in existence when an application for an interim injunction is made.[62]

---

initial *Mareva* injunction order was granted by Drake J. over the telephone. See also *Kelly v British Broadcasting Corporation* [2001] 2 W.L.R. 253. Such applications seem to be more frequent in England in the course of family disputes, as in the *Kelly* case.

[57] [1984] 1 W.L.R. 1025; [1984] 3 All E.R. 111.
[58] [1984] 1 W.L.R. 1025 at 1030; [1984] 3 All E.R. 111 at 116.
[59] It appears anecdotally that at least two injunctions have been granted over the telephone in this jurisdiction.
[60] See Ch.1, Domestic Jurisdiction, para.1–93 as to the form of pleadings used pursuant to which an injunction may be sought.
[61] See the dictum of Finlay C.J. in *Caudron v Air Zaire* [1985] I.R. 716 at 721; [1986] I.L.R.M. 10 at 21.
[62] In *Irish Family Planning Association v Youth Defence* [2004] 2 I.L.R.M. 19, the plaintiff obtained an interim injunction against the defendants restraining them from trespassing on its

It was recognised by the Supreme Court in the case of *B v Governor of the Training Unit Glengarriff Parade Dublin*[63] that in urgent ex parte applications for interim injunctions Chancery judges have, on occasions, when the Central Office is closed and the extreme urgency of the position requires it to be done, accepted an undertaking on behalf of the plaintiff to issue a plenary summons (or other document as appropriate) as soon as the office is open.[64] Of assistance in this regard is the decision of Nourse J. in the case of *PS Refson & Co Ltd v Saggers,*[65] in which he set out the forms, according to circumstances, the undertaking should be given, viz.:

> "(a) 'forthwith to issue a writ of summons in the form of the said draft writ'; or (b) 'forthwith to issue a writ of summons claiming relief in the form of the said draft indorsement with or without other relief'; or (c) 'forthwith to issue a writ of summons claiming relief substantially similar to that hereinafter granted with or without other relief.'"[66]

7–52 However, it should be endeavoured to at least have a draft form of originating document which can be shown to the judge. This should be entitled: "In the matter of an intended action between", followed by the usual form of wording and layout.

7–53 The undertaking given to the court should not be treated lightly. In the *Refson* case, Nourse J. cautioned that:

> "In a case where there has been a breach of an undertaking to issue the writ expeditiously it is well within the power of the court to disallow the plaintiff costs which would normally be awarded to him or to order him to pay costs which would normally be borne by the defendant."[67]

(ii) Ex parte Motion

7–54 If an application is being made ex parte in the High Court, there is clearly no party on notice and, as such, a notice of motion is not an appropriate document upon which to bring the application for interim relief. However, an ex

property, and the following day a plenary summons and a notice of motion claiming interlocutory injunctions issued. In the context of *Mareva* orders, see *Fourie v Le Roux* [2007] 1 W.L.R. 320; [2007] 1 All E.R. 1087, and the analysis of the case by Capper, "Asset Freezing Orders—Failure to State the Cause of Action" (2007) 26 C.Q.J. 181.

63   [2002] 2 I.L.R.M. 161.
64   [2002] 2 I.L.R.M. 161 at 172. See also *Thorneloe v Skoines* (1873) L.R. 16 Eq. 126.
65   [1984] 1 W.L.R. 1025; [1984] 3 All E.R. 111.
66   [1984] 1 W.L.R. 1025 at 1030; [1984] 3 All E.R. 111 at 115.
67   [1984] 1 W.L.R. 1025 at 1029; [1984] 3 All E.R. 111 at 114. Referred to in *Canada Trust Co v Stolzenberg (No. 2)* [2002] 1 A.C. 1 and *Kloeckner & Co AG v Gatoil Overseas Inc.* [1990] 1 Lloyd's Rep. 177.

parte motion should be drafted. The purpose of such notice, which takes the form of a notice of motion, but is entitled "ex parte motion" or similar, is to in essence set out for the benefit of the court exactly what reliefs are being sought. In terms of any order made, the court can then simply grant, deny, or grant with modifications, any or all of the reliefs sought.

7–55 One suggested way of drafting an ex parte notice is to adapt the usual wording for a notice of motion. Rather than the phrase "Take notice that on the [date] …", the words "Take notice that" can be dropped. A suggested alternative formulation would then read:

> "On the [date] … at 11 o'clock in the forenoon, or at the first available opportunity thereafter, counsel on behalf of [party] will apply ex parte to this Honourable Court, sitting at the Four Courts, Inns Quay, Dublin 7 for the following orders: [insert orders sought]."

7– In practical terms, it does not appear to concern judges unduly if the words "notice of motion" appear on the face of the motion.

7–56 In the Circuit Court, an ex parte docket must be completed. These are available from the registrar in the court, or alternatively at Form 27 of Schedule B in the Schedule of Forms to the Rules of the Circuit Court, the material part of which reads:

> "I desire to apply to the Court on . . . . or on the next opportunity thereafter for an order on behalf of the Plaintiff/Defendant to the following effect:
>
> The documents on which the application is based are as follows: . . . . (State the nature of the documents relied upon) as referred to in the affidavit of   filed the   day of   ."

(iii) Grounding Affidavit

7–57 The basic principles applicable to drafting an affidavit grounding an interlocutory application also apply to an interim application, viz. setting out the facts giving rise to the action as well as the facts giving rise to the motion for injunctive relief in as comprehensive a manner as possible. As has been considered in the context of interlocutory applications,[68] the relevant applicable principles set out in the *Campus Oil* case will have to be addressed as far as possible, with any other matters which will assist the court in coming to its determination also included.

---

[68] See Ch.6, Interlocutory Applications, para.6–219.

7–58 More specifically in the context of an application for an interim injunction, it is important that such an affidavit specifies the matter which has led to the urgency underpinning the application, as this is the fundamental basis for an interim application.

7–59 Although an affidavit should not in the normal course contain hearsay evidence, in *M v D*,[69] Moriarty J. suggested that in ex parte applications:

> "it is the established usage of the courts that some appreciable measure of hearsay evidence is considered acceptable in affidavits filed on behalf of parties."[70]

7–60 Furthermore, specific statutory provisions may allow for hearsay evidence, such as, for example, s.8 of the Proceeds of Crime Act 1996.[71] Other than in such specific statutory circumstances, the inclusion of hearsay evidence is permitted by RSC Ord.40 r.4, which provides that:

> "Affidavits shall be confined to such facts as the witness is able of his own knowledge to prove, and shall state his means of knowledge thereof, except on interlocutory motions, on which statements as to his belief, with the grounds thereof, may be admitted. The costs of any affidavit which shall unnecessarily set forth matters of hearsay or argumentative matter, or copies of or extracts from documents, shall not be allowed."[72]

7–61 However, in *Collen Construction Ltd v BATU*,[73] albeit in the context of an application for an interlocutory injunction, Clarke J. cautioned that no reliance should ordinarily be placed on hearsay attributed to unnamed persons.

Sworn Before Application

7–62 In the normal course, an affidavit grounding the application for injunctive relief should be sworn before an application is made. In that regard, RSC Ord.40 r.20 states that:

---

[69] [1998] 3 I.R. 175.

[70] [1998] 3 I.R. 175 at 178. However, per Rigby L.J. in *Re Young JL Manufacturing Co Ltd* [1900] 2 Ch. 753 at 755 "… when a deponent makes a statement on his information and belief, he must state the ground of that information and belief."

[71] See generally, Ch.11, Specific Statutory Injunctions, para.11–113. See generally, the dictum of Moriarty J. in *M v D* [1998] 3 I.R. 175 at 178. See also the case of *Murphy v GM* [2001] 4 I.R. 113 at 155, in which stated in relation to the Proceeds of Crime Act 1996 that: "Nor is the provision for the admission of hearsay evidence of itself unconstitutional: it was a matter for the Court hearing the application to decide what weight should be given to such evidence. The Court is satisfied that there is no substance in these grounds of challenge to the constitutionality of the legislation", per Keane C.J. See also *McKenna v TH*, unreported, Supreme Court, November 26, 2006.

[72] See RCC Ord.25 r.3.

[73] unreported, High Court, Clarke J., May 15, 2006.

"Except by leave of the Court no order made *ex parte* in Court founded on any affidavit shall be of any force unless the affidavit on which the application was made was actually made before the order was applied for, and produced or filed at the time of making the application."[74]

7–63 Even if a sworn affidavit has not been filed in the Central Office, it should be filed in court, as it will be the basis for the evidence which the court has heard. In extremis, however, and with the leave of the court, as provided for in RSC Ord.40 r.20, oral evidence could be offered to the court in the normal way, with the party offering such evidence also giving an undertaking to immediately reduce their evidence to writing and to file that affidavit as soon as practicable. A court will be very slow to sanction such an approach, for it is inevitably difficult to capture the detail, emphases and nuances of oral submissions fully and accurately in an affidavit prepared subsequently.

(e) Guiding Principles and Rules

7–64 Due to the fact that interim injunctions are generally applied for on an ex parte basis, the courts have developed a number of principles and rules which are designed to ensure that a judge hearing the application in the absence of one of the parties, or proposed parties, to an action has before the court sufficient information on which to base a decision. These principles have been referred to as the "triple safeguard", and are set out by Judge L.J. in *St George's Healthcare NHS Trust v S*[75]:

"An interim injunction is granted *ex parte* only in exceptional circumstances and then only subject to the triple safeguards of:
1. The duty of full and frank disclosure,
2. The cross undertaking in damages[76] which is required as a matter of course, and
3. The right of the party enjoined to apply to vary or discharge the *ex parte* order.
If an interim declaration were a remedy known to English law it could hardly be obtainable without these safeguards being put in place."[77]

7–65 These will now be considered in more detail, with particular emphasis on the question of full and frank disclosure.

---

[74] See RCC Ord.25 r.9 which deals with filing, as distinct from swearing, of an affidavit after a judge has heard an application.

[75] [1998] 3 W.L.R. 936.

[76] The English term for the more familiar "undertaking as to damages" as used in this jurisdiction.

[77] [1998] 3 W.L.R. 936 at 966, as cited by Kelly J. in *Adams v DPP*, unreported, High Court, Kelly J., April 12, 2000 and *Ryanair Ltd v Aer Rianta cpt*, ex tempore, High Court, Kelly J., January 25, 2001.

(f) Full and Frank Disclosure

7–66 The potential for injustice arising from the granting of an interim order on inaccurate, incomplete or even invented information is fully acknowledged by the courts.[78] It is clear that the courts are also fully aware that ex parte procedures may be abused out of spite or for tactical purposes.[79] The courts will thus exercise great care when granting any form of ex parte relief.

(i) Uberrimae Fides

7–67 An application made ex parte must be made *uberrimae fides*—with the utmost of good faith.[80] In *Balogun v Minister for Justice*,[81] Smyth J. refused the relief sought, stating that the application before him was, "yet again":

> "an *ex parte* application which had I been given the facts now on affidavit I would have viewed in a different manner. Either selective facts were made known to the legal advisors, or there was a complete failure before counsel was instructed to critically analyse instructions so that the duty and obligation to observe good faith with the Court on an *ex parte* application could be observed."

7–68 In the circumstances, Smyth J. awarded costs to the respondents, commenting that "frankness and truth by the Applicant would as a matter of probability have avoided all these proceedings."

7–69 The requirement for full and frank disclosure is a key one. In *Brennan v Lockyer*,[82] Kennedy C.J. stated that an affidavit which does not fully recite the relevant facts but avers as a fact what is really a conclusion of fact "is not such an honest disclosure of facts as the court should act upon."[83]

(ii) Obligation on Legal Advisers

7–70 There is a consequent obligation upon legal advisers in advising their clients and presenting a case to the court, with Smyth J. reiterating in *Balogun v Minister for Justice*[84] the words of Donaldson M.R. in *Re: C.*[85] In that case the Master of the Rolls had stated that:

---

[78] *Goold v Collins* [2005] 1 I.L.R.M. 1 at 11, per Hardiman J.
[79] *Goold v Collins* [2005] 1 I.L.R.M. 1 at 11, per Hardiman J.
[80] See, inter alia, *McDonogh v Davies* (1875) I.R. 9 C.L. 300 at 302, per Palles C.B. and *State (Vozza) v District Justice O'Floinn* [1957] I.R. 227 at 325 and 251, per Davitt P. and Kingsmill Moore J. respectively. See also *R. v Kensington Income Tax Commissioners* [1917] 1 K.B. 486. See generally Brown "Enforcement—Full and Frank Disclosure" (2005) 155 N.L.J. 272.
[81] unreported, High Court, Smyth J., March 19, 2002.
[82] [1932] I.R. 100.
[83] [1932] I.R. 100 at 108.
[84] unreported, High Court, Smyth J., March 19, 2002.
[85] [1990] 1 Fam. 26.

"the fundamental duty of members of the legal profession is to assist the courts in the administration of justice regardless of the views or interests of their clients."[86]

(iii) The Golden Rule

7–71 The need for full and frank disclosure was characterised as "the golden rule" by Browne-Wilkinson V.C. in the case of *Tate Access Floors Inc. v Boswell*.[87] The Vice Chancellor stated that:

"No rule is better established, and few more important, than the rule (the golden rule) that a plaintiff applying for *ex parte* relief must disclose to the court all matters relevant to the exercise of the court's discretion whether or not to grant relief before giving the defendant an opportunity to be heard. If that duty is not observed by the plaintiff, the court will discharge the *ex parte* order and may, to mark its displeasure, refuse the plaintiff further *inter partes* relief even though the circumstances would otherwise justify the grant of such relief."[88]

7–72 There is therefore a clear obligation on parties moving an application for an interim injunction to make full disclosure of all facts relevant to the application, even where such facts may in fact militate against the granting of an interim order. In *McKenna v DC*,[89] Clarke J. observed that the obligation to make full disclosure was:

"a *quid pro quo* for the entitlement of the applicant to obtain what are, frequently, very onerous orders, without affording the person affected by those orders an opportunity to be heard."[90]

7–73 While this is of course correct, one commentator has fairly observed that in practical terms it is "wholly unrealistic to expect an applicant to put forward an adequate argument for his opponent's case."[91] This leads to the question of what in fact should be disclosed.

---

[86] [1990] 1 Fam. 26 at 36.
[87] [1991] Ch. 512; [1991] 2 W.L.R. 304; [1990] 3 All E.R. 303.
[88] [1991] Ch. 512 at 532; [1991] 2 W.L.R. 304 at 319; [1990] 3 All E.R. 303 at 316; cited with approval by Clarke J. in *Bambrick v Cobley* [2006] 1 I.L.R.M. 81 at 86.
[89] unreported, High Court, Clarke J., May 26, 2006.
[90] See also, *JRM Sports Ltd v Football Association of Ireland*, unreported, High Court, Clarke J., January 31, 2007.
[91] A.A.S. Zuckerman, "Interlocutory Remedies in Quest of Procedural Fairness" (1993) 56 M.L.R. 325 at 335, citing *Amanuel v Alexander Shipping Co* [1986] Q.B. 404 and *Columbia Picture Industries v Robinson* [1987] Ch. 38; [1986] 3 All E.R. 338.

(iv) Facts to Disclose

7–74 The obvious question arising out of the need for candour is what facts
should be disclosed to the court such that it can exercise its discretion. In this
regard, Lord O'Hagan L.C. cautioned in the case of *Atkin v Moran*[92] that:

> "The party applying is not to make himself the judge of whether a particular
> fact is material or not. If it is such as might in any way affect the mind of the
> court it is its duty to bring it forward."

7–75 However, the obligation to make full and fair disclosure is not unqualified,
and in *Bambrick v Cobley*,[93] which concerned an application for a *Mareva*
injunction,[94] Clarke J. referred to the *Brink's Mat* case and noted that:

> "I am also mindful of the fact that the courts have noted (for example in
> *Brink's Mat Limited v Elcombe* [1988] 3 All E.R. 188) that in particular in
> heavy commercial cases the borderline between material facts and non-
> material facts can be a somewhat uncertain one and that, without discounting
> the heavy duty of candour and care which falls upon persons making *ex parte*
> applications, the application of the principle of disclosure should not be
> carried to extreme lengths."[95]

7–76 Clarke J. proceeded to identify the test by reference to which materiality
should be judged as being one of:

> "whether objectively speaking the facts could reasonably be regarded as
> material with materiality to be construed in a reasonable and not excessive
> manner."[96]

7–77 There is no reason to suppose this dictum should not have a wider
application beyond "heavy commercial cases".

7–78 The courts have also acknowledged that applications for interim relief are
often prepared in haste and under considerable time pressures. In the case of
European Paint Importers Ltd v O'Callaghan,[97] Peart J. rejected the contention
that there had been a lack of candour, and accepted that "[t]here will inevitably
in applications for interim relief be some haste in the preparation of affidavits
and exhibits." In accepting this, he also stated that it is inevitable that there may
later be found to be some shortcomings in such papers, but made reference to

---

[92]   [1871] I.R. 6 E.Q. 79.
[93]   [2006] 1 I.L.R.M. 81.
[94]   As to which, see further, Ch.8, Commercial Inunctions.
[95]   [2006] 1 I.L.R.M. 81 at 87.
[96]   [2006] 1 I.L.R.M. 81 at 87.
[97]   unreported, High Court, Peart J., August 10, 2005.

such shortcomings going to something "much more fundamental" than what was before him.

7-79 The key criterion identified by Peart J. was that the process of seeking an injunction had "been abused to the extent of obtaining an order under a false pretence." As such, it is clear that a question as to whether there has been a lack of candour will, in the first instance, have to be determined on a case-by-case basis. Secondly, the effect of such lack of candour will have to be analysed in order to establish whether there has been an abuse, such that the court may identify that an order has been obtained under false pretences. If this is the case, there can be serious consequences for the party found not to have acted with candour.[98]

(v) Principles Relevant to Full and Frank Disclosure

7-80 One of the leading authorities in relation to disclosure in this context is the case of *Brink's Mat Ltd v Elcombe*[99] in which Ralph Gibson L.J. listed seven principles relevant to the duty of full disclosure on an ex parte application. These principles, which bear setting out in full, along with the cases cited by Ralph Gibson L.J. in support of each proposition, are[100]:

> "(1) The duty of the applicant is to make 'a full and fair disclosure of all the material facts'[101];
>
> (2) The material facts are those which it is material for the judge to know in dealing with the application as made: materiality is to be decided by the court and not by the assessment of the applicant or his legal advisers[102];
>
> (3) The applicant must make proper inquiries before making the application ... The duty of disclosure therefore applies not only to material facts known to the applicant but also to any additional facts which he would have known if he had made such inquiries;

---

98   See para.7–86.
99   [1988] 1 W.L.R. 1350; [1988] 3 All E.R. 188. See also *Gadget Shop Ltd v Bug Com Ltd* [2000] All E.R. 799.
100 [1988]1 W.L.R. 1350 at 1366; [1988] 3 All E.R. 188 at 192.
101 Citing *R. v Kensington Income Tax Commissioners* [1917] 1 K.B. 486 at 514, per Scrutton L.J. It has also been held in the case of *Commercial Bank of the Near East Plc v P* [1989] N.L.J.R. 645 that there is an ongoing obligation to bring any subsequent material change in circumstances to the attention of the court.
102 Citing *R. v Kensington Income Tax Commissioners* [1917] 1 K.B. 486 at 504, per Lord Cozens-Hardy M.R., the latter citing *Dalglish v Jarvie* (1850) 2 Mac. & G. 231 at 238 and *Thermax Ltd v Schott Industrial Glass Ltd* [1981] F.S.R. 289 at 295, per Browne-Wilkinson J. See also *Curacao v Harkisandas* [1992] 2 Lloyd's Rep. 186, in which Hirst J. stated that the applicant's solicitors reached a decision not to disclose a point "with complete sincerity and integrity, but I am bound to say in my view it was mistaken. The court is completely dependant in ex parte applications on complete, full and frank disclosure, whatever the nature of the relief sought."

(4) The extent of the inquiries which will be held to be proper, and therefore necessary, must depend on all the circumstances of the case including (a) the nature of the case which the applicant is making when he makes the application; and (b) the order for which application is made and the probable effect of the order on the defendant[103]; ... and (c) the degree of legitimate urgency and the time available for the making of inquiries[104];

(5) If material non-disclosure is established the court will be 'astute to ensure that a plaintiff who obtains [an ex parte injunction] without full disclosure ... is deprived of any advantage he may have derived by that breach of duty'[105];

(6) Whether the fact not disclosed is of sufficient materiality to justify or require immediate discharge of the order without examination of the merits depends on the importance of the fact to the issues which were to be decided by the judge on the application. The answer to the question whether the non-disclosure was innocent, in the sense that the fact was not known to the applicant or that its relevance was not perceived, is an important consideration but not decisive by reason of the duty on the applicant to make all proper inquiries and to give careful consideration to the case being presented;

(7) Finally, it 'is not for every omission that the injunction will be automatically discharged. A locus poenitentiae may sometimes be afforded.'[106] The court has a discretion, notwithstanding proof of material non-disclosure which justifies or requires the immediate discharge of the ex parte order, nevertheless to continue the order, or to make a new order on terms."[107]

(vi) Continuing Obligation After Order Obtained

7–81 In the case of *Network Telecom (Europe) Ltd v Telephone Systems International Inc.*,[108] Burton J. held that the duty to give full and frank disclosure continued where, after the order had been obtained but before it had been served, "significant facts" occurred, and the order relates to: (a) service out of the jurisdiction; and (b) the bringing of a foreigner into the jurisdiction. However, it would appear that the duty to make full and frank disclosure goes beyond those specific circumstances. In the earlier case of *Commercial Bank of the Near East Plc v A*,[109] Saville J. had held that as long as the proceedings remained on an ex parte basis there was a duty on the applicant to bring to the court's attention any new or altered facts or matters which would have been

---

[103] Citing *Columbia Picture Industries Inc. v Robinson* [1987] Ch. 38.
[104] *Bank Mellat v Nikpour* [1985] F.S.R. 87 at 92, per Slade L.J.
[105] per Donaldson L.J. in *Bank Mellat v Nikpour* [1985] F.S.R. 87 at 91, citing Warrington L.J. in
R. v Kensington Income Tax Commissioners [1917] 1 K.B. 486 at 509.
[106] per Lord Denning M.R. in *Bank Mellat v Nikpour* [1985] F.S.R. 87 at 90.
[107] per Glidewell L.J. in *Lloyds Bowmaker Ltd v Britannia Arrow Holdings Plc* [1988] 1 W.L.R.
1337 at 1343; [1988] 3 All E.R. 178 at 183.
[108] [2004] 1 All E.R. (Comm) 418.
[109] [1989] 2 Lloyd's Rep. 319.

disclosed to the court had they pertained when the application was made. This is a view which presumably would commend itself to the courts in this jurisdiction.

(vii) Obligation at the Interlocutory Stage

7–82 It has been observed that the obligation of full and frank disclosure is essentially diminished at the interlocutory stage. Instead, the obligation at that stage is not to knowingly mislead the court.[110] The rationale for this is that, at the interlocutory stage, the defendant is now generally in a position to present his own case.

(g) Undertaking as to Damages

7–83 As with applications for interlocutory injunctions, in bringing an application for an interim injunction a plaintiff must be in a position to provide an undertaking as to damages.[111] Indeed, the practice of providing undertakings as to damages was originally only inserted in ex parte orders for injunctions.[112] Undertakings as to damages and their role in securing an injunction is discussed in greater detail in Ch.6, Interlocutory Applications.

7–84 Such an undertaking is given to the court by counsel acting for the party seeking the injunction.[113] As with applications for interlocutory injunctions, it is not sufficient to offer a limited undertaking, and a court must also be satisfied that the plaintiff would be able to honour such an undertaking, with plaintiffs on occasion required to show that they have the financial means to honour the undertaking.[114]

7–85 In *Cheltenham and Gloucester Building Society v Ricketts*,[115] Peter Gibson L.J., discussing the practice of the court on the enforcement of undertakings as to damages, made particular reference to the risk of injustice in circumstances where an injunction has been granted ex parte.

(h) Consequence of a Lack of Full and Frank Disclosure /Discharge

7–86 In the normal course, if there has not been full and frank disclosure during an ex parte application for an interim injunction, it is open to the party affected,

---

110 Gee, *Commercial Injunctions*, 5th edn (London: Thomson Sweet & Maxwell, 2004), p.247.
111 See also, Ch.5, Perpetual Injunctions, in which the enforcement of an undertaking as to damages is considered.
112 per Jessel M.R. in *Smith v Day* (1882) 21 Ch D 421 at 423.
113 There is no obligation to give such an undertaking on affidavit: see *Harding v Cork Co Council,* ex tempore, High Court, Kelly J., February 28, 2006. However, it is invariably the practice to see a paragraph at the end of an affidavit offering such an undertaking.
114 See *Westman Holdings Ltd v McCormack* [1992] 1 I.R. 151 at 158, per Finlay C.J.
115 [1993] 1 W.L.R. 1545 at 1554; [1993] 4 All E.R. 276 at 284.

generally the defendant, to seek to have the order discharged.[116] Of course, it may not be until a later date that the defendant actually becomes aware of the basis on which the application was made.[117] It was held by the Court of Appeal in *Behbehani v Salem*[118] that it makes no difference whether a court would have come to the same conclusion had all the facts been fully disclosed.

7–87 The importance of compliance with the "golden rule" is highlighted by the decision of McCracken J. in *Production Association Minsk Tractor Works and Belarus Equipment (Ireland) Limited v Saenko*.[119] In that case an application for an interlocutory injunction was refused on a number of grounds, including the fact that after an interim order was granted it was conceded in a replying affidavit that over £95,000 of a total of £300,000 was in fact paid into an account of the first named plaintiff; McCracken J. observed that "this must have been known to the plaintiffs when the original affidavit was sworn." In *TMG Group Ltd v Al Babtain Trading*,[120] Keane J. stated that:

> "The granting of an interlocutory injunction is always a matter for the discretion of the court and I am far from saying that, in a case where it could be shown that the court had been seriously and deliberately misled on an *ex parte* application for an interim injunction, the court in the exercise of its discretion might not properly refuse an interlocutory injunction on that ground alone."[121]

7–88 It is clear that the consequences of non-disclosure are not automatic, based on the dictum of Glidewell L.J. in the case of *Lloyds Bowmaker Limited v Britannia Arrow Holdings Limited* in the context of a *Mareva* injunction[122]:

> "Certainly on the more recent authorities it is my view that the High Court would have a discretion to grant a second *Mareva* order, and it may well be

---

[116] See generally, *Brink's Mat Ltd v Elcombe* [1988]1 W.L.R. 1350; [1988] 3 All E.R. 188 and *Behbehani v Salem* [1989] 1 W.L.R. 723; [1989] 2 All E.R. 143, in which Woolf L.J. endorsed the views expressed in *Brink's Mat Ltd*.

[117] As happened in *Bambrick v Cobley* [2006] 1 I.L.R.M. 81 where the plaintiff's holidays and a family bereavement had led to the papers not being served in the usual manner.

[118] [1989]1 W.L.R. 723; [1989] 2 All E.R. 143.

[119] unreported, High Court, McCracken J., February 25, 1998. The attitude of the courts to being misled in general terms is encapsulated in the observations of Hardiman J. in the case of *Shelly Morris v Bus Atha Cliath* [2003] 1 I.R. 232, a personal injuries case.

[120] [1982] I.L.R.M. 349.

[121] [1982] I.L.R.M. 349 at 357.

[122] [1988] 1 W.L.R. 1337; [1988] 3 All E.R. 178, *cf. R v Kensington Income Tax Commissioners* [1917] 1 K.B. 486, which suggests that discharge is automatic, Warrington L.J. stating (at 509) that where an ex parte application has been granted on foot of an inaccurate grounding affidavit, the beneficiary of the court's relief "will be deprived of any advantage he may have already obtained by means of the order which has thus, wrongly, been obtained by him". See also *Ali & Fahd Shobokshi Group Ltd v Noneim* [1989] 2 All E.R. 404, in which deliberate non-disclosure of material facts led to an automatic discharge.

that this court would have a discretion to preserve the *status quo* in the meantime pending such an application, or a discretion itself to grant a second *Mareva* order".[123]

7–89 However, in the same case Dillon L.J. stated, in relation to the procedural aspect of this, that:

"I find it a cumbersome procedure that the court should be bound, instead of itself granting a fresh injunction, to discharge the existing injunction and stay the discharge until a fresh application is made, possibly in another court, and the court which is asked to discharge the injunction should not simply, as a matter of discretion in an appropriate case, refuse to discharge it if it feels that it would be appropriate to grant a fresh injunction. That leaves me to think that there is a discretion in the court on an application for discharge."[124]

7–90 Clarke J. indicated in *Bambrick v Cobley*[125] that he preferred the approach of Dillon L.J. as set out above. He held that the court has a discretion to refuse to grant the interlocutory injunction and to discharge the interim injunction already granted although it "is not necessarily obliged to do so".[126]

7–91 Summarising the position as considered in *Bambrick*, Clarke J. set out the factors which would be "most likely to weigh heavily with the court" in considering whether to exercise its discretion to discharge the order granted:

"1. The materiality of the facts not disclosed.
2. The extent to which it may be said that the plaintiff is culpable in respect of a failure to disclose. A deliberate misleading of the court is likely to weigh more heavily in favour of the discretion being exercised against the continuance of an injunction than an innocent omission. There are obviously intermediate cases where the court may not be satisfied that there was a deliberate attempt to mislead but that the plaintiff was, nonetheless, significantly culpable in failing to disclose.
3. The overall circumstances of the case which led to the application in the first place."[127]

---

[123]   [1988] 1 W.L.R. 1337 at 1346; [1988] 3 All E.R. 178 at 185.
[124]   [1988] 3 All E.R. 178 at 187; *cf. Yardley & Co Ltd v Higson* [1984] F.S.R. 304 in which it had been suggested that a court may discharge the first injunction if problems exist in relation to material facts, and a second injunction granted. In *Dormeuil Freres SA v Nicolian International (Textiles) Ltd* [1998] 1 W.L.R. 1362. Browne-Wilkinson V.C. suggested that dealing with potentially complex issues at the interlocutory stage was a concern and, as such, the appropriate time to consider a discharge was at the trial of the substantive matter, a view which has been trenchantly criticised: see Courtney, *Mareva Injunctions* (Dublin: Butterworths, 1988), p.314, who states that making a defendant wait until the trial of the action to apply for a discharge seems a "preposterous distortion of the scales of justice".
[125]   [2006] 1 I.L.R.M. 81.
[126]   In relation to the duration of the order, see para.7–108.
[127]   [2006] 1 I.L.R.M. 81 at 89. See also, *McKenna v DC*, unreported, High Court, Clarke J., May

(i) Short Service

7–92 It may well be that a judge hearing an application for an interim injunction will, if the circumstances so require, refuse to grant the order sought ex parte and give liberty for short service of a notice of motion,[128] thus allowing a defendant to be represented and heard at an application.[129] Alternatively the judge may grant the injunction on an interim basis and fix a return date, again providing for short service. In either case, the applicant for the injunction should serve the notice of motion as appropriate, with the affidavit grounding the application for the interim injunction also grounding the application for the interlocutory injunction. If additional facts come to light, or existing facts need to be expanded upon, a supplemental affidavit may also be sworn in advance of the interlocutory hearing.

7–93 It may also be the case that a notice of motion and grounding affidavit seeking an interlocutory injunction have already been issued out of the Central Office and given a return date, but that circumstances are such that the party seeking the injunction is now seeking it on an accelerated basis. In such circumstances, a party will generally make an application to a Chancery judge seeking an earlier return date, together with liberty for short service of any supporting documentation as necessary.

7–94 There is no formal rule which prescribes what documents must be brought to court when seeking short service. As has been seen in the context of interlocutory applications,[130] the normal practice is to bring to court:

- a draft notice of motion for interlocutory relief; this is usually entitled "Notice of Motion for the Sitting of the Court", with spaces left for the insertion of the relevant return dates by the court registrar if short service is granted by the court;
- a copy of the affidavit grounding the application for interlocutory relief.

(j) Refusal to Grant

7–95 If an application for an injunction is refused on an ex parte basis, it is not open to a party to "shop around" other courts until such time as they find a judge who may be willing to grant the injunction. Instead, an appeal should be brought from that refusal.[131] The only circumstances in which a party may come

---

26, 2006 and *JRM Sports Ltd v Football Association of Ireland*, unreported, High Court, Clarke J., January 31, 2007.

[128] See Ch.6, Interlocutory Applications, para.6–211.

[129] As happened, for example, in *Study Group International Ltd v Millar*, unreported, High Court, Peart J., March 28, 2002.

[130] See Ch.6, Interlocutory Applications, para.6–213.

[131] See para.7–132.

back before the courts with the ex parte application is if there has been a material change in circumstances subsequent to the initial application, such that a judge is essentially being asked to determine what amounts to a different matter.

E. THE HEARING OF THE APPLICATION AND RELATED MATTERS

1. Appearance by the Defendant

7–96 Although an interim injunction is often dealt with on an ex parte basis, it may be the case that, having been alerted that an application is being made, a defendant may appear in court, indicate that s/he has only just been informed of the application and ask for matter to be returned for a few days time. Such a position would generally need to accompanied by an undertaking not to continue with a given activity.[132] The breach of such an undertaking can lead to sanctions.[133] Alternatively, a party may appear in court and participate in the application on a without-prejudice basis pending further instructions and/or consideration of the matter.

7–97 In *Graham v Campbell*,[134] the question arose as to whether, once an appearance has been entered, a party may still seek an injunction on an ex parte basis. James L.J, delivering the judgment of the court, stated that:

> "a Defendant who has had notice of motion for an injunction which he is willing and ready to meet, ought not to have that injunction issued against him *ex parte*."[135]

7–98 However, the peculiarity in that case was that an earlier formal motion for an injunction had not been heard due to the "pressure of business in the Court". It is not a dictum which has found favour with the courts subsequently.

7–99 In *Beese v Woodhouse*,[136] Davies L.J. disapproved of the dictum of James L.J. in *Graham*. He observed that if the court takes the view that:

> "irreparable damage may be done to the plaintiff by not preventing the continuance of the alleged nuisance or whatever wrongdoing it may be by the defendant plainly, in my view, the judge has jurisdiction to grant an *ex parte* injunction in such circumstances."[137]

---

[132] Securing such an undertaking may of itself be of tactical value to a plaintiff, thus justifying the bringing of the application in the first place, certainly in the short term.
[133] See Ch.12, Breach of an Injunction Order.
[134] (1878) 7 Ch D 490.
[135] (1878) 7 Ch D 490 at 493.
[136] [1970] 1 W.L.R. 586.
[137] [1970] 1 W.L.R. 586 at 590.

2. Nature and Form of the Order

7–100 Based on the wording of RSC Ord.50 r.6(2), an order "may be made either unconditionally or upon such terms and conditions as the Court thinks just".[138] As with injunction orders obtained at any stage of proceedings, the terms of the order must be certain and definite.[139]

7–101 In the case of *WEA Ltd v Visions Channel 4 Ltd*,[140] Sir John Donaldson M.R. had to consider the effect of ex parte orders. Noting that they were essentially provisional in nature, he stated that such orders are:

"made by the judge on the basis of evidence and submissions on one side only. Despite the fact that the applicant is under a duty to make full disclosure of all relevant information in his possession, whether or not it assists his application, this is no basis for making a definitive order and every judge knows this. He expects at a later stage to be given an opportunity to review his provisional order in the light of the evidence and argument adduced by the other side and in so doing he is not hearing an appeal from himself and in no way feels inhibited from discharging or varying his original order."[141]

7–102 There are also a number of express and implied terms and conditions upon which a court will grant relief.

(a) Terms and Conditions

7–103 The terms and conditions upon which a court will grant relief on an ex parte interim basis were considered by Munby J. in *W v H*.[142] Framed in the context of a family matter in the English courts, Munby J. indicated that he was not attempting to formulate any rule of practice applicable in all cases. However, his suggestions as to the relevant terms and conditions upon which a court might grant interim relief merit setting out, as from a common sense perspective they would appear equally relevant in this jurisdiction:

" (i) any *ex parte* order containing injunctions should set out on its face, either by way of recital or in a schedule, a list of all affidavits, witness statements and other evidential materials read by the judge;

(ii) the applicant's legal representatives should whenever possible liaise with the associate with a view to ensuring that the order as drawn contains this information;

---

[138] See RCC Ord.20 r.3, which appears to be broadly equivalent.
[139] See generally, Ch.5, Perpetual Injunctions, and the dictum of Joyce J. in *Attorney General v Staffordshire County Council* [1905] 1 Ch. 336.
[140] [1983] 1 W.L.R. 721; [1983] 2 All E.R. 589.
[141] [1983] 1 W.L.R. 721 at 727; [1983] 2 All E.R. 589 at 593.
[142] [2001] 1 All E.R. 300 at 318.

    (iii) on receipt of the order from the court the applicant's legal repre-
sentatives should satisfy themselves that the order as drawn correctly
sets out the relevant information and, if it does not, take urgent steps to
have the order amended under the slip rule; and

    (iv) the applicant's legal representatives should respond forthwith to any
reasonable request from the party injuncted or his legal representatives
either for copies of the materials read by the judge or for information
about what took place at the hearing."

7–104 Munby J. also indicated that "persons injuncted *ex parte* are entitled to
be given, if they ask, proper information as to what happened at the hearing."[143]
Dealing with what information was required, he suggested that:

"At the very least they are entitled to be told, if they ask, (a) exactly what
documents, bundles or other evidential materials were lodged with the court
either before or during the course of the hearing and (b) what legal authorities
were cited to the judge. Given this, it would obviously be prudent for those
acting for applicants in such cases to keep a proper note of the proceedings,
lest they otherwise find themselves embarrassed by a proper request for
information which they are unable to provide."[144]

7–105 In *Kelly v BBC*,[145] Munby J. referred to his decision in *W v H* and
highlighted two further points which he believed needed to be considered.
Again, although not binding in this jurisdiction, there is much to commend these
points from a practical perspective. The two points are:

"First, there may of course be cases—and the present was just such a case—
where the urgency is such that there is no time to prepare comprehensive
evidence in proper form. In such a case the court must—and will—act upon
the information provided by counsel. But in every such case there should, as
it seems to me, be an undertaking to swear and file an affidavit as soon as
possible ...

    The second point derives from the elementary principle of natural justice,
that if one party wishes to place evidence or other persuasive material before
the court the other parties must have an opportunity to see that material and
to address the court about it. One party may not make secret communications
to the court. It follows that it is wrong for a judge to be given material at an
ex parte, or without notice, hearing which is not at a later stage revealed to the
persons affected by the result of the application."[146]

---

[143] [2001] 1 All E.R. 300 at 318.
[144] [2001] 1 All E.R. 300 at 318.
[145] [2001] 1 All E.R. 323.
[146] [2001] 1 All E.R. 323 at 359. Although Munby J. recognised that the second of these
principles was qualified to an extent when dealing with children.

7–106 It was further held by Pumfrey J. in *Cinpres Gas Injection Ltd v Melea Ltd*[147] that where a party sought an ex parte interim injunction, it was the responsibility of counsel and solicitors to take a full note of what was said. There is considerable merit in such an approach. It is very easy in practice to depart from the material contained in an affidavit and to effectively put a gloss on it. This cannot really be tested by a court, and may be prejudicial to a party against whom an injunction is granted. In the circumstances, it seems that parties should be either confined to reading what is in the affidavit grounding the application and no more, or alternatively undertaking at the outset of the application to have a contemporaneous note of the application made. Such a note could then be made available to the party against whom the injunction is granted.

7–107 Related to this, Courtney has identified terms and conditions which are implied into an ex parte *Mareva* interim injunction order.[148] The terms and conditions which apply more generally to interim orders obtained on an ex parte basis are[149]:

- notifying any party affected by the order of its terms[150];
- not using the information obtained for any collateral purpose[151];
- to stamp and issue the originating document, affidavit and other court documents as necessary.

(b) Duration of the Order

7–108 As observed by Kelly J. in *Fitzpatrick v Commissioner of An Garda Síochána*,[152] injunctive relief granted on an ex parte application is of an interim nature. As such, there is also imposed upon a successful applicant an obligation to apply for an interlocutory injunction on notice to the respondent within a short period of time.

7–109 The courts have always been concerned to ensure that the interference effected by an injunction is as limited in its duration as is practicable.[153] This is

---

[147] *Times Law Reports*, December 21, 2005.
[148] See Ch.8, Commercial Injunctions, para.8–104.
[149] Courtney, *Mareva Injunctions* (Dublin: Butterworths, 1998), p.335.
[150] For example, in *Minister for Arts, Heritage, the Gaeltacht and the Islands v Kennedy* [2002] 2 I.L.R.M. 94, an interim injunction was granted against the first named defendant prohibiting him from engaging, commencing or continuing any works of any nature or kind on lands which constituted a special area of conservation in Co Kerry. It was further ordered that the plaintiff's solicitor be at liberty to notify the making of the order by telephone, letter and fax by any member of the Wildlife Service or of the Garda Síochána or the solicitor.
[151] See Ch.8, Commercial Injunctions, para.8–106.
[152] [1996] E.L.R. 244.
[153] per Keane C.J. in *Keating v Crowley* [2002] 2 I.R. 744 at 759; [2003] 1 I.L.R.M. 88 at 102.

particularly so as the interference may well be with a right which the defendant is entitled to exercise without such interference That being so, interim injunctions are generally granted on such terms that they continue until a defined date, usually the next motion day.[154] The court will abridge time for the service of a notice of motion in order to ensure that the defendant is heard in a matter of days. There is usually a further qualification that a defendant may apply to court to discharge the order on giving a defined period of notice, often 24 hours.[155] With the hearing of the interlocutory motion, the interim injunction automatically expires.[156]

7–110 An injunction may be dissolved by order of the court prior to the day on which it is fixed to expire, but it does not extend beyond the date of expiry.[157] However, an interim order may be continued beyond the defined date, usually by consent between the parties or, if necessary, by order of the court in the absence of consent.

(c) Effect of the Order

(i) Name and Reputation

7–111 The courts have considered the extent to which it is likely that a view might be formed which is adverse to the good name or reputation of a party on the basis that he or she had been the subject of an ex parte order. Although this was specifically in the context of barring orders,[158] it is of wider application to note that the courts have given short shrift to such a suggestion of damage to a party's good name or reputation by virtue of granting an ex parte order, and have taken the view that any person forming such a view "would be acting

---

[154] Although in *Arisukwu v Minister for Justice, Equality and Law Reform*, unreported, Supreme, March 9, 2006, in the context of an attempted deportation, an injunction was granted at 6.30 pm, to continue until 11am the following morning.

[155] See, for example, *Countyglen Plc v Carway* [1995] 1 I.L.R.M. 481. Outside the legal term, a judge will generally have to exercise their discretion in determining the duration of an interim order, but the relative frequency of vacation sittings and the fact that a duty judge is always available mean that the timescale involved is usually very short. For example, in *Premier Dairies v Doyle* [1996] 1 I.L.R.M. 363, Johnson J. granted four interim injunctions to the plaintiffs on September 11, 1995 (during the summer vacation). On September 13, the defendants unsuccessfully applied to Johnson J. to set aside one of the four injunctions. The hearing of the interlocutory application went ahead before Kinlen J. on September 20, 21 and 22, with a reserved judgment delivered on September 29. See also *Fitzpatrick v Commissioner of An Garda Síochána* [1996] E.L.R. 244.

[156] *Keating v Crowley* [2002] 2 I.R. 744 at 759; [2003] 1 I.L.R.M. 88 at 102, per Keane C.J.

[157] *Bolton v London School Board* 7 (1878) Ch D 766.

[158] There is a significant distinction between the statutory jurisdiction of the District Court to grant barring orders and the jurisdiction enjoyed by the courts of Chancery to grant injunctions in civil cases, particularly in relation to the severity and effect of an ex parte barring order. See *Keating v Crowley* [2002] 2 I.R. 744; [2003] 1 I.L.R.M. 88. See generally, Ch.11, Specific Statutory Injunctions, para.11–143.

unreasonably in the legal sense of that term" and that such a conclusion would be "logically and legally insupportable, would fly in the face of common sense and would be most unjust."[159]

(ii) No Wrongful Injunction

7–112 The expression "wrongful injunction" is sometimes used in relation to an injunction secured on an interim basis but where a party subsequently loses the full trial. However, Jacob L.J. pointed out *in SmithKline Beecham Plc v Apotex Europe Ltd (No. 2)*[160] that the expression was used "for convenience and want of a better term" and that the party who lost the full trial was not regarded as a wrongdoer.

(d) Prompt Prosecution of Proceedings

7–113 When injunctive relief is granted on an ex parte basis there is a need to prosecute the substantive proceedings—for example, by delivering a statement of claim and dealing with attendant issues and matters—in a prompt manner.[161]

7–114 The need to prosecute proceedings promptly was considered by Finnegan P. in *Criminal Assets Bureau v PS*.[162] The President emphasised that the entitlement to have an injunction discharged due to delay is more likely where an interim injunction obtained on an ex parte basis is concerned, as opposed to at the interlocutory stage.

7–115 In *DJS Meats Ltd v Minister for Agriculture and Food*,[163] the plaintiff had obtained an interim injunction, with the application for an interlocutory injunction taking 10 months to bring before the court. No pleadings had been delivered subsequent to the issuing of the plenary summons and the entry of an appearance. On that basis, Lynch J. continued the interim injunction for a limited period of weeks, conditional on the expedition of proceedings.

7–116 In granting an interim injunction, most judges will in fact give directions in relation to the delivery of pleadings, or will incorporate the date(s) for delivery of proceedings into the interim injunction order. By so doing, the party who has secured the interim injunction will now be subject to a timetable agreed with, or imposed by, the court and, as such, there should in principle be few issues arising in terms of prosecuting proceedings.

---

[159] per Hardiman J. in *Goold v Collins* [2005] 1 I.L.R.M. 1 at 11.
[160] [2007] Ch. 71 at 83; [2006] 3 W.L.R. 1146 at 1157.
[161] See *Hytrac Conveyors v Conveyors International* [1982] 3 All E.R. 415 in the context of an application for an *Anton Piller* order.
[162] unreported, High Court, Finnegan P., April 12, 2002.
[163] unreported, High Court, Lynch J., February 17, 1993.

3. Costs

7–117 The costs of an application for an interim injunction are, in the normal course, reserved for the trial judge to determine at the conclusion of the substantive hearing. If the interim injunction is discharged without more at the interlocutory stage, a determination as to costs might be made at that juncture.

7–118 At the substantive hearing, if costs have been reserved, they are generally awarded to the successful party. However, the importance of full and frank disclosure at the ex parte stage is emphasised by the case of *Balogun v Minister for Justice*.[164] In that case costs were awarded to the respondent at the interlocutory stage on the basis that frankness and truth by the applicant would as a matter of probability have avoided all the proceedings.

7–119 An interesting argument in relation to the awarding of reserved costs was put forward in the case of *Murnaghan v Markland Holdings Ltd*.[165] In that case, Laffoy J. had found, inter alia, that the plaintiff could have, but did not, try to resolve the problems which he encountered without resorting to the remedy of an interim injunction. In the circumstances, it was submitted on behalf of the first named defendant that the plaintiff should not be allowed the reserved costs of, inter alia, the applications for interim and interlocutory injunctions. Laffoy J. agreed with the submission, and took the view that, "the plaintiff should not be awarded the reserved costs of the application for the interim injunction."[166]

7–120 However, Laffoy J. did award the costs reserved at the interlocutory injunction stage to the plaintiff on the basis that the construction works complained of which formed the kernel of the case had caused damage to property and "the plaintiff was entitled to pursue the remedy he sought on notice to the defendants."

4. Breach of an Interim Injunction

7–121 There are a variety of remedies available to a party when an injunction has been breached, and these are considered in detail in Ch.12, Breach of an Injunction. Such remedies are applicable to breaches of all forms of injunction[167] and simply because an injunction is interim in nature does not in any way diminish the availability of remedies in relation to an alleged breach.

---

[164]   unreported, High Court, Smyth J., March 19, 2000.
[165]   [2005] 2 I.L.R.M. 161.
[166]   [2005] 2 I.L.R.M. 161at 167.
[167]   See the dictum of Lavery J. in *Gore-Booth v Gore-Booth* (1962) 96 I.L.T.R. 32 at 36.

5. Discharge

7–122 Once an interim injunction has been granted, a party is entitled to apply for its discharge. This term tends to be used interchangeably with variations on "dissolution", "vacation" and "setting aside".[168] In *Bambrick v Cobley*,[169] Clarke J. pointed out that in practice an application for discharge will come on for hearing at the same time as an application for an interlocutory injunction. It makes sense from a practical perspective to deal with the matter at this juncture, as both parties are in court and a judge can consider both sides of any application. However, with the hearing of the interlocutory motion, the interim injunction automatically expires.[170]

(a) Grounds for a Discharge

7–123 A party may seek a discharge on the basis of a lack of full and frank disclosure on the part of the applicant for the injunction. However, other arguments which may be put forward in support of a discharge include the fact that an application may be an abuse of the court's processes,[171] or that an application is vexatious and oppressive having regard to the pertinent facts.[172]

(b) Time Which Must Elapse

7–124 There is no prescribed length of time which must pass before the discharge of an interim injunction can be sought. Indeed, applications to discharge have been made on occasion on the same day as the interim order was made.[173] However, it is often provided for in an interim injunction order that a

---

[168]   It would appear that nothing material turns on whichever term is used, but "discharge" is more frequently used in the context of an application brought in light of a lack of full and frank disclosure; "setting aside" tends to be more commonly used in the context of a successful appeal.

[169]   [2006] 1 I.L.R.M. 81.

[170]   *Keating v Crowley* [2002] 2 I.R. 744 at 759; [2003] 1 I.L.R.M. 88 at 102, per Keane C.J.

[171]   The inherent jurisdiction of a court to strike out proceedings as being an abuse of process in appropriate cases is exercised "only with great caution", per Keane J. in *McCauley v McDermott* [1997] 2 I.L.R.M. 486. See generally the observation of Scarman L.J. in *Goldsmith v Sperrings Ltd* [1977] 2 All E.R. 566 at 582 that the plaintiff's purpose "has to be shown to be not that which the law by granting a remedy offers to fulfil, but one which the law does not recognise as a legitimate use of the remedy sought." For a comprehensive review of the jurisdiction to strike out, in the context of specific performance proceedings which involved a related injunction, see *Claystone Ltd v Larking Ltd*, unreported, High Court, Laffoy J., March 14, 2007. See also Delany & McGrath, *Civil Procedure in the Superior Courts*, 2nd edn (Dublin: Thomson Round Hall, 2005), Ch.14.

[172]   An argument made in *Sweeney v National University of Ireland Cork t/a Cork University Press* [2001] 1 I.L.R.M. 310.

[173]   See, for example, *Maguire v Drury* [1995] 1 I.L.R.M. 108, in which the interim order made by Kinlen J. was discharged by O'Hanlon J. on the day it which had been granted and a further interim order made.

defendant may apply to court to discharge the order on giving a defined period of notice, often 24 hours; in other words, the application to discharge must be made with the other party present in court, or at least on notice that such an application is being made. However, in the case of *London City Agency (JCD) Ltd v Lee*,[174] Megarry J. suggested that an application to vary or discharge an injunction may be made on an ex parte basis where there are sufficiently cogent grounds to support such an application. However, he added the rider that "[i]f time permits, it is plainly preferable that any such application should be made upon due notice."[175]

(c) Parties

7–125 It is also at the court's discretion whether to discharge an injunction as against all the named parties or in respect of certain parties only. This will, of course, depend on who actually brings the application for discharge and the particular circumstances of a given case.[176]

(d) Cross Examination

7–126 If necessary, a party who has sworn an affidavit in support of an injunction may be cross-examined on the contents of the affidavit at the hearing for a discharge, particularly if that hearing is to be treated as the hearing of the action. RSC Ord.40 r.1, which deals with any "petition, motion, or other application" requires an application to be to the court if the attendance of a deponent for cross-examination is required. Witnesses may also give oral evidence.[177]

(e) Agreement Between the Parties/Variation

7–127 The party who has sought and secured the interim injunction may also come to an agreement with the party against whom the injunction is granted to discharge the interim injunction subject to certain undertakings being given. In practical terms, the parties are more likely to agree to the variation of an injunction order (although such agreement is in no way a precondition of

---

174 [1970] Ch. 597; [1970] 2 W.L.R. 136.
175 [1970] Ch. 597 at 599; [1970] 2 W.L.R. 136 at 138. There is old authority to suggest that an interim order obtained ex parte by suppression of a material fact may be discharged without notice of motion to discharge *Boyce v Gill* 64 L.T.N.S. 824. See also, *Wimbledon Local Board v Croydon Rural Sanitary Authority* (1886) 32 Ch D 421.
176 See, for example, *Murnaghan v Markland Holdings Ltd* [2005] 2 I.L.R.M. 161, in which an interim injunction granted against the first defendant was vacated, but that against the second defendant continued (albeit that the second defendant was at that stage effectively out of the picture, having gone into voluntary liquidation).
177 In the case of *Attorney General v X* [1992] I.L.R.M. 401, the parents of X, a 14-year-old schoolgirl allegedly raped by her friend's father, contested the making of the interim orders. That hearing was treated as the hearing of the action and oral evidence was given.

seeking variation; a party against whom an order has been made may also apply on notice to have an order varied).

(f) Applying for a Discharge before Appealing

7–128 In *Voluntary Purchasing Groups Inc. v Insurco International Ltd*,[178] McCracken J. acknowledged the risks inherent in granting ex parte relief and stated that in the interests of justice it is essential that an ex parte order may be reviewed, particularly in circumstances where it had been made in the absence of the parties affected by it, who did not have the opportunity to present their side of the case or to correct errors in the original evidence or submissions before the court.

7–129 It was held in the English case of *WEA Records Ltd v Visions Channel 4 Ltd*[179] that a defendant should not appeal against the granting of an ex parte injunction without first applying for a discharge; the appeal is then from the refusal to discharge. It was also held in *WEA Records* that to appeal directly from the ex parte order is an abuse of process. Whilst there does not appear to be such an explicit dictum from the courts in this jurisdiction, there are rules of court dealing with setting aside an order obtained ex parte. Rules of the Superior Courts Ord.52 r.3 provides that:

> "In any case the Court, if satisfied that the delay caused by proceeding by motion on notice under this Order would or might entail irreparable or serious mischief, may make any order *ex parte* upon such terms as to costs or otherwise and subject to such undertaking, if any, as the Court may think just; and any party affected by such order may move to set it aside."[180]

7–130 In practice, the usual approach is to return to the judge who granted the injunction ex parte and to seek to have that injunction discharged. It is unlikely that, for example, the Supreme Court would be particularly receptive to an appeal seeking a discharge in circumstances where an attempt had not first been made to have the injunction discharged by the High Court judge who granted it.

7–131 The only circumstances in which an appeal might be brought from the granting of an interim injunction[181] before a discharge is sought would be if an injunction has been secured in the Circuit Court. In circumstances where it is not possible to contact a Circuit Court judge in order to deal with an application for discharge, there would appear to be no obstacle to appealing to a High Court judge in such circumstances. This would presumably be subject to explaining to

---

178 [1995] 2 I.L.R.M. 145 at 147.
179 [1983] 1 W.L.R. 721.
180 See RCC Ord.64.
181 As distinct from the refusal of such an order. See para.7–95.

the High Court judge why a discharge was not sought before the appeal was brought.

6. Appeal

7–132 An appeal lies from the Circuit to the High Court and from the High Court to the Supreme Court, encompassing orders sought ex parte, and more particularly the refusal of such orders.

(a) Circuit to High Court

7–133 Rules of the Superior Courts Ord.61 r.9 provides that the notice of appeal from the refusal of an ex parte application by the Circuit Court "shall be a two days' notice", with no service required. Pursuant to RSC Ord.61 r.6, an appeal does not operate as a stay of execution in relation to the decision appealed from, unless ordered otherwise by the Circuit judge or the High Court judge in Dublin.

(b) High to Supreme Court

7–134 By virtue of RSC Ord.58 r.13:

> "Where an *ex parte* application has been refused in whole or in part by the High Court an application for a similar purpose may be made to the Supreme Court *ex parte* within four days from the date of such refusal, or within such enlarged time as the Supreme Court may allow."

7–135 An appeal shall not operate as a stay of execution in relation to the decision appealed from, unless ordered otherwise by court.[182]

7. Relationship to the Interlocutory Application

7–136 As pointed out by McCracken J. in the High Court in the case of *O'Callaghan v Disciplinary Tribunal*,[183] there is no rule in the High Court that a judge who grants an interim injunction may not hear the later interlocutory injunction application. This is because, as pointed out by Geoghegan J. in the Supreme Court in the same case, "[t]he nature of the decision to be made the second time round is quite different from the nature of the decision made on the first occasion."[184]

---

[182] RSC Ord.58, r.18. See generally, Delany & McGrath, *Civil Procedure in the Superior Courts*, 2nd edn (Dublin: Thomson Round Hall, 2005), Ch.20.
[183] [2002] 1 I.L.R.M. 89.
[184] [2002] 1 I.L.R.M. 89 at 94.

7–137 It should also be noted that simply because an application for an injunction on an interim basis has failed, this does not preclude an application being brought on an interlocutory basis in the normal way. Of course, if the interim application has failed, the reasons for such a failure would have to be very carefully reviewed before embarking on an interlocutory application. Failure at the interim stage should not in any way prejudice the substantive hearing for a perpetual injunction as the latter will in the normal course be determined with substantially more evidence before the court.[185]

---

[185] See the dictum of Clarke J. in *O'Brien v AON Insurance Managers (Dublin) Ltd*, unreported, High Court, Clarke J., January 14, 2004.

CHAPTER 8

COMMERCIAL INJUNCTIONS

A. INTRODUCTION

8–01 The development of *Mareva* injunctions, *Anton Piller* orders and *Bayer* orders,[1] which freeze assets, preserve evidence and restrict travel respectively, bears witness to the flexible nature of the injunction. None of these orders were known to the courts before the 1970s. These injunctions are frequently sought in the context of what might broadly be termed commercial litigation and are collectively referred to as "commercial injunctions". Although each is a standalone remedy, they are often sought in combination with each other. For convenience, they are therefore treated together in a single chapter. Each order will be considered in turn, both in terms of its development and range and the applicable tests employed when applying for such an injunction. As each is generally sought on an ex parte basis, reference should also be made to the Ch.7, Interim Injunctions, specifically the applicable considerations when an injunction is sought on an ex parte basis.

B. *MAREVA* INJUNCTION

1. Overview[2]

8–02 A *Mareva* injunction[3] was first granted in 1975 and is named after the eponymous case determined by the Court of Appeal in London, *Mareva*

---

[1] There appears to be no formal reason why *Mareva* injunctions are generally known as such, rather than as *Mareva* orders, in circumstances where in general usage the terms *Anton Piller* orders and *Bayer* orders are commonplace. One possible explanation is that traditionally a *Mareva* injunction has more in common with the traditional understanding of the remit of an equitable injunction, whereas *Anton Piller* and *Bayer* orders go, as will be seen, beyond such a traditional understanding. However, since the introduction of the Civil Procedure Rules (CPR) in England in 1999, the a *Mareva* injunction is now known as a freezing order. Perhaps the dropping of the word "injunction" and the use of the word "order" is a reflection of the expansion of the *Mareva* injunction such that it too now has a remit which goes beyond the traditional understanding of the form and effect of an equitable injunction.

[2] For an extremely clear and comprehensive treatment of *Mareva* injunctions, see generally, Courtney, *Mareva Injunctions* (Dublin: Butterworths, 1998). See also Gee, *Commercial Injunctions*, 5th edn (London: Thomson Sweet & Maxwell, 2004) and Hoyle, *Freezing and Search Orders*, 4th edn (London: Informa, 2006). As noted by Lord Hoffman in the 4th edn of *Commercial Injunctions*, "The *Mareva* was a response to the use of the one-ship company registered in Liberia with directors in Sark and a bank account in Liberia."

[3] Known as a Freezing Order in England since the introduction of the Civil Procedure Rules (CPR) in 1999.

Compania Naviera SA v International Bulk Carriers SA.[4] It is an ancillary relief
and is not a cause of action in itself.[5] A *Mareva* injunction, when granted, is
directed towards a defendant whom it is feared may remove, conceal or
dissipate his assets prior to any attempt to enforce a judgment against him. As
such, it is of great value to a plaintiff in that it orders the defendant to preserve,
and not to dissipate or conceal, his assets up to the predicted value of the claim.
A *Mareva* injunction may be granted in advance of the substantive trial of an
action, but also after judgment if there is a risk that assets will be removed in
order to avoid execution of judgment.[6]

(a) An Ancillary Order

8–03 A *Mareva* injunction is an ancillary order and, as such, there will
generally have to be substantive proceedings in being[7]—or about to come into
being—in aid of which the injunction is actually being sought.[8]

(b) Freezes Assets

8–04 In practical terms, a *Mareva* injunction freezes the assets of the party
against whom it is granted.[9] Those assets are most commonly, though not
exclusively, bank accounts.[10] It prevents that party from dealing with those
assets, such that they cannot be put beyond the reach of the party seeking relief
before judgment is satisfied.[11] As observed by Courtney,[12] the novelty of the

---

[4] [1975] 2 Lloyd's Rep. 509. Its creation was described (somewhat self-servingly) by Lord
    Denning, its creator, as "the greatest piece of judicial law reform in my time": Lord Denning,
    The Due Process of Law (London: Butterworths, 1980), p.134.
[5] *Caudron v Air Zaire* [1985] I.R. 716; [1986] I.L.R.M. 10; *Siskina (Owners of cargo lately laden
    on baord) v Distos SA* [1979] A.C. 210; [1977] 3 W.L.R. 818; [1977] 3 All E.R. 803.
[6] *Orwell Steel Ltd v Asphalt and Tarmac (UK) Ltd* [1984] 1 W.L.R. 1097.
[7] See *Fourie v Le Roux* [2007] 1 W.L.R. 320; [2007] 1 All E.R. 1087.
[8] See *Caudron v Air Zaire* [1986] I.L.R.M. 10. But see Ch.2, Extraterritorial Jurisdiction,
    para.2–78 as to the effect of s.13 of the Jurisdiction of Courts and Enforcement of Judgments
    Act 1998.
[9] In *Countyglen v Carway* [1995] I.R. 208 at 218, Murphy J. did not accept the argument that a
    Mareva injunction should not be granted on the basis of its impingement on a party's
    constitutional property rights; see in particular Arts 40.3.2 and 43. See generally Hogan &
    Whyte, *J.M. Kelly: The Irish Constitution*, 4th edn (Dublin: Butterworths, 2003).
[10] The word "assets" has included, inter alia, cargo on board a ship (*Clipper Maritime Co Ltd of
    Monrovia v Mineralimportexport* [1981] 1 W.L.R. 1262; [1981] 3 All E.R. 664); ships themselves
    (*The Rena K* [1979] Q.B. 377; [1978] 3 W.L.R. 431; [1979] 1 All E.R. 397); machinery (*Rasu
    Maritima SA v Perusahaan Pertambangan Minyak Dan Gas Bumi Negara ("The Pertamina")*
    [1977] 3 W.L.R. 518; [1978] Q.B. 644; [1977] 3 All E.R. 324) and *TDK Tape Distributor (UK) Ltd
    v Videochoice* [1986] 1 W.L.R. 141; [1985] 3 All E.R. 345 (a life assurance policy) and *Allen v
    Jambo Holdings Ltd* [1980] 1 W.L.R. 1252; [1980] 2 All E.R. 502 (aircraft).
[11] Section 35(2) of the Family Law Act 1995 and s.37(2) of the Family Law (Divorce) Act 1996
    provide the power to grant relief in domestic situations in order to prevent assets being put
    beyond the reach of a party seeking to satisfy judgment.
[12] Courtney, *Mareva Injunctions* (Dublin: Butterworths, 1998), p.5.

Mareva injunction is that it restrains a defendant from dealing with its own assets even though the plaintiff has no proprietary interest in those assets.[13] As such, it is an exception to the rule in *Lister v Stubbs*,[14] which:

> "establishes the general proposition that a Plaintiff cannot prevent a Defendant from disposing of his assets *pendente lite* merely because he fears that by the time he obtains judgment in his favour the Defendant will have no assets against which the judgment can be enforced."[15]

8–05 A *Mareva* injunction does not create any rights in the assets frozen.

(c) Enforcement by a Financial Institution

8–06 That it is often bank accounts which are frozen highlights another advantage of a *Mareva* injunction, namely that enforcement can be effected by a financial institution. Such an institution would have "nothing to gain and all to lose"[16] in flouting a *Mareva* injunction.[17] Once an order is made, notice is in the normal course given immediately to the relevant bank(s).[18] However, there is a qualification to the granting of orders in so far as they affect banks. In *GPA Group Plc v Bank of Ireland*,[19] Keane J. gave effect to a policy enunciated by Kerr J. in *Harbottle Ltd v National Westminster Bank Ltd*[20] that it should only be in exceptional cases that the courts will interfere with the machinery of irrevocable obligations assumed by banks such as, for example, payment on foot of a letter of credit.[21] If the court were to interfere in such products, the machinery and commitments of banks would be undermined, and "trust in international commerce could be irreparably damaged."[22]

---

[13] In relation to the question of proprietary interests, see *Rex Pet Foods Ltd v Lamb Brothers (Dublin) Ltd*, unreported, High Court, Finlay P., August 26, 1982.

[14] (1890) 45 Ch D 1. That it is an exception is clear from the dictum of Sir Robert Megarry V.C. in *Barclay Johnson v Yuill* [1980] 1 W.L.R. 1259 at 1266; [1980] 3 All E.R. 190 at 195.

[15] per McWilliam J. in *Powerscourt Estates v Gallagher* [1984] I.L.R.M. 123 at 126.

[16] per Courtney, "Civil Arrest and Injunction to Restrain An Absconding Defendant From Leaving the Jurisdiction Part 1" (1990) 8 I.L.T. 200 at 200.

[17] See the consideration below of whether a bank may be found liable in negligence for breach of a *Mareva* injunction, as considered by the House of Lords in the case of *Commissioners of Customs and Excise v Barclays Bank Plc* [2006] 3 W.L.R. 1; see para.8–113.

[18] A bank is also entitled to an indemnity from the plaintiff against the costs of compliance with the order, which may be significant, particularly in circumstances where the existence of an account is known, but not the details of the account such as the relevant branch, account number etc. See *Z Ltd v A-Z* [1982] Q.B. 558; [1982] 2 W.L.R. 288; [1982] 1 All E.R. 556.

[19] [1992] 2 I.R. 408.

[20] [1978] Q.B. 146 at 155.

[21] See also, Ch.10, General Application, para.10–191.

[22] per Kerr J. in *Harbottle Ltd v National Westminster Bank Ltd* [1978] Q.B. 146 at 155.

(d) Not Designed to Give Security

8–07 A *Mareva* injunction is not intended to give a plaintiff security in advance of judgment being delivered. Rather, it is designed to prevent a defendant defeating the recovery of a judgment in the plaintiff's favour through the dissipation or removal of assets.[23]

8–08 In his decision in *Bambrick v Cobley*,[24] Clarke J. noted that a plaintiff is not entitled to security for every claimed liability. He observed that a *Mareva* injunction:

> "is not intended to provide plaintiffs with security in respect of all claims in relation to which they may be able to pass an arguability test. The true basis of the jurisdiction is the exercise by the court of its inherent power to prevent parties from placing their assets beyond the likely reach of the court in the event of a successful action."[25]

(e) Courts Alert to Abuse

8–09 Applications for *Mareva* injunctions can clearly lead to abuse; the granting of an order can put considerable pressure on a defendant to effectively provide some security for the plaintiff. There is clearly a reputational and business risk involved as well for the party against whom such an order is granted.[26] As such, the courts will be alert to speculative attempts to secure *Mareva* injunctions.

(f) Assets Within and Outside the Jurisdiction

8–10 Whilst *Mareva* injunctions were initially used to prevent foreign defendants from removing their assets from the jurisdiction, by 1980 they were extended by the courts in England to defendants residing within the jurisdiction.[27] A *Mareva* injunction may now also be granted in respect of assets outside the jurisdiction, subject to certain provisos.[28] Furthermore, although evolved in the

---

[23] See the comments of Scott L.J. in *Polly Peck v Nadir* [1992] 4 All E.R. 769 at 782.

[24] [2006] I.L.R.M. 81.

[25] [2006] I.L.R.M. 81 at 90.

[26] Although the courts have given short shrift to a suggestion of damage to a party's good name or reputation by virtue of granting an ex parte order (per Hardiman J. in *Goold v Collins* [2005] 1 I.L.R.M. 1 at 11), it would seem that in the context of *Mareva* injunctions, this statement must be qualified.

[27] See, *Barclay Johnson v Yuill* [1980] 1 W.L.R. 1259 at 1267; [1980] 3 All E.R. 190 at 197, in which Megarry V.C. stated that in his view the *Mareva* doctrine had shed "all the possible limitations of its origin".

[28] *Babanaft International Co SA v Bassatne* [1990] Ch. 13; [1989] 2 W.L.R. 232; [1989] 1 All E.R. 433. See also *Republic of Haiti v Duvalier* [1990] 1 Q.B. 202; [1989] 2 W.L.R. 261; [1989] 1 All E.R. 456; *Chartered Bank v Daklouche* [1980] 1 All E.R. 205; *Barclay-Johnson v Yuill* [1980] 1 W.L.R. 1259; [1980] 3 All E.R. 190.

context of commercial proceedings, the grant of a *Mareva* injunction is not confined to commercial cases.[29] As stated by Kerr L.J. in *Z Ltd v A-Z*[30]:

> "The jurisdiction is … clearly capable of general application, and I would not wish to see any limitation put on it in relation to the nature or subject matter of the proceedings."[31]

8–11 This section will consider the development and effect of *Mareva* injunctions, and will be followed by a consideration of the relevant elements in bringing an application before a court for a *Mareva* injunction.

2. Development of the *Mareva* Injunction

8–12 It was originally settled law that a creditor could do nothing until judgment to prevent foreign defendants from removing assets from the jurisdiction. The prevailing view was that it would be a "fearful authority" for a court to restrain a defendant from dealing with his assets.[32]

8–13 Two cases decided in England in 1975 changed this approach. The first was that of *Nippon Yusen Kaisha v Karageorgis*.[33] In that case the Court of Appeal held that where there is a strong prima facie case that a plaintiff is entitled to money from a defendant and that defendant is within the jurisdiction, and that the plaintiff believes the defendant may remove his assets from the jurisdiction, the court may grant an injunction on an ex parte basis restraining the defendant from removing such assets. Lord Denning M.R. referred to the fact that the court had been told that, "an injunction of this kind has never been granted before."[34] Notwithstanding this, however, the Master of the Rolls held that:

> "It seems to me that we should revise our practice. There is no reason why the High Court or this court should not make an order such as is asked for here. It is warranted by section 45 of the Supreme Court of Judicature (Consolidation) Act 1925 which says that the High Court may grant a mandamus or injunction or appoint a receiver by an interlocutory order in all cases in which it appears to the court to be just or convenient so to do … Two days ago we granted an injunction ex parte and we should continue it."[35]

---

[29] See, for example, *Allen v Jambo Holdings Ltd* [1980] 1 W.L.R. 1252; [1980] 2 All E.R. 502, a personal injuries case.

[30] [1982] Q.B. 558; [1982] 2 W.L.R. 288; [1982] 1 All E.R. 556.

[31] [1982] Q.B. 558 at 584; [1982] 2 W.L.R. 288 at 305; [1982] 1 All E.R. 556 at 571.

[32] *Mills v Northern Railway of Buenos Aires Co* (1870) LR 5 Ch. App. 621. See also, *Robinson v Pickering* (1881) 16 Ch D 661 and *Lister v Stubbs* [1890] 45 Ch D 1.

[33] [1975] 1 W.L.R. 1093.

[34] [1975] 1 W.L.R. 1093 at 1094.

[35] [1975] 1 W.L.R. 1093 at 1095.

8–14 In that regard, it has been observed in relation to this significant new development in the field of injunctions that there was:

"no further analysis, no reference to previous authority, no acknowledgement that there might be formidable obstacles in way of this change in practice."[36]

8–15 Notwithstanding this, the ability to grant such an injunction order was affirmed shortly afterwards by the Court of Appeal in the case of *Mareva Compania Naviera SA v International Bulk Carriers SA*.[37] The new order also survived its first inter partes challenge in the courts. That was in the case of *Rasu Maritima SA v Perusahaan Pertambangan Minyak Dan Gas Bumi Negara* ("*The Pertamina*").[38] Lord Denning M.R., in explaining the new form of order, made reference to the medieval practice of foreign attachment, by virtue of which:

"if the defendant was not to be found within the jurisdiction of the court, the plaintiff was enabled instantly, as soon as the plaint was issued, to attach any effects of the defendant, whether money or goods, to be found within the jurisdiction of the court."[39]

3. Acceptance in Ireland

8–16 The decision in the *Mareva* case was initially adopted by the High Court in Ireland in the cases of *Powerscourt Estates v Gallagher*[40] and *Fleming v Ranks (Ireland) Ltd.*[41] The Supreme Court considered the granting of a *Mareva* injunction in the later case of *Caudron v Air Zaire*,[42] though on the facts of that case refused to grant the relief sought. However, in the 1995 case of *O'Mahony v Horgan*[43] the Supreme Court did grant a *Mareva* injunction, and also set out a number of useful principles which still inform the approach to *Mareva* injunctions in this jurisdiction.

8–17 The continued development of the *Mareva* injunction in this jurisdiction was referred to by the Supreme Court in the case of *Targe Towing Ltd and Scheldt Towage Co NV v The owners and all persons claiming an interest in the*

---

[36] Capper, "The *Mareva* injunction—From Birth to Adulthood" in *Leading Cases of the Twentieth Century,* O'Dell (ed.) (Dublin: Round Hall, 2000), p.256.
[37] [1975] 2 Lloyd's Rep. 509. It is unclear why it was this second case which bequeathed its name to the injunction granted, a curiosity also evident in relation to *Anton Piller* orders, the eponymous case being the second in which such a form of injunction was granted.
[38] [1977] 3 W.L.R. 518; [1978] Q.B. 644; [1977] 3 All E.R. 324.
[39] [1977] 3 W.L.R. 518 at 525; [1978] Q.B. 644 at 654; [1977] 3 All E.R. 324 at 331.
[40] [1984] I.L.R.M. 123.
[41] [1983] I.L.R.M. 541.
[42] [1985] I.R. 716; [1986] I.L.R.M. 10.
[43] *Re John Horgan Livestock Limited* [1995] 2 I.R. 411; [1996] 1 I.L.R.M. 161.

Vessel "Von Rocks".[44] In that case Keane J. observed that the assets of a debtor within the jurisdiction were regarded as being readily available to satisfy the creditors. He then noted that:

> "In an age of greatly enhanced electronic communications, that is not always the case and hence the remarkable development of the *Mareva* injunction in recent years."[45]

8–18 Four more recent cases, all decided by Clarke J., have helped clarify and refine the basis for applying for a *Mareva* injunction, and are also of great assistance in terms of setting out the procedural requirements in making such an application: *Bambrick v Cobley*[46]; *Tracey v Bowen*[47]; *McCourt v Tiernan*[48]; and *Hughes v Hitachi Koki Imaging Solutions Europe.*[49]

4. Legislative Basis

8–19 The power to grant a *Mareva* injunction is based on s.28(8) of the Supreme Court of Judicature (Ireland) Act 1877[50] and Ord.50 r.6(1) of the Rules of the Superior Courts.[51] *Mareva* injunctions can be sought in the High Court and the Circuit Court.[52]

5. Inherent Jurisdiction

8–20 The inherent jurisdiction of the court to grant a *Mareva* injunction has also been cited in at least two cases in New South Wales, *Turner v Sylvester*[53] and *McKay (Riley) Ltd v McKay.*[54] It was also referred to by Stephen Bellamy

---

[44] [1998] 3 I.R. 41; [1998] 1 I.L.R.M. 481.
[45] [1998] 3 I.R. 41 at 55; [1998] 1 I.L.R.M. 481 at 493.
[46] [2006] 1 I.L.R.M. 81.
[47] [2005] 2 I.R. 528.
[48] unreported, High Court, Clarke J., July 29, 2005.
[49] [2006] 3 I.R. 457. See also, *JRM Sports Ltd v Football Association of Ireland*, unreported, High Court, Clarke J., January 31, 2007, which considers, inter alia, the need for candour at the ex parte stage.
[50] The wording of which is set out in Ch.11, Domestic Jurisdiction.
[51] Which provides that: "the Court may grant a mandamus or an injunction or appoint a receiver, by an interlocutory order in all cases in which it appears to the Court to be just or convenient so to do." See generally, Ch.1, Domestic Jurisdiction.
[52] Whereas previously the power derived in England from s.45(1) of the Supreme Court of Judicature (Consolidation) Act 1925, s.37(1) of the Supreme Court Act 1981 subsequently set out the legislative basis. Under the Civil Procedure Rules, CPR r.25.1(1)(f) now gives the courts the power to grant what are called "freezing injunctions".
[53] (1981) 2 N.S.W.L.R. 295.
[54] (1982) 1 N.S.W.L.R. 264.

Q.C. in the context of a family law dispute in *Re M*.[55] It is certainly arguable
that such inherent power has also been invoked on at least one occasion in this
jurisdiction. In *CAB v McSweeney*,[56] a *Mareva* injunction had been granted on
an ex parte basis restraining the defendant and his wife from dealing with
certain assets. O'Sullivan J. had to determine, inter alia, whether the court has
jurisdiction to grant a *Mareva* injunction given that—as he had already
determined—the legislature had given the plaintiff power to bring plenary
proceedings for the recovery of tax. O'Sullivan J. hinted that the courts did have
an inherent jurisdiction, in so far as he took the view that in the absence of:

"... clear explicit authority ... when the jurisdiction of this Court is invoked
by a Plaintiff which has statutory authority to bring proceedings by way of
plenary summons, then the full jurisdiction of the High Court is invoked and,
as I have already indicated, in my opinion, that jurisdiction includes a power
to grant *Mareva* Injunctions."

6. Extraterritorial Effect

8–21 The power to grant *Mareva* injunctions should be exercised with caution.
The caution required is such that in *Derby & Co Ltd v Weldon (Nos 3 & 4)*,[57]
Lord Donaldson M.R. suggested that:

"a failure or refusal to grant an injunction in any particular case is an exercise
of discretion which cannot, as such, provide a precedent binding upon another
court concerned with another case, save insofar as that refusal is based upon
basic principles applicable in both such cases."[58]

8–22 That decision was delivered at a time when Lord Donaldson M.R. took
the view that the granting of *Mareva* injunctions was a "developing branch of
the law". However, although the jurisdiction to make such injunction orders is
now firmly established, the power to grant *Mareva* injunctions must still be
exercised with caution. This was emphasised by Millett L.J. in *Crédit Suisse
Fides Trust SA v Cuoghi*,[59] a case in which he also made reference to the fact
that the law in this area had developed to such an extent that "the conditions
necessary in order to preserve international comity and prevent conflicts of
jurisdiction have become standardised."[60] As was made clear by Millett L.J., this
caution is required due to the fact that *Mareva* injunctions often have
extraterritorial effect, a point to which the courts in England in particular have
devoted a considerable amount of time.

---

55 [2006] 1 F.L.R. 1031.
56 unreported, High Court, O'Sullivan J., April 11, 2000.
57 [1990] 1 Ch. 65; [1989] 2 W.L.R. 412; [1989] 1 All E.R. 1002.
58 [1990] 1 Ch. 65 at 77; [1989] 2 W.L.R. 412 at 420; [1989] 1 All E.R. 1002 at 1007.
59 [1998] Q.B. 818; [1998] 1 W.L.R. 871; [1997] 3 All E.R. 724.
60 [1998] Q.B. 818 at 824; [1997] 3 W.L.R. 871 at 875; [1997] 3 All E.R. 724 at 728.

(a) Not an Extraterritorial Order

8–23 A *Mareva* injunction operates in personam, as is clear from decisions such as that of Buckley L.J. in *Cretanor Maritime Co Ltd v Irish Marine Management Ltd.*[61] Although in the later decision of the Court of Appeal in *Z Ltd v A-Z*,[62] Lord Denning M.R. found that a *Mareva* injunction operated *in rem*, this view was explicitly rejected by Browne-Wilkinson V.C. in *Attorney General v Newspaper Publishing Plc.*[63] Indeed, it has been observed that it is:

> "inaccurate and dangerously unhelpful to consider this [a *Mareva* injunction] as an extraterritorial order. It is made against a defendant who is subject to the *in personam* jurisdiction of the court, and is thus intra-territorial."[64]

(b) Extraterritorial Considerations

8–24 The approach of the courts is generally to limit a *Mareva* injunction to assets within its territorial jurisdiction, if it appears that such assets are likely to be sufficient to satisfy any judgment. However, as is clear from the case of *Babanaft International Co SA v Bassatne*,[65] the order can be extended—with restrictions—to assets located outside the territorial jurisdiction of the courts. It was also recognised in *Babanaft* that third parties such as banks within the jurisdiction might be in contempt if their offices abroad permitted frozen overseas assets to be dealt with in breach of the terms of the order. In *Babanaft* Nicholls L.J. held that:

> "It would be wrong for an English court, by making an order in respect of overseas assets against a defendant amenable to its jurisdiction, to impose or attempt to impose obligations on persons not before the court in respect of acts to be done by them abroad regarding property outside the jurisdiction. That, self-evidently, would be for the English court to claim an altogether exorbitant, extraterritorial jurisdiction."[66]

8–25 That being so, the Court of Appeal held that a worldwide *Mareva* injunction should only bind a defendant personally. It would only be enforceable against third parties in respect of assets outside the jurisdiction if it was declared enforceable in the country concerned. This became known as a "Babanaft proviso".[67] Of course,

---

61 [1978] 1 W.L.R. 966; [1978] 3 All E.R. 164.
62 [1982] Q.B. 558; [1982] 2 W.L.R. 288; [1982] 1 All E.R. 556.
63 [1987] 3 W.L.R. 942; [1987] 3 All E.R. 276.
64 See Briggs & Rees, *Civil Jurisdiction and Judgments,* 4th edn (London: LLP, 2005), p.462; *cf.* Courtney, who takes the view that "by granting relief on a worldwide basis the court is making an extraterritorial order which intrudes upon the jurisdiction of foreign courts": Courtney, *Mareva Injunctions* (Dublin: Butterworths, 1998), p.268.
65 [1990] Ch. 13; [1989] 2 W.L.R. 232; [1989] 1 All E.R. 433.
66 [1990] Ch. 13 at 44; [1989] 2 W.L.R. 232 at 257; [1989] 1 All E.R. 433 at 453.
67 The term used by Staughton L.J. in *Republic of Haiti v Duvalier* [1990] Q.B. 202 at 217; [1989] 2 W.L.R. 261 at 274; [1989] 1 All E.R. 456 at 467.

the dependency on a declaration of enforceability by a foreign court meant that the proviso actually meant very little in practice. This was recognised by Lord Donaldson M.R. in *Derby & Co Ltd v Weldon (Nos 3 and 4)*,[68] a case in which the Master of the Rolls revised the *Babanaft* proviso. He did so by adding the requirement that persons who were subject to the jurisdiction of the English court with notice of the order were required to prevent breaches of its terms if they were able to do so.

8–26 However, a lacuna emerged; the reality is that it is very often banks which are affected by *Mareva* injunctions. Banks based abroad are not in general terms subject to the jurisdiction of the courts of other countries. The proviso as revised in *Derby* only applied to parties subject to the jurisdiction of the English courts. In the subsequent English case of *Baltic Shipping Co v Translink Shipping Ltd*,[69] Clarke J. accepted that any bank, whether English or foreign, should as a general rule be entitled to the protection of an order of the foreign court before it is required to disclose documents kept at a branch or head office abroad. As such, the "Baltic proviso" was adopted.

8–27 Two general propositions were derived from an analysis of the foregoing cases by Tuckey L.J. in *Bank of China v NMB LLC*[70]:

(i) The limit of the court's territorial jurisdiction and the principle of comity require that the effectiveness of *Mareva* injunctions operating upon third parties holding assets abroad should normally derive only from their recognition and enforcement by the local courts.

(ii) Third parties amenable to the English jurisdiction should be given all reasonable protection.[71]

8–28 However, it has been stressed by the courts in England that it is rare to grant a pre-trial injunction against assets of a defendant on a worldwide basis.[72] As observed by Delany:

"Extraterritorial *Mareva* injunctions are more likely to be granted after judgment has been obtained as the risk that such an order will be made in favour of a party who is wrongly asserting a cause of action is removed and it has been stressed that pre-judgment orders will be granted on a worldwide basis less readily than after trial."[73]

---

[68] [1990] Ch. 65; [1989] 2 W.L.R. 412; [1989] 1 All E.R. 1002.

[69] [1995] 1 Lloyd's Rep. 67, referring to the decision of Hoffmann J. in *Mackinnon v Donaldson, Lufkin & Jenrette Securities Corpn* [1986] Ch. 482.

[70] [2002] 1 W.L.R. 844; [2002] 1 All E.R. 717.

[71] [2002] 1 W.L.R. 844 at 851; [2002] 1 All E.R. 717 at 723.

[72] *Babanaft International Co SA v Bassatne* [1990] Ch. 13 at 28; [1989] 2 W.L.R. 232 at 242; [1989] 1 All E.R. 433 at 440, per Kerr L.J.; *Republic of Haiti v Duvalier* [1989] 2 W.L.R. 261 at 272; [1990] 1 Q.B. 202 at 215; [1989] 1 All E.R. 456 at 466, per Staughton L.J.

[73] Delany, *Equity and the Law of Trusts in Ireland*, 4th edn (Dublin: Thomson Round Hall, 2007), p.594.

8–29 The effect of the various provisos and qualifications is best seen by looking at the wording used in England in the standard CPR/Commercial Court form[74] which in the Guidance Notes under the heading "Parties other than the applicant and respondent" sets out that:

"The terms of this order do not affect or concern anyone outside the jurisdiction of this court until it is declared enforceable by or is enforced by a court in the relevant country and then they are to affect him only to the extent that they have been declared enforceable or have been enforced UNLESS the person is: (i) a person to whom this order is addressed ... or (ii) a person who is subject to the jurisdiction of this court and (a) has been given written notice of this order at his residence or place of business within the jurisdiction of this court and (b) is able to prevent acts or omissions outside the jurisdiction of this court which constitute or assist in a breach of the terms of this order."

(c) Approach of Irish Courts to Extraterritorial Effect

8–30 Earlier decisions such as *Countyglen v Carway*[75] and *O'Mahony v Horgan*[76] would "lead one to think"[77] that the Irish courts have looked on worldwide *Mareva* injunctions with displeasure. However, it was explicitly accepted in Ireland in the case of *Deutsche Bank AG v Murtagh*[78] that the courts in this jurisdiction could grant worldwide injunctions. This view was affirmed in the case of *Bennett Enterprises Inc. v Lipton*.[79] In *Murtagh,* Costello J. stated that the "court has jurisdiction to restrain the dissipation of extraterritorial assets where such an order is warranted by the facts."[80] Noting that the basis on which a *Mareva* injunction is granted is to ensure that a defendant does not take action designed to frustrate subsequent orders of the court, Costello J. observed that it was established in England that a *Mareva* injunction might extend to foreign assets, and stated that "the Irish courts have a similar power in order to avoid the frustration of subsequent orders it may make."[81]

7. Applicable Tests for a *Mareva* Injunction

8–31 Derived from case law, there are a number of key tests which will have to be satisfied before a *Mareva* injunction will be granted:

---

[74] Set out in CPR Pt 25; the Annex to Practice Direction—Interim injunctions, in *Civil Procedure 2001*, Vol.1, para.25PD-015, pp.474–475; and Appendix 5(2) to "The Commercial Court Guide", set out in *Civil Procedure* (2001 edn), Vol.2, para.2C-210, p.425.

[75] [1995] I.R. 208 at 218.

[76] [1995] 2 I.R. 411.

[77] Courtney, *Mareva Injunctions* (Dublin: Butterworths, 1998), p.269.

[78] [1995] 2 I.R. 122; [1995] 1 I.L.R.M. 381.

[79] [1999] 2 I.R. 221; [1999] 1 I.L.R.M. 81.

[80] [1995] 2 I.R. 122 at 131; [1995] 1 I.L.R.M. 381 at 388.

[81] [1995] 2 I.R. 122 at 131; [1995] 1 I.L.R.M. 381 at 388.

- First, the applicant for such an order must demonstrate that he has a substantive cause of action.
- Secondly, he must show that has a good arguable case (which means that an apparently higher threshold is applied to *Mareva* injunctions, rather than the bona fide/serious question test used in other interim and interlocutory applications).[82]
- Thirdly, he must show that the defendant has assets. He must also show that the anticipated disposal of a defendant's assets is for the purpose of preventing a plaintiff from recovering damages and not merely for the purpose of carrying on a business or discharging lawful debts.[83] Whilst in the normal course, assets refers to bank accounts, a number of decisions have accepted that the term "assets" has a much broader reach and can include, inter alia, motor vehicles, objets d'art, valuables and choses in action.[84]
- Fourthly, as with other interlocutory injunctions, the balance of convenience is a relevant factor.
- Finally, the behaviour of the defendant will be considered by the court.

8–32 The adequacy of damages, which is part of the consideration in an interim and interlocutory injunction application generally, is not something which falls for consideration in an application for a *Mareva* injunction, as what the plaintiff is essentially seeking is protection in relation to a possible future award, which does not require a consideration of the adequacy of damages relative to granting or withholding an injunction order.

8–33 These tests will now be considered in more detail.

(a) A Substantive Cause of Action

8–34 The courts have held that a party must have a substantive cause of action before it can seek a *Mareva* injunction (although the effect of s.13 of the Jurisdiction of Courts and Enforcement of Judgments Act 1998, considered in Chapter Two, Extraterritorial Jurisdiction, modifies this to a degree). In *A v B*,[85] Saville J. granted an anticipatory *Mareva*, where the party seeking the order had no pre-existing cause of action. The decision was based on, inter alia, the inconvenience which would be caused if the court did not have the power to grant relief in that form. However, this approach was disapproved of by the Court of Appeal in *Veracruz Transportation Inc. v VC Shipping Co Inc. (The Veracruz)*[86] (although this is a decision regarded by commentators as "unjust").[87] In *Veracruz*, Beldam L.J. noted that the power to grant an injunction where the court

---

[82] See in particular, Ch.6, Interlocutory Applications.
[83] per Hamilton C.J. in *O'Mahony v Horgan* [1995] 2 I.R. 411 at 418.
[84] See para.8–04.
[85] [1989] 2 Lloyd's Rep. 423.
[86] *Times Law Reports*, November 14, 1991.
[87] See, for example, Collins, "The Legacy of the Siskina" (1992) 108 L.Q.R. 175 at 175.

considered it just and convenient so to do was to be read subject to the earlier decision of *Siskina (Cargo Owners) v Distos Compania Naviera SA*.[88] In *Siskina* the House of Lords had held that the right to obtain an interlocutory injunction was not a cause of action which could stand on its own.[89] It could only arise from a pre-existing cause of action against the defendant. It was held that convenience should not be allowed to override the necessity for a pre-existing cause of action.

8–35 In *Department of Social Security v Butler*,[90] the Court of Appeal had to consider the situation whereby the plaintiff had a statutory right, but one "which the High Court has no power to enforce even when both personal and territorial jurisdiction are established." The court ultimately held that it could not grant a *Mareva* injunction in such circumstances, Simon Brown L.J. referring to *Veracruz* to support the court's determination.[91]

8–36 However, in *Fourie v Le Roux*,[92] the House of Lords held that in suitable circumstances a *Mareva* injunction might be, and often was, granted and served on the respondent before substantive proceedings had been instituted. In order to provide suitable protection for the defendant in such circumstances, the Lords held that such protection ought to include directions about the institution of proceedings for substantive relief. Furthermore, "the claimant must have some case in some jurisdiction and must be able to state it with sufficient precision for the issue of proceedings at the time of the original application."[93]

(b) A Good Arguable Case

(i) Development of the Test in England

8–37 The test of demonstrating a "good arguable case" was set out by Lord Denning M.R. in *Rasu Maritima SA v Perusahaan Pertambangan Minyak Dan Gas Bumi Negara (The Pertamina)*.[94] As will be seen below,[95] this test was accepted in this jurisdiction in *O'Mahony v Horgan*.[96]

---

[88] [1979] A.C. 210.

[89] Affirmed in *Zucker v Tyndall Holdings Plc* [1993] 1 All E.R. 124.

[90] [1995] W.L.R. 1528; [1996] 1 F.L.R. 65.

[91] Although Courtney, *Mareva Injunctions* (Dublin: Butterworths, 1998), p.142 suggests that "to say that there is *no* jurisdiction to grant *quia timet* relief (i.e. before a substantive cause of action is currently actionable) may be to go too far." He offers the example of "a real threatened breach of an obligation which is presently enforceable." Whilst this suggestion makes real practical sense, the courts have been slow to endorse such a view (or alternatively have not been faced with what Courtney terms "extreme cases" in which they would have to come to a determination as to whether or not to grant a *quia timet Mareva* injunction.

[92] [2007] 1 W.L.R. 320; [2007] 1 All E.R. 1087.

[93] per Capper, "Asset Freezing Orders—Failure to State the Cause of Action" (2007) 26 C.Q.J. 181.

[94] [1978] Q.B. 644 at 661; [1977] 3 All E.R. 324 at 334, followed in *Farey-Jones (Insurance) Ltd v IFM Funding GmbH*, unreported, Court of Appeal, April 10, 1979.

[95] See para.8–42.

[96] [1995] 2 I.R. 411, 416 and 418. For a detailed review of this point, see Capper, "*Mareva* injunctions: A Distinctively Irish Doctrine?" (1995) 17 D.U.L.J. 110.

8–38 The extent to which an application for a *Mareva* injunction demands a different standard from that usually applied in applications for interlocutory injunctions—a serious/bona fide/fair question to be tried—was considered in *Derby & Co Ltd v Weldon (No. 1).*[97] Parker L.J. stated that in his view:

> "the difference between an application for an ordinary injunction and a *Mareva* lies only in this, that in the former case the plaintiff need only establish that there is a serious question to be tried, whereas in the latter the test is said to be whether the plaintiff shows a good arguable case."[98]

8–39 The use of the formulation "need only establish" in the context of a serious question to be tried would suggest that a "good arguable case" is intended to be a higher standard. Parker L.J. then stated that the difference was incapable of definition. However, it seems clear that a courts' analysis will go beyond simply looking at the question of a "good arguable case", based on the decision in *Ninemia Maritime Corporation v Trave Schiffahrtsgesellschaft mbH und Co KG (The Niedersachsen).*[99] In that case Kerr L.J. stated that:

> "A 'good arguable case' is no doubt the minimum which the plaintiff must show in order to cross what the judge rightly described as the 'threshold' for the exercise of the jurisdiction. But at the end of the day the court must consider the evidence as a whole ..."[100]

8–40 That there is a clear distinction between the threshold criterion set out in *American Cyanamid* and in applications for interim and interlocutory *Mareva* injunctions is also evident from the decision of the Court of Appeal in *Polly Peck International Plc v Nadir (No. 2),*[101] particularly the judgment of Lord Donaldson M.R., as the Master of the Rolls took the view that the *American Cyanamid* guidelines had no relevance to *Mareva* injunctions.

8–41 Reviewing the position in *The Canada Trust Co v Stolzenberg (No. 2),*[102] Nourse L.J. acknowledged in the Court of Appeal that "there may at times have been a measure of confusion between 'good arguable case' and 'serious question to be tried' or the like." He suggested that such expressions "can mean different things to different minds" and, to some at any rate, "there cannot be a serious question to be tried if the plaintiff does not have a good arguable

---

[97]   [1990] Ch. 48; [1989] 1 All E.R. 469.
[98]   [1990] Ch. 48 at 57; [1989] 2 W.L.R. 276 at 283; [1989] 1 All E.R. 469 at 475. The test of a "good arguable case" was also accepted in *Establissement Esefka International Anstalt v Central Bank of Nigeria* [1979] 1 Lloyd's Rep. 445 and *Bakarim v Victoria P Shipping Co Ltd "The Tatiangela"* [1980] 2 Lloyd's Rep. 193.
[99]   [1983] 1 W.L.R. 1412.
[100] [1983] 1 W.L.R. 1412 at 1417.
[101] [1992] 4 All E.R. 769.
[102] [1998] 1 W.L.R. 547 at 572.

case."[103] However, based on other cases, particularly the dictum of Kerr L.J. in *The Niedersachsen,* it would seem that the courts will consider whether there is a "good arguable case", and that this is a different standard to that espoused in *American Cyanamid.* However, this threshold will in general terms not be determinative. The facts of each individual case must be examined as a whole in order to determine whether to grant a *Mareva* injunction.

(ii) Development of the Test in Ireland

8–42 Although the test of a "good arguable case" also applies in this jurisdiction, it is similarly bedevilled by a lack of clarity as to what exactly this means. In this jurisdiction the appropriate test to be applied was considered by Murphy J. in the case of *Countyglen Plc v Carway.*[104] Following the test laid out in *Campus Oil,* he held that there was no requirement that an applicant establish as a probability that his claim would succeed. In so holding, however, Murphy J. referred to the decision of McWilliam J. in *Fleming v Ranks (Ireland) Ltd*[105] in which the court had held that the plaintiff must show that he has a "good arguable case". Murphy J. doubted whether there was any significant difference between the expressions "good arguable case" and a "substantial question to be tried", but held that if such a distinction existed he preferred the latter criterion "as the one approved by the Supreme Court in the *Campus Oil* case although not specifically related to the *Mareva* type injunction." Murphy J. rejected the argument that a plaintiff seeking a *Mareva* injunction must establish as a probability that his claim would succeed. However, Murphy J. then stated that "what can and should be done is to determine that there is a fair, serious question to be tried." As such, the test adopted by him is that which was set out in the *Campus Oil* case. However, it should be noted that ultimately the risk of dissipation of assets appears to have been the crucial consideration in the *Countyglen* case.

8–43 However, in *O'Mahony v Horgan,*[106] the Supreme Court approached the issue on the basis of the appropriate test being a "good arguable case".[107] That being so, the position in Ireland is in essence the same as that in England: a "good arguable case" is the threshold test which must be addressed. However, as with the position in England, the courts concern themselves more with the overall facts of each case[108] and so, perhaps, the question of the distinction, if

---

103   [1998] 1 W.L.R. 547.
104   [1995] 1 I.L.R.M. 481.
105   [1983] I.L.R.M. 541.
106   [1995] 2 I.R. 411 at 416 and 418.
107   Although O'Flaherty J. stated that he would have preferred it if the test was a "clear case", where the claim was "more or less certain", he felt that: "It may now be too late to put that particular clock back." [1995] 2 I.R. 411 at 422.
108   See, for example, *Tracey v Bowen* [2005] 2 I.R. 528 at 532.

any, between "good arguable case", "substantial question to be tried" and other formulations is, in real terms, a matter of semantics.

(c) Assets and the Anticipated Disposal of Assets

8–44 The need to point to assets is relatively self-explanatory. As held by Lord Denning in *Third Chandris*,[109] the existence of a bank account is normally sufficient in terms of being able to point to assets within the jurisdiction. More complex is the question of the anticipated disposal of assets.

(i) Intention a Key Consideration

8–45 In seeking a *Mareva injunction*, it is not enough to show that the assets are likely to be dissipated in the ordinary course of business or in the payment of lawful debts.[110] Intention is the key consideration, as is clear from the Supreme Court decision in *O'Mahony v Horgan*.[111] In that regard the court will consider all the circumstances before it, as direct evidence of a defendant's intention to evade his obligations will rarely be available at an interlocutory stage, as was acknowledged by O'Sullivan J. in *Bennett Enterprises Inc. v Lipton*.[112] The decision in *Bennett* was followed in *Aerospace Limited v Thomson*,[113] with judicial approval also given to a passage from Gee on *Mareva Injunctions and Anton Piller Relief*.[114] This passage stated that:

> "Good grounds for alleging that the Defendants have been dishonest is relevant. Dishonesty is not essential to the exercise of the jurisdiction and there is no need to show an intention to dissipate assets. But if there is a good arguable case in support of an allegation that the Defendant has acted fraudulently or dishonestly (e.g. being implicated in an ingenious scheme for the misappropriation of funds belonging to the Plaintiff) or has acted unconscionably, then it is unnecessary for there to be any specific evidence on risk of dissipation for the court to be entitled to take the view that there is a sufficient risk to justify granting *Mareva* relief. Once this is shown, the limit

---

[109] [1979] 3 W.L.R. 122 at 137; [1979] 2 All E.R. 972 at 984.

[110] *Fleming v Ranks (Ireland) Ltd* [1983] I.L.R.M. 541, 546; *Powerscourt Estates v Gallagher* [1984] I.L.R.M. 123; *Oba Enterprises Ltd v TMC Trading International Ltd*, unreported, High Court, Laffoy J., November 27, 1998.

[111] [1995] 2 I.R. 411; [1996] 1 I.L.R.M. 161, approved by O'Sullivan J. in *Bennett Enterprises Inc. v Lipton* [1999] 1 I.L.R.M. 81 and followed by Laffoy J. in *Oba Enterprises Ltd v TMC Trading International Ltd*, unreported, High Court, Laffoy J., November 27, 1998.

[112] [1999] 2 I.R. 221; [1999] 1 I.L.R.M. 81. Referred to by Clarke J. in *Hughes v Hitachi Koki Imaging Solutions Europe* [2006] 3 I.R. 457.

[113] unreported, High Court, Kearns J., January 13, 1999.

[114] *Gee on Mareva injunctions and Anton Piller Relief*, 4th edn (London: Sweet & Maxwell, 1999), p.198. (The up-to-date reference is Gee, *Commercial Injunctions*, 5th edn (London: Thomson Sweet & Maxwell, 2004), p.356.

of the *Mareva* relief will take into account claims for which the Plaintiff has a good arguable case, including those which do not involve such an allegation. The fact that a Defendant is experienced in intricate sophisticated international transactions involving movements of large sums of money may also indicate that there is a real risk of dissipation."

8–46 In *Tracey v Bowen*,[115] Clarke J. stated that both the *Bennett* and *Aerospace* cases were authority for the proposition that:

"In assessing the risk of dissipation the court is entitled to take into account all the circumstances of the case which can include, in an appropriate case, an inference drawn from the nature of the wrongdoing alleged, which, if fraudulent or unconscionable, may lead to the establishment of a risk that further fraudulent or unconscionable actions will be taken so as to place any assets of the defendant outside the jurisdiction of the court."[116]

8–47 However, it was also clear from his decision in *Tracey v Bowen* that Clarke J. felt that the factors as outlined will be of much greater significance where the only assets of the defendant within the jurisdiction are liquid assets which are capable of being moved about with great ease. This can be contrasted with a situation where a party has real property within the jurisdiction.

(ii) Consideration of all Circumstances

8–48 That the need to consider all the circumstances of the case is important is clear when one considers that at an ex parte application it is very easy for an applicant to highlight their own apprehensions without any real safeguards to prevent against abuse of this.[117] It has been suggested that a preferable model may be one in which *Mareva* injunctions would be:

"limited to a proportion of the claim which, amongst other things, reflects the plaintiff's chances of success. As a condition of obtaining the order, the plaintiff will have to give security to support his cross-undertaking in damages."[118]

---

[115] [2005] 2 I.R. 528 at 532.

[116] The same approach was adopted by Clarke J. in *McCourt v Tiernan*, unreported, High Court, Clarke J., July 29, 2005. See also, *Hughes v Hitachi Koki Imaging Solutions Europe* [2006] 3 I.R. 457.

[117] Zuckerman, "*Mareva* injunctions and Security for Judgment in a Framework of Interlocutory Remedies" (1993) 109 L.Q.R. 432 at 441.

[118] Zuckerman, "Interlocutory Remedies in Quest of Procedural Fairness" (1993) 56 L.Q.R. 325 at 338. It is also suggested that further protection could include an immediate inter partes hearing and "the imposition of serious costs on plaintiffs who fail to justify the asset freezing order at the *inter partes* stage."

(iii) Role of Brussels Convention/Regulation

8–49 The role of the Brussels Convention/Regulation[119] was considered in *Bambrick v Cobley*.[120] In that case Clarke J. stated that where a defendant has readily identifiable assets which are held in a country covered by the Judgments Convention/Regulation, this is a factor which the court can properly take into account in assessing whether there is a real risk that the removal of further assets from Ireland to another country can be said to be "with a view to evading obligations". Clarke J.'s view was that the removal *simplicitur* of assets from this jurisdiction to another jurisdiction can, of itself, be such as to give rise to an inference of a reasonable risk of evasion of obligation. However, that inference would weigh less strongly in a case where the second country is a Convention/Regulation country and where, therefore, in the ordinary course, the judgment of this court would be as enforceable as within Ireland.

(iv) England: Different Test

8–50 This is a significant difference between the approaches of the Irish and English courts. Whereas intention is a key factor for the courts in this jurisdiction to consider, the English courts have demonstrated a tendency to focus on the effect of a defendant's actions rather than his intention. This is evident from cases such as *Ninemia Maritime Corporation v Trave Schiffahrtsgesellschaft mbH und Co KG (The Niedersachsen)*.[121]

(v) Insolvent Companies

8–51 A *Mareva* injunction may be available in relation to an insolvent company. In the case of *Hughes v Hitachi Koki Imaging Solutions Europe*,[122] Clarke J. considered how to deal with an application involving such an entity. It had been established in *O'Mahony v Horgan*[123] that the payment of lawful debts in the course of an ongoing business should not give rise to any inference sufficient to justify the grant of a *Mareva* injunction. In *Hughes*, Clarke J. felt that there was, "at least in principle", the need to give separate consideration to

---

[119] See Ch.2, Extraterritorial Jurisdiction.

[120] [2006] 1 I.L.R.M. 81.

[121] [1983] 1 W.L.R. 1412 at 1423; [1984] 1 All E.R. 398 at 404, citing *Etablissement Esefka International Anstalt v Central Bank of Nigeria* [1979] 1 Lloyd's Rep. 445 at 448, per Lord Denning M.R; *Third Chandris Shipping Corporation v Unimarine S.A.* [1979] Q.B. 645 at 669 per Lord Denning M.R.; *Montecchi v Shimco (UK) Ltd* [1979] 1 W.L.R. 1180 at 1183 per Bridge L.J.; *Barclay-Johnson v Yuill* [1980] 1 W.L.R. 1259 at 1265 per Sir Robert Megarry V.C. and *Prince Abdul Rahman bin Turki al Sudairy v Abu-Taha* [1980] 1 W.L.R. 1268 at 1273, per Lord Denning M.R. See also the comments of Capper, "*Mareva* injunctions: A Distinctively Irish Doctrine?" (1995) 17 D.U.L.J. 110 at 117.

[122] [2006] 3 I.R. 457, Clarke J. referring to his earlier decisions in *Tracey* and *McCourt*.

[123] [1995] 2 I.R. 411; [1996] 1 I.L.R.M. 161.

an insolvent corporate entity. Referring to his earlier decision in the case of *McLoughlin v Lannon*,[124] Clarke J. stated that:

> "in an appropriate case, it may be open to a plaintiff to seek *Mareva* relief where it can be shown that an insolvent company intends to deal with its assets in a manner which would prevent those assets being dealt with in accordance with the provisions of the Companies Acts."[125]

8–52 In acknowledging that such a remedy was available in principle, Clarke J. also emphasised that:

> "the primary means available in law for the enforcement of any such entitlement is to seek to place the company in liquidation so that the assets would, then, be dealt with by the liquidator in accordance with corporate insolvency law."[126]

In saying this, however, he also noted that it may not be possible for the plaintiff to seek to have the company put into liquidation, or that liquidation might not be appropriate, and that in such circumstances a plaintiff might be entitled to seek a *Mareva* injunction.

(d) The Balance of Convenience

8–53 As with an application for other interim and interlocutory injunctions, the balance of convenience is a factor to be taken into consideration by the court.[127] To some degree, however, the balance of convenience will be considered by default when the court is considering the assertion that there is a risk that assets will be removed or disposed of. In so far as there exist any points which may impact on the balance of convenience, it appears from the decision of Murphy J. in the case of *Countyglen Plc v Carway*[128] that factors such as hardship and inconvenience will be relevant to the court's consideration of whether to grant a *Mareva* injunction.

(e) Behaviour of the Defendant

8–54 In *Aerospace Ltd v Thomson*,[129] Kearns J. held that a court was entitled to take into account all the circumstances of the case, including inferences from

---

[124] unreported, High Court, Clarke J., July 21, 2006. Also referring to the Supreme Court decision in *Re Frederick Inns Limited* [1994] I.L.R.M. 387 which concerned, inter alia, the duties of directors in a winding-up.
[125] [2006] 3 I.R. 457 at 464.
[126] [2006] 3 I.R. 457 at 464.
[127] See Ch.6, Interlocutory Applications, para.6–127.
[128] [1995] 1 I.R. 208 at 218; [1995] 1 I.L.R.M. 481 at 489.
[129] unreported, High Court, Kearns J., January 13, 1999, approving *Gee on Mareva injunctions and Anton Piller Relief*, 4th edn (London: Sweet & Maxwell, 1999), p.198. See Gee, *Commercial Injunctions*, 5th edn (London: Thomson Sweet & Maxwell, 2004), p.356. See also, *Bennet Enterprises Inc. v Lipton* [1999] 2 I.R. 221.

the wrongdoing alleged on the part of the defendant that further fraudulent or unconscionable action might be taken to place his assets outside the jurisdiction of the court. However, the weight to be attached to such considerations is clearly something which will be determined on a case-by-case basis.[130]

C. APPLYING FOR A *MAREVA* INJUNCTION

1. Introduction

8–55 Although a *Mareva* injunction may be applied for on an inter partes basis, the reality is that most applications for *Mareva* injunctions are made on an ex parte basis. This is because serving notice of a motion returnable on a future date could lead to the dissipation or disposal of assets prior to such motion being heard by the court. The general principles applicable to ex parte applications are thus of equal relevance in the context of applying for *Mareva* injunctions.[131] Ex parte applications are provided for in RSC Ord.52 r.3, which states that:

> "In any case the Court, if satisfied that the delay caused by proceeding by motion on notice under this Order would or might entail irreparable or serious mischief, may make any order *ex parte* upon such terms as to costs or otherwise and subject to such undertaking, if any, as the Court may think just; and any party affected by such order may move to set it aside."[132]

2. Ex parte Applications

8–56 The general practical procedural aspects of ex parte applications are considered in Ch.7.[133] The following documents should in the normal course be brought to court when the application is being made to the High Court for a *Mareva* injunction:

- an ex parte motion (or notice of motion as appropriate if the application is on notice);
- a grounding affidavit setting out the relevant information.[134]

8–57 Due to a *Mareva* injunction being an ancillary order, there will have to be substantive proceedings in being in aid of which the injunction is actually being

---

[130] In *Tracey v Bowen* [2005] 2 I.R. 528 Clarke J. held that such considerations were of less weight in the case before him, as the defendant seemed to have had real property within the jurisdiction apparently sufficient to meet the plaintiff's claim.

[131] Reference should also be made to Ch.7, Interim Applications.

[132] See RCC Ord.20 r.2.

[133] See para.7–34.

[134] In the Circuit Court an ex parte docket and grounding affidavit should be drafted. See Ch.7, Interim Applications.

sought.[135] Therefore, if an originating summons, motion or petition is not already in being, this should in the first instance be drafted.[136] This is the basis of a substantive action and, as such, it is not appropriate to seek interim or interlocutory *Mareva* relief therein.

8–58 If the writ or motion is not in existence when the application for a *Mareva* injunction is made, it should be endeavoured to at least have a draft form in court. In *Fourie v Le Roux*,[137] the House of Lords held that in suitable circumstances a *Mareva* injunction order might be, and often was, granted and served on the respondent before substantive proceedings had been instituted.

8–59 If no proceedings are in being, a claim for substantive relief should at a minimum be formulated and entitled "in the intended matter of", "in the intended action between", or similar formulation. If time permits, a draft order might also be brought into court which the judge hearing the matter can then adapt or adopt if granting the *Mareva* injunction.

8–60 In the normal course the application will be dealt with on affidavit only, with no direct oral evidence. Although the general rule is that an affidavit should not contain hearsay evidence, RSC Ord.40 r.4 provides that in interlocutory motions statements of belief, together with the grounds for such belief, may be admitted. The affidavit should be sworn by the plaintiff or his representative, although in extremis a solicitor may swear the affidavit. However, there is an obvious difficulty in terms of a solicitor's means of knowledge and, as such, this practice should be avoided.

(a) Guiding Principles

8–61 As with any interim injunctions applied for on an ex parte basis, the courts are alive to the potential for injustice arising from the granting of an interim order on inaccurate, incomplete or even invented information.[138] That being so, a number of principles and rules have been developed, designed to ensure that a judge hearing the application in the absence of one of the parties, or proposed parties, to an action has before the court sufficient information on which to base a decision.[139]

---

[135] See *Caudron v Air Zaire* [1985] I.R. 716; [1986] I.L.R.M. 10.
[136] Although Keane J. suggested in *Re Greendale Developments Ltd* [1998] 1 I.R. 8 at 32 that *Mareva* relief might be appropriate only on foot of a plenary summons. See in that regard Ch.1, Domestic Jurisdiction, para.1–93. Courtney takes the view that a consideration of the Rules of the Superior Courts does not support Keane J.'s suggestion: Courtney, *Mareva Injunctions* (Dublin: Butterworths, 1998), p.296.
[137] [2007] 1 W.L.R. 320; [2007] 1 All E.R. 1087.
[138] *Goold v Collins* [2005] 1 I.L.R.M. 1 at 11, per Hardiman J.
[139] See generally, Ch.7, Interim Applications.

8–62 In the case of *O'Mahony v Horgan*,[140] Hamilton C.J. approved of the criteria which had been adopted by Murphy J. in the High Court. These had themselves been derived from the criteria set out by Lord Denning in *Third Chandris Shipping Corporation v Unimarine SA*.[141] The criteria, which will be considered in detail in turn, are:

> "1. The plaintiff should make full and frank disclosure of all matters in his knowledge which are material for the judge to know.
> 2. The plaintiff should give particulars of his claims against the defendant, stating the grounds of his claims and the amount thereof and fairly stating the points made against it by the defendant.
> 3. The plaintiff should give some grounds for believing that the defendant had assets within the jurisdiction. The existence of a bank account is normally sufficient.
> 4. The plaintiff should give some grounds for believing that there is a risk of the assets being removed or dissipated.
> 5. The plaintiff must give an undertaking in damages, in case he fails."[142]

(b) Full and Frank Disclosure

8–63 As has been seen in considering applications for interim injunctions,[143] the courts are alive to the potential for injustice arising from the granting of an interim order on inaccurate, incomplete or invented information. The need for full and frank disclosure is a key consideration in the context of an application for a *Mareva* injunction. This is encapsulated by the dictum of Donaldson L.J. in *Bank Mellat v Nikpour*,[144] in which he referred to the rule requiring full disclosure as being of the most fundamental importance:

> "particularly in the context of the Draconian remedy of the *Mareva* injunction. It is in effect, together with the *Anton Piller* order, one of the Law's two 'nuclear' weapons. If access to such a weapon is obtained without the fullest and frankest disclosure. I have no doubt at all that it should be revoked."[145]

8–64 Given that *Mareva* injunctions are often sought in the context of large commercial cases, the words of Clarke J. in *Bambrick v Cobley*[146] bear repetition:

---

[140] [1995] 2 I.R. 411. And as set out by Clarke J. in *Bambrick v Cobley* [2006] 1 I.L.R.M. 81.
[141] [1979] Q.B. 645 at 668; [1979] 3 W.L.R. 122 at 137; [1979] 2 All E.R. 972 at 984.
[142] [2006] 1 I.L.R.M. 81 at 86. See also Judge L.J.'s "triple safeguard" in *St George's Healthcare NHS Trust v S* [1998] 3 W.L.R. 936.
[143] See Ch.7, Interim Applications.
[144] [1985] F.S.R. 87.
[145] [1985] F.S.R. 87 at 92.
[146] [2006] 1 I.L.R.M. 81.

"I am also mindful of the fact that the courts have noted (for example in *Brink's Mat Limited v Elcombe* [1988] 3 ALL E.R. 188) that in particular in heavy commercial cases the borderline between material facts and non-material facts can be a somewhat uncertain one and that, without discounting the heavy duty of candour and care which falls upon persons making *ex parte* applications, the application of the principle of disclosure should not be carried to extreme lengths."[147]

8–65 Materiality was, according to Clarke J., to be "construed in a reasonable and not excessive manner".[148]

(i) Ongoing Obligation

8–66 It was held in the case of *Commercial Bank of the Near East Plc v P*[149] that there is an ongoing obligation to bring any subsequent material change in circumstances to the attention of the court.

(ii) Consequences of Non-Disclosure

8–67 As with applications for interim injunctions generally,[150] a lack of full and frank disclosure may lead to the discharge of the injunction order granted.[151]

(iii) Revisiting a Decision or an Appeal

8–68 The question of the consequence of a lack of full and frank disclosure was considered, albeit arising out of somewhat unusual circumstances, in the case of *McMorrow v Morris*.[152] The background facts to the case were somewhat convoluted. In essence, Smyth J. granted a *Mareva* injunction in circumstances where the defendants elected not to tender any evidence, despite Smyth J.'s "invitation and accommodation to do so." As such, the case was somewhat different to a straightforward ex parte application; in fact the defendants were represented in court but declined to make a draft affidavit available to the court. The defendants sought and were granted leave to issue a motion to (re)appear before Smyth J. It was argued that there was a failure to make full disclosure of all material facts on the part of the plaintiff. However, Smyth J. took the view that he was not entitled to "revisit and review his own decision on so substantive an issue." He felt that to do so would "in reality be to entertain an appeal by way

---

[147] [2006] 1 I.L.R.M. 81 at 87.
[148] [2006] 1 I.L.R.M. 81 at 87.
[149] [1989] N.L.J.R. 645.
[150] See Ch.7, Interim Applications.
[151] See *Lloyds Bowmaker Ltd v Britannia Arrow Holdings Ltd* [1988] 1 W.L.R. 1337; [1988] 3 All E.R. 178, as considered by Clarke J. in *Bambrick v Cobley* [2006] 1 I.L.R.M. 81.
[152] ex tempore, High Court, Smyth J., June 13, 2007.

of rehearing." Smyth J. referred to the respective roles of a judge at first instance and a judge of appeal, stating that they were "quite different and respect for the law and the justice system is best observed by a strict, respectful and dutiful observance by both of the difference."

(iv) Non-Disclosure and Statutory Schemes

8–69 It was held by Clarke J. in the case of *McKenna v DC*[153] that he was satisfied in principle that the relevant jurisprudence in the area of *Mareva* injunctions generally, certainly in so far as material non-disclosure was concerned, also applied to applications for *Mareva* injunctions provided for in statute. In that case the statutory provisions concerned were ss.2 and 3 of the Proceeds of Crime Act 1996. It had been argued that the Criminal Assets Bureau, in seeking *Mareva* injunctions under that Act, were not seeking to protect their own commercial interest, but rather were carrying out a public role. However, Clarke J. took the view that whilst this may be relevant to the matters to be disclosed (and by association to the jurisdiction to vacate for material non-disclosure), it did not appear to him to affect the general principles in relation to non-disclosure. In doing so, however, he also noted that the criteria for applying for a statutory *Mareva* injunction are different to those otherwise applied in relation to applications for *Mareva* injunctions.

(v) Particulars of Claim

8–70 The particulars of his claim and the grounds for such particulars must be set out by the party seeking a *Mareva* injunction. It is clear from the decision in *Tracey v Bowen*[154] that, as the primary purpose of an affidavit is to place evidence before the court, when setting out such particulars any contentions material should be set out in unemotive terms. Clarke J. indicated that if it is desired to reduce argument by way of advocacy to writing, this should be done by written submission to the court, rather than contained in "flamboyant language" in an affidavit; the affidavits in question had included phrases such as "wholly unsustainable", "outrageous", "completely unacceptable", "preposterous" and "an extravagant ruse". It was found that other matters were placed on affidavit which were primarily for the purpose of embarrassment rather than because they were matters which were material to the issues before the court.

(vi) Identify any Defence

8–71 As well as giving particulars of his claim, the party seeking the *Mareva* injunction must also identify any defence which he believes may be raised and

---

[153] unreported, High Court, Clarke J., May 26, 2006.
[154] [2005] 2 I.R. 528.

advanced.[155] This is a broad requirement and the duty of disclosure would appear to extend not just to defences which the plaintiff is aware may be raised, but also to defences which the plaintiff reasonably expects may be raised. If, however, there is no substance to a potential defence, such a defence need not be raised.[156]

(vii) Disclosure: Facts or Documents

8–72 There is an important distinction to be made between disclosure of material facts and disclosure of documents. In *National Bank of Sharjah v Dellborg*,[157] the Court of Appeal cautioned against a "growing tendency" to burden judges with large numbers of documents at the ex parte stage. Lloyd L.J. ascribed this to confusion between the obligation to disclose material facts on the ex parte application with the obligation to give discovery of relevant documents in the course of preparation for the trial. Lloyd L.J. indicated that the material facts to be put before the court were those necessary to enable the judge to exercise his discretion properly and fairly between the parties.

(c) Grounds of Belief: Assets Within Jurisdiction

8–73 The question of having grounds of belief that there are assets within the jurisdiction which will be removed is relatively self explanatory.[158]

(d) Undertaking as to Damages

8–74 In bringing an application for a *Mareva* injunction, a plaintiff must be in a position to provide an undertaking as to damages. This is for the same reasons that it is sought in applications for injunctions other than "commercial injunctions", namely aiding the court in abstaining from expressing any opinion upon the merits of the case until the hearing.[159]

8–75 In *Cheltenham and Gloucester Building Society v Ricketts*,[160] Peter Gibson L.J., discussing the practice of the court on the enforcement of undertakings as

---

[155] *Lloyds Bowmaker Ltd v Brittania Arrow Holdings Ltd* [1988] 1 W.L.R. 1337; [1988] 3 All E.R. 178.

[156] *Weston v Arnold* (1873) L.R. 8 Ch. App. 1084 at 1090.

[157] *Times Law Reports*, December 24, 2002.

[158] See para.8–44.

[159] per Lord Diplock in *American Cyanamid v Ethicon Ltd* [1975] A.C. 396 at 407; [1975] 2 W.L.R. 316 at 323; [1975] 1 All E.R. 504 at 510, citing *Wakefield v Duke of Buccleuch* (1865) 12 L.T. 628. The origins of the practice of requiring such an undertaking are set out in *Chappell v Davidson* (1856) 8 De G.M. & G. 1 at 2. See also the dictum of Finlay C.J. in *Westman Holdings Limited v McCormack* [1992] 1 I.R. 151 at 158. See generally, Ch.6, Interlocutory Applications.

[160] [1993] 1 W.L.R. 1545; [1993] 4 All E.R. 276.

to damages given by the successful applicant for an interlocutory injunction when subsequently the injunction is shown to have been wrongly granted, made particular reference to the risk of injustice when an interlocutory injunction has been granted ex parte. In relation to *Mareva* injunctions, he stated that:

> "such injunctions can have the effect of ruining a thriving business or of otherwise causing substantial loss to the respondent and were vividly described by Donaldson L.J. in *Bank Mellat v Nikpour* [1985] FSR 87, 92 as being, with the *Anton Piller* order, one of the law's 'two "nuclear" weapons.' The courts are properly concerned lest these weapons are used inappropriately and the undertaking in damages provides a salutary potential deterrent against their misuse."[161]

(i) A Worthwhile Undertaking

8–76 It may be the case that a plaintiff may not be able to give an undertaking as to damages which satisfies the court, namely a "worthwhile" undertaking as to damages. This was the point which fell for consideration in *Allen v Jambo Holdings Ltd*,[162] with Shaw L.J. stating that, "questions of financial stability ought not to affect the position in regard to what is the essential justice of the case as between the parties."[163]

8–77 In *Moloney v Laurib Investments Ltd*,[164] Lynch J. acknowledged the injustice which would arise in not granting a *Mareva* injunction simply because the plaintiff's undertaking would be, as he described it, "worthless", although in refusing to grant the *Mareva* relief sought, Lynch J. did in fact appear to have regard to the fact that the undertaking would be worthless.[165]

8–78 The extent to which a limited undertaking may be provided was touched upon in *O'Mahony v Horgan*.[166] Murphy J. in the High Court had capped a liquidator's undertaking as to damages. O'Flaherty J. in the Supreme Court suggested that he did not think it right in principle that such a limit should be placed on an undertaking. Hamilton C.J. reserved the matter for future consideration whilst suggesting that he was inclined to agree with O'Flaherty J.'s view in that regard.[167]

---

[161] [1993] 1 W.L.R. 1545 at 1554; [1993] 4 All E.R. 276 at 284.
[162] [1980] 1 W.L.R. 1252; [1980] 2 All E.R. 502.
[163] [1980] 1 W.L.R. 1252 at 1257; [1980] 2 All E.R. 502 at 505.
[164] unreported, High Court, Lynch J., July 20, 1993.
[165] Even if the plaintiff's parents (the plaintiff was 15 when she had suffered severe injuries, leaving her paralysed from the waist down) were to join in giving the undertaking, this was not sufficient due to the potential losses which would be suffered by the defendant company if they successfully defended the action after the grant of an interlocutory injunction.
[166] [1995] 2 I.R. 411.
[167] See Ch.6, Interlocutory Applications, para.6–108.

8–79 As has been seen,[168] the matter has been more definitively resolved in England, and in the case of *Re DPR Futures*[169] it was held that the joint liquidators concerned should not be required to provide an unlimited undertaking in damages.

(ii) Enforcement of the Undertaking

8–80 The enforcement of an undertaking as to damages by way of an inquiry as to damages operates on the same principles as apply to a "non-commercial" interlocutory injunction. This is considered in greater detail in Ch.5, Perpetual Injunctions. In *Financiera Avenida v Shiblaq*,[170] Lloyd L.J. stated that ordinary principles of the law of contract apply both as to causation and as to *quantum*.[171]

3. Form of the Order

8–81 A *Mareva* injunction is prohibitory in nature and the order granting an injunction will be worded accordingly. The terms of a *Mareva* injunction usually prevent a party from "disposing of" or "dealing with" assets. A party must:

> "do what he reasonably can to preserve the asset. He must not assist in any way in the disposal of it. He must hold it pending further order …"[172]

8–82 However, due to the potentially drastic nature of the order, a number of safeguards are usually built in to such an order. These will be considered in turn.

(a) Maximum Sum

8–83 An injunction should not be expressed in wider terms than the plaintiff's right, although it has been acknowledged by the courts that some leeway may be required in that regard.[173] A court will generally provide for some form of maximum sum to be inserted in the order (for example, the value of the plaintiff's claim or an amount approximate thereto). It is unusual for a court to make an order for a *Mareva* injunction without inserting some financial limit in the order. In *Z Ltd v A-Z*,[174] Kerr L.J. held that a *Mareva* injunction without such

---

168 See Ch.6, Interlocutory Applications, para.6–106.
169 [1989] 1 W.L.R. 778.
170 *Times Law Reports*, January 14, 1991.
171 Although the difficulties involved in certain inquiries are clear from *Universal City Studios Incorporated v Mulligan (No. 3)* [1999] 3 I.R. 407, specifically in that case in the context of an infringement of copyright.
172 per Lord Denning M.R. in *Z Ltd v A-Z* [1982] 2 W.L.R. 288 at 296; [1982] Q.B. 558 at 574; [1982] 1 All E.R. 556 at 563.
173 See, for example, *Spectravest Inc. v Aperknit Ltd* (1988) 14 F.S.R. 161 at 174.
174 [1982] Q.B. 558; [1982] 2 W.L.R. 288; [1982] 1 All E.R. 556.

limits could not be justified other than in "exceptional" cases.[175] However, an order can be varied if necessary and such financial limit may be revisited by the court upon such an application.

(b) Ordinary Living Expenses

8–84 Provision should be made for the ordinary living expenses of the defendant. What was meant by such expenses was considered by Skinner J. in *TDK Tape Distributor (UK) Ltd v Videochoice*.[176] He held that they meant "ordinary, recurrent expenses involved in maintaining the subject of the injunction in the style of life to which he is reasonably accustomed".[177] There may also be a legal expenses proviso[178] inserted in the order, as well as an ordinary business expenses proviso.[179] It has also been recognised that a variation of such an order to make such a proviso may be required.[180]

8–85 What a court will seek to avoid is a situation where the granting of a *Mareva* injunction would prevent a company trading. In *Moloney v Laurib Investments Ltd*,[181] Lynch J. accepted that to grant the injunction sought would prejudice the rights of bona fide creditors of the defendant company, by preventing the company from availing itself of the opportunity available to it to dispose of a building which was the company's only asset. This would appear to be a logical approach.

(c) Duration

8–86 An order for a *Mareva* injunction generally lasts until judgment is given or a further order is made by a court and may, if necessary, be continued after judgment.[182]

8–87 It is also standard practice for a court upon an application for a *Mareva* injunction (and indeed in *Anton Piller* applications, which may well be sought in conjunction with a *Mareva* injunction, and which are considered below) to

[175]   [1982] Q.B. 558 at 589; [1982] 2 W.L.R. 288 at 310; [1982] 1 All E.R. 556 at 575.
[176]   [1986] 1 W.L.R. 141 at 146; [1985] 3 All E.R. 345 at 349.
[177]   In *PCW (Underwriting Agencies) Ltd v Dixon* [1983] 2 All E.R. 697, Lloyd J. held that the lifestyle of the defendant was key in judging ordinary living expenses.
[178]   See, for example, *TDK Tape Distributor (UK) Ltd v Videochoice* [1986] 1 W.L.R. 141; [1985] 3 All E.R. 345.
[179]   Although it is often difficult to quantify business expenses which may be incurred. For an example of a case in which such a proviso was included, see *Polly Peck International Plc v Nadir* [1992] 4 All E.R. 769.
[180]   See para.8–121.
[181]   unreported, High Court, Lynch J., July 20, 1993.
[182]   *Stewart Chartering Ltd v C and O Managements SA* [1980] 1 W.L.R. 460; *Elwyn (Cottons) Ltd v Pearle Designs Ltd* [1989] I.R. 9; [1989] I.L.R.M. 162.

include a term which enables a defendant, against whom the order has been made in his absence, to have the opportunity to have the order discharged at the very earliest opportunity.[183]

4. Ancillary Orders

(a) Disclosure Orders

8–88 Disclosure orders are orders ancillary to a *Mareva* injunction. They require a defendant to disclose his/her assets, by means of swearing an affidavit to such effect. Costello J. referred to the power of the courts to make such orders in *Deutsche Bank AG v Murtagh*,[184] albeit that this was in the context of assets outside the jurisdiction.[185]

(b) Disclosure/Spouses and Related Companies

8–89 One issue which arises from time to time is that a defendant discloses that his spouse or a related company has assets, whereas he does not have such assets, or at least no significant assets. Bean has identified four methods by which this is dealt with in England[186]:

- A spouse[187] or company[188] is joined as a second defendant.
- An injunction can be granted against a spouse who is not a defendant on the grounds that there is a good arguable case that assets in her name are in reality those of the defendant.[189]
- A company is enjoined from aiding and abetting a breach by a defendant of an injunction order against him.[190]
- A company is enjoined from directing or procuring the disposal or charging of assets by the company.[191]

---

[183] See *Re Capital Expansion v Development Corporation Ltd*, *The Times*, November 30, 1992, as referred to in *McMorrow v Morris*, ex tempore, High Court, Smyth J., June 13, 2007. As explained by Clarke J. in *McKenna v DC*, unreported, High Court, Clarke J., May 26, 2006, the Proceeds of Crime Act 1996 confers a statutory entitlement, at s.2(2), to make such an application.

[184] [1995] 2 I.R. 122; [1995] 1 I.L.R.M. 381. See also *Bennett Enterprises Ltd v Lipton* [1999] 2 I.R. 221. In *Countyglen v Carway* [1995] 1 I.R. 208 an order for discovery was made in relation to assets within the jurisdiction. Section 245 of the Companies Act 1963, as amended, may also be of relevance in the context of disclosure.

[185] [1995] 2 I.R. 122 at 131; [1995] 1 I.L.R.M. 381 at 388.

[186] Bean, *Injunctions*, 9th edn (London: Thomson Sweet & Maxwell, 2007), p.129.

[187] *C Inc. v L* [2001] 2 Lloyd's Rep. 113.

[188] *TSB Private Bank International SA v Chabra* [1992] 1 W.L.R. 231.

[189] *SCF Finance Co Ltd v Masri* [1985] 1 W.L.R. 876.

[190] *Hubbard v Woodfield* (1913) 57 S.J. 729.

[191] *Re A Company* [1985] B.C.L.C. 333.

8–90 The obvious issue arising in relation to the first of these scenarios is that there is no cause of action against the party joined as the second defendant, a point made in the case of *TSB Private Bank International SA v Chabra*.[192] In that case the second defendant was joined of the court's own motion. However, Mummery J. observed that the "special feature" of the case was that on the evidence before the court there was a good arguable case that:

> "assets apparently vested in the name of the company are, in fact, beneficially the property of [the first defendant] and that it is open to the plaintiff to argue that the company was nothing more than the alter ego of [the first defendant]."[193]

8–91 As such, the question of joining a party to the action against whom there is no substantive cause of action will be at the discretion of the court and a "special feature" such as was identified in *Chabra* would have to be identified.

(c) Bankers' Books Evidence Act 1879[194]

8–92 In the case of *A v C*,[195] Robert Goff J. made reference to a very practical problem in relation to the exercise of the court's jurisdiction to grant *Mareva* injunctions. A defendant may have more than one asset within the jurisdiction, such as a number of bank accounts. However, the plaintiff will not know how much is in each account. Nor will the different banks know what is in the other banks' accounts. Without such knowledge, "it is difficult, if not impossible, to operate the *Mareva* jurisdiction properly."[196] That being so, Robert Goff J. accepted that a court could make an order for discovery or interrogatories in order to ensure that the *Mareva* jurisdiction is properly exercised. He also made reference to the Bankers' Book Evidence Act 1879, stating that:

> "But, if the asset is a bank balance, the court, if it holds that the plaintiff is entitled to discovery in respect of that balance, may exercise its power under section 7 of the Bankers' Books Evidence Act 1879 and order that the plaintiff be at liberty to inspect and take copies of any entries in the bankers' books."[197]

8–93 Section 7 of the Bankers' Books Evidence Act 1879 provides as follows:

> "On the application of any party to a legal proceeding a court may order that such party be at liberty to inspect and take copies of any entries in a banker's book for any of the purposes of such proceedings. An order under this section

---

[192] [1992] 1 W.L.R. 231.
[193] [1992] 1 W.L.R. 231 at 239.
[194] See generally, Dunne & Davies "The Bankers' Books Evidence Acts, 1879 and 1959" (1997) 2(7) Bar Rev. 297.
[195] [1981] Q.B. 956; [1981] 2 W.L.R. 629; [1981] 2 All E.R. 126.
[196] [1981] Q.B. 956 at 960; [1981] 2 W.L.R. 629 at 633; [1981] 2 All E.R. 126 at 351.
[197] [1981] Q.B. 956 at 960; [1981] 2 W.L.R. 629 at 633; [1981] 2 All E.R. 347 at 352.

may be made either with or without summoning the bank or any other party, and shall be served on the bank three clear days before the same is to be obeyed, unless the court otherwise directs."

8–94 The purpose of the Act was explained by Murphy J. in the case of *O'C v D*,[198] in which he explained that:

> "Again it must be recognised that the purpose of the Bankers' Books Evidence Act was to facilitate the proof of evidence contained in books used by bankers in the day to day conduct of their profession. Presumably the removal of such crucial documentation for the purposes of litigation might create considerable inconvenience. I would assume that it was for that reason that the legislature permitted, subject to important safeguards, the substitution of secondary evidence."[199]

(i) Manner of Application

8–95 The Act does not prescribe the manner of an application, and there are conflicting authorities in that regard. In the old case of *Arnott v Hayes*,[200] Cotton L.J. held that the Act provided the jurisdiction to make an order on foot of the Act ex parte. However, he qualified this by observing that, "under ordinary circumstances I think it better that the person whose account is to be looked at should be served."[201] Bowen L.J. agreed, saying that a judge should be careful about making ex parte orders, but had the jurisdiction to do so.

8–96 The decision in *L'Amie v Wilson*[202] would suggest, however, that other than in "very exceptional cases", the motion should be on notice to the party whose account is to be inspected and to the bank holding that account. However, it was accepted that s.7 gives discretion to the court to order inspection either with or without notice to the bank concerned and any other party concerned. In the later Irish case of *Staunton v Counihan*,[203] Dixon J. referred to *L'Amie*, and stated that:

> "The usual practice is to serve notice only on the party whose account is sought to be inspected and this, in my opinion, is sufficient."[204]

8–97 Although the various authorities are somewhat inconsistent, the more prudent course would be to bring an application pursuant to the Bankers' Books

---

[198] [1985] I.R. 265.
[199] [1985] I.R. 265 at 274. See also the dictum of Lindley M.R. in *Pollock v Garle* [1898] 1 Ch. 1 at 4, as referred to by Lord Keith in *Douglas v Pindling* [1996] 3 W.L.R. 242 at 249.
[200] (1887) 36 Ch. D. 731.
[201] (1887) 36 Ch. D. 731 at 736.
[202] [1907] 2 I.R. 130.
[203] (1957) 92 I.L.T.R. 32.
[204] (1957) 92 I.L.T.R. 32 at 34.

Evidence Act on notice to both the party whose account is to be inspected and to the bank holding that account. However, "exceptional" circumstances may dictate that putting the bank on notice is not an option. It will be for a court to assess the impact of such circumstances, but it is certainly arguable that, all other things being equal, an applicant should not be penalised for not putting the bank on notice if the circumstances militate against it.

8–98 From a practical perspective it may also be the case that an order under the Bankers' Books Evidence Act may be sought at the end of an application for a *Mareva* injunction,[205] or indeed as one of the reliefs on such an application. As a *Mareva* injunction is generally applied for on an ex parte basis, it may well be that a bank will not be on notice by default.

8–99 At a more general level, referring to the decision of Murphy J. in *O'C v D*,[206] Barrington J. observed in the case of *Larkins v National Union of Miners*[207] that there was:

> "nothing in the Bankers' Books Evidence Acts or in Mr. Justice Murphy's decision to circumscribe the power of the High Court, in an appropriate case, to order the production or inspection of any of a bank's books, documents or computer printouts."[208]

8–100 This would tend to suggest that the courts have a considerable degree of discretion in general terms when dealing with such applications.

(d) Tracing Orders

8–101 A tracing order may also be appropriate by way of ancillary order to a *Mareva* injunction. A tracing order allows a party to trace assets in relation to which he claims he has been wrongfully deprived.[209] Tracing takes on two forms. The first is common law tracing, described by Millet J. in the case of *Agip (Africa) v Jackson*[210] in the following terms:

> "The common law has always been able to follow a physical asset from one recipient to another. Its ability to follow an asset in the same hands into a changed form was established in *Taylor v Plumer*, 3 M. & S. 562. In following the plaintiff's money into an asset purchased exclusively with it, no

---

[205]   As happened in *Chemical Bank v McCormack* [1983] I.L.R.M. 350.
[206]   [1985] I.R. 265.
[207]   [1985] I.R. 671. In *Jennison v Baker* [1972] 2 Q.B. 52; [1972] 2 W.L.R. 429; [1972]1 All E.R. 997, the court looked to see whether the disobedience was "flagrant and overt".
[208]   [1985] I.R. 671 at 696.
[209]   See generally, Keane, *Equity and the Law of Trusts in the Republic of Ireland* (London: Butterworths, 1988), Ch.2. See also, O'Dell, "Tracing" (1999) 21 D.U.L.J. 131.
[210]   [1990] Ch. 265; [1989] 3 W.L.R. 1367; [1992] 4 All E.R. 385.

distinction is drawn between a chose in action such as the debt of a bank to its customer and any other asset: *In re Diplock* [1948] Ch. 466, 519. But it can only follow a physical asset, such as a cheque or its proceeds, from one person to another. It can follow money but not a chose in action. Money can be followed at common law into and out of a bank account and into the hands of a subsequent transferee, provided that it does not cease to be identifiable by being mixed with other money in the bank account derived from some other source: *Banque Belge pour l'Etranger v Hambrouck* [1921] 1 K.B. 321."[211]

8–102 However, there is also an equitable aspect to tracing, described by Lord Greene M.R. in *Re Diplock*[212] as "a more metaphysical approach".[213] As explained by Lord Greene, equity:

"found no difficulty in regarding a composite fund as an amalgam constituted by the mixture of two or more funds each of which could be regarded as having, for certain purposes, a continued separate existence. Putting it in another way, equity regarded the amalgam as capable, in proper circumstances, of being resolved into its component parts."[214]

8–103 A tracing order is of assistance as an ancillary order to a *Mareva* injunction, as is clear from cases such as *Chase Manhattan Bank NA v Israel-British Bank (London) Ltd*[215] in which an order was made in circumstances where the defendant had received moneys belonging or due to the plaintiff in breach of a fiduciary order.

5. Other Undertakings

8–104 Based on the wording of RSC Ord 50 r.6(2), the *Mareva* injunction order "may be made either unconditionally or upon such terms and conditions as the Court thinks just".[216] In the specific context of a *Mareva* injunction, the following undertakings have been identified by Courtney[217]:

- notifying any party affected by the order of its terms[218];

---

[211] [1990] Ch. 265 at 285; [1989] 3 W.L.R. 1367 at 1381; [1992] 4 All E.R. 385 at 398.
[212] [1948] Ch. 465; [1948] 2 All E.R. 318.
[213] [1948] Ch. 465 at 520; [1948] 2 All E.R. 318 at 345.
[214] [1948] Ch. 465 at 520; [1948] 2 All E.R. 318 at 345.
[215] [1981] Ch. 105.
[216] See Ch.1, Domestic Jurisdiction, para.1–49.
[217] Courtney, *Mareva Injunctions* (Dublin: Butterworths, 1998), p.335.
[218] For example, in *Minister for Arts, Heritage, the Gaeltacht and the Islands v Kennedy* [2002] 2 I.L.R.M. 94, an interim injunction was granted against the first-named defendant prohibiting him from engaging, commencing or continuing any works of any nature or kind on lands which constituted a special area of conservation in Co Kerry. It was further ordered that the plaintiff's solicitor be at liberty to notify the making of the order by telephone, letter and fax by any member of the Wildlife Service or of the Garda Síochána or the solicitor.

- paying reasonable costs and expenses of third parties (not the defendants) in complying with the order[219];
- notifying third parties of their right to seek a variation of the order[220];
- notifying third parties in the event of the order being discharged;
- not using the information obtained for collateral purposes; and
- stamping and issuing originating documents, affidavits and other court documents as necessary.

8–105 Further undertakings have been identified as necessary and appropriate in relation to an application for worldwide *Mareva* injunctive relief. These are[221]:

- not to commence foreign proceedings or to use information disclosed about foreign assets in foreign proceedings[222];
- not to seek foreign enforcement without leave;
- not to transfer assets without the leave of the court.

8–106 If it is proposed to take any action which may breach one of those undertakings, an application should be made to the court dealing with the matter in that regard. For example, a party may wish to trace monies on the basis of information obtained in the context of a *Mareva* application. It is arguable that such information should not be used without the permission of the court, given that tracing is, effectively, a collateral remedy. As such, the more prudent approach is to seek the leave of the court to use any information for a defined purpose.[223]

6. Enforcement Abroad

8–107 The issue of enforcement abroad arises from the courts' concerns about the risks of oppression caused by a potential proliferation of foreign proceedings to enforce worldwide *Mareva* injunctions; the courts want to ensure that the granting of a worldwide *Mareva* injunction is not oppressive. In *Derby & Co v Weldon (No. 1)*,[224] the plaintiffs offered an undertaking not to seek to enforce

---

[219] See *Z Ltd v A-Z* [1982] Q.B. 558 at 586; [1982] 2 W.L.R. 288 at 307; [1982] 1 All E.R. 556 at 564. In *Guinness Peat Aviation (Belgium) NV v Hispania Lineas Areas SA* [1992] 1 Lloyd's Rep. 190, a distinction was drawn between losses arising out of grant of the order and those arising out of complying with the order.

[220] *Guinness Peat Aviation (Belgium) NV v Hispania Lineas Areas SA* [1992] 1 Lloyd's Rep 190.

[221] Courtney, *Mareva Injunctions* (Dublin: Butterworths, 1988), p.339.

[222] See *Tate Access Floors Inc. v Boswell* [1991] Ch. 512; [1991] 2 W.L.R. 304; [1990] 3 All E.R. 303.

[223] By analogy, a party giving an implied undertaking not to use any documents discovered for a purpose unconnected with the proper conduct of the proceedings in question should seek, by way of motion, the leave of the court to be released from such an undertaking: See generally, Abrahamson, Dwyer & Fitzpatrick, *Discovery & Disclosure* (Dublin: Thomson Round Hall, 2007), p.197.

[224] [1990] Ch. 48; [1989] 2 W.L.R. 276; [1989] 1 All E.R. 469.

the *Mareva* injunction abroad without the permission of the court. The decision of the English Court of Appeal in *Dadourian Group International Inc. v Simms*[225] has provided some guidance as to how a court should exercise its discretion when considering whether to permit a party to enforce a worldwide *Mareva* injunction. It also considered the position of a party seeking such an order in a foreign jurisdiction by commencing proceedings there. As noted by Arden L.J., one of the primary reasons for giving permission to enforce a *Mareva* injunction abroad is that in a given case it is the way in which a worldwide *Mareva* injunction:

> "is most likely to be rendered effective to safeguard the position of the applicant in relation to assets which exist, or are thought to exist in the relevant jurisdiction."[226]

8–108 The eight guidelines suggested by the Court of Appeal are worth setting out at length (the term WFO refers to a "Worldwide Freezing Order"):

> "Guideline 1. The principle applying to the grant of permission to enforce a WFO abroad is that the grant of that permission should be just and convenient for the purpose of ensuring the effectiveness of the WFO, and in addition that it is not oppressive to the parties to the English proceedings or to third parties who may be joined to the foreign proceedings.
>
> Guideline 2. All the relevant circumstances and options need to be considered. In particular consideration should be given to granting relief on terms, for example terms as to the extension to third parties of the undertaking to compensate for costs incurred as a result of the WFO and as to the type of proceedings that may be commenced abroad. Consideration should also be given to the proportionality of the steps proposed to be taken abroad, and in addition to the form of any order.
>
> Guideline 3. The interests of the applicant should be balanced against the interests of the other parties to the proceedings and any new party likely to be joined to the foreign proceedings.
>
> Guideline 4. Permission should not normally be given in terms that would enable the applicant to obtain relief in the foreign proceedings which is superior to the relief given by the WFO.
>
> Guideline 5. The evidence in support of the application for permission should contain all the information (so far as it can reasonably be obtained in the time available) necessary to enable the judge to reach an informed decision, including evidence as to the applicable law and practice in the foreign court, evidence as to the nature of the proposed proceedings to be

[225] [2006] 1 W.L.R. 2499; [2006] 3 All E.R. 48.
[226] [2006] 1 W.L.R. 2499 at 2503; [2006] 3 All E.R. 48 at 56.

commenced and evidence as to the assets believed to be located in the jurisdiction of the foreign court and the names of the parties by whom such assets are held.

Guideline 6. The standard of proof as to the existence of assets that are both within the WFO and within the jurisdiction of the foreign court is a real prospect, that is the applicant must show that there is a real prospect that such assets are located within the jurisdiction of the foreign court in question.

Guideline 7. There must be evidence of a risk of dissipation of the assets in question.

Guideline 8. Normally the application should be made on notice to the respondent, but in cases of urgency, where it is just to do so, the permission may be given without notice to the party against whom relief will be sought in the foreign proceedings but that party should have the earliest practicable opportunity of having the matter reconsidered by the court at a hearing of which he is given notice."[227]

8–109 Similar guidance has not yet featured in any written decisions from the courts in this jurisdiction, though were they to do so—and it is submitted that there is considerable merit in the guidelines as set out—there are a number of points arising from the guidelines.[228] The granting of permission to take proceedings abroad to enforce a worldwide *Mareva* injunction is discretionary. In *Dadourian*, Arden L.J. referred to the discretion being exercised in a way that was "just and convenient", and also referred to judges having "maximum flexibility" in terms of the circumstances in which an order will be made, and the terms thereof. It is also clear that the circumstances of each individual case will be considered by the courts in coming to their determination. The courts also need to be satisfied that there is a "real prospect that something will be gained by starting proceedings abroad."[229] The courts in England also need to be satisfied that there is a risk of dissipation of the assets in relation to which the claimant wishes to bring the foreign proceedings. The extent to which this guideline would be of relevance in an Irish context is arguable; as has been seen, intention is the key consideration and, as such, it is likely that were an Irish court to adopt the guidelines it would vary this requirement to incorporate a reference to intention.

8–110 Although the guidelines recognise that an application should normally be made on notice but that permission may be given ex parte in cases of

---

[227] [2006] 1 W.L.R. 2499 at 2502; [2006] 3 All E.R. 48 at 55.
[228] The guidelines are themselves analysed in detail in the decision of Arden L.J. Also analysed in Carey, "Worldwide *Mareva* injunctions, Protections and Recent English Guidance" (2007) 3(1) J.C.P.P. 2. See also Rutherford "Frozen Over" (2006) 156 N.L.J. 837.
[229] [2006] 1 W.L.R. 2499 at 2505.

urgency, it is clear that the ability of a party to move quickly could well be somewhat hindered by the number of proofs which they would have to satisfy.

8–111 It should also be noted that Arden L.J. stated that the guidelines set out above "should not be treated as exclusive of any other matter which in the particular circumstances of an individual case needs to be considered."[230]

7. Breach of an Order

8–112 As with any other form of injunction order, there may be a breach of a *Mareva* injunction. Parties breaching such orders will be found to be in contempt of court.[231]

(a) Breach by Third Parties

8–113 The question of the position of a third party which, having been notified of the existence of a *Mareva* injunction, nevertheless allows assets which it holds to be dissipated has been addressed in England. In *Commissioners of Customs and Excise v Barclays Bank Plc*,[232] the House of Lords considered the extent to which a third party—in that case a bank—could be held liable in negligence for allowing the dissipation of assets subject to a *Mareva* injunction.[233] The Lords determined, applying the test in *Caparo v Dickman*,[234] that there was no breach of a duty of care in such circumstances (that being so, there was no consideration of what would constitute reasonable care). They held that there had been no assumption of responsibility and the case was in no way analogous to any established duty of care. How the Irish courts would approach a similar case remains to be determined but, as has been observed, the fact that the Court of Appeal and House of Lords came to different conclusions in the *Barclays Bank* case "points up the fact that this issue involves a delicately balanced value judgment."[235]

(b) Solicitors/Proceeds of Sale

8–114 The specific issue of a firm of solicitors paying the proceeds of sale to its client, which client was subject to a *Mareva* injunction requiring it not to

---

[230] [2006] 1 W.L.R. 2499 at 2508.
[231] See generally, Ch.12, Breach of an Injunction Order.
[232] [2006] 3 W.L.R. 1. Analysed by Ryan and Ryan, "*Mareva* Injunctions, Third Parties and the Law of Negligence" (2006) C.L.P. 13(10) 252. See also Lewis, "Indeterminate Liability" (2006) 156 N.L.J. 1236. The Court of Appeal decision is reviewed by Tinkler, "The Bank, the Thief, the Freezing Order—but Whose Duty?" (2005) 155 N.L.J. 82.
[233] As to the issue of third parties being in contempt of court in such circumstances, see Ch.12, Breach of an Injunction Order.
[234] [1990] 2 W.L.R. 358; [1990] 2 A.C. 605.
[235] Ryan and Ryan, "*Mareva* Injunctions, Third Parties and the Law of Negligence" (2006) C.L.P. 13(10) 252 at 257.

reduce its assets below a specified sum, was litigated in *Twohig v Bank of Ireland*.[236] The plaintiff claimed that in handing over such a sum the solicitor was assisting its client to dissipate its assets within the jurisdiction, thereby contravening the *Mareva* injunction which had been granted. The Supreme Court held that simply handing over money to a party against whom a *Mareva* injunction had been granted, increasing the amount of their assets, could not conceivably be a breach of an order requiring the defendant not to reduce his assets below a specified sum. It also held that solicitors have no right to withhold money from their client, and that their duty was to their client to pay over the monies which they owed him.

8–115 This is consistent with the decision of the Court of Appeal in *Law Society v Shanks*,[237] in which it was stated that apart from *Z Ltd v A-Z*[238] there was no authority for the proposition that a *Mareva* injunction prevents anybody handing the asset over to the owner of the asset.[239] However, the court acknowledged that if the assets were being handed over simply to facilitate the defendant in dissipating that asset, a different view might prevail.

8. Appeal[240]

8–116 A *Mareva* injunction granted by the Circuit Court may be appealed to the High Court and a High Court injunction appealed to the Supreme Court.

(a) Circuit to High Court

8–117 Rules of the Superior Courts, Ord.61 deals with the practical aspect of appeals from the Circuit to the High Court, which are brought by way of notice of appeal. The notice must be served on the relevant parties[241] and lodged[242] within 10 days from the pronouncement of the order appealed against. Rules of the Superior Courts Ord.61 r.9 provides that the notice of appeal from the refusal of an ex parte application by the Circuit Court "shall be a two days' notice", with no service required. Pursuant to RSC Ord.61 r.6, an appeal does not operate as a stay of execution in relation to the decision appealed from, unless ordered otherwise by the Circuit judge or the High Court judge in Dublin.

---

[236] unreported, Supreme Court, November 22, 2002.
[237] [1988] 1 F.L.R. 504.
[238] [1982] Q.B 558; [1982] 2 W.L.R. 288; [1982] 1 All E.R. 556.
[239] See also, *Bank Mellat v Kazmi* [1989] 2 W.L.R. 613.
[240] See Ch.5, Perpetual Injunctions, para.5–80.
[241] RSC Ord.61 r.2.
[242] RSC Ord.61 r.3.

(b) High to Supreme Court

8–118 An appeal from the High to the Supreme Court must be brought by way of notice of appeal as provided for by RSC Ord.58. It is a 10-day notice and must be served within 21 days from the passing and perfecting of the order appealed against.[243] Pursuant to RSC Ord.58 r.4, the notice of appeal "shall in every case state the grounds of appeal and the relief sought."

8–119 By virtue of RSC Ord.58 r.13:

> "Where an *ex parte* application has been refused in whole or in part by the High Court an application for a similar purpose may be made to the Supreme Court *ex parte* within four days from the date of such refusal, or within such enlarged time as the Supreme Court may allow."

8–120 An appeal shall not operate as a stay of execution in relation to the decision appealed from, unless ordered otherwise by court.[244]

9. Variation of a *Mareva* injunction

8–121 A *Mareva* injunction has of course the capacity to cause considerable hardship, and so a court may vary such an injunction in order to allow a party access to funds to discharge living expenses and legal fees.[245] However, a defendant must do more than simply state that money is owed, as is clear from the decision of Robert Goff J. in *A v C*.[246]

8–122 It was also accepted in *Iraqi Ministry of Defence v Arcepey Shipping Co SA (The Angela Bell)*[247] that a variation or qualification could be imposed on a *Mareva* injunction in order to enable a third party creditor of the defendant to be repaid.

8–123 An application to vary or discharge a *Mareva* injunction is made on notice and grounded upon an affidavit. Such an application for variation is generally made if the defendant needs to make a payment to a third party in circumstances where such payment is not being made with a view to frustrating future judgment granted to the plaintiff.

---

[243] RSC Ord.58 r.3. It is possible for the Supreme Court to abridge the relevant time limits by virtue of RSC Ord.58 r.3(3).

[244] RSC Ord.58 r.18. See generally, Delany & McGrath, *Civil Procedure in the Superior Courts*, 2nd edn (Dublin: Thomson Round Hall, 2005), Ch.20.

[245] *DPP v EH*, unreported, High Court, Kelly J., April 22, 1997. See also, s.6(1) of the Proceeds of Crime Act 1996 which contains an equivalent statutory provision, as considered in Ch.11, Specific Statutory Injunctions, para.11–132.

[246] [1981] 2 All E.R. 126.

[247] [1980] 2 W.L.R. 488; [1981] Q.B. 65; [1980] 1 All E.R. 480.

(a) Discharge of an Order

8–124 Rules of the Superior Courts Ord.52 r.3 provides that where the court makes an order ex parte, "any party affected by such order may move to set it aside."[248] The courts have an inherent jurisdiction, in the absence of an express statutory provision to the contrary, to discharge (often referred to as dissolution, vacation or setting aside) an order made ex parte on the application of any party affected by that order.[249] A discharge is often sought when it is claimed that the plaintiff did not satisfy the relevant and necessary proofs for the granting of a *Mareva* injunction; that not all facts were disclosed on an ex parte application or that there has been a failure to comply with any undertaking given to the court. There is no prescribed length of time which must pass before the discharge of an interim injunction can be sought, and each case will be considered on its own merits. The question of discharge and the circumstances in which a discharge will be granted have been considered in greater detail in Ch.7, Interim Applications.

(b) Third Parties

8–125 A third party may also seek to have a *Mareva* injunction discharged or varied.[250] In *Galaxia Maritime SA v Mineral Import Export (The Eleftherios)*[251] a *Mareva* injunction had been granted restraining the defendants from removing from the jurisdiction their assets, in particular cargo laden on board a motor vessel owned by a third party. The practical implication of this was that the ship would have to remain in port for as long as the order endured. On the application of the ship's owners, the *Mareva* injunction was discharged. The Court of Appeal held that it could take into account the effect on third parties when dealing with applications for *Mareva* injunctions.

8–126 However, in the Irish case of *Criminal Assets Bureau v Mc S*,[252] the appellant, who was both a notice party and wife of the defendant in the proceedings, failed in her appeal in which she contended that the *Mareva* injunction granted had at some stage ceased to exist or, if it had continued in existence, it was not binding on her as she was not a party to the proceedings. She also referred to the effect on her and her family and the difficulty it was causing in daily living. The Supreme Court rejected the appeal, but on the basis

---

[248] See RCC Ord.64.
[249] See *Voluntary Purchasing Groups Inc. v Insurco International Ltd* [1995] 2 I.L.R.M. 145 at 147.
[250] *Cretanor Maritime Co Ltd v Irish Marine Management Ltd* [1978] 1 W.L.R. 966; [1978] 3 All E.R. 164, in which a debenture-holder successfully applied for the discharge of a *Mareva* injunction on the basis that the debenture-holder was a secured creditor whose rights ranked in priority to the plaintiff's.
[251] [1982] 1 W.L.R. 539; [1982] 1 All E.R. 796.
[252] unreported, Supreme Court, January 30, 2002.

that she had not put before the court any material which would justify a discharge. The case is thus of limited precedential value in terms of third parties generally.

(c) Applications Post Judgment

8–127 An application for a *Mareva* injunction can also be made once a judgment has been handed down by a court.[253] As has been noted, applications for worldwide *Mareva* injunctions are usually made at such a point.[254]

10. Related Statutory Orders

8–128 There are a number of statutory provisions which have the same effect as a *Mareva* injunction, in that they freeze assets for the same reason as the *Mareva* injunction was developed, in order to ensure that those assets cannot be put beyond the reach of the party seeking relief before judgment is satisfied. It is not proposed to consider these in any detail, as they are self-contained statutory provisions which must be considered on their own terms.[255] These provisions are[256]:

- Company Law Enforcement Act 2001, s.55;
- Taxes Consolidation Act 1997, s.908(4);
- Proceeds of Crime Act 1996, ss.2 and 3;
- Family Law (Divorce) Act 1996, s.37(2);
- Family Law Act 1995, s.35(2); and
- Criminal Justice Act 1994, s.24(1).

D. *Anton Piller* Order

1. Introduction

8–129 The preservation of key evidence, ensuring that trials are not frustrated due to lack of evidence, is a key factor in litigation. The *Anton Piller* order,[257] the second of the law's two "nuclear weapons",[258] is essentially a form of

---

[253] *Stewart Chartering v C & O Managements SA (The Venus Destiny)* [1980] 1 W.L.R. 460; [1980] 1 All E.R. 718.

[254] See para.8–28.

[255] See generally, Ch.11, Specific Statutory Injunctions.

[256] The provisions in force at the time of the publication of the book are identified by Courtney, *Mareva Injunctions* (Dublin: Butterworths, 1998), Ch.3.

[257] Now known as a "Search Order" in England since the introduction of the Civil Procedure Rules in 1999.

[258] per Donaldson L.J. in *Bank Mellat v Nikpour* [1985] F.S.R. 87 at 92.

mandatory injunction[259] which allows a plaintiff to take evidence from a defendant's premises.

8–130 An *Anton Piller* order is ancillary to the substantive cause of action, and does not represent a cause of action in itself. It is an in personam order.[260] Although it provides for the taking of evidence from a premises, it does not give the right to enter a premises, and the defendant's permission must be obtained in that regard. In practical terms, an *Anton Piller* order is of use primarily in cases involving intellectual property, such as copyright infringements and the use of trade secrets, although it is not in any way confined to such cases.

8–131 The essence of an *Anton Piller* order is surprise[261] and the order is as such sought on an ex parte basis. It is granted in very limited circumstances.[262]

2. Development

8–132 First invoked in *EMI Ltd v Pandit*,[263] it was the second case in which the injunction ordered was granted, *Anton Piller KG v Manufacturing Processes Ltd*,[264] which bequeathed its name to the order. Given that such an order is rarely granted, there is considerably less case law in relation to *Anton Piller* orders than in relation to *Mareva* injunctions. In particular, there are very few written judgments dealing with *Anton Piller* orders in this jurisdiction and regard must be had to the consideration of such orders by the English courts for guidance. In broad terms, the criteria upon which such orders are granted have remained constant since its inception, and the contribution of the courts since then has been primarily focused on the terms of the order.

3. Acceptance in Ireland

8–133 The *Anton Piller* order inveigled itself quietly into domestic jurisprudence, and to the extent that it is considered in reported judgments, various cases make reference to *Anton Piller* orders which had been granted at the ex parte stage, without going into the details of their granting.[265] The case of

---

[259] See *EMI v Pandit* [1975] 1 W.L.R. 302 at 308; [1975] 1 All E.R. 418 at 424, per Templeman J.; Snell, *Equity*, 31st edn (London: Thomson Sweet & Maxwell, 2005), p.420 refers to such an order being a hybrid between a disclosure order and an injunction.

[260] per Scott J. in *Altertext Inc. v Advanced Data Communications Ltd* [1985] 1 W.L.R. 457 at 462; [1985] 1 All E.R. 395 at 399.

[261] per Smyth J. in *Microsoft Corporation v Brightpoint Ireland Ltd* [2001] 1 I.L.R.M. 540 at 545.

[262] In *EMI Ltd v Pandit* [1975] 1 W.L.R. 302 at 307; [1975] 1 All E.R. 418 at 424, Templeman J. stated that an *Anton Piller* order should only be granted "where circumstances are exceptional".

[263] [1975] 1 W.L.R. 302; [1975] 1 All E.R. 418.

[264] [1976] Ch. 55; [1976] 2 W.L.R. 162; [1976] 1 All E.R. 779.

[265] See, for example, *Orion Pictures Corp. v Hickey*, unreported, High Court, Costello J., January 18, 1991.

Microsoft Corporation v Brightpoint Ireland Ltd[266] clearly acknowledges the existence of *Anton Piller* orders in this jurisdiction, and rehearses a number of the applicable tests, but does not refer to any previous case as the basis for their acceptance in Ireland. The case certainly goes some way towards dealing with the key tests, although not in as detailed a fashion as it might have done. Nonetheless, it appears that the Irish courts have been willing to make *Anton Piller* orders as necessary.[267]

8–134 The power to grant an *Anton Piller* order is based on s.28(8) of the Supreme Court of Judicature (Ireland) Act 1877[268] and Ord.50 r.6(1) of the Rules of the Superior Courts.[269]

4. Extraterritorial Effect

8–135 It was held in *Cook Industries Inc. v Galliher*[270] that the court had jurisdiction to grant an order for inspection of a property outside the jurisdiction, although such power must be exercised with circumspection.[271] As with *Mareva* injunctions, the ability to grant such inspection derives from the in personam nature of the *Anton Piller* order.

5. Applicable Tests for an *Anton Piller* Order

8–136 There are a number of elements involved in applying for an *Anton Piller* Order, as derived from case law. Once there is a substantive cause of action:

- The party applying must show a very strong prima facie case.
- Actual or potential damage must be very serious.
- There must be clear evidence that the defendant has in his possession vital documents or materials, and that there is a real possibility that he may dispose of or destroy such material.
- There must also be no infringement of any right to claim privilege against self-incrimination.

8–137 These will be considered in turn.

---

[266] [2001] 1 I.L.R.M. 540.
[267] See, for example, *Jobling-Purser v Jackman*, ex tempore, High Court, Carroll J., July 27, 1999 and *JN v TK* [2003] 2 I.L.R.M. 40.
[268] The wording of which is set out in Ch.1, Domestic Jurisdiction, para.1–30.
[269] Such power is derived in England from s.7 of the Civil Procedure Act 1997.
[270] [1979] Ch. 439; [1978] 3 W.L.R. 637; [1978] 3 All E.R. 945.
[271] See also, *Altertext Inc. v Advanced Data Communications Ltd* [1985] 1 W.L.R. 457 at 462.

(a) Strong Prima Facie Case

8–138 The standard to be met when applying for an ex parte *Anton Piller* order is higher than that usually required at the interim and interlocutory stage of other injunction applications.[272] In *Microsoft Corporation v Brightpoint Ireland Ltd*,[273] Smyth J. referred to there being strong prima facie evidence of dishonest conduct by the defendants which indicated a strong probability that they would be likely to destroy records relevant to the action.[274] A strong prima facie case is the relevant applicable test. This is higher than both the *Campus Oil* bona fide test and the test used in applications for *Mareva* injunctions of a "good arguable case", and echoes the test used pre-*American Cyanamid* and *Campus Oil*.

(b) Serious Actual or Potential Damage

8–139 This point is relatively self-explanatory; the damage concerned will be considered on the facts of each individual case, and the circumstances of each party considered.

(c) Possession of Documents

8–140 The plaintiff must also provide clear evidence that the defendant has in its possession incriminating documents or materials, and that there is a real possibility that it may dispose of or destroy such material before any application inter partes can be made.[275]

8–141 It was held in the English case of *AB v CDE*[276] that the risk of disposal or destruction may be inferred if there is evidence that the defendant has been engaging in "nefarious activity", a point accepted in Ireland in the *Microsoft* case.

(d) Protection from Self-Incrimination

8–142 The claim to the privilege against self-incrimination in relation to *Anton Piller* orders was considered in *Rank Film Distributors Ltd v Video Information Centre*,[277] in which the House of Lords upheld a claim to such privilege.[278] Through legislative intervention in England the position is that the right to resist discovery on the ground of self-incrimination applies where there is a serious risk of prosecution for conspiracy.[279]

---

[272] See generally, Chs 6 and 7, Interim Applications and Interlocutory Applications respectively.
[273] [2001] 1 I.L.R.M. 540.
[274] Referring to *Tate Access Floors Inc. v Boswell* [1991] Ch. 512; [1991] 2 W.L.R. 304; [1990] All E.R. 303.
[275] See *Anton Piller KG v Manufacturing Processes Ltd* [1976] 1 All E.R. 779 at 784, per Ormrod L.J.
[276] [1982] R.P.C. 509.
[277] [1982] A.C. 380; [1981] 2 W.L.R. 668; [1981] 2 All E.R. 76.
[278] See also, *Universal Thermosensors v Hibben* [1992] 1 W.L.R. 840; [1992] 3 All E.R. 257.
[279] *Tate Access Floors Inc. v Boswell* [1991] Ch. 512 at 517; [1991] 2 W.L.R. 304 at 315; [1990]

E. Applying for an *Anton Piller* Order

1. Introduction

8–143 As with *Mareva* injunctions, most applications for *Anton Piller* orders are made on an ex parte basis due to the urgency inherent in such applications. The terms of RSC Ord.52 r.3 are of relevance in that they provide for the making of ex parte applications. Reference is made to the key principles in relation to such ex parte applications as considered in the context of *Mareva* injunctions[280] and to Ch.7, Interim Applications, which deals with the practical aspects and issues arising out of ex parte applications in greater detail.[281]

8–144 As with applications for a *Mareva* injunction, there must be full and frank disclosure in the grounding affidavit and, if necessary in court, of all relevant matters.[282] It is for the court and not the plaintiffs or their advisers to determine the question of relevance.[283] It has been held that an affidavit in support of an application for an *Anton Piller* order should thus err on the side of excessive disclosure.[284]

2. Hearing *In Camera* or Limitation on Publication

8–145 There is a clear risk that by making an application for an *Anton Piller* order in open court, the element of surprise which is usually necessary to ensure such order is given full effect is dissipated. As such, a party seeking an *Anton Piller* order may seek to invoke the provisions of s.45(1)(a) of the Courts (Supplemental Provisions) Act 1961 to have the matter dealt with *in camera*. However, it is clear from the decision of Smyth J. in *Microsoft Corporation v Brightpoint Ireland Ltd*[285] that it is not of the essence that an ex parte application for an *Anton Piller* order should be heard *in camera*. Smyth J. referred to the constitutional obligation in Art.34.1 that:

---

3 All E.R. 303 at 312. See also, *Universal City Studios Inc. v Hubbard* [1984] 1 Ch. 225; [1984] 1 All E.R. 661. For a more general discussion in relation to self-incrimination, see Leonowicz, "The Privilege Against Self-Incrimination Part I" (2005) 23 I.L.T. 55; Part II (2005) I.L.T. 77.

[280] See para.8–55.

[281] See para.7–34.

[282] See para.8–63.

[283] per Smyth J. in *Microsoft Corporation v Brightpoint Ireland Ltd* [2001] 1 I.L.R.M. 540 at 550.

[284] *Columbia Picture Industries Inc. v Robinson* [1986] 3 All E.R. 338, as accepted in *Microsoft Corporation v Brightpoint Ireland Ltd* [2001] 1 I.L.R.M. 540 at 546.

[285] [2001] 1 I.L.R.M. 540.

"Justice shall be administered in courts established by law by judges appointed in the manner provided by the Constitution, and, save in such special and limited cases as may be prescribed by law, shall be administered in public."

8–146 He acknowledged that there were statutory exceptions to this, and that there were also rare occasions where in the interests of justice and for good and proper reason a judge may direct a hearing *in camera*.

8–147 Notwithstanding the fact that Smyth J. rejected the contention in *Microsoft Corporation v Brightpoint Ireland Ltd*[286] that it is of the essence that an ex parte application for an *Anton Piller* order should be heard *in camera*, he held that in exercising its inherent jurisdiction a judge sitting in open court may direct or limit or inhibit publication of the order made in open court. Smyth J. acknowledged that the publication of the existence and contents of an *Anton Piller* order in advance of its execution could weaken or deprive it of the element of surprise.

3. Form of the Order

8–148 An *Anton Piller* order should, in the first place, specify the premises to be searched,[287] as well as the parties authorised to carry out such a search.[288] As such an order may be subject to abuse,[289] there are usually a number of provisions built into the order in an attempt to prevent such abuse. In *Universal Thermosensors Ltd v Hibben*,[290] Sir Donald Nicholls V.C. set out a number of such provisions, which provide very useful guidance:

- An order should normally contain a term that before complying with the order the defendant may obtain legal advice, provided this is done forthwith.
- If the order is to be executed at a private house, and it is at all likely that a woman may be in the house alone, the solicitor serving the order must be, or must be accompanied by, a woman.
- In general *Anton Piller* orders should expressly provide that, unless it is seriously impracticable, a detailed list of the items being removed should be prepared at the premises before they are removed, and that the defendant should be given an opportunity to check this list at the time.

---

[286] [2001] 1 I.L.R.M. 540.
[287] *Protector Alarms v Maxim Alarms Ltd* [1978] F.S.R. 442.
[288] *Vapormatic Co Ltd v Sparex Ltd* [1976] 1 W.L.R. 939.
[289] See *Columbia Picture Industries Inc. v Robinson* [1987] Ch. 38; [1986] 3 W.L.R. 542; [1986] 3 All E.R. 338 and *Lock International Plc v Beswick* [1989] 1 W.L.R. 1268; [1989] 3 All E.R. 373.
[290] [1992] 1 W.L.R. 840; [1992] 3 All E.R. 257.

- An order may frequently contain an injunction restraining those on whom they are served from informing others of the existence of the order for a limited period. This is to prevent one defendant from alerting others to what is happening.
- Orders should provide that, unless there is good reason for doing otherwise, the order should not be executed at business premises save in the presence of a responsible officer or representative of the company or trader in question.
- Consideration should be given to devising some means, appropriate to the facts of the case, to avoid a situation whereby one party can himself search the offices of a competitor.[291]

8–149 An *Anton Piller* order may also by its terms limit the number of people who can have access to a specified premises. For example, in *Columbia Picture Industries Inc v Robinson*,[292] a limit of four people other than a solicitor was specified.

4. Ancillary Orders: *Norwich Pharmacal/Megaleasing* Orders

8–150 An ancillary order which is often sought in conjunction with an *Anton Piller* order is a *Norwich Pharmacal* order.[293] Derived from the case of *Norwich Pharmacal Co v Customs and Excise Commissioners*,[294] such orders provide that a party who has not committed any wrong himself may be required to disclose the identity of wrongdoers known to him. This is based on the principle, as accepted in this jurisdiction in the case of *MegaLeasing (UK) Ltd v Barrett*[295] that the courts should aid in obtaining all information relevant and necessary to the true determination of facts.[296]

5. Undertakings

8–151 It was emphasised in *Manor Electronics v Dickson*[297] that procedural undertakings included in ex parte orders should be scrupulously honoured. In *Universal Thermosensors Ltd v Hibben*,[298] the Vice Chancellor suggested, acknowledging the attendant costs of an *Anton Piller* order, that when making such orders judges should give serious consideration to the desirability of providing, by suitable undertakings and otherwise:

[291] [1992] 1 W.L.R. 840 at 860; [1992] 3 All E.R. 257 at 275.
[292] [1987] Ch. 38; [1986] 3 W.L.R. 542; [1986] 3 All E.R. 338.
[293] See generally, Abrahamson, Dwyer & Fitzpatrick, *Discovery & Disclosure* (Dublin: Thomson Round Hall, 2007), p.177. The case also deals with a party's entitlement to seek discovery as a substantive relief in proceedings.
[294] [1974] A.C. 133; [1973] 3 W.L.R. 164; [1973] 2 All E.R. 943.
[295] [1992] 1 I.R. 219; [1993] I.L.R.M. 497.
[296] See also, *International Trading Ltd v Corporation of Dublin* [1974] I.R. 373.
[297] *Times Law Reports*, February 8, 1990.
[298] [1992] 1 W.L.R. 840; [1992] 3 All E.R. 257.

(a) that the order should be served, and its execution should be supervised, by a solicitor other than a member of the firm of solicitors acting for the plaintiff in the action;

(b) that he or she should be an experienced solicitor having some familiarity with the workings of *Anton Piller* orders, and with judicial observations on this subject;

(c) that the solicitor should prepare a written report on what occurred when the order was executed;

(d) that a copy of the report should be served on the defendants; and

(e) that in any event and within the next few days the plaintiff must return to the court and present that report at an inter partes hearing, preferably to the judge who made the order.

8–152 Recognising that these procedures add considerably to the costs of executing an *Anton Piller* order, the Vice Chancellor stated that the plaintiff should be responsible for paying the fees of the solicitor in question. This was to be without prejudice to a decision as to whether such costs should ultimately be borne in whole or in part by the defendant against whom the order was secured.

8–153 However, a word of caution must be sounded in relation to undertakings: in his decision in *Microsoft* Smyth J. rejected the defendant's submissions on implied undertakings on that basis that to accept them would be to:

> "seek to import into this jurisdiction the legal rights duties and responsibilities in England and Wales where legislative and rule provisions deal with the type of undertakings spoken of."[299]

8–154 This being the case, in terms of identifying any undertakings, it is important that they are not solely derived from "legislative and rule provisions" in England. Derived from various reported cases both from this jurisdiction and from England, the following are the undertakings which are generally required when applying for an *Anton Piller* order in this jurisdiction.

(a) Undertaking as to Damages

8–155 If the court accedes to an application for an *Anton Piller* order, the usual undertaking as to damages will be required of the plaintiff.[300]

---

[299] [2001] 1 I.L.R.M. 540 at 550. However, those submissions are not recorded in the report of the judgment.

[300] Considered in Ch.6, Interlocutory Applications, para.6–76. See, in the context of *Anton Piller* orders, *Vapormatic Co Ltd v Sparex Ltd* [1976] 1 W.L.R. 939 at 940.

(b) Rapid Execution of an Order

8–156 Although not necessarily an express undertaking, speed is of the essence in executing an *Anton Piller* order, and in *Jobling-Purser v Jackman*,[301] Carroll J. vacated an *Anton Piller* order in part on the basis that the order was so old that it would be unjust to allow the persons named in it to enter and search the defendant's premises.

(c) Issuing of Proceedings

8–157 Again, although not necessarily an express undertaking, it is incumbent upon the party securing the *Anton Piller* order to cause proceedings to be issued as soon as possible in circumstances where they are not yet in existence. In *Hytrac Conveyors Ltd v Conveyors International Ltd*,[302] Lawton L.J. had to consider a situation in which there had been an attempt to procure an *Anton Piller* order, yet a significant number of weeks passed without any statement of claim being delivered. In observing that a party should deliver its statement of claim within the time specified in rules of court, unless otherwise ordered, Lawton L.J. cautioned that, in the context of an accusatorial procedure:

> "Those who make charges must state right at the beginning what they are and what facts they are based on. They must not use *Anton Piller* orders as a means of finding out what sort of charges they can make."[303]

8–158 This dictum was echoed by Denham J. in the case of *Irish Family Planning Association v Youth Defence*,[304] in which she stated—albeit not in the context of an *Anton Piller* order—that, "those who make charges must state right at the beginning what they are and what facts they are based upon." *Anton Piller* orders are not to be used as a means of finding out what sort of charges can be made.[305]

(d) Use of Documents Disclosed

8–159 In the normal course, documents discovered as part of inter partes litigation are subject to an undertaking that they will not be used other than for the purposes of the litigation at hand.[306] However, in *Roussel v Farchepro*

---

[301] ex tempore, High Court, Carroll J., July 27, 1999.
[302] [1983] 1 W.L.R. 44; [1982] 3 All E.R. 415.
[303] [1983] 1 W.L.R. 44 at 47; [1982] 3 All E.R. 415 at 417.
[304] [2004] 1 I.R. 374 at 383.
[305] See also the decision of the High Court in Northern Ireland in *Group 4 Securitas (Northern Ireland) v McIldowney* [1997] N.I.J.B. 23.
[306] *Ambiorix Ltd v Minister for the Environment (No. 1)* [1992] 1 I.R. 277 at 286, per Finlay C.J.; *Home Office v Harman* [1983] 1 A.C. 280 at 304; [1982] 2 W.L.R. 338; [1982] 1 All E.R. 532, per Lord Diplock and *Crest Homes Plc v Marks* [1987] A.C. 829 at 860, per Lord Oliver. See generally, Abrahamson, Dwyer & Fitzpatrick, *Discovery & Disclosure* (Dublin: Thomson Round Hall, 2007), Ch.17.

Ltd,[307] Kelly J. suggested that documents disclosed on foot of an *Anton Piller* order "may fall to be approached differently from documents disclosed as part of the ordinary process of discovery in *inter partes* litigation."[308]

8–160 Although he did not have to deal with that aspect of the case on the facts, Kelly J. referred to the decision of *Jade Engineering Ltd v Antiference Window Systems*[309] in order to explain such an approach. In that case, Jacob J. had observed that:

> "When one is concerned with the protection of intellectual property rights, one often has a chain of different suppliers and the court has long held that a legitimate purpose can be their pursuit. So leave is given to use the information other than for the exact action before the court, to pursue others concerned with the infringement of the same right."[310]

8–161 It thus appears that the ability to vary the usual undertaking in relation to the use of documents depends on the circumstances of each individual case.

(e) Preservation and Return of Documents

8–162 There should be an undertaking from the plaintiff's solicitor to preserve and return all original documents to the defendant as soon as possible.[311] If the ownership of any article taken from a premises is in dispute, there must be an undertaking from the plaintiff's solicitor to return the articles to the defendant's solicitors for safekeeping on their undertaking to retain them in a safe place.

6. Service and Execution of the Order

(a) Service

8–163 The *Anton Piller* order should be served by a solicitor.[312] It is often recorded in an *Anton Piller* order that the defendant may seek legal advice before any items are removed from its premises.

(b) No Forcible Entry

8–164 Although an *Anton Piller* order is phrased in such a way that it allows for entry by the plaintiff or its representatives into the defendant's premises, a

---

[307] [1999] 3 I.R. 567.
[308] [1999] 3 I.R. 567 at 572.
[309] [1996] 23 F.S.R. 461.
[310] [1996] 23 F.S.R. 461 at 466.
[311] *Manor Electronics v Dickson, Times Law Reports*, February 8, 1990.
[312] *Vapormatic Co Ltd v Sparex Ltd* [1976] 1 W.L.R. 939 at 940.

plaintiff cannot forcibly enter such premises. As explained by Scott J. in *Bhimji v Chatwani*,[313] it is:

> "fundamental to the theory of *Anton Piller* type orders that a civil court in civil proceedings has no power to give one citizen the right to enter a house or premises of another citizen."[314]

8–165 He explained that such orders are in personam orders directed to the defendants, by which the defendants are ordered to allow entry and to allow search. As such, the right of the plaintiff (and his solicitor) to enter and search derives from the defendant's permission, and the court does not have the power to confer such a right. This is a consideration with particular resonance in this jurisdiction due to the constitutional provisions in relation to property.[315]

(c) Report to the Court

8–166 The solicitor concerned may also in general terms have to provide a report to the court on the execution of the order. Specifically, it has been held in England and accepted in Ireland that it is essential for a solicitor who is executing an *Anton Piller* order at a defendant's premises to make a detailed record of the material to be removed from the premises. Scott J. summarised the position in this regard in *Columbia Picture Industries v Robinson*, in the following terms[316]:

> "… it [is] essential that a detailed record of the material taken should always be required to be made by the solicitors who execute [an *Anton Piller* order] before the material is removed from the respondent's premises. So far as possible, disputes as to what material was taken, the resolution of which depends on the oral testimony and credibility of the solicitors on the one hand and the respondent on the other hand, ought to be avoided. In the absence of any corroboration of a respondent's allegation that particular material … was taken, a solicitor's sworn and apparently credible denial is likely always to be preferred. This state of affairs is unfair to respondents. It ought to be avoided so far as it can be."[317]

8–167 The *Columbia Pictures* case represented a turning point in the English courts' willingness to grant *Anton Piller* orders, with Scott J. stating that the

---

[313] [1991] 1 W.L.R. 989; [1991] 1 All E.R. 705.

[314] [1991] 1 W.L.R. 989 at 993; [1991] 1 All E.R. 705 at 708.

[315] See Arts 40.3.2 and 43. See generally, Hogan & Whyte, *J.M. Kelly: The Irish Constitution*, 4th edn (Dublin: Butterworths, 2003).

[316] [1987] Ch. 38; [1986] 3 W.L.R. 542; [1986] 3 All E.R. 338.

[317] [1987] Ch. 38 at 76; [1986] 3 W.L.R. 542 at 570; [1986] 3 All E.R. 338 at 371, as cited with approval by Smyth J. in *Microsoft Corporation v Brightpoint Ireland Ltd* [2001] 1 I.L.R.M. 540 at 549.

balance had been allowed "to swing much too far in favour of claimants", taking the view that, *"Anton Piller* orders have been too readily granted and with insufficient safeguards for respondents."[318]

8–168 In the *Microsoft* case, Smyth J. found in relation to *Columbia Pictures* that the "law in this issue is very properly put". He also suggested that the furnishing of a list of goods taken might have been sensible, and that it was "a courtesy that should have been accorded between officers of the Court."[319]

7. Refusal to Comply with an Order/Contempt

8–169 If entry is refused, the plaintiff's primary recourse is to bring an application to have a defendant found in contempt of court.[320] The plaintiff's solicitor will accordingly be required to give an undertaking to the court to explain the meaning of the order to the person upon whom it is served, and that there may be an entitlement to claim the privilege against self-incrimination.

8–170 If the defendant is in a position whereby it does not want to allow entry, it can in the first instance seek legal advice, although the amount of time taken to secure and act upon such advice is a relevant consideration.[321] There is also the risk that a defendant may be found guilty of contempt in such circumstances.[322] It is also open to a defendant to bring an urgent application to set the *Anton Piller* order aside. As explained by Sir John Donaldson M.R. in *WEA Records Ltd v Visions Channel 4 Ltd*[323]:

> "[The defendants] could, if they had wished, have refused immediate compliance and instead have made an urgent application to have the order set aside. This, in my judgment, is implicit in the final paragraph of the order which I have just read. However, I must emphasise, as did Buckley L.J. in *Hallmark Cards Inc. v Image Arts Ltd* [1977] 3 F.S.R. 150, that defendants who take this line do so very much at their peril. If they succeed in getting the order discharged, all well and good. But if they fail, they will render themselves liable to penalties for contempt of court."[324]

---

[318] [1986] 3 W.L.R. 542 at 570; [1987] Ch. 38 at 76; [1986] 3 All E.R. 338 at 371.
[319] *Microsoft Corporation v Brightpoint Ireland Ltd* [2001] 1 I.L.R.M. 540 at 549.
[320] See generally, Ch.12, Breach of an Injunction Order.
[321] See *Bhimji v Chatwani* [1991] 1 W.L.R. 989; [1991] 1 All E.R. 705.
[322] See para.8–172.
[323] [1983] 1 W.L.R. 721; [1983] 2 All E.R. 589.
[324] [1983] 1 W.L.R. 721 at 725; [1983] 2 All E.R. 589 at 592. See also, *Wardle Fabrics Ltd v G Myristis Ltd* [1984] F.S.R. 263 at 271.

8. Liberty to Seek a Discharge

8–171 Liberty will generally be given to apply to have an *Anton Piller* order discharged. However, echoing the decision in *WEA Records*, Scott J. observed in *Columbia Picture Industries Inc. v Robinson*[325] that if a party does not consent to entry and search of his premises:

> "he is at risk of committal to prison for contempt of court. This is so even if the reason for his refusal to consent is his intention to apply to have the order discharged."[326]

8–172 As is clear from the decision in *Wardle Fabrics Ltd v G Myristis Ltd*,[327] the breach of an order amounts to contempt even if the order is subsequently set aside (notwithstanding Sir John Donaldson M.R.'s dictum in *WEA Records* that if an order is discharged, this is "all well and good"). This is appropriate given that if a party commits a breach it does so without knowing whether an order may subsequently be set aside. As will be seen, this ensures that the dignity of the court is not offended and the administration of justice not interfered with.[328]

8–173 Another option available to a party against whom an *Anton Piller* order has been made is to seek to have the claim to which the order is ancillary dismissed.[329]

9. Variation and Setting Aside of Orders

8–174 A return date will generally be included in an order made on an ex parte basis. The significance of having such a return date was considered by Scott J. in *Columbia Picture Industries*. He observed that:

> "The significance of the return date is that it provides a fixed date on which the respondent, if so advised, can apply to *vary* or *set aside* [the order first made]. It does not, in my judgment, preclude a respondent who does not take advantage of the return date from applying subsequently."[330]

---

[325] [1987] Ch. 38; [1986] 3 All E.R. 338.

[326] [1986] 3 W.L.R. 542 at 566; [1987] Ch. 38 at 71; [1986] 3 All E.R. 338 at 367. See also, Capper, "The Duties of a Plaintiff With an *Anton Piller* Order" (1998) 49 N.I.L.Q. 210.

[327] [1984] F.S.R. 263.

[328] See the analysis of this area of the law carried out by Finnegan P. in *Shell E & P Ireland v McGrath*, unreported, High Court, Finnegan P., April 7, 2006. See generally, Ch.12, Breach of an Injunction Order.

[329] See the case of *Group 4 Securitas (Northern Ireland) Ltd v McIldowney* [1997] N.I.J.B. 23; for a commentary on this, see Capper, "The Duties of a Plaintiff With an *Anton Piller* Order" (1998) 49 N.I.L.Q. 210.

[330] [1987] Ch. 38 at 86.

8–175 In *Microsoft Corporation v Brightpoint Ireland Ltd*,[331] Smyth J. expressed the view that a court should be most responsive to an application defendant/respondent in an appropriate case without waiting for the return date (with or without "liberty to apply") because of the nature of an *Anton Piller* order. He dismissed as "spurious science" the contention that:

> "the Defendant was not entitled to go before the Court under the order of Quirke J. until the return day, and the Defendant had to apply *ex parte* to seek the relief it wished to have."[332]

10. Applications Post-Judgment

8–176 An application for an *Anton Piller* order can also be made post-judgment.[333]

11. Related Statutory Orders

8–177 There are a number of statutory provisions which provide for search and seizure. Self-contained and identified purely for the sake of completeness, these provisions are looked at in further detail in Ch.11, Specific Statutory Injunctions[334]:

* Copyright and Related Rights Act 2000, s.132;
* Copyright and Related Rights Act 2000, s.143(1); and
* Industrial Designs Act 2001, s.62(1).

12. Rolling *Anton Piller* Orders

8–178 Sometimes referred to as "Metallica" Orders[335] or John and Jane Doe Orders,[336] rolling *Anton Piller* Orders are something of an evolving jurisdiction in the common law world; they are primarily of use against street vendors and other transient vendors, and are obtained against unnamed defendants. They generally last up to a renewable one-year period.

---

[331] [2001] 1 I.L.R.M. 540.

[332] [2001] 1 I.L.R.M. 540 at 551.

[333] *Distributori Automatici SpA v Holford General Trading Co Ltd* [1985] 1 W.L.R. 1066; [1985] 3 All E.R. 750.

[334] See para.11–66.

[335] Due to their acceptance in New Zealand in the case of *Tony Blain Pty Ltd v Splain* [1994] F.S.R. 497, in which an order was secured against named and unnamed defendants to restrain the sale of pirated copyright material outside various concert venues when the band Metallica were performing. Also accepted in Australia in the case of *Tony Blain Pty Ltd v Jamison* (1996) 26 I.P.R. 8.

[336] See generally, Berryman, "Recent Developments in the Law of Equitable Remedies: What Canada Can Do For You" [2002] V.U.W. L. Rev 3.

8–179 Due to the fact that such orders are obtained against unnamed defendants, they would probably not be accepted by the courts in this jurisdiction at present. As has been considered in Ch.3, Standing,[337] under the existing Irish Rules of the Superior Courts it would appear that, in principle, the courts will approach the question of unknown respondents based on the same principles as considered in the old English cases of *Friern Barnet* and *Re Wykeham Terrace*,[338] and refuse an injunction sought against an unnamed defendant. Although this renders a consideration of Rolling *Anton Piller* orders somewhat academic in so far as this jurisdiction is concerned,[339] they are nonetheless of some general interest as they highlight the flexibility and usefulness of the injunction as a remedy.

(a) Definition

8–180 Rolling *Anton Piller* orders were described in the Canadian case of *Fila Canada Inc. v Doe*[340] by Reed J. in the following terms:

> "The order which is sought is what is known as a 'rolling' *Anton Piller* order. As is obvious from the style of cause, when these orders are obtained from the Court neither the identity nor the address of the persons against whom they will be executed are known. On some occasions, one or two persons may be identified as named defendants but they will have no necessary connection to the Jane and John Does against whom the order will be executed. The known defendants are allegedly infringing intellectual property rights belonging to the plaintiff but in different places, at different times and in different circumstances. These 'rolling' orders can be distinguished from defendant-specific *Anton Piller* orders. While defendant-specific *Anton Piller* orders may also include Jane and John Doe defendants, in general, the latter will be connected to the named defendants, for example, by being an employee of the defendant or a supplier of the alleged counterfeit goods of the defendant."[341]

8–181 As can be seen from this definition, there are a number of features to such orders:

---

[337] See para.3–61.
[338] See RSC Ord.9. r.1 and R.C.C. Ord.11 r.6, which provide that service of any summons must be effected by personal service where reasonably practical, unless otherwise specified by the Rules.
[339] Although it is noted in Clark, *Irish Copyright and Design Law* (Dublin: Tottel, 2006), p.F/31 that such an order was obtained "in proceedings brought by a prominent Irish artist to restrain the distribution of unauthorised merchandise outside a concert venue". There is no further detail in relation to this case, and it is unclear how the question the granting of an order against an unnamed defendant was addressed.
[340] [1996] 3 F.C. 493.
[341] As set out in Berryman, "Recent Developments in the Law of Equitable Remedies: What Canada Can Do For You" [2002] V.U.W. L. Rev 3.

- They are sought against persons unknown.
- There may be named defendants, but there is no requirement for there to be a connection between these named defendants and the persons unknown against whom the order is sought.
- There is an infringement of the plaintiff's property rights, but the time, place and circumstances of such infringements are different.

8–182 Such orders have been accepted in England. In the case of *EMI Records Ltd v Kudhail*,[342] in England the plaintiff successfully obtained an interlocutory injunction against the named defendant and "all other persons engaged in the trade of selling tapes bearing the trade-name 'Oak Records'", on the basis that the named defendant was a representative of the class of copyright and trade mark infringers. Although the basis for this decision was a representative defendant action,[343] it appears to have the same effect as a rolling *Anton Piller* order.

(b) Protections

8–183 The protections developed by the courts in Canada in relation to such orders, as summarised by Berryman,[344] are:

- The court should be given adequate time to review the motion and supporting documentation.[345]
- The plaintiff should provide evidence of numerous and widespread infringements. The supporting affidavit evidence should show the geographical extent of the infringement so that the order can be drawn to cover a particular area or the entire country.[346]
- A rolling order should not authorise execution against an unnamed party occupying residential premises.[347]
- Before granting a rolling order it is desirable that the plaintiff provides specific instances of infringement against a named defendant. In this way it is hoped that the validity of the plaintiff's substantive legal claim to hold intellectual property rights will be tested.[348]

---

[342] [1985] F.S.R. 36.
[343] See Ch.3, Standing, para.3–48.
[344] Berryman, "Recent Developments in the Law of Equitable Remedies: What Canada Can Do For You" (2002) V.U.W. L. Rev 3.
[345] *Fila Canada Inc. v Doe* [1996] 3 F.C. 493.
[346] *Fila Canada Inc. v Doe* [1996] 3 F.C. 493.
[347] *Nike Canada Ltd v Jane Doe* (1999) 2 C.P.R. (4th) 501.
[348] *Columbia Pictures Industry Ltd v John and Jane Doe* (October 2, 2000) T-1270-00 (FCTD).

F. *Bayer* Order/Writ *Ne Exeat Regno*

1. Introduction

8–184 A *Bayer* Order, a "novel" order[349] in 1986, was named after the case in which it was developed, *Bayer AG v Winter*.[350] The order restrains a party from leaving the jurisdiction. The jurisdiction to make such orders derives from the requirement to make court orders effective. It is not a freestanding order, but rather an ancillary order.[351] It usually also requires, as a reasonable and ancillary order, that the party enjoined delivers up their passport.

8–185 Given the right to travel enshrined in the Constitution,[352] a *Bayer* Order is prima facie a breach of such right. It should only be sought and granted, as held by Kearns J. in *O'Neill v O'Keeffe*,[353] in "exceptional and compelling circumstances".[354] For the same reason, the duration of a *Bayer* order is usually very short.

2. Development

8–186 In the *Bayer* case, the defendants were alleged to be distributing counterfeit insecticide on a worldwide basis, purporting to be a product of the plaintiffs. The plaintiffs sought and obtained a *Mareva* injunction and an *Anton Piller* order, but feared the first defendant would evade the effect of such orders by leaving the jurisdiction. They thus sought the relief of the court. The Court of Appeal held it had jurisdiction to make such an order, by virtue of s.37(1) of the Supreme Court Act 1981.[355] The court also had regard to the decision in *Smith v Peters*,[356] in which Jessel M.R. said that there was no limit to the practice of the court with regard to interlocutory applications:

> "so far as they are necessary and reasonable applications, ancillary to the due performance of its functions, namely, the administration of justice at the hearing of the case. I know of no other limit. Whether they are or are not to be granted must of course depend on the special circumstances of the case."[357]

---

[349] per Fox L.J. in *Bayer AG v Winter* [1986] 1 W.L.R. 497 at 502; [1986] 1 All E.R. 733 at 735.
[350] [1986] 1 W.L.R. 497; [1986] 1 All E.R. 733.
[351] per Wilson J. in *B v B* [1998] 1 W.L.R. 329.
[352] See Art.40.4. See Hogan & Whyte, *J.M. Kelly: The Irish Constitution*, 4th edn (Dublin: Butterworths, 2003), p.1466 for a consideration of the right to travel.
[353] [2002] 2 I.R. 1 at 7; [2003] 2 I.L.R.M. 40 at 45.
[354] Approving *Lennon v Ganley* [1981] I.L.R.M. 84, which dealt with, inter alia, the right to travel.
[355] Which provides that, "the High Court may by order (whether interlocutory or final) grant an injunction or appoint a receiver in all cases in which it appears to the court to be just and convenient to do so."
[356] (1875) L.R. 20 Eq. 511.
[357] (1875) L.R. 20 Eq. 511 at 512.

8–187 The flexibility provided by interlocutory injunctions is again evident from this dictum, as indeed was the recognition of the *Bayer* order itself. Explaining in *Bayer* that the court had a wide discretion to do what appears to be "just and reasonable" in the circumstances of the case, Fox L.J. stated in relation to that discretion that it should be exercised:

> "according to established principles, and the particular matter with which we are concerned at the moment, namely of an injunctional restraint on a person leaving the jurisdiction, is not one on which there appears to be previous authority. It is clear however that the law in relation to the grant of injunctive relief for the protection of a litigant's rights pending the hearing of an action has been transformed over the past ten years by the *Anton Piller* and *Mareva* relief which has greatly extended the law on this topic as previously understood so as to meet the needs of justice.
>
> Bearing in mind we are exercising a jurisdiction which is statutory, and which is expressed in terms of considerable width, it seems to me that the court should not shrink, if it is of opinion that an injunction is necessary for the proper protection of a party to the action, from granting relief, notwith-standing it may, in its terms, be of novel character."[358]

8–188 In granting the relief sought, Fox L.J. also noted that the order should be of very limited duration and should be no longer "than is necessary to enable the plaintiffs to serve the *Mareva* and *Anton Piller* orders which they have obtained and endeavour to obtain from the defendant the information which is referred to in those orders."

3. Acceptance in Ireland

8–189 As observed by Kearns J. in *O'Neill v O'Keeffe*,[359] the jurisdiction to make a *Bayer* order "derives from the requirement to make court orders effective and is analogous to disclosure orders in aid of *Mareva* relief".[360] Kearns J. noted that the Irish statutory provision which corresponded with s.37(1) of the 1981 Act was s.28(8) of the Supreme Court of Judicature Act (Ireland) 1877 which, as has been seen,[361] provides that:

> "A *mandamus* or an injunction may be granted or a receiver appointed by an interlocutory order of the court in all cases in which it shall appear to the court

---

[358] *Bayer AG v Winter* [1986] 1 W.L.R. 497 at 502; [1986] 1 All E.R. 733 at 736. As cited by Kearns J. in the later Irish case of *O'Neill v O'Keeffe* [2002] 2 I.R. 1; [2003] 2 I.L.R.M. 40. In coming to its decision, the court placed considerable reliance on the decision in *House of Spring Gardens Ltd v Waite* [1985] F.S.R. 173 at 183.

[359] [2002] 2 I.R. 1; [2003] 2 I.L.R.M. 40.

[360] [2002] 2 I.R. 1 at 6; [2003] 2 I.L.R.M. 40 at 45.

[361] See Ch.1, Domestic Jurisdiction, para.1–30.

to be just or convenient that such order shall be made, and any such order may be made either unconditionally or upon such terms and conditions as the court shall think just …"

8–190 The plaintiffs in *O'Neill v O'Keeffe* had invested a significant amount of money with the defendants. The plaintiffs became increasingly concerned at the lack of information they were receiving, nor could they get their money returned by the first named defendant. The first plaintiff became apprehensive that his investment monies either had been, or were in the process of being, dissipated or misappropriated. As far as the first plaintiff was concerned, if the defendant was not restrained from leaving the jurisdiction the first-named plaintiff would be unable to get the information he required which was necessary to his case and any order for cross-examination would be frustrated.

8–191 Having reviewed the relevant case law, in making the *Bayer* Order sought, Kearns J. expressed himself happy to adopt the criteria for granting such relief as enumerated in the text *Mareva Injunctions*,[362] wherein the author stated that such an order should only be granted where:

- The court is satisfied that there is a probable cause for believing that the defendant is about to absent himself from the jurisdiction with the intention of frustrating the administration of justice and/or an order of the court.
- The jurisdiction should not be exercised for punitive reasons; a defendant's presence should be required to prevent a court hearing or process or existing order from being rendered nugatory.
- The injunction ought not to be granted where a lesser remedy would suffice.
- The injunction should be interim in nature and limited to the shortest possible period of time.
- The defendant's right to travel should be out-balanced by those of the plaintiff and the proper and effective administration of justice.
- The grant of the injunction should not be futile.

4. Writ *Ne Exeat Regno*[363]

8–192 There are various views as to whether a *Bayer* order is a form of the old writ "*ne exeat regno*",[364] an extension of same or a different remedy altogether.

---

[362] Courtney, *Mareva Injunctions* (Dublin: Butterworths, 1998), p.457.

[363] See generally, Gee, *Commercial Injunctions*, 5th edn (London: Thomson Sweet & Maxwell, 2004), p.649 and Layton and Mercer, *European Civil Practice Volume 1*, 2nd edn (London: Thomson Sweet and Maxwell, 2004), p.154. See also s.7 of the Debtors Act (Ireland) 1872, available to a "legal" creditor, whereas the writ of *ne exeat regno* is available to an "equitable" creditor. See in this regard the analysis by Courtney, "Civil Arrest and Injunction to Restrain An Absconding Defendant From Leaving the Jurisdiction Part 1" (1990) I.L.T. 200.

[364] Which broadly translates as "not to leave the country".

The writ *ne exeat regno* prevents a party leaving the jurisdiction with their assets. In *Felton v Callis*,[365] Megarry J. examined the nature of the writ, and recognised that such a writ still existed, but took the view that the Court of Chancery issued a writ where a debt was equitable, but by analogy to the requirements of s.6 of the Debtors Act 1869.[366]

8–193 However, the writ focused on the fact that a defendant's absence from the jurisdiction would hinder the plaintiff in the prosecution of an action. This is distinct from the defendant's absence hampering the ability to give effect to the enforcement of court orders. In *Allied Arab Bank Ltd v Hajjar*,[367] Leggatt J. rejected the argument that the writ *ne exeat regno* could be used as an aid to enforcing a *Mareva* injunction.

G. APPLYING FOR A *BAYER* ORDER

1. Introduction

8–194 As with both *Mareva* injunctions and *Anton Piller* orders, most applications for *Bayer* Orders are made on an ex parte basis, and reference is made to the key principles in relation to such ex parte applications as considered in the context of *Mareva* injunctions and in relation to ex parte applications generally.[368]

8–195 The plaintiff's solicitors will also usually have to give an undertaking to keep in their custody any passport or travel documents delivered up.

8–196 Provision is made in RSC Ord.40 r.21 for copies of the affidavits grounding an application for a *Bayer* order to be furnished to any party affected, in the following terms:

> "Where an injunction or order not to leave the jurisdiction has been granted or made, the party applying for such injunction or order shall furnish copies of the affidavits grounding the same to any party affected thereby upon demand and payment therefor at the rate specified in Order 117."

---

[365] [1969] 1 Q.B. 200; [1968] 3 W.L.R. 951.
[366] Citing *Colverson v Bloomfield* (1885) 29 Ch D 341, per Stirling J. Section 6 provides that: "Where the plaintiff in any action ... in which ... the defendant would have been liable to arrest, proves at any time before final judgment by evidence on oath, to the satisfaction of a judge ... that the plaintiff has good cause of action against the defendant to the amount of £50 or upwards, and that there is probable cause for believing that the defendant is about to quit England unless he be apprehended, and that the absence of the defendant from England will materially prejudice the plaintiff in the prosecution of his action, such judge may ... order such defendant to be arrested ..."
[367] [1988] Q.B. 787; [1988] 2 W.L.R. 942; [1987] 3 All E.R. 39.
[368] See para.8–55 and Ch.7, Interim Applications.

2. Form of the Order

8–197 Given that a *Bayer* order represents a breach of the constitutional right to travel, it should be granted for as limited a period as possible. In practical terms, this will generally be the period within which it takes for a *Mareva* injunction and *Anton Piller* order to be served. However, as with the application for a non-commercial injunction, an undertaking may be provided in lieu of a *Bayer* order being sought not to leave the jurisdiction, with the same penalties attaching for the breach of such an undertaking as they would for the breach of an injunction order.[369]

3. Variation and Discharge

8–198 In the *Bayer* case, Fox L.J. stated that if the making of *Bayer* Order caused embarrassment or hardship to a party, he could apply to the courts forthwith, on evidence, to ask that it be varied or discharged.[370]

4. Related Statutory Orders

8–199 There are also statutory mechanisms available to prevent a party leaving the jurisdiction, albeit that these can generally only be invoked in relatively limited circumstances. In that regard, two pieces of legislation are of relevance:

- Companies Act 1963, ss.245(8) and s.247; and
- Bankruptcy Act 1988, ss.9[371] and 23.[372]

---

[369] See Ch.12, Breach of an Injunction Order.
[370] [1986] 1 W.L.R. 497 at 502; [1986] 1 All E.R. 733 at 737.
[371] *See Re W Cochrane* (1875) 9 I.L.T.R. 192.
[372] See generally, Sanfey and Holohan, *Bankruptcy Law and Practice in Ireland* (Dublin: Round Hall, 1991).

CHAPTER 9

EMPLOYMENT

A. INTRODUCTION

9–01 The employment relationship has historically been, and continues to be, treated in a very different way from other contractual relationships. There are three key features of the employment relationship which differentiate it from other contractual relationships, particularly in the context of injunctions: the first is the traditional view taken by the courts that the employment relationship is one based on trust and confidence.[1] Secondly, in relation to termination, the notion of unacceptable repudiation has underpinned the approach of the courts. Thirdly, ongoing supervision is often required to ensure that an injunction order is being complied with.

9–02 In recent years the term "employment injunction"[2] has taken on a meaning (and life) of its own, with a considerable number of applications being made to the courts to prevent the purported termination of an employment relationship. However, it is not just purported termination which has been considered by the courts; they have also had to consider requests for injunctions in the context of the advertisement of existing positions, disciplinary procedures, investigations, sick pay and to restrain the suspension of employees. These will all be considered in turn. However, it is necessary to firstly consider the features of the employment relationship which mean that it needs to be treated somewhat separately from other injunction applications.[3] The practical and procedural aspects of applying for an injunction are covered in Chs 5, 6 and 7, dealing with Perpetual Injunctions, Interlocutory and Interim Applications respectively.

B. THE EMPLOYMENT RELATIONSHIP

9–03 As set out above, there are three features of the employment relationship which ensure that it is treated differently in law from other contractual relationships. These will be considered in turn.

---

[1] See generally, Delany, "Employment Injunctions: the Role of Mutual Trust and Confidence" (2006) 28 D.U.L.J. 363.

[2] Also referred to as the "anti-dismissal injunction".

[3] See generally, Redmond, *Dismissal Law in Ireland* (Dublin: Tottel, 2007), p.173.

1. Trust and Confidence

9–04 The courts have traditionally shown an unwillingness to force people to work together in circumstances where those people do not want to. As Geoffrey Lane L.J. stated in the case of *Chappell v Times Newspapers Ltd*[4]:

"If one party has no faith in the honesty or the loyalty of the other, to force him to serve or to employ that other is a plain recipe for disaster."[5]

9–05 Similarly, in the earlier case of *Page One Records Ltd v Britton*,[6] the manager of a pop group was refused an injunction enjoining the group in question from changing to a new manager in breach of contract. In refusing the injunction, Stamp J. held that to grant the injunction would force the group to have to employ a manager in whom they did not have trust and confidence.

9–06 The decision of Laffoy J. in the case of *Berber v Dunnes Stores*,[7] a case which concerned a claim for, inter alia, breach of contract, highlights the role trust and confidence have to play in the employment relationship. Laffoy J. had to consider how an implied term of mutual trust and confidence is breached. She accepted the correct approach as being that set out in the English case of *Mahmud v Bank of Credit and Commerce International SA*.[8] In that case, Lord Steyn made reference to an article in which it was stated that:

"In assessing whether there has been a breach, it seems clear that what is significant is the impact of the employer's behaviour on the employee rather than what the employer intended. Moreover, the impact will be assessed objectively."[9]

9–07 Lord Steyn accepted this as reflecting "classic contract law principles" and adopted the statement.[10] In *Berber*, Laffoy J. also referred to Lord Steyn's dictum that:

"The implied obligation extends to any conduct by the employer likely to destroy or seriously damage the relationship of trust and confidence between the employer and the employee."

---

[4] [1975] I W.L.R. 482; [1975] 2 All E.R. 233.
[5] [1975] I W.L.R. 482 at 506; [1975] 2 All E.R. 233 at 244.
[6] [1968] 1 W.L.R. 157; [1967] 3 All E.R. 822. See also, *Warren v Mendy* [1989] 1 W.L.R. 853; [1989] 3 All E.R. 103.
[7] unreported, High Court, Laffoy J., October 24, 2006. Analysed in Callanan, "Mutual Trust and Confidence in the Workplace—A Concept or an Obligation?" (2007) 4 E.L.R. 9.
[8] [1998] A.C. 20; [1997] 3 W.L.R. 95; [1997] 3 All E.R. 1.
[9] Brodie, "Recent cases, Commentary, The Heart of the Matter: Mutual Trust and Confidence" (1996) 25 I.L.J. 121 at 121.
[10] [1998] A.C. 20 at 47; [1997] 3 W.L.R. 95 at 110; [1997] 3 All E.R. 1 at 16.

9–08 She held this to be the correct approach.

9–09 The role the relationship of trust and confidence has to play in the context of injunctions is considered in more detail below.[11] Based as it is on trust and confidence, courts have generally been slow to intervene to prolong an employment relationship which has broken down.

2. Unacceptable Repudiation

9–10 Another important feature of the employment relationship in the context of injunctions is the concept of unacceptable repudiation. This is best explained by looking at one of the leading cases in relation to unacceptable repudiation, the English case of *Dietman v Brent London Borough Council.*[12] *Dietman* involved a situation where an employee of the defendant council sued the council for having summarily dismissed her for, inter alia, gross misconduct. She claimed damages for wrongful dismissal, a declaration that the dismissal was invalid, and an injunction restraining the council from acting upon the decision to dismiss her. She also alleged that even if she had been grossly negligent, her conduct did not amount to gross misconduct within the terms of her contract of employment.

9–11 In the course of his judgment, Hodgson J. had to consider whether a wrongful dismissal terminates a contract of employment or whether the contract remains in force until that repudiatory breach is accepted by the employee. He first noted that in the case of *Robert Cort & Son Ltd v Charman*,[13] Browne-Wilkinson J. had said that:

> "There have been two views as to how repudiation affects a contract of employment and there is a long-standing difference of judicial opinion on the point. The first view (which we will call 'the unilateral view') is that contracts of service provide an exception to the general law and that a repudiation of a contract of employment puts an end to the contract at once without any acceptance of the repudiation by the other party. The other view ('the acceptance view') is that the general law applies and acceptance of repudiation is necessary to put an end to a contract of employment. In our judgment, it is still not established which of these two views is the correct one."[14]

9–12 Reviewing the relevant authorities in *Dietman* to highlight the difference of opinion, Hodgson J. held that he preferred those cases which had rejected the "unilateral view". He concluded that in a proper case the court can, where there

---

[11] See para.9–18.
[12] [1987] I.C.R. 737.
[13] [1981] I.C.R. 816.
[14] [1981] I.C.R. 816 at 819.

has been a wrongful dismissal, "prevent, by injunction, the implementation of that dismissal until, for instance, the proper procedures laid down in the contract have been followed."[15]

9–13 The concept of unacceptable repudiation is an important one to consider in the context of any purported termination in this jurisdiction as well. It was addressed by Costello J. in the case of *Industrial Yarns v Greene*.[16] In that case, Costello J. endorsed the approach of the English courts in the case of *Gunton v Richmond-upon-Thames London Borough Council*,[17] a case subsequently referred to with approval in *Dietman*. In *Industrial Yarns*, Costello J. held that:

> "At common law that repudiation would not automatically bring the contract of employment to an end; the employee is free to accept that the repudiation has terminated the contract or not to do so."[18]

3. Ongoing Supervision

9–14 The need for ongoing supervision of an employment relationship when an injunction is granted is an important factor which is relevant in the context of employment contracts.[19] This is a derivative of the general equitable rule that it is deemed inappropriate to grant orders for specific performance if they cannot be effectively supervised or if they require constant supervision, a rule which is not confined to employment cases.[20] An example of the consideration of this rule can be seen in the case of *Lift Manufacturers Ltd v Irish Life Assurance Co Ltd*,[21] in which the plaintiff applied for an interlocutory injunction to restrain the defendants from nominating another sub-contractor to do work. Although McWilliam J. granted the injunction sought, he noted that the basis for the rule that specific performance of a contract for services cannot be decreed was that the court cannot oversee the performance of the services.

---

[15] [1987] I.C.R. 737 at 755. Applying the dicta of Sir Robert Megarry V.C. in *Thomas Marshall (Exports) Ltd v Guinle* [1978] I.C.R. 905 at 917 and 921; Buckley L.J. in *Gunton v Richmond-upon-Thames London Borough Council* [1980] I.C.R. 755 at 771 and Templeman L.J. in *London Transport Executive v Clarke* [1981] I.C.R. 355 at 368. See also *Rigby v Ferodo* [1988] I.C.R. 29.

[16] [1984] I.L.R.M. 15.

[17] [1981] Ch. 448; [1980] 3 W.L.R. 714; [1980] 3 All E.R. 577.

[18] [1984] I.L.R.M. 15 at 21.

[19] See, for example, *Powell Duffryn v Steam Coal Co v Taff Vale Ry Co* (1874) L.R. 9 Ch. 331 in relation to difficulties arising concerning enforcement and supervision. However, it is not exclusive to employment contracts, as is evident from cases such as *Co-operative Insurance Society Ltd v Argyll Stores (Holdings) Ltd* [1998] A.C.1; [1997] 2 W.L.R. 898; [1997] 3 All E.R. 297, a case which concerned the attempted enforcement of a covenant to carry on a business.

[20] See generally, Ch.4, Equitable and General Principles, para.4–56.

[21] [1979] I.L.R.M. 277.

However, he also stated that where there did not appear to be any reason for the court to oversee such performance, the rule was not applicable.[22]

9–15 Bearing in mind the influence of these three key features, what is termed the "employment injunction" will now be considered.

C. THE EMPLOYMENT INJUNCTION

1. Introduction

9–16 The need to seek an "employment injunction" in the strict sense arises when a party is purportedly dismissed from their employment.[23] For this reason it is often referred to as an "anti-dismissal" injunction. This section will look at the tests to be applied when an injunction is sought on an interim/interlocutory basis, as this is usually the point at which such an injunction will be considered given the obvious urgency of the situation. As with interlocutory injunctions generally, case law evidences a distinction between the tests applicable to prohibitory interlocutory injunctions and mandatory interlocutory injunctions. At the outset, however, it should be cautioned "that the questions surrounding the anti-dismissal injunction are complex and not amenable to simple formula."[24]

9–17 Before considering these tests, it is proposed to consider in greater detail the question of trust and confidence and how it impacts upon employment injunctions. In the courts in this jurisdiction, this point has effectively segued into a consideration of whether, at a minimum, a party's salary should be paid pending the resolution of any dispute with their employer.

2. Trust and Confidence

9–18 As has been seen above,[25] the courts have traditionally been unwilling to force people to work together in circumstances where those people do not want to. The 1972 decision by the Court of Appeal in the case of *Hill v CA Parsons & Co Ltd*[26] marked the starting point for a somewhat different approach. In that case the plaintiff was granted an injunction by the Court of Appeal in

---

[22] [1979] I.L.R.M. 277 at 280.

[23] For an excellent overview of the conceptual basis of the anti-dismissal injunction, see Horan, "Employment Injunction: Current Status and Future Developments" (2005) 1 E.L.R. 8. For an overview of recent cases and developments, see O'Sullivan, "The Employment Injunction revisited" (2007) 12(4) Bar Rev. 157.

[24] per Horan, "Employment Injunction: Current Status and Future Developments" (2005) 1 E.L.R. 8 at 13.

[25] See para.9–04.

[26] [1972] Ch. 305; [1971] 3 W.L.R. 995; [1971] 3 All E.R. 1345.

circumstances where he refused to join a trade union and was, in consequence, given one month's notice of termination of employment. His interlocutory application for an injunction restraining the defendants from implementing their notice of termination failed. However, his appeal was allowed; in considering the application, the Court of Appeal had regard, inter alia, to the "exceptional circumstances" of the parties' relationship, whereby the employer did not in fact want to terminate the employment relationship, but was put under pressure by the union concerned.

9–19 Although the decision in *Hill* was initially considered to be a case which should be confined to its own facts,[27] in the key case of *Irani v Southampton and South-West Hampshire Health Authority*,[28] the court granted the injunction sought. In doing so, it rejected the submission that there was a clear rule that the courts would not grant specific performance of a contract of employment and that there were no special circumstances which would justify a departure from the rule. Warner J. specifically referred to the decision in *Hill* to justify his views. Similarly, in the case in *Powell v London Borough of Brent*[29] Ralph Gibson L.J. stated that:

> "Having regard to the decision in *Hill v Parsons* and to the long standing general rule of practice to which *Hill v Parsons* was an exception, the court will not by injunction require an employer to let a servant continue in his employment, when the employer has sought to terminate that employment and to prevent the servant carrying out his work under the contract, unless it is clear on the evidence not only is it otherwise just to make such a requirement but also that there exists sufficient confidence on the part of the employers in the servant's ability and other necessary attributes for it to be reasonable to make an order."[30]

9–20 The degree of confidence required was also considered by Ralph Gibson L.J. in the same case. He held that it was to be judged:

> "by reference to the circumstances of the case, including the nature of the work, the people with whom the work must be done and the likely effect upon the employer and the employer's operation if the employer is required by injunction to suffer the Plaintiff to continue in the work."[31]

---

[27] See, for example, the comments of Sir John Donaldson P. in *Sanders v Ernest A Neal Ltd* [1974] 3 All E.R. 327 at 333 in which he referred to character of the decision in *Hill* as being "unusual, if not unique". In *Lauritzencool AB v Lady Navigation Inc.* [2005] 1 W.L.R. 3686 at 3694; [2006] 1 All E.R. 866 at 873, Mance L.J. referred to *Hill* and *Irani* as "exceptional cases".

[28] [1985] I.C.R. 590.

[29] [1988] I.C.R. 176.

[30] [1988] I.C.R. 176 at 194.

[31] [1988] I.C.R. 176 at 194.

9–21 In *Robb v London Borough of Hammersmith and Fulham*,[32] Morland J. went even further and rejected the submission that unless trust and confidence remains, an injunction to preserve the contract of employment should never be granted (albeit that that case centred primarily on the applicability of fair procedures to a disciplinary process).

3. The Position in Ireland/"*Fennelly* payments"

9–22 That the courts in this jurisdiction have recognised that there are exceptions to the principle that the courts will not order specific performance of an employment contract is clear from the case of *Fennelly v Assicurazioni Generali Spa*.[33] The plaintiff in *Fennelly* had a contract with the defendant employer for a fixed period of 12 years, a somewhat unusual contract. Arising out of a serious downturn in business, the defendant sought to terminate the plaintiff's contract. Costello J. held that in view of the "very special circumstances" in the case before him, he would require the plaintiff to be paid his salary and bonus under his contract and recognised that:

> "a court should not require an employer to take on an employee where serious difficulties have arisen between them or where there is no work for the employee, but in this case the parties have obviously the highest regard for one another. I will take an undertaking that the plaintiff will be prepared to carry out such duties as the defendants will ask of him until trial. If they would make use of him until the trial of the action, the plaintiff should attend and carry out such duties as they give him. They might prefer not to give him any duties and put him on leave of absence, that is for the defendant, but they must continue to pay his salary until the trial and I require the plaintiff to give an undertaking as to damages."[34]

9–23 Approaching the matter in this way, and making provision for the payment of salary, has led to the coining of the phrase a "*Fennelly* payment".[35] In *Gee v The Irish Times*,[36] McCracken J. observed that the courts have traditionally been very loath to grant specific performance of a contract of employment, although he noted that there have been exceptions to this rule.

---

[32] [1991] I.C.R. 514.

[33] (1985) 3 I.L.T. 73.

[34] The quotation is extracted from *Gee v The Irish Times* [2001] E.L.R. 249, in which McCracken J. expressed himself satisfied that "the accuracy of the quotation I will make can be relied on." See also, *Boland v Phoenix Shannon Plc* [1997] E.L.R. 113; *Phelan v BIC (Ireland) Ltd* [1997] E.L.R. 208; *Harte v Kelly* [1997] E.L.R. 125; *Lonergan v Salter-Townshend* [2000] E.L.R. 15 and *Moore v Xnet Information System Limited* [2002] I.L.R.M. 278, all of which dealt with wrongful dismissal.

[35] See, for example, the dictum of Clarke J. in *Cahill v Dublin City University*, unreported, High Court, Clarke J., February 9, 2007.

[36] [2001] E.L.R. 249.

9–24 In much the same way as attempts were made to confine *Hill* to its own facts in England, it has been argued that the decision in *Fennelly* was an "exceptional" one.[37] In *Orr v Zomax Ltd,*[38] having considered the question of whether a common law claim for damages for wrongful dismissal and the statutory claim for unfair dismissal are mutually exclusive,[39] Carroll J. observed that in both the *Hill* and *Fennelly* cases "it was emphasised that there were either 'special' or 'exceptional' circumstances and also there was no loss of trust in the employee."[40] In the case before her, she held that:

> "the plaintiff cannot seriously hope that he will be re-instated in employment where the defendant is unwilling to take him back and has no place for him. Therefore his remedy, if he is successful, is in damages."[41]

9–25 However, other cases decided subsequent to *Fennelly* suggest that the "exceptions" have been extrapolated and expanded to contemplate situations in which it is in the "interests of justice" to make an order for what amounts to specific performance. This appears implicit in the case of *Shortt v Data Packaging,*[42] in which Keane J. restrained the defendant company from purporting to terminate the plaintiff's appointment as its managing director and stated that:

> "damages are not an adequate remedy where the Plaintiff will have to await the trial of the action in circumstances where he is totally without remuneration and where a trial will inevitably be some time away. Any loss sustained by the Defendant will be adequately met by the Plaintiff's undertaking. The balance of convenience is also in favour of the granting of an injunction pending the hearing in order to preserve the *status quo.*"[43]

9–26 The interests of justice had a more specific role to play in the case of *Phelan v BIC (Ireland) Ltd.*[44] In that case Costello P. again recognised the established principle of not granting specific performance in employment cases,

---

[37] See, for example, the comments of Macken J. in *Lonergan v Salter-Townshend* [2000] E.L.R. 15 at 27, although Macken J. acknowledged that in subsequent cases "the same relief has been granted". In *Maha Lingham v The Health Service Executive*, unreported, Supreme Court, October 4, 2005, Fennelly J. did not apply *Fennelly* as the defendant was not "making any allegation of improper conduct so it is not the case and it is not contended that the results of natural justice apply."

[38] [2004] 1 I.R. 486.

[39] And finding that they were, following the Supreme Court in *Parsons v Iarnród Éireann* [1997] E.L.R. 203, "underlined" by the House of Lords in *Johnson v Unisys Ltd* [2003] 1 A.C. 518; [2001] 2 W.L.R. 1076; [2001] 2 All E.R. 801.

[40] [2004] 1 I.R. 486 at 495.

[41] [2004] 1 I.R. 486 at 494.

[42] [1994] E.L.R. 251.

[43] [1994] E.L.R. 251 at 256.

[44] [1997] E.L.R. 208.

but granted interlocutory relief notwithstanding that the plaintiff would not be destitute. Having explained that a contract of employment is a contract of personal service and that this underpins the general principle that the courts do not grant injunctions in employment termination situations, the President stated:

> "But there has been a strong body of judgments and authorities that this old rule should be subject to qualifications and in a number of cases the courts have granted interlocutory relief where it was in the interest of justice to do so."[45]

9–27 In *Harte v Kelly*,[46] Laffoy J. noted that the affidavits filed disclosed a total breakdown of trust and confidence between the two shareholders of the company, the plaintiff and the first named defendant. Notwithstanding this, Laffoy J. granted the order sought, and indeed referred to the fact that:

> "the entitlement to the type of order granted in the *Fennelly* case is not limited to a situation in which the Plaintiff can establish that he will face penury if such an order is not made."[47]

9–28 There has been a criticism of these decisions on the basis that:

> "The failure on the part of the courts to analyse in a detailed way some of these points [viz. destitution, trust and confidence and the adequacy of damages] resulted, it is respectfully suggested, in the granting of injunctions in a number of cases where that should not have happened. Applications for injunctions became very regular and there is no doubt that the application for interlocutory relief at a time when it seemed that it would always be granted, became a significant strategic or tactical manoeuvre on the part of dismissed employees."[48]

9–29 Whatever about the merits or otherwise of cases in which injunctions were granted, it is certainly fair to say that interim and interlocutory injunction applications did become very regular, and were often motivated by tactical considerations as much as anything else. However, the courts have been alive to this and, as will be seen,[49] a more stringent line has been adopted in more recent cases such as *Bergin v Galway Clinic Doughiska Ltd.*[50] That said, the courts have to date resiled from unwinding more recent jurisprudence and reverting to the old common law position that an:

---

[45] [1997] E.L.R. 208 at 211.

[46] [1997] E.L.R. 125.

[47] [1997] E.L.R. 125 at 130.

[48] Mallon, "The Employment Injunction", *Employment Law Conference 2006* (Dublin: Thomson Round Hall), p.19.

[49] See para.9–61.

[50] unreported, High Court, Clarke J., November 2, 2007.

"employer was entitled to give that notice [of termination] so long as he complied with the contractual obligation of reasonable notice whether he had good reason or bad for doing it."[51]

4. Summary

9–30 In so far as it is possible to summarise concisely the development of the law in this area, one such helpful summary was provided by Clarke J. in the case of *Yap v Children's University Hospital Temple Street Ltd.*[52] The plaintiff in that case was a consultant paediatrician. Although fit for work, she had not returned to work following illness, due to the circumstances in which she would be required to work. This was what might be termed an ambitious application, in so far as the plaintiff was effectively asking the court to deal with aspects of the running of the defendant hospital.

9–31 The plaintiff applied for an interlocutory injunction requiring that the defendant hospital pay her salary and associated benefits pending the trial of her action. Clarke J. refused the injunction sought. In doing so, he noted that the courts have been reluctant to make orders which amount to (indirect) specific performance of a contract of employment. He explained that the reason for this was that:

"It is not the function of the Courts to deal with the day-to-day operation of contracts of employment, and the Courts would be required to almost act in an industrial relations role if the Courts were to make orders as to precisely how contracts of employment were to work. Therefore there are very limited circumstances in which the Court will intervene to force a continuation of a contract of the employment particularly where there is a serious controversy."[53]

9–32 The limited circumstances identified by Clarke J. in *Yap* in which a court might intervene are:

- cases in which the issue between the parties is technical rather than going to the relationship between employer and employee, e.g. redundancy;
- cases in which, as a matter of the contract of employment between an employer and employee, the employee is entitled to be paid even though not working, such as in the case of sick pay, or where there is a suspension, but pay can only be withdrawn where "very severe" accusations are being made.[54]

---

[51] Per Fennelly J. in *Maha Lingham v Health Service Executive*, unreported, Supreme Court, October 4, 2005.
[52] [2006] 4 I.R. 298.
[53] [2006] 4 I.R. 298 at 301.
[54] [2006] 4 I.R. 298 at 301.

9–33 However, in *Yap,* Clarke J. summarised the position by stating that, "the general rule is that pay follows work."[55]

5. Interlocutory Prohibitory Injunctions

9–34 The courts have, as in other applications for interim and interlocutory prohibitory injunctions, had recourse in general terms to the principles set out in *American Cyanamid/Campus Oil* when considering applications for injunctions in the context of the employment relationship.[56] In *Lonergan v Salter-Townshend,*[57] Macken J. set out what she referred to as being, in "shorthand terms", the relevant tests to be satisfied in order for a plaintiff to succeed in an application for interlocutory relief, namely that he must establish (i) that there is a serious issue to be tried[58]; (ii) that damages would not be an adequate remedy; and (iii) that the balance of convenience favours the granting of an injunction rather than its refusal. She also observed that it is only where all of these requirements are evenly balanced between the parties that the court considers the relative strengths and weaknesses of the claims made by the plaintiff and the defendant.[59]

9–35 As will be seen,[60] however, in the case of *Bergin v Galway Clinic Doughiska Ltd,*[61] Clarke J. suggested that in cases of purported termination, injunctions sought on foot of such termination will be in the nature of mandatory, rather than prohibitory, injunctions and, as such, will admit of a higher standard in terms of demonstrating a strong case, rather than a fair question to be tried.

9–36 In the case of *Garrahy v Bord na gCon,*[62] the plaintiff sought an interlocutory injunction preventing the appointment of a full-time regulation manager on the grounds that it was effectively an attempt to force the plaintiff out of his employment.[63] The defendant sought to argue that the consideration of the normal *Campus Oil* principles did not apply in the case before the court

---

[55]   [2006] 4 I.R. 298 at 302.
[56]   See *Evans v IRFB Services (Ireland) Ltd* [2005] 2 I.L.R.M. 358 at 361, per Clarke J.
[57]   [2000] E.L.R. 15.
[58]   Although Macken J. recognised that use of the word "fair" was frequently used. In his decision in *O'Donnell v Chief State Solicitor* [2003] 14 E.L.R. 268, Kelly J. effectively reversed the formula, as was enunciated by Lord Diplock in *American Cyanamid v Ethicon Ltd* [1975] A.C. 396; [1975] 2 W.L.R. 316; [1975] 1 All E.R. 504, viz. whether this was "a case in which a vexatious or frivolous claim is being made?"
[59]   [2000] E.L.R. 15 at 25. See generally, Ch.6, Interlocutory Applications.
[60]   See para.9–61.
[61]   unreported, High Court, Clarke J., November 2, 2007.
[62]   [2002] 3 I.R. 566.
[63]   See also, *Evans v IRFB Services (Ireland) Ltd* [2005] 2 I.L.R.M. 358.

and that an injunction should not be granted in the context of an employment contract. In doing so he referred to the decision in *Reynolds v Malocco*,[64] a case which had concerned an alleged libel. In that case, Kelly J. had held that the *American Cyanamid/Campus Oil* principles had "a wide but not universal application". Kelly J. had also stated that:

> "One such type of case arises in the field of contracts of employment. Normally courts will not grant an injunction to restrain breaches of covenant in a contract of employment if that would amount to indirect specific performance of such contract or would perpetuate a relationship based on mutual trust which no longer exists."[65]

9–37 However, O'Higgins J. rejected the contention that he should not apply the *Campus Oil* principles, holding that the concept of no injunction being granted in defamation cases, dependent as it is on the right of free speech, could not be legitimately transferred to the case before him. He also observed that the dictum of Kelly J. related to cases concerning wrongful dismissal for the most part—which cases could potentially involve ongoing supervision—and might not apply when dealing with an appointment; the *Garrahy* case concerned an application for an injunction to prevent the appointment of a full-time regulation manager.

9–38 The elements of the *Campus Oil* guidelines, as applied in the case of prohibitory interlocutory employment injunctions, will now be considered.

(a) The Campus Oil Guidelines

(i) Serious Issue to Be Tried

9–39 In considering whether there is a serious issue to be tried, factors which a court may have to confront include whether a purported termination is in breach of contract; whether it is in breach of fair procedures; whether a dismissal is ultra vires; whether there has been a breach of a specific statutory provision; or whether there has been a breach of constitutional rights.[66] These

---

[64] [1999] 2 I.R. 203.

[65] [1999] 2 I.R. 203 at 209. It was reported in the *Irish Times* of February 2, 2008 that the chief executive and chief financial officer of Payzone were granted injunctions restraining the company from dismissing them from their posts pending the outcome of full legal proceedings. This was on the basis that Clark J. held the executives' case was among those "rare cases" where the breach of contract was so clear and the defence to the case so "devoid of merit" that the court should grant the injunctions. She also said the two executives were deprived of constitutional justice and fair procedures.

[66] See generally, the judgment of Hardiman J. in the case of *Maguire v Ardagh* [2002] 1 I.R. 385 at 657, in particular his consideration of the powers of a committee, the findings of fact which such a committee may make and a committee's power to cross-examine, referring (at 672) to the case of *Re Haughey* [1971] I.R. 217 at 263.

considerations will, on their face, be relatively straightforward and will turn on the facts of each individual case. However, one area which has generated a significant amount of case law in the context of there being a serious issue to be tried is the question of whether an employee is bringing a claim for wrongful dismissal or unfair dismissal, and the remedies appropriate to the nature of the claim.

Wrongful Dismissal or Unfair Dismissal

9–40 In general terms, a claim for wrongful dismissal is one which is made at common law, based on the contract for employment, and in relation to which damages will be sought. A claim for unfair dismissal will be dealt with by means of a statutory mechanism, in effect a hearing before the Employment Appeals Tribunal (EAT).

9–41 In the case of *Parsons v Iarnród Éireann*,[67] it was held that employees must choose between suing at common law, or else claiming relief under the applicable legislation, namely the Unfair Dismissals Act, which could ultimately lead to a hearing before the EAT. The Supreme Court held in *Parsons* that any equitable relief was in aid of a common law remedy only, and had no existence independent of such a remedy.

9–42 The decision in *Parsons* was followed by Murphy J. in *Philpot v Ogilvy and Mather Ltd*[68] and by Murphy J. in *Davis v Walshe*.[69] In the latter case it was held that where a claim for damages was not made, there could be no separate declaratory and injunctive relief of an interlocutory nature as sought by the plaintiff. Murphy J. confirmed that such equitable relief had no independent existence apart from a claim for damages for wrongful dismissal. He further held that the application before him was not an application pursuant to an action for wrongful dismissal.

9–43 The case of *Orr v Zomax Ltd*[70] produced a similar outcome. The plaintiff applied for an injunction restraining the purported termination of his employment by reason of redundancy. He also sought an order that the defendant continue to pay his salary pending the trial of the action. Carroll J. held that the common law claim for damages for wrongful dismissal and the statutory claim for unfair dismissal are mutually exclusive. She found that the plaintiff was seeking to introduce a new obligation under the common law on the employer to act reasonably and fairly in the case of wrongful dismissal. Referring to both the *Parsons* case and the House of Lords decision in *Johnson*

---

[67] [1991] E.L.R. 203.
[68] [2000] 3 I.R. 206.
[69] [2003] 14 E.L.R. 1.
[70] [2004] 1 I.R. 486.

v Unisys Ltd,[71] Carroll J. found that it was not open to the plaintiff to argue that the principles applicable under the statutory scheme should be imported into the common law, that there was no fair issue to be tried and that damages were an adequate remedy.

(ii) Damages as an Adequate Remedy

9–44 On one view, a party's salary is generally readily quantifiable, and so it would seem at first blush that it would be very easy to quantify any damages as necessary. As such, the assumption would be that damages will always be an adequate remedy in an employment context. However, there are two reasons accepted by the courts as to why this is not so. The first concerns a situation where a party's salary is their only source of income, with the associated consequences for day-to-day living. The second concerns the wider—and effectively intangible—implications of being dismissed, including such factors as job satisfaction, ability to find a similar job and so on.

Salary as a Sole Source of Income
9–45 In so far as a party's salary from their employer may be their only source of income, it is unlikely that damages will ever adequately compensate an employee if an injunction is not granted.

9–46 In *Murphy v ACC Bank Plc*,[72] O'Sullivan J. held that the plaintiff had made out a case that a substantial question fell to be tried at the hearing of the action, namely whether the defendant complied with its procedures. However, he further held that he did not think that damages were an adequate remedy given that the plaintiff's only source of income was his salary from the defendant, and also given his financial obligations to the members of his family.[73]

9–47 Similarly, in the case of *Harte v Kelly*,[74] Laffoy J. granted an injunction on the basis that it would be unjust to leave the plaintiff without his salary pending the trial of the action, and merely with a prospect of an award of damages. She felt that the entitlement to an order providing for the payment of salary is not limited to situations where the plaintiff can establish that he will face penury if such an order is not made.[75]

---

[71] [2003] 1 A.C. 518; [2001] 2 W.L.R. 1076; [2001] 2 All E.R. 801. The case was cited in *Garrahy v Bord na gCon* [2002] 3 I.R. 566 at 578, with O'Higgins J. stating that the decision had "nothing to say concerning the damages asserted by the plaintiff as likely to occur in default of an injunction in the present case, nor can I see that it has any application by analogy."

[72] unreported, High Court, O'Sullivan J., February 4, 2000.

[73] Following *Harte v Kelly* [1997] E.L.R. 125.

[74] [1997] E.L.R. 125, following Keane J. in *Shortt v Data Packaging* [1994] E.L.R. 251. See also, *Boland v Phoenix Shannon* [1997] E.L.R. 113.

[75] [1997] E.L.R. 125 at 130. See para.9–27.

9–48 It thus seems that in general terms it is not necessary to demonstrate that a party applying for an injunction will face penury if not granted an injunction. In *O'Donnell v Chief State Solicitor*,[76] Kelly J. found that damages would not provide an adequate remedy and stated that:

> "The plaintiff is in receipt of a comparatively modest salary with a wife and family to support. To have to await a trial months hence would on the evidence before me do an injustice to him and his family."[77]

9–49 However, that this is an area which must be approached with a degree of caution is evident from the case of *Orr v Zomax Ltd.*[78] In her judgment, Carroll J. noted that in the case of *Gee v The Irish Times*[79] McCracken J. had "referred to the 'well established practice' of continued payment of salary pending trial." Without specifying that she was referring to *Gee*, Carroll J. referred to the fact that:

> "cases where there is no suggestion of any breakdown of trust or confidence have no relevance to this case; likewise where there is alleged breach of a fixed term contract."[80]

Intangible Implications

9–50 The issue of damages has arisen not just in the context of payment of salary, but also loss of reputation when dismissed. This was touched upon by Lord Loreburn L.C. in *Addis v Gramphone*.[81] In that case, the Lord Chancellor stated that an employee cannot secure compensation for "the loss he may sustain from the fact that his having being dismissed of itself makes it more difficult for him to obtain fresh employment."[82]

9–51 However, Carroll J. held in the case of *Foley v Aer Lingus Group*[83] that damage to reputation is compensatable by an award of damages.[84] A gloss was put on this by O'Higgins J. in *Garrahy v Bord na gCon*,[85] in which he observed that while loss of reputation could be compensated by an award of damages, this did not mean that damages were an adequate remedy in all such cases.[86]

---

[76] [2003] 14 E.L.R. 268.
[77] [2003] 14 E.L.R. 268 at 272. In relation to damages, see also, *Lift Manufacturers Ltd v Irish Life Assurance Co Ltd* [1979] I.L.R.M. 277.
[78] [2004] 1 I.R. 486 at 495.
[79] unreported, High Court, McCracken J., June 27, 2000.
[80] [2004] 1 I.R. 486 at 496.
[81] [1909] A.C. 488.
[82] [1909] A.C. 488 at 491.
[83] [2001] E.L.R. 193.
[84] See also, *Marsh v National Autistic Society* [1993] I.C.R. 453.
[85] [2002] 3 I.R. 566.
[86] [2002] 3 I.R. 566 at 573.

9–52 From a practical perspective, it would seem to be arguable that factors such as job satisfaction, the ability to find equivalent work—particularly in more senior, specialised jobs—and other such factors could have a role to play in arguing that damages would not be an appropriate remedy.

(iii) Balance of Convenience

9–53 As with any other type of interlocutory application, the balance of convenience falls to be considered on the facts of each individual case. It is at this stage that the question of trust and confidence will also be considered as necessary.

9–54 The balance of convenience was a decisive factor in *Foley v Aer Lingus Group*.[87] Carroll J. held that the damage to a company—the then national airline—left without a chief executive indefinitely would far outweigh the potential damage to an employee. She thus found that the balance of convenience lay in favour of refusing the relief sought.

9–55 Another example of the way in which the balance of convenience comes into play based on the individual circumstances of a case is evident in the decision in *Courtney v Radio 2000 Ltd*.[88] In that case, Laffoy J. held that the balance of convenience lay in favour of granting an injunction preventing the defendant from dismissing the plaintiff radio presenter until the trial of the action, on the basis that the position of broadcaster, being a "high profile occupation", was in a special category. Laffoy J. took the view that the case was one in which it could be said that exceptional circumstances in fact warranted an injunction as the appropriate remedy.

9–56 The concept of a "special" occupation also informed the Court of Appeal decision in *Warren v Mendy*,[89] in which it was held that an injunction should not be granted against a third party which would effectively indirectly lead to the specific enforcement of a contract of employment. In the course of his judgment, Nourse L.J. made an important remark of more general application, namely that in the context of contracts for personal services "inseparable from the exercise of some special skill or talent":

> "the court ought not to enforce the performance of the negative obligations if their enforcement will effectively compel the servant to perform his positive obligations under the contract. Compulsion is a question to be decided on the facts of each case, with a realistic regard for the probable reaction of an

---

[87] [2001] E.L.R. 193.
[88] unreported, High Court, Laffoy J., July 22, 1997.
[89] [1989] 1 W.L.R. 853.

injunction on the psychological and material, and sometimes the physical, need for the servant to maintain the skill or talent."[90]

9–57 Whilst decided in the context of dispute about boxing, there should be no reason why a person may not have a "special skill or talent" in the context of, for example, manufacturing and industry.

(iv) Status Quo

9–58 In attempting to maintain the status quo pending the trial of an action, the courts have directed payment of the employee's salary and emoluments; prohibited the implementation of the termination of the employment; and prohibited the filling of the employee's position.[91]

6. Interlocutory Mandatory Injunctions

9–59 As is the case in any injunction application, a mandatory interlocutory injunction attracts a higher standard in relation to the issue to be tried. This is clear from the decision in the case of *Maha Lingam v Health Service Executive*,[92] in which Fennelly J. held that:

> "the implication of an application of the present sort is that in substance what the plaintiff/appellant is seeking is a mandatory interlocutory injunction and it is well established that the ordinary test of a fair case to be tried is not sufficient to meet the first leg of the test for the grant of an interlocutory injunction where the injunction sought is in effect mandatory. In such a case it is necessary for the applicant to show at least that he has a strong case that he is likely to succeed at the hearing of the action. So it is not sufficient for him to simply show a *prima facie* case, and in particular the courts have been slow to grant interlocutory injunctions to enforce contracts of employment."[93]

9–60 As such, in seeking a mandatory interlocutory injunction, an employee must demonstrate in the first instance that he has a strong case that he is likely to succeed at the substantive hearing of the action.

---

[90] [1989] 1 W.L.R. 853 at 867.
[91] See, for example, *Shortt v Data Packaging Ltd* [1994] E.L.R. 251 and *Phelan v BIC (Ireland) Ltd* [1997] E.L.R. 208.
[92] unreported, Supreme Court, October 4, 2005.
[93] Referred to in *Naujoks v National Institution of Bioprocessing Research and Training Ltd*, unreported, High Court, Laffoy J., November 14, 2006.

7. Mandatory or Prohibitory Injunction

9–61 It is important to analyse whether the injunction sought is in fact prohibitory or mandatory. For example, in *Bergin v Galway Clinic Doughiska Ltd*,[94] Clarke J. held that an employment injunction is to all intents and purposes mandatory even though it may be expressed in a negative form. In so holding, he also rejected the argument that in circumstances where it is alleged that there is a breach of fair procedures, the appropriate standard is a fair question to be tried. In Clarke J.'s view there was no difference between an alleged breach of fair procedures and an alleged failure to honour a fixed-term contract for a full period. That being so, he held that if a higher standard, namely a strong case, was required to be shown for one, it was equally applicable to the other. This is clearly a significant development, which should lead parties to consider the strength of their case carefully before embarking on applications for interim or interlocutory relief.

8. Reinstatement or Payment

9–62 It is important to note that, in injuncting a purported dismissal, there may be a distinction between reinstatement and payment, with the courts more likely to order payment of salary but not reinstatement.[95]

9. Statutory Office-Holders

9–63 The position of statutory office-holders admits of somewhat different considerations. This is evident from the decision of the Supreme Court in *Garvey v Ireland*.[96] Although the case did not concern an application for an injunction, it nonetheless sets out a number of important considerations in relation to statutory office-holders.

9–64 The plaintiff in *Garvey* was the Commissioner of the Garda Síochána. Section 6(2) of the Police Forces Amalgamation Act 1925 provides that the Commissioner of the Garda Síochána shall be appointed by the Government and that, while holding that office, the Commissioner "may at any time be removed" by the Government. The plaintiff received a letter from the Government informing him that he was being removed from office unless he resigned within

---

[94] unreported, High Court, Clarke J., November 2, 2007.
[95] See, for example, *Moore v Xnet Information System Ltd* [2002] I.L.R.M. 278; *Fennelly v Assiscurazioni Generali Spa* (1985) 3 I.L.T. 73; *Shortt v Data Packaging* [1994] E.L.R. 251; *Boland v Phoenix Shannon* [1997] E.L.R. 113; *Harte v Kelly* [1997] E.L.R. 125; *Phelan v BIC (Ireland) Ltd* [1997] E.L.R. 208 and *Sheehy v Ryan*, unreported, High Court, Peart J., August 29, 2002.
[96] [1981] I.R. 75.

a two-hour period. The plaintiff was not aware that his removal was being considered. He brought a High Court action in which he claimed, inter alia, a declaration that, in exercising the power of removal conferred by s.6(2) of the 1925 Act the Government was bound to comply with the requirements of natural justice and of constitutional justice. The Supreme Court held that the plaintiff was a holder of an office and was not employed under a contract of employment. It also held that the guarantee of fair procedures provided by Art.40.3 of the Constitution applied to the exercise by the Government of the power of removal conferred by s.6(2) of the 1925 Act. In the circumstances it held that the purported removal of the plaintiff was void, as the Government had not informed the plaintiff of the reason for his removal. It had also failed to give him an opportunity to make representations in that regard.

9–65 In the course of his judgment in *Garvey*,[97] O'Higgins C.J. made reference to the English case of *Malloch v Aberdeen Corporation*.[98] In that case Lord Wilberforce had set out an important principle in relation to statutory office-holders, in the following terms:

> "In *Ridge v Baldwin* [[1964] A.C. 40, 65] my noble and learned friend, Lord Reid, said: 'It has always been held, I think rightly, that such an officer' (sc. one holding at pleasure) has no right to be heard before being dismissed.' As a general principle, I respectfully agree: and I think it important not to weaken a principle which, for reasons of public policy, applies, at least as a starting point, to so wide a range of the public service. The difficulty arises when, as here, there are other incidents of the employment laid down by statute, or regulations, or code of employment, or agreement. The rigour of the principle is often, in modern practice, mitigated for it has come to be perceived that the very possibility of dismissal without reason being given—action which may vitally affect a man's career or his pension—makes it all the more important for him, in suitable circumstances, to be able to state his case and, if denied the right to do so, to be able to have his dismissal declared void. So, while the courts will necessarily respect the right, for good reasons of public policy, to dismiss without assigned reasons, this should not, in my opinion, prevent them from examining the framework and context of the employment to see whether elementary rights are conferred upon him expressly or by necessary implication, and how far these extend."[99]

9–66 The importance of these decisions and the particular position of statutory office-holders is evident from the decision of Clarke J. in the case of *Cahill v Dublin City University*.[100] The plaintiff in that case was an associate professor

---

[97]   [1981] I.R. 75 at 93.
[98]   [1971] 1 W.L.R. 1578; [1971] 2 All E.R. 1278.
[99]   [1971] 1 W.L.R. 1578 at 1597; [1971] 2 All E.R. 1278 at 1295.
[100] unreported, High Court, Clarke J., February 9, 2007.

in the defendant university. Further to discussions with the President of the university, in which the plaintiff indicated that he would move to a rival university, the plaintiff received a letter which purported to give him three months' notice of termination of his contract of employment. At the hearing of the action Clarke J. found that the plaintiff's purported dismissal was contrary to s.25(6) of the Universities Act 1997.[101] That section provided for certain procedures to be followed prior to dismissal. It also provided for tenure, from which the plaintiff benefited.

9–67 Clarke J. made reference to the fact that:

> "where it is established that a suspension or dismissal of an academic office holder is in breach of the provisions of the 1997 Act, the court should lean in favour of making an order which would restore the academic concerned to their duties."

9–68 Acknowledging that the situation may be different as between office-holders governed by that Act and the situation which might "ordinarily obtain" in relation to contracts of employment, Clarke J. also held that:

> "what the court is required to do is to lean in favour of such a position. There may well be, on the facts of any individual case, practical reasons why it may not be possible to make an effective order which would preserve the entitlement of the person concerned to perform their academic duties."

9–69 This again evidences a degree of caution on the part of the courts in terms of intervening to force a continuation of a contract of employment. However, in practical terms, it is usually easier for a holder of a statutory position to secure an injunction if there has been a breach of statutory procedure.

9–70 Based on the foregoing, it is always important to establish whether a party is employed pursuant to statute and, if so, to consider the applicable statutory provision which governs termination. Such provisions may provide for procedures which might otherwise not apply in the case of a person employed other than pursuant to statute.

D. Other Employment-Related Injunctions

1. Introduction

9–71 It is not only the purported termination of employment contracts which gives rise to injunction applications. A number of issues arising out of

---

[101] Considering, inter alia, the decision in *Garvey v Ireland* [1981] I.R. 75.

employment contracts and related applications for injunctions can be identified, including issues which arise post-termination. These can broadly be grouped under the following general headings:

1. advertisement of existing positions;
2. disciplinary procedures and hearings;
3. investigations;
4. sick pay; and
5. suspension.

9–72 Each of these will be considered in turn. The question of injunction applications being brought post termination of a contract of employment will be considered in the next section.[102]

2. Advertisement of Existing Positions

9–73 As has been seen in the case of *Garrahy v Bord na gCon*,[103] the plaintiff in that case, believing that the purported appointment of a full-time regulation manager was effectively an attempt to force him out of his employment, sought an injunction to prevent the appointment. The case of *Harkins v Shannon Foynes Port Company*[104] dealt with a similarly unusual situation. The plaintiff formed the opinion that a new position being advertised by the defendant company, for whom he worked, would in effect absorb or subsume his own existing position. He thus sought an order restraining the defendant from advertising the position of Harbour Engineer, however styled. In granting the injunction sought, O'Sullivan J., in considering the balance of convenience, expressed the view that it was clear that if the defendant was permitted to continue making the appointment advertised, the plaintiff's position at the trial would be devalued, possibly irretrievably, in a way that might not be compensated.[105]

9–74 In the case of *Powell v Brent London Borough Council*,[106] the plaintiff was selected for a post with the defendant, only for the post to be re-advertised when another candidate for the post challenged the plaintiff's appointment. The Court of Appeal held that there was a triable issue as to whether the defendant was intending to break the plaintiff's contract by re-advertising the post concerned, and also held that damages would not be an adequate remedy.

9–75 Related to these, in *Evans v IRFB Services (Ireland) Ltd*,[107] the plaintiff sought to restrain the appointment of a new head of its rugby department on foot

---

[102] See para.9–106.
[103] *Garrahy v Bord na gCon* [2002] 3 I.R. 566; see para.9–36.
[104] [2001] E.L.R. 75.
[105] See also, *Garrahy v Bord na gCon* [2002] 3 I.R. 566 at 572, in which O'Higgins J. remarked in relation to *Harkins* that "there are striking similarities between that case and the present one."
[106] [1988] I.C.R. 176.
[107] [2005] 2 I.L.R.M. 358.

of an internal reorganisation, on the basis that to do so might breach his existing contract of employment. In considering the question of damages being an adequate remedy, Clarke J. observed that the height of the plaintiff's entitlement:

> "subject to the question of the balance of convenience, must necessarily, be for an order in terms similar to that granted in *Garrahy* which would preclude or limit the making of an appointment to the job of head of the rugby department pending the trial of the action."[108]

9–76 Clarke J. then found, after considerable analysis, that the balance of convenience favoured the making of such an order.

3. Disciplinary Procedures and Hearings

9–77 Whilst a plaintiff may seek an injunction in order to prevent a disciplinary procedure from proceeding, or alternatively to prevent the implementation of its findings, an injunction will not automatically issue in such circumstances. A number of key considerations concern the courts, including fair procedures, the constitution of a disciplinary board, particulars of allegations made and representation. The point at which an application for an interlocutory injunction is made is also a relevant factor. Importantly, a word of caution was sounded obiter by Fennelly J. in the case of *Traynor v Ryan*,[109] in which he referred to the "regrettable tendency" in some employment cases to "treat procedural safeguards as the real battlefield in preference to facing the substance of complaints in accordance with an agreed procedure."[110] The overarching message from *Traynor* is clear: semantics and procedural issues should not be viewed as the springboard from which to launch injunction applications.

(a) Fair Procedures/Natural Justice

9–78 Fair procedures and compliance with the rules of natural justice are a key consideration in relation to the employment relationship,[111] particularly so in the context of disciplinary hearings.[112]

---

[108] [2005] 2 I.L.R.M. 358 at 364.

[109] [2003] 2 I.R. 568. Referred to in *Rajpal v Robinson*, unreported, High Court, Kearns J., May 7, 2004.

[110] [2003] 2 I.R. 568 at 578. See also, *Wright v Board of Management of Gorey Community School*, unreported, High Court, O'Sullivan J., March 28, 2000 which concerned the suspension of schoolboys, who based their claim on unfair procedures.

[111] In relation to fair procedures generally, see *Re Haughey* [1971] I.R. 217, particularly the dictum of O'Dalaigh C.J. at p.264, approved of in various cases such as *Glover v BLN Ltd* [1973] I.R. 388 and *Gallagher v Revenue Commissioners (No.2)* [1995] 1 I.R. 55. See also, *Gunn v Bord an Cholaiste Naisisiunta Ealaine is Deartha* [1990] 2 I.R. 168.

[112] See, for example, *Glover v BLN Ltd* [1973] I.R. 388. See also *Joyce v Minister for Health and Children*, unreported, High Court, O'Neill J., July 30, 2004. It was reported in the *Irish Times*,

9–79 This was a point emphasised by Clarke J. in the case of *Carroll v Bus Átha Cliath/Dublin Bus*,[113] in which the plaintiff bus driver sought to injunct a disciplinary process initiated in relation to two complaints made against him. Clarke J. referred to the fact that employees cannot be dismissed as a matter of contract save for good reason such as incapacity, stated misbehaviour, redundancy or the like. He considered that it was this development which had given rise to an emphasis on fair procedures and compliance with the requirements of natural justice. Summarising the position, Clarke J. held that:

> "If the stated reason for seeking to dismiss an employee is an allegation of misconduct then the courts have, consistently, held that there is an obligation to afford that employee fair procedures in respect of any determination leading to such dismissal. That does not alter the fact that an employer may still, if he is contractually free so to do, dismiss the employee for no reason. It simply means that where an employer is obliged to rely upon stated misconduct for a dismissal or, where not so obliged chooses to rely upon stated misconduct, the employer concerned is obliged to conduct the process leading to a determination as to whether there was such misconduct in accordance with many of the principles of natural justice."[114]

9–80 The onus is on the party seeking the injunction to demonstrate that there has been a lack of fair procedures. In *McEvoy v Bank of Ireland*,[115] Laffoy J. refused the injunctions sought, as the plaintiff had not established that there was a fair issue to be tried, namely that the disciplinary process concerned was so flawed that it would be appropriate for the court to prohibit the process continuing. Laffoy J. also noted that the plaintiff's application was premature in that she had two further appeals available to her under the disciplinary process in operation.[116]

9–81 The extent to which fair procedures have been followed, will clearly have to be considered on the facts of each individual case, a point made by Shanley J. in *Vogel v Cheeverstown House Ltd.*[117] The decision in *Vogel* is noteworthy in that Shanley J. also held that the ordinary principles for interlocutory injunctions did not apply in "exceptional cases" such as the one before him, which concerned a complaint of sexual abuse against the plaintiff by the resident of a

---

May 5, 2006 that Bridget Conway, the President's Protocol Officer, had failed in an attempt to secure an injunction halting a disciplinary inquiry against her. As reported, Feeney J. found that Ms Conway had not made out a case establishing that the disciplinary process was so flawed as not to protect her rights to fair procedures and natural justice.

[113] [2005] 4 I.R. 184. See also, *O'Donoghue v South Eastern Health Board*, unreported, High Court, Macken J., September 5, 2005.

[114] [2005] 4 I.R. 184 at 209.

[115] unreported, High Court, Laffoy J., January 26, 2006.

[116] See also para.9–91.

[117] [1998] 2 I.R. 496.

centre for persons with mental handicaps. The defendant had established a committee to investigate the claim, but that committee had decided that the complainant would not be available for examination and cross-examination at the inquiry on account of her condition. The plaintiff sought an interlocutory injunction to restrain the defendant from commencing the disciplinary hearing without affording him an opportunity to cross-examine the complainant. In the circumstances Shanley J. refused the relief sought, but granted an injunction restraining the defendant from commencing the disciplinary hearing pending the holding of a validation exercise (in essence, a review by an appropriately qualified person such as a psychologist or a psychiatrist) by a nominee of the plaintiff.

(b) Constitution of Board

9–82 Inevitably, a situation may arise where a party reasonably fears bias and injustice in terms of the constitution of a hearing committee. In *O'Neill v Beaumont Hospital Board*,[118] the Supreme Court granted an injunction preventing certain members of the board from participating in a meeting concerning the plaintiff's retention as a consultant. However, it did not restrain a meeting of the board.

9–83 When putting together such a board, an organisation must adhere to its disciplinary rules.[119] This was a point emphasised in *Carroll v Bus Átha Cliath/Dublin Bus*,[120] in which Clarke J. observed that unless a court was satisfied that all reasonable possibilities for empanelling such a board had been exhausted, it was likely that the court would make an order precluding the conduct of the disciplinary hearing until the board was properly constituted.

(c) Particulars of Allegations

9–84 In *Mooney v An Post*,[121] Barrington J., referring to the fact that what fair procedures demand will depend upon the terms of employment and the circumstances surrounding a proposed dismissal, observed that the minimum an employee is entitled to is to be informed of the charge against him and to be given an opportunity to answer it and to make submissions.[122]

9–85 The importance of this is also evident from the case of *Murphy v ACC Bank Plc*,[123] in which the plaintiff was dismissed by the defendant bank, but

---

[118] [1990] I.L.R.M. 419.
[119] This presupposes of course that the organisation has such rules in place. That they might not gives rise to separate considerations.
[120] [2005] 4 I.R. 184.
[121] [1998] E.L.R. 238.
[122] [1998] E.L.R. 238 at 248, referred to with approval by Laffoy J. in *Maher v Irish Permanent Plc* [1998] E.L.R. 77 at 87.
[123] unreported, High Court, O'Sullivan J., February 4, 2000.

claimed that in breach of the disciplinary procedure he was not informed of the complaint against him. On the plaintiff's application for an interlocutory injunction, O'Sullivan J. held that the plaintiff had made out a case that a substantial question fell to be tried at the hearing of the action, namely whether the defendant complied with its procedures.

(d) Representation and Witnesses[124]

9–86 A question which often confronts the courts is the extent to which a party at a disciplinary hearing may have legal or other representation, and whether witnesses may be called to give evidence at the hearing on his behalf.[125]

9–87 In *Maher v Irish Permanent Plc (No. 1)*,[126] the plaintiff was suspended pending an investigation into an allegation of sexual misconduct made against him. He was ultimately informed that he was to be dismissed. Laffoy J. found that the plaintiff was entitled to be furnished with statements made by staff members in advance of the relevant oral hearing dealing with the matter, but that he was also entitled to be legally represented at the hearing. She consequently made an order restraining the defendant from taking any further steps to terminate the plaintiff's employment save in accordance with the defendant's disciplinary procedures and in accordance with natural justice. As is clear from this decision, an employee may be entitled to be legally represented at the hearing. However, it is important to emphasise the word "may"; each case will have to be dealt with on its own facts in that regard.

9–88 That legal representation, or more specifically lack thereof, will not automatically lead to the entitlement to an injunction, is clear from the case of *O'Neill v Iarnród Eireann*.[127] Finlay C.J. stated that he was not satisfied, having regard to all the circumstances of the case, that there were any prima facie grounds for suggesting that the respondent had acted in breach of natural justice in failing to allow the applicant to be legally represented at the hearings. Barr J. made an even more general statement in relation to representation in *Aziz v Midland Health Board*[128] when he held that "there is no general right to legal representation at quasi-judicial disciplinary hearings such as those in the present case."[129]

---

[124] As to the sources of the right to legal representation at a disciplinary hearing, see generally, Farrell, "Opening the Door to Injunctions?—Refusing Legal Representation at Disciplinary Hearings" (2006) 3(1) I.E.L.J. 7.

[125] See *Maguire v Ardagh* [2002] 1 I.R. 385 at 672, specifically Hardiman J.'s consideration of the powers of a committee, the findings of fact which such a committee may make and a committee's power to cross-examine, referring to the case of *Re Haughey* [1971] I.R. 217 at 263.

[126] [1998] E.L.R. 77.

[127] [1991] E.L.R. 1.

[128] [1995] E.L.R. 48.

[129] [1995] E.L.R. 48 at 58.

9–89 Even where there is an entitlement to legal representation, the employer may, through his conduct, render such representation ineffective, leading to a claim for an injunction. This was the case in *Cassidy v Shannon Castle Banquets and Heritage Ltd,*[130] in which Budd J. found that although the plaintiff was entitled to have his solicitors present at meetings at which a claim of unwanted sexual advances made against him was investigated, the efficacy of the solicitor:

> "was nullified because the defendant prevented her having an effective role by denying her the statements and the opportunities to make representations and submissions."[131]

9–90 Related to this is the ability of a party to call witnesses at a hearing.[132] In *Carroll v Bus Átha Cliath/Dublin Bus,*[133] Clarke J. accepted that the right to have a witness give evidence on a party's behalf at a disciplinary hearing constituted a fundamental right to fair procedures. An issue had arisen in that case in that the proposed witness had been certified sick for work, and so the defendant took issue with his appearing as a witness. Clarke J. dismissed this objection, holding quite sensibly that there are situations in which a person may not be fit to attend work but still be fit to give evidence.

(e) Timing

9–91 The point at which an interlocutory injunction is sought may also be a relevant consideration for the courts. The courts will be keeping a watchful eye out for applications which are premature in the context of any remedies available.

9–92 Timing was a relevant consideration in *Morgan v Trinity College Dublin.*[134] In that case the plaintiff sought an interlocutory injunction restraining the third named defendant, the chair of a disciplinary panel, from holding a disciplinary hearing. Kearns J. refused the injunction sought, and held, inter alia, that the plaintiff's complaints were premature as all matters could have been dealt with fairly before the disciplinary panel.

9–93 In *Carroll v Bus Átha Cliath/Dublin Bus,*[135] Clarke J. stated that a court should be reluctant to intervene in an incomplete disciplinary process, especially

---

[130] [2000] E.L.R. 248.
[131] [2000] E.L.R. 248 at 271.
[132] The Employment Appeals Tribunal has held that a party should be allowed call witnesses at a disciplinary hearing: See, for example, U.D. 367/88 *Gearon v Dunnes Stores*; U.D. 69/197 *Moran v Bailey Gibson Ltd.*
[133] [2005] 4 I.R. 184.
[134] [2004] 15 E.L.R. 235.
[135] [2005] 4 I.R. 184.

at the interlocutory stage. This was a point he repeated in his decision in *Bergin v Galway Clinic Doughiska Ltd.*[136] In the latter case, Clarke J. wanted to avoid a situation developing where recourse "might well be had to the courts at many stages in the course of what would otherwise be a relatively straightforward and expeditious set of disciplinary proceedings." However, in *Carroll* Clarke J. also held that where an employer had, in clear and unequivocal terms, indicated that procedures would be followed which would be manifestly unfair, the court might intervene as appropriate. Clarke J. felt that this was particularly apposite where the degree of prejudice which the employee concerned would suffer in the event of an adverse finding at the particular stage in the process in respect of which the complaint was made would be great and unlikely to be substantially reversed by a finding of a court made after the process had come to an end. He stated that it is:

> "a basic tenet of the rules of fair procedures that a person should not be required to embark upon a process affecting their rights (which a disciplinary hearing which may give rise to removal from employment clearly is) without having at least a reasonable account of the complaint which they are asked to answer."[137]

9–94 Clarke J. granted the interlocutory injunction sought, restraining the defendant company from holding a hearing until such time as they provided particulars of the allegations made and allowed the plaintiff's witnesses to attend the hearing.

9–95 In *Becker v Board of Management of St Dominic's Secondary School*,[138] Clarke J. held that a court should only intervene in the course of an uncompleted disciplinary process in a "clear case", and that it should not be invited to intervene at a "variety of stages". Such intervention should only occur, according to Clarke J., in cases where a step or act had been taken in the process which could not be cured and which was "manifestly at variance with the entitlement to fair procedures". He also observed that it should not be assumed that unfairness will occur in the future.

9–96 The emphasis is thus on a party contemplating bringing an injunction application—and his legal advisers—to ensure that all internal mechanisms available to them have been exhausted prior to initiating legal proceedings.

4. Investigations

9–97 In the normal course, an investigation will precede a disciplinary hearing. In *O'Brien v AON Insurance Managers (Dublin) Ltd*,[139] an internal investigation

---

[136] unreported, High Court, Clarke J., November 2, 2007.
[137] [2005] 4 I.R. 184 at 191.
[138] unreported, High Court, Clarke J., April 13, 2006.
[139] unreported, High Court, Clarke J., January 14, 2004.

was carried out into the plaintiff's conduct. The investigators made certain allegations of misconduct and recommended disciplinary proceedings. The plaintiff sought an interlocutory injunction to restrain those disciplinary proceedings, making a series of complaints concerning the procedures followed by the investigators. In refusing the relief sought, Clarke J. held that even if there were infirmities in the methodology of the investigators, the recommendations did not amount to a sanction. As such, the rights to fair procedures did not arise.[140] This is clearly an issue which will have to be dealt with on a case-by-case basis and will require detailed, practical analysis.

5. Sick Pay

9–98 The question of whether an employee has a right to be paid a salary until the trial of an action in circumstances where the illness which results in his being out of work is the employer's fault was considered in *Mullarkey v Irish National Stud Company Ltd.*[141] That case involved the seeking of two injunctions requiring the plaintiff's salary to be paid to him pending trial, notwithstanding the fact that he was not working due to illness. It was alleged that that illness was directly related to the situation which obtained at his place of work.

9–99 As summarised by Kelly J., the plaintiff's argument was that although he had been out sick longer than the period within which he could be paid whilst on sick leave, his salary should be paid until trial regardless of contractual entitlements. Kelly J. rejected the argument that the fact that it was alleged that the plaintiff's work situation had given rise to the illness concerned meant that the plaintiff was entitled to be paid. In doing so he distinguished two cases cited in support of the argument, namely *Charlton v His Highness, The Aga Kahn's Stud*[142] and *Rooney v Kilkenny*.[143] He felt that the latter two cases involved the court identifying the existence of an implied term entitling the plaintiff to sick leave for a reasonable time. Neither of them decided that because of the wrongdoing of an employer an employee injured by such acts or omissions was ipso facto entitled to be paid a salary until the trial of an action for damages.

9–100 However, Kelly J. did find that on balance a fair case had been made out by the plaintiff that a reasonable time, in the context of a management employee with the defendant, is one which involves a period of full pay whilst on sick leave greater than that of 13 weeks. This was particularly so as the defendant operated in the public sector and the pension scheme concerned was a state one.

---

140 Applying *Morgan v Trinity College* [2003] 3 I.R. 157.
141 unreported, High Court, Kelly J., June 30, 2004.
142 unreported, High Court, Laffoy J., December 22, 1998.
143 [2001] E.L.R. 129.

Kelly J. was also satisfied that damages would not be an adequate remedy, as the plaintiff had ongoing financial obligations which he would fail to meet. Kelly J. thus found the balance of convenience to be in favour of granting an injunction. The terms of the employee's contract will clearly be a crucial factor in such circumstances.

6. Suspension

9–101 An employee may find themselves suspended by their employer, and the question thus arises as to the extent to which the employee can obtain an injunction preventing such suspension.[144] Whilst there may be a popular perception that suspension is in some way a "lesser" issue than a dismissal, as is clear from the decision of the Supreme Court in *Rajpal v Robinson*[145] a suspension can be an extremely serious development, with Hardiman J. making reference to "the drastic nature of the decision to suspend without pay".[146] He also referred to the fact that the suspension in issue was:

> "quite clearly punitive in its effect on the surgeon suspended. It is calculated to place him in a position of humiliation and disadvantage. On the one hand it compromises his ability to pay his ordinary liabilities and to support himself and those for whom he is responsible in the standard to which they are accustomed. It undermines his credit worthiness. It radically and dramatically transforms his position as a self supporting member of the community. It can be of long and indefinite duration. It stigmatises him in the eyes of medical colleagues, patients and such members of the wider community as become aware of it. In a rural area this is probably a substantial group. It puts a major obstacle in the way of his obtaining alternative employment or developing a private practice. It constitutes a financial disaster, a grave blow, possibly irrecoverable, to reputation and a gross professional humiliation."[147]

9–102 A similar view is evident in England. In the case of *Mezey v South West London and St Georges Mental Health Trust*,[148] Sedley L.J. was faced with the argument that a suspension was a "neutral act" which preserved the employment relationship. He rejected this proposition, and stated that a suspension:

---

[144] An alternative is to adopt the somewhat Jesuitical approach of asking someone to "stay away" from work; they are not suspended as such, but nor do they report to work. See, for example, the article headed "Merrill Lynch tells 20 staff to 'stay away' for e-mailing porn", *The Irish Times*, June 23, 2006.

[145] [2005] 3 I.R. 385.

[146] [2005] 3 I.R. 385 at 396.

[147] [2005] 3 I.R. 385 at 396.

[148] [2007] I.R.L.R. 244.

"changes the *status quo* from work to no work, and it inevitably casts a shadow over the employee's competence. Of course this does not mean that it cannot be done, but it is not a neutral act."[149]

9–103 The decision in *Rajpal* is certainly more forceful in relation to suspension than that in the earlier High Court case of *Yeates v Minister for Posts and Telegraphs*.[150] In *Yeates*, the plaintiffs claimed, inter alia, an injunction restraining the defendants from continuing the purported suspension of their employment by the defendant, as well as a mandatory injunction ordering the defendants to pay the salary and emoluments to which the plaintiffs claimed they were entitled. The plaintiffs also claimed an injunction directing the defendant Minister to terminate the suspension of each plaintiff and to restore each of them to the position he held before the date when they were suspended.

9–104 Kenny J., refusing the grant of an interlocutory injunction, observed that the plaintiffs had only been suspended, not dismissed, which he found to be of "critical importance".[151] A second point fatal to the application was the fact that Kenny J. felt that damages would be an adequate remedy, and that assessment of such damages would be easy, "for they will be the amount which the plaintiffs would have been paid if they had not been suspended."[152] Kenny J. also took the view that to restore the plaintiffs to their positions would in effect be to order specific performance of a contract for personal services.[153]

9–105 The decision in *Martin v Irish Nationwide Building Society*[154] is more in keeping with the tenor of *Rajpal* in its approach to suspensions. In the High Court Macken J. concluded that the plaintiff had established a fair question to be tried in relation to a suspension which had "gone on for too long", and that he would suffer irreparable loss and damage if she did not grant an injunction reinstating him as a branch manager at one of the defendant building society's branches. Based on *Rajpal*, it is crucial to consider the effect of suspending a party, which should in no way be treated lightly or as a neutral act in the context of an employment relationship.

---

149 [2007] I.R.L.R. 244 at 245.
150 [1978] I.L.R.M. 22. See also, *Flynn v An Post* [1987] I.R. 68.
151 [1978] I.L.R.M. 22 at 24.
152 [1978] I.L.R.M. 22 at 25.
153 The decision was delivered a number of years before *Fennelly v Assicurazioni Generali Spa* (1985) 3 I.L.T. 73, and thus Kenny J. was able to state without qualification that "it is settled law that the courts never specifically enforce a contract for personal services".
154 [2001] 1 I.R. 228.

E. Post-Termination

1. Introduction

9–106 Many contracts of employment will contain a clause in restraint of trade or preventing the dissemination of confidential information. Employers can, on that basis, seek to prevent their now former employees from acting for a competitor within a defined time frame, commonly achieved by what is known as a "restraint of trade" clause. Alternatively, and where appropriate, an employer may try to secure an injunction to prevent the dissemination of confidential information, often referred to as "trade secrets". Each of these will be considered in turn, although they are closely linked in that a restraint of trade clause may be designed to prevent the dissemination of trade secrets.

2. Restraint of Trade/Restrictive Covenants

9–107 It has been suggested that there is no doctrinal barrier to judicial activism in the area of restrictive covenants, where individuals have been restrained from breaching their contracts and entering into commitments with other parties.[155] In other words, a person may not be forced to work for an employer, but can be prevented from working for another one.[156]

9–108 Employers will often seek to restrict employees from competing against them once they have left their employment, and will seek to injunct a (now former) employee from so competing. In *Kerry Co-Operative Creameries Ltd v An Bord Báinne*,[157] O'Flaherty J. in the Supreme Court adopted the definition of restraint of trade contained in Cheshire, Fifoot & Furmston's *Law of Contract*[158]:

> "A contract in restraint of trade is one by which a party restricts his future liberty to carry on his trade, business or profession in such manner and with such persons as he chooses. A contract of this class is *prima facie* void, but it becomes binding upon proof that the restriction is justifiable in the circumstances as being reasonable from the point of view of the parties themselves and also of the community.

---

[155] Horan, "Employment Injunction: Current Status and Future Developments" (2005) 1 E.L.R. 8 at 9, giving the examples of in *Lumley v Wagner* (1852) De G.M. &G. 604, 42 E.R. 687 and *Warner Brothers Pictures Incorporated v Nelson* [1937] 1 K.B. 209.

[156] See the comments to this effect by O'Flaherty J. in *Capital Radio Productions Ltd v Radio 2000 Ltd*, ex tempore, Supreme Court, May 26, 1998.

[157] [1991] I.L.R.M. 851.

[158] The definition is from p.380 of the 11th edn. The up-to-date reference is Cheshire, Fifoot & Furmston's, *Law of Contract*, 15th edn (Oxford: OUP, 2006), p.517.

Such has long been the legal effect of two familiar types of contract. First, one by which an employee agrees that after leaving his present employment he will not compete against his employer, either by setting up business on his own account or by entering the service of a rival trader. Secondly, an agreement by the vendor of the goodwill of a business not to carry on a similar business in competition with the purchaser."[159]

9–109 The theory underlying the restraint of trade in the more specific context of employment was considered by the Privy Council in the case of *Stenhouse Australia Ltd v Phillips*,[160] in which it was held that:

"The accepted proposition that an employer is not entitled to protection from mere competition by a former employee means that the employee is entitled to use to the full any personal skill or experience even if this has been acquired in the service of his employer: it is this freedom to use to the full a man's improving ability and talents which lies at the root of the policy of the law regarding this type of restraint. Leaving aside the case of misuse of trade secrets or confidential information ... the employer's claim for protection must be based upon the identification of some advantage or asset inherent in the business which can properly be regarded as, in a general sense, his property, and which it would be unjust to allow the employee to appropriate for his own purposes."[161]

9–110 As stated by O'Flaherty J. in *Kerry Co-Operative Creameries Ltd v An Bord Báinne Co-Operative Ltd*[162]:

"A restraint may be imposed more readily and more widely upon the vendor of a business in the interests of the purchaser, than upon an employee in the interests of an employer."[163]

9–111 Courts will have to consider the individual circumstances of each case in relation to restraints of trade, and an unduly restrictive and wide-ranging clause is likely to fall foul of an application for an injunction. For example, the defendant in *Murgitroyd and Co v Purdy*[164] was a patent attorney who, upon terminating his employment with the plaintiff company set up in competition with the plaintiff, contrary to a clause in his employment contract. He argued

[159] See generally, *Esso Petroleum Co Ltd v Harpers Garage (Stourport) Ltd* [1968] A.C. 269 for an overview of the history of restraint of trade. See also, *Mulligan v Corr* [1925] 1 I.R. 169 at 175, per FitzGibbon J.
[160] [1974] A.C. 391; [1974] 2 W.L.R. 134; [1974] 1 All E.R. 117.
[161] [1974] A.C. 391 at 400; [1974] 2 W.L.R. 134 at 138; [1974] 1 All E.R. 117 at 122.
[162] [1991] I.L.R.M. 851.
[163] [1991] I.L.R.M. 851 at 875. See also, *Schroeder Music Publishing Co Ltd v Macaulay* [1974] 3 All E.R. 616 at 623, per Lord Diplock.
[164] [2005] 3 I.R. 12. See also, the Circuit Court case of *Oates v Romano* (1950) 84 I.L.T.R. 161.

that the non-competition clause in question was unenforceable as a restraint of trade. Clarke J. agreed, taking the view that the restriction on all competition which was provided for in the non-competition clause was too wide. He stated that:

"Covenants against competition by former employees are never reasonable as such. They may be upheld only where the employee might obtain such personal knowledge of, and influence over, the customers of his employer as would enable him, if competition were allowed, to take advantage of his employer's trade connections... The prohibition in this case on all competition is too wide. A prohibition on dealing with (in addition to soliciting of) customers of the plaintiff would, in my view, have been reasonable and sufficient to meet any legitimate requirements of the Plaintiff. The wider prohibition which restricts dealing with those who might be, but are not, such customers is excessive."[165]

9–112 Restraint of trade clauses should also be limited in subject-matter, duration and geographical extent. For example, in *Mulligan v Corr*,[166] the Supreme Court refused to enforce a restraint of trade clause in a contract between a solicitor and his former apprentice by virtue of which the (now qualified) apprentice was not to practise within 30 miles of defined areas. However, in *Murgitroyd* Clarke J. held that a clause which applied to all of Ireland did not of itself make it unreasonable in the context of the number of patent attorneys operating in Ireland. He also held that, having regard to the "specialised nature" of the business, a restraint period of 12 months was not unreasonable.

9–113 If a restraint of trade clause is relatively short in a temporal sense, it may make more sense for a court to suggest dealing with any interlocutory injunction application as the hearing of the matter, as a resolution will generally effectively dispose of the action.

(a) Implied Terms

9–114 The question of an implied term restricting competition was considered by the Court of Appeal in *Wallace Bogan & Co v Cove*.[167] Leggett L.J. held that employers could protect goodwill by an express covenant in "reasonable restraint of trade", but held that there was no such protection if the employers "do not bother to exact an express covenant".[168]

---

[165] See also, *European Chemical Industries Ltd v Bell* [1981] I.L.R.M. 345; and *European Paint Importers v O'Callaghan*, unreported, High Court, Peart J., August 10, 2005.
[166] [1925] 1 I.R.169.
[167] [1997] I.R.L.R. 453, referred to in *The Pulse Group Ltd v O'Reilly*, unreported, High Court, Clarke J., February 17, 2006.
[168] [1997] I.R.L.R. 453 at 455.

(b) Garden Leave

9–115 The use of a contractual clause providing for what is commonly termed "garden leave" is an attempt to deal with the problems arising from former employees working for a competitor. By virtue of such a clause, the employee does not undertake any work for his existing employer for a defined period, but is still on the employer's payroll. Although such clauses do not appear to have been considered in any detail in any reported Irish cases,[169] the Court of Appeal in England held in *Provident Financial Group Plc v Hayward*[170] that there was a discretion to enforce such a garden leave clause if there was a real prospect of serious damage to the soon to be former employers.[171]

3. Confidential Information[172]

9–116 Linked to restraint of trade is the fact that many contracts of employment will contain a confidentiality clause preventing an employee from disclosing any confidential information when they have left their employment. However, such clauses must be viewed in the light of the well-known English decision of the Court of Appeal in *Faccenda Chickens v Fowler*,[173] in which the court refused to protect confidential information after the employment relationship had ended if such information fell short of being in the nature of a trade secret.[174]

9–117 In *Cantor Fitzgerald Ltd v Wallace*,[175] the High Court in England held that an employer could not claim a proprietary interest and protect for itself the customer connection an employee built up during the course of employment, where such a connection arose as a result of an employee's personal qualities. In the circumstances, the court did not grant an injunction preventing bond

---

[169] Although their existence and use has been acknowledged: see, inter alia, *Brightwater v Allen*, ex tempore, High Court, Laffoy J., May 12, 2005 and *Orr v Zomax Ltd* [2004] 1 I.R. 486. See also, the Employment Appeals Tribunal decisions in U.D. 751/2006 *Finn v AON Insurances Managers (Dublin) Ltd*; U.D. 339/2005 *Malone v Timac Albatross Ltd* and P.W. 82/2002 *Pierce v Core Air Conditioning Ltd.*

[170] [1989] 3 All E.R. 298.

[171] See also, *Evening Standard v Henderson* [1987] I.C.R. 588 and *Credit Suisse Asset Management Ltd v Armstrong* [1996] I.C.R. 882.

[172] See generally, Kimber, "Restrictive covenants in employment law" (2006) 3(3) I.E.L.J. 85. See also, Lavery, *Commerical Secrets The Action for Breach of Confidence in Ireland* (Dublin: Round Hall, 1996).

[173] [1987] Ch. 117.

[174] It was held in the English case of *Hivac Ltd v Park Royal Scientific Instruments Ltd* [1946] Ch. 169 that an injunction could lie, not just against the employee, but also the party who purported to employ him in a position which could lead to the misuse of confidential information, the new employers being exposed to the allegation that they had induced a breach of contract.

[175] [1992] I.R.L.R. 215.

dealers from working in a competing business after the termination of their employment terminated.

9–118 Disclosure of information was central to the case of *Norbrook Laboratories v Mountford*.[176] The plaintiff had employed the defendant as a senior chemist on a two-year contract, as part of which the defendant was obliged to sign a confidentiality and ownership of inventions agreement. The defendant's employment with the plaintiff subsequently terminated, following which she took up employment with a wholly-owned subsidiary of competitors of the plaintiff. The plaintiff sought interlocutory injunctions restraining the defendant from using or disclosing any confidential information obtained during the course of her employment with the plaintiff, or engaging in any activity or employment in the course of which she might be expected or required to use or disclose such confidential information. Crucially, the defendant and her new employer offered undertakings to the plaintiff with respect to breaches of confidentiality. In refusing the relief sought, McCracken J. held, first, that to succeed it would have to be shown that it could reasonably be anticipated that an employee would be required or would disclose confidential information. In the light of the undertakings offered by the defendant and her employer, he did not accept that there was a reasonable anticipation that this would occur. McCracken J. also found that damages would not be an adequate remedy to either party. He held that the balance of convenience alone must be considered, and that the undertakings offered by the defendant must be taken into account in that exercise. In the circumstances, he found that the undertakings had shifted the balance of convenience in favour of refusing the injunction.

9–119 Summarising the state of the law in *The Pulse Group Ltd v O'Reilly*,[177] and referring to the *Faccenda Chickens* case, Clarke J. held that in the absence of an express term in a contract of employment, the only enduring obligation on the part of an employee after his employment has ceased is one which precludes the employee from disclosing a trade secret.

9–120 In so far as the courts may grant injunctions in order to protect trade secrets, some cases require a demonstration to the court that the information in question is in the nature of a trade secret which merits protection. In the English case of *Mainmet Holdings Plc v Austin*,[178] Lionel Swift Q.C., sitting as a deputy judge of the High Court, found that there was no evidence of specific trade secrets being contained in either of two reports received by the defendant, the former managing director of the second named plaintiff. In the circumstances it was held that there was no serious question to be tried in relation to breach of confidence, and the court discharged the ex parte injunction which had been

---

[176]   [2001] E.L.R. 189.
[177]   unreported, High Court, Clarke J., February 17, 2006.
[178]   [1991] F.S.R. 538.

granted to the plaintiffs.[179] The information must also be such that it can be defined in a meaningfully precise way.[180] The English courts have also rejected the defence that information which had been copied could be legitimately pieced together.[181]

9–121 The granting of an injunction will of course depend to a degree on the extent to which the information has already been used and the extent to which the granting of such an injunction would actually provide real protection.[182]

---

[179] An interlocutory injunction was refused in *Austin Knight (UK) Ltd v Hinds* [1994] F.S.R. 52 as Vinelott J. took the view the view that the defendant had neither taken with her nor misused any confidential documents upon leaving her employment with the plaintiff.

[180] *Lock International Plc v Beswick* [1989] 1 W.L.R. 1268; [1989] 3 All E.R. 373.

[181] *Johnson & Bloy v Wolstenholme Rink* [1987] I.R.L.R. 499.

[182] See, for example, *Seager v Copydex* [1967] 1 W.L.R. 923; [1967] 2 All E.R. 415 and *Speed Seal Products Ltd v Paddington* [1985] 1 W.L.R. 1327; [1986] 1 All E.R. 91.

CHAPTER 10

GENERAL APPLICATION

A. INTRODUCTION

10–01 The purpose of this chapter is to look at various different areas of the law in which injunctions have been sought and granted, identifying any key features or special factors relevant to injunctions in those different areas. It seeks to identify important cases, but does not purport to definitively catalogue every decided case related to injunctions in a given area, for cases will invariably turn on their own facts.[1] In so far as there are common principles underlying the case law, reference should be made to Chs 5, 6 and 7, which deal with Perpetual Injunctions, Interlocutory and Interim Applications respectively, and in which are considered the practical and procedural aspects of bringing applications for injunctions. The overarching applicable equitable and general principles are dealt with in Chapter Four.

10–02 Each area of law in this chapter is considered in a discrete section on an alphabetical basis. The wide spread of material covered by the general term "tort" has led to the distillation of subjects which come within that term into individual sections.[2] For ease of reference, matters relating to what might be termed "publication", viz. breach of confidence, defamation and privacy, are treated as a section in their own right. The law concerning injunctions in the areas of planning and development law, industrial relations, intellectual property law, proceeds of crime and family law is primarily based on specific statutory provisions. As such, these areas are dealt with in Ch.11, Specific Statutory Injunctions.

10–03 There are also a number of areas such as banking and immigration law which do not contain a substantial body of case law deriving from injunction applications, although merit consideration. These have been grouped together in a final section under the heading "other areas". This is not intended to in any way diminish their importance. It is simply a recognition that other areas of the law contain a much greater volume of cases dealing with injunctions, or contain cases which set out key legal principles which merit consideration.

---

[1] It is much less an attempt to comprehensively set out the applicable general law. Reference should be made to textbooks dealing with each particular area for a much fuller exposition of the law as necessary; these will be identified as appropriate.

[2] viz. Passing Off, Nuisance, and Trespass.

B. ARBITRATION

1. Introduction[3]

10–04 There are a number of circumstances in which an injunction may be sought in the context of an arbitration agreement. It has been suggested that injunctions may be sought in aid of an arbitration agreement, in addition to an arbitration agreement and in breach of an arbitration agreement.[4] Within that context, there are three circumstances in practice which the courts have considered: the first is when an injunction is sought to prevent an arbitration going ahead. The second is whether seeking an injunction in plenary proceedings should prevent a matter going to arbitration. A third question with which the courts have been faced is whether they can injunct the enforcement of an arbitral award. These particular issues will be considered in turn.

10–05 There are two legislative provisions which are of relevance in relation to injunctions sought in the context of arbitration. Section 22(1) of the Arbitration Act 1954 sets out various protective orders which a court can make in order to preserve the status quo between the parties. In that regard, s.22(1)(h) makes express provision for interim injunctions. Section 5(1) of the Arbitration Act 1980 makes provision for the staying of court proceedings in circumstances where an application is made to do so by a party to an arbitration agreement who seeks to have the matter referred to arbitration.

2. Injuncting an Arbitration

10–06 It is possible to seek an injunction to prevent an arbitration taking place. For example, in *Dun Laoghaire-Rathdown Co. Council v Shackleton*,[5] the plaintiff local authority sought an interlocutory injunction to prevent the first defendant, a statutory arbitrator, from embarking on an arbitration to hear a claim for assessment of compensation in relation to certain lands. A tribunal of inquiry was investigating the circumstances surrounding the re-zoning of those lands. It was claimed that in the circumstances of the case any award made by an arbitrator would constitute unjust enrichment if it was found by the tribunal that monies had been paid to effect the re-zoning in question.

10–07 In granting the interlocutory injunction sought, and having gone through the elements of the *Campus Oil* guidelines, O'Sullivan J. held that the plaintiff had demonstrated an arguable case of unjust enrichment, and that the balance

---

[3] See Stewart, *Arbitration: Commentary and Sources* (Dublin: First Law, 2003), p.36 and Sutton & Gill, *Russell on Arbitration*, 22nd edn (London: Thomson Sweet & Maxwell, 2003), p.308.

[4] Stewart, *Arbitration: Commentary and Sources* (Dublin: First Law, 2003), p.36.

[5] unreported, High Court, O'Sullivan J., January 23, 2002.

of convenience favoured the granting of the injunction sought. O'Sullivan J. also stated that he had had regard to public interest considerations in the case, specifically the question of the tribunal's investigation.[6] However, the Supreme Court held on appeal that the injunction "should never have been granted".[7] That was on the basis that:

> "the plaintiffs have entirely failed to show that there is any question to be tried between the parties in these proceedings, in the manner in which they have framed their proceedings."

3. Staying Plenary Proceedings

10–08 Section 5(1) of the Arbitration Act 1980 reads:

> "If any party to an arbitration agreement, or any person claiming through or under him, commences any proceedings in any court against any other party to such agreement, or any person claiming through or under him, in respect of any matter agreed to be referred to arbitration, any party to the proceedings may at any time after an appearance has been entered, and before delivering any pleadings or taking any other steps in the proceedings, apply to the court to stay the proceedings, and the court, unless it is satisfied that the arbitration agreement is null and void, inoperative or incapable of being performed or that there is not in fact any dispute between the parties with regard to the matter agreed to be referred, shall make an order staying the proceedings."

10–09 In other words, a party may in general terms apply to have plenary proceedings stayed in order that a matter may be referred to arbitration pursuant to an arbitration agreement, provided that no "step" has been taken. It was made clear in *O'Dwyer v Boyd*[8] that the courts have very limited discretion to refuse an application to stay proceedings in the circumstances set out in s.5(1), provided that the application for the stay had been made at the right time, viz. "before delivering any pleadings or taking any other step in the proceedings".[9]

(a) An Injunction as a Step

10–10 As can be seen from the wording of s.5, a key consideration is whether a "step" has been taken in proceedings, such that proceedings should not be stayed and a matter remitted to arbitration. The question of what constitutes a

---

[6] As to which, see generally, Ch.4, Equitable and General Principles, para.4–72.
[7] ex tempore, Supreme Court, June 17, 2002, per Keane C.J.
[8] [2003] 1 I.L.R.M. 112.
[9] See, for example, *O'Flynn v Bord Gais* [1982] I.L.R.M. 324; *Williams v Artane Service Station Ltd* [1991] I.L.R.M. 893; *Kavanagh v Artane Service Station Ltd*, unreported, High Court, Flood J., November 19, 1993.

step was considered in, inter alia, *O'Dwyer v Boyd*,[10] with Geoghegan J. in the Supreme Court referring to a passage from *Halsbury's Laws of England*[11] which reads:

> "The applicant must have taken no step in the proceedings after acknowledgment of service. A step in the proceedings is an act which both invokes the jurisdiction of the court and which demonstrates the applicant's election to allow the action to proceed. An applicant may take what would otherwise be a step if he makes it clear that that act is done without prejudice to his right to apply for a stay."[12]

10–11 The question arose in *MacCormack v Monaghan Co-Operative Agricultural and Dairy Society Ltd*[13] as to whether the seeking of an injunction constituted a step for the purposes of s.5(1). In that case the rather unusual facts were that the plaintiff issued a plenary summons and sought an interlocutory injunction. He then attempted to stay his own proceedings to have the matter referred to arbitration. O'Hanlon J. refused to stay the proceedings on the grounds that an interlocutory injunction had been obtained, holding that this constituted a step in the proceedings. The case must be treated with a degree of caution, however; it has been argued that the plaintiff's actions constituted an abuse of process.[14] As such, it seems better to view the case as turning on its own facts. This is particularly so in view of the decision reached in the later case of *Telenor Invest AS v IIU Nominees Ltd.*[15]

10–12 In *Telenor*, the parties to the proceedings were all shareholders in the telecoms company Esat Digifone Ltd. The plaintiff sought an interlocutory order directing the first defendant to take steps to cause its nominees on the board of directors of Esat Digifone to resign. Alternatively, it sought to restrain the nominees from acting pending the determination of a dispute between the parties in relation to the minimum shareholding required in order to have nominees on the board of directors. The first defendant sought to stay all

---

[10] [2003] 1 I.L.R.M. 112.

[11] 4th edn reissue, Vol.2, para.627.

[12] [2003] 1 I.L.R.M. 112 at 119.

[13] [1988] I.R. 304.

[14] See Hutchinson, "Staying Litigation Pending Arbitration" (1994) C.L.P. 133 for a review of this case, including the suggestion that the case was decided on its own particular facts. See also, *Kavanagh v Artane*, unreported, High Court, Flood J., November 19, 1993, in which Flood J. found himself compelled to grant an order pursuant to s.5, but referred disapprovingly to, inter alia, the defendants,' "action in approbating and reprobating in relation to applying to the Court for injunctive relief and the mandatory Order for the Plaintiff to deliver possession of the premises and their abandonment of the said proceedings at a point in time where they had effectively forcibly taken possession of the premises in question."

[15] unreported, High Court, O'Sullivan J., July 20, 1999. For an analysis of the case, see Kennedy, "Injuncting the Arbitral Process" (2000) 5(4) Bar Rev. 211.

proceedings by the plaintiff on the basis that the dispute between them was the subject of an arbitration agreement. The plaintiff argued, inter alia, that even if s.5 of the 1980 Act did apply, the court had jurisdiction under s.22(1)(h) of the Arbitration Act 1954 to grant the relief sought by way of injunction. That provision reads:

> "(1) The Court shall have, for the purpose of and in relation to a reference, the same power of making orders in respect of –
>
> ...
>
> (h) interim injunctions or the appointment of a receiver,
>
> as it has for the purpose of and in relation to an action or matter in the Court."

10–13 Finding that there was a substantial question to be tried in relation to the interpretation and application of the relevant shareholders' agreement, O'Sullivan J. granted the injunction sought. Applying the *Campus Oil* principles, his decision turned on the key fact that the disadvantage which the plaintiff would suffer as a 49 per cent shareholder in Esat Digifone was incapable of being compensated by damages; this outweighed any damage which might be suffered by the first defendant. O'Sullivan J. also stayed the proceedings in order that the matter might go to arbitration.

10–14 It is therefore clear from the *Telenor* decision that a court may both grant interim relief pursuant to s.22(1)(h) of the Arbitration Act 1954, as well as granting a stay so that the matter can be referred to arbitration.

4. Restraining the Enforcement of an Award

10–15 It is rare for the courts to restrain the making of an award by an arbitrator. An example of the courts' unwillingness in that regard is the case of *Elkinson v Kelly*.[16] An injunction was sought by the plaintiff to restrain an official assignee in bankruptcy from acting upon, or seeking to enforce, an arbitration award. The plaintiff had entered into a contract with a firm of building contractors, which contract contained an arbitration clause. A dispute arose about the amount payable under the contract. However, the builders brought a petition for arrangement under the Bankruptcy Acts. Having secured the protection of the court, an order was subsequently made confirming the resolution of creditors accepting the petitioners' proposals "to vest as fully as in bankruptcy the entire of the petitioners' estate and effects" in the official assignee in bankruptcy. The official assignee referred the matter to arbitration, and an award was made. This award had been made in the absence of the plaintiff, who claimed that no rights under the contract passed to the official

---

[16] [1946] I.R. 248.

assignee. She also argued that even if any rights did pass, the arbitration clause was merely a personal agreement and was revoked by bankruptcy. The third strand of her argument was that she had validly revoked the submission to arbitration and that, accordingly, there was no jurisdiction to arbitrate. However, Overend J. held that the official assignee was entitled to the benefit of the arbitration clause. That being so, he refused the application for the injunction.

10–16 A similar issue arose in England in the case of *The Oranie and the Tunisie*.[17] It was held in that case that an injunction to restrain the making of an award by an arbitrator when the arbitration in question has already taken place may be granted in exceptional cases. However, it has quite correctly been observed that the party seeking such an injunction is likely to be open to an accusation of delay[18]; no less than in other areas of the law, general and equitable principles are equally applicable in relation to injunctions sought in the context of arbitration.[19]

C. COMPANY LAW

1. Introduction[20]

10–17 There are a number of different areas of company law in which injunctions have had a role to play. In most cases when the injunction is sought on an interlocutory basis, the courts will apply the *Campus Oil* principles,[21] although a notable exception to this is an application to restrain a winding-up petition. As has been seen in the context of commercial injunctions,[22] there are also statutory remedies which are available in aid of issues arising in the context of company law. For example, s.55 of the Company Law Enforcement Act 2001 creates a statutory injunction which freezes the assets of directors or other officers of a company. The various areas in which injunctions have been sought will be considered in turn.

---

[17] [1960] 1 Lloyd's Rep. 477.
[18] Sutton & Gill, *Russell on Arbitration*, 22nd edn (London: Thomson Sweet & Maxwell, 2003), p.309. Although, as per the analysis in Chapter Four, Equitable and General Principles, para.4–28, it will generally be necessary to show that it would be unjust to grant the injunction sought due to the delay.
[19] See generally, Ch.4, Equitable and General Principles.
[20] See generally, the enduringly excellent and comprehensive Courtney, *The Law of Private Companies*, 2nd edn (Dublin: Butterworths, 2002).
[21] See generally, Ch.6, Interlocutory Applications.
[22] See Ch.8, Commercial Injunctions.

2. General Application

(a) Removal of a Director

10–18 Section 182(1) of the Companies Act 1963 provides that a company "may by ordinary resolution remove a director before the expiration of his period of office." Pursuant to s.182(7), compensation or damages may be sought by the director so removed.

10–19 The question of whether an injunction should be granted to prevent the removal of a director was considered in some detail by the Supreme Court in the case of *McGilligan v O'Grady*.[23] In that case a petition was brought under s.205 of the Companies Act 1963. That section deals with circumstances in which a party claims that the powers of the directors of a company are being exercised in a manner oppressive to him or any of the members, or in disregard of his or their interest as members.[24] Section 205(3) provides that:

> "If, on any application under subs. (1) or subs. (2) the court is of opinion that the company's affairs are being conducted or the directors' powers are being exercised as aforesaid, the court may, with a view to bringing to an end the matters complained of, make such order as it thinks fit, whether directing or prohibiting any act or cancelling or varying any transaction or for regulating the conduct of the company's affairs in future, or for the purchase of the shares of any members of the company by other members of the company or by the company and in the case of a purchase by the company, for the reduction accordingly of the company's capital, or otherwise."

10–20 *McGilligan* concerned, in general terms, an investment under the Business Expansion Scheme. Proceedings were issued seeking an interlocutory injunction restraining the removal of the first plaintiff as a director of the third defendant, a company called Premier International Merchandising Ltd. It was also sought to restrain the third defendant from becoming involved in manufacturing. A petition was then brought pursuant to s.205 of the Companies Act 1963, under which it was claimed that the affairs of the third defendant were being conducted in a manner oppressive to the plaintiffs and in disregard of their interests.

10–21 In the High Court, O'Donovan J. granted an injunction preventing, inter alia, the defendants from removing the first plaintiff as a director of the third and fourth defendants.

---

[23] [1999] 1 I.R. 346; [1999] 1 I.L.R.M. 303.

[24] In *Re Via Networks Ireland Ltd* [2002] 2 I.R. 47 at 57, the Supreme Court dismissed a petition seeking relief pursuant to s.205(1) of the Companies Act 1963. Keane C.J. held, that if there is an arbitration clause in a shareholders' agreement, a shareholder entering into such an agreement is expressly waiving the right to have issues that arise between the parties arising out of the shareholders' agreement litigated in any forum other than the arbitral tribunal; see *Re Vocam Europe Ltd* [1996] B.C.C. 396.

(i) Application of Campus Oil Principles

10–22 On appeal, Keane J. in the Supreme Court made it clear that the court could grant interlocutory relief in the circumstances as outlined. As Keane J. observed:

> "Why then should the Court on an application for an interlocutory injunction be unable to restrain the company from removing a director pending the hearing of a petition under section 205 where he has established that there is a serious question to be tried as to whether his exclusion from the affairs of the company constitutes conduct which would entitle shareholders to relief under section 205?"[25]

10–23 The Supreme Court approached the matter on the basis that the *Campus Oil* principles were applicable.[26] In the words of Keane J.:

> "If it is desirable, in accordance with the principles laid down in the *American Cynamid Co.* and *Campus Oil* cases, to preserve the plaintiffs' rights pending the hearing of the s.205 proceedings and the balance of convenience does not point to a different conclusion, I see no reason why interlocutory relief should not be granted."[27]

10–24 In approaching the matter on this basis, Keane J. found that the balance of convenience was in the plaintiff's favour. He felt that if the plaintiff was excluded from participation in the board meetings of the third defendant and was denied the financial information and audited accounts pending the hearing of the s.205 petition, the asset base of the company could be seriously damaged. He also held that the efficacy of the winding-up order to which the plaintiffs might ultimately have been entitled would be significantly affected. As against that, he did not believe that the interests of the defendants would be seriously affected by the affording of the financial information in question, or by the presence of the first plaintiff at board meetings.

---

[25] [1999] 1 I.R. 346 at 362; [1999] 1 I.L.R.M. 303 at 319. See the decision of Laffoy J. in *Feighery v Feighery*, unreported, High Court, Laffoy J., February 25, 1998. In that case Laffoy J. referred to *Bentley-Stevens v Jones* [1974] 1 W.L.R. 638, in which Plowman J. refused to grant an interlocutory injunction in a case where disputes arose between the three shareholders in a company which ran a nursing home and two of the shareholders sought to remove the third shareholder as a director.

[26] See generally, Ch.6, Interlocutory Applications. See also the case of *Re Ural Hudson Ltd*, unreported, High Court, Finlay Geoghegan J., January 9, 2005, which concerned proceedings under s.205. Finlay Geoghegan J. was satisfied that the *Campus Oil* principles were applicable in determining whether or not to grant the injunction sought. The injunction was to prevent the paying out or disposal of any party of a sum arising from an execution process until after the determination of the s.205 proceedings.

[27] [1999] 1 I.R. 346 at 362; [1999] 1 I.L.R.M. 303 at 319.

10–25 That the relief granted was not that sought in the substantive proceedings was not an obstacle to the granting of such relief. In that regard, Keane J. cited the example of a *Mareva* order, in which the relief granted was often not that sought in the substantive proceedings.[28]

(b) Exclusion from Meetings

10–26 In the case of *Coubrough v James Panton & Co Ltd*,[29] the plaintiff sought, inter alia, an order restraining the defendant from excluding him from meetings of the board of directors of the defendant company. This exclusion took effect after a resolution had been passed purporting to remove him and other directors (the others subsequently being re-elected) from the board of the company. At the trial of the action, Budd J. held the resolution to be invalid. He also held that the plaintiff had the right to attend meetings of the board of directors and that, as such, the defendants should be restrained by injunction from excluding the plaintiff from such meetings and from otherwise preventing or interfering with the exercise of his powers and duties as such director.[30]

(c) Access to Books of Account

10–27 A director's right of access to books of account may be enforced by injunction. This is clear from the decision of *Healy v Healy Homes Ltd*.[31] In that case Kenny J. also held that in exercising his right to inspect his company's books of account pursuant to s.147(3) of the Companies Act 1963, a company director is entitled to be accompanied by an accountant and to make copies of such documents. Although s.147 is now repealed and replaced by s.202 of the Companies Act 1990, the same principles continue to apply, as appears clear from the decision of Smyth J. in the case of *Brosnan v Sommerville*,[32] decided after the introduction of the 1990 Act.

(d) Shareholdings

10–28 Injunctions may also be sought in relation to shareholdings in a company. There are, in broad terms, three areas in which the courts have had to consider granting injunctions in connection with shareholdings.

---

[28] See Ch.8, Commercial Injunctions.
[29] [1965] I.R. 272.
[30] Applying *Pulbrook v Richmond Consolidated Mining Company* (1878) 9 Ch D 610.
[31] [1973] I.R. 309.
[32] unreported, High Court, Smyth J., October 3, 2006.

(i) Shareholders Dispute

10–29 The case of *Telenor Invest AS v IIU Nominees Ltd*[33] involved a dispute over a shareholders' agreement. As has been seen,[34] the plaintiff sought an interlocutory injunction to prevent the first named defendant's nominees on the board of the second named defendant, Esat Digifone Ltd, from acting as such pending the resolution of a dispute between the plaintiff and the first named defendant. That dispute centred on the provisions of the applicable share-holders' agreement. At issue was whether a shareholding below a certain threshold was such that the first named defendant was obliged to seek the resignation of its board members from the board of the second named defendant. Applying the *Campus Oil* guidelines, O'Sullivan J. granted the interlocutory injunction sought. He held that damages would not be an adequate remedy; the disadvantage which the plaintiff would suffer as a 49 per cent shareholder in Esat Digifone was incapable of being compensated by damages, and this outweighed any damage which might be suffered by the first defendant. O'Sullivan J. also held that the balance of convenience favoured the granting of an interlocutory injunction to the plaintiff pending the resolution of the dispute.

(ii) Allotment of Shares

10–30 In the context of an allotment of shares, an injunction was refused in the case of *Afric Sive Ltd v Oil & Gas Exploration Plc*.[35] Costello J. declined to grant the interlocutory injunction sought to prevent the allotment of shares under a rights issue without this offer extending to the plaintiffs so that they could take up an allotment of 200,000 of the new shares. He found the balance of convenience was against the granting of an injunction.

(iii) Voting Rights

10–31 Injunctions may be granted in relation to the exercise of voting rights. In the case of *O'Gorman v Kelleher*,[36] Carroll J. granted an interlocutory injunction restraining the first named defendant from exercising his voting rights in respect of disputed shares contrary to the interests of the plaintiff. She held that the voting rights attached to the shares were being used to oust the first named plaintiff. Carroll J. took the view that if an unpaid vendor of shares were to vote deliberately so as to damage the purchaser, or contrary to the interests of the purchaser, the beneficial owner, he should be restrained by the court.

---

[33] unreported, High Court, O'Sullivan J., July 20, 1999.
[34] See para.10–12 in the context of Arbitration.
[35] unreported, High Court, Costello J., May 10, 1988.
[36] ex tempore, High Court, Carroll J., July 19, 1999.

(e) Receivership

10–32 It may be necessary for a receiver to seek an injunction from the court in order to obtain a statement of affairs. In the case of *Somers v Kennedy*,[37] the defendants failed to comply with requests from the receiver to be furnished with a statement of affairs. The receiver successfully applied to the High Court seeking a mandatory injunction compelling the submission and verification of a statement of affairs.

10–33 The wide range of areas in which an injunction order may be deployed in the area of company law is evident from the case of *McGowan v Gannon*.[38] In that case the sale of a company's factory premises by the defendant receiver was restrained by injunction in circumstances where there was a divergence of valuations of the premises on both sides.

(f) Winding Up[39]

10–34 Winding-up petitions are generally brought on foot of an outstanding debt, pursuant to s.214 of the Companies Act 1963, or an application seeking remedies for oppression under s.205 of the Companies Act 1963. Section 213 of the Companies Act 1963 provides that "a company may be wound up if … (e) the company is unable to pay its debts". Section 214 of the 1963 Act sets out the circumstances in which a company is deemed unable to pay its debts.

10–35 If a debt is bona fide disputed, a winding-up petition is not a legitimate means of enforcing payment of such debt. If a company, "in good faith and on substantial grounds", disputes liability in respect of the debt claimed, then the petition will in normal circumstances be restrained. This is clear from the leading case in the area, the decision of Keane J. in *Truck and Machinery Sales Ltd v Marubeni Komatsu Ltd*.[40] This area, and the decision in *Truck and Machinery Sales* in particular, bear a degree of analysis due to the displacement of the *Campus Oil* principles when considering applications for interlocutory injunctions.

---

[37] [1998] 1 I.R. 1.

[38] [1983] I.L.R.M. 516.

[39] See generally, Courtney, *The Law of Private Companies*, 2nd edn (Dublin: Butterworths, 2002), p.1443 and Canniffe, "Restraining a Creditor's Winding Up Petition—The Position Since *Truck and Machinery Sales Ltd v Marubeni Komatsu Ltd*" (1997) 4(2) C.L.P. 30.

[40] [1996] 1 I.R. 12 at 24, Keane J. citing *Mann v Goldstein* [1968] 1 W.L.R. 1091 and *Stonegate Securities v Gregory* [1980] Ch. 576, both of which were adopted in *Re Pageboy Couriers Ltd* [1983] I.L.R.M. 510. *Truck and Machinery* was approved in, inter alia, *Coalport Building Company Ltd v Castle Contracts*, unreported, High Court, Laffoy J., January 19, 2004 and *Meridien v Eircell*, unreported, Supreme Court, May 10, 2001.

(i) Test of Good Faith and Substantial Grounds

10–36 The test of "good faith and substantial grounds" derives from the English case of *Re a Company*.[41] In that case an application was brought by a company seeking to restrain the advertising of a winding-up petition in circumstances in which the debt allegedly due by the company to the petitioner was disputed. Hoffmann J. made an order restraining the advertising of the petition. In the course of his judgment he said that:

> "It is agreed that in order to restrain advertisement, I must be satisfied on the evidence before me that it would appear on the hearing of the petition that the debt is disputed in good faith and on substantial grounds."[42]

10–37 A fuller exposition of the rationale behind a determination as to whether or not to restrain a winding-up petition was provided, again by Hoffmann J., in the later case of the same appellation, *Re a Company*.[43] Hoffmann J. stated that:

> "It does seem to me that a tendency has developed, possibly since the decision in *Cornhill Insurance Plc. v Improvement Services Ltd* [1986] BCLC 26 to present petitions against solvent companies as a way of putting pressure on them to make payments of money which is *bona fide* disputed rather than to invoke the procedures which the rules provide for summary judgment. I do not for a moment wish to detract from anything which was said in the *Cornhill Insurance* case, which indeed followed earlier authorities, to the effect that a refusal to pay an undisputed debt is evidence from which the inference may be drawn that the debtor is unable to pay. It was, however, a somewhat unusual case in which it was quite clear that the company in question had no grounds at all for its refusal. Equally it seems to me that if the court comes to the conclusion that a solvent company is not putting forward any defence in good faith and is merely seeking to take for itself credit which it is not allowed under the contract, then the court would not be inclined to restrain the presentation of the petition. But, if, as in this case, it appears that the defence has a prospect of success and the company is solvent, then I think that the court should give the company the benefit of the doubt and not do anything which would encourage the use of the Companies Court as an alternative to the RSC O.14 procedure."[44]

(ii) Non-Applicability of *Campus Oil* Principles

10–38 In *Truck and Machinery Sales* Keane J. had to consider the applicable test in determining whether or not to grant the injunction sought to restrain the

---

[41] [1992] B.C.L.C. 633.
[42] [1992] B.C.L.C. 633 at 634. As referred to by Morris J. in *Clandown v Davis* [1994] 2 I.L.R.M. 536.
[43] [1992] B.C.L.C. 865.
[44] [1992] B.C.L.C. 865 at 868.

petition in question. He determined that since the application to restrain the presentation of a winding-up petition involves the exercise by a creditor of his right of access to the courts (a right which he held "should not be inhibited save in exceptional circumstances"),[45] the normal *Campus Oil* principles did not apply.[46] Keane J. also referred to the distinction between the restraint of an alleged violation of a plaintiff's right—the usual circumstances in which an injunction is sought—and the situation before him, in which a creditor's right to bring a petition was threatened by injunction. In other words, it was a third party's right which would be affected by any injunction order granted.

(iii) A Prima Facie Case of Abuse of Process

10–39 In refusing the injunction order sought in *Truck and Machinery Sales*, Keane J. stated that the jurisdiction to restrain a petition should only be exercised "where the plaintiff company has established at least a *prima facie* case that its presentation would constitute an abuse of process."[47] Keane J. also held that abuse can be prima facie established in most instances where it can be proved that the petition is bound to fail, or at least that there is a suitable alternative remedy. In other words, if there is a bona fide dispute as to the debt, a petition could constitute an abuse of process. If so, an injunction order would appear not to be appropriate. It should be noted that Keane J. appears to have made no distinction in his decision between restraining the advertisement of a petition and the actual bringing of a petition.[48]

10–40 That an application to restrain the presentation of a winding-up petition should be treated with caution is also clear from *Truck and Machinery Sales*. Keane J. referred to the English decision of *Bryanston Finance Ltd v De Vires (No. 2)*,[49] in which it had been held that a putative petitioner should not be restrained from exercising his right to petition "except on clear and persuasive grounds".

---

[45] [1996] 1 I.R. 12 at 27.
[46] [1996] 1 I.R. 12 at 27. Approved by the Supreme Court in *Meridian Communications Ltd v Eircell Ltd*, unreported, Supreme Court, May 10, 2001 (reasons for the order of the court dated April 27, 2001).
[47] [1996] 1 I.R. 12 at 27.
[48] See Canniffe, "Restraining a Creditor's Winding Up Petition—The Position Since *Truck and Machinery Sales Ltd v Marubeni Komatsu Ltd*" (1997) 4(2) C.L.P. 30. She observes that the view that the two are separate applications such that an injunction may be granted in one but not the other was not looked upon with favour by McWilliam J. in *Re Murph's Restaurant* [1979] I.L.R.M. 141 at 143. Lynch, Marshall and O'Ferrall, *Corporate Insolvency and Rescue* (Dublin: Butterworths, 1996), suggest at p.35 that the two are separate applications which are not co-dependent.
[49] [1976] 1 Ch. 63.

(iv) Disputed Balance

10–41 If indebtedness is admitted, but a balance of the amount claimed as due and owing is disputed, a creditor should not normally be restrained from presenting a winding-up petition.[50]

(g) *Statutory Provisions*

10–42 There are also a number of specific statutory provisions which either provide explicitly for injunctions in the context of company law, or alternatively provide the basis upon which an injunction application can be based. These provisions include:

- Section 8(2) of the Companies Act 1963 makes provision for a member or holder of debentures of a company to restrain the company from doing any act or thing which the company has no power to do, in other words, an ultra vires act.[51]
- Section 245(8) of the Companies Act 1963[52] gives the courts power to summon a person for examination.
- Section 247 of the Companies Act 1963 provides for the arrest[53] of contributories and officers of a company.[54]
- Section 371 of the Companies Act 1963, which deals with the general duty to comply with the relevant provisions of company legislation.[55]
- Section 55 of the Company Law Enforcement Act 2001 creates a statutory injunction which freezes the assets of directors or other officers of a company.[56]

---

[50] *Truck and Machinery Sales Limited v Marubeni Komatzo Ltd* [1996] 1 I.R. 12 at 24, per Keane J.
[51] See MacCann, *Companies Acts 1963–2006* (Dublin: Tottel, 2007), p.43. See, for example, the old cases of *Smith v Croft (No. 2)* (1860) 8 H.L. Cas. 712; *Hoole v Great Western Railway Co.* (1867) 3 Ch. App. 262; *Spokes v Grovenor Hotel Co* [1897] 2 Q.B. 4.
[52] As inserted by s.126 of the Companies Act 1990.
[53] A step which was described as a "strong one", per Page Wood V.C. in *Re Imperial Mercantile Credit Company* [1867] L.R. 5 Eq. 264 at 265.
[54] In *Re J Ellis Pharmaceuticals Ltd*, *Irish Times*, August 13, 1988, "Man is ordered to stay in State", Blayney J. granted an order restraining the managing director of the company concerned from leaving the jurisdiction until he had been examined pursuant to s.245 of the Companies Act 1963. See also *Re Mark Synnott (Life and Pensions) Brokers Ltd*, *Irish Times*, July 4, 1991 (wherein reference is made to a "surrender passport order") and *Re Oriental Credit Ltd* [1988] Ch. 204; [1988] 2 W.L.R. 172.
[55] See MacCann, *Companies Acts 1963–2006* (Dublin: Tottel, 2007), p.630.
[56] O'Reilly, "Freezing Orders Under Section 55 of the Company Law Enforcement Act 2001" (2002) 9(5) C.L.P. 109 at 109 notes that an order under s.55 is "similar in effect but wholly different in operation" to a *Mareva* injunction. Summarising the effect of s.55, O'Reilly observes (at p.112) that: "Section 55 is available to a litigant in limited circumstances only. It should not be confused with an equitable injunction. In practice it will assist in the prosecution of claims against miscreant company officers."

D. Constitutional Law

1. Introduction[57]

10–43 The courts are prepared to grant an injunction to protect a right under the Constitution as they would to protect any other right. The basis upon which an injunction may be sought if there has been an infringement of a party's constitutional right was considered by Walsh J. in *Meskell v Coras Iompair Éireann*.[58] In the course of his judgment he stated that:

> "It has been said on a number of occasions in this Court, and most notably in the decision in *Byrne v Ireland*, that a right guaranteed by the Constitution or granted by the Constitution can be protected by action or enforced by action even though such action may not fit into any of the ordinary forms of action in either common law or equity and that the constitutional right carries within it its own right to a remedy or for the enforcement of it. Therefore, if a person has suffered damage by virtue of a breach of a constitutional right or the infringement of a constitutional right, that person is entitled to seek redress against the person or persons who have infringed that right."[59]

10–44 A *quia timet* injunction may also be sought in the context of constitutional proceedings, as is clear from cases such as *East Donegal Co-Operative Livestock Mart Ltd v Attorney General*.[60] In that case, referring to the fact that rights guaranteed by the Constitution should be protected by the provisions of the Constitution, Walsh J. in the Supreme Court stated that such provisions:

> "must enable the person invoking them not merely to redress a wrong resulting from an infringement of the guarantees but also to prevent the threatened or impending infringement of the guarantees and to put to the test an apprehended infringement of these guarantees."[61]

10–45 As has been seen in Ch.4, Equitable and General Principles,[62] a court will not make an order which is futile or unenforceable. This applies equally to injunctions made in order to protect constitutional rights in the same way as it applies to injunctions made in the protection of rights arising under private law, a point confirmed in the case of *Attorney General v X*.[63]

---

[57] See generally, Hogan & Whyte, *J.M. Kelly: The Irish Constitution*, 4th edn (Dublin: Butterworths, 2003).
[58] [1973] I.R. 121.
[59] [1973] I.R. 121 at 132.
[60] [1970] I.R. 317.
[61] [1970] I.R. 317 at 338. See also, *Curtis v Attorney General* [1985] I.R. 458 at 462.
[62] See para.4–53.
[63] [1992] I.L.R.M. 401.

2. General Application

(a) Validity of a Statute

10–46 It was held in *Pesca Valentia Ltd v Minister for Fisheries*[64] that, in an appropriate case, a party may invoke the jurisdiction of the courts to restrain the operation of a statutory provision pending a challenge to its constitutional validity. The Supreme Court rejected the contention that the courts should never grant an interlocutory injunction which in effect prohibited—even for a temporary period—the exercise of a statutory power contained in a post-Constitution statute. In so holding, Finlay C.J stated that:

> "It is, as has been so frequently stated, the duty of the courts to protect persons against the invasion of their constitutional rights or against unconstitutional action. It would seem wholly inconsistent with that duty if the Court were to be without power in an appropriate case to restrain by injunction an action against a person which found its authority in a statutory provision which might eventually be held to be invalid having regard to the Constitution. In particular, it seems to me that this power must exist in an appropriate case where the form of action is under a penal section and involves conviction of and the imposition of a penalty for the commission of a criminal offence."[65]

10–47 However, in *Grange Development Ltd v Dublin Co. Council (No. 4)*,[66] Murphy J. cautioned that there was an "enormous onus which lies on anybody who seeks to establish that an Act of the Oireachtas is invalid having regard to the provisions of the Constitution."[67]

10–48 An injunction was refused in the case of *Gilligan v Special Criminal Court*.[68] The plaintiff had been convicted in the Special Criminal Court in respect of offences of importing a controlled substance and possession for the purpose of sale or supply. An inquiry into whether the plaintiff benefited from drug trafficking was pending before the Special Criminal Court. The plaintiff sought an interlocutory injunction against the DPP on the grounds that he wished to challenge certain statutory provisions. This was refused. The Supreme

---

[64] [1985] I.R. 193; [1986] I.L.R.M. 68. Applied in, inter alia, *Carrigaline Community Television Broadcasting Co Ltd v Minister for Transport, Energy and Communications* [1994] 2 I.R. 359.
[65] [1985] I.R. 193 at 201; [1986] I.L.R.M. 68 at 72, based on the court's earlier decision in *State (Llewellyn) v Ua Donnchacha* [1973] I.R. 151. *Pesca Valentia* was subsequently applied in, inter alia, *Beara Fisheries and Shipping Ltd v Minister for the Marine* [1987] I.R. 413 and *Carrigaline Community Television Broadcasting Co Ltd v Minister for Transport, Energy and Communications* [1994] 2 I.R. 359. See also, *Nova Media Services Ltd v Minister for Posts and Telegraphs* [1984] I.L.R.M. 161 at 169.
[66] [1989] I.R. 377.
[67] [1989] I.R. 377 at 383.
[68] [2001] 4 I.R. 655.

Court found that although serious issues had been raised, the case was "wholly unlike" *Pesca Valentia*.[69] It observed that the damage that would be done to the plaintiffs by the maintenance of the proceedings against them in *Pesca Valentia* would have been irremediable. In *Gilligan,* Keane C.J. took the view that if the legislation in question was ultimately found to be unconstitutional, or to have been operated by the Special Criminal Court in an unconstitutional manner, the plaintiff would be entitled to redress for any damage suffered.

10–49 Each case will fall to be determined on its merits. As has been seen in the context of locus standi/standing,[70] the plaintiff in the case of *Crotty v An Taoiseach*[71] sought an injunction to prevent the Government from ratifying the Single European Act. He argued that the European Communities (Amendment) Act 1986 was not constitutional. Barrington J., finding that the Single European Act could enter into force and become constitutionally unassailable, determined that the balance of convenience was ultimately in favour of granting the injunction. He granted the interlocutory injunction sought in order to preserve the status quo.[72]

(b) Right to Earn Livelihood

10–50 The invasion of constitutional rights in the context of breaches of the Road Transport Act 1932 was considered in some detail in two cases, *Parsons v Kavanagh*[73] and *Lovett v Gogan*.[74] In *Parsons*, O'Hanlon J. had found that:

> "the constitutional right to earn one's livelihood by any lawful means carries with it the entitlement to be protected against any unlawful activity on the part of another person or persons which materially impairs or infringes that right."[75]

10–51 He thus granted the injunction sought to prevent the operation of an unlicensed passenger bus service.

---

[69] [2001] 4 I.R. 655 at 660.
[70] See Ch.3, Standing, para.3–06.
[71] [1987] I.R. 713.
[72] However, see *Slattery v An Taoiseach* [1993] 1 I.R. 286, in which an (ultimately unsuccessful) attempt was made to stop a referendum on the Maastricht Treaty. Hederman J. held that there could be "no injunction against the Government to prevent them from carrying out the directions of the Oireachtas."
[73] [1990] I.L.R.M. 560 at 566.
[74] [1995] 3 I.R. 132; [1995] 1 I.L.R.M. 12.
[75] [1990] I.L.R.M. 560 at 566. See also, *Yeates v Minister for Posts and Telegraphs* [1978] I.L.R.M. 22 and the reference therein to "the constitutional right to earn a livelihood" and the dictum of Walsh J. in *Murphy v Stewart* [1973] I.R. 97 in relation to the right to work. In *O'Connor v Williams* [2001] 1 I.R. 248 Barron J. refused the relief sought by the plaintiffs on the basis that the implementation of the applicable criminal law was the most appropriate remedy in the circumstances.

10–52 Subsequently, in *Lovett v Gogan* Finlay C.J., similarly dealing with an unlicensed motor coach passenger service, held that the plaintiff was entitled to an injunction if he could establish that it was the only way of protecting him from the threatened invasion of his constitutional rights.[76]

(c) Dissolution of Dáil Éireann

10–53 In the case of *O'Malley v An Taoiseach*,[77] an ex parte application for interim injunctive relief was brought in an attempt to restrain the Taoiseach from advising the President of Ireland to dissolve Dáil Éireann, pending the enactment of legislation by the Oireachtas revising Dáil Éireann constituencies. Hamilton P. refused the relief sought. He held, inter alia, that the constitutional duty of dissolving Dáil Éireann vests in the President of Ireland, and that the President is not answerable to any court for the exercise and performance of that duty. He found that the courts have no jurisdiction to place any impediment in the way of the President in the matter, a matter he found to be the sole prerogative of the President.

(d) Dissemination of Information

10–54 In the case of *Society for the Protection of Unborn Children (Ireland) Ltd v Grogan*,[78] Finlay C.J. stated that the application brought seeking an interlocutory injunction was in the nature of an application to restrain an activity which had been clearly declared by the court to be unconstitutional and therefore unlawful. He held that such activity could assist and was intended to assist in the destruction of the right to life of an unborn child, a right acknowledged and protected under the Constitution.[79] In *Attorney General (SPUC) v Open Door Counselling Ltd (No. 2)*,[80] the Supreme Court granted a perpetual injunction preventing the defendants from, inter alia, disseminating information in regard to the obtaining of abortions outside the jurisdiction.

3. Interlocutory Considerations

10–55 The *Campus Oil* principles apply when considering an application for an interlocutory injunction in the context of a constitutional right.[81] Finlay C.J. held in *Pesca Valentia Ltd v Minister for Fisheries*[82] that he was not satisfied that

---

[76] [1995] 3 I.R. 132 at 142; [1995] 1 I.L.R.M. 12 at 20.
[77] [1990] I.L.R.M. 461.
[78] [1989] I.R. 753; [1990] I.L.R.M. 350.
[79] [1989] I.R. 753 at 764; [1990] I.L.R.M. 350 at 356.
[80] [1994] 2 I.R. 333; [1994] 1 I.L.R.M. 256.
[81] As to which, see Ch.6, Interlocutory Applications.
[82] [1985] I.R. 193; [1986] I.L.R.M. 68. Applied in, inter alia, *Carrigaline Community Television Broadcasting Co Ltd v Minister for Transport, Energy and Communications* [1994] 2 I.R. 359.

"there is any special principle applicable to an application for an interlocutory injunction of this kind."[83] Particular consideration has been given to the question of the balance of convenience in the context of constitutional rights.

(a) The Balance of Convenience

10–56 In the case of *Society for the Protection of Unborn Children (Ireland) Ltd v Grogan*[84] Finlay C.J. had stated in relation to the balance of convenience that he was satisfied that:

> "where an injunction is sought to protect a constitutional right, the only matter which could properly be capable of being weighed in the balance against the granting of such a protection would be another competing constitutional right."[85]

10–57 As observed by Kelly J. in *Controller of Patents, Designs and Trademarks v Ireland*,[86] the presumption of constitutionality must be weighed in the balance both when deciding whether there is a serious issue to be tried, and also where the balance of convenience lies.[87]

10–58 However, in the case of *Foley v Sunday Newspapers Ltd*,[88] Kelly J. rejected the submission that once a plaintiff seeks an injunction to protect a constitutional right the balance of convenience is recalibrated so as to permit only the consideration of another competing constitutional right. He observed that, "to apply this approach could give rise to injustice and abuses of process."[89] Kelly J. found that the dictum of Finlay C.J. did not have universal application regardless of the facts. In the *SPUC* case, the activity which the defendants were intending to pursue had been determined to be unlawful having regard to Art.40 of the Constitution. Kelly J. was concerned that:

> "A formulaic assertion of a claim to protect a constitutional right without any analysis of the background against which it was made being open to the court and an ability only to consider on the balance of convenience a competing constitutional right could give rise to considerable injustice."

10–59 This was particularly having regard to the strong guarantees in relation to freedom of expression in the Constitution.[90]

---

83 [1985] I.R. 193 at 201; [1986] I.L.R.M. 68 at 72.
84 [1989] I.R. 753; [1990] I.L.R.M. 350.
85 [1989] I.R. 753 at 765; [1990] I.L.R.M. 350 at 357.
86 [2001] 4 I.R. 229.
87 [2001] 4 I.R. 229 at 237.
88 [2005] 1 I.R. 88.
89 [2005] 1 I.R. 88 at 101.
90 Referring to the decision of O'Hanlon J. in *Maguire v Drury* [1994] 2 I.R. 8; [1995] 1 I.L.R.M.

E. CONTRACT LAW

1. Introduction[91]

10–60 As has been seen, contracts of employment attract particular considerations in terms of the granting or otherwise of an injunction.[92] Employment contracts apart, once a valid contract is in force[93] a guiding principle is that the courts will grant an injunction to enforce a particular negative promise in the agreement.[94] Specific performance may be used to seek the performance of a positive obligation.[95] However, what seems to be a relatively straightforward distinction is not always entirely clear. Furthermore, as noted by Halsbury:

"In the case of a positive contract, the court will sometimes import a negative covenant not to do anything inconsistent with the contract, and grant an injunction to restrain the breach of this implied covenant."[96]

10–61 As will be seen, the applicable test at the interlocutory stage has also been the subject of some discussion and it would seem that the law is not firmly resolved one way or the other in that respect.

2. General Application

10–62 The general principles applicable to contracts can be divided into a consideration of circumstances where a negative promise is contained in a contract and circumstances where it is sought to enforce a positive obligation.

(a) Negative Promise

10–63 The general approach of the courts is that the granting of an injunction to enforce a negative promise in an agreement does nothing more than sanction what the parties concerned have already contracted for. As such, the parties have the right to have such a promise enforced.[97] In *Irish Shell Ltd v Elm Motors Ltd,*[98]

---

108 as an example of the importance of freedom of expression. Kelly J. also made reference to Art.10 of the European Convention on Human Rights.

91 See generally, McDermott, *Contract Law* (Dublin: Butterworths, 2001); Clark, *Contract Law*, 4th edn (Dublin: Round Hall Sweet and Maxwell, 1998) and *Chitty on Contracts Vol. I General Principles*, 29th edn (London: Thomson Sweet & Maxwell, 2004).

92 See Ch.9, Employment.

93 See *Central Meat Products Co Ltd v Carney* [1944] Ir. Jur. Rep. 34, in which an injunction was refused as no enforceable contract existed between the plaintiffs and the defendant.

94 *Lumley v Wagner* (1852) 1 De G.M. & G. 604.

95 See Ch.1, Domestic Jurisdiction, para.1–55. See generally, *Widowerhood Chemical Co v Hardman* [1891] 2 Ch. 416; *Mortimer v Beckett* [1920] 1 Ch. 571.

96 *Halsbury's Laws of England* Vol. 24 (reissue), para.899.

97 See, inter alia, *National Provincial Bank of England v Marshall* (1888) 40 Ch D 112.

98 [1984] I.R. 200; [1982] I.L.R.M. 519.

Costello J. took the view that the parties concerned had contracted with their eyes open. He felt that "it is the courts duty to see that that contract which in my judgment is an enforceable one, is carried out."[99] In so saying, Costello J. had regard to the statement of Lord Cairns L.C. in *Doherty v Allman*.[100] In that case, the Lord Chancellor had stated that:

> "If parties, for valuable consideration, with their eyes open, contract that a particular thing shall not be done, all that a court of equity has to do is to say, by way of injunction, that which the parties have already said by way of covenant, that the thing shall not be done; and in such cases the injunction does nothing more than give the sanction of the process of the court to that which is the contract between the parties. It is not then a question of the balance of convenience or inconvenience or of the amount of damage or of injury—it is the specific performance, by the court, of that negative bargain which the parties have made, with their eyes open, between themselves."[101]

10–64 However, it was made clear in *Shaw v Applegate*[102] that the statement in *Doherty* must be applied having regard to the considerations in each individual case and that wider discretionary considerations must be applied when an injunction of a mandatory nature is sought.[103]

(b) *Implying a Negative Stipulation*

10–65 It was held in the old case of *Wolverhampton and Walsall Railway Co v London and North-Western Railway Co*,[104] that if a contract contains no express stipulation of a negative nature, a court may in fact imply such a stipulation, having regard to the substance of the agreement.[105]

(c) *Positive Obligations*

10–66 In *Braddon Towers Ltd v International Stores Ltd*,[106] Slade J. observed that:

> "for many years practitioners have advised their clients that it is the settled and invariable practice of the court never to grant mandatory injunctions requiring persons to carry on business."[107]

---

99   [1984] I.R. 200 at 217; [1982] I.L.R.M. 519 at 532.
100 (1878) 3 App. Cas. 709.
101 (1878) 3 App. Cas. 709 at 720.
102 [1977] 1 W.L.R. 970 at 975, per Buckley L.J.
103 See, for example, *Shepherd Homes Ltd v Sandham* [1971] Ch. 340; [1970] 3 W.L.R. 348; [1970] 3 All E.R. 402.
104 (1873) L.R. 16 Eq. 433 at 440, per Lord Selborne.
105 See, for example, *Metropolitan Electric Supply Co v Ginder* [1901] 2 Ch. 799. See also *Irish Shell Ltd v Elm Motors Ltd* [1984] I.R. 200; [1982] I.L.R.M. 519.
106 (1987) 1 E.G.L.R. 209.
107 (1987) 1 E.G.L.R. 209 at 213. Referred to by Lord Hoffmann in *Co-Operative Insurance v Argyll Stores Ltd* [1998] A.C. 1; [1997] 2 W.L.R. 898; [1997] 3 All E.R. 297.

10–67 As explained by Spry, this is because when positive obligations of a contract are sought to be enforced, discretionary factors such as hardship are much more relevant.[108]

3. Interlocutory Considerations

10–68 The principles set out in *Doherty v Allman*[109] were also applied at the interlocutory stage in the case of *Dublin Port and Docks Board v Brittania Dredging Co Ltd.*[110] In that case, O'Dalaigh C.J. pointed out that the court was not concerned to examine either the balance of convenience or the amount of damage; the parties had entered into a negative covenant and it was the court's duty to hold the defendants to their bargain pending the trial. However, in the later case of *TMG Group Ltd v Al Babtain Trading and Contracting Co.*[111] Keane J. distinguished the facts before him from those in *Brittania Dredging*. He took the view that O'Dalaigh C.J. had not laid down any general principles in the latter case to the effect that:

> "in all cases where the plaintiff establishes a *prima facie* case[112] of a breach of a negative stipulation in a contract, the court could disregard any question of the balance of convenience between the parties."

10–69 Keane J. felt that O'Dalaigh C.J.'s observations were:

> "clearly confined to a case where one party to a contract was proposing to act in breach of a negative covenant ... in circumstances where the court was not satisfied on the evidence that they were entitled to do so."

10–70 These views were subsequently endorsed by McCarthy J. in *Irish Shell Ltd v Elm Motors Ltd.*[113]

10–71 Nonetheless, in *Irish Shell Ltd v JH McLoughlin (Balbriggan) Ltd,*[114] Clarke J. had regard to the *Dublin Port and Docks* approach as a factor to be

---

[108] Spry, *The Principles of Equitable Remedies*, 6th edn (London: Sweet and Maxwell, 2001), p.586.

[109] (1878) 3 App. Cas. 709.

[110] [1968] I.R. 136.

[111] [1982] I.L.R.M. 349.

[112] [1982] I.L.R.M. 349 at 353. The use of the term "prima facie" predated the consideration of what the appropriate test should in fact be in the *Campus Oil* case; see Ch.6, Interlocutory Injunctions, para.6–36.

[113] [1984] I.R. 200. In *Premier Dairies v Doyle* [1996] 1 I.L.R.M. 363 O'Flaherty J. appeared to accept that if he had not been dealing with ss.4 and 5 of the Competition Act 1991, a "rather complex piece of legislation", he would have found the case to come within the *Brittania Dredging* principles, but there appears to be little other judicial support for suggesting that *Brittania Dredging* might in fact have set down general principles applicable to breaches of negative covenants.

[114] unreported, High Court, Clarke J., August 4, 2005.

taken into account in the grant of an interlocutory injunction. A relevant consideration in that regard was that in that case a permanent injunction might have been of little benefit if obtained at trial having regard to the purpose for which the covenant concerned had supposedly been entered into.

10–72 It thus appears that the *Doherty/Dublin Port and Docks* approach is the one preferred by the courts at present in general terms, but that the specific terms of the contract before the court in each case will ultimately determine the approach which the court should take.

F. CRIMINAL LAW

1. Introduction

10–73 A burgeoning area of the law concerns applications in relation to the prosecution of alleged criminal offences. As part of the process of judicial review, injunctions are often sought to prevent such prosecution or further prosecution. Whilst the area of criminal law in general terms is a specialised, relatively self-contained area, which merits entirely separate treatment,[115] some of the key areas in which injunctions are sought will be set out.

2. Rationale for an Injunction

10–74 It was explained in *DPP v PO'C*,[116] a case concerning alleged sex offences, that:

> "the correct way to proceed in cases such as this is by way of prohibition where the court is an inferior court, and by way of injunction against the Director of Public Prosecutions where the prosecution is in the Central Criminal Court."

10–75 The rationale for this approach included the fact that:

> "From a procedural and practical point of view also, orders of prohibition and injunctions allow a framework within which issues of fact can be determined, and in delay cases issues of fact are of primary importance, as the applicant must not only show delay, but must also show prejudice, which is a pure question of fact."

---

[115] See generally, Charleton, McDermott & Bolger, *Criminal Law* (Dublin: Butterworths, 1999).
[116] unreported, Court of Criminal Appeal, January 27, 2003, McCracken J. giving the judgment of the court.

10–76 It was held by Geoghegan J. in the Supreme Court in the case of *BF v DPP*[117] that where no judge was named as a respondent to the proceedings, the appropriate order was for an injunction restraining the Director of Public Prosecutions from proceeding further with the prosecution concerned, rather than an order of prohibition.

3. General Application

(a) Stopping Criminal Prosecutions

10–77 The starting point for a consideration of attempts to stop criminal prosecutions is the basic principle that the right to trial with reasonable expedition is an essential feature of the law.[118] The court must determine between vindicating the rights of the accused person, by prohibiting the trial, and upholding the continued prosecution of the accused in the common good.[119] The key factors which must be taken into account by the court were identified by McKechnie J. in the case of *BJ v DPP*[120]:

- Where, due to delay, the right to a fair trial is prejudices, the appropriate remedy to vindicate a person's constitutional right is by way of an order of prohibition or injunction.[121]
- An accused person has a right to have a trial with reasonable expedition.[122]
- An accused person's right to a trial in due course of law must include, not only the concept but also the implementation of fairness right throughout that process.
- There is no statutory time limit on the institution of a prosecution in respect of serious crime.
- Where delay is an issue, a consideration of whether it is complainant delay or prosecutorial delay will arise; the former involves delay by the complainant in initiating a complaint, the latter involves the delay in actually prosecuting the person concerned. An examination of the reasons for this also arise, as the nature of the crime itself, without more, could not be a reason for a court's refusal to grant relief, if otherwise it was appropriate to so do. As will be seen, it is the effect of the delay, as distinct from the fact of the delay itself, which is often the key consideration.

---

[117] [2001] 1 I.R. 656.
[118] See *DPP v Byrne* [1994] 2 I.R. 236.
[119] See, for example, *TH v DPP*, unreported, High Court, McKechnie J., March 9, 2004. The Supreme Court decision is reported at [2006] 3 I.R. 520.
[120] unreported, High Court, McKechnie J, February 12, 2002. The dismissed appeal is reported at [2003] 4 I.R. 525.
[121] McKechnie J. citing *State (O'Connell) v Fawsitt* [1986] I.R. 362.
[122] See *DPP v Byrne* [1994] 2 I.R. 236 and *Knowles v Malone*, unreported, High Court, McKechnie J., April 6, 2001.

- If, on an analysis of the relevant material, it is shown that there is a real risk of an unfair trial, then its continuation will be stopped. Such an analysis would include consideration of the rights of society, such as those which stem from its responsibility to invoke due process for all its citizens.
- Each case, both the general and specific, must ultimately depend on its individual circumstances with the result that any list of factors which must be considered, no matter how detailed, cannot be conclusive.
- There is a category of cases, however which are called "special cases" and which require additional analysis. This category includes allegations involving child sexual abuse.[123]

(i) Criminal or Civil Case

10–78 As is clear from the decision of Abbott J. in *Murray v Commission to Inquire into Child Abuse*,[124] a distinction must be drawn between civil and criminal cases in relation to delay, in that:

> "the balance between the right to a fair trial and the right of the public and the complainant to have the complaint heard are brought into balance in a context which is much different and favours the respondent much more than in civil cases and indeed much more again than in the case of a respondent before the Committee."[125]

(ii) Prosecutorial Delay

10–79 The question of prosecutorial delay was considered in the case of *PM v Malone*.[126] Keane C.J. made reference to the balancing exercise required in circumstances where prosecutorial delay is alleged. He stated that:

> "The essential issue for resolution is, accordingly, as to whether the stress and anxiety caused to the applicant as a result of the violation of his constitutional right to a reasonable expeditious trial justifies the prohibition of the trial proceeding at this stage. If this were a case in which it could be said that his ability to defend himself had been impaired and, as a result, there was a real and substantial risk of an unfair trial then, as pointed out by Denham J. in *D. v D.P.P.* [1994] 2 I.R. 465, the applicant's right to a fair trial would necessarily outweigh the community's right to prosecute. Where, as here, the violation of the right has not jeopardised the right to a fair trial, but has caused unnecessary stress and anxiety to the applicant, the court must engage in a balancing process. On one side of the scales, there is the right of the accused

---

[123]   See the dictum of Finlay C.J. to this effect in *Hogan v President of the Circuit Court* [1994] 2 I.R. 513 at 521; *DPP v G* [1994] 1 I.R. 58 and *B v DPP* [1997] 3 I.R. 140.
[124]   [2004] 2 I.R. 222.
[125]   [2004] 2 I.R. 222 at 302.
[126]   [2002] 2 I.R. 560.

to be protected from stress and anxiety caused by an unnecessary and inordinate delay. On the other side, there is the public interest in the prosecution and conviction of those guilty of criminal offences. In all such cases, the court will necessarily be concerned with the nature of the offence and the extent of the delay."[127]

10–80 This dictum is clear on its own terms as to the factors which a court will take into account when considering the issue of prosecutorial delay.

(iii) "Special Cases"

10–81 As identified by McKechnie J. in *BJ v DPP*,[128] there is a category of "special cases" which require additional analysis. These are child sexual abuse cases, the special position of which was noted by Finlay C.J. in the case of *G v DPP*.[129]

Effect of Delay

10–82 As is clear from the key decision of the Supreme Court in the case of *H v DPP*,[130] the test to be applied in such cases to determine if there would be a fair trial is whether there is a real or serious risk that the applicant, by reason of the delay, would not obtain a fair trial, or that a trial would be unfair as a consequence of the delay. The Supreme Court also recast the relevant applicable test, holding that it was no longer necessary for the court to inquire into the reasons for the delay or whether the accused had exercised dominion over the complainant or to make assumptions as to the truth of the complaints. The question of the effect of the delay became central.

10–83 In the course of his judgment in *H*, Murray C.J. traced the development of the law in this area, referring to *B v DPP*,[131] *D v DPP*[132] and *PC v DPP*.[133] Those cases considered both the reasons for delay, as well as the effect of the delay.[134] This was well articulated by Keane J. in *PC v DPP*,[135] in which he stated that:

"Manifestly, in cases where the court is asked to prohibit the continuance of a prosecution on the ground of unreasonable delay, the paramount concern of

---

[127] [2002] 2 I.R. 560 at 581. See also the decision of Kearns J. in *PM v DPP* [2006] 3 I.R. 172.
[128] unreported, High Court, McKechnie J., February 12, 2002. The Supreme Court decision is reported at [2003] 4 I.R. 525.
[129] [1994] 1 I.R. 374 at 380. See also, *Hogan v President of the Circuit Court* [1994] 2 I.R. 513.
[130] [2006] 3 I.R. 575. See also, *PT v DPP*, unreported, Supreme Court, July 31, 2007.
[131] [1997] 3 I.R. 140.
[132] [1994] 2 I.R. 465.
[133] [1999] 2 I.R. 25.
[134] *Guihen v DPP* [2005] 3 I.R. 23.
[135] [1999] 2 I.R. 25.

the court will be whether it has been established that there is a real and serious risk of an unfair trial: that, after all, is what is meant by the guarantee of a trial 'in due course of law'. The delay may be such that, depending on the nature of the charges, a trial should not be allowed to proceed, even though it has not been demonstrated that the capacity of the accused to defend himself or herself will be impaired. In other cases, the first inquiry must be as to what are the reasons for the delay and, in a case such as the present where no blame can be attached to the prosecuting authorities, whether the court is satisfied as a matter of probability that, assuming the complaint to be truthful, the delay in making it was referable to the accused's own actions.

If that stage has been reached, the final issue to be determined will be whether the degree to which the accused's ability to defend himself has been impaired is such that the trial should not be allowed to proceed. That is a necessary inquiry, in my view, in every such case, because, given that the finding that the delay is explicable by reference to the conduct of the accused is necessarily grounded on an assumption as to the truth of the complaint, it follows that, in the light of the presumption of innocence to which he is entitled, the court asked to halt the trial must still consider whether the degree of prejudice is such as to give rise to a real and serious risk of an unfair trial".[136]

Revised Test Summarised

10–84 In holding in *H* that it was no longer necessary to consider the reasons for the delay, Murray C.J. summarised by restating the relevant test as being:

> "whether there is a real or serious risk that the applicant, by reason of the delay, would not obtain a fair trial, or that a trial would be unfair as a consequence of the delay. The test is to be applied in light of the circumstances of the case."[137]

10–85 He concluded by saying:

> "In this case the developing jurisprudence as to delay in bringing a prosecution for offences of child sexual abuse was considered by the court. I am satisfied that in general there is no necessity to hold an inquiry into, or to establish the reasons for, delay in making a complaint. The issue for a court is whether the delay has resulted in prejudice to an accused so as to give rise to a real or serious risk of an unfair trial. The court does not exclude wholly exceptional circumstances where it would be unfair or unjust to put an accused on trial."[138]

---

[136] [1999] 2 I.R. 25 at 68. The question of the inhibition of the complainant was considered in *PL v Buttimer* [2004] 4 I.R. 494 and *DD v DPP* [2004] 3 I.R. 172. See also, *PC v DPP* [1999] 2 I.R. 25.

[137] [2006] 3 I.R. 575 at 620.

[138] [2006] 3 I.R. 575 at 622.

10–86 Where wholly exceptional circumstances are involved, precedents are of relatively limited value and the court will have to consider a case on its own merits. This is clear from the subsequent dictum of Denham J. in the Supreme Court in the case of *PT v DPP*.[139]

(b) Road Traffic Offences

10–87 An injunction may be sought by way of judicial review restraining prosecution or further prosecution in relation to certain road traffic offences. For example, in the case of *Landers v DPP*,[140] the interventions of a District Court judge were found to have prevented a trial in accordance with constitutional requirements. The question before Kearns J. was whether it would be fair in the exceptional circumstances of the case, or a proper exercise of the court's discretion, to remit the matter for a further trial before the District Court. The exceptional circumstances included the fact that the hearing of the prosecution against the applicant had taken most of the day in the District Court, with a large number of civilian and Garda witnesses called by the prosecution. The interventions by the District Court Judge and the nature of those interventions had been found by O'Caoimh J. to have prevented a trial in accordance with constitutional requirements. Kearns J. took the view that it would not be proper to remit the matter for a further trial. In reviewing the case as a whole, Kearns J. was of the view that the "overall unfairness" of the original District Court hearing was such as to persuade him to make the injunction order sought. Kearns J. also held that the failure of the applicant to seek to injunct the respondent from further attempting to prosecute him in an earlier set of judicial review proceedings did not preclude him from seeking that form of relief in a second set of proceedings. This was in circumstances where it was reasonable for both the applicant and his legal advisers to take the view, based on existing jurisprudence and the unusual facts of the particular case, that a fresh prosecution of the applicant would not be sought.

(c) Preservation of Evidence

10–88 Attempts have been made to seek to injunction to stop a prosecution on the basis that potential evidence has not been preserved. In *Murphy v DPP*,[141] the applicant's solicitors requested access to a car involved in an incident less than five weeks after the initial charges, and while the car was in the possession of the Gardaí. The Gardaí initially informed the applicant's solicitor that the car was available for inspection, but a week later they allowed an insurance company to remove the vehicle, before it had been examined on behalf of the applicant or the Gardaí themselves. Lynch J. granted an injunction restraining

---

[139]   unreported, Supreme Court, July 31, 2007.
[140]   [2004] 2 I.R. 363.
[141]   [1989] I.L.R.M. 71.

the DPP from proceeding. Applying the principles set out in *Dillon v O'Brien*,[142] he stated that evidence relevant to guilt or innocence must, so far as is necessary and practicable, be kept until the conclusion of the trial, with an accused person to be afforded every reasonable opportunity to inspect all material evidence which is under the control and power of the prosecuting authorities in order adequately to prepare his defence. Removing evidence, as in *Murphy*, amounted to a breach of the rule of fair procedures in that it deprived the applicant of the reasonable possibility of rebutting the evidence proffered against him.[143]

(i) Real and Serious Risk of Unfair Trial

10–89 In *Braddish v DPP*,[144] Hardiman J. made clear that it was the duty of the Gardaí, arising from their unique investigative role, to seek out and preserve all evidence having a bearing or potential bearing on the issue of guilt or innocence, although acknowledged that such a duty had to be interpreted realistically on the facts of each case.[145]

10–90 It is important that an applicant seeking to injunct a prosecution can show a real and serious risk of an unfair trial by virtue of evidence not having been preserved. This is clear from, inter alia, *McGrath v DPP*.[146] In that case the applicant sought an injunction restraining further prosecution of her under s.53 of the Road Traffic Act 1961. She contended that the breaking up of the motorcycle which had been driven by the person who had died as a result of the collision between the applicant's car and the motorcycle had deprived her of evidence relevant to the preparation of her defence. The injunction was refused on the basis that a duty on the Gardaí to keep evidence relevant to guilt or innocence so far as it is necessary or practicable until the end of the trial could not be precisely or exhaustively defined in words of general application. It had to be interpreted realistically on the facts of each case and could not be interpreted as requiring the Gardaí to engage in disproportionate commitment of manpower.[147] Applying *R. (Ebrahim) v Feltham Court*,[148] Murphy J. held that the applicant had not shown that, on the balance of probabilities, she would suffer serious or any prejudice to the extent that no fair trial could be held.

---

142   (1887) 20 L.R. 300.
143   Applying *State (Healy) v Donoghue* [1976] I.R. 300; *cf. Rogers v DPP* [1992] I.L.R.M. 695, in which O'Hanlon J. refused an injunction on the facts.
144   [2001] 3 I.R. 127.
145   [2001] 3 I.R. 127 at 133 and 135. See also, *Dunne v DPP* [2002] 2 I.L.R.M. 241; *Bowes v DPP* [2003] 2 I.R. 25.
146   unreported, High Court, Murphy J., December 20, 2001.
147   Following *Murphy v DPP* [1989] I.L.R.M. 71 and *Braddish v DPP* [2001] 3 I.R. 127.
148   [2001] 1 W.L.R. 1293.

4. Prosecution by the Director of Public Prosecutions

10–91 By virtue of s.2(5) of the Prosecution of Offences Act 1974, the Director of Public Prosecutions is independent in the performance of his functions, and has a discretion as to whether or not to prosecute. In *State (McCormack) v Curran*,[149] Walsh J. observed that the actions of the DPP are not outside the scope of review by the courts and stated that if the DPP:

> "oversteps or attempts to overstep his function he can, if necessary, be restrained by injunction but I do not think any step he takes or any action or omission which is *ultra vires* can be of the nature of orders which attract certiorari. A failure to perform his statutory duties could however be the subject of mandamus."[150]

G. EUROPEAN LAW

1. Introduction

10–92 Under Irish law a party may seek an injunction to enforce the provisions of European Community law which is directly effective.[151] Community law rights are to be vindicated in accordance with domestic procedure rules.[152]

10–93 One issue which is less certain is the test to be applied in the context of interim and interlocutory injunctions when a challenge is brought to a Community measure.

2. Enforcing the Provisions of Community Law

10–94 The position of the courts in this jurisdiction when a provision of the Treaty of Rome is to be enforced, and the implications in terms of interlocutory injunctions, was considered by Keane J. in the High Court in the case of *Campus Oil Ltd v Minister for Energy (No. 2)*.[153] He stated that he accepted:

> "entirely the obligation of the court to enforce not merely the Constitution of Ireland and the laws of this State, but also the provisions of the Treaty, being

---

[149] [1987] I.L.R.M. 225 at 238.
[150] Referred to in *H v DPP* [1994] 2 I.R. 589; [1994] 2 I.L.R.M. 285.
[151] See, for example, *Dunlea v Nissan (Irl) Ltd*, unreported, High Court, Barr J., May 24, 1990. See also *R. v Secretary of State for Transport, Ex p. Factortame Ltd (No 2.)* [1991] 1 A.C. 603; [1991] 1 All E.R. 70.
[152] See Case 158/80 *Rewe Handelsgesellschaft Nord mbH v Hauptzollamt Kiel* [1981] E.C.R. 1805 at 1841.
[153] [1983] I.R. 88; [1984] I.L.R.M. 45.

also part of the law of the State. However, that does not preclude the court from continuing to exercise its traditional jurisdiction in relation to the granting of interlocutory injunctions where the applicant raises a fair question as to whether a particular right he asserts is being violated and where both the balance of convenience between the parties and the desirability of preserving the status quo are in favour of granting such relief. To depart from that principle would be not merely contrary to well-settled authority, but might also hinder the objects of the Treaty itself and institutions established thereunder since it would seem proper that, in an appropriate case, the status quo should be preserved by interlocutory order so far as is consistent with the rights of the parties, pending the determination of the issue in question by the Court of Justice of the European Communities. Support for this view of the law is to be found in the decision of the Court of Justice in *Hoffman La-Roche v Centrafarm*."[154]

10–95 As has been held by the European Court of Justice (ECJ), it is for the domestic legal system of each Member State to determine the procedural conditions governing actions at law intended to ensure the protection of the rights which citizens have from the direct effect of community law.[155]

10–96 In *Martin v An Bord Pleanála*,[156] O'Sullivan J held, following the decision in *Pesca Valentia Ltd v Minister for Fisheries*,[157] that in such circumstances, on an interlocutory application the applicable principles are those enunciated by the Supreme Court in *Campus Oil*, notwithstanding that the matter concerned European Directives.

3. Challenging Community Law

10–97 The applicable test would appear, however, to be different where a ruling is sought from the ECJ in circumstances where it is claimed that a Community measure is invalid.[158]

10–98 Article 186 of the Treaty confers the power to prescribe any interim measures. The case of *Atlanta Fruchthandelsgesellschaft mbH v Bundesamt für Ernährung und Forstwirtschaft*[159] concerned a dispute before a national court as

---

[154] [1983] I.R. 88 at 100; [1984] I.L.R.M. 45 at 55.
[155] Case C–33/76 *Rewe-Zentral Finanz AG v Landwirtschaftskammer für das Saarland* [1976] E.C.R. 1989.
[156] unreported, High Court, O'Sullivan J., July 24, 2002.
[157] [1985] I.R. 193; [1986] I.L.R.M. 68. Applied in, inter alia, *Carrigaline Community Television Broadcasting Co Ltd v Minister for Transport, Energy and Communications* [1994] 2 I.R. 359.
[158] See generally Wyatt and Dashwood, *European Union Law*, 5th edn (London: Sweet and Maxwell, 2006), p.217. See also Anderson and Demetriou, *References to the European Court* (London: Sweet and Maxwell, 2002), p.206.
[159] Case C–465/93 [1995] E.C.R. I–3761. See also, Joined Cases C–143/88 and C–92/89 *Zuckerfabrik Suederdithmarschen and Zuckerfabrik Soest* [1991] E.C.R. I–415.

to the legality of a Regulation in the context of an action brought against a national implementing measure. Two questions were raised for the consideration of the ECJ, one of which concerned the appropriate test to be applied when adopting interim measures.

10–99 It was held by the ECJ that Art.189 of the Treaty:

> "does not preclude national courts from granting interim relief to settle or regulate the disputed legal positions or relationships with reference to a national administrative measure based on a Community regulation which is the subject of a reference for a preliminary ruling on its validity."

10–100 In the earlier case of *Zuckerfabrik Suederdithmarschen and Zuckerfabrik Soest*,[160] the ECJ had held[161] that interim measures could be adopted only if the factual and legal circumstances relied on by the applicants are such as to persuade the national court that "serious doubts"[162] exist as to the validity of the Community Regulation on which the contested administrative measure is based.

10–101 In *Atlanta*, the court again referred to "serious doubts", stating that:

> "For the national court to be able to order such interim relief, it must entertain serious doubts as to the validity of the Community act and state them in its decision."

10–102 The use of the phrase "serious doubts" would suggest that the test to be used by the national courts is in fact not the usual *Campus Oil* test. It would appear to be a higher standard than a bona fide/fair question test. This point appeared to be accepted by the House of Lords in the case of *R. v Secretary of State for Health, Ex p. Imperial Tobacco Ltd*.[163] It has been suggested that such a test stops the over-hasty grant of interim orders, the granting of which could prejudice uniform application of Community law.[164]

H. JUDICIAL REVIEW

1. Introduction

10–103 Order 84 r.25 of the Rules of the Superior Courts provides that any interlocutory application may be made to the court in proceedings for judicial review. It reads:

[160] [1991] E.C.R. I–415.
[161] para.23.
[162] para.33.
[163] [2000] 2 W.L.R. 834.
[164] See generally, Wyatt and Dashwood, *European Union Law*, 5th edn (London: Sweet and Maxwell, 2006), p.217.

"1. Any interlocutory application may be made to the court in proceedings in an application for judicial review. In this rule 'interlocutory application' includes an application for an order under Order 31, or Order 39, rule 1 or for an order dismissing the proceedings by consent of the parties'."

10–104 It has been accepted by the courts that the use of the phrase "interlocutory application" in Ord.84 r.25(1) is sufficiently wide to encompass an application for an injunction on foot of an application for judicial review.[165] However, as pointed out by Barr J. in *Murphy v Turf Club*,[166] the jurisdiction of the court to grant an injunction on an application for judicial review is confined to the review of activities of a public nature.[167]

2. Seeking an Injunction Prior to Seeking Leave

10–105 In *Harding v Cork Co. Council*,[168] Kelly J. accepted that the court had jurisdiction to grant an injunction prior to granting leave to apply for judicial review. This was based on both RSC Ord.84 r.25, and by reference to the court's inherent jurisdiction to make such an order. In that regard, Kelly J. followed the decision of the House of Lords in the English case of *M v Home Office*,[169] in which Lord Woolf had quoted from note 53/1-14/24 to *The Supreme Court Practice 1993*:

> "Where the case is so urgent as to justify it [the judge] could grant an interlocutory injunction or other interim relief pending the hearing of the application for leave to move for judicial review. But, if the judge has refused leave to move for judicial review he is *functus officio* and has no jurisdiction to grant any form of interim relief. The application for an interlocutory injunction or other interim relief could, however, be renewed before the Court of Appeal along with the renewal of the application to move for judicial review."[170]

---

[165] *Harding v Cork Co Council* [2006] 1 I.R. 294; [2006] 2 I.L.R.M. 392. As explained by Kelly J. in that case: "The definition which follows from the first sentence of O. 84, r. 25(1) is inclusive and not exclusive. Rules of court ought not to be construed as to give rise to an absurd result." It was reported in the *Irish Times* of February 1, 2008 that Cardinal Desmond Connell had secured leave from the High Court to bring a judicial review challenge (reported in the *Irish Times* of February 12, 2008 as subsequently having been withdrawn) to the Dublin Diocesan Commission of Investigation's handling of the discovery of documents which it is claimed are legally privileged. An interim injunction was also secured restraining the Commission from examining the documents in question. See also RSC Ord.84 r.18(2).

[166] [1989] 1 I.R. 171.

[167] [1989] 1 I.R. 171 at 175. Following *Law v National Greyhound Racing Club Ltd* [1983] 3 All E.R. 300.

[168] [2006] 1 I.R. 294; [2006] 2 I.L.R.M. 392.

[169] [1994] 1 A.C. 377; [1993] 3 All E.R. 537.

[170] [1994] 1 A.C. 377 at 423; [1993] 3 All E.R. 537 at 565. See also, *YD (Turkey) v Secretary of State for the Home Department* [2006] 1 W.L.R. 1646, also cited by Kelly J. in *Harding*.

10–106 Kelly J. stated that the position in this jurisdiction was exactly the same. He felt that the court must have such jurisdiction, "otherwise the whole exercise embarked upon by the applicant could be rendered futile."[171]

3. Interlocutory Considerations

10–107 An application for leave for judicial review is generally made ex parte in accordance with the provisions of RSC Ord.84 r.20(2). As noted by Keane C.J. in *McDonnell v Brady*,[172] the usual threshold for granting leave to seek judicial review is "relatively low". In *Smart Mobile Ltd v Commission For Communications Regulation*,[173] Kelly J. observed that it was at least arguable that:

> "the standard of proof that has to be achieved on an application for an interim injunction is, if anything, higher than the standard which has to be achieved for leave to apply for Judicial Review using the criteria specified in the decision of the Supreme Court in *G. v D.P.P.*"[174]

10–108 In practical terms, the "standard of proof" on an interim or interlocutory injunction is that based on the *Campus Oil* principles. This is clear from the decision of the Supreme Court in *Garda Representative Association v Ireland*.[175] In other words, the legal principles upon which an injunction is granted on an application for judicial review are the same as those used in a non-judicial review context.

10–109 In *O'Brien v Moriarty*,[176] the applicant sought, by way of ancillary relief, an interlocutory injunction restraining the respondent tribunal from conducting a proposed public hearing pending the determination of the application for judicial review. In granting the interlocutory injunction sought, Fennelly J. noted that in *McDonnell v Brady*,[177] the court had held that the normal criteria in respect of the grant of an interlocutory injunction applied to an application of the type before it in *O'Brien*.

10–110 In *Seery v An Bord Pleanála*,[178] Finnegan J. reiterated that on an application for interlocutory injunctive relief a court would not attempt to

---

[171] [2006] 1 I.R. 294 at 300; [2006] 2 I.L.R.M. 392 at 397.
[172] [2001] 3 I.R. 588.
[173] unreported, High Court, Kelly J., March 13, 2006.
[174] *G v DPP* [1994] 1 I.R. 374.
[175] unreported, Supreme Court, December 18, 1987. See also, inter alia, *Fitzpatrick v Commissioner of An Garda Síochána* [1996] E.L.R. 244 and *Birmingham v Birr UDC* [1998] 2 I.L.R.M. 136, in which it was accepted that this is the correct position.
[176] [2005] 2 I.L.R.M. 161; [2005] 2 I.L.R.M. 321.
[177] [2001] 3 I.R. 588.
[178] [2001] 2 I.L.R.M. 151.

resolve conflicts of fact or questions of law, or otherwise evaluate the strength or weakness of the respective positions of the parties, and that it would not do so in the context of a judicial review either.[179]

I. LAND LAW

1. Introduction

10–111 Injunctions are frequently sought and granted in relation to rights and obligations coming within the broad rubric of land law. The range of such rights and obligations is considerable. A flavour of the cases involving such rights will be provided, including the granting of injunctions in relation to land law at the interlocutory stage.

2. General Application

10–112 The areas in which injunctions have been granted in relation to rights coming within the area of land law covers a broad spectrum, as is evident from the following non-exhaustive set of cases. The cases set out provide examples of the areas in relation to which injunctions have been granted.

(a) Compliance with a Covenant

10–113 Once a party can point to a valid covenant, he may be able to enforce it by means of an injunction. The covenant in question in the case of *Whelan v Madigan*[180] was for peaceable use and enjoyment of land. The plaintiffs sought, inter alia, injunctions to restrain the defendant from interfering with their peaceable enjoyment of the properties let to them. Granting the injunctions sought, Kenny J. found that if the defendant was not restrained by an injunction, he would be likely to continue "his campaign to get the defendants out by other means of intimidation".[181] In the case of *Gaw v CIE*, the plaintiff was granted a mandatory injunction by Dixon J. to enforce the execution of repairs in accordance with a covenant.[182] In *Sibra Building Co. Ltd v Ladgrove Stores Ltd*,[183] the plaintiff sought to enforce a restrictive covenant relating to the sale of alcohol from a shopping centre for as long as certain parties owned a public house in operation opposite the shopping centre. Keane J. granted the injunction sought. Finding that the sale of alcohol from a supermarket within the shopping

---

[179]   [2001] 2 I.L.R.M. 151 at 154.
[180]   [1978] I.L.R.M. 136. See also, *Coillte Teo v Kelly*, unreported, Circuit Court, Kenny J., March 3, 1998; *Lapedus v Glavey* (1965) 99 I.L.T.R. 1; *Calders v Murtagh* [1939] Ir. Jur. Rep. 19.
[181]   [1978] I.L.R.M. 136 at 144.
[182]   *Gaw v CIE* [1953] I.R. 232.
[183]   [1998] 2 I.R. 589.

centre did come within the terms of the restrictive covenant, the Supreme Court dismissed the appeal, and also rejected the contention that the covenant breached the terms of s.4(1) of the Competition Act 1991, which was then in force.

10–114 In general terms, when an interlocutory injunction is sought in the context of a dispute involving land, the *Campus Oil* principles will be applied by the courts.[184] For example, in the case of *Carrick v Morton*,[185] the plaintiff sought an interlocutory injunction prohibiting the defendant from continuing to carry out the construction of a dwelling house on land the subject of a restrictive covenant. In granting the injunction, Kelly J. applied the *Campus Oil* principles. He found that there was a serious issue to be tried, and that the balance of convenience lay in granting the interlocutory injunction. Kelly J. found that if the plaintiff was ultimately successful, the house would have to be removed; if the defendant was successful, the damages which the plaintiff must undertake to pay would be adequate compensation for the delay or any additional costs incurred.

(b) Vacation of Property or Lands

10–115 In *Feehan v Leamy*,[186] the plaintiff sought an injunction, including an interlocutory injunction, directing the defendant to vacate and to cease to trespass on certain lands, as well as damages for trespass. In granting the injunctive relief sought, Finnegan J. had to consider the question of dispossession.[187] He found that the plaintiff exercised all the rights of ownership which he wished to, pending the determination by, ultimately, the Supreme Court, of the question of title in relation to the lands.

10–116 The *Campus Oil* principles were applied at the interlocutory stage in *ICC Bank Plc v Verling*.[188] In that case Lynch J. granted the mandatory interlocutory injunction sought, requiring the defendants to vacate certain premises; Lynch J. held that the undertaking as to damages given by the plaintiff was such that it would be sufficient to compensate the second and third named defendants if the interlocutory injunction was granted and those defendants ultimately won the action. However, he found that if the interlocutory injunction was refused, the plaintiff would suffer substantial loss and it had not been established that any of the defendants would be in a position to make good that loss.

---

[184] See Ch.6, Interlocutory Applications.
[185] unreported, High Court, Kelly J., June 13, 2002.
[186] unreported, High Court, Finnegan J., May 29, 2000.
[187] Referring to the cases of *Murphy v Murphy* [1980] I.R. 183 and *Seamus Durack Manufacturing Ltd v Considine* [1987] I.R. 677.
[188] [1995] 1 I.L.R.M. 123.

10–117 However, in *Barnaton Investments Ltd v O'Leary*,[189] Peart J. refused an application for an interlocutory injunction requiring the defendant to vacate the plaintiff's premises from which the defendant operated a restaurant. It was argued that the premises had been assigned to the defendant in contravention of the terms of a lease. In refusing the application, Peart J. found that any loss which the plaintiff might suffer could be adequately compensated for in damages, and that in any event the balance of convenience lay in favour of refusing the relief sought so that the restaurant which the defendants operated could continue to trade while the proceedings were brought to trial and determined.

(c) Right of Way

10–118 In so far as easements are concerned, it has been commented that, "the equitable remedy of an injunction often provides the best remedy for a disturbance of an easement or *profit à prendre.*"[190] In *Smeltzer v Fingal County Council*,[191] Costello J. made an order prohibiting the defendant from carrying out the proposed development until there was compliance with the statutory procedures relating to the extinguishment of a public right of way. However, an application in relation to an easement was refused by Peart J. in the case of *Frank Towey Ltd v Dublin County Council*,[192] based on his interpretation of an agreement concerning access from a dual carriageway.

(d) Right to Light[193]

10–119 Injunctions are also frequently sought in relation to the right to light, although in general terms the courts will consider awarding damages rather than an injunction in such cases.[194] In the case of *Leeds Industrial Co-Operative Society v Slack*,[195] it was held that where an action was brought for an injunction

---

[189]   unreported, High Court, Peart J., July 30, 2004.

[190]   Bland, *The Law of Easements and Profits a Prendre* (Dublin: Round Hall Sweet & Maxwell, 1997), p.317.

[191]   [1998] 1 I.R. 279; [1998] 1 I.L.R.M. 24. See also, *Dwyer Nolan Developments Ltd v Kingscroft Developments Ltd* [1999] 1 I.L.R.M.141 and *Fortin v Delahunty*, unreported, High Court, Quirke J., January 15, 1999.

[192]   unreported, High Court, Peart J., March 16, 2005.

[193]   See generally, Bland, *The Law of Easements and Profits a Prendre* (Dublin: Round Hall Sweet & Maxwell, 1997), Ch.4.

[194]   See Craig, "The Right to Light" (2006) 156 N.L.J. 1868 who suggests, based on cases such as *MidTown Ltd v City of London Real Property Company Ltd* [2005] E.W.H.C. 33 that there has been an increasing reluctance to enforce rights to light by injunction, certainly in England. See generally, *Deakins v Hookings* (1994) 9413 Estates Gazette 133, as analysed by Galligan, "When the Price is Light" (1995) 2(2) I.P.E.L.J. 70. See also, *Mackey v Scottish Widows Fund Life Assurance Society* (1877) I.R. 11 Eq. 541; *Carr-Saunders v Dick McNeil Associates Ltd* [1986] 1 W.L.R. 92.

[195]   [1924] A.C. 851.

to restrain an obstruction of ancient lights, and it was found that, when completed, the defendant's buildings would cause an actionable obstruction to the plaintiff's lights, but that no such obstruction had yet taken place, the court had jurisdiction to award damages in lieu of an injunction. In the case of *McGrath v Munster and Leinster Bank Ltd*,[196] the plaintiff was the lessee of office premises in a building in Dublin. The defendants proceeded to enlarge and rebuild portion of their adjoining premises, diminishing the light in the plaintiff's premises. The plaintiff brought an action claiming an injunction to restrain the defendants from building and for damages. Dixon J. held that she was entitled to damages in lieu of an injunction, as the light entering her office had been substantially diminished. Commenting on this type of situation, Keane identifies a "more indulgent approach" on the basis that the law:

> "has had to balance the degree of inconvenience caused to the plaintiff against the natural reluctance to order the removal of a building upon which money and labour have been expended and which may be in an urban area where new building is sometimes virtually impossible without causing some diminution in another person's right."[197]

(e) Restraint on Entry

10–120 The plaintiff in the case of *Griffin v Bleithin*[198] sought an injunction to restrain the defendant from entering upon the portion of a strip used by the plaintiff to access a garage, the plaintiff asserting that he had entered into adverse possession of that strip of land. Quirke J. granted the relief sought after an examination of the facts surrounding the possession of the land in question.[199]

(f) Non-Derogation from Grant[200]

10–121 Barron J. explained the doctrine of derogation of grant in the case of *Connell v O'Malley*[201] in the following terms:

> "The doctrine of derogation from grant imposes implied obligations which arise where the owner of land disposes of part of it while retaining the balance. The most usual application is in relation to easements, but it is not

---

[196] [1959] I.R. 313.
[197] Keane, *Equity and the Law of Trusts in the Republic of Ireland* (London: Butterworths, 1988), p.212.
[198] [1999] 2 I.L.R.M. 182.
[199] See also, *Perry v Woodfarm Homes Ltd* [1975] I.R. 104.
[200] See generally, Bland, *The Law of Easements and Profits a Prendre* (Dublin: Round Hall Sweet & Maxwell, 1997), p.209.
[201] unreported, High Court, Barron J., July 28, 1983. See also *Kennedy v Elkinson* (1937) 71 I.L.T.R. 153.

limited to the creation of easements by implied grant. The obligations which are implied depend upon the particular nature of the transaction and arise from the presumed intention of the parties."[202]

10–122 The plaintiff in that case sought, inter alia, various injunctions in relation to the defendant's obstruction of a passage to the plaintiff's land in circumstances where the defendant, knowing that the plaintiff was to develop the land as a building site, sold the land to the plaintiff. Barron J. found that there was a clear derogation from grant by the actions of the defendant and granted the relief sought.

(g) Restriction on User

10–123 The case of *Dublin (South) City Markets Co v McCabes Ltd*[203] offers an example of how an injunction may be used in aid of a restriction on user. The defendant, which carried on business as a fishmonger, was the lessee of premises situated in the Dublin (South) City Markets. The plaintiffs complained to the defendants about dampness on the ceiling of the roof of vaults directly underneath the premises leased by the defendant. It was held, inter alia, that on a true construction of the lease, the licence which the defendant had to carry on the trade mentioned in the lease was subject to a covenant restricting the defendant from carrying on that trade in such a manner as to offend against the terms of a clause in the lease. As observed by Budd J.:

"Contrary to the defendants' contentions it seems to me that the authorities show that a breach of covenant is a sufficient ground for the Court to interfere by way of injunction without the necessity of showing damage to the reversion."[204]

10–124 An interesting feature of the case was the observation by Budd J. that:

"It did also seem to me to be suggested at one stage of the proceedings that I ought not to grant an injunction because the plaintiff's experts were unable to swear positively that the remedies they suggested would definitely stop the trouble. That seems to amount to a contention that an injunction cannot go unless the plaintiffs' expert witnesses are almost prepared to guarantee the success of their suggested remedies."[205]

---

[202] See also, inter alia, the dictum of Cotton L.J. in *Birmingham, Dudley and District Banking Co. v Rose* 38 Ch D 295 at 308 and *Harmer v Jumbil (Nigeria) Tin Area Ltd* [1921] 1 Ch. 200 at 225, per Younger L.J.

[203] [1953] I.R. 283.

[204] [1953] I.R. 283 at 310.

[205] [1953] I.R. 283 at 317.

10–125 However, Budd J. sensibly rejected this contention on the basis that plaintiffs were not bound to suggest any remedy at all.

(h) Waste

10–126 Waste involves any act which results in a change to land, even if the waste concerned actually improves the land. Courts will grant injunctions in relation to waste,[206] although damages are often a more appropriate remedy in such circumstances.[207] Furthermore, where there is an instance of ameliorating waste, the courts are much slower to grant an injunction in such a situation.[208] As observed by Lord O'Hagan in the case of *Doherty v Allman*[209]:

> "The waste with which a Court of Equity … ought to interfere, should not be ameliorating waste, not trivial waste. It must be waste of an injurious character—it must be waste of not only an injurious character, but of a substantially injurious character, and if either the waste be really ameliorating waste—that is a proceeding which results in benefit and not in injury—the Court of Equity … ought not to interfere to prevent it."[210]

(i) Fishing Rights[211]

10–127 In *Tennent v Clancy*,[212] the defendant's use of canoes on a river and lakes which adjoined both his and the plaintiff's properties was the subject of an injunction application by the plaintiff, on the basis that such use was alleged to interfere with the plaintiff's fishing rights. Costello J. granted the injunction sought, on the basis that the title adduced by the plaintiffs expressly established that the plaintiffs owned the bed and soil of the river and lakes in question. As a result, they enjoyed a corporeal right to fishing.[213]

(j) Unlawful Obstruction

10–128 The wide range of matters which may be addressed by way of an application for an injunction is evident from the case of *Massereene v Murphy*.[214] The defendant owned a premises bounded by a river. He erected on

---

[206] See *Dunsany v Dunne* (1864) 15 Ir. Ch. R. 278; *Re Pigott's Trusts* [1919] 1 I.R. 23.

[207] *Shaftesbury v Wallace* [1897] 2 I.R. 381.

[208] *Craig v Greer* [1899] 1 I.R. 258.

[209] (1878) 3 App. Cas. 709.

[210] (1878) 3 App. Cas. 709 at 724.

[211] See generally, Bland, *The Law of Easements and Profits a Prendre* (Dublin: Round Hall Sweet and Maxwell, 1997), Ch.9.

[212] [1987] 1 I.R. 15; [1988] I.L.R.M. 214.

[213] Costello J. referring to the English case of *Rawson v Peters* (1972) 116 S.J. 884 in which Lord Denning M.R. had said that the plaintiffs' fishing rights were an incorporeal hereditament. See also, *Maude v Murphy* [1934] I. R. 394 and *Wills Trustees v Cairngorm Canoeing and Sailing School Ltd* (1976) S.C. 30.

[214] 65 I.L.T.R. 193; *cf. Doona v O'Donoghue* [1957] Ir. Jur. Rep. 85 and *O'Brien v Kearney* [1995] 2 I.L.R.M. 232.

his own half of the river bed concrete piers and steel stanchions for the purpose of supporting a building. This in essence caused the diversion of an appreciable quantity of water away from the defendant's half of the river bed and over to the plaintiff's half. The court held that the piers and stanchions constituted an unlawful obstruction and diversion of the waters of the river. In the circumstances, an injunction was therefore granted compelling the defendant to remove them.

J. NUISANCE

1. Introduction

10–129 O'Higgins C.J. suggested in the case of *Connolly v South of Ireland Asphalt Co*[215] that an actionable nuisance is incapable of exact definition. He proceeded, however, to state that the term nuisance "contemplates an act or omission which amounts to an unreasonable interference with, disturbance of, or annoyance to another person in the exercise of his rights."[216] Whilst statute may prescribe certain forms of nuisance, the two main classes of nuisance at common law are public nuisance and private nuisance.[217] The former, involving interference with the rights of the public, is generally protected by the Attorney General acting on behalf of the public in bringing the appropriate litigation.[218] A private nuisance, involving unreasonable interference with a person's right to the quiet and peaceful enjoyment of their property, can be the subject of an injunction application by that person. There is old authority which suggests that if the nuisance in question is both public and private in character, the individual suffering the particular nuisance may bring an action, as may the Attorney General on behalf of the public.[219]

2. General Application

10–130 The Supreme Court defined the parameters of the law of private nuisance in the case of *Hanrahan v Merck Sharp & Dohme*[220] in the following terms:

---

[215] [1977] I.R. 99.
[216] per O'Higgins C.J. in *Connolly v South of Ireland Asphalt Co* [1977] I.R. 99 at 103.
[217] For an overview of some of the older cases relating to nuisance generally, see Pugh and Brittenden, "A Sobering Thought for Business?" (2004) 154 N.L.J. 570. See also, McMahon & Binchy, *The Irish Law of Torts*, 3rd edn (Dublin: Butterworths, 2000), Ch.24.
[218] See further, Ch.3, Standing, para.3–35. Cases concerning public nuisance include *Attorney General v Mayo Co Council* [1902] 1 I.R. 13 and *Attorney General (Boswell) v Rathmines and Pembroke Joint Hospital Board* [1904] 1 I.R. 161.
[219] *Attorney General v UK Telegraph Co Ltd* (1861) 30 Beav. 287.
[220] [1988] I.L.R.M. 629.

"It is clear from the authorities on the law of nuisance that what an occupier of land is entitled to as against his neighbour is the comfortable and healthy enjoyment of the land to the degree that would be expected by an ordinary person whose requirements are objectively reasonable in all the particular circumstances. It is difficult to state the law more precisely than that."[221]

10–131 In that case the plaintiffs owned a farm a small distance from the defendant's factory. The nuisance complained of was the emission of toxic gases from the factory. Henchy J., delivering the judgment of the court, held that:

"To provide a basis for the award of damages for private nuisance, the plaintiffs have to show that they have been interfered with, over a substantial period of time, in the use and enjoyment of their farm as a result of the way the defendants conducted their operations in the factory. The plaintiffs do not have to prove want of reasonable care on the part of the defendants. It is sufficient if it is shown that what they complain of was suffered by them as occupiers of their farm in consequence of the way the defendants ran their factory."[222]

10–132 The onus of proof is on the party asserting that he has sustained damage by reason of a nuisance to establish such damage and that it was caused by the alleged nuisance.[223] As was made clear by Gannon J. in the case of *Halpin v Tara Mines Ltd*,[224] it is:

"no defence to such a claim that the activities complained of were carried out with the highest standard of care, skill and supervision and equipment or that such activities are of great public importance and cannot conveniently be carried out in any other way."

10–133 It is important to note that the fact that planning permission has been granted does not prevent development from giving rise to tortious liability under the law of nuisance.[225]

10–134 Injunctions have been granted in a range of cases involving an alleged nuisance, and frequently arise in cases concerning halting sites. These include *County Meath VEC v Joyce*,[226] which concerned an unauthorised halting site next to school grounds, and allegations of trespass on the grounds, disruption of

---

[221] [1988] I.L.R.M. 629 at 634.
[222] [1988] I.L.R.M. 629 at 633.
[223] *Halpin v Tara Mines Ltd*, unreported, High Court, Gannon J., February 16, 1976.
[224] *Halpin v Tara Mines Ltd*, unreported, High Court, Gannon J., February 16, 1976.
[225] *Convery v Dublin County Council* [1996] 3 I.R. 153 at 173.
[226] [1997] 3 I.R. 402.

classes by loud noise, quarrelling and shouting and general obstreperous behaviour, intimidation, the disposal of rubbish on school grounds, as well as the state of the halting site itself.[227]

3. Interlocutory Considerations

10–135 In the case of *Patterson v Murphy*,[228] Costello J. held that injunctive relief is granted on well-established principles in cases of nuisance. Although the case was determined prior to that in *Campus Oil*, it would seem sensible that the *Campus Oil* principles should be equally applicable. Importantly, however, Costello J. held in that case that when an infringement of the plaintiffs' right and a threatened further infringement to a material extent has been established, the plaintiff is prima facie entitled to an injunction. Costello J. also acknowledged that there may be circumstances depriving the plaintiff of this prima facie right, but held that generally speaking the plaintiff will only be deprived of an injunction in very exceptional circumstances. In other words, the threatened repetition of a nuisance would seem to weight the judicial scales heavily towards granting an injunction.

K. Passing Off

1. Introduction[229]

10–136 A number of cases which have defined the contours of the law relating to interlocutory injunctions generally in fact arose in the specific context of actions for passing off.[230] For example, cases such as *B & S Ltd v Irish Auto Trader Ltd*[231] and *Curust Financial Services Ltd v Loewe-Lack-Werk*[232] are important in terms of the wider principles which they set out in relation to interlocutory injunctions.[233] Before looking at the interlocutory applications of injunctions in passing-off actions, the more general aspects of such injunctions will be set out.

---

[227] See *Vitalograph (Ireland) Ltd v Clare County Council*, unreported, High Court, Kelly J., April 23, 1997, which concerned an unauthorised halting site beside the industrial estate. See also, *Page Motors Ltd v Epsom and Ewell Borough Council* 80 L.G.R. 337 and *Sedleigh Denfield v O'Callaghan* [1940] A.C. 880, both referred to in *Vitalograph*. See also, *Lind v Tipperary County Council*, unreported, High Court, November 9, 1990 and *Harrington Confectioners Ltd v Cork City Council*, unreported, High Court, Gilligan J., July 5, 2005, cases which also concerned halting sites.

[228] [1978] I.L.R.M. 85.

[229] See generally, Clark and Smyth, *Intellectual Property Law in Ireland*, 2nd edn (West Sussex: Tottel, 2005).

[230] See generally, Ch.6, Interlocutory Applications.

[231] [1995] 2 I.R. 142; [1995] 2 I.L.R.M. 152.

[232] [1994] 1 I.R. 450.

[233] See also, *Polycell Products Ltd v O'Carroll* [1959] Ir. Jur. Rep. 34.

2. General Application

10–137 An action for passing off can be brought to protect a wide range of interests.[234] These include descriptive names,[235] place names,[236] packaging and get-up[237] and designs.[238]

10–138 The key elements to establish passing off were set out by Lord Oliver in the case of *Reckitt & Colman Products Ltd v Borden Inc.*[239] The plaintiff must establish:

> "a goodwill or reputation attached to the goods or services which he supplies in the mind of the purchasing public by association with the identifying 'get-up' (whether it consists simply of a brand name or a trade description, or the individual features of labelling or packaging) under which his particular goods or services are offered to the public, such that the get-up is recognised by the public as distinctive specifically of the plaintiff's goods or services. Secondly, he must demonstrate a misrepresentation by the defendant to the public (whether or not intentional) leading or likely to lead the public to believe that goods or services offered by him are the goods or services of the plaintiff. Whether the public is aware of the plaintiff's identity as the manufacturer or supplier of the goods or services is immaterial, as long as they are identified with a particular source which is in fact the plaintiff. For example, if the public is accustomed to rely upon a particular brand name in purchasing goods of a particular description, it matters not at all that there is little or no public awareness of the identity of the proprietor of the brand name. Thirdly, he must demonstrate that he suffers or, in a *quia timet* action, that he is likely to suffer damage by reason of the erroneous belief engendered by the defendant's misrepresentation that the source of the defendant's goods or services is the same as the source of those offered by the plaintiff."[240]

10–139 This definition has been approved by the Irish courts in cases such as *DSG Retail Ltd v PC World Ltd.*[241]

---

[234] See generally, *Slazenger & Sons v Spalding & Bros* [1910] 1 Ch. 257.

[235] Considered, inter alia, in *DSG Retail Ltd v PC World Ltd*, unreported, High Court, Laffoy J., January 13, 1998.

[236] *Muckross Park Hotel Ltd v Randles*, unreported, High Court, Barron J., November 10, 1992.

[237] *Reckitt & Colman Products Ltd v Borden Inc.* [1990] 1 W.L.R. 491; [1990] 1 All E.R. 873.

[238] See *Adidas Sports Schuhfabriken Adi Dassler KA v Charles O'Neill & Co* [1983] I.L.R.M. 112, in which O'Higgins C.J. held that a three stripe design which appeared on Adidas products was not associated exclusively with Adidas in the public mind.

[239] [1990] 1 W.L.R. 491; [1990] 1 All E.R. 873.

[240] [1990] 1 W.L.R. 491 at 499; [1990] 1 All E.R. 873 at 880. See also the definition suggested by Lord Diplock in *Warnink (Erven) BV v J Townend & Sons (Hull) Ltd* [1979] 3 W.L.R. 68; [1979] A.C. 731; [1979] 2 All E.R. 927, as referred to by McCracken J. in *Smithkline Beecham Plc v Antigen Pharmaceuticals Ltd* [1999] 2 I.L.R.M. 190.

[241] unreported, High Court, Laffoy J., January 13, 1998.

10–140 A number of points arise from this definition. First, as accepted by Kinlen J. in the case of *An Post v Irish Permanent Plc*,[242] the matter which has to be established is whether people are likely to be deceived.[243] It is not necessary to establish an actual instance of deception.[244] Furthermore, as made clear by Laffoy J. in *Guinness Ireland Group v Kilkenny Brewing Co Ltd*,[245] it is not necessary to demonstrate an intention to defraud; as stated by Laffoy J., "the defendant's state of mind is wholly irrelevant to the existence of the cause of action of passing off".[246]

10–141 Secondly, an action for passing off is not restricted to a trader representing the goods of another party as his own. It extends to the deceptive use of a descriptive term, in order to protect the goodwill in the descriptive term enjoyed by those entitled to use it.[247] Applying the dicta from *C & A Modes v C & A (Waterford) Ltd*,[248] Kinlen J. also held in *An Post* that in considering whether to grant an interlocutory injunction, the court should bear in mind that the purpose of the passing-off action was to prevent unfair competition caused by a party seeking to gain commercial advantage from creating confusion in the public mind between its own trading activities and those of another party, with such confusion calculated to operate to the detriment of the goodwill of the other party. Based on the decision of Laffoy J. in *DSG Retail Ltd v PC World Ltd*,[249] following *C & A Modes*, foreign goodwill may also be identified and recognised in Ireland.

3. Interlocutory Considerations[250]

10–142 In cases involving passing off, a key consideration at the interlocutory stage is generally the question of the balance of convenience, as distinct from

---

242   [1995] 1 I.R. 140; [1995] 1 I.L.R.M. 336.
243   See also, *B & S Ltd v Irish Auto Trader Ltd* [1995] 2 I.R. 142; [1995] 2 I.L.R.M. 152 and *Private Research v Brosnan* [1995] 1 I.R. 534.
244   Applying *Muckross Park Hotel Ltd v Randles*, unreported, High Court, Barron J., November 10, 1992.
245   [1999] 1 I.L.R.M. 531.
246   [1999] 1 I.L.R.M. 531 at 536. See also, *C & A Modes v C & A (Waterford) Ltd* [1976] I.R. 195 at 214, per Kenny J. However, Clark and Smyth, *Intellectual Property Law in Ireland*, 2nd edn (West Sussex: Tottel, 2005), p.527 make the sensible observation that: "Proof that the defendant intended to appropriate the plaintiff's reputation is clearly of probative value."
247   per Kinlen J. in *An Post v Irish Permanent Plc* [1995] 1 I.R. 140; [1995] 1 I.L.R.M. 336, considering *Bollinger v Costa Brava Wine Co Ltd* [1960] Ch. 262; *Vine Products Ltd v MacKenzie & Co Ltd* [1969] R.P.C. 1; *John Walker & Sons Ltd v Henry Ost & Co Ltd* [1970] 1 W.L.R. 917 and *Warnink BV v Townend & Sons (Hull)* [1979] A.C. 731. See also, *Guinness Ireland Group v Kilkenny Brewing Co Ltd* [1999] 1 I.L.R.M. 531. As to the difference between "goodwill" and "reputation", see *Muckross Park Hotel Ltd v Randles*, unreported, High Court, Barron J., November 10, 1992.
248   [1976] I.R. 195.
249   unreported, High Court, Laffoy J., January 13, 1998.
250   A comprehensive and extremely useful review of the applicable principles in the context of

the adequacy of damages[251] (although the latter will sometimes be considered as an element of the former).[252] This is clear from the dictum of Costello J. in *Three Stripe International Ltd v Charles O'Neill & Co Ltd*[253] and later cases such as *DSG Retail Ltd v PC World Ltd.*[254] An application of the *Campus Oil* principles will generally lead to a finding of uncompensatable damage, although this must of course be approached on a case-by-case basis. The fact that property rights are at issue in an action for passing off is an important consideration; it is frequently almost impossible to quantify goodwill which has been built up in a name or brand. As remarked by Clarke J. in *Jacob Fruitfield Food Group Ltd v United Biscuits (UK) Ltd*,[255] "a claimant's goodwill is a property right which should not lightly be taken to be capable of being diminished or interfered with in return for damages."

10–143 In *Mitchelstown Co-Operative Agricultural Society Ltd v Golden Vale Products Ltd*,[256] Costello J. referred to the "axiom" that in most passing-off actions damages are not an adequate remedy for a successful plaintiff. A similar point was made by Laffoy J. in *DSG Retail Ltd v PC World Ltd.*[257] In that case she made reference to "the normal axiom in passing off actions, that damages would not be an adequate remedy for the plaintiff." However, these dicta must be treated with caution: in *Jacob Fruitfield Food Group Ltd v United Biscuits (UK) Ltd*[258] Clarke J. rejected the suggestion that these cases established that there was a rule of law to the effect that:

> "a plaintiff will suffer uncompensatable damages if an injunction is refused even though the plaintiff has established a fair case to be tried and that the balance of convenience will, therefore, almost always require that an interlocutory injunction be granted in those circumstances."

interlocutory injunctions in the field of infringements of trademarks was carried out by Clarke J. in the case of *Metro International SA v Independent News & Media Plc* [2006] 1 I.L.R.M. 414. Although the case concerned an alleged infringement of trademarks, Clarke J. made a number of helpful observations in relation to passing off, and also dealt with a number of cases arising in the context of passing off.

[251] As to the role of damages, see *Westman Holdings Ltd v McCormack* [1992] 1 I.R. 151.

[252] See *Symonds Cider v Showerings (Ireland) Ltd* [1997] 1 I.L.R.M. 481. In the case of *Metro International SA v Independent News & Media Plc* [2006] 1 I.L.R.M. 414 at 423, Clarke J. suggested that it was a question of "semantics" rather than "substance" whether the question of adequacy of damages and the weighing up of balance of convenience are viewed as two separate tests, or as one in which the former is a significant part of the latter.

[253] [1988] 1 I.R. 144 at 148, per Costello J.

[254] unreported, High Court, Laffoy J., January 13, 1998.

[255] unreported, High Court, Clarke J., October 12, 2007.

[256] unreported, High Court, Costello J., December 12, 1985.

[257] unreported, High Court, Laffoy J., January 13, 1998. Both *Mitchelstown* and *DSG Retail* were referred to by Clarke J. in *Metro International SA v Independent News & Media Plc* [2006] 1 I.L.R.M. 414.

[258] unreported, High Court, Clarke J., October 12, 2007.

10–144 Instead, he summarised the position, derived from earlier decisions, as being that:

> "a proper application of the principles applicable to a consideration of the balance of convenience and the adequacy of damages will normally, in a passing off case, lead to the conclusion that the plaintiff will suffer uncompensatable damages and that the balance of convenience will favour the grant of an injunction. The factors which lead to such a conclusion may vary from case to case."

10–145 It bears repeating that, as has been seen in the context of interlocutory applications generally, it was held in *Curust Financial Services Ltd v Loewe-Lack-Werk*[259] that difficulty—as opposed to complete impossibility—in the assessment of such damages is not a ground for characterising the awarding of damages as an inadequate remedy.[260]

L. Publication

1. Introduction

10–146 Within the broad rubric of publication, this section considers three aspects arising out of publication: breach of confidence; defamation and the related issue of prior restraint of publication; and privacy. As will be seen, applications for interlocutory injunctions for defamation in particular have given rise to very particular considerations in this area.

2. Breach of Confidence[261]

10–147 The tort of breach of confidence is a common law tort that protects private information conveyed in confidence. As described by Shanley J. in the High Court in *National Irish Bank Ltd v RTÉ*[262]:

---

[259] [1994] 1 I.R. 450 at 468, per Finlay C.J. See generally, the analysis of this case by Delany, (1993) 15 D.U.L.J. 228. See also the Supreme Court decision in *Ó'Murchú t/a Talknology v Eircell Ltd,* unreported, Supreme Court, February 21, 2001.

[260] See also, *Mantruck Services v Ballinlough Electrical Refrigeration Co Ltd* [1992] 1 I.R. 351; *Mitchelstown Co-Op Ltd v Société des Produits Nestlé SA*, unreported, Supreme Court, October 26, 1988 and *Sweeney v National University of Ireland Cork t/a Cork University Press* [2001] 1 I.L.R.M. 310.

[261] See generally, Lavery, *Commercial Secrets The Action for Breach of Confidence in Ireland* (Dublin: Round Hall Sweet & Maxwell, 1996), especially Ch.9, Remedies. See also, Toulson and Phipps, *Confidentiality* (London: Thomson Sweet & Maxwell, 2006). An excellent overview of the then state of the law in relation to both breach of confidence and privacy is contained in a paper by McCullough, "What do Privacy Laws Protect?" Bar Council, July 14, 2006.

[262] [1998] 2 I.R. 465; [1998] 2 I.L.R.M. 196.

"Where a person in whom confidential information reposes discloses that information to the detriment of the party who has confided in him, he commits the tort of breach of confidence."[263]

10–148 The law in relation to confidential information "is independent of contract".[264] It applies to both purely personal and to non-commercial information.[265] Before looking at the applicable criteria when seeking an injunction for breach of confidence, it is proposed to set out the parameters of the doctrine of breach of confidence.

(a) Breach of Confidence Defined

10–149 In the important case of *House of Spring Gardens Ltd v Point Blank*,[266] the first to deal with the subject in any great detail in this jurisdiction, Costello J. reviewed various English decisions dealing with the circumstances from which an obligation of confidence may be deduced. He focused on a number of more recent decisions. The first of these was *Saltman Engineering Co v Campbell Engineering Co.*[267] In the course of his decision in that case, Lord Greene stated that:

"The main part of the claim is based on breach of confidence, in respect of which a right may be infringed without the necessity of there being any contractual relationship. I will explain what I mean. If two parties make a contract, under which one of them obtains for the purpose of the contract or in connection with it some confidential matter, even though the contract is silent on the matter of confidence the law will imply an obligation to treat that confidential matter in a confidential way, as one of the implied terms of the contract; but the obligation to respect confidence is not limited to cases where the parties are in a contractual relationship."[268]

10–150 Lord Greene also observed that:

"The information, to be confidential, must, I apprehend, apart from contract, have the necessary quality of confidence about it, namely, it must not be something which is public property and public knowledge."[269]

---

[263] unreported, High Court, Shanley J., March 6, 1998. The Supreme Court decision is reported at [1988] 2 I.R. 465; [1998] 2 I.L.R.M. 196. See also, *Coco v A N Clark (Engineers) Ltd* [1969] R.P.C. 41 at 47, per Megarry J., as referred to in *Mahon v Post Publications Ltd* [2007] 2 I.L.R.M. 1 at 21.

[264] As explained by Fennelly J. in the case of *Mahon v Post Publications Ltd* [2007] 2 I.L.R.M. 1 at 20.

[265] *Mahon v Post Publications Ltd* [2007] 2 I.L.R.M. 1 at 20, per Fennelly J.

[266] [1984] I.R. 611.

[267] [1963] 3 All E.R. 413.

[268] [1963] 3 All E.R. 413 at 414.

[269] [1963] 3 All E.R. 413 at 415.

10–151 Costello J. also referred to the case of *Terrapin Ltd v Builders' Supply Co. (Hayes) Ltd.*[270] It was held in *Terrapin* that a person receiving information in confidence is not allowed to use that information as a spring-board for activities detrimental to the person who made the confidential communication. The third case which Costello J. referred to was that of *Seager v Copydex.*[271] In *Seager* Lord Denning M.R. explained that the law in this area did not depend on an implied contract. Rather, it depended on "broad principle of equity that he who has received information in confidence shall not take unfair advantage of it."[272]

10–152 Costello J. observed, on the basis of his review of the English authorities, that there was no "simple test" for deciding what circumstances will give rise to an obligation of confidence.[273] Observing that the court was effectively being asked to enforce a "moral obligation",[274] Costello J. found that, on the facts before him, there had been a breach of confidence.[275]

10–153 Having reviewed these earlier decisions, in *Mahon v Post Publications Ltd,*[276] Fennelly J. summarised "the contours of the equitable doctrine of confidence" in the following terms:

> "1. The information must in fact be confidential or secret: it must, to quote Lord Greene, "have the necessary quality of confidence about it;"[277]
> 2. It must have been communicated by the possessor of the information in circumstances which impose an obligation of confidence or trust on the person receiving it;
> 3. It must be wrongfully communicated by the person receiving it or by another person who is aware of the obligation of confidence."[278]

10–154 The growing influence of the European Convention on Human Rights has led in England to a move away from the necessity of confidence or trust in recent years; the nature of the information concerned itself may provide a sufficient basis for a breach of confidence action.[279] Although the Convention

---

[270] [1960] R.P.C. 128. See *Cranleigh Precision Engineering Ltd v Bryant* [1965] 1 W.L.R. 1317.
[271] [1967] 1 W.L.R. 923; [1967] 2 All E.R. 415.
[272] [1967] 1 W.L.R. 923 at 931; [1967] 2 All E.R. 415 at 417. See also, *Fraser v Evans* [1969] 1 Q.B. 349; [1968] 3 W.L.R. 1172.
[273] [1984] I.R. 611 at 662.
[274] [1984] I.R. 611 at 663.
[275] The appeal to the Supreme Court, also reported at [1984] I.R. 611. In the course of his judgment, O'Higgins C.J. made reference to Costello J.'s review of the various authorities and, in relation to the conclusions the trial judge had drawn from them, O'Higgins C.J. stated that the agreed entirely with the views of Costello J. [1984] I.R. 611 at 696.
[276] [2007] 2 I.L.R.M. 1.
[277] per Lord Greene in *Saltman Engineering Co v Campbell Engineering Co* [1963] 3 All E.R. 413.
[278] [2007] 2 I.L.R.M. 1 at 22.
[279] See, for example, *Campbell v MGN Ltd* [2004] 2 A.C. 457. See also *Imutran Ltd v Uncaged*

has a role to play in this jurisdiction, the impact of the Constitution must also be factored into consideration.[280]

(b) Private or Public Confidences

10–155 The case of *Attorney General for England & Wales v Brandon Book Publishers Ltd*[281] is important for its consideration of the distinction between public and private confidences. The plaintiff in *Brandon Book Publishers* sought to restrain the publication of a book written by a deceased member of the British Secret Service. The book did not involve a private confidence or trade information, but rather information shared between a government and a private individual.

10–156 Carroll J. took the view that a distinction should be drawn between a government and a private person.[282] Referring to the case of *Commonwealth of Australia v John Fairfax & Sons Ltd*,[283] she found it a correct statement of the law to say that it may be a sufficient detriment to the citizen that disclosure of information relating to his affairs will expose his actions to public discussion and criticism. However, Mason J. had also observed that "it can scarcely be a relevant detriment to the government that publication of material concerning its actions will merely expose it to public discussion and criticism."[284] Mason J. had concluded in *John Fairfax* that unless it is likely that the public interest would be injured by disclosure, it would not be protected. Turning to the authorities closer to home, Carroll J. found various English authorities to be of no assistance in relation to the matter before her. This was on the basis that considerations in England in relation to the public interest were different to considerations in Ireland. She found that the considerations which applied in this jurisdiction were, inter alia, that the public interest in this jurisdiction was

---

Campaigns Ltd [2001] 2 All E.R. 385 and *Cream Holdings Ltd v Banerjee* [2005] 1 A.C. 253; [2004] 3 W.L.R. 918. As to the impact of human rights legislation and an increasing emphasis on the freedom of the press, see McFarlane, "Privacy's Death Knell?" (2007) 157 N.L.J. 1134. See generally, Kelleher, *Privacy and Data Protection Law in Ireland* (Dublin: Tottel, 2006). In this jurisdiction, the Data Protection Acts 1988 to 2003 must also be considered. See para.10–194 in relation to breaches of the European Convention on Human Rights Act 2003.

[280] In the case of *Kennedy v Ireland* [1987] I.R. 587 at 592 Hamilton P. recognised that: "Though not specifically guaranteed by the Constitution, the right of privacy is one of the fundamental personal rights of the citizen which flow from the Christian and democratic nature of the State. It is not an unqualified right. Its exercise may be restricted by the constitutional rights of others, by the requirements of the common good and is subject to the requirements of public order and morality."

[281] [1986] I.R. 597; [1987] I.L.R.M. 135.

[282] It was held in *Duchess of Argyll v Duke of Argyll* [1967] Ch. 302; [1965] 2 W.L.R. 790; [1965] 1 All E.R. 611 that communications between a husband and wife gave rise to an obligation of confidence.

[283] (1980) 147 C.L.R. 39.

[284] (1980) 147 C.L.R. 39 at 51.

not affected by publication; there was no breach of confidentiality in a private or commercial setting and there was no absolute confidentiality where the parties were a government and a private individual. On this basis, Carroll J. held that no cause of action had been shown. In the circumstances, she held that the balance of convenience lay with the right of the defendant to exercise its constitutional right to publish. Such a right could not be measured in money terms.

(c) Interlocutory Applications

10–157 In general terms, the *American Cyanamid/Campus Oil* principles apply to an application for an injunction based on breach of confidence,[285] although this is subject to an element of qualification.[286] It is of course necessary in the first instance to demonstrate that the information concerned is confidential.[287]

10–158 In an interlocutory application for an injunction based on breach of confidence, the factors which a court will consider when looking at the balance of convenience include the long-term effect on goodwill[288] and the extent to which the defendant has invested in the relevant information.[289] The extent to which the information central to the injunction application has actually been used is also often a factor in considering whether to grant the injunction.[290]

10–159 However, some doubt was cast on the use of the *Campus Oil* principles in *National Irish Bank Ltd v RTÉ*.[291] In that case, an interim injunction was granted to the plaintiff banks restraining the defendant from publishing confidential information relating to them and to their customers. The information which the defendant sought to publish related to the operation by National Irish Bank and a company called Clerical Medical International of a particular scheme of insurance. Shanley J. discharged the ex parte injunction which had been granted to the plaintiffs. The plaintiffs appealed to the Supreme Court.

10–160 On the facts before it, the Supreme Court, dismissing the appeal, acknowledged that the consequences which would result from either the granting or the withholding of the injunction would essentially be irreparable. As observed by Keane J.:

---

[285] *Aksjeselskapet Jotul v Waterford Iron Founders Ltd,* unreported, High Court, McWilliam J., November 8, 1977.

[286] See *National Irish Bank Ltd v RTÉ* [1988] 2 I.R. 465; [1998] 2 I.L.R.M. 196; see para.10–159.

[287] See *Mainmet Holdings Plc v Austin* [1991] F.S.R. 538 at 544, per Lionel Swift Q.C.

[288] *Boots Co Ltd v Approved Prescription Services Ltd* [1988] F.S.R. 45.

[289] *Aksjeselskapet Jotul v Waterford Iron Founders Ltd,* unreported, High Court, McWilliam J., November 8, 1977.

[290] See, for example, *Seager v Copydex* [1967] 1 W.L.R. 923; [1967] 2 All E.R. 415; *Coco v AN Clark (Engineers) Ltd* [1969] R.P.C. 41.

[291] [1998] 2 I.R. 465; [1998] 2 I.L.R.M. 196.

"If no injunction is granted, the relationship of confidentiality will be at once destroyed. If, on the other hand, disclosure is restrained until the trial of the action, the role of RTÉ in transmitting news as it happens will be seriously inhibited."[292]

10–161 That being so, Keane J. took the view that the usual criteria to be applied when considering the granting or withholding of an interlocutory injunction were of "limited relevance".[293] The key question was in essence whether the defendants had established a public interest in the disclosure of the information which outweighed the public interest in confidentiality and, if so, the extent of the disclosure which was legitimate. In the circumstances, it seems that the *National Irish Bank* case turned on its own very specific facts. In the normal course, it would seem that the better approach would be to apply the *Campus Oil* principles when an interlocutory injunction is being sought.

10–162 In granting an injunction on an interlocutory basis, the courts will often consider the period for which such an injunction should be granted. An interlocutory injunction is usually granted until the hearing of the substantive action. However, the courts have recognised that in granting an interlocutory injunction based on an alleged breach of confidence, they may have regard to the length of time it would take a party to develop or acquire the information which they are alleged to have received in breach of confidence. This is often referred to as a "spring board" injunction.[294] As such, the injunction may be granted for this period of time only, rather than until the date of the substantive hearing.[295]

(d) Remedies

10–163 In extreme cases concerning breach of confidence, the court may grant an order for delivery up or destruction of documents. Such an order provides that any product which has been created or developed as a result of information obtained in breach of confidence can be delivered back to the plaintiff, or in the alternative destroyed.[296]

3. Defamation

10–164 As noted by Gee,[297] before the Judicature Acts[298] the Court of Chancery would not restrain a libel.[299] This was because the court granted

---

292 [1998] 2 I.R. 465 at 484; [1998] 2 I.L.R.M. 196 at 209.
293 [1998] 2 I.R. 465 at 484; [1998] 2 I.L.R.M. 196 at 209.
294 See *Terrapin Ltd v Builders & Supply Co (Hayes) Ltd* [1967] R.P.C. 375.
295 As was done in *Roger Bullivant v Ellis* [1987] F.S.R. 172.
296 See, for example, *Peter Pan Manufacturing Corp v Corset Silhouette* [1963] I.P.R. 457.
297 Gee, *Commercial Injunctions*, 5th edn (London: Thomson Sweet & Maxwell, 2004), p.5.
298 See Ch.1, Domestic Jurisdiction, para.1–28.
299 *Prudential Assurance Co v Knottt* (1875) 10 L.R. Ch. App. 142.

injunctions to protect property rights. Libel did not come within these rights; the court could not know what would be regarded as libellous before there had been a verdict of a jury. However, as has been seen, the Judicature Act (Ireland) 1877 confers jurisdiction on the High Court to grant injunctions in all cases where it appears just and convenient to do so.[300] Nonetheless, the courts are still very reluctant to grant interlocutory injunctions in cases of defamation. This is due to the importance attached to the unspecified right to freedom of communication guaranteed by Art.40.3 of the Constitution and the right of free speech, guaranteed by Art.40.6.1 of the Constitution.[301] As explained by Keane J. in *Oblique Financial Services Ltd v The Promise Production Co. Ltd*[302]:

> "Article 40.6.1 is concerned not with the dissemination of factual information, but the rights of the citizen, in formulating or publishing convictions or opinions, or conveying an opinion; and the rights of all citizens, including conveying information, arises in our law, not under Article 40.6.1 but under Article 40.3.1."[303]

(a) Emphasis on Freedom of Expression

10–165 The emphasis which the courts place on freedom of expression is also evident from the case of *Cullen v Toibin*.[304] In that case the plaintiff sought an injunction to prevent publication of material on the grounds that it was likely to interfere with a criminal trial. Barrington J. took the view that the court was entitled to grant such an injunction.[305] However, the Supreme Court allowed the appeal. It held that the courts should only interfere with the freedom of the press and of communication guaranteed in Art.40.6 of the Constitution where this was necessary for the administration of justice. The Supreme Court further held that since publication of the article could not possibly prejudice the objective determination by the Court of Criminal Appeal of pure issues of law, there was no basis for the granting of the injunction in the case.[306]

(b) Impact of the European Convention on Human Rights

10–166 The courts' reluctance to grant such injunctions has been fortified by Art.10 of the European Convention for the Protection of Human Rights and Fundamental Freedom. Article 10(1) provides that:

[300] See generally, Ch.1, Domestic Jurisdiction.
[301] See *Attorney General v Paperlink* [1984] I.L.R.M. 373 at 381 and *Murphy v IRTC* [1999] 1 I.R. 12 at 24. See generally, Hogan & Whyte, *J.M. Kelly: The Irish Constitution*, 4th edn (Dublin: Butterworths, 2003).
[302] [1994] 1 I.L.R.M. 74.
[303] [1994] 1 I.L.R.M. 74 at 78.
[304] [1984] I.L.R.M. 577.
[305] Citing *DPP v Irish Press Ltd*, unreported, High Court, Finlay P., December 15, 1976.
[306] However, false and fraudulent misrepresentations which are likely to mislead the public may

"1. Everyone has the right to freedom of expression. This right shall include freedom to hold opinions and to receive and impart information and ideas without interference by public authority and regardless of frontiers. This article shall not prevent States from requiring the licensing of broadcasting, television or cinema enterprises."[307]

10–167 The case of *Mahon v Post Publications Ltd*[308] has already been looked at above in the context of a consideration of breach of confidence.[309] The case is also important in the instant context for what it has to say about the impact of the European Convention on Human Rights on domestic law in the context of publication.[310] The case concerned the publication in a Sunday newspaper of material that had been circulated by the Planning Tribunal to various parties in advance of public hearings, which material was supposed to remain confidential until those hearings. Both the High and Supreme Courts, the latter by a majority, denied the injunction sought by the tribunal to restrain parties from publishing such confidential material in the future while such information remained confidential. Speaking as part of the majority in the Supreme Court, Fennelly J. referred to the fact that:

"The right of freedom of expression extends the same protection to worthless, prurient and meretricious publication as it does to worthy, serious and socially valuable works. The undoubted fact that news media frequently and implausibly invokes a public interest to cloak worthless and even offensive material does not affect the principle."[311]

10–168 In finding that the tribunal had not established any legal justification for its claim of confidentiality, Fennelly J. reached this conclusion by considering whether the restrictions provided for in Art.10(2) of the European Convention on Human Rights should be allowed. Article 10(2) provides that:

"The exercise of these freedoms, since it carries with it duties and responsibilities, may be subject to such formalities, conditions, restrictions or penalties as are prescribed by law and are necessary in a democratic society,

---

be restrained by injunction if sought by the Attorney General: see *Attorney General (O'Duffy) v Myddletons Ltd* [1907] 1 I.R. 471.

[307] See *Venables v News Group Newspapers Ltd* [2001] Fam. 430 in relation to the exceptions in Art.10(2), Butler Sloss P. citing with approval the observations of Munby J. in *Kelly v BBC* [2001] 1 All E.R. 323 about the need for proper evidence rather than inviting the court to make assumptions.

[308] [2007] 2 I.L.R.M. 1.

[309] See para.10–153.

[310] A comprehensive overview of the impact of the Convention and associated case law is contained in a paper by McCullough, "Recent Decision in the Law Relating to Freedom of Speech" (Bar Council, December 8, 2007).

[311] [2007] 2 I.L.R.M. 1 at 13.

in the interests of national security, territorial integrity or public safety, for the prevention of disorder or crime, for the protection of health or morals, for the protection of the reputation or the rights of others, for preventing the disclosure of information received in confidence, or for maintaining the authority and impartiality of the judiciary."

10–169 Fennelly J. found, based on the wording of Art.10(2), first that any such restriction must be "prescribed by law". Secondly, it must be "necessary" in a democratic society, to promote an interest set out in Art.10(2). It must therefore be proportionate.[312] It is clear from the foregoing that the courts are willing to analyse freedom of expression in the context of the tests set out in the European Convention on Human Rights.[313]

(c) Interlocutory Considerations

10–170 One of the "special categories" identified where the *Campus Oil/ American Cyanamid* guidelines, "even if satisfied, do not result in an interlocutory injunction being granted"[314] is the rule that unless there are exceptional circumstances, no prior restraint will be imposed on publication, unless it is clear that no defence will succeed at trial in relation to a claim arising out of publication. This is referred to as the rule in *Bonnard v Perryman*,[315] a rule which highlights the importance put on free speech. In the words of Lord Coleridge C.J.:

> "The importance of leaving free speech unfettered is a strong reason in cases of libel for dealing most cautiously and warily with the granting of interim injunctions ... The right of free speech is one which it is for the public interest that individuals should possess, and, indeed, that they should exercise without impediment, so long as no wrongful act is done; and, unless an alleged libel is untrue, there is no wrong committed; but, on the contrary, often a very wholesome act is performed in the publication and repetition of an alleged libel. Until it is clear that an alleged libel is untrue, it is not clear that any right at all has been infringed ..."[316]

---

[312] As to proportionality, see the dictum of Lord Hope in *R. v Shayler* [2003] 1 A.C. 247 at 281; [2002] 2 W.L.R. 754 at 783; [2002] 2 All E.R. 477 at 506. See also the dictum of Lord Nicholls in *Attorney General v Punch Ltd* [2003] 1 A.C. 1046 at 1055; [2003] 2 W.L.R. 49 at 57; [2003] 1 All E.R. 289 at 297 in relation to the necessity for clarity and certainty in relation to an injunction order, as referred to by Fennelly J. [2007] 2 I.L.R.M. 1 at 30.

[313] The provisions of the European Convention on Human Rights also had a role to play in the context of a claim of journalistic privilege in the case of *Mahon v Keenan*, unreported, High Court, October 23, 2007 (currently under appeal). See also the decision of Matthews J. in the Circuit Court in *People (DPP) v Redmond*, unreported, Circuit Court, Matthews J., April 25, 2007, which concerned the extent to which a criminal court can give directions in relation to the scope of permissible media reporting prior to a trial.

[314] per Kelly J. in *Foley v Sunday Newspapers Ltd* [2005] 1 I.R. 88 at 98.

[315] *Bonnard v Perryman* [1891] 2 Ch. 269.

[316] *Bonnard v Perryman* [1891] 2 Ch. 269 at 284. *Khashoggi v IPC Magazines Ltd* [1986] 1

10–171 Within this context, as explained by Kelly J. in the case of *Reynolds v Malocco t/a "Patrick"*,[317] "damages are the normal remedy for defamation and injunctions are not".[318] This view is evident from the case of *Connolly v RTÉ*.[319] The plaintiff had sought an injunction to prevent the defendant from using film taken at a checkpoint during a campaign against drunk driving. She complained that the footage taken, coupled with a voiceover about drunk driving, defamed her. In considering the balance of convenience, Carroll J. stated that she had to take into account the right to freedom of expression balanced against the plaintiff's right to a good name and reputation in the light of the law on injunctive relief in defamation cases. Refusing to grant the interlocutory injunction sought, Carroll J. stated that, in circumstances where there was no immediate danger of the footage being (re-)used, and the defendant indicated that it would co-operate in bringing the matter to an early trial, it was preferable "in the circumstances of this case that the alleged libel which is contested should be tried by a jury rather than that an injunction should issue."[320]

(d) Displacement of Campus Oil Guidelines

10–172 The importance of free speech in effect trumps the *Campus Oil* guidelines. It requires a much higher standard when seeking an injunction in a defamation action, namely the need to show that there is no doubt but that the words published are defamatory. This is clear from, inter alia, the case of *Reynolds v Malocco t/a "Patrick"*.[321] In that case, Kelly J. made reference to the granting of an injunction in a libel action as being "a jurisdiction of a delicate nature", and the fact that "the court must be circumspect to ensure that it does not unnecessarily interfere with the right of freedom of expression".[322] Approving the case of *Sinclair v Gogarty*,[323] which itself had approved and followed *Bonnard v Perryman*,[324] Kelly J. held that where a person seeks an interlocutory injunction to restrain the publication of defamatory statements, he

W.L.R. 1412; [1986] 3 All E.R. 577 and *Holley v Smyth* [1998] 2 W.L.R. 742 at 756, in which Auld L.J. stated that: "Where there is a defence or claim of justification the discretion is further guided by the rule in *Bonnard v Perryman* that it is not normally just or convenient to grant relief unless the plaintiff has proved that the libel is plainly untrue."

317 [1999] 2 I.R. 203; [1999] 1 I.L.R.M. 289.
318 [1999] 2 I.R. 203 at 218; [1999] 1 I.L.R.M. 289 at 302.
319 [1991] 2 I.R. 446.
320 [1991] 2 I.R. 446 at 448.
321 [1999] 2 I.R. 203; [1999] 1 I.L.R.M. 289. See generally the analysis of this case by Cox, "Tort-Prior Restraint-Injunctions-Defamation" (1998) 20 D.U.L.J. 246.
322 [1999] 2 I.R. 203 at 218; [1999] 1 I.L.R.M. 289 at 302. See the judgment of Lord Esher M.R. in *Coulson v Coulson* (1887) 3 T.L.R. 846. See generally, *Barrett v Independent Newspapers Ltd* [1986] I.R. 13; [1986] I.L.R.M. 601.
323 [1937] I.R. 377.
324 See also, *Fraser v Evans* [1969] 1 Q.B. 349 and *Herbage v Pressdram Ltd* [1984] 2 All E.R. 769, which also approved the rule in *Bonnard v Perryman*, as cited by Kelly J. in *Foley v Sunday Newspapers Ltd* [2005] 1 I.R. 88 at 99.

must establish "not merely that he has raised a serious issue concerning the words complained of, but that there is no doubt that they are defamatory."[325] This was a view confirmed by Kelly J. in the case of *Foley v Sunday Newspapers*.[326] In the latter case Kelly J. also observed that in the English case of *Greene v Associated Newspapers Ltd*[327] it was held that the Human Rights Act 1998 had not changed the rule.

10–173 Kelly J. proceeded to hold in *Reynolds*, approving the case of *Cullen v Stanley*,[328] that where a defendant intends to plead justification, the court will generally not grant an interlocutory injunction to restrain publication. This is subject to the caveat that the plea must have some substance or prospect of success on the evidence adduced by the defendant. This avoids the situation which could arise whereby a defendant could effectively oust the ability of a court to intervene by way of injunction in an appropriate case "by the simple expedient of expressing an intention to plead justification at the trial of the action."[329] In practical terms, the basis for a plea of justification would have to be set out in any affidavit replying to an application for an interlocutory injunction,[330] although it does not appear necessary in the normal course to go any further and, for example, formally exhibit material upon which such a plea is based. It was suggested by Charleton J. in the case of *Cullen v Sunday Newspapers Ltd*[331] that, in the context of an application being brought against a newspaper, it might be sufficient for a newspaper to, as necessary, explain the basis of the plea of justification by reference to material which it can be averred is confidential.

10–174 In *Reynolds*, Kelly J. preferred not to set out in a hard and fast manner any factors which could influence the discretion. However, having regard to the circumstances, and in particular to the virtual impossibility of recovering any sum awarded if the plaintiff was successful at the hearing of the defamation action due to, inter alia, the financial position of the various defendants, Kelly J. exercised his discretion to grant the injunction sought in *Reynolds*.

---

[325] [1999] 2 I.R. 203 at 209; [1999] 1 I.L.R.M. 289 at 294. Characterised by Charleton J. in *Cullen v Sunday Newspapers Ltd,* ex tempore, High Court, Charleton J., December 14, 2007 as "the highest test known to non-mandatory injunctions in civil law".

[326] [2005] 1 I.R. 88.

[327] [2005] Q.B. 972; [2005] 3 W.L.R. 281; [2005] 1 All E.R. 30.

[328] [1926] I.R. 73.

[329] [1999] 2 I.R. 203 at 212; [1999] 1 I.L.R.M. 289 at 297. As observed by Clarke J. in *Cogley v RTÉ* [2005] 2 I.L.R.M. 529 at 535, one of the key issues in *Reynolds* relate to whether a mere assertion by a defendant that he intended to raise a plea of justification was, of itself, sufficient. Clarke J. observed that this was "a proposition for which there was some authority in the United Kingdom".

[330] By default, that justification might be pleaded means that an ex parte interim injunction application is entirely unsuitable in such circumstances. The better approach is to seek short service of an interlocutory motion.

[331] ex tempore, High Court, Charleton J., December 14, 2007.

10–175 Defamation in the context of publication also arose—in part—in the decision of Clarke J. in *Cogley v RTÉ*,[332] which concerned a programme to be broadcast by the defendant concerning alleged irregularities in the operation of a nursing home.[333] The plaintiff director of the nursing home sought an interlocutory injunction to prevent the broadcast of the programme on the basis that she would be defamed by it if it was to be broadcast. In refusing the injunction sought, Clarke J. held that in an interlocutory application in which a plaintiff seeks prior restraint of the broadcast of material on the grounds that it is defamatory, it must be clear from the evidence available at the interlocutory stage that the plaintiff will ultimately succeed at trial. He stated, consistent with the approach of Kelly J. in *Reynolds*, that not only must the plaintiff raise a serious issue concerning the words complained of, but that it must be shown that there is "no doubt" that the impugned words are defamatory. On the facts before him, Clarke J. held that the possible outcome of the defamation claim was not clear.

10–176 Having examined the decision in *Reynolds*, as well as reviewing the general *Campus Oil* principles, Clarke J. then appeared to go a step further in stating that:

> "The defendant may succeed in defending the action for any one of a number of reasons. For example the words or materials intended to be broadcast or published may not be found to be defamatory in the first place. Though defamatory the words may be shown, to the extent that they are defamatory, to be justified. There may on the facts of appropriate cases be possible defences of qualified privilege or, possibly, a public interest defence although the availability and parameters of such a defence in this jurisdiction have yet to be clearly established.[334] I am satisfied that the reference in the authorities to a clear case means a case where it is clear that the plaintiff will succeed and where, therefore, it is equally clear that none of the possible lines of defence which may be open to a defendant could reasonably succeed."[335]

10–177 It is certainly arguable that in saying this, Clarke J. has opened up the possibility that not only a substantiated averment that justification will be pleaded to meet a claim of alleged defamation will essentially defeat a claim for

[332] [2005] 4 I.R. 79; [2005] 2 I.L.R.M. 529.
[333] There were in fact two claims brought; one in the context of defamation, one arising out of an alleged breach of privacy, namely secret filming inside a nursing home. Clarke J. took the view that such filming might constitute a breach of privacy, citing the New Zealand case of *TV3 Network Services Ltd v Fahy* (1999) 2 N.Z.L.R. 129.
[334] Although see the subsequent ruling of Charleton J. in the case of *Leech v Independent Newspapers (Ireland) Ltd*, unreported, High Court, Charleton J., June 27, 2007, which would suggest that such a defence is available in this jurisdiction. See also the earlier case of *Hunter v Gerald Duckworth & Co Ltd*, unreported, High Court, O'Caoimh J., July 31, 2003.
[335] [2005] 4 I.R. 79 at 86; [2005] 2 I.L.R.M. 529 at 536.

an interlocutory injunction. He also seems to suggest that defences such as qualified privilege or, possibly, public interest, might be pleaded by way of defeating an application for an interlocutory injunction.[336]

(e) Undertaking as to Damages

10–178 It is arguable that a consideration of the question of an undertaking as to damages[337] is of limited value in an interlocutory application concerning an alleged defamation. Common sense would suggest that it is very difficult to establish what loss might be caused to, for example, a newspaper were it not allowed to publish a particular article or piece. However, as was stated by Finlay C.J. in the case of *Curust Financial Services Ltd v Loewe-Lack-Werk*,[338] albeit in the context of an assessment of the plaintiff's damages:

> "Difficulty, as distinct from complete impossibility, in the assessment of such damages should not, in my view, be a ground for characterising the awarding of damages as an inadequate remedy."[339]

(f) Proposed Changes

10–179 Pursuant to s.32 of the Defamation Bill 2006, it is proposed to incorporate an injunction into statute, on an interim, interlocutory and perpetual basis. Section 32 provides that:

> "(1) The High Court, or where a defamation action has been brought, the court in which it was brought, may, upon the application of the plaintiff, make an order prohibiting the publication or further publication of the statement in respect of which the application was made if in its opinion—
>   (a) the statement is defamatory, and
>   (b) the defendant has no defence to the action that is reasonably likely to succeed.
>   (2) Where an order is made under this section it shall not operate to prohibit the reporting of the making of that order provided that such reporting does not include the publication of the statement to which the order relates.
>   (3) In this section 'order' means—
>   (a) an interim order,
>   (b) an interlocutory order, or
>   (c) a permanent order."

---

[336] This seems to be the approach taken in relation to fair comment on a matter of public interest in the English case of *Fraser v Evans* [1969] 1 Q.B. 349 at 360; [1968] 3 W.L.R. 1172 at 1178; [1969] 1 All E.R. 8 at 10 by Lord Denning M.R. As to privilege, see *Harakas v Baltic Mercantile and Shipping Exchange Ltd* [1982] 1 W.L.R. 958; [1982] 2 All E.R. 701.

[337] As to which, see Ch.6, Interlocutory Applications, para.6–76.

[338] [1994] 1 I.R. 450. See generally the analysis of this case by Delany, (1993) 15 D.U.L.J. 228.

[339] [1994] 1 I.R. 450 at 468, disagreeing with the determination of Barron J. in the High Court that, "damages which are not readily susceptible to accurate measurements are not usually an

10–180 The proposed section would appear to reflect in statutory terms the approach of the courts as set out in, inter alia, *Reynolds v Malocco*.[340]

4. Privacy[341]

10–181 It is clear that the importance of freedom of speech also underpins the courts' slowness to grant interlocutory injunctions in relation to a breach of privacy when publication is in issue.[342] In the case of *R. v Central Independent Television Plc*[343] Hoffmann L.J. stated that:

> "The motives which impel judges to assume a power to balance freedom of speech against other interests are almost always understandable and humane on the facts of the particular case before them. Newspapers are sometimes irresponsible and their motives in a market economy cannot be expected to be unalloyed by considerations of commercial advantage. Publication may cause needless pain, distress and damage to individuals or harm to other aspects of the public interest. But a freedom which is restricted to what judges think to be responsible or in the public interest is no freedom. Freedom means the right to publish things which government and judges, however well motivated, think should not be published. It means the right to say things which 'right-thinking people' regard as dangerous or irresponsible. This freedom is subject only to clearly defined exceptions laid down by common law or statute …"[344]

(a) Constitutional Guarantee

10–182 An important factor in this jurisdiction is that the right to privacy is one of the unspecified personal rights guaranteed by the Constitution.[345] In the case of *Maguire v Drury*,[346] the High Court was asked to restrain the publication of material relating, in general terms, to the breakdown of a marriage. This was in order to save the minor children of a marriage from the distress it was alleged the publication would cause. O'Hanlon J. stated that it "seems desirable that it

---

appropriate remedy." See also, *Mantruck Services v Ballinlough Electrical Refrigeration Co Ltd* [1992] 1 I.R. 351.

[340] The explanatory memorandum accompanying the Bill simply states that: "Section 32 sets out the grounds on which a court may grant or refuse an order prohibiting the publication or further publication of defamatory matter."

[341] In relation to privacy, see McCullough, "What do Privacy Laws Protect?" (Bar Council, July 14, 2006).

[342] Privacy may also arise in the context of intrusion on personal privacy (s.10 of the Non Fatal Offence against the Person Act 1997, which creates the criminal offence of harassment) and (mis)appropriation of somebody's image for trading purposes.

[343] [1994] 3 W.L.R. 20.

[344] [1994] 3 W.L.R. 20 at 30.

[345] *McGee v Attorney General* [1974] I.R. 284 at 322, per Budd J.

[346] [1994] 2 I.R. 8; [1995] 1 I.L.R.M. 108.

should be left to the legislature, and not to the courts to 'stake out the exceptions to freedom of speech'."[347] He felt that to restrain publication as sought would represent:

> "a new departure in our law, for which, in my opinion, no precedent has been shown, and for which I can find no basis in the Irish Constitution, having regard, in particular, to the strongly-expressed guarantees in favour of freedom of expression in that document."[348]

10–183 O'Hanlon J. also expressed the concern that by granting the relief sought, "the interlocutory injunction could be used effectively to encroach in a significant manner on the freedom of the press."[349] In the circumstances, he refused the interlocutory injunction sought, as there was no fair case to be tried.

10–184 In *Domican v Axa Insurance Ltd*,[350] an interlocutory injunction was sought by the plaintiff to prevent the defendant insurance company from interfering with the solicitor/client relationship between the plaintiff and his solicitor by communicating directly with him in connection with his personal injuries action against a party insured by the defendant. Clarke J. dismissed the plaintiff's claim. He found that it had not been established that there had been a breach of the plaintiff's constitutional right to privacy or his right to privacy guaranteed by the European Convention on Human Rights. He also held that, given the nature of the relationship between the parties, it was necessary that there be some communication. He found that the plaintiff had failed to establish that his right to privacy extended to the narrow question of the manner in which communication with him was to be conducted.

M. TRESPASS

1. Introduction

10–185 Trespass involves wrongful conduct which causes a direct injury. The most common form of injunction concerning trespass is in relation to trespass to land.[351] Injunctions may also be sought in relation to trespass to the person[352]

---

[347] [1994] 2 I.R. 8; [1995] 1 I.L.R.M. 108 at 116.

[348] [1994] 2 I.R. 8 at 17; [1995] 1 I.L.R.M. 108 at 116.

[349] [1994] 2 I.R. 8 at 18; [1995] 1 I.L.R.M. 108 at 116.

[350] unreported, High Court, Clarke J., January 19, 2007.

[351] See generally, *Moore v Attorney General (No. 3)* [1930] I.R. 471; *Irish Shell v John Costello Ltd* [1984] I.R. 511; *Flanagan v Mulhall* [1985] I.L.R.M. 134; *Dwyer Nolan Developments Ltd v Dublin Co Council* [1986] I.R. 130; *Cork Co Council v Burke*, unreported, High Court, Peart J., August 15, 2005 and *AGS (ROI) Pension Nominees v Madison Estates*, unreported, High Court, Lavan J., July 25, 2007 (injunction refused as the plaintiffs had failed to established a stateable case).

[352] *O'Boyle v Attorney General* [1929] I.R. 558. Trespass to the person can be sub-divided into

and in relation to trespass to goods.[353] Whilst injunctions sought on a perpetual basis admit of no particular considerations which are peculiar to the area of trespass, the same cannot be said in relation to injunctions relating to trespass sought on an interlocutory basis.

2. General Principles

10–186 As observed by Laffoy J. in the case of *Dwyer Nolan Developments Ltd v Kingscroft Developments Ltd*,[354] it is not necessary to prove damage in the case of trespass.

10–187 Defences to an action for trespass include consent; the defence of a person or property; or lawful authority. However, it is important to note that pursuant to s.4 of the Occupiers' Liability Act 1995, an occupier of a premises must not injure a trespasser or damage their property intentionally, nor must he act with reckless disregard for the person or the property of the person.[355] This is subject to the modification of an occupier's duty towards entrants as set out in s.5 of the Act.

3. Interlocutory Considerations

10–188 As has been seen,[356] where a plaintiff clearly has good title and the defendant's trespass is indisputable, an interlocutory injunction will generally be granted as a matter of course. As stated by Balcombe L.J. in the case of *Patel v WH Smith (Eziot) Ltd*[357]:

> "It seems to me that, first, *prima facie* a landowner whose title is not in issue is entitled to an injunction to restrain trespass on his land whether or not the trespass harms him."[358]

---

assault, battery and false imprisonment. See generally, McMahon & Binchy, *The Irish Law of Torts*, 3rd edn (Dublin: Butterworths, 2000), Ch.22 (Trespass to the person) and Ch.23 (Trespass to land).

[353] *Sligo Corporation v Gilbride* [1929] I.R. 351; *Wymes v Tehan* [1988] I.R. 717.

[354] unreported, High Court, Laffoy J., February 9, 2007.

[355] For the position adopted by the courts in relation to trespass generally prior to the introduction of the Act, see cases such as *Purtill v Athlone UDC* [1968] I.R. 205 and *McNamara v ESB* [1975] I.R. 1; *Keane v ESB* [1981] I.R. 44 and *Smith v CIÉ* [1991] 1 I.R. 314.

[356] See Ch.6, Interlocutory Applications, para.6–163.

[357] [1987] 1 W.L.R. 853; [1987] 2 All E.R. 569.

[358] [1987] 1 W.L.R. 853 at 858; [1987] 2 All E.R. 569 at 573. See also, *Hampstead & Suburban Properties Ltd v Diomedus* [1969] 1 Ch. 248; [1968] 3 W.L.R. 990; [1968] 3 All E.R. 545, in which a defendant was in clear breach of a binding covenant. This should be distinguished from cases where liability is arguable: *Texaxo Ltd v Mulberry Filling Station Ltd* [1972] 1 W.L.R. 814.

10–189 In *Keating & Co. Ltd v Jervis Shopping Centre Ltd*,[359] Keane J. repeated almost verbatim Balcombe L.J.'s dictum.[360] If evidence is put forward in an attempt to establish that a party has a right to do what would otherwise be deemed a trespass, the court will proceed on the basis of the *American Cyanamid/ Campus Oil* principles. In *Dublin Corporation v Burke*,[361] Geoghegan J. observed that he was:

> "extremely doubtful that there would even be a *prima facie* case for an injunction where a defendant with some back-up evidence (if ultimately accepted) is alleging an actual tenancy in the premises and the plaintiff is for all practical purposes merely sceptical of the truth of the allegation."[362]

N. OTHER AREAS

10–190 There are a number of other areas of the law in which injunctive relief has played a important role, although perhaps not to the same extent in terms of either volume of case law or the establishment of any particularly unusual principles. These areas, each of which will be considered in turn, are:

1. banking;
2. education;
3. human rights;
4. immigration;
5. landlord and tenant;
6. partnership.

1. Banking

10–191 Specific statutory provisions have been introduced in relation to injunctions in the context of banking.[363] Injunction applications in relation to banking are not confined to the specific areas detailed in the legislation, however. One particular area which has given rise to detailed consideration in both this jurisdiction and in England is the question of performance bonds. As has been noted by Breslin,[364] there is a reluctance on the part of the Irish courts to interfere with performance bonds and letters. As such, the decided case law

---

[359] [1997] 1 I.R. 512.
[360] [1997] 1 I.R. 512 at 518. In relation to the construction of a contract, see *Fellowes & Son v Fisher* [1976] Q.B. 122; [1975] 3 W.L.R. 184 and *Associated British Ports v Transport and General Workers' Union* [1989] 1 W.L.R. 939 at 979.
[361] unreported, Supreme Court, October 9, 2001.
[362] Cited by Carroll J. in *Dublin City Council v McGrath*, unreported, High Court, Carroll J., March 12, 2004.
[363] See Ch.11, Specific Statutory Injunctions, para.11–162.
[364] See Breslin, *Banking Law*, 2nd edn (Dublin: Thomson Round Hall, 2006), p.423.

would suggest that at the interlocutory stage, in order to persuade a court to injunct an issuing bank from paying a beneficiary, the party seeking the injunction must go beyond demonstrating a serious arguable case.[365] This is evident from, inter alia, the case of *GPA Group Plc v Bank of Ireland*,[366] in which Keane J. cited a passage from the judgment of Kerr J. in *Harbottle Ltd v National Westminster Bank Ltd*,[367] Kerr J. had stated that:

> "It is only in exceptional cases that the courts will interfere with the machinery of irrevocable obligations assumed by banks. They are the life-blood of international commerce. Such obligations are regarded as collateral to the underlying rights and obligations between merchants at either end of the banking chain. Except possibly in clear cases of fraud of which the bank have notice, the courts will leave the merchants to settle their disputes under the contracts by litigation or arbitration ... The courts are not concerned with their difficulties to enforce such claims; these are risks which the merchants take. In this case the plaintiffs took the risk of the unconditional wording of the guarantees. The machinery and commitments of banks are on a different level. They must be allowed to be honoured, free from interference by the courts. Otherwise, trust in international commerce could be irreparably damaged."[368]

10–192 As pointed out by Keane J., the Supreme Court adopted a similar approach in the case of bills of exchange in *Walek & Co. KG v Seafield Gentex*.[369] He refused the interlocutory injunction sought as he felt that it would defeat policy considerations if the court was to make an order enjoining the bank from payment until the final disposal of the action in circumstances where:

> "the question as to whether the Bank is obliged to make payment depends solely on the construction of the letter of credit and the documents furnished by the party seeking payment."[370]

2. Education

10–193 The issue of the State being compelled by way of mandatory injunction to provide educational services has been a high-profile area of litigation in recent years.[371] However, the decision of the Supreme Court in *TD v Minister*

---

[365] See *Deutsche Ruckversicherung AG v Walbrook Insurance Co Ltd* [1996] 1 All E.R. 791 at 801 per Staughton J. and *Solo Industries UK Ltd v Candar Bank* [2001] 1 W.L.R. 1800 at 1813, per Mance L.J.
[366] [1992] 2 I.R. 408.
[367] [1978] Q.B. 146 at 155.
[368] Also cited by Keane J. in *Hibernia Meats Ltd v Ministère de l'Agriculture et de la Revolution Agraire*, unreported, High Court, Keane J., February 16, 1984.
[369] [1978] I.R. 167.
[370] [1992] 2 I.R. 408 at 424.
[371] See generally, O'Mahony, "A New Slant on Education Rights and Mandatory Injunctions" (2005) 27 D.U.L.J. 363, in which the relevant cases are reviewed.

for Education,[372] which held that mandatory injunctions of this nature dealt with matters of policy and, as such, amounted to a breach of the separation of powers, has meant that this is an area is which injunctions are much less likely to be granted. That said, subsequent to *TD*, in *Cronin v Minister for Education*[373] Laffoy J. granted an interlocutory mandatory injunction compelling the Minister for Education to provide the plaintiff with educational facilities pending the substantive determination of the litigation in question. A key consideration was the fact that the injunction order was limited to the particular needs of the plaintiff, and merely extended a programme which the Minister for Education had already sanctioned, as distinct from requiring the implementation of a range of new facilities.

3. Human Rights

10–194 The role and impact of the European Convention on Human Rights has already been considered in the context of publication in broad terms.[374] A related question is the extent to which an injunction may be sought in relation to a breach of the European Convention on Human Rights and the European Convention on Human Rights Act 2003. This specific issue is a matter which does not appear to have been fully addressed by the courts in this jurisdiction, although it has been considered. In the case of *O'Donnell v South Dublin County Council*,[375] the plaintiffs suffered from a syndrome which caused the body's inability to develop, resulting in physical complications. An order was sought from the court requiring the defendant to provide accommodation deemed suitable to the third named defendants' needs, including a wheelchair-accessible caravan with indoor wheelchair-accessible shower and toilet, adequate sanitary facilities and central heating. It was claimed that the defendant county council was in breach of its statutory duties to the plaintiffs, as well as in breach of their constitutional rights and their rights under the European Convention on Human Rights, specifically Arts 3 and 8 thereof. The plaintiffs also claimed damages under the 2003 Act.

10–195 Article 3 of the Convention provides that, "no-one shall be subjected to torture or to inhuman or degrading treatment or punishment." Article 8 provides that:

> "1. Everyone has the right to respect for his private and family life, his home and his correspondence.

---

[372]   [2001] 4 I.R. 259.
[373]   [2004] 3 I.R. 205.
[374]   See para.10–166.
[375]   unreported, High Court, Laffoy J., May 22, 2007.

2. There shall be no interference by a public authority with the exercise of this right except such as is in accordance with the law and is necessary in a democratic society in the interests of national security, public safety or the economic well-being of the country, for the prevention of disorder or crime, for the protection of health or morals, or for the protection of the rights and freedom of others."

10–196 In finding that there had been a breach of Art.8, Laffoy J. also held that "the only remedy which the court can provide for the breach it has found of article 8 of the Convention is an award of damages." At first blush, this might suggest that an injunction would not be available in such circumstances. However, it is important to note that Laffoy J. qualified her statement by stating that this remedy was being provided "on the basis of the plaintiffs' claim as formulated". It is arguable that on the basis of a Contracting State's obligations under the European Convention on Human Rights, an injunction should be available in appropriate circumstances. In that regard, an analogy can be drawn with the State's obligations in respect of European law, as considered above.[376]

4. Immigration

10–197 Injunctions are often sought in the context of judicial review proceedings in the context of attempts to deport parties from the State. In seeking declarations in relation to their entitlement to stay in the State, applicants will often seek a stay pursuant to RSC Ord.84 r.20(7)(a), or an interim and/or interlocutory injunction restraining the respondents from acting adversely to the rights of the applicant pending the determination of the proceedings.

10–198 That the courts have jurisdiction to grant interlocutory relief in judicial review proceedings is clear from the terms of RSC Ord.84 r.25.[377] As was made clear in decisions such as *Malsheva v Minister for Justice, Equality and Law Reform*,[378] the approach to be taken on such an application for interlocutory relief is to have regard to the *Campus Oil* principles. In most such cases, it will be usual that damages would be an adequate remedy, and so a key focus will be the question of the balance of convenience.

10–199 However, it was stressed in the case of *PF v Minister for Justice, Equality and Law Reform*,[379] in which an injunction was sought "restraining the respondent from failing to readmit the second named applicant to this

---

[376] See para.10–92.
[377] See para.10–103. See also RSC Ord.84 r.18(2).
[378] ex tempore, High Court, Finlay Geoghegan J., July 25, 2003.
[379] unreported, High Court, Murphy J. January 23, 2004.

jurisdiction and from failing to take all steps necessary to secure such readmission", that it is important to bring such applications at the correct time. In *PF*, Murphy J. observed that the applicants were out of time in relation to the relevant deportation order and that, as such "there would seem to be no fair question to be tried even if the court were to allow the amendment to the grounds."

5. Landlord and Tenant

10–200 Injunctions have been granted in a number of areas in the context of the relationship between landlord and tenant. The three main areas in which they have been granted are in relation to breaches of convenants[380]; to provide for peaceable re-entry[381]; and to prevent breaches of sub-leases.[382] Injunctions have also been granted in relation to wrongful distress,[383] which involves the seizure of a person's goods without a court order allowing such seizure. Frequently such goods belong to a tenant and are removed by a landlord in essence as a security against payment of rent.

(a) Quia Timet Injunctions

10–201 *Quia timet* injunctions have also been granted in the context of landlord and tenant disputes. In *Whelan v Madigan*,[384] such an injunction was granted in relation to an alleged campaign of intimidation. That case is also of note in that Kenny J. observed that where a lease does not contain a covenant for quiet enjoyment, such a covenant cannot be implied when the tenant is in arrears in rent.

10–202 However, a *quia timet* injunction was refused in *McCrane v Louth Co. Council*[385] in relation to the proposed development of a rubbish dump. Seemingly influencing the court was the fact that a report had been commissioned by the defendant county council in relation to the suitability of the site and to its development and management.

---

[380] *Goldfarb v Williams* [1945] I.R. 433; *Solomon v Red Bank Restaurant Ltd* [1938] I.R. 793; *Whelan v McKinley* (1921) 56 I.L.T.R. 21. In *Whelan v Cork Corporation* [1991] I.L.R.M. 19 Murphy J. refused to grant an injunction to restrain breaches of restrictive covenants in a lease on the basis that when a lessee enlarges his interest under s.8 of the Landlord and Tenant (Ground Rents) (No. 2) Act 1978, then by virtue of s.28 of the Act, all covenants subject to which the lessee held the land ceased to have effect.

[381] *Sweeney (FG) Ltd v Powerscourt* [1984] I.R. 501. Although see *McGill v S* [1979] I.R. 283, in which Gannon J. held that a bare licensee had no ground for seeking an injunction to prevent the licensor requiring him to leave the premises concerned.

[382] *Enock v Lambert Jones Estates Ltd* [1983] I.L.R.M. 532.

[383] *Cassidy v Foley* [1904] 2 I.R. 427.

[384] [1978] I.L.R.M. 136.

[385] unreported, High Court, O'Hanlon J., December 9, 1983.

(b) Application of Campus Oil Guidelines

10–203 The *Campus Oil* guidelines are in the normal course applied to landlord and tenant disputes in the context of applications for interlocutory injunctions. However, it was held on an application for an interlocutory injunction in the case of *The Right Honourable The Lord Mayor, Aldermen and Burgesses of Dublin v Burke*[386] that the balance of convenience will be in favour of refusing an interlocutory injunction where a solid property right might be lost by the grant of the injunction. In the Supreme Court, Geoghegan J. also observed that he was "extremely doubtful" that there is even a prima facie case for an injunction if a defendant has backup evidence of a tenancy and a plaintiff "is for all practical purposes merely sceptical of the truth of the allegation."

6. Partnership

10–204 An injunction may be granted against a partner who acts in breach of his fiduciary duties as a partner,[387] or in breach of the partnership agreement in more specific terms.[388] The goodwill of a partnership may also be protected by injunction.[389]

---

[386] unreported, Supreme Court, October 9, 2001. For an analysis of this case, see Courtney, "Landlord and Tenant Update" (2002) 7(1) C.P.L.J. 20.

[387] *Anderson v Wallace* (1826) 2 Mol. 540.

[388] *Morris v Colman* (1812) 18 Ves. Jr. 437. As noted by Twomey, *Partnership Law* (Dublin: Butterworths, 2000), p.468, based on the decision in *Floyd v Cheney* [1970] 1 All E.R. 446, an injunction can be granted even if the partnership is a partnership at will.

[389] *Gargan v Ruttle* [1931] I.R. 152.

CHAPTER 11

SPECIFIC STATUTORY INJUNCTIONS

A. INTRODUCTION

11–01 The general ability of the courts to grant equitable injunctions is based primarily on s.28(8) of the Supreme Court of Judicature Act (Ireland) 1877.[1] However, statute has a further role to play in the context of injunctions. Various pieces of legislation make provision for the granting of injunctions in defined areas and circumstances. This is both explicit—in the sense of using the term "injunction" in the legislation—and also implicit, in that provision can be made for orders which amount to injunctions.[2] Where such injunctions are provided for in statute, the legislation adopts, in general terms, one of two approaches: it either makes provision for an application for an injunction based on the breach of a particular statutory provision or set of circumstances,[3] or it provides for a self-contained code,[4] which will govern the application for, and granting of, an injunction order. For ease, such injunctions will be referred to in this work as "specific statutory injunctions".

11–02 Some of these legislative provisions have already been referred to in the context of other areas of the law.[5] It is not practicable to identify each and every area of the law in which a statutory injunction or similar order is provided for. The purpose of this chapter is to identify the key principles which must be considered when dealing with statutory injunctions, and in doing so to examine their relationship to equitable injunctions. Different areas of the law in which specific statutory provision is made for injunction or injunction-style orders will then be looked at, starting with the area of planning and development law. This will be followed by an overview of the area of industrial relations law, which demonstrates how prescriptive legislation can be in terms of injunctions. By way of contrast, the legislative provisions related to intellectual property law will then be looked at, as these are more descriptive, rather than prescriptive, in form. The Proceeds of Crime Act is also reviewed. This is because, on its face, the Act appears to provide for both interim and interlocutory injunctions. However, that particular piece of legislation has been subject to scrutiny by the courts in relation to the real nature of these injunctions. The resulting case law

---

[1] See Ch.1, Domestic Jurisdiction, para.1–30.
[2] See, for example, s.160 of the Planning and Development Act 2000. See para.11–12.
[3] See para.11–66, dealing with intellectual property.
[4] See *Mahon v Butler* [1997] 3 I.R. 369 at 377; [1998] 1 I.L.R.M. 284 at 290.
[5] See, for example, Ch.8, Commercial Injunctions.

is of interest in so far as it demonstrates that whilst it may appear that legislative provision is made for certain types of injunction, these must be approached with caution. The provision for what amount to injunction orders by the District Court—not a court with equitable jurisdiction—in the area of family law will then be looked at before some of the statutory provisions in which injunctions are provided for will be identified. However, reference should be made to specialist texts—which will be identified in each individual section as appropriate—in such areas for more detailed analysis and consideration of how such injunctions are applied for and the considerations which inform their granting or otherwise.

B. General Considerations

1. Role of Equitable Considerations

11–03 The main consideration overarching all forms of specific statutory injunction is the question as to whether equitable considerations play their normal role.[6] The role of equity in the context of a specific statutory remedy can be broken down into two questions. The first is whether, if a statutory remedy is provided for, there co-exists the right to seek an equitable injunction. The second is whether general equitable principles have a role to play in a court's determination as to whether or not to grant a specific statutory injunction.

(a) Co-Existence of Equitable Remedy

11–04 The first of these two questions was dealt with by the Supreme Court in the case of *Mahon v Butler*.[7] In the context of a consideration of s.27 of the Local Government (Planning and Development) Act 1976,[8] Denham J. held in *Mahon v Butler*[9] that the court had no jurisdiction to expand that particular statute by invoking the court's equitable jurisdiction. She held that any discretion in that regard was within the ambit of the section only.[10] She thus refused to grant a *quia timet* injunction, as this was not provided for in the applicable legislation. It would therefore seem that, if a statute prescribes an exclusive remedy, the court is not at liberty to grant an injunction on an equitable basis.[11]

---

[6] See generally, Ch.4, Equitable and General Principles.

[7] [1997] 3 I.R. 369; [1998] 1 I.L.R.M. 284.

[8] See para.11–12, below.

[9] [1997] 3 I.R. 369; [1998] 1 I.L.R.M. 284, overturning Costello P. and rejecting the argument that the court had an equitable jurisdiction to issue a *quia timet* injunction under s.27, based on an analysis of the wording of s.27(1), which referred to events which occurred in the present or past, but not to future events. This lacuna was addressed by the provisions of s.160 of the Planning and Development Act 2000. See generally, Flynn, "Pop Concerts and Planning" (1997) 4(4) I.P.E.L.J. 127.

[10] per Denham J. in *Mahon v Butler* [1997] 3 I.R. 369 at 377; [1998] 1 I.L.R.M. 284 at 290.

[11] cf. *Attorney General v Ashbourne Recreation Ground Co.* [1903] 1 Ch. 101 at 107.

11–05 Such an approach is consistent with the English decision of *Department of Social Security v Butler*.[12] In the Court of Appeal Simon Brown L.J. stated the relevant law as that found in *Halsbury's Laws of England*[13]:

> "Where it is the intention of a statute, as disclosed by its scope and by its wording, that a special remedy provided by it should be the only one for enforcing a particular obligation created by the statute, the result may be to exclude or restrict the inherent or ordinary jurisdiction of the courts and to send a person wishing to enforce the obligation to an administrative body, to arbitration or to some particular court or tribunal only. A statute should not be construed so as to take away the jurisdiction of superior courts unless it does so by express words or necessary implication."[14]

11–06 In *McKenna v EH*,[15] Finnegan J. had to deal with the question of whether the injunctive reliefs provided for in the Proceeds of Crime Act 1996 were in the nature of ancillary or substantive relief. He referred to the test for the grant of an injunction in aid of a statute as used by Ungoed-Thomas J. in the case of *Duchess of Argyll v Duke of Argyll*,[16] namely whether the statute concerned manifests an intention to confer a civil right on the plaintiff. If it does, "the possibility of an injunction arises".[17] Finnegan J. also referred to the Australian case of *King v Goussetis*.[18] In that case it was held that the appropriate test for determining whether or not an injunction should be granted "is to have regard to the nature, scope and terms of the statute—it is a question of statutory interpretation whether an injunction should be granted or not." In other words, each statute must be interpreted on its own terms in order to establish whether it provides for an injunction and, by extension, whether such a remedy is intended to be exclusive.

11–07 Summarising the position, Spry identifies a number of matters which may assist in arriving at a view as to what the statute intends, viz.:

---

12 [1995] W.L.R. 1528.
13 4th edn, Vol. 44, p.594, para.946.
14 As cited in *Butler* [1995] W.L.R. 1528 at 1542. The cases cited by Halsbury in this regard include *Attorney General v Ashbourne Recreation Ground Co.* [1903] 1 Ch. 101; *Yorkshire Miners' Association v Howden* [1905] A.C. 256; *Attorney General v Wimbledon House Estate Co. Ltd* [1904] 2 Ch. 34; *Carlton Illustrators v Coleman & Co Ltd* [1911] 1 K.B. 771; *A.G. v Lewes Corp.* [1911] 2 Ch. 495, and *Bradbury v London Borough of Enfield* [1967] 1 W.L.R. 1311; [1967] 3 All E.R. 434.
15 [2002] 1 I.R. 72; [2002] 2 I.L.R.M. 117. Reference was also made to the fact that it is the function of procedural law to give effect to the intent of the Oireachtas, and that the courts must construe the Rules widely. See also, *McKenna v RM* [2003] 3 I.R. 1 in relation to s.3 of the Proceeds of Crime Act 1996.
16 [1967] Ch. 302; [1965] 2 W.L.R. 790; [1965] 1 All E.R. 611.
17 [2002] 1 I.R. 72 at 81; [2002] 2 I.L.R.M. 117 at 125.
18 [1986] 5 N.S.W.L.R. 89.

> "the nature of the right that has been created by the statutory instrument in question, the probable efficacy of the penalty or remedy set out if it were an exclusive procedure, the nature of the tribunal before which material statutory proceedings are to be taken ... any restriction of the class of persons who are entitled to avail themselves of the statutory procedure and the appropriateness of that procedure effectively to prevent future breaches ... "[19]

11–08 He also suggests when considering the extent to which a statutory remedy is exclusive, that it is necessary to ask more precisely whether or not there has been an exclusion or denial of the particular remedy sought.[20]

(b) Role of Equitable Considerations

11–09 The dictum of Denham J. in *Mahon* deals with situations where in effect a party seeks an equitable injunction where provision is already made in statute as to how a particular situation must be remedied. However, this is distinct from the question of whether the courts may have regard to equitable considerations in coming to their determinations when dealing with a specific statutory injunction. The point was not specifically addressed by Denham J. in *Mahon*. As will be seen,[21] the courts appear to have had no difficulty, on an application for a statutory injunction, having regard to general and equitable principles and concepts such as delay, clean hands and so on.[22]

2. Res Judicata

11–10 In the case of *Lipschitz v Tierney*,[23] it was held by Murnaghan J. that a statutory injunction cannot be negated or defeated by the operation of a previous judgment, or by the operation of the principles of res judicata or estoppel.[24]

11–11 With these basic points in mind, it is now proposed to look at various areas in which specific statutory provisions have been enacted in terms of injunctions, starting with the area of planning and development law.

---

[19] Spry, *The Principles of Equitable Remedies*, 6th edn (London: Sweet and Maxwell, 2001), p.367.
[20] Spry, *The Principles of Equitable Remedies*, 6th edn (London: Sweet and Maxwell, 2001), p.365.
[21] See in particular para.11–24.
[22] See Ch.4, Equitable and General Principles.
[23] [1959] 1 I.R. 144.
[24] Citing *Griffiths v Davies* [1943] K.B. 618 at 621 and *Bradshaw v M'Mullan* [1920] 2 I.R. 412 at 425.

C. Planning and Development Law

1. Introduction[25]

11–12 Section 160 of the Planning and Development Act 2000 provides the statutory basis for what is commonly termed the "planning injunction", even though the word "injunction" does not in fact specifically appear in the wording of s.160. As observed by Barrington J. in *Avenue Properties Ltd v Farrell Homes Ltd*[26] in relation to s.27 of the Local Government (Planning and Development) Act 1976,[27] the section which s.160 replaced:

> "The term "injunction" is not used in section 27 but it is clear that the Order contemplated by the section is an order in the nature of an injunction whether restraining or mandatory. The reference to 'interim' and 'interlocutory' orders in section 27(3) appears to reinforce this interpretation."

11–13 Under s.160, relief is available where development has been or is being carried out without planning permission or where an unauthorised use is being made of land. Section 27 was frequently referred to as a "fire brigade" section.[28] Its purpose was considered by Keane J. in the case of *Dublin Corporation v McGowan*.[29] Keane J. observed that the section was intended to deal with an urgent situation requiring immediate action rather than a situation where an unauthorised development was completed a number of years previously. The same purpose underlies s.160, and in *Leen v Aer Rianta cpt*,[30] McKechnie J. confirmed that case law in relation to the discretionary nature of s.27 had been carried over to s.160 of the 2000 Act.[31]

2. Planning and Development Act 2000, Section 160

11–14 Section 160(1) of the Planning and Development Act 2000 provides for injunctive relief to be granted on the application of any person where unauthorised development has been carried out, is being or is likely to be carried out. It reads:

---

[25] For a comprehensive overview of the "planning injunction", see Simons, "Planning Injunctions: section 160" (2004) J.S.I.J. 199 and also his authoritative work on planning, *Planning and Development Law,* 2nd edn (Dublin: Thomson Round Hall, 2007).

[26] [1982] I.L.R.M. 21 at 26.

[27] As substituted by s.19(4) of the Local Government (Planning and Development) Act 1992.

[28] per Keane J. in *Dublin Corporation v McGowan* [1993] 1 I.R. 405 at 411.

[29] [1993] 1 I.R. 405 at 411.

[30] [2003] 4 I.R. 394, considering *O'Connor v Frank Harrington Ltd,* unreported, High Court, Barr J., May 28, 1987.

[31] A problem was identified in *Dublin County Council v Kirby* [1985] I.L.R.M. 325, namely that under s.27 of the Local Government (Planning and Development) Act 1976, the High Court was given jurisdiction to make both prohibitory and mandatory orders if the developer had

"Where an unauthorised development has been, is being or is likely to be carried out or continued, the High Court or the Circuit Court may, on the application of a planning authority or any other person, whether or not the person has an interest in the land, by order require any person to do or not to do, or to cease to do, as the case may be, anything that the Court considers necessary and specifies in the order to ensure, as appropriate, the following:

(*a*) that the unauthorised development is not carried out or continued[32];

(*b*) in so far as is practicable, that any land is restored to its condition prior to the commencement of any unauthorised development;

(*c*) that any development is carried out in conformity with the permission pertaining to that development or any condition to which the permission is subject."

11–15 The purpose of s.160 was expressed by Peart J. in *Mountbrook Homes Ltd v Oldcourt Developments Ltd*[33] as being to ensure in the public interest that development was carried out in a proper manner, in accordance with permission duly granted.

11–16 It is proposed to look at each of the specific elements of the planning injunction in turn. Before doing so, it is important to consider the issue of who has the standing to bring an application under s.160, as the rules in this regard are different to those which normally pertain to parties seeking an injunction order. This will be followed by a brief consideration of the circumstances in which a court has jurisdiction to entertain an application brought pursuant to s.160.

3. Standing and Jurisdiction

(a) Applicant

11–17 What was unusual, and indeed innovative, when s.27 of the 1976 Act was introduced was that by its terms any member of the public, regardless of whether that person had any interest in the land in question or suffered damage as a result of the particular development, could bring an application under the section. In other words, it was not necessary to demonstrate an interest in order to establish locus standi, or standing, in the normal way.[34] As stated by

---

obtained planning permission. If the developer had not, the court had prohibitory powers only. This was remedied by the enactment of the Local Government (Planning and Development) Act 1992; see s.19(4).

[32] The concept of "unauthorised development" is defined in s.2 of the Planning and Development Act 2000. However, a court may not, in a s.160 application, review, alter or set aside a decision of the planning authority regarding the granting or withholding of permission: See, *The Right Honourable The Lord Mayor Aldermen and Burgesses of Dublin v Garland* [1982] I.L.R.M. 104

[33] unreported, High Court, Peart J., April 22, 2005.

[34] See Ch.3, Standing.

Barrington J. in *Avenue Properties Ltd v Farrell Homes Ltd*,[35] the intention of the section was that the Planning Acts "should be policed not only by the Planning Authority but also by individual citizens."[36] In the case of *Leen v Aer Rianta cpt*,[37] McKechnie J. observed that the motive of the applicant was irrelevant to his standing to bring proceedings under s.160, although it was "highly relevant" to the exercise of the court's discretion in considering what relief it might grant him.

(b) Respondent

11–18 The parties who should be named as respondents are those against whom orders are sought.[38] In the normal course, this would be the owners or occupiers of the land in question.[39]

(c) Onus

11–19 There is no express provision as to the onus of proof contained in s.160. The most logical interpretation to be derived from the wording of s.160 would be that the onus is on the applicant to show that the development comes within the terms of s.160, and that it is not in any way exempted, such that an injunction cannot be granted under s.160.[40]

(d) Jurisdiction

11–20 It is important to establish that a court has jurisdiction to deal with a matter under s.160. For example, in *Loughnane v Hogan*,[41] Blayney J. refused to make the orders sought under s.27, on the basis that the jurisdiction of the court under s.27(1) was limited to prohibiting the continuance of a development or unauthorised use which has been commenced without the required planning permission. However, once the building was completed there was no longer any development being carried out within the meaning of s.27(1)(a) of the Act. Accordingly, the court had no jurisdiction to order its removal.[42] Based on

---

[35] [1982] I.L.R.M. 21.

[36] [1982] I.L.R.M. 21 at 26.

[37] [2003] 4 I.R. 394.

[38] See RSC Ord.103 r.8 and RCC Ord.56 r.3(3)(b), which provide for orders against "a person whose identity is unknown".

[39] In the case of *Dublin County Council v Elton Homes Ltd (In Liquidation)* [1984] I.L.R.M. 297 it was held that it would be inappropriate to make an order against a company in liquidation or its directors, who were now functus officio.

[40] See *Callan v Boyle Quarries Ltd*, unreported, High Court, Murphy J., March 20, 2007, in which Murphy J. held that where objective, credible evidence is adduced in relation to the matter at hand, the court may have regard to the absence of available evidence from, inter alia, the respondent.

[41] [1987] I.R. 322.

[42] Applying *Dublin Co Council v Kirby* [1985] I.L.R.M. 32.

McKechine J.'s acceptance in *Leen v Aer Rianta cpt*[43] that case law determined under s.27 carried over to the s.160 regime, there would appear to be no reason why this view as to jurisdiction should not still prevail.

4. Potential Defences

11–21 It is a full defence to an application under s.160 to show that the development is exempted.[44] In that regard, s.4 of the 2000 Act sets out 12 specific instances of development which is exempted, including, but not limited to, development of land for agricultural purposes; development a by a county council in its functional area; and development consisting of the use of any structure or other land within the curtilage of a house for any purpose incidental to the enjoyment of the house. It will clearly be up to the court to determine in each case in which it is argued whether or not a development is "exempted".[45] Other defences include demonstrating that there is no development taking place, that there is existing planning permission for such a development or that established use can be shown.[46] It is also important to bear in mind that the s.160 remedy is a discretionary one; as will be seen below, there are a number of factors which a court will consider in determining whether or not to exercise its discretion.

5. Discretionary Remedy

11–22 Section 27 afforded the court a wide discretion as to whether or not to grant an injunction. One of the reasons for this was identified by Barrington J. in the case of *Stafford v Roadstone Ltd*,[47] in which he stated that:

> "it seems to me, that if a person who is not the planning authority and who has no interest in the lands can apply for an injunction under section 27 then it is all the more important that the High Court should have a wide discretion on the question of whether or not to issue an injunction."[48]

---

[43] [2003] 4 I.R. 394, considering *O'Connor v Frank Harrington Ltd*, unreported, High Court, Barr J., May 28, 1987.

[44] See Simons, "Planning Injunctions: Section 160" (2004) 4(2) J.S.I.J. p.213/214.

[45] See, for example, *Smyth v Colgan* [1999] 1 I.R. 548.

[46] See generally in relation to defences Keeling, "Defending s.160 Planning Injunctions" (2004) I.P.E.L.J. 54.

[47] [1980] I.L.R.M. 1. See also, *Dublin Corporation v Mulligan*, unreported, High Court, Finlay P., May 6, 1980; *Dublin Corporation v Kevans*, unreported, High Court, Finlay P., July 14, 1980; *Dublin Corporation v Garland* [1982] I.L.R.M. 104 and *Furlong v AF & GW McConnell Ltd* [1990] I.L.R.M. 48.

[48] [1980] I.L.R.M. 1 at 19.

11–23 Also relevant, according to Barrington J., was the fact that a breach might be "innocent or technical" and could be put right by an application for planning permission. In the case of *Wicklow Co. Council v Forest Fencing Ltd*,[49] Charleton J. observed that when a court is exercising its jurisdiction under s.160, it "would not exercise its equitable powers in relation to matters which are trivial".

(a) Equitable and General Considerations

11–24 In the case of *White v McInerney Construction Ltd*,[50] Blayney J. endorsed in the Supreme Court the idea that there was such a wide discretion. He specifically rejected the contention that in so far as there was discretion, it should only be exercised in a particular way, namely to ensure compliance with the Planning Acts. Blayney J. found such a proposition to be "wholly inconsistent" with the wider discretion afforded the court under s.27.[51] In relation to how the discretion should be exercised, Blayney J. cited with approval the decision of Barrington J. in the case of *Avenue Properties Ltd v Farrell Homes Ltd.*[52] In *Avenue Properties*, Barrington J. had referred to the fact that, when exercising its discretion, the court should "be influenced, in some measure, by the factors which would influence a court of equity in deciding to grant or withhold an injunction."[53]

11–25 The impact of equitable and general principles is also evident in the case of *Morris v Garvey.*[54] Henchy J. referred to the correct approach to be taken to s.27(2), which empowered the High Court to order any person to do or cease to do anything necessary to ensure that the conditions of a planning permission were observed. He set out a number of "exceptional circumstances" which would be required before a court would refrain from making an order to ensure that a development is carried out in conformity with the relevant provisions. These factors included "genuine mistake, acquiescence over a long period, the triviality or mere technicality of the infraction, gross or disproportionate hardship, or suchlike extenuating or excusing factors".[55]

11–26 The decision in *Morris* appeared to narrow down the scope of the factors which the court could take into account. However, in *Leen v Aer Rianta cpt*,[56] McKechnie J. held that the discretionary nature of the old s.27 had been carried through to s.160. He reviewed the decision in *Morris* and made it clear that

---

[49] unreported, High Court, Charleton J., July 13, 2007.
[50] [1995] 1 I.L.R.M. 374.
[51] [1995] 1 I.L.R.M. 374 at 381. See also, *Grimes v Punchestown Development Co Ltd* [2002] I.L.R.M. 409.
[52] [1982] I.L.R.M. 21.
[53] [1982] I.L.R.M. 21 at 26. See generally, Ch.4, Equitable and General Principles.
[54] [1983] I.R. 319; [1982] I.L.R.M. 177.
[55] [1983] I.R. 319 at 324; [1982] I.L.R.M. 177 at 180.
[56] [2003] 4 I.R. 394.

Henchy J. did not intend the illustrations set out in that case to be exhaustive, on the basis that every court must decide each case on the individual facts and circumstances surrounding it. McKechnie J. then set out a number of matters to which "particular attention" should be given. In observing that "the courts have tended to individualise each case and decide it accordingly", he held that every court must decide each such case on the individual facts and circumstances surrounding it. In that context, and based on the facts before him, the matters which McKechnie J. set out were:

- the conduct, position and personal circumstances of the applicant;
- the question of delay and acquiescence;
- the conduct, position and personal circumstances of the respondent;
- the public interest.[57]

11–27 These will be considered in turn, as it would seem that they have a wider application.

(i) Conduct and Position of the Applicant

11–28 If a court takes a view that the applicant has not acted in good faith, it may deny the relief sought under s.160. For example, in *O'Connor v Frank Harrington Ltd*,[58] an applicant who was being financed by a competitor of the respondent, and who had not disclosed that fact, was refused relief for that reason. Barr J. determined that the applicant had not come to court with clean hands.[59] He felt that the application under the section was "seriously misleading". He referred to the fact that the "primary motivation" for the application "had not been disclosed". However, in *Fusco v Aprile*,[60] Morris P. held that the fact that the applicant was himself in breach of planning control did not per se disentitle him to relief, on the basis that he had disclosed that fact.

11–29 In relation to a party's conduct, prejudice arising from that conduct is a factor which the courts may consider. In *PM Cantwell v McCarthy*,[61] Murphy J. had regard to the fact that the absence of prejudice was a factor which the court could take into account.

(ii) Delay and Acquiescence[62]

11–30 Certain time limits are provided for in the 2000 Act within which a section 160 application must be made. In essence, a section 160 application may

---

[57] [2003] 4 I.R. 394 at 410.
[58] unreported, High Court, Barr J., May 28, 1987.
[59] See generally, Ch.4, Equitable and General Principles, para.4–13.
[60] unreported, High Court, Morris P., June 6, 1997.
[61] unreported, High Court, Murphy J., November 1, 2005.
[62] See generally, Ch.4, Equitable and General Principles, para.4–21.

not be brought after the expiration of a period of seven years from the date of commencement of the development, or after the expiration of a period of seven years from the date of expiration of the planning permission.[63]

11–31 There are a number of cases in which an application brought within the time limit may be refused on the grounds that the court feels that there has been delay which would warrant such a refusal. In *Dublin Corporation v Mulligan*,[64] Finlay P. stated that:

> "If an applicant to the Court could be said to be guilty of laches and delay quite clearly as in any other proceedings seeking an injunction he might and should be disentitled to relief."

11–32 In the case of *Dublin Corporation v Lowe*,[65] Morris P. also accepted that unreasonable delay on the part of an applicant could be regarded as acquiescence. However, in *Mason v KTK Sand and Gravel Ltd*,[66] Smyth J. had regard to the fact that the applicant's solicitors had written to the respondents before the use complained of. As such, he was prepared to overlook the objection that the applicant had delayed. In *Sweetman v Shell E & P Ireland Ltd*,[67] Smyth J. referred to the applicant's delay, but this was one of six factors identified by Smyth J. in refusing the relief sought. One of the other factors was the applicant's failure to respond promptly to the replying affidavits, leaving on the court file a large number of complaints concerning the development in question which were "wholly unwarranted".

11–33 Despite these decisions, however, the extent to which delay has a role to play in section 160 applications was viewed by McKechnie J. in *Leen* as not being "quite clear".[68] This was on the basis that it was unclear whether delay could ever, in itself, be a ground for refusing relief when otherwise the application is within s.160, and this is a matter which appears to remain unresolved. Based on the relevant case law arising out of delay generally,[69] it would seem that not only must there be delay, but that such delay means that it would be unjust to grant an injunction to the plaintiff.

(iii) Conduct and Position of the Respondent

11–34 It has been held in a number of cases that if a respondent has acted bona fide in the belief that development was authorised, this is a factor in favour of

---

[63] Under the previous legislation, the time period was five years.
[64] unreported, High Court, Finlay P., May 6, 1980.
[65] unreported, High Court, Morris P., February 4, 2000.
[66] unreported, High Court, Smyth J., May 7, 2004.
[67] unreported, High Court, Smyth J., March 14, 2006.
[68] [2003] 4 I.R. 394.
[69] See Ch.4, Equitable and General Principles, para.4–21.

withholding relief. For example, in *Mountbrook Homes Ltd v Oldcourt Developments Ltd*,[70] even though there had been delay in complying with the condition on the part of the respondent, Peart J. refused to make the "draconian order" to stop the development in question.[71] In *Grimes v Punchestown Development Company*,[72] Herbert J. considered as a relevant factor in exercising his discretion to refuse to grant relief that there was:

> "evidence of a *bona fide* belief in the respondents, in the solicitors for the respondents and in the officials of the planning authority that planning permission was not needed in respect of this venture."[73]

11–35 The fact that based on this the respondents had incurred enormous costs in progressing this venture was also a factor referred to by Herbert J.

11–36 By way of contrast, in *Dublin Corporation v O'Dwyer Brothers Mount St Ltd*,[74] Kelly J. took the view that the owners and operators of a nightclub had demonstrated an attitude of disruptive behaviour and evasiveness towards their planning obligations. As such, he refused to put a stay on the order granted, as doing so would "only enable such operators to further enhance their profit from an unlawful development".

(iv) The Public Interest

11–37 There has been considerable discussion in the context of injunctions generally as to the extent to which third party interests can be taken into account.[75] Based on the dictum of McKechnie J. in *Leen* as set out above,[76] it appears clear that in the context of section 160 applications the public interest is a relevant factor for the court to consider.[77] In *Stafford v Roadstone Ltd*,[78] Barrington J. held that the court is entitled to look "not only at the convenience of the parties but at the convenience of the public"[79] when a member of the public comes forward as a "watchdog of the public"[80] under s.27. This view was

---

[70] unreported, High Court, Peart J., April 22, 2005.
[71] Following *Dublin Corporation v McGowan* [1993] 1 I.R. 305. In *McGowan*, Keane J. had also referred to the "draconian" power of s.27, holding that it was not appropriate to use it in a case such as that before him, in which the respondents had acted bona fide, albeit on the basis of a mistaken impression gained from a less than thorough inquiry as to planning conditions.
[72] [2002] 1 I.L.R.M. 401.
[73] [2002] 1 I.L.R.M. 401 at 414.
[74] unreported, High Court, Kelly J., May 2, 1997.
[75] See generally, Ch.4, Equitable and General Principles, para.4–72.
[76] See para.11–26.
[77] See also, *Sweetman v Shell E & P Ireland Ltd*, unreported, High Court, Smyth J., March 14, 2006.
[78] [1980] I.L.R.M. 1.
[79] [1980] I.L.R.M. 1 at 19.

adopted by McKechnie J. in *Leen*.[81] McKechnie J. identified a number of other cases in which the position of third parties had been looked at.[82] He also made reference to other issues of a public nature such as the potential environmental impact of a development,[83] but cautioned that it would be "unhelpful, unnecessary and ... probably impossible" to identify what public interest considerations should be taken into account in this area.

11–38 Another example of the role of the public interest is the case of *Johnson & Staunton Ltd v Esso Ireland Ltd*.[84] In that case an application to discharge an injunction was refused in the High Court by Costello J. on the basis that it was in the public interest:

> "that illegal developments should be halted until the court has had an opportunity to examine all the circumstances of the case to see whether there are any reasons why it should not permanently stop the development."[85]

11–39 In *Curley v the Mayor Alderman and Burgesses of the City of Galway*,[86] Kelly J. found that the respondent was guilty of a deliberate and conscious violation of a particular planning permission and also that for an eight-month period it deliberately and consciously perpetrated an illegality. Notwithstanding this, however, he granted a stay on the execution of his order on public convenience grounds.

(v) Other factors

11–40 The fact that it is very difficult to set out the relevant principles with any more specificity, and that a lot will turn on the facts of an individual case, is highlighted by the decision in *Westport UDC v Golden*.[87] In that case, Morris P. dealt with two alleged breaches of the planning acts. In the first instance he was satisfied that the respondent deliberately set out to disregard planning procedures and constructed a roof, knowing "full well" that the same would constitute an unauthorised development. The President affirmed an order of the Circuit Court without a stay. However, he was more lenient in relation to the

---

[80] [1980] I.L.R.M. 1 at 19.

[81] unreported, High Court, McKechnie J., 31 July 2003.

[82] *Dublin County Council v Sellwood* [1981] I.L.R.M. 23; *White v McInerney Construction Ltd* [1995] 1 I.L.R.M. 374, *Mahon v Butler* [1998] 1 I.L.R.M. 284 and *Blainroe Estates Management Company Ltd v IGR Blainroe Ltd*, unreported, High Court, Geoghegan J., March, 18, 1994).

[83] Referring to *Irish Wildbird Conservancy v Clonakilty Golf and County Club Ltd*, unreported, High Court, Costello J., July 23, 1996.

[84] [1990] 1 I.R. 289.

[85] [1990] 1 I.R. 289 at 295.

[86] unreported, High Court, Kelly J., December 11, 1998.

[87] [2002] 1 I.L.R.M. 439.

second instance—the stripping out of an old restaurant and the installation of a new facility in its place—on the basis that whilst he believed that the respondents had "carried out this work in the full knowledge of the fact that there was at the very least a grave danger that they were in contravention of the planning laws and have ignored the applicant's suggestions that there should be consultation", he felt that it was "in the interests of all parties" to put a stay on the order so that the respondents could take steps to "regularise their position".

11–41 In summary, there are a number of other identifiable factors which the courts have had regard to in exercising their discretion whether to grant or refuse the injunction sought. These include, although are not confined to, disproportionate hardship,[88] the attitude of the planning authority to the development in question (at least when proceedings are taken by a private citizen),[89] the purpose of the development,[90] the trivial nature of the breach in question[91] and the fact that the developer has received professional advice.[92]

11–42 As is clear from the foregoing, the courts have a very wide discretion when it comes to the granting or otherwise of an order under s.160.[93] It should be re-emphasised, however, that the factors which the courts have taken into account do not form part of a finite list; there may be other factors as yet unenumerated by the courts which will play a key role in determining whether or not an injunction will be granted under s.160.[94]

---

[88] See *Avenue Properties v Farrell* [1982] I.L.R.M. 21, in which Barrington J. declined to grant an order under s.27 because it would have been "unduly harsh and burdensome to grant an injunction notwithstanding the fact that the respondents are formally in the wrong".

[89] See *White v McInerney Construction Ltd* [1995] 1 I.L.R.M. 374. See also, *O'Connor v Frank Harrington Ltd*, unreported, High Court, Barr J., May 28, 1987; *Mahon v Butler* [1997] 3 I.R. 369; [1998] 1 I.L.R.M. 284; *Grimes v Punchestown Development Company* [2002] 1 I.L.R.M. 401 and *Sweetman v Shell E & P Ireland Ltd*, unreported, High Court, Smyth J., March 14, 2006.

[90] See *Dublin Corporation v Maiden Poster Sites* [1983] I.L.R.M. 48.

[91] See *Avenue Properties v Farrell Homes* [1982] I.L.R.M. 21; *Dublin County Council v Mantra Investments Ltd* [1980] 114 I.L.T.R. 102; *Grimes v Punchestown Developments Company Ltd* [2002] 1 I.L.R.M. 409; *Mountbrook Homes Ltd v Oldcourt Developments Ltd*, unreported, High Court, Peart J., April 22, 2005 and *O'Connell v Dungarvan Energy Ltd*, unreported, High Court, Finnegan J., February 22, 2001, the latter citing Lord Denning in *Lever (Finance) Ltd v Westminster Corporation* [1973] All E.R. 496.

[92] See *Altara Developments Ltd v Ventola Ltd*, unreported, High Court, O'Sullivan J., October 6, 2005.

[93] See the comment of Smyth J. to this effect in *Sweetman v Shell E & P Ireland Ltd*, unreported, High Court, Smyth J., March 14, 2006.

[94] For example, in some cases, the fact that retention planning permission has been applied for may be taken into account by the court in determining whether to adjourn the proceedings pending the outcome of such an application. However, see *Monaghan County Council v Brogan* 1987 I.L.R.M., in which the court rejected the putative defence that obtaining planning permission would be a matter of formality. See also, *Dublin County Council v Tallaght Block Company* [1983] I.L.R.M. 534 in which the respondent's application for retention permission had been refused.

6. Bringing an Application

11–43 Proceedings in a section 160 application are, in the normal course, commenced by way of an originating Notice of Motion and grounding affidavit, as specified by s.160(3). They are usually dealt with on the basis of affidavit evidence.[95] However, as is clear from the decision of Peart J. in *Limerick County Council v Tobin Sand and Gravel*,[96] there does not seem to be any reason why a court cannot order such directions as to pleadings and mode of trial as may be appropriate where it is necessary or desirable to do so. As stated by Peart J.:

> "it appears that a Defence put forward by the Respondent is one where oral evidence, and even pleadings and discovery are necessary or desirable, there does not seem to be any reason why the Court cannot order such directions as to pleadings and mode of trial as may be appropriate, and certainly there could in my view be no question that the planning authority could be non-suited as it were, having commenced its application by the method provided for in s.160, merely because the respondent raises a matter by way of defence which for its determination requires either pleadings or oral evidence."

11–44 For example, it has been held that where novel questions of law or complex factual questions have to be resolved, it may be necessary to proceed other than by way of a section 160 application.[97] However, as noted by Simons, this leads to the practical problem that "there is no obvious alternative form of proceedings available".[98] He observes that the Planning and Development Act 2000 criminalises unauthorised development. As such, the bringing of proceedings by way of plenary summons could cause a potential issue in relation to standing, as it is normally only the Attorney General who can seek an injunction in aid of a breach of the criminal law.[99]

11–45 Although there is no formal rule as to who should swear the grounding affidavit, in the normal course it will be sworn either by a member of the planning enforcement staff in an appropriate case, or else a party suitably qualified in planning matters, on behalf of the applicant. The affidavit should contain sufficient material to demonstrate to the court that, in essence,

---

[95] *Cork Corporation v O'Connell* [1982] I.L.R.M. 505. A court may not accept new points previously not addressed in the affidavits during the course of the hearing per Costello J. in *South Dublin Co Council v Balfe*, unreported, High Court, Costello J., November 3, 1995.

[96] unreported, High Court, Peart J., August 13, 2005.

[97] See *Mahon v Butler* [1997] 3 I.R. 369 at 379; [1998] 1 I.L.R.M. 284 at 292, per Denham J. and *Waterford County Council v John A. Wood Ltd* [1999] 1 I.L.R.M. 217 at 224, per Murphy J. See also, *Ryan v Roadstone Dublin Ltd*, unreported, High Court, O'Donovan J., March 6, 2006.

[98] See Simons, *Planning and Development Law*, 2nd edn (Dublin: Thomson Round Hall, 2007), p.308.

[99] See Ch.3, Standing, para.3–35.

development has been or is being carried out without planning permission or that an unauthorised use is being made of land, and that the land is not exempted development.[100]

11–46 A respondent to an application brought under s.160 will invariably seek to file a replying affidavit, dealing with the points raised in the grounding affidavit. It is crucial that any points which a respondent wishes to make are contained in the replying affidavit, as only evidence contained in the affidavits may be relied upon.[101] There would appear to be no rule precluding a further exchange of replying affidavits as necessary, and indeed it is usually the case that further replies will in fact be filed.

11–47 As is the case with injunctions in general, an undertaking may be offered to the court rather than an injunction being granted.[102] If an injunction order is granted, a stay may be granted on such an order.[103]

7. Interlocutory Applications

11–48 Interlocutory injunctions are provided for under s.160(3)(a) of the Planning and Development Act 2000 which reads:

> "An application to the High Court or the Circuit Court for an order under this section shall be by motion and the Court when considering the matter may make such interim or interlocutory order (if any) as it considers appropriate."

11–49 There is little reported case law on the application of this subsection. In a somewhat different context, namely seeking a stay on any further consideration of a planning appeal pending the determination of a challenge by way of judicial review to its appeal, O'Sullivan J. held in *Martin v Bord Pleanála*[104]

---

[100] See *Dublin Corporation v Sullivan*, unreported, High Court, Finlay P., December 21, 1984; *Dublin Corporation v Regan Advertising* [1989] I.R. 61; *Carroll v Brushfield Ltd*, unreported, High Court, October 9, 1992 and *Ryan v Roadstone Dublin Ltd*, unreported, High Court, O'Donovan J., March 6, 2006. See also, *Westport UDC v Golden* [2002] 1 I.L.R.M. 439. In *Dillon v Irish Cement*, unreported, Supreme Court, November 26, 1986 (distinguished in the *Westport* case), Finlay C.J. considered that in the particular circumstances of that case and by reason of the "unique exemption" claimed, the onus was on the respondent.

[101] See *South Dublin County Council v Balfe*, unreported, High Court, Costello J., November 3, 1995.

[102] *State (Fitzgerald) v An Bord Pleanála* [1985] I.L.R.M. 117.

[103] See, for example, *Furlong v AF & GW McConnell Ltd* [1990] I.L.R.M. 48; *County Meath Vocational Education Committee v Joyce* [1994] 2 I.L.R.M. 210; *The Right Honourable The Lord Mayor Aldermen and Burgesses of Dublin v Garland* [1982] I.L.R.M. 104 and, *Curley v the Mayor Alderman and Burgesses of the City of Galway*, unreported, High Court, Kelly J., December 11, 1998. Post the 2000 Act, see *Westport UDC v Golden* [2002] 1 I.L.R.M. 439.

[104] unreported, High Court, O'Sullivan J., July 24, 2002.

that on any application for an interlocutory injunction, the court must apply the *Campus Oil* principles. By extension, it would seem appropriate to apply these principles to an application under s.160(3)(a).

11–50 The question of the adequacy of damages in such applications has already been touched upon in Ch.6, Interlocutory Applications.[105] In *Dunne v Dun Laoghaire Rathdown Co. Council*,[106] the plaintiffs applied for an interlocutory injunction to prevent the defendant from removing, as part of a road-building scheme, parts of a monument on lands which the defendant owned. Hardiman J. observed, in considering the application of the *Campus Oil* guidelines, that:

> "As to adequacy of damages, I cannot see how, in a case where no damages are claimed and where the right asserted is a public right, it can be said that damages would be an adequate remedy to the plaintiffs."[107]

11–51 In an application under s.160, damages are not part of the remedy which will be claimed by the applicant.

11–52 In relation to the adequacy of damages from the respondent's perspective, the matter is somewhat more complicated. It appears, in short, that the courts will require an undertaking as to damages. As with such an undertaking generally, the rationale for this is that it:

> "aided the court in doing that which was its great object, viz. abstaining from expressing any opinion upon the merits of the case until the hearing."[108]

11–53 In *Dublin County Council v Crampton*,[109] Finlay J. dealt with this issue by holding that the section 27 injunction had the characteristics of an equitable injunction. As such, he felt that an undertaking as to damages was appropriate. In *Mahon v Butler*,[110] considering the question of whether the order which had been sought in the High Court was interlocutory or final in nature, Denham J. observed in the Supreme Court that "[s]uch an undertaking is required as a matter of course where the court is asked to grant an interlocutory injunction."[111]

---

[105] See para.6–109.
[106] [2003] 1 I.R. 567.
[107] [2003] 1 I.R. 567 at 580.
[108] per Lord Diplock in *American Cyanamid Co v Ethicon Ltd* [1975] A.C. 396 at 407; [1975] 2 W.L.R. 316 at 323; [1975] 1 All E.R. 504 at 510, citing *Wakefield v Duke of Buccleuch* (1865) 12 L.T. 628.
[109] unreported, High Court, Finlay J., March 10, 1980.
[110] [1997] 3 I.R. 369; [1998] 1 I.L.R.M. 284.
[111] [1997] 3 I.R. 369 at 378; [1998] 1 I.L.R.M. 284.

11–54 Consistent with this, in *Limerick Co. Council v Tobin*,[112] Peart J. indicated that a claim might be brought for damages by the respondent in the event that it would ultimately be found that the interlocutory injunction should not have been granted.

11–55 In relation to a consideration of the balance of convenience on an interlocutory application, it has been noted that "the planning authority will have a natural advantage in that it will usually be asserting a public interest in restraining the alleged unauthorised development."[113]

D. INDUSTRIAL RELATIONS

1. Introduction

11–56 The Industrial Relations Act 1990 underpins the seeking of an injunction in the context of an industrial relations dispute. Prior to the enactment of the 1990 Act it was quite common for employers to neutralise legitimate industrial action by going to court to apply for an interim injunction to restrain picketing.[114] It has been commented in that regard that the injunction "has long been regarded as possibly the most powerful weapon an employer can use against employees if there is a trade dispute."[115] In an effort to address this, the 1990 Act sets out specific provisions in relation to the application for, and granting of, injunctions. This section will consider these provisions and associated case law.

2. Industrial Relations Act 1990

11–57 As a starting point, the Act benefits those in the relationship of employer and employee; an independent contractor is not entitled to the protection of the Act.[116]

11–58 Fundamental to the way in which the 1990 Act deals with injunction applications is s.14. This section sets out comprehensive provisions on the holding of secret ballots, which had not been provided for in the Trade Disputes Act 1906, the legislation which preceded the 1990 Act.[117] By virtue of s.14, the

---

[112] unreported, High Court, Peart J., August 15, 2005.

[113] See Simons, *Planning and Development Law*, 2nd edn (Dublin: Thomson Round Hall, 2007), p.317.

[114] See the comments of Keane J. in *Nolan Transport (Oaklands) Ltd v Halligan*, unreported, High Court, Keane J., March 22, 1994.

[115] Purcell, "Industrial Relations, the Right to Picket and Restrictions of Right to Injunction" (1998) 3(5) Bar Rev. 239 at 242.

[116] This point also applied to the Trade Disputes Act 1906. See the decision of Costello J. in *Lamb Brothers Dublin Ltd v Davidson* [1978] I.L.R.M. 226.

[117] The 1906 Act was repealed by the 1990 Act.

rules of every trade union must contain these provisions in relation to secret ballots. As will be seen, s.14 is directly linked to s.19(1) of the 1990 Act, the latter section governing the right to apply for an injunction. That right is contingent upon a secret ballot being held in accordance with the rules of a trade union.

(a) Section 14: Secret Ballot

11–59 Section 14(2)(a) of the 1990 Act provides that:

> "the union shall not organise, participate in, sanction or support a strike or other industrial action without a secret ballot, entitlement to vote in which shall be accorded equally to all members whom it is reasonable at the time of the ballot for the union concerned to believe will be called upon to engage in the strike or other industrial action".

11–60 The onus of establishing that the provisions of s.14 have been complied with was considered by Keane J. in the case of *Nolan Transport (Oaklands) Ltd v Halligan*.[118] Dealing with the matter on the basis of a "first impression" and without the benefit of authority, he held that such onus is on the person resisting the injunction application, believing this to be "crucial to the operation of the section". A similar view was expressed by Murphy J. in the Supreme Court. He stated that if a "significant statutory benefit is conferred on one litigant at the expense of another upon express statutory terms, the benefit should not be available if the terms are not fulfilled."[119]

11–61 In other words, it is the trade union which must show that s.14 has been complied with if it seeks to resist an injunction application brought by an employer. In *Nolan Transport*[120] Keane J. referred to the need for evidence of sufficient weight to indicate that s.14 had been complied with.[121] In *Daru Blocklaying Ltd v BATU*,[122] Kelly J., in refusing the injunctive relief sought, found that whilst the defendant trade union had put the result of a ballot in evidence before the court, it had not discharged the onus required to demonstrate a full and complete compliance with s.14.

---

[118]   unreported, High Court, Keane J., March 22, 1994.
[119]   [1999] 1 I.R. 128 at 158.
[120]   unreported, High Court, Keane J., March 22, 1994.
[121]   In *G & T Crampton Ltd v BATU*, unreported, High Court, Laffoy J., November 20, 1997, Laffoy J. referred to the fact that there had been a "bald assertion" that a ballot had been carried out in accordance with the rules of the union, although on the facts of the case, did not need to express any view on whether such assertion was sufficient.
[122]   [2002] 2 I.R. 619; [2003] 1 I.L.R.M. 227.

(b) Section 19: Granting an Injunction

11–62 Once the provisions of s.14 have been complied with, s.19(2) of the 1990 Act deals with the circumstances in which the court may—or, more specifically, may not—grant an injunction. That provision reads:

> "Where a secret ballot has been held in accordance with the rules of a trade union as provided for in s.14, the outcome of which or, in the case of an aggregation of ballots, the outcome of the aggregated ballots, favours a strike or other industrial action and the trade union before engaging in the strike or other industrial action gives notice of not less than one week to the employer concerned of its intention to do so, a court shall not grant an injunction restraining the strike or other industrial action where the respondent establishes a fair case that he was acting in contemplation or furtherance of a trade dispute."

11–63 Described as an "unusual and special situation", the object of s.19(2) was stated by Keane J. in the High Court decision in *Nolan Transport (Oaklands) Ltd v Halligan*[123] as being:

> "to ensure that in cases where there is at least a fair case that the trade union was acting in contemplation or furtherance of a trade dispute, such injunctions should not be granted where they would have been previously granted on the basis of irreparable damage which would not be remediable by an award of damages."

11–64 The key test thus is as set out in the legislation, namely that there shall be no injunction granted if the respondent establishes a "fair case" that he was acting in contemplation or furtherance of a trade dispute. As Keane J. noted in *Nolan Transport*, such considerations would "otherwise not apply" if they had not been provided for in legislation. If the respondent can satisfy the test set out in s.19(2), then he benefits from the protection of the legislation. Of course, in protecting the party establishing such a fair case, the legislation is also depriving an employer of a common law protection to which he would normally have recourse.[124]

11–65 Where a defendant is not entitled to rely on s.19 of the 1990 Act, the matter falls to be considered on the basis of the usual *Campus Oil* principles. This was made clear by Laffoy J. in the case of *G & T Crampton v BATU*[125] and

---

[123] unreported, High Court, Keane J., March 22, 1994.

[124] A point which, it has been suggested, raises a constitutional difficulty: See Byrne & Binchy, *Annual Review of Irish Law 1990* (Dublin: Round Hall, 1991), p.354.

[125] unreported, High Court, Laffoy J., November 20, 1997. See the critique of the Supreme Court decision in the same case by Costello, "Trade Union Law—The Labour Injunction and the Burden of Proof" (1997) 19 D.U.L.J. 197.

by McCracken J. in *Malincross Ltd v BATU*.[126] In that regard, there would appear to be no conflict with *Mahon v Butler*,[127] in so far as s.19 provides for procedural steps in relation to seeking an injunction, rather than setting out substantive provisions in relation to the seeking of an injunction order. There is nothing suggesting that a consideration of equitable principles should not be considered if s.19 cannot be relied on.

E. INTELLECTUAL PROPERTY

1. Introduction[128]

11–66 The four main categories encompassed by the term "intellectual property" are patents, trade marks, copyright and industrial designs. Over the past two decades, legislation has been introduced and updated to modernise the intellectual property regime in this jurisdiction. In the context of injunctions, these statutes are of interest in that, in broad terms, they simply state that injunctions are available in relation to various breaches or threatened breaches. In some cases they specify who may bring the application for an injunction, but beyond that they do not prescribe any particular rules or procedures for the bringing of such applications. What is notable is the contrast between the lack of detail in these statutory provisions and the more thorough provisions of the Planning and Development Act 2000 and the Industrial Relations Act 1990, as considered above.[129] This emphasises the different ways in which legislation addresses the question of specific statutory injunctions.

11–67 Case law in the area of intellectual property arises from substantive injunction applications, rather than in relation to the legislation itself; the legislation in essence is descriptive rather than prescriptive. In fact it is the related area of the tort of passing off which has generated a considerable volume of case law,[130] which cases go to the heart of the principles underlying the granting of, in particular, injunctions on an interlocutory basis.[131]

11–68 It is proposed to look at the key provisions of the relevant statutes in so far as they relate to injunctions. There are two purposes to this: first, to set out

---

[126] [2002] 13 E.L.R. 78.
[127] See para.11–04.
[128] See generally, Clark and Smyth, *Intellectual Property Law in Ireland*, 2nd edn (West Sussex: Tottel, 2005).
[129] See paras 11–12 and 11–56.
[130] Section 7(2) of the Trade Marks Act 1996 provides that: "No proceedings shall lie to prevent or recover damages for the infringement of an unregistered trade mark as such; but nothing in this Act shall affect the law relating to passing off." As such, the common law relating to passing off is not affected by the 1996 Act.
[131] Considered in Ch.10, General Application, para.10–136.

the provisions in their own right; but, secondly, to highlight the different approaches which can be taken by the legislature in terms of how it addresses injunctions in statute.

2. Industrial Designs Act 2001

11–69 The term "design" is set out in s.2 of the Industrial Designs Act 2001 as meaning:

> "the appearance of the whole or a part of a product resulting from the features of, in particular, the lines, contours, colour, shape, texture or materials of the product itself or its ornamentation ..."

11–70 The 2001 Act contains two sections which simply provide that an injunction can be sought as appropriate in given circumstances. A third section provides for a situation in which a court should not grant an injunction. The essentially descriptive nature of these sections is evident from the explanatory memorandum which accompanied what was the Industrial Designs Bill 2000, and which stated that the relevant chapter, Ch.8, within which these sections are set out, "lists the civil remedies available under this Bill to registered proprietors and others in respect of registered designs." Provision is also made for an *Anton Piller*-style order.[132] The relevant sections are as follows:

(a) Section 57: Infringement

11–71 Section 57(3), which concerns infringement actionable by the registered proprietor, provides that:

> "In an action for infringement of the design right under this section, all relief by way of damages, injunction, account of profits or otherwise is available to the plaintiff as it is available in respect of the infringement of any other property right."

11–72 In other words, s.57(3) simply provides that in the case of an infringement of a design right, a party may, inter alia, seek an injunction to protect such a property right. The section does not prescribe the means of applying for such an injunction or the factors which have to be considered by a court in coming to a determination in relation to the granting or otherwise of an injunction. As such, regard should be had to the normal considerations in applying for an injunction.[133]

---

[132] See Ch.8, Commercial Injunctions, para.8–129.
[133] See, inter alia, Ch.4, Equitable and General Principles; Ch.5, Perpetual Injunctions, and Chs 6 and 7, Interlocutory and Interim Applications respectively.

(b) Section 58: Innocent Infringement

11–73 A similar approach is evident in s.58(3), which deals with innocent infringement. That section provides that:

> "Nothing in this section shall affect the power of the appropriate court to grant an injunction in any proceedings for the infringement of the design right in a registered design."

(c) Section 60: Undertaking to Take a Licence

11–74 The focus of s.60(1)(a) is somewhat different: it provides that no injunction shall be granted against a defendant:

> "Where, in proceedings for infringement of the design right in a design in respect of which a licence is available as of right, the defendant undertakes to take a licence on such terms as may be agreed or, in default of agreement, settled by the Controller."

11–75 In other words, a party seeking to bring an injunction application in relation to an alleged infringement of a design right must clarify whether a defendant is prepared to take a licence as set out. The wording of the section would appear to suggest, however, that in reality proceedings may be in being before the defendant gives such an undertaking. This will clearly have cost implications which will have to be addressed by a court. However, once such an undertaking is given, the court cannot then grant an injunction.

(d) Section 62: Seizure of Infringing Products or Articles

11–76 Section 62(1) of the Act provides that an *Anton Piller*-style order may be granted by the court if the terms of that section are met, namely that the registered proprietor of a design has reasonable grounds for believing that there are being hawked, carried about or marketed infringing products or articles. However, in contrast to an *Anton Piller* order,[134] such order is made by the District Court, and will authorise a member of the Garda Síochána to seize without warrant the products or articles and to bring them before the District Court.

3. Copyright and Related Rights Act 2000

11–77 As explained by Clark and Smyth:

---

[134] See Ch.8, Commercial Injunctions See para.8–129.

"While copyright is clearly an individual right given to a human person in order to encourage and recognise the economic and cultural benefits of creating new works, the nature of copyright is in fact a collection of separate rights, the most important being rights to authorise or control physical reproduction of the work and public performance of the work."[135]

11–78 As with the Industrial Designs Act 2001, the provisions of the Copyright and Related Rights Act 2000 are primarily descriptive in the context of making provision for the granting of an injunction. The following provisions are set out to again demonstrate the descriptive nature of the 2000 Act in so far as injunctions are concerned.

(a) Section 127: Infringement

11–79 Placed in the context of Ch.9 of the 2000 Act, which is headed "Remedies: Copyright Owner", s.127(2) of the 2000 Act is very similar to s.57(3) of the Industrial Designs Act 2001.[136] It provides that:

"In an action for infringement of the copyright in a work under this section, all relief by way of damages, injunction, account of profits or otherwise is available to the plaintiff as it is available in respect of the infringement of any other property right."[137]

11–80 It would seem, as with the 2001 Act, that regard should be had to the normal considerations in applying for an injunction.[138]

(b) Section 129: Construction of a Building

11–81 Section 129 deals specifically with the issue of constructing buildings.[139] It provides that in an action for infringement of the copyright in respect of the construction of a building no injunction or other order shall be made after the construction of the building has begun, or requiring the building to be demolished.

---

[135] Clark and Smyth, *Intellectual Property Law in Ireland*, 2nd edn (West Sussex: Tottel, 2005), p.182.

[136] See para.11–71.

[137] See generally, *Sweeney v National University of Ireland Cork trading as Cork University Press* [2001] 2 I.R. 6 and *Universal City Studios Inc. v Mulligan (No.2)* [1999] 3 I.R. 392 (decided under the Copyright Act 1963).

[138] See, inter alia, Ch.4, Equitable and General Principles; Ch.5, Perpetual Injunctions, and Chs 6 and 7, Interlocutory and Interim Applications respectively.

[139] "Building" is defined in s.2 of the 2000 Act as including "any structure".

(c) Section 130: Undertaking to Take a Licence

11–82 Section 130(1) is very similar in terms to s.60(1)(a) of the Industrial Designs Act 2001.[140] It provides that no injunction shall be granted against a defendant where that defendant undertakes to take a licence on such terms as may be agreed or, in default of agreement, settled by the controller.

(d) Section 132: Seizure of Infringing Copies

11–83 Section 132 of the Copyright and Related Rights Act 2000 provides for specific search and seizure provisions. In that regard it has the flavour of an *Anton Piller*-style order. However, s.132(1) provides that the owner of a copyright may apply to the District Court in respect of any infringement which he believes is taking place. As such, this is quite clearly different from a normal equitable injunction, which cannot be granted by the District Court. Furthermore, in contrast to an *Anton Piller* order, whereby the order will specify the parties authorised to carry out any search, pursuant to s.132, the court may authorise a member of the Garda Síochána to seize without warrant the copies, articles or devices and to bring them before the District Court.[141]

(e) Section 137: Breach of Moral Rights

11–84 Although the concept is not without some controversy, Clark & Smyth explain that:

> "copyright, or the *droit d'auteur*, is seen as an author's right, based upon an act of creation by the author or artist. The work thus produced is seen as a part of the identity, personality or integrity of the author or artist and, as such, subject to economic *and* moral laws."[142]

11–85 Moral rights are covered by s.137(3) of the 2001 Act, which again simply provides that a court may grant an injunction in relation to any breach under s.109 (integrity right) unless there has been a sufficient disclaimer dissociating the person entitled to the right from the treatment of the work.

---

[140] See para.11–74.

[141] See also s.133, by virtue of which, where it would be impractical to apply to the District Court, the copy, article or device may be seized and detained by the copyright owner or a designated representative thereof where the copy, article or device is found being hawked, carried about or marketed.

[142] Clark and Smyth, *Intellectual Property Law in Ireland*, 2nd edn (West Sussex: Tottel, 2005), p.390.

(f) Section 138: Moral Rights and Buildings

11–86 Section 138 mirrors s.129 of the 2000 Act[143] in relation to a claim made for a breach under s.107 (paternity right)[144]; s.109 (integrity right)[145]; or s.113 (false attribution of work), in that no injunction order may be made to prevent the completion of a building which has already been begun, or to require the demolition of a building.

(g) Section 143: Search Warrants and Seizure

11–87 Section 143(1) of the 2000 Act deals with search warrants and seizures. Having heard information on oath, a District Court may issue a warrant authorising a member of the Garda Síochána to enter and search the premises specified in the warrant and to seize any goods in relation to which it is suspected there is an offence being—or about to be—committed under s.140 of the Act.

11–88 It has been suggested that the use of s.143 is in many ways preferable to seeking an *Anton Piller* order.[146] This is because it does not involve the copyright owner in any significant expense and entry can be enforced. A criminal prosecution may also be more effective in bringing an end to breaches rather than a civil action for damages, particularly as a defendant may not be in a position to pay such damages.

(h) Section 303: Performers' Property Rights

11–89 Section 303 deals with owners of performers' property rights, At subs.(2) it is provided again that a court may, inter alia, grant an injunction in relation to the infringement of such rights. Section 305(1) mirrors s.130(1) of the 2000 Act in that it provides that when an undertaking is given by a defendant to take a licence, no injunction should be granted in such circumstances.

(i) Section 319(3): Integrity Rights[147]

11–90 Again, within the overall context of performers' moral rights, s.319(3) provides that an "appropriate court" may grant an injunction prohibiting any

---

[143] See para.11–81.
[144] Defined in s.107(1) as "the right to be identified as the author and that right shall also apply in relation to an adaptation of the work".
[145] Defined in s.109(1) as "the right to object to any distortion, mutilation or other modification of, or other derogatory action in relation to, the work which would prejudice his or her reputation and that right shall also apply in relation to an adaptation of the work".
[146] See Delany, *Equity and the Law of Trusts in Ireland*, 4th edn (Dublin: Thomson Round Hall, 2007), p.606.
[147] Defined in s.109(1) as "the right to object to any distortion, mutilation or other modification of, or other derogatory action in relation to, the work which would prejudice his or her reputation and that right shall also apply in relation to an adaptation of the work."

rights conferred by s.311 (integrity right)[148] unless there is a sufficient disclaimer in relation to that right.

4. Trade Marks Act 1996[149]

11–91 The provisions of the Trade Marks Act 1996 were derived from the first Council Directive 89/104/EC of December 21, 1988 to approximate the laws of the Member States relating to trade marks.

11–92 In the case of *Jaguar Cars Ltd v Controller of Patents*,[150] Clarke J. adopted the test laid down by O'Sullivan J. in the case of *Montex Holdings Ltd v Controller of Patents*[151] as to ownership of a trade mark. As stated by O'Sullivan J.:

> "I further accept that the test of ownership in the mark is that ownership vests in the party first using it in this jurisdiction. In this I am following Morritt L.J., in *Al Bassam Trade Mark* [1995] R.P.C. 511 at p. 522, where he said:—
>
>> 'Accordingly it is necessary to start with the common law principles applicable to questions of the ownership of unregistered marks. These are not in doubt and may be shortly stated. First the owner of a mark which had been used in conjunction with goods was he who first used it. Thus in *Re Nicholson & Sons Ltd's Application* (1931) 48 R.P.C. 227 at page 253 Lawrence L.J. said:—
>>
>>> "The cases to which I have referred (and there are others to the like effect) show that it was firmly established at the time when the Act of 1875 was passed that a trader acquired a right of property in a distinctive mark merely by using it upon or in connection with his goods irrespective of the length of such user and of the extent of his trade and that such right of property would be protected by an injunction restraining any other person from using the mark".' "[152]

---

[148] Defined in s.311(1) as "the right to object to any distortion, mutilation or other modification of, or other derogatory action in relation to, his or her performance or a recording thereof, which would prejudice his or her reputation."

[149] A comprehensive and extremely useful review of the applicable principles in the context of interlocutory injunctions in the field of infringements of trademarks was carried out by Clarke J. in the case of *Metro International SA v Independent News & Media Plc* [2006] 1 I.L.R.M. 414.

[150] [2006] 1 I.R. 607 at 611.

[151] [2000] 1 I.R. 577.

[152] [2000] 1 I.R. 577 at 586.

11–93 Section 14(2) of the Trade Marks Act 1996 provides that a person:

> "shall infringe a registered trademark if that person uses in the course of trade a sign where because ...
> '(b) the sign is similar to the trademark and is used in relation to goods or services identical with or similar to those for which the trademark is registered, there exists a likelihood of confusion on the part of the public which includes the likelihood of association of the sign with the trademark.' "

11–94 As observed by McCracken J. in *Smithkline Beecham Plc v Antigen Pharmaceuticals Ltd*,[153] s.14 introduced a totally new concept into the definition of infringement, namely the idea of association.[154] Given its genesis in an EU Council Directive, the jurisprudence of the European Court of Justice (ECJ) is of some relevance. In particular, in the case of *Sabel BV v Puma AG*[155] the ECJ referred to how "confusion" may be inferred, and stated, referring to the tenth recital in the preamble to the Directive that:

> "the appreciation of the likelihood of confusion 'depends on numerous elements and, in particular, on the recognition of the trademark on the market, of the association which can be made with the used or registered sign, of the degree of similarity between the trademark and the sign and between the goods or services identified'. The likelihood of confusion must therefore be appreciated globally, taking into account all factors relevant to the circumstances of the case.
>
> That global appreciation of the visual, aural or conceptual similarity of the marks in question must be based on the overall impression given by the marks, bearing in mind, in particular, their distinctive and dominant components."[156]

11–95 It is this second paragraph which is of relevance in determining whether or not there is an element of confusion.

(a) Section 18: Infringement

11–96 Infringement is defined at s.14(1) of the 1996 Act in the following terms:

> "A person shall infringe a registered trade mark if that person uses in the course of trade a sign which is identical with the trade mark in relation to goods or services which are identical with those for which it is registered."[157]

---

[153] [1999] 2 I.L.R.M. 190.
[154] See also the remarks of Clarke J. in the case of *Metro International SA v Independent News & Media Plc* [2006] 1 I.L.R.M. 414 at 420.
[155] Case C–251/95 [1997] E.C.R. I–6191.
[156] See paras 22 and 23.
[157] See also the other provisions of s.14.

11–97 Section 18(2) of the 1996 Act is almost identical to s.127(2) of the Copyright and Related Rights Act 2000. It simply provides that:

> "In an action for infringement of a registered trade mark all such relief by way of damages, injunctions, accounts or otherwise shall be available to the proprietor as is available in respect of the infringement of any other property right."

11–98 Again, it appears that regard should be had to the normal considerations in applying for an injunction, given that the section does not prescribe the means of applying for such an injunction or the factors which have to be considered by a court in coming to a determination in relation to the granting or otherwise of an injunction.

(b) Section 24: Groundless Threats

11–99 Section 24(2)(b) provides that an injunction may be sought from the court[158] to prevent the continuation of threats in circumstances where there are groundless threats of infringement proceedings. In short, s.24 provides that a party may seek an injunction from the High Court when he can show, first, that he is faced with a threat of trade mark infringement proceedings and, secondly, that there has been no such infringement.[159] The onus of proof is on the defendant, pursuant to s.24(3), which provides that the plaintiff shall be entitled to relief upon satisfying the relevant proofs. Subsection 3 also provides that it is a defence to show that there is actual infringement.[160]

(c) Section 61: Well-Known Trade Marks

11–100 The Paris Convention is the Paris Convention for the Protection of Industrial Property of March 20, 1883, as amended.[161] Section 61 deals with well-known trade marks. Section 61(2) reads as follows:

> "Subject to section 53, the proprietor of a trade mark which is entitled to protection under the Paris Convention as a well-known trade mark shall be entitled to restrain by injunction the use in the State of a trade mark which, or the essential part of which, is identical or similar to the proprietor's mark, in relation to identical or similar goods or services, where the use is likely to cause confusion."

---

158   Defined in s.2 of the 1996 Act as the High Court.
159   In a detailed article on the section, Lambert, "Section 24 of the Trade Marks Act 1996—A New Remedy for Groundless Threats" (1999) 6 C.L.P. 293 at 294 notes that the first part of these proofs "should be the easier satisfied", but that this second proof "may prove more difficult".
160   The equivalent English section was considered in the case of *Trebor Bassett Ltd v The Football Association* [1997] F.S.R. 211.
161   See s.60 of the 1996 Act.

(d) Section 62: Country Emblems

11–101 Section 62 deals with the specific issue of the national emblems of certain countries. Reference is made within the context of s.62 to flags, armorial bearings or other state emblems, official signs or hallmarks, national flags and other state emblems and official signs or hallmarks. Section 62(6) provides that where:

> "the authorisation of the competent authorities of a Convention country is or would be required for the registration of a trade mark, those authorities shall be entitled to restrain by injunction any use of the mark in the State without their authorisation."[162]

(e) Section 63: Emblems of International Organisations

11–102 Section 63 is very similar to s.62, except that it covers emblems of certain international intergovernmental organisations. Section 63(4) provides that where:

> "the authorisation of an international organisation is or would be required for the registration of a trade mark, that organisation shall be entitled to restrain by injunction any use of the mark in the State without its authorisation."

(f) Section 65: Proprietor in a Convention Country

11–103 Section 65 covers situations where an application for registration of a trade mark is made by a person who is an agent or representative of a person who is the proprietor of the mark in a Convention country and the application is made without the proprietor's authorisation. In such circumstances, s.65(4) provides that the proprietor may apply to the court[163] for an injunction.

(g) Section 97: State Emblems

11–104 Section 97 provides that the relevant government Minister can apply to the courts for an injunction to prevent the unauthorised use of the State emblems of Ireland.[164]

---

[162] A "Convention Country" is defined at s.60 of the Act as being a country which is a party to the Paris Convention for the Protection of Industrial Property of March 20, 1883, as amended or supplemented by any protocol to that Convention which is for the time being in force in the State.

[163] Defined in s.2 of the 1996 Act as the High Court.

[164] Defined in s.2 of the 1996 Act as "any emblem notified as such under Article 6ter of the Paris Convention".

5. Patents Act 1992

11–105 The Patents Act 1992, as amended by the Patents (Amendment) Act 2006, enabled effect to be given to the European Patent Convention in national law. Again, the provisions of the Act dealing with injunctions are in essence descriptive in nature, and do not specify in detail the requirements for bringing an injunction application. There are three main sections in relation to injunctions in the Act.

(a) Section 47: Infringement

11–106 Section 47 provides that:

> "Civil proceedings for infringement of a patent may be brought in the Court by the proprietor of the patent in respect of any act of infringement which he alleges he is entitled."

11–107 Pursuant to s.47(1)(a), such proceedings may include a claim for "an injunction restraining the defendant from any apprehended act of such infringement."

11–108 As defined by s.2 of the Act, "court" refers to the High Court. However, pursuant to s.66(5), certain proceedings may be brought in the Circuit Court, irrespective of the amount of the claim involved.[165] Section 66 concerns actions for infringement in relation to short-term patents, defined in s.63 as:

> "a patent the term of which shall be ten years in lieu of the term provided for by or under section 36 in respect of a patent granted under Part II."

11–109 The usual term for a patent is 20 years. The short-term patent was devised, according to the explanatory memorandum accompanying the Bill which ultimately became the 1992 Act, "in the interests of the small inventor who may find that a full term patent is unnecessary for his particular invention."

11–110 Lower official fees apply in relation to a short-term patent, and so it seems entirely sensible that any litigation in respect of a short-term patent could be dealt with by the Circuit Court. Section 66(1) also essentially provides[166] for certain protections in relation to the holders of short-term patents, in so far as it requires any party proposing to institute proceedings against the holder of a short-term patent to make a request to the Controller of Patents, Designs and Trade Marks to cause a search to be undertaken in relation to the invention and a report of the results of the search to be prepared.

---

[165] per s.66(4).
[166] Subject to a qualification in s.66(3).

(b) Section 53: Groundless Threats

11–111 Similar to s.24 of the Trade Marks Act 1996, s.53(2)(b) of the Patents Act makes provision for an injunction against the continuation of groundless threats of infringement proceedings.

(c) Section 68: Undertaking to Take a Licence

11–112 As with s.130(1) of the Copyright and Related Rights Act 2000 and s.160(1)(a) of the Industrial Designs Act 2001, s.68(2)(c)[167] of the Patents Act 1992 provides that no injunction shall be granted against a defendant where that defendant undertakes to take a licence on such terms as may be agreed or, in default of agreement, settled by the controller.

F. Proceeds of Crime

1. Introduction

11–113 The Proceeds of Crime Act 1996, amended by the Proceeds of Crime (Amendment) Act 2005, was designed to enable the High Court to make orders for the preservation of disposal of property classified as being the "proceeds of crime".[168] It provides for "some unique remedies and some unique procedures"[169] which remedies and procedures are equivalent to, and include, injunctions. The purpose of considering certain provisions of the 1996 Act, as amended, in some detail is to set out how the legislature purports to deal with interim and interlocutory applications for injunctions by way of statute, and how the courts subsequently interpret those provisions in the context of a wider understanding of what is meant by interim and interlocutory relief.

2. Proceeds of Crime Acts 1996[170]

11–114 Before considering the provisions of the 1996 Act which deal with injunction-style orders, it is first necessary to consider whether proceedings under the 1996 Act are civil or criminal in nature, and the associated issues arising from this.

---

[167] As amended by r.47 of the Patents Rules 1992 (S.I. No. 179 of 1992).
[168] The Act essentially supersedes the Criminal Justice Act 1994 in relation to the freezing of assets.
[169] per Geoghegan J. in *McKenna v AF* [2002] 2 I.L.R.M. 303 at 306.
[170] See generally, Murphy, "Tracing the Proceeds of Crime: Legal and Constitutional Implications" (1999) 9(2) I.C.L.J. 160.

(a) Civil or Criminal Proceedings

11–115 The first case in which the Irish courts considered whether proceedings under the Proceeds of Crime Act 1996 are properly categorised as civil proceedings was *Gilligan v Criminal Assets Bureau*.[171] In that case McGuinness J. stated that an action under the Proceeds of Crime Act 1996 "is strictly speaking an action '*in rem*' rather than '*in personam*'." She took the view that the seizure of the proceeds of crime "could well be viewed in the light of a reparation rather than punishment or penalty."[172] However, McGuinness J. ultimately categorised proceedings under the 1996 Act as forfeiture proceedings. In doing so, she relied upon the decision of the Supreme Court in *Attorney General v Southern Industrial Trust Ltd*,[173] which "undoubtedly establishes that legislation providing for forfeiture is not necessarily criminal in nature".[174] McGuinness J. thus classified the proceedings as civil proceedings, to which the civil standard of proof on the balance of probabilities should be applied.[175]

11–116 The issue as to whether proceedings under the 1996 Act are civil or criminal in character arose again for consideration in *Murphy v GM*.[176] In that case an interim order freezing the property concerned was made under s.2, followed by an interlocutory order under s.3, along with an order appointing a receiver pursuant to s.7 of the Act. Keane C.J. stated that:

> "The effect of the statutory scheme ... is to freeze property which senior members of the gardaí suspect of representing the proceeds of crime for an indefinite period."

11–117 However, he also pointed out the possibility that the process might ultimately result in the forfeiture of the property.[177] On this basis, he followed the decision of the Supreme Court in *Southern Industrial Trust Ltd*. He concluded that proceedings under ss.2 and 3 of the Act are akin to civil in rem forfeiture proceedings. Keane C.J. acknowledged that the making of an order under the Act is dependent on a finding that some criminal activity has taken place, but concluded that the proceedings were nonetheless civil in character because the 1996 Act provides for the civil forfeiture of the proceeds of crime.

---

[171] [1998] 3 I.R. 185; that case involved an (unsuccessful) challenge of the constitutionality of the 1996 Act.

[172] [1998] 3 I.R. 185 at 218.

[173] (1957) 94 I.L.T.R. 161, in which High Court held that forfeiture provisions contained in the Customs (Temporary Provisions) Act 1945 were civil proceedings.

[174] [1998] 3 I.R. 185 at 223.

[175] [1998] 3 I.R. 185 at 224.

[176] [2001] 4 I.R. 113.

[177] [2001] 4 I.R. 113 at 137.

11–118 A similar approach was adopted in *McKenna v GWD*.[178] The principal issue before the Supreme Court in that case was whether the 1996 Act applied to the proceeds of crime committed outside of the State, rather than property outside of the State that represents the proceeds of crime committed in Ireland. Fennelly J. held that there was no question of the Proceeds of Crime Act 1996 having extra-territorial effect; it had effect only within the boundaries of the State. As such, he concluded that it had no application to the proceeds of activities outside of the State that are crimes under foreign law.

11–119 With that general background in mind, it is now proposed to consider the individual sections which make provision for what amount to injunction orders.

(b) Section 2: An "Interim" Order

11–120 Section 2 of the Proceeds of Crime Act 1996[179] provides that a member of the Garda Síochána not below the rank of chief superintendent, or a specially authorised officer of the Revenue Commissioners, may apply to the court for a *Mareva*-type order.[180] Such an order freezes a person's property for a period of 21 days. However, it must be shown to the satisfaction of the court on an ex parte application that the person is in possession or control of specified property and that the property constitutes directly or indirectly proceeds of crime.[181] Its value must also be not less than the euro equivalent of £10,000. This is described in the act as an "interim" order.

11–121 In *McKenna v MB*,[182] Finnegan P. observed that s.2 made no reference to the procedure to be adopted by the court. In particular it did not purport to circumscribe the practice of the court or the power of the court to regulate its own procedures. In the circumstances, the President felt that the court was entitled to adopt the procedure which it had traditionally adopted in the case of applications for interim injunctions and to apply them to applications pursuant to s.2.

(c) Section 3: An "Interlocutory" Order

11–122 Section 3(1) of the 1996 Act[183] is described on its terms as an "interlocutory" order. Although s.3 appears, on its face, to provide for a

---

[178] [2004] 2 I.R. 470.
[179] As amended by s.4 of the Proceeds of Crime (Amendment) Act 2005.
[180] See Ch.8, Commercial Injunctions, para.8–02.
[181] A detailed consideration of whether various property constituted "proceeds of crime" is contained in the decision of Finnegan P. in *McKenna v SD*, unreported, High Court, Finnegan P., May 8, 2006.
[182] unreported, High Court, Finnegan P., May 26, 2005.
[183] As amended by s.5 of the Proceeds of Crime (Amendment) Act 2005.

statutory interlocutory injunction, the Supreme Court held in the case of *McKenna v AF*[184] that an order under s.3 of the 1996 Act is not truly interlocutory in character in the sense of being ancillary to substantive relief. Rather, it is a free-standing substantive remedy and imposes a complete embargo on any dealing with property.[185] As explained by Geoghegan J., the jurisdiction to grant such an injunction derives from s.28(8) of the Judicature Act (Ireland) 1877. That section by its terms does not use the expression "interlocutory injunction" but rather "interlocutory order". As observed by Geoghegan J., however:

> "it is well known to all lawyers that 'an interlocutory order' within the meaning of the Judicature Act and of the Rules of the Superior Courts in their various forms over the years means an order which is not a final order."[186]

11–123 Geoghegan J. found that s.3 orders are final orders even though they can be discharged. They are not just temporary orders. He held that no significance was to be attached to the label used in the Act which suggested that such orders were interlocutory in nature. In confirming that a s.3 order is not interlocutory in nature, Fennelly J. found the interlocutory injunction to be the closest equivalent type of interlocutory order and, in that context, found s.3 to lack a number of the essential attributes of an interlocutory injunction. However, Fennelly J. also observed that s.3 confers power on the High Court to make a *Mareva* order. Nonetheless, he held that the s.3 remedy was substantive in nature for a number of reasons. This included the fact that it was a free-standing substantive remedy; it was not ancillary to an order to be made in the future and the court does more than determine that there is a fair issue to be tried, in so far as it must determine that the subject property represents the proceeds of crime.

11–124 That s.3 does not have the characteristics of an interlocutory injunction as normally understood was also made clear in the decision of Finnegan J. in *McKenna v EH*.[187] However, he went a step further and suggested that the interim injunction provided for in s.2 did not have the characteristics of interim relief as normally understood either. This appears to be somewhat at odds with the dictum of Geoghegan J. in the Supreme Court in *McKenna v AF*.[188] Geoghegan J. had taken the view that the name "an interim order" as used in s.2 was "genuinely descriptive" and gave rise "to no great difficulty".[189]

---

184 [2002] 2 I.L.R.M. 303.
185 It was held by the Supreme Court in *McKenna v D* [2004] 2 I.L.R.M. 419 at 432 that an order under s.3 "is not, in any normal sense, an order of forfeiture. It would do violence to the language of s.3 to hold that it effects a forfeiture."
186 Citing Jessel M.R. in *Re Stockton Iron Furness Co.* (1879) 10 Ch D 334 at 349. The Master of the Rolls had stated that, "the rules appear to contemplate two classes of orders: final orders which determine the rights of the parties, and orders which do not determine the rights."
187 [2002] 2 I.L.R.M. 117.
188 [2002] 2 I.L.R.M. 303.
189 [2002] 2 I.L.R.M. 303 at 307.

11–125 In *McKenna v AF*,[190] Geoghegan J. also held that, for proceedings initiated under s.3, the appropriate method for doing so was by way of plenary summons and that, as such, a statement of claim would have to be delivered in the normal manner.[191]

(i) Orders Sui Generis

11–126 In the case of *McKenna v EH*,[192] Finnegan J. undertook an analysis of the provisions of the 1996 Act, specifically ss.2 and 3. As has been seen,[193] Finnegan J. referred to the the test set out in the case of *Duchess of Argyll v Duke of Argyll*,[194] namely whether the statute concerned manifests an intention to confer a civil right on the plaintiff. He also referred to the Australian case of *King v Goussetis*,[195] in which it was held that the appropriate test for determining whether or not an injunction should be granted, "is to have regard to the nature, scope and terms of the statute—it is a question of statutory interpretation whether an injunction should be granted or not."

11–127 Applying these tests to the Proceeds of Crime Act, Finnegan J. held that the Act created a statutory right to an injunction to preserve the assets said to be the proceeds of crime. He found that it:

> "was not necessary that the statute should do so as in the ordinary course the court would have jurisdiction to grant interim and interlocutory injunctions in aid of the statutory right created by the Act in s.4, the right to have a disposal order made."

11–128 He also observed that the Act did not regard "the orders pursuant to ss.2 and 3 as identical in nature to an ordinary interim or interlocutory injunction in so expressly providing for them". Finnegan J. made reference to the provision for the evidence which must be adduced in order to obtain the injunctions, and to the fact that the injunctions as set out were removed from the "ordinary régime" as laid down in *Campus Oil*.

11–129 Finnegan J. ultimately concluded that the injunctions provided for under ss.2 and 3 of the Proceeds of Crime Act were not ancillary, but rather

---

[190] [2002] 2 I.L.R.M. 303.
[191] Also holding that even if an order under s.3 was a genuine interlocutory order in the ordinary sense of the term, there would still be a requirement to deliver a statement of claim, although not necessarily before the application for the interlocutory injunction had been determined. See *McKenna v Monandbon*, unreported, High Court, Finnegan P., November 20, 2006 in relation to the making of an order pursuant to s.3.
[192] [2002] 1 I.R. 72; [2002] 2 I.L.R.M. 117.
[193] See para.11–06.
[194] [1967] Ch. 302; [1965] 2 W.L.R. 790; [1965] 1 All E.R. 611.
[195] [1986] 5 N.S.W.L.R. 89.

were *sui generis*. This analysis by Finnegan J. is quite compelling, though it does leave open the question of whether s.2 in particular is in fact an interim order in the sense as normally understood, which would appear to be what Geoghegan J. held in *McKenna v AF*.[196]

(d) Section 4: Disposal Order

11–130 Section 4 of the 1996 Act[197] provides that where an interlocutory order has been in force for not less than seven years in relation to specified property, the court, on application to it by the applicant, may make a "disposal" order. It was held in *McKenna v AF*[198] that an application for a disposal order is not to be equated to the trial of the action with the application for an order under s.3 regarded as an application for an interlocutory order.

11–131 Pursuant to s.4(9),[199] an application under s.4(1) may be made by originating motion.

(e) Section 6: Other Orders

11–132 An application may be brought under s.6(1) of the 1996 Act,[200] which allows a court to make such orders as it considers appropriate in relation to property the subject of an interim or interlocutory order. It may do so if it considers it essential for the purpose of enabling the person affected by the order to discharge reasonable living and other necessary expenses, including legal expenses, in or in relation to proceedings under the Act. This is similar to orders which may be made in relation to *Mareva* injunctions.[201] Section 6(1) reads as follows:

> "At any time while an interim order or an interlocutory order is in force, the court may, on application to it in that behalf by the respondent or any other person affected by the order, make such orders as it considers appropriate in relation to any of the property concerned if it considers it essential to do so for the purpose of enabling—
> (a) the respondent or that other person to discharge the reasonable living and other necessary expenses (including legal expenses in or in relation to proceedings under this Act) incurred or to be incurred by or in respect of the respondent and his or her dependants or that other person ..."

---

[196] [2002] 2 I.L.R.M. 303.
[197] As amended by s.6 of the Proceeds of Crime (Amendment) Act 2005.
[198] [2002] 2 I.L.R.M. 303.
[199] Added to the 1996 Act by s.6 of the Proceeds of Crime (Amendment) Act 2005.
[200] As amended by s.8 of the Proceeds of Crime (Amendment) Act 2005.
[201] See Ch.8, Commercial Injunctions, para.8–84.

11–133 In *DPP v EM*,[202] Kelly J. had to deal with an application under s.24 of the Criminal Justice Act, which was a similar provision, and accepted an analogy between the relevant restraint order and a *Mareva* injunction. In determining the approach which the court should take, Kelly J. had regard to the decision of Robert Goff J. in *A v C (No. 2)*.[203] In that case it was held that the court could qualify a *Mareva* injunction in circumstances where the defendant could satisfy the court that the assets the subject of the injunction were required for a purpose which did not conflict with the policy underlying the *Mareva* jurisdiction. However, Robert Goff J. also held that he could not accept that, "in normal circumstances a defendant can discharge that burden of proof simply by saying, 'I owe somebody some money'."[204] Rather, the defendant had to demonstrated that he did not have any other assets available out of which the debt would be paid.

(f) Section 16B(1)(a): Corrupt Enrichment

11–134 Section 16B(1)(a) of the Act[205] defines corrupt enrichment as follows:

"A person is corruptly enriched if he or she derives a pecuniary or other advantage or benefit as a result of or in connection with corrupt conduct, wherever the conduct occurred."

11–135 By virtue of s.16B(1)(b), this includes:

"Any conduct which at the time it occurred was an offence under the Prevention of Corruption Acts 1889 to 2001, the Official Secrets Act 1963 or the Ethics in Public Office Act 1995."

11–136 Section 16B(4) is of relevance in the context of injunctions. It provides for an ex parte application for interlocutory relief, in the following terms:

"In any proceedings under this section the Court may, on application to it *ex parte* in that behalf by the applicant, make an order prohibiting the defendant or any other person having notice of the order from disposing of or otherwise dealing with specified property of the defendant or diminishing its value during a period specified by the Court."

11–137 Section 16B(5) provides that an affidavit and/or oral evidence from a member or authorised officer stating that they believe that the defendant is in possession of property acquired through corrupt conduct shall be evidence

---

[202] ex tempore, High Court, Kelly J., April 22, 1997. See also, *MFM v MB* [1999] 1 I.L.R.M. 540.
[203] [1981] Q.B. 961; [1981] 2 W.L.R. 634; [1981] 2 All E.R. 126.
[204] [1981] Q.B. 961 at 963; [1981] 2 W.L.R. 634 at 636; [1981] 2 All E.R. 126 at 127.
[205] As inserted by the s.12 of the Proceeds of Crime (Amendment) Act 2005.

provided the court is satisfied that there are reasonable grounds for this belief. Section 16B(6) provides that, on application, the court may make an order directing the defendant to file an affidavit specifying the property owned by the defendant, or the income or sources of income of the defendant, or both such property and such income or sources. Section 16B(6)(b) provides that such an affidavit is not admissible in evidence in any criminal proceedings against the defendant of their spouse, except for perjury proceedings arising from statements in the affidavits.

11–138 The standard of proof required to determine any question arising in proceedings under the section as to whether a person has been corruptly enriched and, if so, by how much, "shall be that applicable in civil proceedings", as provided for by s.16B(8).

11–139 Order 136 of the Rules of the Superior Courts provides that an application for an order under s.16B(2) shall be by originating notice of motion and grounding affidavit.

G. FAMILY LAW

1. Introduction

11–140 Injunctions have been used as a remedy in the area of family law in a number of situations such as, for example, to restrain a party from breaching a non-molestation clause,[206] or against assault and battery.[207] In *Lett v Lett*,[208] an injunction was sought in relation to a promise not to bring proceedings for past misconduct. In *Conway v Conway*,[209] Kenny J. granted an injunction restraining a husband from entering the family home because of his "outrageous" conduct, notwithstanding his entitlement to a half share in the family home. Previously, the same judge refused to grant an injunction in the case of *Cullen v Cullen*[210] sought by a father to prevent his sons trespassing on various lands, on the basis, inter alia, that injunctions should not govern the relations between fathers and sons.

11–141 Shatter identifies four types of injunction which were most commonly sought in the area of family law, viz.[211]:

---

[206] See *Sanders v Rodway* (1852) 16 Beav. 207; see also, *Patel v Patel* (1988) 18 Fam. Law 395.
[207] See *Egan v Egan* [1975] Ch. 218.
[208] [1906] 1 I.R. 618.
[209] [1976] I.R. 254, considering *Gurasz v Gurasz* [1969] 3 W.L.R. 482.
[210] 1962 I.R. 269.
[211] Shatter, *Family Law*, 4th edn (Dublin: Butterworths, 1997), p.879.

- to restrain a defendant from attending at, or near, or entering a residence[212];
- to restrain a defendant from molesting, assaulting or putting in fear the plaintiff and dependent children;
- a mandatory injunction compelling a party to vacate a home or other property in which they are resident;
- an injunction to prevent a defendant taking children out of the custody of the plaintiff or out of the jurisdiction.[213]

11–142 However, the use of equitable injunctions in the sense in which they are commonly understood has largely been rendered unnecessary due to a number of different statutory provisions in the area of family law (albeit that, as pointed out by Shatter, the injunction "may be given a new lease of life in relation to cohabitees").[214]

11–143 It is not proposed to consider these in any detail; the purpose of focusing on family law in the instant context is to consider how a piece of legislation may in fact essentially diminish the need for equitable injunctions. A second point of interest is the fact that under the relevant family law legislation, the District Court, which is not a court with equitable jurisdiction, may make orders which amount to injunctions in all but name. Legislation can also supplement the position of parties to a family law action; for example, s.35(2) Family Law Act 1995 and s.37(2) of the Family Law (Divorce) Act 1996 both provide for *Mareva*-style injunction orders in the context of family law proceedings.[215]

11–144 The key piece of legislation which effectively supersedes the need to apply for an injunction on an equitable basis is the Domestic Violence Act 1996, which regulates spousal violence and misconduct.[216] That Act enables defined

---

212 See *F v F*, unreported, High Court, Murphy J., May 20, 1982, in which Murphy J. said that an injunction at common law restraining a spouse from entering the matrimonial home "should be granted or withheld on the same grounds as those specified in s.22 of the Family Home (Maintenance of Spouses and Children) Act 1976". See Binchy, *A Casebook on Irish Family Law* (Oxford: Professional Books, 1984), p.299.

213 See generally, *RW v CC* [2005] 1 I.L.R.M. 142 in which Finlay Geoghegan J. held, inter alia, that there were "a number of significant differences between such an injunction and the barring order at issue in *Keating v Crowley*" [2002] I.R. 744.

214 Shatter, *Family Law*, 4th edn (Dublin: Butterworths, 1997), p.877.

215 See generally, Ch.8, Commercial Injunctions. See also s.11(c) of the Judicial Separation and Family Law Reform Act 1989; in *AS v GS* [1994] 2 I.L.R.M. 68, Geoghegan J. in the High Court found that this section, (which provides for "the protection of the family home or of any moneys realised from the conveyance of any interest in the family home") "is analogous to an interlocutory injunction in that it is open to a party affected at the final hearing to establish that the applicant was never in fact entitled to an order under s.11(c)."

216 The genesis of the relevant provision being s.22 of Family Home (Maintenance of Spouses and Children) Act 1976, as enlarged by s.2 of the Family Law (Protection of Spouses and Children) Act 1981; *McA v McA* [1981] I.L.R.M. 361; s.3(1) of the 1981 Act introduced the "protection order".

categories of persons to apply for and obtain from the Circuit Court or the District Court four forms of order, viz. a barring order, an interim barring order, a protection order and a safety order. It is the forms of barring order and protection order which have, in essence, displaced the need for injunctions. This section will consider the key provisions of the 1996 Act in so far as it concerns barring orders, protection orders and associated case law.

2. Barring Orders

11–145 Section 3(1) of the 1996 Act specifies the category of persons who may apply for and obtain barring orders, with s.3(2)(a) providing that a court may make a barring order, on the application of such a person, where:

> "it is of the opinion that there are reasonable grounds for believing that the safety or welfare of the applicant or any dependent person so requires."

11–146 Pursuant to s.4 of the Act, the court may make an interim barring order where it:

> "is of the opinion that there are reasonable grounds for believing that—
> (a) there is an immediate risk of significant harm to the applicant or any dependent person if the order is not made immediately, and
> (b) the granting of a protection order would not be sufficient to protect the applicant or any dependent person ..."

11–147 Barring orders and interim barring orders may be made by the District Court, with the Circuit Court entitled to make such orders on appeal.

11–148 In *CC v Early*,[217] MacMenamin J., reviewing the effect of an interim barring order, made reference to the decision of the Supreme Court in *Keating v Crowley*.[218] In the course of his judgment in the latter case, Keane C.J. had referred to the "draconian consequences" of the making of such an order. MacMenamin J. noted that it is a criminal offence to breach such an order, even if the order should never have been granted. He pointed out that:

> "The granting of an interim order in the absence of the defendant may in such cases crucially tilt the balance of the entire litigation against him or her to an extent which may subsequently be difficult to redress."

---

[217] unreported, High Court, MacMenamin J., April 28, 2006.
[218] [2002] I.R. 744.

3. Protection Orders

11–149 Related to s.4 is s.5 of the Act, which provides for the making of protection orders and reads:

> "If, on the making of an application for a safety order or a barring order or between the making of such an application and its determination, the Court is of the opinion that there are reasonable grounds for believing that the safety or welfare of the applicant for the order concerned or of any dependent person so requires, the Court may by order (in this Act referred to as a Protection Order) direct that the respondent to the application—
>
> (a) Shall not use or threaten to use violence against, molest or put in fear the applicant or that dependent person, and
>
> (b) If he or she is residing at a place other than the place where the applicant or that dependent person resides, shall not watch or beset the place where the applicant or that dependent person resides, and the Court may make the Protection Order subject to such exceptions and conditions as it may specify."

11–150 Protection orders are often sought as a first step towards ultimately securing a barring order.

4. Bringing an Application

(a) Barring Orders

11–151 Section 4(3) of the 1996 Act provides for ex parte applications for interim barring orders:

> "(a) An interim barring order may be made *ex parte* where, having regard to the circumstances of the particular case, the court considers it necessary or expedient to do so in the interests of justice."

11–152 The application is grounded on an affidavit and various directions are provided for in s.4 in relation to what must happen and the steps to be taken once such an order is granted. Protection orders can also be made ex parte.

11–153 Order 59 r.6 of the District Court Rules provides for the manner in which a barring order may be applied for, depending on the point at which it is sought, including by means of an ex parte application.

11–154 Section 16(1) of the 1996 Act provides that civil proceedings under the Act are to be heard otherwise than in public.[219]

---

[219] As to whether a "McKenzie friend" may appear in court in light of this provision, see *RD v McGuinness* [1999] 2 I.R. 411; [1999] 1 I.L.R.M. 549.

(b) Protection Orders

11–155 Section 5(1) of the 1996 Act provides that:

> "If, on the making of an application for a safety order or a barring order or between the making of such an application and its determination, the court is of the opinion that there are reasonable grounds for believing that the safety or welfare of the applicant for the order concerned or of any dependent person so requires, the court may by order (in this Act referred to as a "protection order") direct that the respondent to the application—
>
> (a) shall not use or threaten to use violence against, molest or put in fear the applicant or that dependent person, and
>
> (b) if he or she is residing at a place other than the place where the applicant or that dependent person resides, shall not watch or beset the place where the applicant or that dependent person resides,
>
> and the court may make the protection order subject to such exceptions and conditions as it may specify."

11–156 In other words, the point at which the application for a protection order is brought is related to the bringing of an application for a barring order. Order 59 r.7 of the District Court Rules provides for the manner in which a protection order may be applied for, depending on the point at which it is sought, including by means of an ex parte application.

H. GENERAL LEGISLATIVE PROVISIONS

11–157 The following chronological list, which does not purport to be comprehensive, identifies a number of legislative provisions which concern injunctions. The purpose of setting out a list is twofold: first, to illustrate the range of areas in which injunctions are provided for by statute and/or statutory instrument, or indeed where they are not permitted in specific circumstances.[220]

11–158 Secondly, the purposes of such a list is to provide a starting point from which to identify whether an injunction should be sought on the normal equitable basis, or whether a statutory provision governs such an application and indeed requires a party to proceed on foot of the statutory process rather than on the basis of a common law or equitable jurisdiction.[221]

---

[220] As has been seen, for example (see para.11–74), s.60(1)(a) of the Industrial Designs Act 2001, which provides that: "Where, in proceedings for infringement of the design right in a design in respect of which a licence is available as of right, the defendant undertakes to take a licence on such terms as may be agreed or, in default of agreement, settled by the Controller—(a) no injunction shall be granted against the defendant."

[221] It should be noted that there are a number of statutory instruments which also make provision for injunctions in areas concerning matters such as genetically modified organisms, life and non-life assurance and semiconductor products.

11–159 However, it should be noted that many of these provisions are effectively descriptive and simply provide that an injunction may be sought by a designated party rather than setting out any particular criteria as to the basis on which such an injunction should be granted, in much the same way as those related to intellectual property, as considered above.

11–160 Other provisions are more prescriptive, such as s.57CP of the Central Bank Act 1942, as inserted by s.16 of the Central Bank and Financial Services Authority of Ireland Act 2004. That section specifies who may seek an injunction, the basis on which it may be sought and specifically excludes a requirement for an undertaking as to damages on the part of the Financial Services Ombudsman.

11–161 A word of caution should be sounded in that statute often makes provision for an injunction without actually using the term "injunction", as is the case in relation to planning injunctions pursuant to s.160 of the Planning and Development Act 2000, as considered above.[222]

11–162 Some of the relevant sections of legislation which make provision for injunctions (excluding those already considered above) are:

- Social Welfare and Pensions Act 2005, s.35 (amending s.90 of the Social Welfare (Consolidation) Act 1993)[223];
- Central Bank and Financial Services Authority of Ireland Act 2004, ss.16 (inserting s.57CP into the Central Bank Act 1942), and 27 (substituting Pt V of the Central Bank Act 1997)[224];
- Competition Act 2002, ss.14(5)(a), 26(2) and 32(4)(a)[225];
- Communications Regulations Act 2002, s.53(19);
- Equal Status Act 2000,[226] s.23(3);

---

[222] See also reg.13 of European Communities (Protection of Consumers in Respect of Contracts Made by Means of Distance Communication) Regulations 2001 (S.I. No. 207 of 2001), as amended by European Communities (Protection of Consumers in Respect of Contracts Made by Means of Distance Communication) (Amendment) Regulations 2005 (S.I. No. 71 of 2005). See also the English Stop Now Orders (EC Directive) Regulations 2001, analysed in McCalla, "Stop Now Orders" (2001) 151 N.L.J. 751.

[223] As inserted by s.39 of the Social Welfare Act 1996.

[224] As pointed out by Breslin, *Banking Law*, 2nd edn (Dublin: Thomson Round Hall, 2006), p.12. It should be noted that where an injunction is granted under this provision, the Financial Services Ombudsman is not required to give an undertaking as to damages. He also notes that no provision is made for a quia timet injunction under the inserted s.74 of the Central Bank Act 1997, and IFSRA must wait for a person against whom an injunction is obtained to actually breach the injunction.

[225] In relation to agreements, decisions and concerted practices, see generally, *Irish Sugar v Parlon*, unreported, High Court, O'Donovan J., November 29, 2001, in which the *Campus Oil* principles were applied at the interlocutory stage. Abuse of a dominant position was considered by Carroll J. in *A& N Pharmacy Ltd v United Drug Wholesale Ltd* [2001] 4 I.R. 259.

[226] As amended by the Equality Act 2004.

- Qualifications (Education and Training) Act 1999, s.65(2);
- Arbitration (International Commercial) Act 1998, s.7(1);
- Employment Equality Act 1998,[227] ss.10(5), 65(1), 85(5)[228];
- Plant Varieties (Proprietary Rights) (Amendment) Act 1998, s.21(1)[229];
- Credit Union Act 1997, s.125(4);
- Universities Act 1997, s.52(2);
- Pensions (Amendment) Act 1996, s.39 (amending s.90 of the Pensions Act 1990);
- International Common Fund for Commodities Act 1982, Sch.1, Art.42(3);
- Plant Varieties (Proprietary Rights) Act 1980, ss.4(5), 18(3);
- Mines and Quarries Act 1965, s.32(4);
- Arbitration Act 1954, ss.22(1),[230] 39(1).

---

[227] As amended by the Equality Act 2004.
[228] See, in relation to all three sections, Circuit Court Rules (Employment Equality Act 1998) 2004.
[229] See Plant Varieties (Farm Saved Seed) Regulations 2000.
[230] See Ch.10, General Application, para.10–12.

CHAPTER 12

BREACH OF AN INJUNCTION ORDER

A. INTRODUCTION

12–01 An injunction order is an order of the court, which must be strictly complied with.[1] When granting an injunction order, "the court does not contemplate that it will be disobeyed."[2] Until such time as an injunction order is discharged,[3] a court may find that a person breaching that order is in contempt of court.[4] This is the case regardless of whether the injunction order is interim,[5] interlocutory or final in nature,[6] and whether the order has been granted by the Circuit or Superior Courts. As was made clear by McCracken J. in *Donegal County Council v Ballantine*,[7] if there is a breach of an injunction order, the proper procedure is not to reapply to the court for a further injunction, but to bring proceedings for contempt.[8]

12–02 The seriousness of such proceedings was underlined by Peart J. when he stated in *Adebayo v Commissioner of An Garda Síochána*[9] that:

> "the deliberate disobedience of a Court Order is a matter of the utmost gravity, and in an appropriate case where that element of deliberateness or culpability is present, the Court must not hesitate to exercise its undoubted jurisdiction to penalise severely the contempt ..."

---

[1] *Cooke v Cooke* [1919] 1 I.R. 227 at 239, per Sir James Campbell C.

[2] *South Bucks District Council v Porter* [2003] 2 A.C. 558 at 580; [2003] 2 W.L.R. 1547 at 1564; [2003] 3 All E.R. 1 at 19, per Lord Bingham, citing *Re Liddell's Settlement Trusts* [1936] Ch. 365 at 373 and *Castanho v Brown & Root (UK) Ltd* [1981] A.C. 557 at 574.

[3] See the dictum of Lord Donaldson M.R. in *Johnson v Walton* [1990] 1 F.L.R. 350 at 352.

[4] This chapter deals with the issues related to contempt in so far as they relate to injunctions. For a more thorough review of contempt of court, reference should be made to publications such as Borrie & Lowe, *The Law of Contempt*, 3rd edn (London: Butterworths, 1996); Arlidge, Eady & Smith, *On Contempt* (London: Sweet & Maxwell, 1999); Miller, *Contempt of Court* (Oxford: Clarendon Press, 2000). See also the Law Reform Commission's *Consultation Paper on Contempt of Court* (July 1991) and associated *Report on Contempt of Court* (LRC 47–1994) and the Australian Law Reform Commission's *Report on Contempt* ALRC 35 (1987).

[5] See *Clarke v Smith* (1914) 48 I.L.T.R. 244.

[6] See the dictum of Lavery J. in *Gore-Booth v Gore-Booth* (1962) 96 I.L.T.R. 32 at 36. See also, *Eastern Trust Co v McKenzie Mann & Co Ltd* [1915] A.C. 750 at 760, per Sir George Farwell.

[7] unreported, High Court, McCracken J., March 20, 1998.

[8] However, as is clear from the same case, if there is doubt in relation to the order, the parties should have sought "liberty to apply" so that they may come back to court to clarify the extent or application of the order.

12–03 In such circumstances, an application can be brought seeking to have that person—the alleged contemnor—found to be in contempt of court and sanctioned accordingly.

12–04 In punishing for contempt what the court is doing is punishing for interference with the administration of justice. As explained by Costello J. in *Council of the Bar of Ireland v Sunday Business Post Ltd*,[10] contempt of court is not:

> "an offence against the dignity of the court. It is an interference with the administration of justice. And in punishing for contempt what the court is doing is punishing for such interference."[11]

12–05 It has been stated that if the law of contempt is applied where the court is faced with novel circumstances, it is not the case that the law is being widened in its application, rather that it is merely a "new example of its application".[12] This chapter deals with situations in which an injunction is breached, and the consequences arising out of such a breach.

12–06 Having regard to the provisions of Art.34.3.1 of the Constitution, which deals with the jurisdiction of the courts, it is clear that the High Court has full jurisdiction to deal with breaches of injunctions.[13] The Circuit Court deals with breaches of injunctions granted in the Circuit Court,[14] and the Rules of the Circuit Court contain a number of provisions in relation to contempt of court. For ease, it is proposed to consider the issues arising in relation to breaching an injunction and associated remedies on the basis of the Rules of the Superior Courts and case law of the High and Supreme Courts. Where there are equivalent rules in the Circuit Court Rules, or issues arising which are peculiar to the Circuit Court, these will be noted.

12–07 At the outset, it should be emphasised that this is an area which in many instances is marked by a lack of definitive guidelines and consequent number of anomalies and uncertainties.[15] Furthermore, many of the principles applied in

---

9   unreported, High Court, Peart J., October 27, 2004.
10 unreported, High Court, Costello J., March 30, 1993.
11 See also the dictum of Lord President Clyde in *Johnson v Grant* (1923) S.C. 789 at 790 and the dictum of Sir John Donaldson MR in *Attorney General v Newspaper Publishing Plc* [1988] Ch. 333 at 368; [1987] 3 All E.R. 276 at 299.
12 per Sir John Donaldson M.R. in *Attorney General v Newspaper Publishing Plc* [1988] Ch. 333 at 368; [1987] 3 All E.R. 276 at 299.
13 See *Attorney General v O'Ryan* [1946] I.R. 70 which involved an unsuccessful challenge to the jurisdiction of the High Court to act in respect of a contempt of the Circuit Court, referred to with approval by Gavan Duffy P. in *Attorney General v Connolly* [1947] I.R. 213 at 222.
14 Although the Circuit Court does not have the jurisdiction to deal with breaches of orders of the High Court.
15 In the case of *Desmond v Glackin* [1992] I.L.R.M. 490, O'Hanlon J., in the context of

relation to breach of an injunction were developed in the wider context of civil contempt, then subsequently applied in the more narrow context of breaches of injunctions; it is thus an area which must be approached with a degree of caution.

12–08 This chapter will look firstly at the nature of contempt and the purpose of the remedies for contempt, before turning to the different parties who might breach an injunction and the implications of who the contemnor is. The practicalities of an application for remedies for a breach, along with the hearing of such applications, will then be considered.

B. THE NATURE OF CONTEMPT

1. Introduction

12–09 Contempt may, in general terms, be civil or criminal in nature. The distinction has historically been an important one. The nature and purpose of the remedies available in each case is different. There are also procedural differences arising between the two. However, the distinction between the two has been blurred in a number of more recent cases, leading some to question whether such a distinction still has any ongoing relevance.

2. Nature and Purpose of the Remedies

(a) Introduction

12–10 The breach of an injunction by a party will prima facie give rise to a civil contempt. However, there is some lingering uncertainty as to whether a party in contempt for disobedience of the terms of an injunction order is in fact liable to be punished for civil or criminal contempt.

(b) Distinction Between Civil and Criminal Contempt

12–11 The distinction between civil and criminal contempt was explained by Ó Dálaigh C.J. in the case of *Keegan v de Burca*[16]:

---

statements made during the course of a radio interview, made reference to the "present state of considerable confusion and uncertainty which exists in relation to the law of contempt of court". The recommendations of the Law Reform Commission's *Report on Contempt of Court* (LRC 47–1994) have never been acted upon on a structured formal basis. A private member's Contempt Bill 1995 was withdrawn from the Dáil on June 27, 1996. See 467 *Dáil Debates*.

[16]   [1973] I.R. 223.

"Criminal contempt consists in behaviour calculated to prejudice the due course of justice, such as contempt in *facie curiae*, words written or spoken or acts calculated to prejudice the due course of justice or disobedience to a writ of *habeas corpus* by the person to whom it is directed—to give but some examples of this class of contempt. Civil contempt usually arises where there is a disobedience to an order of the court by a party to the proceedings and in which the court has generally no interest to interfere unless moved by the party for whose benefit the order was made."[17]

12–12 This explanation would suggest that the breach of an injunction order is in the nature of a civil contempt.[18] However, notwithstanding the apparently clear dictum of Ó Dálaigh C.J., the distinction between civil and criminal contempt has caused the courts some difficulties, leading to a struggle to articulate "clear principles in this area".[19] In order to better understand whether contempt in the context of injunctions is civil or criminal in nature, the distinction between the punishment which each attracts is of relevance.

(c) Contempt and Punishment

12–13 In the case of *Australian Consolidated Press Ltd v Morgan*,[20] it was stated in relation to committal[21] (and sequestration[22]) that:

"They are used primarily to compel obedience rather than to punish disobedience; for equity acts in personam, and historically the purpose of the processes of the Court of Chancery was to rectify and reform the conscience of the wrongdoer."[23]

12–14 In the case of *Keegan v de Burca*,[24] Ó Dálaigh C.J., referring to the Supreme Court's earlier decision in *Re Haughey*,[25] explained that:

"Criminal contempt is a common law misdemeanour and, as such, is punishable by both imprisonment and fine at discretion, that is to say without statutory limit, its object is punitive."[26]

---

[17] [1973] I.R. 223 at 227. See also the decision of Finlay P. in *State (Commins) v McRann* [1977] I.R. 78, 89 and the dictum of Diplock L.J. in *Attorney General v Times Newspapers Ltd* (which related to reporting on the "thalidomide" cases in England) [1974] A.C. 273 at 307; [1973] 3 W.L.R. 298 at 316; [1973] 3 All E.R. 54 at 71.

[18] See O'Donnell, "Some Reflections on the Law of Contempt" [2002] 2 J.I.S.J. 88 at 91 and Courtney, *Mareva Injunctions and Related Interlocutory Orders* (Dublin: Butterworths, 1998), p.478.

[19] Law Reform Commission's *Consultation Paper on Contempt of Court* (1991), p.177.

[20] (1965) 112 C.L.R. 483.

[21] See para.12–100.

[22] See para.12–131.

[23] (1965) 112 C.L.R. 483 at 498.

[24] [1973] I.R. 223.

[25] [1971] I.R. 217.

[26] [1973] I.R. 223 at 227.

12–15 The Chief Justice explained that civil contempt:

"Is not punitive in its object but coercive in its purpose of compelling the party committed to comply with the order of the court, and the period of committal would be until such time as the order is complied with or until it is waived by the party for whose benefit the order was made."[27]

12–16 This dictum appears to make clear the fact that civil contempt—including the breach of an injunction—will attract a period of indefinite imprisonment, until such time as a person indicates that they are willing to purge their contempt and comply with the injunction order concerned.

12–17 However, in *Shell E. & P. Ireland v McGrath*,[28] Finnegan P. held that in so far as Ó Dálaigh C.J. had held in both *Keegan* and *Re Haughey* that:

"the objective in imposing imprisonment for civil contempt was coercive and not punitive I have regard to the facts of each of those cases. In each case he was concerned with criminal contempt and for that reason I regard his definition of civil contempt to be *obiter*."[29]

12–18 The President also held that:

"Committal for civil contempt is indefinite but in practice after an appropriate period if committal is not having its desired coercive effect it will be appropriate to release the contemnor. However it may not be just or fair in every case that the contemnor should thereby escape a punishment."[30]

12–19 Based on this dictum, it seems that punishment for civil contempt should in the first instance be viewed as coercive, and involve indefinite imprisonment. However, the courts will be alive to the fact that such coercion may not be effective, and in the circumstances may have to look at other remedies.

12–20 A pragmatic approach is also evident in the context of the procedural distinction between civil and criminal contempt.

3. Procedural Distinction

12–21 In cases of criminal contempt the court will, in the normal course, move of its own volition.[31] It may do so at any time. In cases of civil contempt the

---

[27] [1973] I.R. 223 at 227.
[28] [2007] 1 I.R. 671 (more popularly known as the "Rossport Five" case).
[29] [2007] 1 I.R. 671 at 687.
[30] [2007] 1 I.R. 671 at 688.
[31] *Re the Youghal Election Petition* (1869) I.R. 3 C.L. 537.

court only moves at the instance of the party whose rights are being infringed and who has obtained a court which he seeks to have enforced.[32] Therefore, in the case of an injunction it is the party who has obtained the injunction who must come to court in order to seek to have the order enforced. This is probably the most significant distinction between civil and criminal contempt. However, as with the different rationales for punishment there has been blurring of this distinction, most recently accepted by Finnegan P. in *Shell E. & P. Ireland v McGrath.*[33]

12–22 By way of background, in *Churchman v Joint Shop Stewards' Committee of the Workers of the Port of London*,[34] Lord Denning M.R. suggested that:

> "It may be that in some circumstances the court may be entitled, on sufficient information being brought before it, to act on its own initiative in sending a contemnor to prison."[35]

12–23 Such a course was in fact adopted in *Phonographic Performance Limited v Amusement Caterers (Peckham) Ltd.*[36]

12–24 A similar approach was evident in *Clarke v Chadburn*,[37] in which Sir Robert Megarry V.C. observed that there appeared to be a clear case for "considering whether there should be some relaxation by the courts of their present restraint on themselves in enforcing their orders in cases where these are being openly flouted and the administration of justice is being brought into disrespect,"[38] but that such a power was effectively be a residual power, to be exercised in exceptional cases.

12–25 In *Shell E. & P. Ireland v McGrath*,[39] Finnegan P., referring to the fact that commital by way of punishment likewise should be the last resort, and should only be engaged where there has been "serious misconduct", also acknowledged that the court might move of its own volition in appropriate circumstances. Referring to such punishment, the President stated that:

---

[32] per Finlay P. in *State (Commins) v McRann* [1977] I.R. 78 at 89. See also the dictum of Ó Dálaigh C.J. in *Keegan v de Burca* [1972] I.R. 223 at 227.

[33] unreported, High Court, Finnegan P., April 7, 2006.

[34] [1972] 1 W.L.R. 1094; [1972] 3 All E.R. 603.

[35] [1972] 1 W.L.R. 1094 at 1100; [1972] 3 All E.R. 603 at 608.

[36] [1963] Ch. 195.

[37] [1985] 1 W.L.R. 78.

[38] [1985] 1 W.L.R. 78 at 83.

[39] unreported, High Court, Finnegan P., April 7, 2006.

"in litigation concerning exclusively private rights this will usually occur only at the request of the Plaintiff. Circumstances may exist which cause the Court to act on its own motion … However where the interest of the public in general is engaged or where there is a gross affront to the Court it would be appropriate for the Court to proceed of its own motion to ensure that its orders are not put at nought."

12–26 As with the nature and purpose of the remedy of committal, so too it appears that the procedural distinction between civil and criminal contempt has been blurred by the courts. This leads to the question of whether the distinction between civil and criminal contempt has any real relevance at this juncture.

4. Ongoing Relevance of the Distinction

12–27 The Canadian Supreme Court in *Videotron Ltée v Industries Microlec Produits Electroniques Inc.*[40] identified the issue which lies at the heart of the matter. It observed that one of the sources of confusion is that there has always been a punitive element in civil contempt as well as criminal contempt.[41] This view has been adopted by the Law Reform Commission which has observed, in considering the role of the intervention of the courts in the context of contempt, that:

"there are some cases classically characterised as civil contempt where the court's intervention can not credibly be perceived as serving a coercive function."[42]

12–28 Similarly, the Commission identified "some instances of criminal contempt where the appropriate—or, at all events, an appropriate—judicial response might appear to be of coercive rather than a punitive nature."[43]

12–29 The apparently artificial distinction between civil and criminal contempt is evidenced by reference to a highly unsatisfactory problem which arises from alleging that third parties are in breach of an injunction.

---

[40] (1993) 96 D.L.R. (4th) 376.

[41] See *Comet Products v Hawkex Plastics* in which Lord Denning M.R. notes that the civil contempt concerned partook of the nature of a criminal charge, with the defendant liable to be punished for it. [1971] 2 Q.B. 67; [1971] 1 W.L.R. 1287; [1971] 1 All E.R. 1141.

[42] Citing the example of a person ordered not to destroy a document who may do so nonetheless; in such circumstances, as the document cannot be restored, coercion is ineffective, whereas punishment may seem desirable. See Law Reform Commission's *Consultation Paper on Contempt of Court* (1991) p.177.

[43] The example is given of the refusal by a witness to answer a question in the absence of any privilege.

5. The Position of Third Parties

12–30 Breach of an injunction by a third party can be viewed as prejudicing the due course of justice, a mark of criminal contempt identified by Ó Dálaigh C.J. in *Keegan v de Burca*.[44] However, it ultimately still constitutes disobedience of a court order, albeit not by a party to the proceedings. It would appear somewhat strange that a defendant who breached an injunction was treated as having committed a civil contempt, with anyone who aided and abetted him—or indeed was involved in an "interference in the course of justice"[45]—being charged with a criminal contempt.

6. Statutory Change in England

12–31 The Phillimore Committee, which was established in England to consider the law relating to contempt of court, advocated a fixed term of imprisonment for contemnors. Pursuant to the report, by virtue of the Contempt of Court Act 1981 in England, an indeterminate sentence for contempt is now no longer possible.[46] Although there is no such specific legislation in this jurisdiction, by virtue of Ord.44 r.2 of the Rules of the Superior Courts (RSC), an order for committal directs that, upon his arrest, the person against whom the order is directed is to be lodged in prison until he purge his contempt and is discharged pursuant to further order of the court. However, the Rules of the Superior Courts would appear to contemplate committal for a definite period, or at a minimum do not prevent it: RSC Ord.44 r.4 provides that once the alleged contemnor is before the court upon an order for attachment, he may be committed to prison for a definite period to be specified in the order.[47]

7. Attempted Re-Classification

12–32 The classification of contempt into civil and criminal categories was described by Salmon L.J. in *Jennison v Baker*[48] as "unhelpful and almost meaningless".[49] Similarly, in *Attorney General v Newspaper Publishing Plc*.[50]

---

[44] [1973] I.R. 223. See also, *Council of the Bar of Ireland v Sunday Business Post Ltd*, unreported, High Court, Costello J., March 30, 1993.

[45] per Lord Atkinson in *Scott v Scott* [1913] A.C. 417 at 456.

[46] See the Phillimore Committee, Report of the Committee on Contempt of Court (1974) Cmnd. 5794, para.172. A maximum period of two years in prison is provided for in the 1981 Act.

[47] Although in practice most applications are for attachment and committal, a curious anomaly arises in that it seems that a person attached may, consequent upon that attachment, be committed to prison for a definite period for contempt. A fixed period does not appear to be applicable where a person is committed under RSC Ord.44 r.2 without first having been attached.

[48] [1972] 2 Q.B. 52; [1972] 2 W.L.R. 429; [1972]1 All E.R. 997.

[49] [1972] 2 Q.B. 52 at 61; [1972] 2 W.L.R. 429 at 434; [1972]1 All E.R. 997 at 1002. In that case, as summarised by Finnegan P. in *Shell*, "it is clear from the judgment that the Court saw no objection to committal being imposed for civil contempt by way of punishment."

[50] [1988] Ch. 333; [1987] 3 All E.R. 276.

Sir John Donaldson M.R., whilst acknowledging that contempt had traditionally been classified under the two different heads of "civil contempt" and "criminal contempt", questioned the value of this classification in modern times. The Master of the Rolls based his suggestion on the fact that the classification tends to mislead rather than assist. This was on the basis that the standard of proof in each is the same, namely the criminal standard, and the fact that there were common rights of appeal. He further suggested a re-classification in the following terms:

> "(a) conduct which involves a breach, or assisting in the breach, of a court order and (b) any other conduct which involves an interference with the due administration of justice, either in a particular case or, more generally, as a continuing process, the first category being a special form of the latter, such interference being a characteristic common to all contempts."[51]

12–33 The Master of the Rolls elucidated the distinction between the two categories of his reclassification when he explained that the distinction between the two categories was based on the idea that:

> "in general conduct which involves a breach, or assisting in the breach, of a court order is treated as a matter for the parties to raise by complaint to the court, whereas other forms of contempt are in general considered to be a matter for the Attorney General to raise."[52]

8. The Constitutional Aspect

12–34 The foregoing would tend to suggest that it may be sensible to abolish the distinction between civil and criminal contempt. However, circumstances peculiar to this jurisdiction would suggest that such a course is unlikely. It has been observed that the distinction will probably not be displaced "by reason of the constitutional distinction between criminal matters and civil matters" in this jurisdiction.[53] More specifically, it has been suggested that the need to draw a distinction between civil and criminal contempt was to avoid a challenge bring brought:

> "to avoid the argument ... that, since a person could end up in prison and could only be committed there if proof was provided beyond a reasonable doubt, in truth, civil contempt was so criminal in nature that the safeguards provided for under the Constitution for criminal trails should apply."[54]

---

[51] [1988] Ch. 333 at 362; [1987] 3 All E.R. 276 at 294, citing Lord Diplock in *Attorney General v Leveller Magazine Ltd* [1979] A.C. 440 at 449.

[52] See further, Miller, *Contempt of Court* (Oxford: Clarendon Press, 2000), pp.113–115.

[53] Courtney, *Mareva Injunctions and Related Interlocutory Orders* (Dublin: Butterworths, 1998), p.477.

[54] O'Donnell, "Some Reflections on the Law of Contempt" [2002] 2 J.I.S.J. 88 at 117, suggests

12–35 It would appear that for, inter alia, constitutional considerations, the distinction between civil and criminal contempt may not formally be displaced. Rather than developing what could be viewed as an artificial distinction in relation to the substantive distinction, it has also been suggested that the better approach may be to accept that all contempt is in fact sui generis.[55] The other way in which the courts have attempted to tackle the issue is to sub-divide civil contempt into two categories, namely mere civil contempts and contumacious civil contempts.

9. Sub-Division of Civil Contempt

12–36 In *Larkins v National Union of Miners*,[56] Barrington J. referred to the approach of the English courts in relation to this division of civil contempt. He cited a passage from Arlidge and Eady on *The Law of Contempt*[57] which set out this division, and which explained that contumacious civil contempts involved:

> "not merely disobedience to the court's order but some form of defiance of the court's authority, with the result that the matter ceases to be a mere matter between private litigants but calls in question the authority of the court."[58]

12–37 Barrington J. also referred to the dictum of Cross J. in *Phonographic Performance Ltd v Amusement Caterers*.[59] In that case, Cross J. had referred to *Halsbury's Laws of England*, and to a situation where "there has been wilful disobedience to an order of the court and a measure of contumacy on the part of the defendants".[60] In such circumstances, Cross J. held that civil contempt bore a twofold character:

that this was "unfortunate" and suggests that "[l]ogically, the distinction is deeply unpersuasive". See also, Courtney, *Mareva Injunctions and Related Interlocutory Orders* (Dublin: Butterworths, 1998), p.478. The distinction is also of some relevance in the context of a consideration of legal aid and potentially in terms of whether the provisions of the European Convention on Human Rights might have a role to play.

55 O'Donnell, "Some Reflections on the Law of Contempt" [2002] 2 J.I.S.J. 88 at 118. Arlidge, Eady & Smith, *On Contempt* (London: Sweet & Maxwell, 1999), p.142. Note that the Court of Appeal in *Morris v Crown Office* [1970] 2 Q.B. 114 based its decision on the proposition that contempt of court was a misdemeanour, but one for which the procedure is sui generis, as distinct from being a wrong sui generis.

56 [1985] I.R. 671. In *Jennison v Baker* [1972] 2 Q.B. 52; [1972] 2 W.L.R. 429; [1972]1 All E.R. 997, the court looked to see whether the disobedience was "flagrant and overt".

57 Arlidge and Eady on *The Law of Contempt* (1982 edn), p.57. The discussion as to the distinction between different forms of contempt generally now appears at Arlidge and Eady on *The Law of Contempt* (London: Sweet & Maxwell, 1999), pp.121 et seq.

58 [1985] I.R. 671 at 685.

59 [1964] Ch. 195; [1963] 3 W.L.R. 898. See also, *Steiner Products Ltd v Willy Steiner Ltd* [1966] 1 W.L.R. 986, *Jennison v Baker* [1972] 2 Q.B. 52; [1972] 2 W.L.R. 429; [1972]1 All E.R. 997 and *Re Grantham v Vegetable and Potato Merchants Ltd* [1972] 1 W.L.R. 559.

60 [1964] Ch. 195 at 198; [1963] 3 W.L.R. 898 at 900.

"implying as between the parties to proceedings merely a right to exercise and a liability to submit to a form of civil execution, but as between the party in default and the state a penal or disciplinary jurisdiction to be exercised by the court in the public interest."

In other words, not only could civil contempt be subdivided, the nature of the remedies which would be attracted for "contumacious" civil contempts could be penal in nature.

12–38 This found an echo in the decision of Finnegan P. in *Shell E. & P. Ireland v McGrath*,[61] wherein the President concluded that:

"committal for contempt is primarily coercive its object being to ensure that Court orders are complied with. However in cases of serious misconduct the Court has jurisdiction to punish the contemnor. If the punishment is to take the form of imprisonment then that imprisonment should be for a definite term."[62]

12–39 In the *Larkins* case, the distinction in character between the forms of civil contempt proved crucial. Barrington J. accepted that there was such a distinction made in the English courts and held that:

"the contempt of which the union was convicted falls into the category of contumacious civil contempt and that it touched not only issues between the parties but on the whole question of the maintenance of the rule of law in the United Kingdom."[63]

12–40 However, Barrington J. did not have to deal directly with the issue as to whether he believed that the distinction should be recognised in the Irish courts as well; his judgment dealt with the nature of a contempt in so far as it related to an order of the courts in England.[64] That said, he certainly did nothing to dispel the notion that, in an appropriate case, the Irish courts might adopt a similar approach.

10. Transfer of Civil Contempt

12–41 Although not referred to by Barrington J., the Canadian case of *Pojé v Attorney General of British Columbia*[65] evidences a similar approach to that in

---

[61] [2007] 1 I.R. 671.
[62] [2007] 1 I.R. 671 at 687.
[63] [1985] I.R. 671 at 688.
[64] The key issue was whether the order in question was penal in nature; if it was, then the claim brought by the sequestrators' concerned would fail as "sequestration is not an appropriate penal measure".
[65] [1953] 2 D.L.R. 785.

Phonographic Performance, although Kellock J. referred to conduct being transferred from the "realm of mere civil contempt … into the realm of a public depreciation of the authority of the Court tending to bring the administration of justice into scorn."[66] McLachlin J. was even more explicit in *United Nurses of Alberta v Attorney General for Alberta*[67] when stating that a civil contempt could become criminal in character. He stated that:

> "a civil contempt is not converted to a criminal contempt merely because it attracts publicity … but rather because it constitutes a public act of defiance of the court in the circumstances where the accused know, intended or was reckless as to the fact that the act would publicly bring the court into contempt."[68]

12–42 Although probably more theoretical than practical, there is clearly a distinction between sub-dividing civil contempt, thereby giving it a "twofold character" and transferring or converting civil contempt into the realm of criminal contempt. However, both bear witness to attempts by the courts to ensure that, effectively, the punishment fits the crime. In the context of the constitutional position in Ireland, a somewhat ambiguous civil contempt of a "twofold character" may appear to be more palatable than the idea of "converting" contempt, although it remains to be seen how the courts will develop the jurisprudence in this area. That there is a need for some overall review would appear clear.

C. Parties Capable of Breaching an Injunction Order

1. Introduction

12–43 An injunction generally takes effect upon its pronouncement.[69] It is in the normal course addressed to a party to the proceedings, usually the defendant.[70] The injunction will normally be worded using a formula which encompasses a phrase enjoining "the defendant, his servants or agents". If that party has notice that an injunction has been made[71] and breaches that injunction, provided the terms of the order were clear,[72] he may be found to be in contempt

---

[66] [1953] 2 D.L.R. 785 at 795.
[67] [1992] 89 D.L.R. 609.
[68] [1992] 89 D.L.R. 609 at 637.
[69] *Z Ltd v A-Z* [1982] Q.B. 558; [1982] 2 W.L.R. 288; [1982] 1 All E.R. 556. It may, however, be stayed or suspended: see Ch.5, Perpetual Injunctions, para.5–77.
[70] See *Marengo v Daily Sketch and Sunday Graphic Ltd* [1948] 1 All E.R. 406.
[71] See generally in relation to the requirements for notice, *Duff v Devlin* [1924] 1 I.R. 56. See also, *Ex p. Langley* (1879) 13 Ch D 110.
[72] See *Iberian Trust Ltd v Founders' Trust and Investments Company Ltd* [1932] 2 K.B. 87. See also, *Redland Bricks Ltd v Morris* [1970] A.C. 652; [1969] 2 W.L.R. 1437; [1969] 2 All E.R. 576 and *Hackett v Baiss* (1875) L.R. 20 Eq. 494.

of court. In *R. v Freeman's Journal Ltd*,[73] Gibson J. made it clear that an order of the court "cannot be treated as disobeyed if its substance is not known."[74] In *Council of the Bar of Ireland v Sunday Business Post Ltd*,[75] Costello J. went further in stating that a contempt may also occur through a "reckless failure to ascertain the legal consequences of a court order" just as much as from a deliberate flouting of such an order.

12–44 Whilst it is clear that a defendant named in an injunction may be in contempt of court in breaching that injunction, the courts have also had to consider, in the context of breaches of injunctions, the position of companies, their officers and employees, that of third (or non-) parties and that of parties based outside the jurisdiction. The basic proposition is that an order is binding on any person having notice of the making of that order.[76]

2. Breach of an Undertaking Given in Lieu of an Injunction Order

12–45 A party who has given an undertaking to a court in lieu of an injunction order being made is under the same obligation to abide by the terms of the undertaking as they would be if it was an injunction. In *Biba Ltd v Stratford Investments Ltd*,[77] Brightman J. stated that "I think it would be a pity to disturb that practice by giving a lesser quality to an undertaking than to an injunction."[78] For example, in the case of *Re H, a Bankrupt*,[79] the defendant undertook to give up possession of lands by a certain date. This undertaking was not complied with, and as a result the defendant was found by O'Byrne J. to be guilty of contempt of court.[80] An undertaking may also be given on behalf of a company,[81] subject to its being properly authorised.[82] However, it has been held

---

[73] [1902] 2 I.R. 82.

[74] [1902] 2 I.R. 82 at 91.

[75] unreported, High Court, Costello J., March 30, 1993.

[76] See generally, *Smith-Barry v Dawson* (1891) 27 L.R. Ir. 558; *Avory v Andrews* 30 W.R. 564 and *Scott v Scott* [1913] A.C. 417.

[77] [1973] 1 Ch. 281; [1972] 3 W.L.R. 902; [1972] 3 All E.R. 1041.

[78] [1973] 1 Ch. 281 at 287; [1972] 3 W.L.R. 902 at 907; [1972] 3 All E.R. 1041 at 1045. See also, *Hussain v Hussain* [1986] 2 W.L.R. 801; [1986] 1 All E.R. 961; [1986] Fam. 134 and *Witham v Holloway* (1995) 183 C.L.R. 525. In *D v A & Co* (1900) 1 Ch. 484, it was held that undertakings given in an action are enforced by committal, not by attachment.

[79] (1936) 70 I.L.T.R. 199.

[80] See also, *Re H, An Arranging Debtor* I.R. 11 Eq. 106 at 334 (1877); *Re M & R, Arranging Debtors* 30 I.L.T.R. 137 (1896); *Re Birt, An Arranging Debtor* [1906] 2 I.R. 452. Miller sets out examples cases in which there were breaches of undertakings not to molest a person, to carry out building works, to take down a fence, to limit publication of television schedules and not to infringe patent rights: Miller, *Contempt of Court* (Oxford: Clarendon Press, 2000), pp.638–639.

[81] *Biba Ltd v Stratford Investments Ltd* [1973] 1 Ch. 281; [1972] 3 W.L.R. 902; [1972] 3 All E.R. 1041.

[82] See Courtney, *Mareva Injunctions and Related Interlocutory Orders* (Dublin: Butterworths, 1998), p.506.

that if, by mistake, an undertaking has been provided in a more extensive form than was intended, the court will not enforce that undertaking by committal.[83]

(a) A Clear Undertaking

12–46 An injunction must be clear in order to be found to be in contempt for the breach of such an order.[84] The same principle applies to an undertaking.[85] In *Irish Shell v J. H. McLoughlin (Balbriggan) Ltd*,[86] Clarke J. refused an application for attachment and committal and also refused to discharge the injunction concerned. This was on the basis that he felt it would be inappropriate to imply undertakings or to construe indications or commitments as being undertakings, unless the matter referred to was specifically given in the form of an undertaking and noted in the court order.

3. Liability of Different Parties

12–47 The extent to which each of the various parties identified above may be found liable for the breach of an injunction, and issues peculiar to each of them, will be considered in turn. Many of the decisions which consider the liability of various parties are English. However, in the absence of a significant number of equivalent Irish decisions, the principles established in those English cases can certainly be viewed as being of strong persuasive value.[87]

(a) The Party Named in the Injunction

12–48 It is clear from the decision of the Supreme Court in *Moore v Attorney General (No.1)*[88] that an injunction, which is in the nature of an execution, will only be granted in personam. It will not in general terms be granted against any person not a party to an action.[89]

---

[83] *Mullins v Howell* (1879) 11 Ch D 763.
[84] *Federal Bank of the Middle East v Hadkinson* [2000] 1 W.L.R. 1695; *Iberian Trust Ltd v Founders' Trust and Investments Company Ltd* [1932] 2 K.B. 87.
[85] *Redwing Ltd v Redwing Forest Products Ltd* (1947) 177 L.T. 387.
[86] unreported, High Court, Clarke J., December 19, 2005.
[87] Subject to the caveat that the provisions of the Contempt of Court Act 1981 apply in that jurisdiction.
[88] [1930] I.R. 471 at 486, per Kennedy C.J.
[89] Albeit that the courts in England have sometimes had recourse to an injunction *contra mundum*, which applies as against the population at large. See further, Ch.3, Standing, in which it is submitted that such orders are unlikely to find favour with the Irish courts under the existing Rules of Court. The old case of *Hope v Carnegie* (1868) L.R. 7 Eq. 254 is authority for the proposition that if an injunction is granted against a married couple, and one of the couple breaches the injunction, the other spouse will not be held liable for such a breach in the absence of complicity.

(i) Proper Notice of the Order

12–49 An application in relation to contempt can be brought against the person against whom the injunction order is made, subject to that person having proper notice of the terms of an injunction.[90] As was clearly stated by Warrington J. in *Stancomb v Trowbridge Urban District Council*[91]:

> "If a person or a corporation is restrained by injunction from doing a particular act, that person or corporation commits a breach of the injunction and is liable for process of contempt, if he or it in fact does the act, and it is no answer to say that the act was not contumacious in the sense that, in doing it there was no direct intention to disobey the order."[92]

12–50 The same basic principles apply to undertakings. In *Ronson Products Ltd v Ronson Furniture Ltd*,[93] it was held that the failure to serve on an individual the order containing a negative undertaking was not a bar to proceedings against that individual for its breach, as he was fully aware of it. Different considerations should be applied to positive undertakings, however, as the putative contemnor must be in a position to know exactly what is required to be done, even in circumstances where he is the one giving the undertaking.[94]

(ii) Accepted Propositions

12–51 A number of propositions have been accepted by the courts in England as to the circumstances in which an individual may be found to have breached an injunction order:

- It has been held that a party's motive in breaching the order is irrelevant.[95] Intent of the party, unless otherwise stated on the face of the order, was viewed as not relevant to a consideration of whether there has been a breach of an injunction order.[96] However, as has been seen,[97] the courts may recognise that there has been "contumacious" civil contempt, in which case intent must be of some relevance in so far as such contempt requires wilful disobedience.

---

[90] In *McClure v McClure* [1951] I.R. 137, it was held by Maguire J. on an appeal to the High Court that a defendant should not be committed for non-compliance with an order which was not served upon him within the time limited by the order for compliance with its terms.

[91] [1910] 2 Ch. 190.

[92] [1910] 2 Ch. 190 at 194. See also, *Knight v Clifton* [1971] Ch. 700 at 721.

[93] [1966] Ch. 603; [1966] 2 W.L.R. 1157; [1966] 2 All E.R. 381.

[94] See generally, Arlidge, Eady & Smith, *Contempt* (London: Sweet & Maxwell, 1999), pp.787–788.

[95] per Lord Sterndale M.R. in *R v Poplar Borough Council (No. 2)* [1922] 1 K.B. 95 at 103.

[96] per Sachs L.J. in *Knight v Clifton* [1971] Ch. 700 at 721; [1971] 2 All E.R. 378 at 393.

[97] See para.12–36.

- The burden of proof when impossibility is pleaded rests on the defendant.[98]
- It is not open to a party to plead that he "did his best", notwithstanding that the order was not complied with.[99] However, some judges have demonstrated a reluctance to resort to redress for contempt without having explored other options, and will generally take a realistic view when there is difficulty complying with an injunction.[100]
- The fact the defendant may have obtained professional advice and acted on it is not a defence to a charge of contempt, although this may be a factor which can be taken into account by a court.[101]

12–52 Specific provision is made in the Rules of the Superior Courts in relation to the breach of a mandatory injunction. It is clear from the terms of RSC Ord.41 r.8 of the Rules that a party named in such an order is bound by its terms, with an endorsement to that effect required by the Rules.

(iii) Mental Illness

12–53 The issue of whether mental illness may be a bar to an order for committal for contempt was considered in the case of *State (H) v Daly*.[102] However, O'Higgins J. found that "whatever degree of mental illness the prosecutor suffered it was not such as rendered him incapable of knowing fully what he was doing." He also stated that he was doing so "without considering further whether in such circumstances mental illness may be a bar to an order for committal."[103] The point does not appear to have been further considered in any written judgments. This is obviously a sensitive matter which is presumably best dealt with on a case-by-case basis.

---

[98] *Lewis v Pontypridd, Caerphilly and Newport Railway Co* (1895) 11 T.L.R. 203. Although see the *dictum* of Sir Raymond Evershed M.R. in *Pride of Derby v British Celanese Ltd* [1953] 1 All E.R. 179 at 197: "Equally, of course, the Court will not impose on a local authority, or on anyone else, an obligation to do something which is impossible, or which cannot be enforced, or which is unlawful", cited by O'Hanlon J. in *Lennon v Ganly* [1981] I.L.R.M. 84.

[99] *Howitt Transport v Transport and General Workers Union* [1973] I.C.R. 1 at 10.

[100] This is particularly so in relation to family proceedings, as evidenced by the decision of Ormrod L.J. in the case of *Ansah v Ansah* [1977] Fam. 138; [1977] 2 W.L.R. 760; [1977] 2 All E.R. 638. However, see *Jones v Jones* [1993] 2 F.L.R. 377, in which Russell L.J. cautioned that Ormrod L.J.'s decision in *Ansah* was not the basis for a general principle that an immediate custodial sentence should not be imposed, irrespective of circumstances. It was held in *Thomason v Thomason* [1985] F.L.R. 214 that the "Draconian powers" to imprison or fine which may have to be invoked should be regarded as the weapon of the last resort.

[101] *Re Mileage Conference Group of the Tyre Manufacturers' Conference Ltd's Agreement* [1966] 1 W.L.R. 1137; [1986] 2 All E.R. 849.

[102] [1977] I.R. 90.

[103] [1977] I.R. 90 at 97.

(b) Servants and Agents

12–54 That the servants and agents of an individual named in an injunction order may also be amenable to the jurisdiction of the court is clear from the decision of *Gore-Booth v Gore-Booth*.[104] In that case, Lavery J. held that any "intelligible construction" of the order concerned must "extend its operation to the servants or agents of the Committee through whom he must act".[105] However, specific considerations apply in relation to directors and employees of corporations, and these will be considered below.

(c) Companies

12–55 Companies may be subject to an injunction order by the courts (or may also give undertakings in lieu of injunction orders).[106] In such a case, the separate legal personality of the company may be disregarded, and an order issued against the company's directors or controlling members in addition to the company itself.[107] It is not a defence for a company to claim that its officers were unaware of the terms of order, or that they failed to realise its terms were being bring broken by their actions.[108] It has also been held in England that a company can be in breach of both an injunction[109] and an undertaking[110] where an employee is acting contrary to express instructions.[111] The position in relation to directors, employees and shareholders of a company will be considered below, but the first matter for consideration are the criteria upon which a company will be found to be in breach of an injunction, set out in RSC Ord.42 r.32.

(i) Wilful Disobedience

12–56 The wording of RSC Ord.42 r.32 of the Rules provides for "wilful" disobedience on the part of a company in relation to a breach of a judgment or order.[112] As to what is to be understood by the term "wilful", the decision of

---

[104] (1962) 96 I.L.T.R. 32.

[105] (1962) 96 I.L.T.R. 32 at 38.

[106] *Biba Ltd v Stratford Investments Ltd* [1973] 1 Ch. 281; [1972] 3 W.L.R. 902; [1972] 3 All E.R. 1041.

[107] Courtney, *The Law of Private Companies*, 2nd edn (Dublin: Butterworths, 2002), p.237.

[108] See *Re Garage Equipment Associations' Agreement* (1964) L.R. 4 R.P. 491; *Re Galvanized Tank Manufacturers Associations' Agreement* [1983] 1 All E.R. 203. In *Re British Concrete Pipe Association's Agreement* [1983] I.C.R. 215, an undertaking given by one company was found to bind the company of which it became a wholly owned subsidiary.

[109] *Re The Supply of Ready Mixed Concrete (No. 2); Director General of Fair Trading v Pioneer Concrete (UK) Ltd* [1995] 1 A.C. 456; [1994] 3 W.L.R. 1249; [1995] 1 All E.R. 135.

[110] It was held in *Re the Agreement of the Mileage Conference Group of the Tyre Manufacturers' Conference Ltd* [1966] 1 W.L.R. 1137; [1966] 2 All E.R. 849 that the breach of an undertaking constitutes a contempt even if it is not wilful.

[111] A view which has been criticised: see further below, in relation to both this and breaches of undertakings by employees, para.12–62.

[112] See RCC Ord.36 r.5, which provides that: "Any judgment or order against a corporation

Lord Wilberforce in *Heatons Transport (St Helens) Ltd v Transport and General Workers Union*[113] appears to represent the position arrived at in England in relation to the term. In delivering his judgement in *Heatons*, Lord Wilberforce approved the earlier case of *Stancomb v Trowbridge UDC*,[114] in which Warrington J. had taken the view that:

> "if a person or corporation is restrained by injunction from doing a particular act, that person or corporation commits a breach of the injunction, and is liable for process of contempt, if he or it in fact does the act, and it is no answer to say the act was not contumacious in the sense that, in doing it, there was no direct intention to disobey the order."[115]

12–57 Warrington J. though that the expression "wilful" was "intended to exclude only such casual or accidental or unintentional acts as I referred to in *Fairclough v Manchester Ship Canal Co.*"[116] This is a fairly broad test, and is obviously reliant on the courts dealing with the facts of the case before them.

12–58 The meaning of "wilfully" was considered by the Supreme Court in *Irish Shell Ltd v Ballylynch Motor Ltd and Morris Oil Company Ltd.*[117] Lynch J., delivering the unanimous judgment of the court, stopped short of providing a definition of the word. However, in finding that the second-named defendant had wilfully disobeyed an earlier court order, he noted that:

> "Nothing whatever was done by the Appellants to check the accuracy and reliability of the assurances given to them by the consignee company ... and to ensure that a delivery of motor fuels to them did not contravene the order ..."

12–59 Reading *Irish Shell* together with *Stancomb*, the position would appear to be that it is not sufficient in the context of dealing with the word "wilful" to argue that there was no direct intention to disobey an order. The only stateable argument which may be put forward would seem to be that an act (or indeed, non-act, as was the case in *Irish Shell*) was "casual or accidental or uninten-

---

wilfully disobeyed may, by leave of the judge, be enforced by an execution order by way of attachment or committal against the directors or other officers thereof, or any of them."

[113] [1973] A.C. 15; [1972] 3 W.L.R. 431; [1972] 3 All E.R. 101.
[114] [1910] 2 Ch. 190.
[115] [1910] 2 Ch. 190 at 194.
[116] Not following the definition of Stirling J. in *Worthington v Ad-Lib Club Ltd* [1964] 3 All E.R. 674. However, *Fairclough* was decided in the context of the then applicable Rules in England which required "wilful" disobedience. The word "wilful" did not appear in the later Rules of the Supreme Court 1965, although the same principles continued to be applied in relation to the use of the word; see, for example, *In re Mileage Conference Group of the Tyre Manufacturers' Conference Ltd's Agreement* [1966] 1 W.L.R. 1137 at 1162; [1966] 2 All E.R. 849 at 861, per Megaw P.
[117] unreported, Supreme Court, March 5, 1997.

tional", as set out in *Stancomb*. "Wilful" appears to cover all behaviour beyond that, and is not to be measured further in terms of degrees of behaviour.[118]

(ii) Liability of a Corporation for Breaches by Employees / Agents

12–60 The House of Lords, in *Heatons Transport (St Helens) Ltd v Transport and General Workers Union*,[119] held that a corporation was responsible for the acts of its agents acting within the scope of their authority.

(iii) Acting Within Authority or Acting in Breach

12–61 The fact that the servant or agent must be acting within the scope of their authority was confirmed in *Director of Fair Trading v Smiths Concrete Ltd.*[120] It was held in that case that whether an employer was bound by an act of its employee depended on the scope of the employee's mandate. In other words, the usual principles of vicarious liability would apply.[121] However, in the House of Lords decision in *Re The Supply of Ready Mixed Concrete (No. 2); Director General of Fair Trading v Pioneer Concrete (UK) Ltd*,[122] which overturned the *Smiths Concrete* decision, it was decided that even in circumstances where employees had been expressly instructed not to enter into an agreement which would breach the injunction in place, an employer could be held liable for breach of an injunction if the employees acted contrary to such instructions.

12–62 It has been argued that such a test of strict liability is inappropriate as a test for determining the liability of an employer for contempt through his servants. This is predicated on the view that an injunction against a person not to do an act by his servants or agents or otherwise is a restraint on the person to whom the injunction is addressed. The liability of an employer for the acts of his servant is personal, not vicarious.[123] Nonetheless, in *MGFM Asia Ltd v Securities Commission*,[124] the Privy Council followed the approach set down by Lord Nolan. It would thus appear that the only defences open to a company charged with contempt in a *Ready Mixed Concrete*-type situation would be to argue either a) that the acts in question were not deliberate but casual or

---

[118] See the case of *Arisukwu v Minister for Justice*, unreported, Supreme Court, March 9, 2006, in which it was argued that for the State to have the intent to deport in face of an ex parte order was a contempt of court. Denham J. held that to have such intent was not incompatible with the court or court proceedings.

[119] [1973] A.C. 15; [1972] 3 W.L.R. 431; [1972] 3 All E.R. 101.

[120] [1991] 4 All E.R. 150.

[121] As to which, see generally, McMahon & Binchy, *Irish Law of Torts*, 3rd edn (Dublin: Butterworths, 2000), especially Ch.43.

[122] [1995] 1 A.C. 456; [1994] 3 W.L.R. 1249; [1995] 1 All E.R. 135.

[123] See Courtney, *Mareva Injunctions and Related Interlocutory Orders* (Dublin: Butterworths, 1998), pp.495–496.

[124] [1995] 2 A.C. 500.

accidental or unintentional (based on the decision in *Stancomb*) or b) that the servants or agents were not acting in course of their employment and/or were engaged in some kind of frolic.[125] Having regard to the context in which *Pioneer Concrete* was decided—against the background of the Restrictive Trade Practices Act 1976[126]—there may be some traction in the argument that regard should also be had to the context against which an order is being sought.

12–63 In this jurisdiction, there does not appear to be any case which follows or espouses the approach in *Ready Mixed Concrete*. That being so, the default position in Ireland would appear to be that an employee must be acting within the scope of his authority in order that a corporation may be found liable for the breach of an injunction by that employee.

Independent Contractors
12–64 It would seem, based on English authority, that where an independent contractor is responsible for the breach of an injunction, unless such a contractor is clearly specified in the injunction order, the defendant corporation is not strictly liable for such actions.[127]

(iv) Position of Company Directors

12–65 The position of company directors requires separate consideration. Rules of the Superior Courts Ord.42 r.32 provides that in relation to a judgment or order against a company wilfully disobeyed, attachment is available as a remedy against "the directors or other officers"[128] of the company, as is an order of sequestration of their property.[129] The relationship between the actions of a company and its directors is thus crucial.

12–66 This relationship was considered in the case of *Sligo Corporation v Cartron Bay Construction Ltd.*[130] Ó Caoimh J. determined in relation to the second and third named respondents, who were the directors of the first-named respondent company, that:

> "Insofar as a company can have a will it must be by those in control of the company. In the instant case the control was in the hands of the second and third Respondents. At the same time it must be recognised that the failure of

---

[125] Borrie & Lowe, *The Law of Contempt*, 3rd edn (London: Butterworths, 1996), p.570.

[126] Discussed in *MGFM Asia Ltd v Securities Commission* [1995] 2 A.C. 500.

[127] *World Wide Fund for Nature v THQ/ Jakks Pacific LLC* [2004] F.S.R. 10 at 161, discussed by Gee, *Commercial Injunctions*, 5th edn (London: Sweet & Maxwell, 2004), p.548.

[128] Section 2 of the Companies Act 1963 provides that directors and the company secretary are encompassed by the word "officer". See RCC Ord.36 r.5.

[129] As to sequestration, see para.12–131.

[130] unreported, High Court, Ó Caoimh J., May 25, 2001.

a corporate entity will not necessarily give rise to a conclusion of wilful default on its part or on the part of its directors."[131]

(v) Extent to Which Directors Cause Breach

12–67 The key test therefore appears to be the extent to which the directors of a company have caused the company to be in default of, and by extension in breach of, an injunction. It was indicated in the case of *Phonographic Performance Ltd v Amusement Caterers (Peckham) Ltd*[132] that under the then applicable rules in England, no proceedings for contempt could be taken against directors unless proceedings could also have been taken against the company.[133] However, where such circumstances existed, proceedings could be taken against both the directors and the company. Referring to the decision of Luxmore J. in *Iberian Trust Ltd v Founders' Trust and Investments Company Ltd*,[134] Cross J. took the view that he did not believe that Luxmoore J.:

> "was intending to say that one could not make an order for the sequestration of the company's property and an order for committal of the directors to prison; what he was saying was that the Plaintiff could not proceed against the directors unless he was in a position to proceed against the company."[135]

12–68 This is relatively self-explanatory; once a party is in a position to proceed against a company, he may also proceed against the directors of the company. In *R. v Poplar Borough Council (No. 2)*,[136] Lord Sterndale M.R. emphasised that if a party seeks to attach individual members of a corporation, their names must be inserted individually in the *rule nisi* for attachment (i.e. the relevant order) with each served individually, although an irregularity in that regard can be waived.

(vi) No Role in Breach

12–69 The question remains of how to deal with directors in circumstances where they have not had a role in the breach concerned. In *Biba Ltd v Stratford Investments Ltd*,[137] it was held that a director had a case to answer in relation to

---

[131] unreported, High Court, Ó Caoimh J., May 25, 2001, p.75.
[132] [1964] 1 Ch. 195; [1963] 3 W.L.R. 898; [1963] 3 All E.R. 493.
[133] See also, *Ronson Products Ltd v Ronson Furniture Ltd* [1966] Ch. 603; [1966] 2 W.L.R. 1157; [1966] 2 All E.R. 381 and *Biba Ltd v Stratford Investments Ltd Biba Ltd v Stratford Investments Ltd* [1973] 1 Ch. 281; [1972] 3 W.L.R. 902; [1972] 3 All E.R. 1041. The directors must also be acting as directors, not as shareholders: *Northern Counties Securities Ltd v Jackson and Steeple Ltd* [1974] 1 W.L.R. 1133; [1974] 2 All E.R. 625.
[134] [1932] 2 K.B. 87; 48 T.L.R. 292.
[135] [1964] 1 Ch. 195 at 202; [1963] 3 W.L.R. 898 at 903; [1963] 3 All E.R. 493 at 498.
[136] [1922] 1 K.B. 95.
[137] [1973] 1 Ch. 281; [1972] 3 W.L.R. 902; [1972] 3 All E.R. 1041; *cf. Director General of Fair Trading v Buckland* [1990] 1 All E.R. 545, in which it was held that a person will not be found liable for contempt merely by virtue of being an officer of a company.

contempt, notwithstanding that he only had a passive role in relation to the breach concerned. Similarly, in *Attorney General for Tuvalu v Philatelic Distribution Corp Ltd*,[138] Woolf L.J. held that where a director of a company is aware of an order he is under a duty to "take reasonable steps to ensure that the order or undertaking is obeyed". Woolf L.J. cautioned that if the director:

> "wilfully fails to take those steps and the order is breached he can be punished for contempt. We use the word 'wilful' to distinguish the situation where the director can reasonably believe some other director or officer is taking those steps."[139]

(vii) No Joint and Several Liability

12–70 An important point in relation to joint and several liability was emphasised in *McMillan Graham Printers Ltd v RR (UK) Ltd*.[140] It was held in that case that it was wrong in principle to impose a fine jointly and severally on a company and on one of its directors; each defendant must be considered separately.

(viii) Position of Shareholders

12–71 In *Northern Counties Securities Ltd v Jackson and Steeple Ltd*,[141] Walton J. had to consider the role of shareholders in circumstances where they might cause a company to be in contempt of court. He found that the shareholders would not be in contempt in such circumstances. In doing so, he made a distinction between directors and shareholders. In relation to shareholders, he held that:

> "When a shareholder is voting for or against a particular resolution he is voting as a person owing no fiduciary duty to the company and who is exercising his own right of property, to vote as he thinks fit. The fact that the result of the voting at the meeting (or at a subsequent poll) will bind the company cannot affect the position that, in voting, he is voting simply in exercise of his own property rights."[142]

---

[138] [1990] 1 W.L.R. 926; [1990] 2 All E.R. 216.
[139] [1990] 1 W.L.R. 926 at 936; [1990] 2 All E.R. 216 at 222. Such an approach is consistent with the development of the law in relation to applications under s.150 of the Companies Act 1990 for the restriction of directors. See, for example, *Re Barings Plc (No. 5) Secretary of State for Trade and Industry v Baker* [1999] 1 B.C.L.C. 433 and *Kavanagh v Delaney* [2005] I.L.R.M. 34 (*Re Tralee Beef & Lamb*).
[140] [1993] T.L.R. 152.
[141] [1974] 1 W.L.R. 1133; [1974] 2 All E.R. 625.
[142] [1974] 1 W.L.R. 1133 at 1144; [1974] 2 All E.R. 625 at 635.

12–72 Walton J. concluded that the shareholders were not abetting the company in question in committing a contempt of court. By convening a meeting and putting a circular before the members, Walton J. felt that the company "will have done its best, and the rest is in the lap of the gods in the shape of the individual decisions of the members."[143]

12–73 However, Walton J. cautioned that it could be otherwise if circumstances arose in which an order was made by the courts upon a company to do something, giving the example of increasing its capital, which would, of necessity, involve the shareholders voting in a particular manner. However, he could not envisage any ordinary situation where such an order would ever be made.

(e) Third Parties/Non-Parties

12–74 The fact that an injunction order may be directed towards one or more named parties does not preclude parties not named in the order from breaching its terms. The basic rule still applies, namely that an order is binding on any person having notice of the making of the order.[144] A third party or non-party who acts contrary to an injunction when they know of its existence and terms can therefore be guilty of contempt.[145] Kennedy C.J. observed in *Moore v Attorney General*[146] that a number of English cases had laid down the principle that a motion to attach a third party is technically wrong because he is not bound by the injunction, but that he may be committed for contempt of court "because he is acting so as to obstruct the course of justice".[147] In practical terms, a court is unlikely to refuse an application for contempt on the basis that it is sought to attach, rather than commit, a third party.

12–75 However, the manner in which a third party may breach an injunction has given rise to considerable judicial discussion, particularly in England. The behaviour of third parties has been considered both in the context of the "aiding and abetting" by a third party of the breach of an injunction and the doing of something which does not constitute "aiding and abetting" in the strict sense,

---

[143] [1974] 1 W.L.R. 1133 at 1145; [1974] 2 All E.R. 625 at 636.
[144] See generally, *Avory v Andrews* (1882) 46 L.T. 279; *United Trading Company v Dale* (1884) 25 Ch D 778; *Smith-Barry v Dawson* (1891) 27 L.R. Ir. 558; *R v Freeman's Journal Ltd* [1902] 2 I.R. 82 and *Scott v Scott* [1913] A.C. 417; *cf. Iveson v Harris* (1802) 7 Ves. Jun. 251 at 256, per Lord Eldon L.C.
[145] See, for example, *Smith-Barry v Dawson* (1891) 27 L.R. Ir. 558, one of the earliest cases to explore this principle in detail. This is so even in circumstances where an injunction may be granted against an unknown person: see *South Cambridgeshire DC v Gammell* [2006] 1 W.L.R. 658.
[146] [1930] I.R. 471 at 486.
[147] Citing *Seaward v Paterson* [1897] 1 Ch. 545; [1895–1899] All E.R. Rep 1127; *Brydges v Brydges* [1909] P. 187 at 191; *Ranson v Platt* [1911] 2 K.B. 291 at 307 and *Scott v Scott* [1913] A.C. 417 at 457.

but "which disables the court from conducting the case in the intended manner, thus interfering with the course of justice".[148] These will be considered in turn.

(i) Aiding and Abetting

12–76 A number of cases have established that a third party can be in contempt for aiding and abetting a breach of an injunction. In *Moore v Attorney General*,[149] Kennedy C.J. had regard to the "ruling of authority" of *Lord Wellesley v Earl of Mornington*,[150] which the Chief Justice held had established that:

> "a person, not a party to a suit in which an injunction has been granted to restrain the doing of certain acts (i.e., a negative injunction), but with full knowledge of the injunction and of the acts forbidden by the order, nevertheless aids and abets in committing a breach of it."[151]

12–77 In confirming that there was no authority for an order enjoining every member of the public,[152] Kennedy C.J. adopted the view set out in *Lord Wellesley*. He stated that a third party aiding and abetting the breach of an injunction is acting so as to "obstruct the course of justice".[153]

(ii) Interfering in the Course of Justice

12–78 The idea that a third party could be found guilty of a breach in circumstances other than simply "aiding and abetting" has been developed by the courts, particularly in the context of newspaper publishing in England. It is now accepted in that jurisdiction that a third party can be found to be in contempt in circumstances where a defendant is not.[154] This idea is based

---

[148] *Attorney General v Times Newspapers Ltd* [1992] 1 A.C. 191; [1991] 2 W.L.R. 994; [1991] 2 All E.R. 398.

[149] [1930] I.R. 471.

[150] [1684] 1 Vern. 266.

[151] [1930] I.R. 471 at 486. See also, *Witham v Holloway* (1995) 183 C.L.R. 525 and *Johnston v Moore* [1965] N.I. 128. See also, *Seaward v Paterson* [1897] 1 Ch. 545; [1895-9] All E.R. Rep 1127, although this was not in fact the sole basis for the decision, as discussed by Eveleigh L.J. in *Z Ltd v A-Z* [1982] Q.B. 558; [1982] 2 W.L.R. 288; [1982] 1 All E.R. 556. *Seaward* concerned a prohibitory injunction, but was viewed as being of more general application, extending to breaches of mandatory orders and undertakings given: *Elliot v Klinger* [1967] 1 W.L.R. 1165; [1967] 3 All E.R. 141.

[152] See Ch.3, Standing, in relation to injunctions *contra mundum*, at para.3–59.

[153] [1930] I.R. 471, 487, having referred to *Seaward v Paterson* [1897] 1 Ch. 545; *Brydges v Brydges and Wood* [1909] P. 187; *Ranson v Platt* [1911] 2 K.B. 291; *Scott v Scott* [1913] A.C. 417 and *Smith-Barry v Dawson* (1891) 27 L.R. Ir. 558.

[154] An extension of the basic principles applicable to third parties described by Spry as "not easy to justify in principle": Spry, *The Principles of Equitable Remedies*, 5th edn (London: Sweet & Maxwell, 1997), p.370. But *cf.* Miller, *Contempt of Court* (Oxford: Clarendon Press, 2000), p.667, who suggests that the application of the law of contempts in such situations is entirely consistent with its underlying rationale, although accepting that this view is "unfashionable in some quarters".

broadly on the notion of interfering in the course of justice, and was endorsed in the key case of *Attorney General v Times Newspapers Ltd.*[155]

12–79 In the *Times Newspapers* case, injunctions had previously been granted against two newspapers restraining them from publishing material from the book "Spycatcher" by a former secret service agent. However, Times Newspapers Ltd, which was not one of the two newspapers against which an injunction had been granted, proceeded to publish extracts from the book. It was quite clear that Times Newspapers was acting independently of the other newspapers, and was not aiding and abetting them in any way. In approving of the concept of "interfering in the court of justice" as the basis for finding a party to be in contempt, Lord Jauncey held that:

> "a person who knowingly acts in a way which will frustrate the operation of an injunction may be guilty of contempt even although he is neither named in the order nor has he assisted the person who is named to breach it."[156]

12–80 He also observed that it would be "extraordinary if orders of the court could be set at nought with impunity by third parties seeking to achieve that end".

(iii) The Floodgates Argument

12–81 Lord Jauncey addressed the floodgates argument arising from such an approach by suggesting that it could only be in a limited type of case that independent action by a third party would have the effect of interfering with the operation of an order to which he was not a party. He gave the example of confidential information as one such instance.

12–82 Lord Jauncey's view appears to have been borne out, with the idea of "interference with the course of justice" in the context of contempt "applied sparingly".[157] In the later case of *Attorney General v Newspaper Publishing*

---

[155] [1992] 1 A.C. 191; [1991] 2 W.L.R. 994; [1991] 2 All E.R. 398. This in fact formed part of a somewhat complex series of cases. A number of different newspapers were involved at different stages of the proceedings, but the relevant case law starts for present purposes with the decision in *Attorney General v Newspaper Publishing Plc* [1988] Ch. 333; [1987] 3 All E.R. 276 in the Court of Appeal (the appeal from Browne Wilkinson V.C.). The Court of Appeal remitted the matter to Millett J., who determined that there had been contempt, which led to a further appeal to the Court of Appeal and ultimately an appeal to the House of Lords, reported as *Attorney General v Times Newspapers Ltd.*

[156] [1992] 1 A.C. 191 at 231; [1991] 2 W.L.R. 994 at 1026; [1991] 2 All E.R. 398 at 426. The application of these principles in the specific context of *Mareva* injunctions and *Anton Piller* orders is comprehensively dealt with by Courtney, *Mareva Injunctions and Related Interlocutory Orders* (Dublin: Butterworths, 1998), pp.500–506.

[157] See, for example, *Re Lonrho Plc* [1990] 2 A.C. 154; [1989] 2 All E.R. 1100.

Plc,[158] Lord Bingham C.J. observed that both parties had accepted that the necessary mens rea for third parties was that stated by Sir John Donaldson M.R. in the "Spycatcher" proceedings, namely that a party "specifically intended to impede or prejudice the administration of justice".[159]

12–83 Whether the Irish courts would adopt the same approach is unclear. Whilst they have certainly accepted that a third party may be in contempt of court both when he is found to have aided and abetted the breach of an injunction, there has never been an explicit extension of the principle beyond this.[160] In principle, there would appear to be nothing to prevent the Irish courts from relying on the idea of interference in the course of justice as a ground for finding a third or non-party in breach of an injunction. In making such a finding, however, a court would have pay due regard to the underlying principle that an injunction fundamentally operates in personam. To go beyond this, and indeed beyond showing that a person aided and abetted the breach of an injunction, it would presumably be necessary to adopt the standard approved of by Lord Bingham C.J. in *Attorney General v Newspaper Publishing Plc*, namely showing "some significant and adverse effect on the administration of justice."[161]

(iv) Aiding/Intermeddling/Interference

12–84 The Canadian courts have approached this area of the law by drawing a distinction between aiding and abetting, inter-meddling and interference in the administration of justice. The difference between these has been summarised in the following manner[162]:

> "The cases in which a non-party has been found guilty of contempt for aiding and abetting are cases where the non-party has acted in collusion with the named party to achieve a single objective. Where the non-party has been found to be inter-meddling, the non-party's intent and objective in participating is not the same as the named party, yet the non-party is aware that his or her actions will further the named party's goal in some respect. In the case of interfering with the administration of justice, the non-party's actions have the same effect as the enjoined conduct regardless of how that may advance the interests of the named party. In this sense, even totally

---

[158] A case which dealt with what were commonly known as the "Arms to Iraq" proceedings, which were separate from the earlier "Spycatcher" proceedings reported by the same title, [1997] 1 W.L.R. 926; [1997] 3 All E.R. 159.

[159] [1988] Ch. 333 at 374; [1987] 3 All E.R. 276 at 304. See also, *Attorney General v Punch Ltd* [2003] 1 A.C. 1046.

[160] Although as seen in *Moore v Attorney General*, Kennedy C.J. did refer, albeit in the context of aiding and abetting, to such conduct being an example of "obstructing the course of justice".

[161] [1997] 1 W.L.R. 926 at 936; [1997] 3 All E.R. 159 at 168.

[162] Berryman, "Recent Developments in the Law of Equitable Remedies: What Canada Can Do For You" (2002) V.U.W. L. Rev. 3.

independent action by the non-party will give rise to contempt if it violates the terms of the injunction."

12–85 Again, this is an area which does not appear to have given rise to any considerable scrutiny by the Irish courts. In so far as the courts in this jurisdiction may seek to find a non-party in contempt, the categorisation could certainly be of some assistance.

D. Applying for Remedies for the Breach of an Injunction Order

1. Introduction

12–86 Contempt of court is unlawful conduct, which conduct attracts a sanction. In *State (Commins) v McRann*,[163] Finlay P. held that Art.34 of the Constitution, which states that justice shall be administered in courts established by law and by judges appointed in accordance with the Constitution, authorised the courts to adjudicate in a summary manner the issue of contempt of court and to impose sanctions in the event of disobedience to their orders.[164]

12–87 The classic remedies for breach of an injunction by an individual are attachment, whereby the individual is brought before the court to answer for the contempt he is alleged to have committed, and committal, which involves the imprisonment of the contemnor. Sequestration is the remedy most often used as against companies which are in breach of an injunction, but is also available as a remedy against an individual for the breach of a mandatory injunction and against company directors. The courts have also had recourse to fines and the use of costs penalties as a means of sanction for breaching an injunction.

12–88 Remedies for breaches of injunctions are discretionary, and a court will usually seek to enforce obedience of the terms of its order in the first instance, rather than granting alternative relief. Courts should also consider the most appropriate approach when the contempt concerned is of a minor or technical nature.[165] For example, in *Dubsky v Drogheda Port Company*,[166] O'Sullivan J., whilst finding that the defendants in question were in breach of an earlier interlocutory order, found that "such breaches … seem to me to fall rather more on the technical side that on the substantive side". He made an order continuing the restraint which had previously been put in place. Furthermore, the courts are

---

[163] [1977] I.R. 78.

[164] Finlay P. referred (at 85) to the decision of the Supreme Court in *Keegan v de Burca* [1973] I.R. 223. The President also referred to *Attorney General v O'Kelly* [1928] I.R. 308; *Re Earle* [1938] I.R. 485 and *Attorney General v Connolly* [1947] I.R. 213.

[165] See *Marshall v Marshall* (1966) 110 S.J. 112; *Smith v Smith* [1988] 1 F.L.R. 179 at 181.

[166] unreported, High Court, O'Sullivan J., February 22, 2000.

always alive to the effect their orders may have. For example, in the case of *Cullen v Cullen*,[167] Kenny J. refused to grant an injunction sought by a father against his sons to prevent them trespassing on the family farm. In doing so, he noted that relations between fathers and sons:

> "should not be governed by the heavy artillery of Court orders, injunctions or the threat of committal to prison, but by respect, affection, honour and the feeling of moral obligation."[168]

2. Determination at the Application

12–89 It has been held in England that a court must determine at the application whether there has been contempt or not. In *Delaney v Delaney*,[169] it was made clear that a party cannot be remanded pending a decision as to whether they are in contempt.[170]

3. An Anticipatory Order

12–90 The question as to whether an order can be made in anticipation of a refusal to comply with the terms of an injunction was touched upon in *Savage v Norton*.[171] The case involved very particular circumstances relating to a stock transfer and an apparent refusal to execute such a transfer. In refusing to make an anticipatory order an order under s.14 of the Judicature Act, 1884, Parker J. noted that he was not deciding that there was no case in which the Court could make an anticipatory order. In *Victoria v Australian Building Construction Employees' and Builders Labourers' Federation*,[172] Gibbs C.J. in the Australian High Court stated that "A superior court which has power to punish contempts, and which also has power to issue injunctions, may grant an injunction to restrain a threatened contempt."[173] Such a situation may arise where, for example, a newspaper threatens to publish material in breach of an injunction. Gee cites the decision in *World Wide Fund for Nature v THQ/Jakks Pacific LLC*[174] as authority for the proposition that a defendant:

---

[167] [1962] I.R. 268.
[168] [1962] I.R. 268 at 290. Two English decisions had been opened to the court, *Waterhouse v Waterhouse* (1905) 94 L.T. 133, and *Stevens v Stevens* (1907) 24 T.L.R. 20. An injunction had in fact been granted in *Stevens*, but the circumstances of that case were held by the court to be "very grave": (1907) 24 T.L.R. 20 at 21.
[169] [1996] Q.B. 387.
[170] Albeit that this was decided in the context of the 1981 English Contempt of Court Act.
[171] [1908] 1 Ch. 290.
[172] (1982) 152 C.L.R. 25.
[173] (1982) 152 C.L.R. 25 at 42.
[174] [2004] F.S.R. 10 at 161.

"has a responsibility when he can foresee the possibility that a servant or agent might act contrary to the terms of an injunction to take all reasonable steps to prevent them from doing so."[175]

4. Sanctions

12–91 The sanctions available to a court for the breach of an injunction will be considered in turn. They are attachment and committal, sequestration of assets, fines, costs orders and alternative remedies under the Rules of Court.

(a) Attachment and Committal

12–92 Although the remedies of attachment and committal are often treated together, they are in fact separate remedies. It was stated in *Cooke v Cooke*[176] that whilst committal was the proper remedy where a prohibited act was done, attachment was the proper remedy for neglecting to do some act ordered to be done.[177] The courts do not appear to have had any great regard for that distinction, and it was also acknowledged by Sir James Campbell C. in *Cooke* that in practice both forms of redress were treated as substantially the same. However, a distinction is made in regard to the rules of procedure applicable to each.[178]

12–93 Rules of the Superior Courts Ord.42 r.7 provides that:

"A judgment requiring any person to do any act other than the payment of money, or to abstain from doing anything, may be enforced by order of attachment or by committal."[179]

12–94 By virtue of RSC Ord.44 r.6, "[t]he court may make an order of attachment where the application is for an order of committal, and *vice versa*."

(i) Attachment

12–95 Under RSC Ord.44 r.1, an order for attachment requires the alleged contemnor to come before the High Court to answer for the contempt he is

---

175 Gee, *Commercial Injunctions*, 5th edn (London: Sweet & Maxwell, 2004), p.548.
176 [1919] 1 I.R. 227, referring to *Callow v Young* 56 L.T. 147.
177 See also, *Re Evans* [1893] 1 Ch. 252.
178 [1919] 1 I.R. 227 at 238. Wylie, *The Judicature Acts (Ireland)* (Dublin: Sealy, Bryers and Walker, 1906), p.606 states that, "the only difference between 'attachment' and 'committal' appears to be that in the former case the delinquent is arrested upon the order of the Court or Judge without the issue of a writ." RSC Ord.70 r.62 deals with attachment "In all matrimonial causes and matters."
179 See RCC Ord.37 r.1.

alleged to have committed.[180] However, in *Cooke v Cooke*,[181] Sir James Campbell C., acknowledging the effectiveness of attachment as a method of securing obedience with a court order, also cautioned that it was:

> "having regard to its punitive consequences, a jurisdiction to be exercised with scrupulous care and caution upon convincing evidence, and only after the fullest and fairest opportunity has been given to the person sought to be attached of making his defence."[182]

12–96 Attachment should in general terms be sought by the party in whose favour the injunction order has been made.[183] An order for attachment is directed to the Commissioner and members of the Garda Síochána. It recites the High Court adjudication that the defendant should be attached on the ground that he was in default in a specified manner, and it commands the Commissioner and members to attach the alleged contemnor so as to have him before the High Court. He is to be brought there:

> "to answer for the contempt which by reason of such default it is alleged he has committed against the High Court, as well as such other matters as shall then and there be charged against him, and further to perform and abide such order as the High Court shall make on his behalf … "[184]

12–97 In other words, the alleged contemnor is brought before the court where he is provided with the opportunity to explain the contempt alleged.

12–98 Rules of the Superior Courts Ord.44 r.4 provides that once the alleged contemnor is before the court, he may be discharged:

> "on such terms and conditions as to costs or otherwise as it thinks fit or commit him to prison for his contempt either for a definite period to be specified in the order, or until he shall purge his contempt and be discharged by further order of the court."[185]

12–99 Officers of a company who were parties to the alleged breach of an injunction may also be attached. By virtue of RSC Ord.42 r.32, where a

---

[180] See RCC Ord.37 r.1, which provides, inter alia, that, "the person entitled to the benefit of such order may serve a notice requiring the person so bound to attend the Court on a day and at an hour to be named in such notice to show cause whey he should not be committed for his contempt in neglecting to obey such order".

[181] [1919] 1 I.R. 227.

[182] [1919] 1 I.R. 227 at 235.

[183] Although see the dictum of Finnegan P. in *Shell E. & P. Ireland v McGrath*, unreported, High Court, Finnegan P., April 7, 2006, para.12–25.

[184] Form 11 in Appendix F, Pt II of the Rules.

[185] The Rules of the Circuit Court appear to contain no directly equivalent provision.

company breaches a judgment or order, the remedies available are, by leave of the court, sequestration against the corporate property, sequestration against the directors' and officers' property, or attachment against the directors or other officers.[186]

(ii) Committal

12–100 Committal involves the summary imprisonment of a contemnor. An order for committal is directed to the Commissioner and members of the Garda Síochána.[187] By virtue of RSC Ord.44 r.2, an order for committal directs that, upon his arrest, the person against whom the order is directed is to be lodged in prison until he purges his contempt and is discharged pursuant to further order of the court.[188] However, the more normal course would be for the party who has obtained the injunction to bring an application for attachment and committal. Attachment would essentially be a precursor to any potential committal, with a party being afforded the opportunity to first appear before a court in order to explain the alleged contempt.

12–101 It is clear that the courts have always taken the view that the power to order committal in the case of the breach of an injunction is one to be exercised with very great care, and all the circumstances of a case will be looked at. In the case of *Gore-Booth v Gore-Booth*,[189] Lavery J. refused to make the order for committal sought, but indicated that the decision was taken "with hesitation and some fear that it may be acting with undue leniency." However, he acknowledged that there were circumstance which, although they did not excuse the conduct of the defendant might, "in some degree, be taken into account in extenuation".[190]

12–102 The exercise of the power to commit should be carefully considered by the court when it is unlikely to produce the desired result and when there is some reasonable alternative course available, even where there has been a clear contempt. This is evident from the case of *Ross Co Ltd v Swan*,[191] which arose out of the occupation of the plaintiff's premises and the defendants' defiance of an injunction to vacate the premises. In considering whether to commit the defendants, O'Hanlon J. stated that:

---

[186] Committal is not explicitly provided for in this regard. See generally RCC Ord.36.
[187] See Form No. 12 in Appendix F, Pt II of the Rules. See RCC Ord.37 r.3.
[188] RCC Ord.37 r.5 simply provides that: "Any person in custody under any order for attachment or committal may apply to the Court for his discharge, on giving notice to the party at whose instance he has been committed of his intention so to apply."
[189] (1962) 96 I.L.T.R. 32.
[190] (1962) 96 I.L.T.R. 32 at 39.
[191] [1981] I.L.R.M. 416

"It is undesirable that the High Court should commit to prison for an indefinite period a person who has no intention of obeying the order of the Court, and who may even welcome the publicity he gains by the making of such an order as a means of furthering his own cause. If no reasonable course is open, then the order may have to be made to vindicate the authority of the Court. If some other reasonable course is open, then it is preferable that it should be adopted."[192]

12–103 O'Hanlon J. held that the "other reasonable course" in the case before him would be for the Gardaí to use the powers of arrest provided for in s.9 of the Prohibition of Forcible Entry and Occupation Act 1971.[193]

12–104 The position in relation to the exercise of the power of committal is well summarised by Kelly, who states that when dealing with cases of civil contempt:

"the High Court may exercise a prudent discretion with an eye to avoiding a course which may be futile and thus counter-productive from the point of view of upholding the Court's own authority."[194]

12–105 This leads to the question of exactly how long a party should be committed for.

Indefinite Period of Committal

12–106 The question of how long a period of committal should be for is not one which has been satisfactorily resolved by the courts in this jurisdiction.[195] Committal is usually ordered for an indefinite period, until such time as contempt has been purged. However, there is the power under the Rules of the Superior Courts to commit for a definite period: RSC Ord.44 r.4 provides that once the alleged contemnor is before the court upon an order for attachment, he may be committed to prison for a definite period to be specified in the order.[196]

---

[192] [1981] I.L.R.M. 416 at 418. O'Hanlon J, applying *Danchevsky v Danchevsky* [1974] 3 All E.R. 934, held that the "other reasonable course" would be for the Gardaí to use the powers of arrest provided for in s.9 of the Prohibition of Forcible Entry and Occupation Act 1971. See also, *Enfield LBC v Mahoney* [1983] 1 W.L.R. 749; [1983] 2 All E.R. 901.

[193] See also, *Enfield LBC v Mahoney* [1983] 1 W.L.R. 749; [1983] 2 All E.R. 901.

[194] Hogan & Whyte, *J.M. Kelly: The Irish Constitution*, 4th edn (Dublin: Butterworths, 2003), p.723.

[195] The Phillimore Committee, which was established in England to consider the law relating to contempt of court, advocated a fixed term of imprisonment for contemnors. Pursuant to the report, by virtue of the Contempt of Court Act 1981 in England, an indeterminate sentence for contempt is now no longer possible: The Phillimore Committee, Report of the Committee on Contempt of Court (1974) Cmnd 5794, para.172. A maximum period of two years in prison is provided for in the Act.

[196] RCC Ord.37 r.4 simply refers to the lodgement of the committal order.

Fixed Period of Committal

12–107 In *Ross Co v Swan*,[197] O'Hanlon J. took the view that he could make a punitive order sending the party in contempt to prison for a fixed period.[198] In that case, in considering whether to commit the defendants, O'Hanlon J. had stated that it would be undesirable to commit to prison for an indefinite period:

> "a person who has no intention of obeying the order of the Court, and who may even welcome the publicity he gains by the making of such an order as a means of furthering his own cause."[199]

12–108 Similarly, in *Flood v Lawlor*,[200] Smyth J. imprisoned the respondent for a fixed period of three months. The ability to commit for a fixed period in the case of the breach of an injunction has never been disavowed by the Irish courts.[201]

12–109 The English case of *Danchevsky v Danchevsky*,[202] decided before the introduction of a fixed period of committal in England in 1981, provides some useful guidance as to when it might be appropriate to set a fixed term of committal. Lord Denning M.R. expressed the difference between fixed term committal and indefinite committal by stating that it seemed to him that:

> "when the object of the committal is punishment for a *past* offence, then, if he is to be imprisoned at all, the appropriate order is for a fixed term. When it is a matter of getting a person to do something in the future—and there is a reasonable prospect of him doing it—then it may be quite appropriate to have an indefinite order against him and to commit him until he does do it."[203]

12–110 There is obvious merit in such an approach, and ultimately it appears that the courts will have significant discretion to determine how best to deal with the alleged breach of injunction when making an order for committal.[204] This is

---

[197] [1981] I.L.R.M. 416 at 417.

[198] [1981] I.L.R.M. 416 at 417. It should be noted, however, that O'Hanlon J. referred, in the context of committal for an indefinite period, to the distinction between committal and an alternative order (such as, for example, a fine or a punitive costs order).

[199] [1981] I.L.R.M. 416 at 418.

[200] ex tempore, High Court, Smyth J., January 15, 2001.

[201] This would seem to sit uneasily with the Law Reform Commission's conclusion that "the balance of the argument is against the introduction of a fixed term of imprisonment to deal with the coercive function of civil contempt. It would introduce an added potential for injustice for no substantial gain." Law Reform Commission's *Consultation Paper on Contempt of Court* (1991), p.385.

[202] [1975] Fam. 17; [1974] 3 All E.R. 934.

[203] [1975] Fam. 17 at 21; [1974] 3 All E.R. 934 at 937.

[204] In *Flood v Lawlor* [2002] 3 I.R. 67 at 80 Keane C.J. observed that in the context of inquisitorial proceedings established by the legislature, "it cannot be that a sentence imposed in respect of a contumelious disregard of the orders of a tribunal and the High Court is coercive only in its

particularly so in circumstances where contemnor is imprisoned, but shows no sign of purging his contempt. A period of indefinite imprisonment would be of little use in coercing a defendant to comply with an injunction.

12–111 This was the situation facing Finnegan P. in *Shell E. & P. Ireland v McGrath*.[205] In that case, five parties were committed to prison for 94 days. The plaintiff subsequently applied to have the injunction which had been breached, and on foot of which the committal had been secured, discharged. Upon this discharge, the contemnors sought their release, even though they were unwilling to purge their contempt and were unwilling to comply with further orders of the court. Although releasing the contemnors, Finnegan P. indicated that he would consider whether, having regard to the contempt found against each of the contemnors and their refusal to purge their contempt, it was appropriate that the court should exercise its punitive powers in respect of any of the contemnors. The contemnors argued that once the injunction had been discharged, the court had no powers to punish them.

12–112 In considering the matter, the President suggested that:

> "Committal for civil contempt is indefinite but in practice after an appropriate period if committal is not having its desired coercive effect it will be appropriate to release the contemnor. However it may not be just or fair in every case that the contemnor should thereby escape a punishment."[206]

12–113 Finnegan P. held that the High Court could make a punitive order sending a contemnor to prison for a fixed period. He noted that such jurisdiction was recognised in two English cases, *Yager v Musa*[207] and *Danchevsky v Danchevsky*.[208] In *Ross Co Ltd v Swan*, O'Hanlon J. had previously viewed the decision in *Danchevsky* as "a correct and prudent one". In coming to his decision, the President also considered the case of *Jennison v Baker*,[209] in which the objectives of imprisonment were considered. Salmon L.J. had stated in *Jennison* that[210]:

> "Of course an injunction is granted and enforced for the protection of the Plaintiff. The Defendant who breaches it is sent to prison for contempt with the object of vindicating (a) the rights of the Plaintiffs (especially the Plaintiff

---

nature." See generally, Murphy, "Contempt for Failure to Make Discovery Following *The Sole Member v Lawlor*" (2002) 7(3) Bar Rev. 160, especially pp.162–164.

[205] [2007] 1 I.R. 671.

[206] [2007] 1 I.R. 671 at 688.

[207] [1961] 2 All E.R. 561.

[208] [1974] 3 All E.R. 934.

[209] [1972] 2 Q.B. 52; [1972] 2 W.L.R. 429; [1972] 1 All E.R. 997.

[210] Having considered the earlier decision of *Seaward v Paterson* [1897] 1 Ch. 545.

in the action) and (b) the authority of the Court. The two objects are in my view inextricably intermixed. Rigby L.J. in *Seaward*'s case pointed out that the Court might well send the Defendant to prison even if a Plaintiff (having applied for attachment) relented and asked that the order in his favour should not be so enforced. The Plaintiff cannot waive the order, but, as a rule the Court will pay attention to his wishes. A stranger who helps the Defendant to breach the injunction is sent to prison, no doubt, as a punishment for contempt but the effect of sending him to prison is also an indirect enforcement of the order which benefits the Plaintiff."[211]

12–114 Finnegan P. took the view that the High Court could, in appropriate cases, commit for contempt for a fixed period in order to vindicate the authority of the court whose order has been disobeyed.

(iii) Applying for an Order of Attachment and/or Committal

12–115 An application for attachment and/or committal is brought by way of notice of motion. It has, however, been recognised in England that a party can be committed on an ex parte application in exceptional circumstances.[212]

12–116 An application for the issue of a writ of attachment is technically different from an application for a committal order. The provisions of RSC Ord.52 r.4 require that every notice of motion for an attachment must state in general terms the grounds of the application. In other words, it is not sufficient to simply seek an order for attachment in the notice of motion, but the actual grounds must be set out. There is no such requirement set out in the Rules of the Superior Courts in relation to a motion to commit.[213] However, in relation to an application for committal, it was stated by Sir John Donaldson M.R. in *Chiltern District Council v Keane*[214] that where an order made covered a wide range of activities the defendant was entitled to know whether the plaintiffs alleged that he was in breach of every single requirement of those orders or of only some of them and, if so, which ones.

12–117 Most applications will be for both attachment and/or committal and, as such, the better course is that the grounds for committal should also be set out in the notice of motion, as distinct from simply seeking committal. Rules of the Superior Courts Ord.44 r.3 provides that:

---

[211] [1972] 2 Q.B. 52 at 61; [1972] 2 W.L.R. 429 at 437; [1972] 1 All E.R. 997 at 1004.

[212] *O'Donovan v O'Donovam* [1955] 1 W.L.R. 1086. See also, *In Warwick Corporation v Russell* [1964] 1 W.L.R. 613; [1964] 2 All E.R. 337. See generally, Cordial, *Consolidated Circuit Court Rules* (Dublin: Thomson Round Hall, 2001, latest release 2006), p.D–107.

[213] See *Cooke v Cooke* [1919] 1 I.R. 227 at 238; *cf.* the then equivalent rule in England, which required a notice of motion to set out with sufficient particularity the grounds for committal.

[214] [1985] 1 W.L.R. 619; [1985] 2 All E.R. 118.

"Save in respect of committal for contempt in the face of the Court or committal under rule 4 [*where a person is brought before the court on attachment*] no order of attachment or committal shall be issued except by leave of the Court to be applied for by motion on notice to the party against whom the attachment or committal is to be directed."[215]

12–118 An application for attachment and/or committal can be brought on a single notice of motion, together with a grounding affidavit.[216] The order sought should, for attachment, be for the Garda Commissioner to attach the party concerned.[217] If committal is also being sought in the same notice of motion, the grounds for an application for committal—i.e. the nature of the breach—should be set out in the notice of motion. Although not prescribed by the Rules, the better practice would be, in the rarer case of an application for committal only, to similarly set out the grounds on which the application is based.

12–119 The grounding affidavit should set out:

- a summary of the action to date;
- the terms of the court order for an injunction sought and obtained;
- a statement that the order was served personally on the defendant, together with the appropriate penal endorsement if warranted[218];
- a statement should be made that the defendant (or other party) remains in breach of the order and the nature of such breach.

12–120 In general, once an appearance has been entered, personal service of documents including notices of motion and affidavits is no longer necessary. However, a motion seeking leave to attach and commit a person is treated differently, and should be served personally due to the standard of proof required on such a motion is the criminal standard, namely beyond reasonable doubt.[219] In the circumstances, strict compliance with all procedural prerequisites is required. For the same reason, the affidavits of service should be filed.[220]

---

[215] See RCC Ord.37 r.2.

[216] Differences between the injunction order and Notice of Motion will not vitiate the application for committal, assuming that such differences are of no major significance: See *Gore-Booth v Gore Booth* (1962) 96 I.L.T.R. 32 at 38, per Lavery J.

[217] RCC Ord.37 r.3 provides that: "Every order of attachment or committal for contempt of Court shall be directed to the Superintendent of the Garda Síochána for the district in which the party to be attached or committed resides ..."

[218] See Ch.5, Perpetual Injunctions, para.5–74. See *Century Insurance Co Ltd v Larkin* [1910] 1 I.R. 91.

[219] See paras 12–34 and 12–123. See *Re Boyle Local Government Election Petition* (1890) 39 I.L.T.R. 243. An affidavit of service should be sworn, setting out the manner, time, date and place where the defendant or alleged contemnor was served.

[220] In *Century Insurance Co Ltd v Larkin* [1910] 1 I.R. 91 it was held that in cases of compulsion, as distinct from restraint, there could be no attachment unless the rules relating to service were

12–121 Mere knowledge on the part of the defendant of the plaintiff's intention to move to commit does not dispense with the necessity of endeavouring to effect personal service. In *Chiltern District Council v Keane*,[221] it was held that the requirements of personal service applied equally to the notification of a new hearing date where there had been an adjournment. An appearance at a hearing to commit does not constitute a waiver of objection on the grounds of either lack of personal service or some other irregularity.[222]

12–122 In summary, before making a committal order, a court must be satisfied that:

- the defendant was served personally with the order of the court;
- the order of the court contained the appropriate penal endorsement warning the defendant that disobedience with the order would render him liable to committal;
- the defendant has breached the order; and
- the notice of motion to commit the defendant was served personally on him.

(iv) Burden and Standard of Proof Required

12–123 As Lavery J. stated in *Gore-Booth v Gore-Booth*, the burden of proof in an application for committal is "squarely on the plaintiffs to show a breach".[223] The standard of proof for committal is the criminal standard, namely beyond reasonable doubt.[224] In *National Irish Bank Ltd v Graham*,[225] Keane J. refused to make an order for committal on the basis that before a court could deprive a person of their liberty for failure to comply with an order of the court, it must be satisfied beyond reasonable doubt that he had in fact committed the alleged contempt.[226] Similarly, in *Cooke v Cooke*, O'Connor L.J. had regard to the consequences of making an order for imprisonment and let common sense

---

complied with, and the fact that a person was in court when an order was made does not dispense with the requirement for service and a proper indorsement.

[221] [1985] 1 W.L.R. 619; [1985] 2 All E.R. 118.

[222] *Mander v Falcke* [1891] 3 Ch. 488. However, it appears that in exceptional circumstances the courts may make a committal order ex parte: see *O'Donovan v O'Donovan* [1955] 1 W.L.R. 1086; [1955] 3 All E.R. 278. Personal service may also not be required where there is an attempt to evade service: see *Bhimji v Chatwani*[1991] 1 W.L.R. 989 at 993, Scott J. referring to Note 52/4/2 in The Supreme Court Practice 1990.

[223] (1962) 96 I.L.T.R. 32 at 35.

[224] In relation to the burden of proof, see generally, McGrath, *Evidence* (Dublin: Thomson Round Hall, 2005), especially Ch.2.

[225] [1994] 1 I.R. 215.

[226] [1994] 1 I.R. 215 at 220. Referred to by Laffoy J. in *Brightwater v Allen*, ex tempore, High Court, Laffoy J., May 12, 2005, albeit that the orders sought in that case were for attachment and sequestration. See also, *Re Bramblevale Ltd* [1970] Ch. 128; [1969] 3 W.L.R. 699; [1969] 3 All E.R. 1062 and *Dean v Dean* [1987] 1 F.L.R. 517.

dictate that "the degree of proof should approximate to that which is required to ensure a conviction in an ordinary criminal case".[227]

(v) Conditional and Suspended Orders of Attachment and Committal

12–124 Conditional orders may also be made in appropriate circumstances. In *Re Hibernia National Review*,[228] Kenny J. held that a conditional order of attachment should be directed to the editor of the newspaper calling upon the editor to show cause why the conditional order should not be made absolute.[229]

12–125 A stay may also be put on an order for committal, as happened in *Flood (Planning Tribunal) v Lawlor*,[230] with Denham J. holding that it was "for the Court to consider the justice of the application of the case."

12–126 It is also possible to suspend an order made pursuant to the breach of an injunction. In another instalment of the litigation in *Flood v Lawlor*,[231] Keane C.J. held that he was:

> "satisfied that a court has jurisdiction to suspend, in whole or part, a sentence of imprisonment imposed in respect of civil contempt and thereafter, in the event of a further contempt, may at its discretion require the party in default to serve some or all of the balance of the sentence."[232]

12–127 The Chief Justice adopted the statement of the law set out by the English Court of Appeal in the case of *Re W(B) (An infant)*.[233] Lord Denning M.R. had stated in that case that:

> "The court has a discretion analogous to a suspended sentence in the criminal courts. Imprisonment is not the inevitable consequence of a breach. The court has a discretion to do what is just in all the circumstances. It can reduce the length of the sentence or can impose a fine instead. It may indeed not punish at all. It all depends on how serious is the breach, how long has the man behaved himself, and so forth."[234]

---

[227] [1919] 1 I.R. 227 at 249. In the context of an *Anton Piller* order, Costello J. also applied the standard of "beyond a reasonable doubt" in *Orion Pictures v Hickey,* unreported, High Court, Costello J., January 18, 1991.

[228] [1976] I.R. 389, in which *Ambard v Attorney General for Trinidad and Tobago* [1936] A.C. 322 and *R. v Evening Standard Co Ltd* [1954] 1 Q.B. 578 were considered.

[229] See also, *Stancombe v Trowbridge Urban District Council* [1910] 2 Ch. 190 and *Phonographic Performance Ltd v Amusement Caterers (Peckham) Ltd* [1964] Ch. 195; [1963] 3 W.L.R. 898; [1963] 3 All E.R. 493.

[230] ex tempore, Supreme Court, August 3, 2001.

[231] [2002] 3 I.R. 67.

[232] [2002] 3 I.R. 67 at 80.

[233] [1969] 2 Ch. 50.

[234] [1969] 2 Ch. 50 at 56. See also, *Lee v Walker* [1985] Q.B. 1191; [1985] 3 W.L.R. 170; [1985]

12–128 Similarly, in *Phonographic Performance Ltd v Amusement Caterers*,[235] Cross J. made the orders for sequestration and committal which the plaintiffs sought, but on their undertaking not to enforce them if within the appropriate time the defendants paid the plaintiffs' costs and the amount owing for licence fees at issue.

12–129 Such a discretion has also been exercised in the Circuit Court. For example, in the case of *O'Donovan v Kirby*,[236] the defendant appeared on a motion for attachment and committal accepting that he was in breach of court orders, and gave an undertaking to abide by those orders. In the circumstances, the court committed the defendant to prison for six months, but suspended the sentence for two years on condition that the defendant enter his bond of £1,000 to be of good behaviour towards all people.

12–130 The circumstances in which a suspension of an order is to be removed require careful consideration, with Ormrod L.J. cautioning in *Ansah v Ansah*[237] that the activation of an order is not an inevitable consequence of a breach of an order during the period of suspension.

(b) Sequestration of Assets

12–131 An order for sequestration of assets is particularly appropriate, though not confined to, cases where an injunction is breached by a corporation or where the contemnor is outside the jurisdiction. It is also available as a remedy against an individual for breach of a mandatory injunction or against company directors. However, it is a remedy which is both "drastic and blunt".[238] In *Larkins v National Union of Miners*,[239] Barrington J. held that sequestration was penal in effect.

12–132 Sequestration was explained by Sir John Donaldson P. in the case of *Con-Mech Ltd v Amalgamated Union of Engineering Workers* as being different from a fine. This is because:

> "If someone is fined the money is lost to him forever. If his assets are sequestered the money remains his but he cannot use it. The money stays in the sequestrator's possession until the court orders what shall be done with it.

1 All E.R. 781 and *Churchman v Joint Shop Stewards' Committee* [1972] 1 W.L.R. 1094; [1972] 3 All E.R. 603.

[235] [1964] Ch. 195 at 198. See also, *Stancomb v Trowbridge Urban District Council* [1910] 2 Ch. 190.

[236] unreported, Circuit Court, McCartan J., May 25, 2001.

[237] [1977] Fam. 138.

[238] Australian Law Reform Commission, *Report on Contempt* A.L.R.C. 35 (1987), para.533.

[239] [1985] I.R. 671 at 688.

The man can come to the court at any time and ask for the money to be returned to him, but if he does so the court will require some explanation of his conduct."[240]

12–133 In general terms, when property is sequestered, a contemnor is deprived of its use, but does not permanently forfeit the property in the normal course.

(i) Corporations

12–134 In *R. v Freeman's Journal Ltd*,[241] the view was expressed that the proper order against a company which has committed a contempt is one directing it to attend and answer in respect of the contempt.[242] As a company can act only through agents, an application to attach the directors of the company may be made, as well as an order for sequestration of their property. Although RSC Ord.42 r.32 provides for sequestration against corporate property, in the normal course an application would be brought for attachment and sequestration.[243] This affords an alleged contemnor the opportunity to explain its or his contempt prior to any order for sequestration being made.

12–135 As previously noted,[244] RSC Ord.42 r.32 of the Rules requires that any disobedience be "wilful" before sequestration may be obtained against the corporate property. This requirement does not appear in the Rules in relation to attachment or committal.[245]

12–136 The principles on which the court acts when asked to sequester the property of a company in such circumstances are:

"the same as those applicable where it is sought to commit a private individual to prison for contempt. In these cases, casual, or accidental and

---

[240] [1973] I.C.R. 620 at 627. See also the dictum of Windeyer J. in *Australian Consolidated Press Ltd v Morgan* (1965) 112 C.L.R. 483 at 501. It should be noted that third parties must cooperate with sequestrators: *Messenger Newspapers Group Ltd v National Graphical Association* [1984] 1 All E.R. 293.

[241] [1902] 2 I.R. 82.

[242] It will also of course be necessary when bringing contempt proceedings against a corporation to demonstrate that the corporation has been properly served; service on companies formed and registered under the Companies Acts 1963–2005 is governed by s.379(1) of the Companies Act 1963.

[243] The Rules of the Circuit Court do not appear to provide specifically for sequestration. However, RCC Ord.33 sets out various execution orders. RCC Ord.36 r.6 provides for distraint. See generally, Glanville, *The Enforcement of Judgments* (Dublin: Round Hall Sweet & Maxwell, 1999) p.18.

[244] See para.12–56.

[245] In relation to which, see para.12–92. Nor is there a requirement for "wilful" disobedience in such circumstances in the Rules of the Circuit Court.

unintentional disobedience to an order of the court is not enough to justify either sequestration or committal; the court must be satisfied that a contempt of court has been committed—in other words, that its order has been contumaciously disregarded".[246]

(ii) Corporations Outside the Jurisdiction

12–137 In the case of *Kutchera v Buckingham*,[247] Henchy J. observed that where the defendant is a limited company, it is nonetheless amenable to the court's jurisdiction if it is registered in this State, even if it only has assets within the State. This is because the court could give effect to its orders by, for example, processes such as the sequestration of the company's assets. A similar approach is evident in the English case of *Hospital for Sick Children (Board of Governors) v Walt Disney Productions Inc.*,[248] in which it was held that the fact that the defendant in question was incorporated in California did not constitute a good ground for refusing to grant an injunction. Lord Denning M.R. took the view that an injunction against a company could be enforced by sequestration of its assets within the jurisdiction,[249] and thus could be granted. Noting that there was no evidence that the defendant had any assets in the jurisdiction, the Master of the Rolls observed that this did not matter, as the defendant "may have assets tomorrow".[250] However, in *Babanaft International v Bassatne*,[251] it was made clear that an injunction should not affect non-parties who are resident abroad.[252]

(iii) Individuals

12–138 As is clear from the provision of RSC Ord.43 r.2, sequestration of assets is also available as a remedy against an individual for breach of a mandatory injunction. RSC Ord.43 r.2 provides that:

> "Where any person is by any judgment or order directed to pay money into court or to do any other act in a limited time, and after due service of such judgment or order refuses of neglects to obey the same according to the

---

[246] Per Stamp J. in *Steiner Products Ltd v Willy Steiner Ltd* [1966] 1 W.L.R. 986 at 991; [1966] 2 All E.R. 387 at 390, following the remarks of the Court of Appeal in *Fairclough v Manchester Ship Canal Co* (1896) 13 T.L.R. 56. See para.12–56.

[247] [1988] I.L.R.M. 501. See Ch.2, Extraterritorial Jurisdiction, para.2–81.

[248] [1968] Ch. 52; [1967] 2 W.L.R. 1250; [1967] 1 All E.R. 1005.

[249] See para.12–131.

[250] [1968] Ch. 52 at 69. Although Harman L.J. suggested that in such a situation there was a burden on the defendants to show that they had no such assets, but had not attempted to show this.

[251] [1990] Ch. 13 at 44; [1989] 2 W.L.R. 232 at 257; [1989] 1 All E.R. 433 at 453, per Nicholls L.J.

[252] See Ch.8, Commercial Injunctions, para.8–24.

exigency thereof, the person prosecuting such judgment or order shall, at the expiration of the time limited for the performance thereof, be entitled, without obtaining any order from the Court for that purpose, to issue an order of sequestration in the Form No 17 in Appendix F, Part II, against the estate and effects of such disobedient person."[253]

12–139 Although sequestration does not involve the liberty of the alleged contemnor, it is nonetheless viewed as a serious matter.[254] In *Larkins v Nation Union of Miners*,[255] Barrington J. held that that the sequestration process, whether civil or criminal in nature and whether coercive or punitive in purpose, was penal in effect, being a process for establishing the authority of the court against a recalcitrant litigant and punishing it for its contempt.

(iv) Issuing an Order for Sequestration

12–140 The Rules of the Superior Courts, specifically RSC Ord.43, set out the circumstances in which orders of sequestration may be issued. Rules of the Superior Courts Ord.43 r.2 states that at the expiration of the time limited for performing the act required by a judgment or order, a person shall be entitled to issue an order of sequestration against the estate and effects of the disobedient person without any order from the court.[256] However, by virtue of RSC Ord.43 r.3, any person entitled to issue an order of sequestration must, before doing so, apply to the Master to approve one or more sequestrators, and obtain directions as to his or their security and accounting.[257] The Master will issue a certificate approving the nominee(s), at which point the order may issue directed to the sequestrator(s).[258]

12–141 The prescribed form of order of sequestration, addressed to the sequestrator or sequestrators, gives him or them:

> "full power and authority to enter upon all the messuages, lands, tenements and real estate whatsoever of the [defendant], and to collect, receive, and

---

[253] Courtney observes that sequestration as a means of enforcing a prohibitory order "is only appropriate where such an order lends itself to multiple future breaches": Courtney, *Mareva Injunctions and Related Interlocutory Orders* (Dublin: Butterworths, 1998), p.522.

[254] A point emphasised in *Steiner Products Ltd v Willy Steiner Ltd* [1966] 1 W.L.R. 986; [1966] 2 All E.R. 387.

[255] [1985] I.R. 671 at 688.

[256] Under RCC Ord.36 r.21: "Where a notice of motion for committal has been served, or an order of committal has been made against a debtor, and is outstanding, an order for execution against the goods of the debtor shall not be issued in the same proceeding except by leave of the Judge, and on such terms as he may impose."

[257] It should be noted that the Master's role is confined to approving the sequestrator and giving directions, and does not encompass giving leave to issue the writ, for which no order of the court is required, per RSC Ord.43 r.2.

[258] One sequestrator only is named in the order, unless the court otherwise directs.

sequester into your hands not only all the rents and profits of his said messuages, lands, tenements and real estate, but also all his goods, chattels, and personal estates whatsoever…".[259]

12–142 The sequestrator(s) must thus acquire all the defendant's real and personal estates, and keep them under sequestration until the defendant does what he was ordered to and clears his contempt, or the High Court makes "other order to the contrary".[260] The acquisition of property by the sequestrator(s) does not convert the property acquired into that of the creditor. Not only does it not confer title, it does not give the creditor a charge over each part of the property acquired.[261]

12–143 The question arose in *Richardson v Richardson*[262] as to whether the sequestors could sell the assets sequestered. Scott Baker J. had to deal with the distinction between sequestrations to enforce orders for the payment of money or fines and sequestrations to enforce other orders of the court such as injunctions. He referred to *Con-Mech (Engineers) Ltd v Amalgamated Union of Engineering Workers (Engineering Section) (No.3)*.[263] In that case, Sir John Donaldson, President of the National Industrial Relations Court, had said that:

> "The distinction between these two processes—seizing property to coerce the contemnor into complying with the court's order and using the assets so seized to satisfy a judgment—has never been of importance in the jurisdiction of the High Court. They are, however, distinct processes."

12–144 The President observed that the court could, if it felt it appropriate, "seize and hold without applying the property in satisfaction of the judgment". He also stated that the court "must do so if the judgment is not of a nature which can be satisfied out of the assets, e.g. an injunctive order".[264]

12–145 However, Scott Baker J. took the view that where otherwise the whole purpose of the sequestration would be defeated, the court was not constrained by ancient practice from using the seized assets in satisfaction of the order.

---

[259] Form No. 17 in Appendix F, Pt II of the Rules.
[260] Form No. 17 in Appendix F, Pt II of the Rules. The Law Reform Commission refer to Borrie & Lowe, *The Law of Contempt*, 3rd edn (London: Butterworths, 1996), p.439 in identifying limits to the range of property which the sequestrators may take and "get into [their] hands": Property of which the defendant merely is a trustee is not within the range of such property, nor is a fund in court which is liable to solicitor's lien in another suit, nor are *choses in action* which are not alienable: Law Reform Commission's *Consultation Paper on Contempt of Court* (July 1991), p.165.
[261] See the dicta of Romer L.C. in *Re Pollard* [1903] 2 K.B. 41 at 47.
[262] [1989] 3 W.L.R. 865; [1989] 3 All E.R. 779; [1989] Fam. 95.
[263] [1974] I.C.R. 464.
[264] [1974] I.C.R. 464 at 467.

12-146 Once contempt has been purged, the assets sequestered will be returned if they have not been used in satisfaction of an order.[265]

(v) Burden and Standard of Proof Required

12-147 The burden of proof in relation to showing that there has been a breach is on the on the plaintiffs and the applicable standard of proof is that of beyond reasonable doubt.

(vi) Conditional and Suspended Orders of Sequestration

12-148 As has been seen, conditional orders may be made in relation to attachment and committal in appropriate circumstances. The same is true in relation to sequestration. As well as dealing with the attachment of its editor, Kenny J. held in *Re Hibernia National Review*[266] that a conditional order of sequestration should be directed to the company which published the newspaper concerned, with the newspaper also being called upon to show cause why the conditional order should not be made absolute.[267]

(c) Fine

12-149 There has been some:

> "uncertainty as to the extent to which the powers of enforcement of courts
> with equitable jurisdiction include the power of fining those who act in breach
> of injunctions or of orders of specific performance."[268]

12-150 However, there are many cases in which it has been held that a fine is the most appropriate remedy for the breach of an injunction such as, for example, *Irish Shell Ltd v Ballylynch Motors Ltd.*[269]

---

[265] See *Sligo Corporation v Cartron Bay Construction Ltd*, unreported, High Court, Ó Caoimh J., May 25, 2001, in which Ó Caoimh J. stated that: "The Order of Sequestration will remain in force until such time as the works set forth in the Order of 1988 have been completed."

[266] [1976] I.R. 389, in which *Ambard v Attorney General for Trinidad and Tobago* [1936] A.C. 322 and *R. v Evening Standard Co Ltd* [1954] 1 Q.B. 578 were considered.

[267] See also, *Stancomb v Trowbridge Urban District Council* [1910] 2 Ch. 190 and *Phonographic Performance Ltd v Amusement Caterers (Peckham) Ltd* [1964] Ch. 195; [1963] 3 W.L.R. 898; [1963] 3 All E.R. 493.

[268] Spry, *The Principles of Equitable Remedies,* 5th edn (London: Sweet & Maxwell, 1997), p.371. It can be argued that because the enforcement of injunctions is a civil matter, and is not in theory penal, a fine is not an appropriate remedy for breach of an injunction. See *Australian Consolidated Press Ltd v Morgan* (1965) 112 C.L.R. 483.

[269] unreported, Supreme Court, March 5, 1997. See also the decision of Cross J. in *Phonographic Performance Ltd v Amusement Caterers (Peckham) Ltd* [1964] Ch. 195 at 200; [1963] 3 W.L.R. 898 at 902; [1963] 3 All E.R. 493 at 497, in which he stated that he could not see the logic of there being no alternative to sending the defendants in question to prison for civil contempt,

12–151 In *Heatons Transport (St Helens) Ltd v Transport and General Workers Union*,[270] a fine was permitted on the basis, according to Lord Wilberforce, that:

> "the effective administration of justice normally requires some penalty for disobedience to an order of a court if the disobedience is more than casual or accidental or unintentional."[271]

12–152 This was consistent with the earlier decision of *Ronson v Ronson*,[272] in which it was held that although there had been breaches of the undertakings on the part of the defendant company in contempt of the order of the court, that they were not so serious as to warrant more than a fine. There would appear to have been no distinction made as to whether a fine was appropriate to both companies as well as individuals.

12–153 In the ex tempore decision of *Flood v Lawlor*, delivered by Smyth J. in the High Court, the individual defendant was committed to prison and fined.[273] The period of committal was to be effectively extended if the fine was not paid by a specified date. In *Curley v The Mayor of Galway*,[274] Kelly J. had no hesitation in imposing a fine given the seriousness of the contempt, in circumstances where the contemnor had apologised and given various undertakings to the court in relation to remedying the situation which had arisen.

12–154 There are in fact two types of fines which a court can have recourse to. The first is a fixed fine, often used to punish a breach which has taken place. However, a fine can also be coercive in nature in so far as a court can indicate to a contemnor or putative transgressor that if they engage in conduct in breach of a court order, the court will fine them at a specified *per diem* rate. The latter fine has been referred to as an "accruing" fine and is both coercive and penal in nature.[275] The Australian Law Reform Commission has elaborated on the distinction, stating that:

> "It is coercive when it is threatened, but penal when it is applied. On this basis, it is distinguishable from the traditional coercive sanctions of indefinite imprisonment and sequestration, which are coercive both when the court

---

and felt that the court must have the power "to impose the lesser penalty of a fine", following *British Motor Trade Association v Hewitt*, *The Times*, June 1, 1951, and *Multiform Displays Ltd v Whitmarley Displays Ltd* [1957] R.P.C. 137.

[270] [1973] A.C. 15; [1972] 3 W.L.R. 431; [1972] All E.R. 1214.

[271] [1973] A.C. 15 at 109; [1972] 3 W.L.R. 431 at 449; [1972] 3 All E.R. 101 at 117.

[272] [1966] Ch. 603; [1966] 2 W.L.R. 1157; [1966] 2 All E.R. 381.

[273] ex tempore, High Court, Smyth J., July 31, 2001. Smyth J. had made an earlier order committing the defendant on January 15, 2001, but not fining him.

[274] unreported, High Court, Kelly J., March 30, 2001.

[275] Australian Law Reform Commission: "Non-Compliance with Court Orders and Undertakings" ALRC Research Paper No. 6 (1987), para.550.

orders the sanction and at the time of actual application. The crucial difference with an accruing fine is that, by the time of the collection of the amounts that have accrued, the original order will most likely have been complied with. At that point, the fine is essentially penal and incurred in respect of past disobedience."[276]

12–155 The Irish Law Reform Commission has taken what appears to be the very pragmatic view that "the courts should have power to order fines, whether as punitive or coercive sanctions, and whether on an accruing basis or otherwise."[277]

12–156 Imposing a fine of any nature would also appear to be consistent with the Rules of the Superior Courts. In the case of attachment, RSC Ord.44 r.4 provides that when a person against whom an order of attachment is directed is brought before the court, that person may be discharged "on such terms and conditions as to costs or otherwise as it thinks fit." This would appear to contemplate the imposition of a fine, or at a minimum not to exclude it. In relation to committal, RSC Ord.44 r.5 provides that a person against whom an order of committal is directed may apply to the court to discharge such order. Where such order is discharged, the court may likewise do so "on such terms and conditions as to costs or otherwise as it thinks fit." This would also appear to provide for the imposition of a fine, though there is something of a fiction involved, in that technically a person would have to be committed before a fine could be imposed. However, once the court has determined that a fine is an appropriate remedy, it is unlikely that the court would engage in an exercise to commit a person, then discharge them immediately and impose a fine. This would also circumvent the requirements of RSC Ord.44 r.5, which provides that an application for discharge must be made by notice on motion to the party at whose instance the order for committal was made.

12–157 As is clear from the foregoing, under the Rules it is for the court to determine whether a fine is an appropriate remedy, and an application would not be brought by the person seeking attachment or committal to also seek a fine.[278] A court will generally grant liberty to apply should the fine not be paid within a specified time.[279]

---

[276] Australian Law Reform Commission: "Non-Compliance with Court Orders and Undertakings" ALRC Research Paper No. 6 (1987), para.550.

[277] Law Reform Commission's *Consultation Paper on Contempt of Court* (July 1991), pp.239 et seq. Although *cf.* the dictum of Ó Dálaigh C.J. in *Keegan v de Burca* [1973] I.R. 223 to the effect that civil contempt, which encompasses breaches of injunctions, is not punitive but coercive.

[278] However, the Law Reform Commission conclude that the District and Circuit Courts should not have the power of imposing unlimited fines for civil contempt: *Report on Contempt of Court* (LRC 47–1994), p.7.

[279] See, for example, *Council of the Bar of Ireland v Sunday Business Post Ltd*, unreported, High Court, Costello J., March 30, 1993, in which the fines were to be paid within one month.

(i) Burden and Standard of Proof Required

12–158 Where the sanction concerned is a fine, it is unclear whether the appropriate standard is in fact beyond all reasonable doubt, although the better view is that it probably is. In *Charlton v Aga Khan*,[280] Budd J. referred to adopting either the standard of being satisfied beyond reasonable doubt or, rather nebulously, "such standard as the Court, with its responsibility, regards as consistent with the gravity of the charge".

(d) Costs

12–159 The courts may also use costs as a sanction for the breach of an injunction. In *Charlton v Aga Khan*,[281] Budd J. had recourse to costs as an alternative to the attachment and/or committal sought. Expressing the view that the courts are always reluctant to impose a prison sentence, Budd J. stated that:

> "although it must be understood that the Court cannot countenance disregard of or defiance of Court Orders. The Court's concern at the defiance of Orders will be reflected in the Orders in respect of costs."

12–160 This approach is consistent with that of the Supreme Court in *Gore-Booth v Gore-Booth*.[282] The defendants in that case, although escaping committal on the basis of the circumstances of the case, were ordered to pay costs in both the High and Supreme Courts.[283] Similarly, in *Ross Co Ltd v Swan*[284] O'Hanlon J., whilst refusing to make an order committing the defendants to prison for contempt of court, awarded the costs of the application to the plaintiff against the defendants served with notice of the application, on a solicitor and client basis.[285] Ultimately, the use of costs as a remedy for contempt would appear to be at the discretion of the court.[286] For example, in *Curley v Mayor of Galway*,[287] Kelly J. made an order for costs "at the highest possible scale" given the material and substantial breaches committed.

---

[280] unreported, High Court, Budd J., February 22, 2000.

[281] unreported, High Court, Budd J., February 22, 2000.

[282] (1962) 96 I.L.T.R. 32 at 36.

[283] See also, *Re Grantham Wholesale Fruit Vegetable and Potato Merchants Ltd* [1972] 1 W.L.R. 559 at 568 in which Megarry J. had regard to the fact that there were passages in *Plating Company v Farquharson* (1881) 17 Ch D 49 which "read literally, strongly condemn motions in which in opening the case counsel says that he asks not for committal but merely for an apology and for payment of his costs", but essentially distinguished *Plating Company* on the basis that there never had been a sufficient case for committal.

[284] [1981] I.L.R.M. 416 at 418.

[285] For a fuller discussion as to the types of costs orders which may be made, see Delany & McGrath, *Practice and Procedure in the Superior Courts*, 2nd edn (Dublin: Thomson Round Hall, 2005), Ch.21.

[286] See the comments at para.12–98 in relation to RSC Ord.44 r.4.

[287] unreported, High Court, Kelly J., March 30, 2001.

However, in that case the contemnor had apologised and given various under-takings to the court in relation to remedying the situation which had arisen. As such, Kelly J. felt that it was not necessary to sequester the defendant's assets or commit the county manager to prison.

(e) Alternative Remedies

(i) Rules of the Superior Courts Ord.42 r.31

12–161 In cases where a mandatory injunction has been granted and not complied with, seeking to have an alleged contemnor attached or committed may ultimately not further the plaintiff's position in real terms in that the act required under the mandatory injunction will still not have been undertaken. In such circumstances, there is provision under the Rules for a remedy which will facilitate the completion of the act. This is set out at RSC Ord. 42 r.31:

> "If a mandamus, granted in an action or otherwise, or a mandatory order, injunction, or judgment for the specific performance of any contract be not complied with, the Court, besides or instead of proceedings against the disobedient party for contempt, may direct that the act required to be done may be done so far as practicable by the party by whom the judgment or order has been obtained, or some other person appointed by the Court, at the cost of the disobedient party, and upon the act being done, the expenses incurred may be ascertained in such manner as the Court may direct, and execution may issue for the amount so ascertained, and costs."[288]

12–162 The application is brought on notice, grounded on an affidavit. In framing the notice and affidavit, two factors are of relevance: firstly, the court must be able to formulate an order as to what must be done. Sometimes this may not be possible, but in the case of *Parker v Camden London Borough Council*,[289] the Court of Appeal dealt with the matter by making an order, the exact terms of which were to be worked out once an investigation had been carried out. Secondly, the ability to ascertain the expenses incurred is important. It should be noted, however, that if the injunction order in question is prohibitory in nature, the provisions of RSC Ord.42 r.31 do not appear to be of assistance.

12–163 A remedy under RSC Ord.42 r.31 does not preclude an application bring made for attachment and/or committal in addition, and it is clear from the wording of the Order that this is a matter which is at the court's discretion.

---

[288] RCC Ord.36 r.26 contains the equivalent provision.
[289] [1986] Ch. 162; [1985] 3 W.L.R. 47; [1985] 2 All E.R. 14, which dealt with the equivalent order in England.

(ii) Other Remedies

12–164 That the foregoing remedies are not necessarily a closed category, would appear to be the import of the decision of Peart J. in *Adebayo v Commissioner of An Garda Síochána*,[290] a habeas corpus application. In that case, having made reference to the court's jurisdiction to supervise its own orders, Peart J. stated that:

> "The Court's inherent jurisdiction is deep enough to ensure that it has the capacity to ensure compliance with its orders. There are occasions when a Court must dig deep into its reserves of inherent jurisdiction in order to fashion an appropriate remedy to meet an unusual situation."

(f) Illegality of Acts in Breach of an Injunction

12–165 In the case of *Clarke v Chadburn*,[291] Sir Robert Megarry V.C. held that not only was wilful disobedience of an order of the court punishable as a contempt, it could also be described as being illegal; those disobeying the order ought not to be able to claim that the acts done in defiance of that order were not tainted by the illegality that produced them. In the words of the Vice Chancellor:

> "It seems to me on principle that those who defy a prohibition ought not to be able to claim that the fruits of their defiance are good, and not tainted by the illegality that produced them."[292]

E. The Hearing of an Application for Remedies

12–166 In principle any judge should be able to hear an application based on an alleged breach of an injunction. However, a number of procedural and evidential issues must be considered in this context.

1. Hearsay

12–167 In *SPUC v Grogan*[293] Carroll J. held that newspaper reports of breaches of an injunction were hearsay evidence and not satisfactory proof of contempt of court for the purpose of committal to prison. A broader view was put forward in *Smithkline Beecham v Antigen Pharmaceuticals Ltd*,[294] in which McCracken J., whilst acknowledging that hearsay evidence may be admissible under certain

---

[290] unreported, High Court, Peart J., October 27, 2004.
[291] [1985] 1 W.L.R. 78; [1985] 1 All E.R. 211.
[292] [1985] 1 W.L.R. 78 at 81; [1985] 1 All E.R. 211 at 213.
[293] [1989] I.R. 753.
[294] [1999] 2 I.L.R.M. 190 at 196.

circumstances in interlocutory applications, cautioned about the dangers of relying on such evidence.[295] As observed by Clarke J. in *Collen Construction Ltd v BATU*[296] in a more general context, whilst it was permissible to include hearsay evidence in affidavits sworn for interlocutory applications, no reliance should ordinarily be placed on hearsay attributed to unnamed persons, as such evidence "could not ... be regarded as meaningful evidence in any proper sense of the term".

2. Evidence and Cross-Examination

12–168 A respondent may, if he wishes, give oral evidence, or evidence by affidavit. The position in relation to cross-examination of a deponent on his affidavit is somewhat unclear, particularly in relation to whether the leave of the court is required. Rules of the Superior Courts Ord.40 r.31, which deals with trial on affidavit, makes provision for the service of notice upon a party who has filed an affidavit requiring the production of the deponent for cross-examination at the trial. However, RSC Ord.40 r.1, which deals with any "petition, motion, or other application" requires an application to be to the court if the attendance of a deponent for cross-examination is required. It would seem that the more prudent view is that the leave of the court should be sought.[297]

3. Factors Taken Into Account

12–169 Injunctions being an equitable remedy, it would appear that in all subsequent applications based on the injunction, equitable factors must still be taken into account in determining the outcome of the application. Thus, for example, it may be the case that laches on the part of the person seeking to enforce an injunction can be taken into account by the court.[298] As stated by Goulding J. in *Easton v Brown*,[299] albeit in the context of specific performance:

> "It is common ground that it is for the plaintiff to explain and excuse the extraordinary delay which has taken place. It is common ground that in exercising its discretion, the court must consider what, at the present time when the discretion is to be exercised, is equitable between the plaintiffs and the defendant."[300]

---

[295] In *Savings and Investment Bank Ltd v Gasco Investments* [1988] Ch. 422; [1988] 2 W.L.R. 1212; [1988] 1 All E.R. 975, hearsay evidence was held to be admissible.

[296] unreported, High Court, Clarke J., May 15, 2006.

[297] See, in relation to the question of cross-examination upon an affidavit in an injunction application, the Court of Appeal decision in *Comet Products UK Ltd v Hawkex Plastics Ltd* [1971] 2 Q.B. 67; [1971] 1 All E.R. 1141.

[298] See Chapter Four, Equitable and General Principles.

[299] [1981] 3 All E.R. 278.

[300] [1981] 3 All E.R. 278 at 281, referring to the decision of O'Bryan J. in the Supreme Court of Victoria in *McKenna v Richey* [1950] V.L.R. 360; [1950] A.L.R. 773.

4. Defences

12–170 It will be for the alleged contemnor to explain their behaviour to the court. However, it is not sufficient to argue that an injunction order should not have been made in the first instance.[301] As stated by Lord Cottenham L.C. in *Chuck v Cremer*[302]:

> "It would be most dangerous to hold that the suitors, or their solicitors, could themselves judge whether an order was null and void—whether it was regular or irregular ... the course of a party knowing of an order which was null and irregular and who might be affected by it was plain. He should apply to the court that it might be discharged. As long as it existed it must not be disobeyed."[303]

5. Retraction or Variation of an Order (Waiver)

12–171 Where an injunction is breached, an order made on foot of such a breach is made at the instigation of a party (generally the plaintiff) to proceedings. That party is free to decide whether to retract an application for an order, or to apply to have the injunction varied.[304] However, once a person or company has been found to be in contempt, they are now in contempt of the court, not the injured party. As such, the matter is beyond the injured party.[305] It is for the court, and only the court, to determine whether and on what terms an order should be discharged.[306] In *Heatons Transport (St Helens) Ltd v Transport and General Workers Union*,[307] Sir John Donaldson P. observed that:

> "Once proceedings for contempt of court have been set in motion it is not open to the parties to settle the matter of contempt. They can certainly settle

---

[301] per Romer L.J. in *Hadkinson v Hadkinson* [1952] P. 285 at 288; [1952] 2 All E.R. 567 at 569. See also, *Isaacs v Robertson* [1985] A.C. 97; [1984] 3 W.L.R. 705; [1984] 3 All E.R. 140; *Johnson v Walton* [1990] 1 F.L.R. 350; [1990] Fam. Law 260; *M v Home Office* [1994] 1 A.C. 377; [1993] 3 W.L.R. 433; [1993] 3 All E.R. 537.

[302] (1846) 1 Coop. T. Cott. 205, cited in *Hadkinson v Hadkinson* [1952] P. 285 at 288; [1952] 2 All E.R. 567 at 569.

[303] (1846) 1 Coop. T. Cott. 205 at 238, as cited in *Hadkinson v Hadkinson* [1952] P. 285 at 288; [1952] 2 All E.R. 567 at 569.

[304] The Law Reform Commission has considered whether what it terms "Waiver and discontinuance" should be permitted in its present form, but ultimately elects in favour of retaining the present system. Law Reform Commission's *Consultation Paper on Contempt of Court* (July 1991), pp.389–392. The issues peculiar to family litigation are considered at pp.392–411 of the Consultation Paper.

[305] In *Jennison v Baker* [1972] 2 Q.B. 52; [1972] 2 W.L.R. 429; [1972] 1 All E.R. 997, it was held that a person may be committed even if an injunction ceases to be effective.

[306] O'Donnell, "Some Reflections on the Law of Contempt" [2002] 2 J.I.S.J. 88 at 92.

[307] [1973] A.C. 15; [1972] 3 W.L.R. 73; [1972] 2 All E.R. 1214.

the dispute which they may have with each other … But as far as the contempt of court is concerned, that is a different matter and one with which we are deeply concerned."[308]

12–172 However, the court will generally pay attention to the wishes of the party bringing the application.[309]

6. Apology by the Contemnor Prior to a Determination

12–173 The courts will treat the breaches on a case-by-case basis, and will have regards to the factors before them. One such factor is the fact that the contemnor may offer an apology for his actions prior to the court arriving at a decision as to how to deal with him. An apology was offered to the court by the defendants in the case of *Little v Cooper (No. 2)*.[310] The defendants also offered an undertaking that they would not commit such a breach in the future. Notwithstanding this, Johnston J. made an order that the defendants be committed. This was on the basis that he was not satisfied with the "reality of the apology", unsupported by affidavits, written statements or an offer of amends to the plaintiff.[311] It is unclear exactly what Johnston J. had in mind when he referred to affidavits or written statements. There is, and would appear that there was at the time, no Rule in force which would require such documents to be produced in the context of offering an apology. However, the basic principle still applies, namely that the court may, if it wishes, accept an apology from the contemnor; such an apology will usually be accepted in conjunction with an undertaking not to further breach the injunction in place or some offer of recompense to the party who had secured the injunction, as the court sees fit.

7. Hearing a Contemnor

12–174 Finnegan P. found in *Shell E. & P. Ireland v McGrath*[312] that there was a well settled rule that a court would not entertain an application by a person who is in contempt of court until he had purged himself of that contempt.[313] One of the cases cited by Finnegan P. in support of this was *Hadkinson v Hadkinson*,[314]

---

[308] [1972] 2 All E.R. 1214 at 1220, which sets out the relevant decision delivered in the See also *Pojé v Attorney General of British Columbia* [1953] 2 D.L.R. 785.

[309] See the dictum of Salmon L.J. in *Jennison v Baker* 1972] 2 Q.B. 52 at 64; [1972] 2 W.L.R. 429 at 437; [1972] 1 All E.R. 997 at 1004.

[310] [1937] I.R. 510.

[311] [1937] I.R. 510 at 512.

[312] [2007] 1 I.R. 671.

[313] Citing *Bettinson v Bettinson* [1965] 1 All E.R. 102; *Hadkinson v Hadkinson* [1952] P. 285; [1952] 2 All E.R. 567; Daniell's *Chancery Practice*, 7th edn, Vol.1, p.725; Oswald on *Contempt of Court*, 3rd edn, p.248; *Taylor v Taylor* 1849 1 M.A.C. & G. 397.

[314] *Hadkinson v Hadkinson* [1952] P. 285; [1952] 2 All E.R. 567.

in which Romer L.J. held that no application to the court by a person found to be in contempt will be entertained until he has purged himself of his contempt.[315] This was subject to specific exceptions, however, such as applying to purge contempt; applying to set aside the order on which contempt was founded; arguing that his actions were not in breach; or to defend himself against subsequent applications. However, Denning L.J. held in the same case that the fact that a party to a cause had disobeyed an order of the court was not of itself a bar to his being heard, but that the court had a discretion to refuse to hear a party. Gee has suggested that the general provisions applicable in hearing a contemnor can now be formulated as follows[316]:

- Not to hear a party is a strong thing to do and must be justified on the facts, and must be a proportionate means of securing a legitimate end.
- A contemnor should not be prevented from making applications in other proceedings.
- A contemnor should not be precluded from defending himself in proceedings.
- A contemnor should not be precluded from making application or advancing an appeal to set aside or vary the order of which he is in contempt.
- A contemnor should not be precluded from defending subsequent proceedings.
- The court has, however, a discretion to refuse to hear a contemnor.[317]

8. Purging Contempt Following Attachment or Committal[318]

12–175 Rules of the Superior Courts Ord.44 rr.4 and 5 provide that a person against whom an order of attachment and committal respectively is directed may apply to the court to discharge that order.[319] A party seeking to purge his contempt will generally come before the court and apologise for his actions and offer an undertaking not to repeat the act that was found to be in contempt. Although the Rules are silent as to whether a specific judge must hear a contemnor, in the normal course the judge who committed the parties, or the judge who has seisin of the substantive matter, will usually deal with such an

---

315 Referring to *Garstin v Garstin* Sw & Tr 73 and *Gordon v Gordon* [1904] P. 163.
316 Gee, *Commercial Injunctions*, 5th edn (London: Sweet & Maxwell, 2004), p.589.
317 Reference is also made to *Golden v UK* (1975) 1 E.H.R.R. 524 which provides for the right to a fair trial, with an implied, albeit not absolute, right of fair access to the courts.
318 As explained by the Australian Law Reform Commission: "Until the Reformation, the Lord Chancellor was generally an ecclesiastic, and his coercive techniques owed much to the Ecclesiastical Courts, where disobedient parties were excommunicated until they obeyed. The religious heritage of the Court of Chancery is preserved today in the terminology of this type of contempt: a contemnor 'purges' his or her contempt, and even after the order has been obeyed a prison term might be necessary by way of 'expiation'." *Report on Contempt* ALRC 35 (1987).
319 See RCC Ord.37 r.5.

application. However, the emphasis which the courts have placed on "the seriousness of depriving a citizen of personal liberty"[320] would seem logically to lead to the view that any judge with appropriate jurisdiction is competent to hear such an application.

12–176 If the court accedes to an application, it may do so on such terms and conditions as to costs or otherwise as it thinks fit. For example, in *Clarke v Smith*,[321] the defendant had been committed for contempt of court for refusal to obey an interim injunction against trespassing on the plaintiff's lands. He subsequently undertook not to repeat the acts complained of and agreed to judgment being entered against him in the action. He also swore that he was unable to pay any of the costs, as he was an unemployed labourer without any means. Dealing with matter, Barton J. was satisfied that if he was to make an order making the payment of costs a condition precedent to discharge, it would be one "which the defendant could not comply with". He thus ordered the discharge of the defendant, leaving the plaintiff to decide how best to enforce the payment of the outstanding costs.

9. Finding Contempt Twice on One Injunction Order/Double Jeopardy

12–177 There is English authority for the proposition that where there is a breach of an order to do a certain act by a certain date in respect of which the contemnor is committed to prison for non-compliance, that breach cannot be the subject matter of a further committal order. In the case of *Kumari v Jalal*,[322] an order was made following a divorce for the return of the goods by a specific day. The defendant failed to comply with the order and consequently served a term of three months' imprisonment. However, upon an appeal by the defendant having been sentenced for a second time due to his ongoing failure to comply with the order, the Court of Appeal held that in such circumstances, the breach cannot be the subject matter of a further committal order. Neill L.J. observed that "[i]f the failure by the alleged contemnor has continued, then it is necessary to go back to the court and obtain a further order."[323] Neill L.J. also had regard to Borrie & Lowe, *The Law of Contempt*[324] and a passage dealing with the case of an offender who repeatedly commits contempts, in which it is stated that:

---

[320] per Geoghegan J. in *Re Earle* [1938] I.R. 485 at 510.

[321] (1914) 48 I.L.T.R. 244.

[322] [1997] 1 W.L.R. 97, referring to *Danchevsky v Danchevsky* [1975] Fam. 17; [1974] 3 All E.R. 934 and *Lamb v Lamb* [1984] F.L.R. 278. A similar point was raised in *Shell E & P Ireland v McGrath*, unreported, High Court, Finnegan P., April 7, 2006, but was not explicitly dealt with in detail by Finnegan P.

[323] [1997] 1 W.L.R. 97 at 101.

[324] Borrie & Lowe, *The Law of Contempt*, 3rd edn (London: Butterworths, 1996), p.630, fn.15.

"If [*the strategy of seeking increasingly longer sentences*] is adopted care should be taken that a fresh order is made on each occasion lest a plea of *autrefois convict* is raised."[325]

10. Appeal

12–178 Where a contemnor is found to have been in breach of an order and in contempt, it is possible to appeal such a decision. The right of appeal exists from both the Circuit Court to the High Court and from the High Court to the Supreme Court.[326]

12–179 The applicable standard required to succeed in an appeal is a high one, and it appears that there must be an error in principle or a "gross miscarriage" identified in order to be successful.[327]

---

[325] See generally, McDermott, *Res Judicata and Double Jeopardy* (Dublin: Butterworths, 1999).

[326] The rules and procedures governing appeals are set out in Ch.5, Perpetual Injunctions, para.5–80. See generally, Delany & McGrath, *Practice and Procedure in the Superior Courts*, 2nd edn (Dublin: Thomson Round Hall, 2005), Ch.20.

[327] per Lavery J. in *Gore-Booth v Gore-Booth* (1962) 96 I.L.T.R. 32 at 36.

INDEX